YESHUA:
THE REBEL WHO
SHOOK THE WORLD

RICHARD TROMBINSKI

ISBN: 143925771X
ISBN-13: 9781439257715
Library of Congress Control Number: 2009909300

DEDICATION

TO EDNA ANNE

My inspiration, strength and support, my best friend and my wife

To Nic and Cheryl

I hope you enjoy this historical novel. It is meant to inform, inspire and entertain. Best Wishes.

Oct 19/2012

PROLOGUE:
THE BIBLE IS WRONG

My name is James and I am the brother of Yeshua. That is his Hebrew name. You know him by his Greek name Jesus. I am the bishop of Jerusalem, leader of his Judaic Christian Synagogue. His modern Judaism is growing within and outside Israel so fast that many countries fear us and are bitterly persecuting us. Yeshua often said our church will grow from the blood of our martyrs.

Even our own Sanhedrin, Jerusalem's old Judaic establishment fears our growing influence. My sources warn me the High Priest Ananas, is planning to charge me with blasphemy. He has never before shown interest in me, except when attacking me for Yeshua's teachings. The apostles and elders of our church fear for my safety and urge me to run. They fear if I stay I will be the next martyr on the High Priest's long list.

For that reason they urge me to write the story of Yeshua for posterity, before it becomes lost to the world. Thirty years have passed since his Crucifixion, and already many of his deeds have become legends, like a mixture of fact and fiction.

• • •

I suppose Yeshua's story starts with his first conflict with the Priests of the Temple. He was thirteen years old when it happened. His parents, Joseph and Miriam, took him to Jerusalem for the bar mitzvah ceremony, our traditional religious rite, whereby a boy becomes a man. After rigorous examination he was declared the best religious scholar ever examined. He recited every passage from the Scriptures from memory; chapter and verse. The leaders of the Sanhedrin met with him, hoping to persuade him to join one of their religious factions. They were about to discover he was a free thinking intellect, a nascent renegade, against all dogma. A bitter argument ensued and they threw him out of the Temple. Greek scholars wrote that at age twelve the boy Jesus had amicable religious discussions in Jerusalem with the priests and scholars.

This is how Yeshua explained it: after the bar mitzvah, the leaders of the Sanhedrin took him to a large dark room of the Temple adjacent to the priests' prayer court. Master Zohar, leader of the ultra-conservative Sadducees led the discussion. He was a stone faced little man with deep lines resembling deep chisel cuts.

"I am Zohar, Chairman of the Sanhedrin when the High Priest is absent," he barked authoritatively, to instill respect and fear in the young man. Then he pointed to the old man beside him with a terse sentence, "Master Gera, leader of the Pharisees." Yeshua waited for Zohar to introduce the young priest sitting beside him, but the old stone face did not, and continued, "We will carry on until the High Priest comes. You are fortunate master Yeshua, for the Sanhedrin decided you were the best scholar…" adding almost inaudibly, "A scholar from Galilee…a first!".

Yeshua heard the snide remark nevertheless stretched his lips in a self-conscious smile of equal doses of contentment, shyness and mistrust. He had been forewarned by rabbi Ezra ben Lebbus, about the Temple priests of Judeah, their contempt for the rustic Galileans and above all not to cross them.

Master Zohar's smirk resembled a sneer as he asked, "Tell me, master Yeshua, what will you be when you grow up?"

"Master Zohar, I just completed the bar mitzvah; our rite into manhood! I am a grown up!" he answered innocently.

Master Gera let out an involuntary chuckle which he quickly stifled. Master Zohar glared at the gratuitous interruption, the lines on his face growing darker.

"Yes, of course, our tradition…I mean have you chosen a line of work?" Zohar sneered with a scornful smile, "Galileans are simple tradesmen or farmers, correct?"

Yeshua ignored the gratuitous remark and answered his first inquiry frankly, "I intend to be the High Priest of this Temple."

The old men exchanged meaningful glances, "We already have a High Priest, his Excellency Ananas…he has four sons and a son in law, master Caiphas. I am sure they are in line for this lofty station", Zohar proclaimed.

Yeshua insisted, "My ancestors are from the House of David… that's King David. I may have a more legitimate claim…" but he stopped remembering the promise the rabbi extracted from him, to avoid arguments at all costs.

"Maybe you do…that's between you and the High Priest. Our intention was to meet with you to assess your character and persuade you to join one of our leading religious sects: Sadducees, we are more conservative but faithful to the scriptures; or the Pharisees, so loose with the holy book that they change with the wind".

"We want you to choose carefully," Master Gera chirped like a street vendor selling his wares.

Yeshua's eyes went from one to the other with trepidation. To choose one meant lasting hatred from the other. Why did rabbi Ben Lebbus not warn him about this? He stuttered lamely, "I'm not familiar…which religion…to choose."

Zohar laughed condescendingly, "You must be confused. There is only one religion. It's the Pharisees' interpretation that makes it seem like two."

Gera interrupted, "Now, now, you promised …"

"It's one religion. But our interpretation is correct. Do you understand?"

Yeshua nodded, "Yes sir," then reconsidered and shook his head, "No, sir…"

Master Gera interjected, "Explain the Sadducees' views, then I'll do mine so he can decide."

Zohar rattled off impatiently, "All right! Sadducees believe in the Lord Adonai. That's it! We do'nt believe in souls, angels, prophets or everlasting life. No miracles, and above all not the popular fraud you peasants call the Messiah."

Gera smiled, "The problem with Sadducees? No imagination. Their sect is a petrified tree; ossified on the outside, and as hard as a stone on the inside – like their hearts. We believe Adonai created angels to communicate with us, and saintly persons to perform miracles…and gave us the annointed Messiah!"

"Sorcery! Witchery! An illusion of an overburdened imagination," Zohar protested gruffly.

Yeshua recognized the arguments for they discussed them in Nazareth in the synagogue. He enjoyed it among friends, but here he sensed all opinions came with dire consequences for a lifetime. He ventured cautiously, "I am to choose the better… dogma?" The old men nodded. "Have you asked Lord Adonai's opinion?"

Surprised by the question they looked at each other in confusion. Zohar recovered first, "What has Lord Adonai got to go with this?"

"It is His religion, His scriptures. If His doctrines confuse you, He ought to clarify Himself."

Zohar found the boy's naiveté hilarious, "Ask Adonai…Sadducees don't need His opinions. We know the answers! Our logic is infallible!"

"Perhaps we should test it?" Yeshua suggested innocently. Zohar fixed his grey eyes on the precocious boy and hesitated before nodding. "Do you admit that Lord Adonai is omnipotent?" the boy continued.

"Everybody knows that," the old man snapped.

"Do you acknowledge Lord Adonai Created everything?" Yeshua asked and Zohar jerked a nod impatiently. "That He created heaven and earth…and the stars…?" The old man sighed, his thin lips stretching into a thin line. "…all creatures on earth?"

The old man lost his patience, "Yes! Yes! Adonai is omnipotent, the Creator… Get on with it."

Yeshua continued calmly, "So you admit there is nothing He cannot create?"

"You are asking the same question," Zohar argued.

Yeshua smiled faintly, "The Pharisees are correct, and you are wrong."

Master Gera exploded with laughter, "Bravo! Master Zohar, admit defeat. You were soundly beaten by a classical display of logic, by a mere child!"

Zohar shouted, "He proved nothing! To say Adonai can create angels and Messiahs is no proof He did it!"

Yeshua raised his hand patiently, "The Scriptures say that an angel of God stopped Abraham from sacrificing his son. And an angel first appeared to Moses in the fire of burning bushes…" he stopped momentarily and saw the old man's eyes open wide as if he had never heard it before. He pressed on, "You must have read that Moses was the first to announce God's promise to send an anointed one: The Messiah?"

"You don't have to draw pictures!" Zohar shouted. Then he demanded smugly, "If angels exist why can't I see them?"

"If one sat across from you, you would deny his existence," the boy pointed to the young priest beside him who nodded emphatically.

"Because there is no one there," Zohar snapped stiffly.

Yeshua looked at the old priest then at the young priest beside him, with disbelief.

The big door opened and they saw his Excellency, Ananas, the High Priest enter donning his rich colorful robe and the breast plate studded with rare jewels. Everyone stood at attention as the newcomer took a place between the two priests, opposite Yeshua and the young priest. He sat down and motioned them to do the same.

"How are you doing with our star scholar?" Ananas asked in a very distinct high pitched voice. Before anyone could answer, he addressed the youth with a smile which did not mask his smugness, "I'm sure our religious leaders have impressed you...not many intellects up in the backwoods of Galilee..?"

Yeshua replied with a disarming smile, "I have had better discourses and less dogma with our simple rabbi...in the backwoods of Galilee your Excellency."

Ananas' smile froze, and his intuition warned him this young man was a trouble maker. Galilee always produced those types, he thought.

Zohar saw the perfect opening and moved in for revenge, "The young pup says he intends to be the new High Priest!" He watched Ananas' face turning red, so aimed his words carefully and threw them like poisoned darts, "He says he is a descendant of King David...therefore has priority to your office...Perhaps you should tender your resignation," he punctuated his sarcasm with a malicious laughter.

Ananas leaned over until he stood almost over the boy, "My resignation? When do you propose to push me out my office you precocious little pup?" His high pitched voice climbed into falsetto threatening to crack.

But Zohar was just beginning, "Your Excellency, he is also a lover of all the superstitious rubbish we abhor: angels, magic...even that fraud Messiah."

Ananas shrieked, "Irreligious libertine: What have you to say?"

Yeshua was so shocked he blurted out, "Tradition says ... the Messiah will...come...to save..."

The High Priest shouted, striking his fist on the table, "The great Messiah! The savior! Liberator of Israel," he spat out sardonically, "just like he did some thirteen years ago. A bright star appeared and everyone was talking about the Messiah's birth. They planned an uprising. It upset King Herod so, he sent out the army to kill all new born children. That's what the Messiah caused!"

Zohar added spitefully, "Today a dozen Messiahs trek the countryside. All promising cures, miracles for a heavy price..."

"Taking the last drachmas from destitute peasants…The Messiah is a fraud on simple peasants!" Ananas concurred.

Yeshua apologized weakly, "People need someone…give them hope."

"Hard work is what they need, not miracles."

The boy tried one last defense, "Master Zohar agreed Lord Adonai can empower the Messiah…"

The High Priest lost all self control, "If a Messiah ever comes to Jerusalem, he will leave on a slab!"

Yeshua froze on the bench. Even master Gera did not dare to interrupt.

Master Zohar moved in for the kill, "Your Excellency is there a way we can nullify this blasphemer's bar mitzvah? Clearly he does not deserve to be part…"

Master Gera interrupted striking the table, "Have you no decency? He earned the right to be part of the congregation."

The High Priest heard enough, "Stop it! Let's not cause dissention over a worthless peasant. Nothing will happen to the Galilean." He turned to Zohar adding apologetically, "How did we miss the Galilean trait? It is his rabbi's fault. Didn't he petition that we allow an outcast to come for the bar mitzvah as well?"

Master Zohar nodded emphatically, "He argued vehemently that we make an exception. Imagine, an outcast in the House of the Lord."

"We'll have to remember him," the High Priest concurred.

At that moment the big door flung open interrupting them. They could discern a man standing in the shaft of light. As the door closed, they saw a bearded stranger coming towards them. Suddenly he stopped, "Yeshua! They said you were here,"

"Father," the boy ran into his father's embrace.

Master Zohar interrupted "Is this your son?"

Joseph gushed proudly, "I see you met him. Is he not a fountain of knowledge?"

"A raging flood," Ananas spat out frostily.

"A bursting dam," Zohar snapped.

"That is what everybody says," Joseph continued. "His mother and I almost reached Nazareth before discovering he was missing. Can you believe that?"

"Pity you remembered," master Zohar muttered into his beard.

Ananas pointed his bony finger at Joseph as he began to stand up, "Take this precocious monster back to Nazareth and never come back. If I ever see either of you again..." his high pitched voice screeched and finally cracked.

Joseph did not wait for him to finish. Seeing the High Priest's veins stand out on his neck, he grabbed the boy, who, while trying to escape ran into his father, both almost tripping, trying to exit. They ran along the dark corridor, out of the building, hardly touching the marble steps going down, grabbed their donkey which waited laden with camping gear. The animal almost toppled when Joseph yanked the lead rope, and they ran through the narrow streets and out of the city gate. They did not slow down until they were many miles from the city walls.

Joseph looked worried and when he spoke he said gruffly, "You will have a lot of explaining to do to the rabbi. Everything points to one of your unprovoked arguments you delight to start..."

He glared sternly at the boy for an explanation. However Yeshua was trying to resolve a much bigger problem. Ever since he could remember he wanted to be the High Priest of the Temple in Jerusalem. His lineage was from the House of David which was royal blood. He had no concept of the office or its responsibilities, only that he represented Lord Adonai. But, today he became bitterly disappointed. They were not representing a Creator or a loving faith. They were greedy for power, and full of prejudiced opinions. For the first time he realized why Esau, his closest friend and an outcast, was refused the bar mitzvah. The decision was not based on love, Judaism or Lord Adonai; it was the prejudice of mean spirited old men.

Yeshua announced to his father, "Father I no longer wish to be the High Priest."

Joseph shrugged his shoulders, "You will have to explain that one to your mother."

Yeshua nodded. He expected she would be disappointed but would understand when he told her. They continued walking for a while when the boy remembered something said back at the Temple, which bothered him. He turned to his father, "Why did the High Priest and master Zohar call the Messiah a fraud?"

joseph stared at his son for a long time, beginning to understand the gist of the argument. He considered carefully before responding, "The wealthy establishment is afraid he may lead a rebellion to liberate Israel."

"Don't they want Israel liberated?"

"The rich, the priests, the merchants, and the tax collectors like the way things are. Oh, outwardly they make a show and lament the loss of their kingdom. But, these wealthy nabobs and money lenders would be quite upset if a real revolution started. If they got liberated the peasants would demand rights and freedoms…" he noticed that the boy showed great interest, so stopped to explain, "Take the tax collector. He has to collect an amount for Rome. Did you know he adds one quarter more just for himself? If we were free that would stop!"

"No wonder they're afraid. They said the he was born about thirteen years ago…That would make him my age…?"

Joseph felt a tingle run up his spine and the small hair rise on his neck. He did not know what to say, so started walking staring directly ahead. But he could feel his son's radiant gaze burning. He could invent an answer, but did not want to lie. Suddenly an idea popped in his head and he blurted out, "We moved to Egypt at the time…" then frantically tried to change the topic, a trick his wife often used, "So what did you say to make them so angry?"

"They were not all angry. The young priest liked my answers."

"What young priest?"

"He sat to my right. You had to see him before you saw me!"

Joseph studied his son, and mentally tried to place every person he saw in that room. Granted he was there but a few moments, yet he remembered everyone except a young priest. He asked, "Explain to me precisely where everyone sat."

"Across from me was master Zohar, the High Priest in the middle and master Gera on the other side. On my right sat the young priest."

Joseph went over it again and again and came up with three persons plus his son, but no priest. Then he thought perhaps he missed him because it was a dark room, and was about to say so when the boy added, "He wore a white cloak and really stood out."

As soon as he said it, Yeshua felt a pain in the pit of his stomach. Did it happen again? Did he imagine a person who really was not there…? Or, that nobody but he could see? He remembered master Zohar pointing to the Priest saying there was nobody there or he'd see him. These strangers only appeared in times of crisis…like guardian angels, he thought. But he decided to drop the matter.

Fortunately the old patriarch also decided not to pursue it. This was not the first time his son mentioned someone that neither he nor his wife Miriam saw. It did not occur often, but when it did, it perturbed him. Not that he suspected his son of suffering illusions. On the contrary he believed the youth did see whom he said he saw. And he believed his son saw a young priest beside him. The trouble was that no one else saw him. Joseph realized it was only a matter of time before this would create great embarrassment, if not trouble, for his son. Therefore, once again, he concluded this was their fault, as parents, for not revealing the true identity to their son.

From the time of the boy's birth Joseph and Miriam argued over the appropriate time to tell him the truth. Joseph wanted to tell him as soon as he could understand it, but his wife disagreed. She contended it was both dangerous and irresponsible to tell the boy too soon. Dangerous to the public for the infant may, in a fit of anger or to amuse himself, inadvertently cause injury to someone. And irresponsible for if the authorities learned of the child's supernatural gifts, they would surely take him away. Emperors' courts, generals' quarters and wealthy lords' castles were full of mystics, astrologers, soothsayers and fortune tellers to foretell the future or perform magic. They could easily kidnap or take the child away by force and put him among the servants for their pleasure.

Joseph sneered at his wife's paranoia until an event proved her correct. The boy was not yet five years old in school when one day he misbehaved and the school master tried to punish him. When he reached out to wring the boy's ear, his arm was caught in an invisible vice grip and began to twist in pain. Then it slowly withered before his eyes. Nobody in town could explain the cause of the strange paralysis-- nobody but Yeshua's parents. They suspected he had something to do with it. They were wrong. Unbeknownst to their son, some invisible force intervened to protect the boy. Nevertheless Miriam pleaded with her son every night to pray for the school master to recover. The boy maintained he was mean and steadfastly refused. The impasse continued for almost a week when he relented and prayed for him. He was cured immediately. The school master had accused the boy of demonic powers causing his paralysis, so he packed his suitcases and fled Nazareth, never to return.

Yeshua asked his mother if his prayers cured him, but she fabricated a story about a brilliant young medicine man passing by and prescribing a miraculous potion.

For thirteen years Joseph and Miriam lived with a blessing, an enigma and fabricated stories. When someone needed a cure, the mother persuaded the boy to pray or go and do something special. After the miracle she invented myriad explanations to explain it. Then the parents argued. That was the only source of friction between them when Joseph threatened to reveal the true identity to the boy.

Today's event revived all the past arguments and made Joseph extremely angry. The arguments with his wife, the threats by the Priests and the name calling against the Messiah caused him to make an impulsive decision: to tell Yeshua the truth that very day! He had the perfect excuse to do it. Today Yeshua became a man with all the rights and responsibilities of an adult. Even in the eyes of Lord Adonai, Yeshua was a man. In the Israeli tradition Adonai would only come in the midst of a congregation composed of ten adults of their faith. From this day Yeshua would be counted as one of the congregants. Therefore, Joseph reasoned he must be told he was the son of God!

Joseph knew he was prone to making impulsive decisions which led to troubles with Miriam, but this time he decided not to back down. His boy was a man, and a man must be told the truth. Moreover he was captivated by the persuasive reasoning of Adonai and the Congregation. A popular old saying went thus: Adonai will not come to nine rabbis, but will to ten street sweepers. Yeshua was counted as an important member of society. Miriam would be swept up by his logic. Moreover, he mused, by the time she would find out the deed would be done.

Once he resolved to tell him everything, he decided to do it promptly and without delay; tonight, after dinner, by the soothing, relaxing camp fire.

With the decision made, he began to plan how to tell him: the blunt statement and get it over with; or spin the entire story, filling it with details, both relevant and irrelevant hoping he would deduce the message. He debated the styles at length and in the end he chose to rely on his instincts and the mood of the moment. He always preferred the impulsive style.

Late afternoon they set up camp, raised the tent, gathered wood and started a fire, cooked dinner, ate it leisurely, cleaned up, and sat back to enjoy the silence of the night under a star studded sky.

But Joseph was not able to relax. After deciding to reveal his son's identity, he could not find a moment of peace. He knew the boy would ask many questions, as he always did, so he spent all the time framing explanations. He expected the boy to refute them as lame excuses and transparent fabrications. He was sure they would end up arguing, make accusations and probably break all communications. The fear of this occurring bothered him until he could not find peace. He thought about it as they walked, then his mind was overwhelmed by it while he poured water into the pot overfilling it and putting out the fire. Then he cut his thumb while peeling potatoes. He almost burnt dinner and did not enjoy one bite of it. He hated cleaning up, and now the infernal noise of the frogs and crickets annoyed him. In short, he was in a foul mood. Angry and confused he wavered and almost favored postponing the decision which infuriated him even more, so he resolved again – for the last time – to tell Yeshua the whole truth! He turned to his son, fixed his eyes on him as he sat daydreaming serenely across the fire. When he called out his baritone voice came unnaturally loud.

"Yeshua!" the loud baritone even stopped the frogs and crickets, as if they too wished to hear the confession. But the boy continued absorbed in his thoughts. "Yeshua!!" the old man called louder still.

The boy sat up surprised, "Yes, father?"

Joseph looked deeply into his son's eyes, "Son there is something… important I wish…must tell you." Then his mind falterd and stared at him blankly.

After a long pause as they sat staring at each other, the boy asked, "Father? Did you wish to say something?"

"The truth," Joseph blurted out. "I must say it… the truth you should have been told long ago…the truth about you… Do you understand?"

Yeshua nodded mechanically, "Yes, father…" but as he contemplated his eye brows furrowed and he started to shake his head, "No, father…"

Joseph continued to gaze at the boy. He kept thinking, the truth, and nothing less…but Yeshua's eyes seemed to radiate a deep light like a distant beacon, and this unnerved the old Patriarch. He stuttered and muttered a few false openings and finally stopped. There seemed to be some interference and slowly in his mind's vision he saw it forming; it was Miriam standing before him looking sternly, disapprovingly…

"Father, do you wish to say something?" Yeshua was curious about the enigmatic opening. "Did you say I have lived a lie all these years?"

Joseph knew he was caught. His mind searched frantically for a plausible explanation hoping something would come up as he muttered, "Well…yes…no…that is not what I want to say…" but he could not think of what he wanted to say. Suddenly an inspiring thought appeared,

"What I really wanted to say, was… Let's not tell anybody what happened back there at the Temple. Why cause unnecessary worry?" He chuckled weakly. "We'll just say that you had a good, long conversation with the priests and scholars of the Sanhedrin…"

Yeshua studied his father for some moments, considered the statement and smiled, nodding, "That is the truth. I did have a good long discussion…" Then he leaned back and returned to his dreams.

Joseph sighed, wiped off the perspiration from his forehead and leaned back. He could still see Miriam's face against the stars, but now she was smiling pleasantly. Then he also began to hear the crackling of the fire, the frogs and crickets and smiled delighted. He had rarely enjoyed a more peaceful, inspirational night.

CHAPTER I - A CRISIS OF FAITH

"Yeshua!"

No Answer.

"Yeshua! Breakfast!"

No answer.

Miriam peered out of the window up to the two rooms on top of the roof but it was still too dark to see. She raised the oil lamp, but its anemic flame did not help. She debated going up to awaken her son but the cool air of the morning made her shiver so she desisted. Instead she turned to her husband sitting on the mats enjoying the warmth of the fire. "Joseph, go up there and give him a shake," she pleaded.

He sighed and yawned, hoping she would go away. When she did not, he mumbled, "Modern youth! They grow so fast, I swear the skin covers their hearing!"

He took her oil lamp and left. At the door he stopped, picked up the broom, and walked back to a spot directly below Yeshua's room. He thrust the end of the broom upwards striking the mud-packed ceiling repeatedly, bellowing with his strong baritone, "Yeshua. Breakfast!"

His yelling jolted Miriam who had started making breakfast, and she stared at him with disbelief. It awoke the youngest children who saw the strange sight; their father attacking the ceiling with the broom. Suddenly it broke through, sending a shower of straw and dust on him. He released it to protect himself, and it remained stuck.

Miriam deadpanned, "Why did I not think of that?"

Joseph glared at her, spat dust and dirt while brushing his hair, and marched to the door, "I'll have to drag his Royal Highness from the cot! When I was his age..." he muttered going out.

Within moments the door opened and Yeshua, a youth almost nineteen years of age entered, carrying an oil lamp in his left hand, a measuring stick, compasses and stylus in his right, and a few pages of papyrus under his arm. He almost collided with the broom, stopped, turned to his mother, his face a question mark.

"Ask your father," she shrugged.

At that moment Joseph re- entered, "He's not in his…" stopping when he saw his son. "Why don't you answer when called?"

Yeshua saw the dust and straw on his father's thick hair, glanced at the broom smirking, "I see…" Then he explained, "I was in my work shed, re-doing the figures, and re-designing the plans." He smiled and offered the bundle under his arm, "Take the papyrus. I think you'll agree; I solved the problems." They sat by the fire, "I redesigned the sailboat completely, taking out the leeboards and giving it a new modern contour." He flipped the papyrus to a page and pointed, "The most modern boat in Galilee?"

They sat on mats of palm fronds covering the ground, while Miriam dished out porridge, poured goat milk and topped it with honey. Then she cut a thick slice of rye bread and poured some oil and vinegar in a small dish for dipping, "Eat while it is hot."

Yeshua watched his father studying the designs, stroking his long salt and pepper beard, smacking his lips, his eyebrows furrowing, all the while mumbling. The youth suspected his father did not understand the drawings, so leaned over pointing, "This is the profile of the boat from bow to stern. Remember how it had two wings on the sides – the leeboards?" He saw the old man shake his head so reminded him, "You called them elephant's ears…Well they are out. See how I made the bottom of the boat deeper? My invention, I'll call the keel. It will work like leeboards."

"You moved the leeboards from the top to the bottom? Why?"

"I took them out entirely. The keel is better!"

The old man studied it for a long time then said with a hint of sarcasm, "Keel! You changed the leeboards and gave it a new name."

Yeshua sighed and tried to explain patiently, "On the top they were hinged, awkward to work, always a danger in a storm. A keel is an integral part of the boat, sturdy, and it will track the course better." He smiled and when he saw the patriarch's eyebrows rise, he added, "I'll fill it with heavy stones!"

Joseph's mouth dropped, "Why? So it will sink?"

"The keel, I'll only fill the keel. The weight will keep it upright…"

Joseph persisted, "Fill it with stones and the first wave will swamp it."

"I redesigned the beem, making the boat wider, and raised the topsides so it will be higher above the water. A full gale won't sink it!"

The old man reconsidered the designs and nodded. It was obvious the youth had thought of everything. He knew he should be proud of him, but he could not hide his disappointment. "So, you don't want to be a carpenter...Have you no respect for our tradition?"

Yeshua raised his hands to the heavens in desperation, "Tradition! All you keep saying is tradition! Where is it written that if the oldest son does not follow his father's trade he failed?" He knew he was hurting him and tried to lessen the pain, "Being a fisherman is more dependable. You admitted carpentry is fickle. You were right. A little misunderstanding and what did your customers do? Cancelled all work orders leaving us destitute. No work, no food: Just like that!"

"They'll be back. They always have in the past," the patriarch said.

"Four times they did this. I was forced to leave school to help the family. Carpentry is serfdom; you eat or starve at the whim of the customers!"

"Don't forget your sermon started this," the old patriarch retorted accusingly. "Were you trying to start a riot in the Synagogue?"

"I had to stir the peasants into action..."

"Start a war with the Romans?"

"No!" Yeshua snapped impatiently. "Our real oppressors are our own Israeli rulers and the priests of the Temple."

"So, you plan to overthrow our moral leaders?"

"They took power from the people and control of their lives. They separated the people from their God. Then, they put priests between them. Now they control everything; politics, religion and economics. And today people cannot utter Yahweh's name on pain of death."

"So you intend to lead them in some insane uprising?"

The young man shook his head, "They pray for a miracle-man to lead them...a Messiah. Why not fight for it ourselves?"

"Utter God's name and they'll charge you with blasphemy" Joseph said.

Yeshua wondered what his parents would say if they knew that he was considering quitting religion altogether ...perhaps even Yahweh?

Miriam worried their discussion was on the brink of an argument, and touched her son's shoulder, "Why don't you two eat while the porridge is hot? My mother said all problems evaporate when the stomach is full."

The two men knew they were tilling the same ground as yesterday, and the previous week since the crisis two months ago. Their positions were entrenched neither of them backing down. So they picked up the bowls and dug in hungrily. They were almost finished when Joseph picked up the papyrus. "The designs are excellent…but, you forgot the most important thing." The old man enjoyed the puzzled look on his son's face, "Mo-ney; money for wood, glue, nails, sails…and all the rest. Where are you going to find money?" He waited before adding, "Carpentry! Carpentry pays well…"

Yeshua could not help a spontaneous laughter, "Carpentry? All you give me to do is sieves. For two treacherous months I manufactured sieves; big sieves, little sieves, sieves for sand, sieves for flour! I will not save one shekel…"

The old man moaned, "I only get meager…copper penny contracts…"

The young man felt guilty for his outburst, took a stick and moved some embers around, "It's my fault! If I had not given that sermon there would not have been a riot. You would still have work, I would be in the lyceum…and…"

Miriam interjected, "It's too late to blame yourself now. Besides, your sermon was…" She searched for a positive expression without success.

Joseph tried to help, "Much of it was wise. The unwise part was…to say it to our congregation. Israelis don't appreciate being told they are narrow minded bigots."

Yeshua conceded, "Like they say: You'll move a pyramid before you change the mind of an Israeli. I have resolved: never to give another sermon in Nazareth!"

"I should say not!" Both parents concurred in perfect unison.

The young man smiled speaking with renewed enthusiasm, "As to money, I have a plan: to sell the rights to the boat to anyone who helps build it, or supply material."

Miriam who was dressing up the two youngest children asked, "Did you forget? No one in Nazareth will speak to us. We're worse than lepers."

The young man smiled expansively, "My friends, masters Marcus, Daniel, Esau and the others will organize the people, material, construction… Esau will manage!"

His parents looked at him apprehensively. "Esau? You want an outcast to manage the project?" Miriam questioned the decision.

"This is his chance to prove himself," Yeshua responded assertively.

"Where money is concerned, Israelis are tighter than the skin on a goat!" Joseph reminded him.

"If that doesn't succeed, I have another project that may prove profitable," The young man grinned coyly. "It's still on a trial basis…"

"The carvings under the canvas in your workshop?" Joseph asked.

"Master El Sharif suggested I do a couple of samples," Yeshua explained. "I hope he approves. He'll take them on the caravan and test the market"

"Is he not overdue? He should have passed through," master Joseph queried.

Yeshua nodded, "Overdue by more than a week. I've noticed before, whenever he returns to Persia he is a few days late."

Yeshua noticed someone peek in, make eye contact then go out again. "Esau has arrived. I want to see him… Thanks for breakfast, mother." He picked up his work and left. Outside the sun was quickly shortening the shadows. The friends nodded without exchanging pleasantries, and went to Yeshua's work shed. Esau was a youth of the same age, a tall fellow who walked stooped and sounded as if constantly pleading.

"Did you want to see me?"

"Yes," Yeshua placed the papyrus on the work bench, then swept his hands over the designs as if introducing royalty, "Feast your eyes on these magnificent designs and confess: they're the most beautiful drawings your eyes ever beheld!"

Esau turned the pages, studying every detail and finally passing judgment, "These are the most beautiful drawings I have every beheld. What is it?"

Yeshua was scandalized, "Don't you recognize a sailboat?" He was shocked when his friend shook his head. He explained every page, "This is called a diagram. It presents the plan of the boat from every angle: here is the profile looking from the starboard side; the bow, the stern; this is the top side; here's the keel."

"Oh!"

Yeshua expanded his dream with enthusiasm, "When we build it, we'll sail the seas, go fishing and sell the catch, then sail for adventures beyond the horizon."

"Hold it! Hold it!" Esau stood back, "Go back…before we went over the horizon. Did you say, 'When we build it?' "

"Just think; no people, no problems! Just the serene blue water and the blue sky..." the young man smiled effusively with a dreamy look in his eyes.

"Me, build a boat?" Esau looked skeptical. "I have never built anything. What do I know about boats? I could not tell the front from...the bow!"

"See? Perfect," Yeshua gushed. "You will be the ideal project manager."

Esau's eyes popped and he mouthed the words without making a sound, "M-me: M-manager? I have never managed anything."

The young man exclaimed ecstatically, "It's uncanny: a blank mind - no preconceived notions, no opinions. It's like a dry sponge sucking up knowledge then teaching the crew...managing, leading and guiding!"

"Whoa! Not so fast! Why do you bother with me: a dry sponge? Why not Marcus? He is a born leader. Full of confidence."

Yeshua put an arm around his shoulder, "Before making the decision, I deliberated and debated everything. You are the best person for the job."

"Really?"

"You are my man!"

Esau was overwhelmed, for he rarely received compliments, "I...I don't know what to say. But, I cannot say no to you. When do we start building - today?"

"There is one minor problem. We don't have any wood...or money to buy it. No material, no glue, or nails... no pitch, canvas, or ropes..."

"What do we have?"

"An idea...and these drawings."

Esau stammered, "I--I take it back. I'll say no to you. Building a boat is tough enough. Building it from nothing calls for a miracle. That's not my domain."

He began to walk away. Yeshua caught up, put his arm around his shoulder to persuade him, "Wait! I have a plan. We'll find people with money, access to material, workers. We'll sell rights to the boat. They'll sail, fish, and dream." When he finished they were walking back to the shed.

"When you say 'We'll find investors', is it the same we who are building it?"

Yeshua nodded. Esau turned to walk out again, "I don't know any people with money, or material. Where to look for them? What to say when I find them?"

Yeshua quickly stood in front blocking his exit, "You won't have to look further than our friends in the lyceum. Masters Marcus, Daniel,

Ahmed…the ultra conservative boys. Sell them the dream; sail the blue waters to far off shores…beyond the sunset. Sell them the adventure, excitement of discovery…Then tell them to buy into their dream."

Esau was tempted, almost persuaded to accept the challenge, but a lifetime of fear gripped him and he mumbled, "I don't know anybody with money…"

Yeshua grinned, "Turn any Israeli upside down, give a shake and it will rain shekels."

The companion asked, "Who shall make up the building crew?"

"School friends; masters Marcus, Ahmed, Daniel…"

Esau moaned, "I'm an outcast. They'll refuse to work with me."

"On this project there will be no outcast. If they don't, others will."

Esau looked at his friend with awe and admiration. He had a way of saying something that made a person feel special, unique. He had an invisible aura that attracted and persuaded everyone around him. They looked into his radiant eyes and believed. He heard a small voice inside say, 'jump, take the chance.' Finally, he took a deep breath and muttered, "I'd like to, but…"

Yeshua hugged him, crushing him with exuberance, "I knew I could count on you! Esau this is the first day of your new life. And, I'll stand by you."

"Do you really believe I can do it?"

"You're the best. You could sell sand to the nomads of the desert," Yeshua roared with enthusiasm, watching his friend. "Starting today after school I'll start teaching you how to construct a boat. Tomorrow you'll teach them"

"Will they listen to…?" But he did not finish.

Yeshua exclaimed, "Their cumulative knowledge about boats can be scribed on a grain of sand. You will appear wiser than Moses, more stately than Abraham. You will stand shoulder to shoulder with the great admiral – NOAH!"

Esau repeated with admiration, "Noah's Ark! That's what I'll be building." Then he queried, "Where did you learn to build a boat?"

"Last year during school holidays I worked for Master Hariph in Capernaum, remember? In daytime I worked for the scribe, in the evenings I walked the shores of the Sea of Galilee. I met an old master shipwright. He could shape a piece of wood into anything. He spent days teaching, explaining, drawing…"

"Does that mean you're not returning to the lyceum?"

The question shook Yeshua and he was not certain how to answer, "I want to...but cannot afford it."

"Exams are only a month away," he said and saw his friend's spirit deflate. "The schoolmaster said you'll be returning any day..."

Yeshua smiled, "Is master Ben Joseph into miracles? I need one."

Esau started to draw random patterns with his sandal in the dust, a sign he wanted to change topics. At last he commented, "That sermon. You should not have..."

The young man interrupted, "That's history...forget it."

But he persisted "Go to the church elders. Plead forgiveness..."

"They banished us although we were not ordered to leave town. They prefer to see us starve slowly."

Esau who grew up apologizing even when he was right could not understand this, but admired his courage. "I'll be off to school", he began to shuffle away with his friend accompanying him. At the gate he murmured with a quivering voice, "Thank you...nobody ever trusted me before."

Yeshua slapped his back, but when he saw his friend leave he noticed a tear drop from his face. He returned to the workshop, donned his apron, picked up a small board with a work order: "Sieves – 35 large; 45 medium; 90 small."

He sighed: how desperately boring this was. But, he had no option, so picked up a round form, adjusted the two ends to a pre-measured mark for small frames and locked it in place. His hands automatically reached for a pile of thin, pre-cut branches, bent one carefully to fit inside the frame, cut off the excess, joined the ends and fastened them. He took the branch out, put another in the frame repeating the work. This gave him two pieces; top and bottom. Between them he placed a precut net, joined the two halves, giving them one twist until they locked. One sieve was completed. It was repetitious, mindless work.

When he first started to make sieves, he picked up a thin branch fastened the ends without giving attention to what he was doing. He continued the repetitious and boring labor while his mind long ago wondered into a world of fantasy. At the end of the day he re-did dozens of sieves because of the atrocious mess he had created. After many days of abysmal failures he feared that unless he found a solution for this mindless work he would go insane.

That inspired him to design a sieve with interchangeable parts that could be fitted into place one way: the correct way. The parts could be fastened without being checked.

After long days of trials and errors he solved the problem and was pleased with the results. He always referred to it as his first miracle. But, he was wrong!

He took it to his father's work shed, certain the patriarch would be pleased to see the new, improved modern sieve. He had visions of soaring profits, and hoped the extra earnings would enable him to return to the lyceum.

Master Joseph was most impressed. He congratulated his son for the superb invention. Then he announced proudly that he would lower the price for manufacturing sieves and corner the market. He was correct. They cornered it so well Yeshua could never keep up with the orders, even if he slaved around the hourglass. He was never more bored or under greater pressure, without a noticeable increase in profits.

By noon he was back to the same drudgery. His daydreaming was constant, and his spirit like the birds of the wild soared over the valleys and the Sea of Galilee. So he started to dream about sailing. That day he did the first drawings of the sailboat.

He thought about the sermon two months ago. He remembered his father asking, "Were you trying to start a riot?"

There was no easy explanation why he did it. It was not an impulsive decision. Like a seed it germinated in his mind for years before it sprouted and took life.

As a child he read the ancient scriptures where the Creator was described as a loving God, close and intimate with the people. Later, authors started describing Him as an Israeli God, a jealous Creator, too quick to punish and slow to love. They changed Him into a tribal God, relevant only to the tribes of Israel. The nation's rulers led the people to wars in the name of this tribal God. Later still, they purported to speak for God, and now forbade them to say His name.

During this transformation of God, there was a major change in the people. Once independent and confident, Israelis became subjugated by the rulers and the priests. They lost their confidence and sense of purpose. Presently they were oppressed by their rulers   in conspiracy with the Romans.

His sermon was to reintroduce the loving Creator back into their lives, and persuade the people to take control of their affairs.

Alas, he did not get a chance to explain himself. The congregants rioted and demanded he be charged and stoned.

He was so stunned that he made two decisions: give up Judaism and to become a fisherman. But, he only confided this decision to a few close friends, and not his parents.

Giving up carpentry was easier. He had been forced to suspend his education before when customers did not pay their bills or there was no work. Fishing would be different. People had to eat, so they would buy all he caught and would have to pay for the fish.

He chuckled at the cruel irony: Israel's most promising scholar relegated to the mindless, uninspiring construction of sieves.

Could he sink lower? He wondered.

He felt saddest for his youngest siblings, for they were punished, yet had done no wrong. Neighbors chased them from their yards. They were verbally abused; rocks were thrown at them, and they were beaten up. Playmates refused to come so they played alone like the kids in leprosy camps.

Only two persons of the thousands in the valley remained steadfast, and stood up courageously to the town regardless of consequences; rabbi Ezra ben Lebbus whom everybody held in low esteem for his simple scholastic ability, and the schoolmaster Ben Joseph. The rabbi proved a valuable ally, stopping the elders from laying blasphemy charges. The school master who was always impressed with Yeshua's scholastic ability, offered to pay for the young man's education so he could graduate from the lyceum. Joseph thanked him but refused charity.

Yeshua's closest friends, stood by him bravely. Alas, they were an assortment of rejects and outcasts, absolutely powerless within the community. He always supported the oppressed and underdogs, and attracted such types.

He was deeply in thought about the events of the past two months and did not hear his name called until the second time.

"Master Yeshua are you there?" he heard a male voice.

Almost simultaneously he saw a schoolmate in the doorway. It was master Marcus, whose nickname was "Greco-Roma-Jew", a handsome lad of eighteen, with a strong physique, exuding confidence. He was the tallest and strongest of Yeshua's friends. His friends teased him because as Israelis his family behaved as chameleons: when Greece conquered the world they adopted the Hellenist culture, and now that Rome was master they were more Roman than the Romans.

Yeshua met him at the door, shook hands, studying his friend closely as he could be volatile. He noticed his friend frowning and decided to pepper him with questions, "Coming from school? How are you? Study anything interesting today?" Marcus nodded stiffly, remaining serious, which warned Yeshua to expect a heated exchange. He tried to avoid confrontation by changing topics, "I was told exams are only a month away…Are you ready? Are you still having problems with abstract courses; geometry, algebra; logic? Can I be of help?"

"I don't want your help!" Marcus refused to take the bait. Then he jumped into the subject troubling him, "I should be the project manager. Am I not the hardest worker?"

"The hardest and the best," the young scholar nodded emphatically.

Marcus did not expect his friend to agree so readily, and for a moment stood confused, before returning to the attack, "So…you admit I am the most qualified?"

"To build it," Yeshua concurred then added judicially, "You will be the perfect lead man. The team will emulate you and work hard. It will make Esau's job as manager easier."

Marcus was perplexed, "Don't you want the best qualified, most confident person to lead the crew?"

"Therein lies the problem. In the matter of qualifications of building boats, you are pretty equal; zero knowledge or experience. An overconfident person will mask his ignorance by confrontation with the crew resulting in poor and unsafe construction."

"I would never do that!"

"But your vanity will. Unsafe construction of a boat does not show up until a storm, with disastrous consequences. So, by not choosing you, I will be saving your life!"

Marcus threw his arms in the air ranting, "I hate it when you argue like that!" He paced back and forth arguing, "I feel you just carved out my heart, for which I should be thankful. Sometimes I feel you don't want to be my friend."

"Friendship brings heavy commitments. A friend should be free to speak the truth, however ugly it sounds, and the other must accept it. And, friends must help friends…"

"This has nothing to do with qualifications, and everything to do with Esau…" He waited for his friend to deny it and when he did not, Marcus continued, "Need I remind you this is about boat building, not building an outcast's confidence?"

"Are they separable?" Yeshua walked up to his friend, "In his case they are one and the same. Esau is depending on your support. And so am I."

"I did not cause his problems. I think I have always treated him fairly, but I refuse to give him special treatment."

Yeshua raised his voice, "Why not? Our religion crushed his confidence, and will do so for the rest of his life. Is it not up to us to help him?"

"How did a simple boat construction become entangled with the country's religion? It's a simple question: the best man for the job — That's me!"

"Unfortunately life is more complex…," Yeshua responded.

"Only around you," Marcus interrupted. "To me the issue is simple: only the strongest survive! The weak can…perish, for all I care."

"Have you noticed the privileged and powerful always say that? Would you say that if you were the outcast?"

"I did not make him an outcast," Marcus defended himself uncomfortably.

"When you support an unjust rule you may as well be its author," the young scholar retorted. They stood facing each other, neither giving way, both realizing they were pushing their friendship to the limit. He decided to try persuasion, "When I told him the news his eyes lit up…with pride and fear. Will you help me, and support him?"

Marcus snarled dryly, "So you lied to him, and now beg me to save your skin…"

"I did not lie! He is sensitive, eager and a great team member: qualities of a leader."

"Those are qualities of a wimp. A leader must be strong and assertive. Demanding! Unrelenting! That's how the Romans conquered the world."

"You're not a Roman. Why do you push their agenda?" Yeshua rebuked him.

Marcus realized that no amount of argument would persuade him, so he kicked the dirt moodily, shuffling away slowly, "Will you forsake all your friends for one outcast?"

Yeshua did not reply. Marcus sighed and turned to leave, hesitating, hoping his friend would have a change of heart. When he saw Esau entering the yard, he quickened his step to the gate. They passed each other hardly nodding in silence.

"Is he the new manager?" Esau inquired not raising his eyes off the ground.

"You won't get off that easy!"

Esau looked up surprised and pleased, "I know he is the better man, but I do not want to give it up…"

"Are you nervous?" The young scholar asked and his friend nodded jerkily. "After lyceum you will start the lessons. Once you learn terms, measurements, angles and the principles, you'll relax. But, I warn you, there will be problems, so be ready."

They were interrupted by voices in the yard. Yeshua looked out and recognized, masters Ahmed and Daniel. "Wait here while I find out what they want."

Ahmed stopped when he saw Yeshua come out, "Good day, my friend. We wanted to be the first to offer our labor on the project."

"After we settle a minor problem first," Daniel corrected him.

"That's right; after we settle a difference of opinion," Ahmed concurred. "Then the sailboat is as good as done."

Daniel interrupted, "You Syrians never get things right. Did you not hear Esau? It will be as big as Noah's Ark, maybe a ship!"

Yeshua glanced at Esau in the shed, who raised his shoulders guiltily. "I am glad you're joining, but it's a sailboat. Esau got carried away with enthusiasm,"

"Is that not what I said? The outcast can't get anything right," Daniel snapped. "If he can't tell a boat from an Ark, what kind of manager will he make?"

"Daniel is right," Ahmed demurred. "You should have chosen Marcus."

"Or either one of us. We know more about boats," Daniel opined.

Master Daniel stopped when he saw Esau come out with the papyrus. They greeted him with a curt nod which he did not acknowledge.

Yeshua took the papyrus, opened it and asked, "What is this drawing?" They studied the design for a few moments, tilting their heads one way, then the other, shaking their heads. Yeshua turned the page, "How about these two?" He held it out and they shrugged their shoulders. He turned to Esau.

"It's the profile of the boat from the starboard side," Esau emphasized the word. Yeshua turned the page, "The design on the top is the view of the bow, the bottom is the stern. To the uninitiated it is the front and back of the boat."

Yeshua folded the papyrus and watched his two friends' reactions.

"I must warn you: I have no money," master Ahmed announced defensively.

Yeshua smirked, "Spoken like a Syrian. Do you know why Syrian coins are thinner than Israelis'? Because you squeeze them tighter."

"Does the wood have to be long, thick...?" master Daniel tried to ease the tension.

"Anything will do," Yeshua replied.

They stood facing each other uneasily shuffling from one foot to the other. The newcomers were about to leave when Daniel turned to Esau, "I'm sorry you heard my comments."

"Do you think it hurts less if you keep your sentiments secret? I prefer prejudices in the open. It hurts less than being ambushed."

Master Daniel tried to deflect the criticism, "I don't think you are the right person for the position, that's all..."

Master Ahmed interjected, "What master Daniel is trying to say is, anyone can memorize a few drawings. But a manager must be...a special person."

"Can an outcast not be that?" Esau countered. "I'm surprised to hear that from a Syrian. Have you forgotten your complaints, 'I'm tired of being called a pagan. I am as good as any of them.'" Then he softened his tone, "When master Yeshua offered me the leadership, I admit, I was frightened. I was uncertain I could do it. But, I wanted it. Then I realized I feared it because all my life my friends encouraged those fears. They accepted me as long as I did not demand equality. No one encouraged me to tackle my fears, except Yeshua. Well, I refuse to live in the shadows. I want to prove I can be like the rest. Forget I'm an outcast and work with me. I need your support."

They looked down embarrassed and confused. Master Daniel was the first to ask, "What did master Marcus decide?"

"He's thinking about it," Esau replied.

Esau did not hide his disappointment, but did not argue. Instead he turned to Yeshua who warned them, "There are few vacancies, and I'm certain the manager will want to fill them right away: first come, first served."

The two friends were concerned but decided to take their chances. They began to leave when master Daniel suddenly turned, "I almost forgot. Four classmates, from the ultra conservative clan, wish to speak with you - out there. They refused to enter the yard."

They walked out to the street where four young Israelis, about seventeen, dressed in similar black robes waited. They bowed to Yeshua and the leader stepped forward, "Esau told us your plan to construct a ship to surpass Noah's Ark..." Yeshua glanced at Esau who blushed and looked away. "We wish to join this great venture..."

Yeshua replied enthusiastically, "Say no more. Presently the project manager seeks fine workers, and you seem excellent for the positions." He smiled confidently at Esau who nodded. Daniel and Ahmed stood back shocked, as Yeshua continued, "If you are not afraid to tackle the intricate profession of shipwrights, it is guaranteed to test your intellect and your mettle..."

Master Ahmed could not stand by watching his position given away, and stepped forward, "You can't give our jobs away." He looked at the four youths, "Sorry, all vacancies are taken, boys." He looked to master Daniel for support but when he did not speak up, the Syrian amended his statement, "At least I am committed."

"Me too," master Daniel stepped forward impulsively, and turned to Yeshua, "Give us a chance to speak to master Marcus. We'll persuade him."

"That's the manager's decision," Yeshua replied.

Master Ahmed announced impulsively, "Master Marcus is in. I'll speak to him." Then he turned to the youths, "Sorry fellows, better luck next time!"

They smiled broadly; happy to have their positions secured, bowed and bid a good day to them, and exited bouncing merrily along the road.

Surprised and shocked the four youths looked to Yeshua who explained, " Do not worry, there will be enough work for everybody."

The leader of the group nodded and said, "We wish to donate all the money we have to help start the project." One of the boys, obviously the treasurer came forward with a pouch of coins and gave it to Esau. "We will collect all the wood we find and bring it here."

"We are pleased to welcome you to the project. But, you must realize this is a sailboat not a ship," Yeshua clarified.

They smiled winking at one another. Before leaving the leader passed close to Yeshua leaned and confided in low voice, "We did not agree with our parents. We enjoyed your sermon."

The others nodded nervously grunting words of encouragement, then marched away quickly. Esau tossed the pouch in the air happily, but Yeshua contemplated the last statement seriously, visibly disturbed.

"I was impressed with your trick to get masters Daniel and Ahmed to join in," Esau chuckled with envy. "Using this group as decoy was a stroke of genius."

"It was no trick," the young scholar replied. "Those four would make excellent workers: eager, cooperative, and no arguments."

Esau handed the pouch to his friend, leaned closer and asked in a low voice, "Have you thought about it any more?" Yeshua stared back, and he clarified himself, "You're not serious about giving up Judaism?"

"Can you blame me? Look at them starving us...in the name of Yahweh...Who needs such a religion?"

"They've been doing it to me all my life, but I have not turned against God." Then he pleaded, "You must not do it. You promised, someday you would build a synagogue, and I would belong there. I was counting on you." He mumbled then turned and left.

Yeshua thought back to the eve of the bar mitzvah, over five years ago, when Esau was told as an outcast he could not go. Yeshua rebelled in sympathy and refused to go too. The outcast pleaded with him to go ahead, and when he grew up to build a church where people like him could belong. How could he have forgotten his promise?

He remembered what the ultra conservative boys said and it bothered him. During the sermon he noticed a clear division along generational and gender lines. While the old patriarchs screamed and threw objects, the younger congregants supported him. The old men jeered, while young ladies cheered. If they did not have him to attack, they might have gone at each other.

His desire to modernize Judaism, return it to the people, meant turning present social values on their heads. It meant he must clash with the establishment, and the religious leaders: in short, old men! The patriarchs wanted status quo because it was to their advantage. They could commit adultery, marry as many women as they desired or divorce their wives at a whim with impunity. The women hated that but were powerless.

Rabbi Ben Lebbus had warned him, "The old patriarchs will destroy everything before compromising. You may be swept up in the violence… and pay with your life."

That sermon shook him to the core. If he pushed his concepts for a Universal Creator, a personal relationship of love with Yahweh, he may rend families asunder: fathers against sons, old against young. That real possibility made him tremble with fear. Give up religion rather than risk an uprising, he concluded. He would become a sailor, a fisherman, even a vagabond, but never a religious leader of men.

Suddenly his youngest siblings, Judas and Salome, eight and six years of age ran by yelling and screaming into the safety of the house. He turned to see the cause while master Joseph came out from his work shed with a piece of lumber. They saw master El Sharif, an old friend and a potentate from Persia. He owned a caravan and traveled between Persia and Egypt. Joseph laughed, his rich baritone echoing beyond the yard. The childrens' shouts and Joseph's laughter brought out curious neighbors who lined up on the streets and roof tops to check out the commotion.

Master Joseph, the inveterate actor, saw the curious Israelis and put on an act speaking unusually loud, "Master El Sharif welcome, my wealthy Persian lord." He turned to the house continuing loudly, "Lady Miriam, our good friend the potentate is here, with servants loaded down with gifts: exotic silks from China, perfumes from India, soaps and jewels. Come and welcome our rich powerful friend."

Miriam rushed out of the house and ran into the Persian's arms who embraced her warmly. The little ones hung onto her dress.

"Welcome, master El Sharif," she greeted him cheerily.

"Lady Miriam, you look younger and more beautiful every time," he held her at his side. With his free arm he embraced her husband, "Look at you, Joseph: healthier and stronger than ever."

Joseph replied with a booming voice, "Never felt better! Our friends, the gentiles, fill our shops with work so we can barely keep up."

El Sharif peeked into the work shops and verified his suspicion: meager work and probably starvation wages. Nevertheless he joined the play-acting, "I confess I have rarely seen your shops so full. Quality work, good profits!" He turned to Miriam, "I brought you lovely gifts from the mysterious orient." He clapped his hands and servants handed her large canvas bags. He announced proudly pulling samples out, "Exotic perfumes from rare flowers, fine soaps for your delicate skin. Also the most colorful silks from China…and your favorites: myrrh and frankincense."

Miriam's emotions overflowed, as she hugged the potentate, "I love these. I'm eternally grateful." He blushed in his white beard.

El Sharif reached into a small bag and brought out two small balls wrapped in cloth, leaned over and gave them to the little ones still hiding behind the mother, "Something special for you: delicious sweets!"

Two little hands reached out, snatching them with the speed of lightning and hid behind the mother again.

"You must thank master El Sharif," Yeshua walked up smiling.

They said a quick "Thank you," but remained hidden.

Yeshua embraced the old friend.

Master Joseph motioned to him, "Come inside enjoy lunch with us."

"Thank you, but I have eaten", he demurred.

"Perhaps a goblet of wine?"

The potentate assented and they entered the house. Lady Miriam went to the far corner, poured some wine from a large jar into a smaller carafe, added some water and brought it, filling their goblets. They sat around the simmering fire.

El Sharif turned to the young scholar, "You are not in school. Is it a religious holiday?"

"No," he replied looking down embarrassed.

"I heard about your sermon," The Persian smiled. "It was the talk of the town in Capernaum."

"They're starved for news if our sermon is the highlight of that place," master Joseph scowled.

"On every corner people argued passionately. You must have shaken the foundation of your synagogue!" El Sharif commented.

"Never saw a more violent reaction," master Joseph volunteered. "I dragged out the family while ducking to avoid missiles flying from every quarter."

"How you exaggerate," Lady Miriam criticized. "I was only struck once!"

In his decades of travelling the potentate knew of no race as passionate about religion as the Israelis. He saw the young scholar's sad face and tried to lift his spirit, "Don't get discouraged. Continue with your ideas. In time they will be accepted…and you'll fly on the wings of an eagle. Alas, your biggest obstacle will be the people of Nazareth."

"Why?" Lady Miriam asked deeply troubled.

"The peasants watched him growing up: a barefoot peasant like them. They'll never see him as a scholar commanding respect," the Persian explained. "Someday when the nations of the world revere him, Nazareth will discover him!"

"Their revenge knew no bounds," the patriarch grumbled. "They cancelled all work demanding their deposits…We're teetering between bankruptcy and slavery!"

"That bad," El Sharif was deeply shocked. "Let me help you." He reached for his money pouch.

The old man shook his head vigorously, "If we go into slavery, it will be only for six years. The seventh, the jubilee year, we'll be free. But, a debt is for life!"

"So that's what your adage means, 'Buy a Jewish slave and you're buying a master'," El Sharif chuckled. Then he became serious, "Don't be a proud fool. This is not a loan. It's a gift!"

"Charity? We don't need charity! We survived crisis before, and will again."

The Persian knew there was little as rigid or passionate as Galilean pride, so opted for diplomatic persuasion, "Master Joseph, you will be doing me a favor. When I die, I'll have no one to leave it to."

"When you die I'll accept the bequest. Now it's charity!" He raised his goblet with a toast, "And I wish you to live another hundred years."

They touched goblets and took a healthy swig.

El Sharif wiped his beard quipping, "Your toast implied I am already a hundred?"

They enjoyed the joke. The Persian pulled out a shiny yellow dagger from his belt, in the shape of a small saber handing it to Joseph, "This saber-dagger is a new design my foundry is manufacturing in Persia."

Joseph took it and admired it, "It is beautiful and heavy. Lovely shine… why yellow? Gold?"

"Bronze. Keeps a sharp edge and is almost as strong as steel. My gift to you." Then he lowered his voice, "In some quarters if you show this saber-dagger, you will get help from the most unexpected places… powerful people."

Joseph was about to accept it when Miriam interjected, "I hope you won't be offended but we cannot take it. We have many knives and with little children..."

"It's dangerous," the potentate nodded. "I understand..."

"Will you join us for dinner tonight?" Master Joseph queried.

Yeshua rejoined, "Please say you will come."

"All right. I'll return." Then he turned to the young scholar, "Did you manufacture the special order I requested?"

"Yes," Yeshua responded. "I have two. Come, and I'll show you."

"Go ahead. Get them ready for inspection. I want a word with your parents."

When Yeshua walked out El Sharif leaned closer lowering his voice, "I bring greetings from the magnate in Babylon and the magi from Syria. They inquire about master Yeshua's progress. Ever since we came to celebrate his birth, we have been impatient to see him fulfill God's plan. Have you told him...?"

Joseph responded eagerly, "As Lord Adonai is my witness; I have always wanted to tell him. But, she argues that he is not ready."

"I was going to..." She started adding timidly, "But the sermon..."

"Nonsense," El Sharif interjected with an assertive tone. "The sooner he is told the better." He leaned closer still, "Did you consider the sermon and the riot as a nudge from above...to get on with it?"

Joseph blurted out enthusiastically, "Yes, we must tell him without delay."

Miriam sighed weakly, "I'll reconsider...seriously..." She looked at them waiting, so she added, "I promise!"

"Help me up. I want to see Yeshua's work." El Sharif held out his arm which master Joseph took. He was almost at the door when lady Miriam grabbed his arm.

"You will not tell him - not now. Promise you won't do it."

Master El Sharif looked at her, gave a non committal smile, turned and left.

When he entered Yeshua's work shed the young man removed the canvas uncovering two elegant wood carvings; one of a young shepherd carrying a young lamb draped around his neck, the other of a fisherman in a sailboat.

Master El Sharif was genuinely impressed. "You have the eyes of an artist, and a chisel with divine touch. I want to order one hundred carvings, and am ready to prepay you…" he pulled out his purse full of gold talents from his belt.

Yeshua put his hand over the old man's arm, "You heard father. No charity. Take these and test the market. If you sell them, then I'll accept your deposit."

The old man shook his head with disbelief, "If I live to be as old as Abraham I will not understand you people: in Persia they are like vultures after my money; here I cannot give it away." He took out two small coins and put them in Yeshua's hand, "Two drachmas for them."

The young scholar showed him the designs of the boat, and was congratulated, "The drawings are self-explanatory, but what I like most is how you solve problems."

When he said he was disillusioned with religion, Master El Sharif tried to give him some encouragement, "Don't let people's reaction discourage you…"

"I'm not discouraged," he interrupted tersely. "I'm seriously considering giving up Judaism… perhaps even Yahweh…"

The potentate turned pale and his eyes opened as wide as saucers as he spluttered, "No! You cannot…" And impulsively he decided the young man must be told. "You… you must not… you have a special…great future…special powers. A…great destiny…God promised…"

"What are you talking about?"

The potentate, never at a loss for words, was clearly shocked, unable to regain control. He vacillated between telling him, and honoring lady Miriam's request. "I told them, 'Tell him…the truth…'" he muttered as he picked up the carvings, and started to leave. But he stopped at the door, "Master Yeshua, someday they'll tell you…Please, forgive them…" and walked out.

Left alone the young scholar contemplated the strange episode and mysterious message. God said-- special powers--great destiny. Why did he speak in riddles? He had long suspected he was different, seeing people no one else did. He had long suspected he had something to do with the school master's withered arm, but was too self conscious to ask.

Now master El Sharif seemed to verify it. But why did his parents not tell him?

Suddenly he realized something he had not considered: if he told them he wanted to give up Yahweh it would crush them. More confused than ever he returned to his sieves.

He assembled four dozen sieves before realizing it was late afternoon. The work proceeded steadily, while he spent the time devising a plan on how to teach Esau. He would teach him to interpret the drawings, organizing and construction, framing, attaching the ribs, keel, stern, and only then explain about steaming and bending planks and so on. At the beginning he would superintend closely, later distancing himself, and encouraging Esau to take the reins of leadership.

· · ·

It was dusk and the sun kissed the roof tops before night fall, when a young lady of seventeen came into the yard, walked to the door and knocked faintly. Masters Joseph and El Sharif sat on the mat by the fire, sipping watered down wine, carrying on an animated conversation without hearing the knock. Judas and Salome came to the door, saw the girl's face in the dark and ran back to tell their mother. Miriam came out carrying an oil lamp and looked at the stranger. She saw a young girl dressed in tattered, dirty rags, and a hood pulled over her head hiding her face.

"What is it you wish?"

The girl raised her arms to pull back the hood, and Miriam saw her hands wrapped in dirty strips of cloth, with blood mixed with pus oozing through. As she slid back the hood, Miriam recognized a young girl with unmistakable signs of leprosy. A part of her nose had been carved, one earlobe was eaten away, and a cavity chipped above her right eye. Her hands were chiseled and two fingers resembled harpy claws.

"Dear lady, I am unclean, I have no family or home. I have not tasted food for two days. I have gone to every home, and you are my last hope. Can you help me? Can you share a morsel, a crumb, anything to help me?"

Miriam responded with sympathy, "We do not have much, but I will give you some bread and vegetable soup."

"Lord Adonai will bless your family, kind lady," she bowed deeply adding, "My name is Anna. I would be pleased to be your servant…I'll clean, wash clothes, sweep… anything…"

Miriam's attention was momentarily diverted when she noticed Yeshua coming out of his work shed with Esau. She answered the girl, "Anna I cannot afford to pay a servant girl."

Anna interjected quickly, "I seek no pay, my lady. I will work for food and a corner to sleep."

Miriam touched her arm reassuringly, "Anna, you need look no further." She turned to her son, "Yeshua, go wash up. Its dinner time and master El Sharif is already here. But, leave the water in the basin as it will be needed."

"Yes, mother" he replied and parted from his friend who left. Then he took his oil lamp to the basin, washed his face and hands, looked into the broken mirror and arranged his hair with his fingers. Coming to the house he barely nodded at the ladies and went inside.

"I'll take that," Miriam took his oil lamp which she handed to Anna. "Go over by the back fence where you'll find a basin and wash up. I'll find you clean clothes and join you presently."

Anna went, set down the oil lamp and started to unravel the cloth strips from her hands and fingers. She took the soap and passed it gingerly over the open wounds. She knew the alkaline would sting and tightened her jaws to help her withstand the pain. She washed and scrubbed repeatedly for she had not washed for days. Suddenly she heard a chunk from her hand fall off and splash in the water. Her heart sank. She knew that meant the sickness was advancing and eating away healthy flesh, causing the waste to fall off. She closed he eyes, and tears ran down her face.

She looked down at her trembling hand, almost too afraid to find out how much she had lost this time. What she saw made her freeze with disbelief. She blinked a few times and brought her hand closer to the light. She stood still as stone. Not only did she not lose further flesh, but, under her very eyes she watched the flesh regenerate and repair itself. Voids and craters were filling, new skin was advancing and covering it, while the scars formed, healed and fell off. She looked at her other hand and saw it mending. She looked into the broken mirror. The scarred face, the cratered nose, the ulcerated ear were almost back to normal, and she saw the lovely unmarked face of her former self staring back.

The sight frightened her. For years she lived the nightmare of leprosy, prayed, cried, and hoped, refusing to accept the evidence of the advancing, incurable curse, until she saw pieces of her young body rot and fall off. She dreamt of miracles, and her dreams showed her mending to the beautiful young lady she used to be. Alas, when she awoke the miracle dissolved and she stared at the scarred face in the mirror. She cried.

Now she was seeing the same sight as before. Was this a cruel, sadistic joke intent on driving her to madness? Would she awaken only to discover the momentary, magical illusion evaporate again? She tried to force herself to awaken, but nothing happened. When she realized she was fully awake, she became frightened. Was she a victim of witchcraft, or some black magic? The lady of the house was too nice, too friendly. The fear possessed her mind and she wanted to scream and run away. She started to turn when a hand touched her shoulder. She jumped with fright falling against the small table almost overturning the basin. She stuttered, "W-who are you? W-what do you want from me?"

"Do not fear, Anna. It is true: you are cured," Miriam whispered tenderly.

Anna held back covering her head, "Leprosy is incurable. What form of sorcery did you perform?"

Miriam consoled her calmly, "Yes, leprosy is not curable. Nevertheless...my son Yeshua washed in this water. You were cured. Do not fear. But, you must promise not to speak of this to anyone...including Yeshua." The girl was too frightened to comprehend it, but as she looked at Miriam's face she trusted her. "Take this dress and change. We'll burn the old one. Then come in and help me serve the meal, and eat with us." Miriam turned and went into the house.

Anna looked into the mirror then inspected her hands again. The truth struck her: she was not dreaming. She was cured. Tears welled in her eyes and rolled down her cheeks. She let herself cry. She was too happy to stop the tears. "Master Yeshua, what Godly powers do you have, that without touching you cured me?" She looked up to the stars whispering, "Yeshua: are you the living Messiah I dreamt about?"

CHAPTER II - THE THRONE

Yeshua rolled out of his cot long before the sun rose, got up and lit the oil lamp. He rarely got up this early, but he wanted to say goodbye to master El Sharif. Coming down he skipped the last few steps, landing on the ground and turned to the basin. Alas, he did not see Anna who was returning from the water well with a full jug on her head. The entire contents rushed on him drenching him from head to the sandals.

"Oh! Master Yeshua! You startled me ..." she apologized.

"Me too," he gurgled through water cascading down his tunic.

"You are totally drenched. And, I put out your oil lamp," she took the jug and rushed about confused, "It was my fault." She handed him the towel.

"My fault entirely," he replied. "I always jump without looking." He broke out in laughter. "I came down to wash, and got a bath in the bargain."

Anna was too worried to share the humor, "Will you forgive me? Please, don't tell lady Miriam," she pleaded.

"Why not? She'll enjoy a good laugh out of it."

"She may terminate my services ..."

"Is that what's worrying you?" Yeshua asked.

"I have nowhere else to go..." she replied timidly.

He finished drying and handed her the towel, "I saw you last night, playing with the children. They adopted you. Consider yourself part of the family."

"From your lips to God's ears, " she murmured full of hope.

"What do you mean you have nowhere to go? Where is your family?"

Anna looked down embarrassed, "It's a very long story..."

He waited and when she did not speak, he crossed his arms, leaned against the workshed leisurely, "The sun has not yet risen. Can your story take longer than a day?"

She smiled shyly and relented, "I am from a small hamlet south of Laish, an only child. My parents were farmers growing, mostly rocks. It's a dry forsaken valley. A few years back I began to be sick…a curse. I became unclean…"

"A leper," he whispered.

She nodded, "Incurable." As she said it she quickly brought her hands up and glanced at them furtively as if to check if the flesh eating curse returned. "My parents became afraid and called the rabbi. He took one look and sentenced my life: I was unclean, untouchable and must leave the hamlet never to return. I was banished to a lepers' colony. After he left, my parents refused to let me go. I was only fourteen." She began to cry silently. "They hoped to get me cured, and searched for doctors. They spent fortunes on medicine, ointments, oils and herbs, but nothing arrested the disease."

"There is no medicine to cure it," he noted.

"One day my parents heard of a holy man, a Messiah, who visited villages and everyone said he performed wonderful miracles. He cured people…"

Yeshua interjected, "And he cured you?"

"He never came to our village and I could not go to him, for I was forbidden to go out in public."

"But you seem cured?"

Anna continued as if she had not heard him, "My parents borrowed fortunes to help me, and when they could not repay, they lost their farm, and were forced to sell themselves into slavery. Their master, knowing he could only own Israeli slaves for six years, took them to Egypt and sold them. I have not seen them since."

He waited for her to go on, but she started to leave. He grabbed her arm, "How were you cured?"

She could not believe he did not know. Then she remembered being warned not to reveal it to anyone. "You mean, you really do not know?" she queried.

"Know what? You were cured, were you not?" he stared at her strangely.

She became confused, not knowing what to say. She stuttered, "Uh? Oh, yes…I was cured… miraculously," and she looked at her hands again.

Yeshua took her hands and inspected them under the early morning sun, "The person who cured you had divine inspiration. Who was the person?"

"Please don't make me say it, master Yeshua," she spluttered in confusion, then added quickly, "But I swear, it wasn't witchery …I have nothing to do with sorcery …"

He smiled reassuringly, "I am certain you don't. The cure has a divine touch. I'll respect your promise, and will not ask again."

She sighed relieved and for the first time relaxed with him. Her intuition told her she could trust him without reservation.

Yeshua started to leave then stopped, "Anna, a word of caution: our family has never had a servant. We may demand too much and treat you as a slave. You are not a slave. You have the right to demand and receive respect." He turned to leave.

"Master Yeshua, do you mean, slaves have no right to be respected?" she called after him.

He saw her teasing smile and realized his blunder. He bowed conceding defeat, ran up the steps, changed into a dry tunic, and ran to the caravan.

· · ·

The town of Nazareth covered the top of three neighbouring hills overlooking the Esdrelon Valley. The hills had much uneven terrain, cliffs with caves which served as dwellings for the homeless, protection for sheep, or cool places to store food. A spring supplied water to the town. From this spring a stream meandered lazily through the valley. The residents called it their river

Joseph's house was on the westerly hilltop, at the perimeter of town. The town's square, business section and the agora — the open market — were on the north hill, and the remaining houses, synagogue and school were on the southern hill. All around the hills and into the valleys were orchards and farms with cypress, olive groves, vineyards and wheat fields. A large swamp area was to the west of the southern hill.

The caravan was ready to leave when Yeshua arrived. El Sharif met him with a broad smile, "Master Yeshua, I was beginning to think you had slept in."

"I would never forgive ...myself, if I let you ...leave without a last ...goodbye", he said between breaths, and fell into the old man's arms, where he remained for awhile. "Which way will you be going?"

"The usual," the potentate sighed: "Jerusalem, Joppa, Gaza, and into Egypt, up to Alexandria, Caesarea and back here. God willing I'll return in six months."

Yeshua knew the caravan's route by heart, but he liked the sound of the exotic names of distant cities and foreign lands. Of these, he only knew Jerusalem with its gigantic Temple, and terrifying memories. His schoolmaster Ben Joseph came from there and told him much about the the holy city. "Some day I will spend a year travelling those places with you ... and see all the cities, and ports...," he sighed longingly.

"It would be a joy to experience the loveliness of the countryside through your eyes. I have done it too often to see its beauty," the Pearsian muttered sadly.

Yeshua told him about Anna, her story and the miraculous cure.

"This girl Anna, when did she arrive?"

"Last night."

"You say she was miraculously cured from leprosy ... Did she say how long ago?"

"No, but I suspect quite recently, for she inspected her hands repeatedly as if in fear the disease may return. I must say, sir, whoever cured her must have been blessed with the touch of God. She has no blemish or a scar - incredible!"

El Sharif stroked his long beard musing, "More than a touch of God, my boy."

Their eyes made contact for one instant, then quicly looked away. Yeshua had many questions, and master El Sharif wanted to tell him much, but neither knew where to begin and stood in awkward silence.

When the Persian turned to leave, Yeshua blurted out impulsively, "I thought about what you said...things troubled for me a long time...I'm different...I have powers...which I don't understand. What you were trying to say?"

"Forget what I said," El Sharif retorted without turning around. "That was an old man rambling. You'll find out soon enough." He started to go, stopped and turned to the young man, pleading, "Don't give up Yahweh."

"Why not? Every time I involve Him in anything I get into trouble," he objected.

"Earth shaking ideas do that. You have a special gift which the people cannot understand. That's why they lash out at you."

"Well I'm tired of their threats."

"They are naïve, and accept the priests' lies," the potentate tried to console him. "They need you to guide, and unite them..." He put his hands on Yeshua's shoulders, "It's your destiny..." He turned away abruptly but stopped and looked over his shoulder beseechingly, "Promise you will not give up Yahweh...do it for my peace of mind."

Yeshua wanted to argue, but when he looked into the old man's eyes he realized how important it was to him. He sighed heavily and murmured, "I promise..."

. . .

The sun was coming over the horizon when Yeshua returned, but at the gate he turned right, and followed a narrow path into the bushes and trees along the ridge for almost one mile to his hide-away place: a small clearing at the foot of an old oak tree overlooking the valley. The small grassy area was surrounded by bushes on three sides except at the brow of the hill from where he had a clear view of the meadow with the meandering river.

The oak tree was a symbol of strength and permanence, a silent sentinel witnessing the comings and goings of dozens if not hundreds of generations before him, and probably as many more after he would be gone. It protected a spot for him to sit, and rest against its sturdy trunk. It gave him protection from the rain, shade from the blistering sun of summer, and the cold north winds of winter.

He sat and leaned on the trunk like an old revered friend, studying the horizon, but the vision in his mind imagined the long road ahead of master El Sharif. He turned to the left admiring the large bush of hibiscus flowers. It was his favorite flower. Its delicate texture, opening its petals to welcome the first rays of sun in the morning, and bloom in a riot of colors; reds, pinks, and white brightened his private area. His favorite was a deep red, almost pulsating with life.

He always came to this place after some important event, to contemplate. Living in this secluded small town was like living on a small isolated island surrounded by a vast mysterious ocean, always wondering what was beyond the horizon.

This morning he thought about master El Sharif, wondering about his travels and adventures in strange lands. What he did not know were the strangest of circumstances that would bring them together again.

· · ·

As Yeshua approached his gate, he saw a half dozen of his friends in a semi-circle listening to Esau explaining something. He came within ear shot and stopped.

"The length of the boat will be fifteen cubits, and the width five," Esau read the drawings, then looked at them. They stared back.

"Is that big, like an ark? Or is it small like a dinghy?" Ahmed asked.

"Neither. It is not too big, and not too small," Esau responded. "It's like a … sailboat!"

They nodded, none the wiser.

"I'll draw a rough sketch," Yeshua quickly volunteered as he drew a straight line in the dusty road. Then he measured fifteen small paces, then five paces perpendicular. "This is the length, and this is the breadth, I'll draw the hull from the bow, along the beam which is the widest part, to the stern: one line on port and one on starboard sides. Across here is the stern."

They looked at it filled with admiration, because for the first time they visualized what they would be building.

Esau took the stick from Yeshua and pointed to the centre line, "This is the length of wood we need for the boat."

"No it is not!" Marcus countered with sarcasm dripping from his lips like honey. "It will be a skinny boat, because that's the centre. The wood will have to be as long as these outer lines. That's the length of the hull." Marcus stood smirking at the opportunity to expose Esau's ignorance. His friends elbowed each other, scoffing and sneering, like a pack of rapacious hyenas.

Yeshua interjected, "The truth is, Marcus is not strictly correct, nor is Esau strictly wrong. We need both lengths, as most planks fall in between the two."

Marcus was visibly deflated, while Esau wisely remained impassive. The boys looked at the small pieces of wood they brought and at the pile lying against the fence. Not one piece was longer than a cubit.

"This is the biggest piece I could find," Daniel grumbled.

"Don't despair," Yeshua tried to sound enthusiastic. "We may be able to use it somewhere, the stern perhaps as support …"

Esau tried to encourage them, "It's only the first day. We'll have better luck … "

Marcus interrupted, "I have not seen wood that long since …ever!"

Yeshua who had been inspecting the wood piled against the fence interrupted, "The important fact to remember is that the wood must not be too weathered and dried. Otherwise it will be like pulp, without strength."

They looked at him blankly, "What exactly do you mean?" Ahmed queried.

"Fresh wood: dried but with good fiber in it," Yeshua replied as the started to search through the pile.

"Why don't you let the project manager explain?" Marcus interjected with a smirk.

His friends sniggered enjoying the ingenious trap he set up for the outcast.

Yeshua knew Marcus came solely for the purpose of creating trouble, and he was equally resolved not to let him succeed. He turned to the group explaining, "Quality of wood is a question of carpentry, so I will answer." He took the piece of wood Marcus brought, held it up high between his fingers and thumb as he spoke, "This is a classic example of useless wood. I am surprised you bothered to pick it up." He pressed it and it snapped. "It is grey right through, as dry as a twig. If you find wood that is grey on the outside, scratch it with a sharp rock, or a nail. Good wood will have a creamy or pinkish color inside. That means the deeper fibers still have strong fibres and elasticity, therefore strength."

"Why do we need to worry about moisture and elasticity?" Daniel asked.

"Esau will explain in due course," Yeshua responded. "Test the wood you brought and find out how much of it is useful."

Most of their wood snapped as easily as Marcus'. "I don't think we'll find good wood in this town," Marcus lamented. "The piece I brought was the best of the lot."

Yeshua shared their pessimism but was careful not to show it.

Ahmed brought humor back to the meeting, "I found a perfect piece of wood: dry but firm, long and thick. Unfortunately my parents wouldn't part with the table."

"This is all very fine," Daniel interrupted the revelry," but are we not forgetting school? We're going to be late."

They waived a quick farewell to Yeshua and left.

Esau remained for a few moments and confided to his friend, "It's clear master Marcus is most unhappy with me as manager, and won't miss a chance to quarrel."

"You're the manager. If he is insubordinate you will have to make a decision."

Esau replied, "He is an excellent worker...and a friend. I had better catch up to the others." He turned and ran.

Yeshua went into the house for breakfast then returned to his shed and the sieves. Although he was not ready to admit defeat, again he wondered if it would be easier to raise the money and purchase the wood instead. After computing in his mind while making sieves, he decided they had a better chance of finding wood than money. There was one plausible solution: his oak tree. But the mere thought was like a stab through his heart. That tree was an old friend, a companion that protected him, a symbol of life. The possibility of losing it unsettled him.

He was concentrating so hard that he did not hear a commotion out on the street. A large crowd was gathering, filling the street all the way to the top of the hill, with people climbing up on their roof tops, and trees, curiously following a rare and disagreeable sight: a visit by the Roman army. Little by little the strange noises began to register in the young scholar's consciousness; horses whinnying, pounding their hoofs on the dirt road, and the sound of chariot wheels. He stopped working, listened for a moment, dropped everything and rushed out. He was astounded by the size of the mob. His parents were already in the middle of the yard wondering where the soldiers were going. Suddenly a sharp order answered them, "COMPANY – HALT." The centurion barked and the unit stopped in front of their gate.

A sharp shock went through the bodies of Joseph's family. Little Jude and Salome who were on the street gawking realized they were coming in, and flew into the yard and into their house, without stopping until they were in the darkest corner in their parents' bedroom.

A legate stood erect in the chariot pulled by two pure white stallions from Hispania. Behind him were six soldiers in two rows led by a centurion. They wore fine looking tunics, breastplates, helmets and were armed with swords. The legate wore a red toga, and he as well as the centurion wore the helmets with a distinct red brush.

Joseph and Miriam looked over the multitude. It seemed most of the town's population surrounded their humble yard and more were arriving. Those who climbed the neighbors' roofs were now invading theirs, making themselves comfortable, sitting down as if they were in the front row of an amphitheatre, impatient for the drama. They knew a visit by Roman soldiers was an omen of disaster foreshadowing a calamity. At the very least a member would be dragged out in manacles, or be summarily executed on the spot. To the spectators this was fodder for many months of discussions.

Joseph and Miriam did not move as the legate entered the gate, followed by the centurion. The soldiers guarded the gate. Miriam grabbed her husband's arm holding it tight, trembling. Yeshua stood on the opposite side by his father.

The legate stopped a couple of paces from them, his eyes swept over the spectators on the roof tops, trees and out on the street. His lips stretched in a shadow of a smile, for he liked a large audience. He stretched to his full height, swept his toga over his shoulder, "Are you master Jospeh, the carpenter?"

Joseph whose normal voice was a rich baritone was unable to utter a sound. He nodded his head stiffly, his beard shaking as he coughed and sputtered managing a squeaky, "This is he...I mean, he is me...I mean, I am he ..."

"Are you Joseph?" The legate demanded.

A tiny sound spluttered, "Yes...Yes..."

The legate reached into his tunic, fumbled and started to pull out a scroll rolled on spindles. Joseph's eyes followed his every move and his mind frantically wondered what he had done wrong. He guessed they came to arrest him for Yeshua's sermon, but he discarded that because Romans rarely became involved in religious disputes. Then he remembered he was abominably late paying taxes, and even further in arrears with the Temple's silver shekel, but he did not see the tax collector. He thought about charges of blasphemy but those were not matters of the empire. Finally he thought he found the problem: the town council must have trumped up false charges to exact revenge and destroy his family. His punishment: Imprisonment, perhaps execution. He felt weak, vulnerable and alone - so totally alone. His wife and eldest son stood by his side, but he knew the Romans only wanted him.

The spectators on the roof saw his worried look and elbowed each other smirking.

Joseph's heart was beating so hard his head ached. He perspired through every pore and his throat was parched. His head felt light and his body so weak he did not hear the legate ask the question. Yeshua nudged him and whispered to answer him which brought his glazing eyes into focus. He saw the legate glaring, waiting for an answer, but did not know what was asked. "Uh... pardon...?" he mumbled weakly.

The legate, who did not appreciate repeating questions asked emphasizing every word, "Are you from the house of David?"

"Whose house?...Oh, yes!...Yes, David, of course, yes!"

The legate unrolled the scroll slowly enjoying the old patriarch's discomfort:

"From HIS EXCELLENCY HEROD ANTIPAS, tetrarch of the provinces of Galilee and Perea,

"To JOSEPH of Nazareth, carpenter, of the HOUSE OF DAVID,

"GREETINGS:
"You are Hereby Ordered to hew, fashion, design and manufacture from the most exotic, elegant and durable woods from within and without the Provinces of the Empire, including mahogany, ebony, oak and such other exotic woods as in your opinion behooves the governor's high station, TWO THRONES for his palaces in the cities of JERUSALEM and AUGUSTEANA.

"Said thrones shall be handsomely decorated with intricate carvings depicting historical events of Israel and the nation's traditions, including a conspicuous bas-relief of the LION OF JUDAH, with the pinnacles supporting the backrest on top of which shall be depicted the SUPREME ROMAN EAGLE.

"Said thrones shall contain imbedded at prominent places in a tasteful manner, interspaced, mother of pearl, precious stones and rare gems which shall be supplied from the tetrarch's private collection.

"A deposit of thirty gold talents is hereby delivered to defray expenses and services. Future payments will be delivered on request.

"Signed under Seal HEROD ANTIPAS"

The legate rolled up the scroll and smiled at Joseph who stood staring ahead without blinking. He was so thoroughly shaken up that, although he heard the message, he did not comprehend a word of it. All he could say with certainty was that he did not hear the words charges, arrest or prison. He should be happy but not certain why.

Yeshua nudged him whispering, "Say something."

The old patriarch leaned to his son mumbling, "What do they want from me?"

The young scholar whispered, "Herod wants you to build two luxurious thrones of exotic wood, inlaid with precious stones. Price is no object."

The old man's eyes brightened, his rosy color returning to his face and his beard parted into a diabolical grin. His eyes swept over the gawking peasants. How fortunate, he thought, that these vultures should witness his sudden meteoric rise, from the depths of hell where they tried to push him, to dizzying heights of unimaginable prosperity. Miriam saw his transformation and guessed devious plans were crystallizing in his mind. The closest spectators who heard the message gasped and "oohed!" with shock and seeing Joseph's grin, recoiled and cowered.

Joseph wanted to make certain everybody heard the message from the tetrarch. He stretched himself to full height measuring his words, "My dear legate, welcome to our humble abode." He bowed deeply and the legate smiled, for he was rarely welcomed in Israeli homes. "I apologize, but, I forgot your name ..."

"Legate Vinicius."

"My dear legate Vinicius, will you honor us with your presence and your centurion, and share a chalice or two of our fine wine?"

"With pleasure master Joseph," the legate was about to put away the scroll.

"Before we go in, I want these good people to understand clearly that his excellency, King Herod, requests that I hew and fashion two thrones..."

"From the most exotic woods of the empire: mahogany, oak and ebony."

"Inlaid with rare gems and precious stones?"

"Rubys, emeralds, opals, the finest from King Solomon's mines...AND PRICE IS NO OBJECT!" The legate announced at the same moment as he pulled out a pouch from his belt, raised it high above his head, spilling gold coins from it to his lower hand, announcing, "GLITTERING GOLD! The purest gold talents of the realm!" Some coins spilled falling to the ground which neither rushed to pick up, for there was an over abundance. The centurion picked them up and handed them to his superior. The legate drawled, "If you need more gold, just ask and I will personally deliver them!"

The spectators gasped and cheered as they saw the gold glitter in the sun, floating through the air. Few saw or had ever held one. The legate handed the pouch to Joseph.

"Where do I sign?" Joseph asked eagerly.

"This is an order. Imperial commands require obedience, not replies," the legate frowned.

As the old man reached for the pouch Yeshua placed a hand on his arm, warning, "Father, what if something goes drastically wrong?"

The legate heard him and broke in gruffly, "Nothing had better go wrong old man. One mistake and Herod will nail your hide to the gate."

They all knew the shadow of Herod Antipas stretched to every corner of the province; so did his vengeance!

The warning sobered him from his euphoria but only for a moment. This was his chance to celebrate, feel free from the yoke he was forced to wear his entire life. He tossed caution to the wind and reached for the gold. Miriam grabbed his hand impulsively and they exchanged glances. He nodded slightly and she smiled, releasing him. He raised it high above his head, and the crowd cheered.

He shouted, "Lady Miriam pour the best wine for our friends legate Vinicius and the centurion," and started for the door. They went inside.

Yeshua started to his shed when he heard his name being called. He looked back.

"Master Yeshua, over here…It's me, Quintus."

He recognized his friend, a Roman soldier about eighteen years of age and went to him briskly, "Quintus? Why did you not come in sooner?" They embraced warmly, "How are you? When did you return from Egypt?"

"Fine, a week ago. When I heard the legate was coming, I offered to lead him."

"Come into my shop. I have many questions about Egypt."

As they walked, Yeshua overheard some Israeli's lamenting as they walked away, "Now master Joseph will have his revenge."

"Woe to all of us", an old man wailed.

"It's too late to cry now," the first man said. "Let's go to the rabbi. Ben Lebbus will know what to do."

"Tell me about Egypt," Yeshua requested.

"It's a fantastic nation, vast and mysterious; richer and more modern than our humble Israel. I was never so impressed!"

"I thought your unit went on training, not on a vacation," Yeshua teased.

"There were generals bent on killing us: never worked, marched or fought so hard in my life," he complained with a pained look, but in the next moment his enthusiasm returned. "Let me tell you; Egypt is full of ancient history…and mystery, and hidden ancient treasures. One had to step gingerly not to trip over a statue of a Pharao, or fall into his tomb." He seemed to be reliving his journey all over again and Yeshua laughed at his friend's exuberance, for he was rarely emotional or dramatic. "In contrast Ethiopia was the exact opposite: miserably humid and hot, barren and austere." The sun baked us every single day."

"How long will you be staying?" Yeshua asked.

"The legate let me bring him here. I'll be returning directly…although I hope to persuade him to let me go visit my father in Capernaum. I have not seen him over six months."

"He's in good health. I visited the centurion often while working for master Hariph."

"Father wrote about your visits. He enjoyed the discussions you two had immensely. Said he learned more about Israeli history and religion that summer than the thirty years living here," Quintus spoke with appreciation. "Thanks for keeping him company. He is quite lonely since mother died, the poor fellow."

"Old? He may be retired, but mentally he is younger than most our age. Full of modern ideas, inquisitive, argumentative but never boring."

"That's how he described you. He said you would make a fine Roman!"

"The centurion was very kind to pay for the construction of that synagogue. Being retired I'm certain he has limited means."

"I'll wager father saved and invested his coins tighter than the Israeli. I'm sure Caesar's face is imprinted in the palm of his hand," Quintus guffawed heartily. Then he lowered his voice, "I suspect at heart he is an Israeli in a Roman's skin."

"He inquired about converting," Yeshua confided in low voice, "but I discouraged it. A circumcision at his advanced age is too dangerous."

"I will never understand a religion based on circumcision," the Roman frowned.

"Ancient tradition: older than the Sphynx and far less useful," the Israeli shook his head. "Judaism needs a total overhaul; torn apart and modernized."

"The Nile will flow upstream before you change this religion," the Roman declared emphatically.

"I should have remembered that two months ago," Yeshua concurred. "I tested new ideas on our congregation and got stoned for it."

"I heard about your sermon in Augusteana. A merchant said he never saw the people so angry...the rabbi had to save you from charges of blasphemy? That could mean getting stoned to death?"

"Yes, but they still had their revenge: by starving us. I was forced to leave school," the Israeli confided with pain in his voice.

"Again? You'll retire before you graduate!" Quintus suddenly brightened up and commented with renewed enthusiasm, "This order to build the thrones should change your fortune. It must have been divine intervention!"

"What do you mean?" Yeshua looked at this friend strangely.

"Think about it. Just when you were most desperate, an order to build a throne...nay, two thrones! Payment in gold!" the Roman, not known for verbalizing, concluded proudly, "It has to be divine intervention."

"You saw too many mummies or else the sun affected your intellect," Yeshua rebuked him. "The Creator has more pressing matters than our trivial problems."

"You're right. Ever since I saw Rabban, the hulk of a man from Egypt, I see divine intervention in anything extra-ordinanary," the Roman tried to explain his reaction, which was more apologetic than persuasive.

"What Egyptian?"

"Rabban, the strongest man I ever saw. He's really an Israeli living in Egypt...I think you call them the diaspora," Quintus' voice suddenly rose dramatically. "He uprooted a gigantic tree over fifty cubits high and a girth this thick." He held out both arms out and around. "He threw it a distance of more than a hundred paces. Do you know the strangest part? His hands never touched the tree."

"How can someone uproot, raise and throw an entire tree without touching it?" Yeshua tried to visiualize it thoroughly astonished."

"I would not believe it, if these very eyes had not seen it."

"How did he do it?" Yeshua asked with skepticism.

"Power of the mind, his manager explained. He stood away from it and concentrated. When he raised his arms the tree was ripped out roots and all. When he heaved his arms forward it flew away."

"His name is Rabban?"

"They call him the Messiah. What is the Messiah?"

The young scholar considered it before answering, "Our prophets foretold that the Creator would send an anointed one to help Israel."

"Is this another Israeli fable purporting that your God will make Israel a great nation?" Quintus smirked sardonically.

"They say the Messiah will make us free."

"After thousands of years of wars, poverty, and slavery, should you not question if you are truly the favored children of God?" he spoke sarcastically, but his friend knew there was much truth in it. "Perhaps you would prosper more with less attention form Him?" Then he added filled with remorse, "Please forgive me, I meant no offence."

"I know. Tell me, can Rabban cure leprosy?"

"No one can cure leprosy ... short of a miracle! He performs super feats, like a circus show but I'm sure that's all. They said he will come to Jerusalem for Passover to destroy the Temple!"

They had both seen the colossal structure made of gigantic stones and shook their heads. Quintus picked up the papyrus from the bench and absent mindedly flipped through the drawings. "Did you design these? Where did you learn that?"

"An old shipwright taught me. I formed a group to build it, and Esau will manage it."

"Esau: the outcast?" Quintus saw him nod, "Are you starting another quarrel with your tradition?"

"Part of the same quarrel: but, it is a moot point. We cannot find wood, and have no money ..."

The Roman sat up interrupting him, "How much wood do you need?"

"The designs show the measurement."

Quintus read it, computed it mentally and smiled, "Look no further. I'll get you enough wood to build not one, but two boats."

"I don't want war booty your army plundered from the countryside," the Israeli retorted tersely.

"Relax. It's not what you think. It's extra wood father has from the construction of the synagogue. His last letter offered it to me. So do him and me a favor and take it."

"Every person who brings something receives an interest in the boat," Yeshua told him.

"I'll accept what the others received…what were they given?"

"The right to use it."

"I'll accept."

Yeshua chuckled at his friend's enthusiasm and willingness to help. He saw a movement outside and saw the legate and the centurion come out arm in arm, singing and trying to dance a jig. "Your officers will need help."

"It's going to be a battle to keep the legate in the chariot. Good-bye til the next time, when I return with the wood." Leaving, he walked up to master Joseph, shook hands hurriedly and left. The old patriarch realized the soldier seemed familiar and turned to his son, "Issh tha' yo' frien'… from…?"

"Quintus, his father is the retired centurion in Capernaurn," Yeshua explained. "He is giving us the wood for the boat."

"Yes, Quintus. He may be Roman, but I alwaysh though' he wash good'nough to be an Israeli," the old patriarch mused. Then he turned to his oldest son, "When you finish the lyceo you can return to order …"

"Your father has had too much wine," Miriam frowned. "He means when you finish this work order you may return to the lyceum." She interlocked her arm with the husband's and gently guided him into the house, "Come, you can sleep off the wine."

Yeshua returned to the sieves and for the first time in months did not hate the work. He did not take a sudden liking to it, but analyzed it with a dash of sentimentality. Sieves were not the depth of hell. Their problem was that they were more like spending an eternity in purgatory: a state of suspension where the intellect withered forever.

It was mid afternoon when he.noticed a shadow roving back and forth by his door. He glanced up and saw his younger brother Simon, about eleven, the shepherd in the family, pacing silently.

"Brother Simon, are you in trouble?" he asked and heard a mumble. "Come tell me about it."

Simon came in with his head down, biting his lower lip, fighting back tears, "Sextus is missing," he confessed. The older sibling searched his memory for such an acquaintance without success. The boy explained, "That's master Isaac's lamb."

"Oh! Where did you lose Sextus?"

"East of town, past the limestone caves," the young boy mumbled into his chin.

Yeshua knew the area well from the days when he was the shepard in the family. He asked, "Is that not the area full of bandits and dangerous beasts?" The boy nodded. "Did father not forbid you to take the sheep there?"

"I followed the other shepherds," he muttered lamely.

"Where is the rest of the flock?"

"Safe in the cave," he motioned to the north.

Yeshua got up and started to prepare to leave, "I'll get my staff. Do you have your sling?" The boy pointed at his pouch. "Projectiles?" He pointed again. "Water?" The boy nodded. "Let's hurry. Every moment is precious."

As usual when Yeshua was in a hurry he took long strides forcing Simon to half jog to keep up. They crossed the hill, descended it and ascended the adjacent neighborhood to the east, passing the biggest mansion in town. He was surprised to see it pretty well finished. It was a monstrous edifice, covering many lots, dwarfing all the little mud houses in town. It was the talk of Nazareth and everybody had an opinion about it, but no one had one scintilla of fact.

Simon asked between breaths, "Let's go in and take a peek? It's pretty well finished... They say the family will move in any day."

"No time. We must press on," the older brother was well aware of the dangers the lamb faced in that rough terrain. Seeing the boy disappointed, he added, "On the way back, if there is still daylight."   S o o n they were at the outskirts of town when Yeshua asked, "How much further?"

"About two miles down that valley," Simon pointed ahead.

The young scholar knew the area and remembered it as very poor for grazing: too rocky, with cliffs and crevices, but excellent to play games of hide and go seek. "Did you enjoy your games today?"

"What do you mean?" Simon blushed.

He saw him turn crimson, and smiled. Simon returned a furtive smile, and they both knew what happened. "But, I kept a close watch on them," the boy defended himself. "Sextus, has always been a troublesome lamb ... a renegade."

"You two should get along marvelously," the older brother teased him.

They chuckled, keeping up the fast pace. About one mile further Simon, who had once again fallen back ran up, "Do you want to explore a real neat cave?"

"I've seen all the caves in these valleys. Some more than once ..."

"Not this one. It is very deep, and it has some tall earthen jars...all closed up, with strange writing on them..."

Yeshua slowed down perceptably, very curious, "What do the writings say?"

"We could not make it out. It's all consonants."

"Ancient Hebrew," he stopped quite interested. "Only they wrote exclusively with consonants. Where are these caves?" He looked where Simon pointed towards some hills and cliffs rising almost vertically to the north. "How far?"

"Past those hills: not far."

Yeshua looked at the sun and knew they had only a few moments. However, he also knew if they were to find the lamb, they must press on.

"Alright, but we have to be fast," and they ran towards the first escarpment, climbed up and over it, descending on the opposite side only to face a steeper grade. Soon Yeshua could discern a cave because he had discovered so many in the past. A few paces further they reached the low entrance. A quick inspection told him that the entrance had been closed with stones set in mortar, plastered over roughly, matching the terrain and making it almost invisible. With the passage of time, rain, wind and changes in seasons the mortar weakened, weathered and finally crumbled.

They stood inside the dark cave until their eyes adjusted. Simon walked to the far corner.

"Be careful. These places are breeding nests for scorpions."

The boy stopped, glanced around carefully and continued gingerly. He disappeared in the black depth, from where his voice echoed, "Here they are."

Yeshua approached slowly until he saw them.

Suddenly Simon let out a gasp, "Yeshua, is that you coming?"

"What's the matter?"

"Your eyes are shinning. It's scary."

He could barely make out ten large vases in the corner. He touched one for texture, shape, smoothness, type of mud used and the wear on it even in the protected environment. He felt the top, "It is plastered over."

"Do you think there are treasures in them: gold and silver?" Simon queried.

Yeshua leaned forward, his forehead almost touching the vase before he could decipher the letters. He rubbed off the dust then blew gently, "Yes, it is Hebrew, the language of our ancestors. Today it is only used by scholars," he explained, excited with the discovery. "No, there are no hidden treasures. Our ancestors were not wealthy like the Persians and Egyptians. You'll only find old parchments of historical events, or religion."

A heavy sigh came from Simon, "How old are they?"

"A thousand years … maybe more," Yeshua guessed.

"That's older than father," the boy commented trying to read. "Why did they write only consonants?"

"Possibly a code so foreigners could not decipher the message."

"Why did they hide it?" Simon still hoped for a treasure trove.

"To save their history. Invaders destroyed the past of people they conquered or falsified it."

"Why?"

"Victors want their version of history. By falsifying it, they undermined them, and within a generation the nation disappeared," Yeshua explained. "You know how important our tradition is to us. If we had conflicting versions, imagine the arguments …and you know Israelis don't need help to start arguments…"

They dusted off a few vases when Yeshua gasped, "Here is the most important one. He read: "YHWH". Add the vowels and it is YAHWEH, God's name."

"Don't say His name. It is forbidden!"

"Yahweh? When they forbade you to say it they cut you off from Him, and made Yahweh their exclusive property," the older brother explained. "Their sneaky plan succeeded better than expected: elevating the priests and lords above you."

The younger brother nodded meaningfully, wondering, "Is that why they threw stones and sandals at you?" He heard his brother grunt, and asked with renewed hope, "How do we know there is no treasure, if we don't break them open, and see for ourselves?"

Yeshua realized his brother and his shepherd friends would not desist until they broke some, if not all to sate their curiosity. He leaned closer to the brother whispering mysteriously, "Ancient people planned for such events. They sprinkled poison powder in some vases. Break it and 'swoosh', it rushes up your nostrils, and you're as stiff as a broomstick! In others they deposited scorpion eggs. Break it and it will crawl up," he scratched his nail up Simon's leg.

The young lad let out a scream, sprang up and ran helter skelter to the distant light. Yeshua ran after him, grabbing him before he toppled over the cliff.

"Did you see that creepy scorpion?" Simon was shaking.

"It's too dark to see until it's on top of you," the older brother remarked.

"Wait 'til I tell my friends about the serpents and the poison," Simon conceded as they resumed their trek, "No one will go into that cave ... ever!"

"I'll write master Hariph to come and take the vases," Yeshua confided, looking up to the heavens hoping for forgiveness for his little lie.

They walked over two more hills arriving to a large, deep valley over two stadia long. "Here is where Sextus went missing," Simon swept his hand over the valley.

Fond memories from his younger days rushed through Yeshua's mind: games of hide and go seek, impromptu races, but mostly, he remembered the boys testing their strength and dexterity with long battles with the staff. "We'll go to that far corner. We'll have a full view and you'll call Sextus."

"He won't hear me," Simon objected, but on further consideration decided he was too desperate to argue. When they they finally arrived to the spot he cupped his hands calling, "SEXTUS! SEXTUS!" His boyish voice disappeared in the hot air and in the next instant returned magnified, louder and deeper, echoing and bouncing from cliff to cliff and into the caves.

"HOLY MOSES! I did not..." the young boy looked startled and pleased. He tried to speak but Yeshua held up his hand, concentrating for a bleat sound. After awhile he signaled and Simon called again, "SEXTUS, HERE BOY." They listened carefully again with disappointing results.

Yeshua pointed to a place further along the ledge, "Let's go to that cypress tree and try again. The echo travels to the other side of the valley there."

"How do you know about all this?" Simon asked as he followed.

"I was the family shepherd when you were crawling," Yeshua chuckled. "After that brother James took over."

When they arrived Simon took a deep breath, called, and they listened as the echo traveled down the cliffs. The older brother knew if they did not receive an answer the lamb may not be alive, or have gone out of the valley and into the hills. They would have better luck finding a grain of rice in the desert...

Suddenly Yeshua's musing was interrupted and his face brightened, "Did you hear that?" He pointed to the left. Simon shook his head. "Call again and listen for it there."

The boy did it, listened and smiled, "It's Sextus!"

"Your lamb is in distress," Yeshua warned. "Let's hurry!"

They skipped from boulder to boulder along the ledge and started leaping downward as they raced to the far corner of the valley. In places worn smooth by rain and wind they slid down over fine powdery sand which acted as grease, skipping down, as friction heated the soles of their sandals. They grabbed tufts of long grass to slow the descent, dragging the staff for steerage. The lamb was bleating, and as they looked to the right, they saw it less than two hundred paces away. They turned and ran towards it. When they arrived at the corner they saw the problem. A few paces below they saw a large flat rectangular rock jutting out of the cliff over the valley. Sextus walked out on it where its front right leg slipped and became caught in a crevice. The lamb pulled at it desperately, getting helplessly stuck. It did not see them coming as its attention was in the opposite direction. When they looked they saw the cause of the lamb's distress: a full grown black panther was moving slowly, stealthily towards the victim.

Yeshua whispered, "I have to reach the lamb before the panther. Get your sling ready. I will distract the animal and when I give a signal you shoot! Hopefully we'll chase it away!"

Simon nodded and started to get the sling ready. They crawled closer to the rock, crouching down low not to be seen by the panther. The animal had its eyes fixed on the lamb and was oblivious or unaware of their presence, moving silently, imperceptibly. Only the reflection of the sun's rays dancing along its rich fur gave evidence that it was moving. The lamb bleated continuously, terrified, becoming hoarse as it squealed desperately, pulling its leg, totally mesmerized by the stalking killer. The boys snuck to within a few paces without the animal realizing their presence.

Yeshua raised his hand slowly whispering, "Stay here. Get the sling ready ..."

"It's ready."

Yeshua took one giant leap and flew through the air aiming for one corner of the rock. At the same instant the panther coiled and leapt to the opposite end. They landed simultaneously. When the big cat saw him, it was startled and stumbled, almost losing its footing, managing to stop on the edge of the rock, struggling to get back on it. It regained its balance and stood up ready to fight the unexpected intruder. Yeshua took advantage of the moment and moved slowly, closer to the lamb. The predator was surprised and angry for it had lost its advantage and would have to fight for the lamb. It let out a blood curdling growl, letting him know that it had no intentions of giving up the meal.

Yeshua held the staff firmly in both hands ready to swing either end at the foe. He knew his only advantage was to keep the panther close to the edge and off balance. He approached cautiously to within one pace from the lamb.

"Quiet Sextus, we are here," he said not removing his eyes from the panther.

The terrified lamb was struggling to get loose, trying to bleat, emitting a hoarse sound and frothing at the mouth. The panther's sole interest was how to beat the human, but it did not rush or approach the lamb. It moved slowly around them, on the very edge of the rock, looking for a chance to attack. It growled continuously, whipping its tail like a nervous snake. Yeshua fixed his eyes on the angry cat and started to speak to it with an amazing calm voice. "Easy, cat, no need to fight and neither of us will get hurt. Why don't we come to an understanding: you go back to your family and we'll take Sextus home. We both will be safe. How about it?"

A radiant light appeared to shine from his dark eyes which captivated the panther. At the same time an aura of brightness appeared around his head from the shoulders up. The animal stopped and gazed at this strange creature and listened to his calming voice, its growling subsiding to a few grunts. Yeshua stood only four paces from the animal ready to defend himself. Slowly he reached forward with the staff, leaning towards the cat. The animal froze but did not attack. In this manner they walked around each other trading places on the rock, neither making an aggressive move. The cat growled and hissed, opened its large jaw exposing huge fangs. Yeshua kept the end of the staff close to its mouth almost touching it. The animal whipped its tail wildly, stretching itself upwards to make itself appear bigger, but did not fold its ears back or coil in preparation to leap. Yeshua knew those were signals of an impending attack. He wondered if it was not hungry enough to fight for the lamb. "Calm down and return to your little ones. We will take Sextus and promise to leave your territory."

The cat hissed and growled, annoyed with the staff so close to its face, and swiped at it with its huge claws. Yeshua sensed the decisive moment arrived: fight or walk away. Fearing if he did not act the panther would find a weakness and attack, he stepped forward, giving the cat a narrow path to escape. With lightning speed he flicked the staff striking the panther's snout sharply, the animal's most sensitive spot. It pulled back letting out a growl from the pit of its stomach, preparing to coil for a leap. But it started to lose its balance, and as it tilted and slipped, loose pebbles fell into the abyss. It scratched and managed to regain its balance. It sprang up in the air and in an acrobatic leap landed facing in the opposite direction, then escaped through the narrow path to the far side of the rock.

Simon screamed, "Yeshua, look out!"

The sound of another voice caught the feline by surprise. It was so busy with this human it did not realize there was another intruder present. It growled at the boy.

"Don't come closer. Get the sling ready."

"It's ready!"

The panther suspected they were planning a concerted attack, took one look at Sextus, and made a decision. It let out the loudest shrieking growl then leapt from the rock onto the ledge of the cliff, jumped over the boulders and disappeared around the corner. Yeshua watched it carefully until it disappeared and he knew it would not pose further danger.

"Help me free Sextus," the young scholar called.

Simon came down still looking over his shoulder to be sure the panther was not returning, held the lamb and tried to calm it down. Yeshua pushed the leg down and forward through the crevice, freeing it, then pressed the bones gently, inspecting it for fractures.

"It is bruised, but there are no breaks," he declared as he lifted the small animal over his head, draping it around his neck. He picked up his staff and looked to the west, "We must hurry before the sun goes down."

During the walk back Simon was so excited by the adventure he could not stay still or keep silent. He relived and recounted the battle, a fight to the death between man and beast, now moving stealthily as the panther, then acting the part of his big brother – the hero – sparring and fighting as courageously as a gladiator, his eyes fixed on the beast, moving in with his staff to crush it. At the conclusion of every play-acting, he asked endless questions. "Yeshua; you were not afraid were you?"

"Only living fools and the dead have no fear."

"But I did not see any fear!"

"Never be afraid to acknowledge fear, but don't be paralyzed by it," the young scholar explained. "Did you see how the panther stretched to make itself bigger? I suspect it too was unsure of itself, but chose to frighten me instead. The truth is that before I leaped down onto the rock, I had already planned my escape, and chose the place where I would battle the animal if combat was inevitable."

"Really? Where?" Simon was flabbergasted.

"About five cubits directly below the rock, there was a large mound of sand and loose gravel. I knew I would be no match for the panther up on the rock or the hard ground. But in a pile of sand it would sink and slip and slide. That would neutralize its agility and I could stand my ground with the staff." Then he added quickly, "Besides, I knew I could count on you with the sling."

The boy smiled proudly nodding. Then he remembered something, "How did you make yourself glow? That really stopped the panther."

"What are you talking about?" Yeshua looked at him strangely.

"Two or three times you had a glow all around your head down to the shoulders ... like a white fire," he searched for words to describe it. "And, I saw the same strange light in your eyes, like I saw in the cave."

Yeshua did not remember anything strange, so shrugged it off, "Probably a reflection from the low sun."

Simon accepted the explanation, "Where did you learn to fight with the staff? I thought only shepherds like me did that...I'm the best in our group, you know?"

"I'm glad to hear it. As a shepherd I took good care of myself in impromptu tournaments. Later James excelled at it. So, you should be today's champion."

Simon beamed, his insides swelling bigger than his outsides.

They walked in silence and Yeshua reflected on what Simon had said; his eyes glowing, and a light shinning over his head? What was this transformation that changed him into a monster?

Yeshua shared the latest news: the visit of the Romans, Herod's order of two thrones, and his good fortune to be returning to the lyceum.

"I am sorry to hear that," the boy sympathized. "Making sieves seemed like so much fun!"

"Simon, how many sieves have you manufactured?"

"Me? None, but watching you make them, I'd love to try my hand at it."

"Brother Simon, this is your lucky day," he put an arm around the boy's shoulders. "An opening is presently available in the sieve factory. Why not apply? You'll never have to suffer inclement weather…or the great outdoors. No more hide and go seek or jousting with staffs. You will sit comfortably in the shed, month after month…forever."

"No thanks," he interrupted in panic. "It's like prison. I'll be a shepherd!"

They returned via the town gate and through the town square, about to turn directly to their street when Simon remembered." Are we not going to the mansion? You said we could go."

Yeshua relented and they turned left towards the gigantic building.

They stood outside the gate admiring the grandest, most opulent edifice in the entire region. It had just been completed but was still vacant. Built on eight regular lots, the main mansion was almost in the middle, sitting sideways to the street, with the front of the building facing the inner yard. The back of the edifice had a sizable back yard which was covered by a gigantic tree. Across from the front of the house and the inner yard stood a smaller building with utility rooms, supply rooms and quarters for servants and slaves.

They tried to enter through the large double gate but it was chained, so they used the smaller gate beside it. Inside they looked for evidence of people, but the place seemed deserted, as silent as a tomb.

They stood in the centre of the yard basking in the wealthy surroundings. They counted five doors leading to different separate rooms.

Every door was of heavy wood carved with motifs of nature and wild animals. The windows, built in local fashion, were narrow and high off the ground to discourage prowlers or thieves. Across the entire front of the house ran a large portico with the roof supported by six light pink marble columns with intricate ornamental designs in the Corinthian style. The floor was a mosaic pavement with interlocking geometric designs and rosette patterns in a riot of colors, of black, white, yellow and red. In front of the central room, on the porch, stood a limestone pedestal table on which rested brand new serving wares, made of bronze, glass and glossy pottery jars and flasks. Under the table sat two large stone jars ready for use.

"Those utensils tell me someone has already moved in," Yeshua whispered to his brother. Their eyes swept every door, the length and breadth of the portico, and across the yard to the servants' quarters. There was no evidence of people.

They returned to admiring the place that reeked of opulance.

Between the columns stood white marble statuettes each about three cubits high, obviously imported from Greece, some of which Yeshua recognized: Zeus, the patriarch of all Greek Gods, with his thunderbolt; Aphrodite, the goddess of love and fertility: Apollo, Mars and others he was neither familiar with nor knew their names.

Simon grinned like a cheshire cat for he knew something his brother did not, "Do you know who the family is who will be moving in here? I do!" he smirked. Yeshua shrugged, "An Israeli prince or the richest Israeli family in the whole country!"

Yeshua rubbed his chin thoughtfully, "Do you know that as a fact?"

"It stands to logic," the boy replied proudly. "My shepherd friends and I all agreed!"

"I think you're all wrong on both counts. Israeli princes prefer seclusion in country homes or ocean fronts. The rich like to rub shoulders with wealthy nabobs, to impress each other. Who can they impress here: a farmer? a carpenter? No, I am certain it will not be Israelis living here."

"Who do you think?"

"A wealthy foreigner," Yeshua declared analytically. "The intriguing question is why would they move here?"

"Why?" Simon's curiosity was at a peak.

"They are hiding. They did something terribly wrong in their country and need to be invisible. So they hide in a one donkey town. "

"Do you mean big time criminals: maybe pirates, or murderers?" Simon's curiosity matched his imagination as his eyes swept over the eerie place with trepidation.

"Probably some heinous crime," the young scholar concluded.

Suddenly a deep voice shattered the silence, "Very impressive deduction. Now that you discovered my secret, I will have to kill you both!" The words echoed through the empty building and amplified onto the yard.

Simon jumped against his brother almost causing him to lose his balance and drop Sextus. The brothers' eyes swept over the yard and the buildings, especially the shadows which grew longer with the low sun.

"Yeshua, let's get out of here," the boy pleaded with a shaky voice. "Tell him we were joking, we did not mean to call them pirates. Tell him we did not touch anything. Please!"

The older brother put one hand on the boy's shoulder, squeezing the staff in the other, as his eyes skimmed over the place for any movement. But, the owner of the sinister voice remained invisible.

Yeshua decided to take his brother's advice, "We meant no disrespect…to you or whoever will live here…We caused no damage to the possessions. We were, simply curious …" He started to push his brother, at the same time holding him from panicking and running. "We will be leaving now. Good bye …"

Simon clung onto his brother's tunic fighting the urge to take flight.

They were at the gate when they heard the deep voice again, "If I ever see you here again I promise you will not walk out alive!"

This time Yeshua identified the direction of the voice, quickly turned and saw a man standing, mostly in the shadows, but sufficiently in the light to discern some recognizable features: a head with rich black hair, the left side of his face had a hideous scar starting at the temple, it ran down through the eye brow, and continued down the cheek and into the chin.

As soon as Yeshua saw him, he retreated into the shadow and disappeared.

They walked out of the yard and continued at a fast pace until they were well away from the mansion, without looking back or exchanging a word. They were almost home when Simon said, "You were right. That man was a foreigner…"

Yeshua nodded but did not respond. He was deep in thought: From whom was the man hiding? What hideous crimes did he commit?

CHAPTER III - SARAH

Yeshua's sister Debborah, age twelve, ran into the yard, up the steps to the roof, peeked into the older brother's room, and seeing that he was not in, she ran down and into his work shed. She saw him sitting at the table with a stylus in hand. "Are you busy?" She asked as she rushed in.

"Yes!"

"Remember that big mansion on the next hill?" she asked. "A family is moving in - foreigners! They're super rich - richest family in Israel!"

He thought of the perfect phrase, dipped the stylus in the ink ready to scribe, muttering, "Humm, that's nice."

Her voice went up an octive, "Do you want to know the best news? They have a girl your age...the most beautiful girl I have ever seen!" He started writing in earnest. "Don't you have anything to say?"

He drawled mechanically, "Hmm, that's nice."

Realizing she had to take drastic action to get his attention, she bumped him dislodging him from the stool.

"Hey, be careful," he objected, dropping the stylus and grabbing the bench.

She smiled for now she had his full attention, "A family is moving into the big mansion, with a lovely girl your age." She looked for the effect her statement made, and when he started to return to writing she pronounced every syllable as if announcing a prize, "SHE – IS – LOV-VE-LY!"

He sighed heavily and gave up, "How do you know they're foreigners?"

Debborah replied proudly, "Their possessions are all in crates caked in thick dust. They traveled a long way." He nodded and she continued, "The girl is truly beautiful ... just for you." Then she added matter-of-factly, "She has a brother my age. Let's go."

He pulled back, "Brother Simon and I were threatened there..."

"Don't let a little misunderstanding stop you. Besides, you'll be with me now ..."

He studied her suspiciously, "You cannot fool me. You want me to do your dirty work: get to know them, win their trust, and ZAP! You nab the boy. I won't be used! Do your own devious deeds!"

She grabbed him pleading, "I admit it, but I was also thinking of you. C'mon. What are you writing that's so important?"

"A letter to master Hariph, with directions to a cave in the hills …"

"That's like describing the hump of one camel in a herd of camels," she scoffed. "Tell him to come here and you will take him."

His eyes lit up, "Right, why did I not think of that?" He quicky wrote it.

She pulled him away and they left. They barely left the yard when neighbors greeted them from every direction. They came to the fence, or out to the road to make small talk. The sudden attention surprised them. They replied timidly and pressed on.

"For two months they avoided us," she said. "Why the sudden change?"

Yeshua responded in a low voice, "The gold coins made us the toast of the town. They think we're rich!"

"Are we rich?"

He chuckled, "Most of the coins will be spent on exotic woods, supplies, glues and rare shells. Herod is a sly fox. He gave enough to appear charitable."

"I was scared when that legate said they'd nail father to the gate," she said.

"Me too! Father is a construction carpenter. Building thrones is for master carpenters and artists."

Debbie waved at a neighbor and whispered, "Hypocrites! I liked them better when they ignored us."

He teased her, "I'll give another sermon - guaranteed to give us peace …"

She reacted frantically, "That's not funny!" Then she added with a grin, "Should you ever get the urge, warn me, so I can leave town for a long, long time. What did you say to make them so angry?"

"Were you not listening?"

"I was busy dodging flying debris. One giant sandal just missed my nose."

"Saul's sandal: smacked my forehead right after master Yacek's walking stick."

"Anyway, why were the congregants so angry?"

"I called them arrogant bigots. The old patriarchs control everything and I want to change that."

"Why do you bother?"

"I was trying to get their attention. I intended to talk about a modern, kinder religion: a Universal God based on love and equality. But I never got that far…"

"You're always trying to change everything," she complained.

"You're right. The people don't want it. I could change the Sahara into a tropical garden before I change Israelis." They continued in silence, each with their thoughts, when he turned to her, "I will tell you a secret which you must not repeat to anyone. I am seriously contemplating giving up Judaism…especially Yahweh."

Her mouth dropped and she bombarded him with questions, "What? Why? When did you get such a foolish notion? Have you thought this through? You can't do that!"

"Why not? Every time I have dealings with Yahweh it is the same: heartaches and strife. Remember when I went to the barmitzvah?"

"Father is still talking about it: my son the scholar achieved the highest grades in the nation. Afterwards he sat with the senior representatives of the Sanhedrin and discussed complex questions of Judaism."

Yeshua laughed heartily, "The truth is that those old men did not represent Judaism or Yahweh, but the wealthy and powerful. The meeting was about controlling everything: God, religion and society."

"Then it was all a…"

"Yes, a lie. Moreover all the years when I went to the rabbis' classes I could never express my views or opinions. It was all about the Book as the Priests in Jerusalem saw Him. I suffered all those years until he allowed me to speak to the people in the synagogue." He sighed deeply finishing almost in a whisper, "I tried to speak of love and almost got lynched. Why should I care about such religion? Who wants such God?"

"Yeshua, you can't do it. It will kill mother," she pleaded, her lips quivering with fear. After some thought, she reconsidered, adding with sympathy, "If your ideas are so important, you shouldn't give up! I'll bet the Messiah would not do it."

"What do you know about the Messiah?" he stared at her surprised.

"Mother talked about him. I think she knows him"

"When was that?" He asked eagerly.

"The day we went to the pools and the women soiled her water hole, so she couldn't wash clothes. She threatened to get the Messiah after them."

"Are you sure that is what she said?"

"She was very clear. She said, `I have a good mind to tell the Messiah to teach them a lesson`. I asked, who? And she repeated 'The Messiah. He could tie them all up with a rope of sand, and give them all a good dunking.' So I asked, 'Is he that strong?' And she replied 'Nothing is impossible to him.' I suggested we go get him."

She stopped for a breath and he asked impatiently, "Did she get him?"

Debborah shook her head, "Mother decided the Messiah had more important work than to meddle in women's silly fights."

He started daydreaming what he would do if he had supernatural powers.

She interrupted his musing, "You must not give up your dreams. You cause troubles because you are different. You analyze and question everything…It's a rare gift. People like you are natural leaders of people."

"Did you come to this conclusion on your own?" he asked suspiciously.

"I overheard rabbi BenLebbus talking to our parents. He said you were a person with a vision…and a special destiny."

They passed the vineyards that grew on terraced areas and entered the area of olive groves when she remembered something important, "Master Benjoseph said you will be returning to the lyceum tomorrow."

Yeshua laughed, "Our school master seems to know everything that happens in our household before we do."

"He is a good schoolmaster and cares about you. He said he misses you."

"Did he really say that?"

"His exact words were 'I cannot wait for that argumentative troublemaker to come back. The lyceum is too docile without his novel opinions. It's sleepwalking. We need him to light some fire under the students.'" She looked ahead and pointed, "There it is: the mansion. Look at all the people gawking." Suddenly she remembered what he had said and asked, "Were you and Simon really threatened there?"

A shadow of a smirk crossed his lips, "A bit late to worry about it now, isn't it?"

"Do you think he meant it?"

"I'm not curious to find out. But, I must say I have an uneasy premonition about the place "

"When you see the beautiful girl you will forget all premonitions. If I wished for an older sister she would be the one. You'll love her like I did the moment I saw her."

As they approached they saw a commotion: a dozen donkies, loaded down with big crates, boxes and large baskets waited to get unloaded. It was like a traveling caravan transporting merchandise to international bazaars. Crates were taken off and new ones brought; servants and slaves scurried into the yard where the crates were opened and the items taken into the mansion. When a luxurious bed was uncrated there were loud "oohs" and "aahs," for not one of the hundred spectators owned a bed, and most had never seen one. The place reeked of opulence: beds, sofas, Roman style reclining couches, chairs, tables, exotic vases, jars, statuettes, full size mirrors, paintings, fine weaved tapestry, robes, cloaks, togas, silks in a riot of colors, uncrated and carted in, in an endless parade into the magnificent edifice.

Yeshua and Debborah stood by the gate, gawking, only to discover they were in the way, and were uncerimoniosly pushed away. As they shuffled off their eyes feasted on the largesse in the yard, their necks stretching as they looked back as if drawn by a magnet. Walking thus he did not see what was coming.

"KABOOM! CRASH! BANG! Oof! Ouch! Tinkle, tinkle, tinkle…!"

Yeshua's first recollection was lying on the dusty road, picking himself up dazed and confused. There was a thick cloud of dust rising, and enveloping him where it remained suspended. Suddenly dozens of small items began to rain down: flasks, vials, jars, tubes and small glasses, boxes, and baskets striking him and bouncing into the thick dust. He heard the tinkling of breaking glass, popping jars and in the distance the echo of laughter from the gawkers who enjoyed the spectacle. His nostrils picked up the scent of rich perfumes mixed with fine dust.

He sat immobilized trying to comprehend what had happened, when he saw through the clouds of dust, sprawled on the road a couple of paces in front, a body sitting up. Only then his memory was able to replay it: he was walking away, looking back when he collided with that body, both flying through the air, baskets full of flasks and vials flying in the air. His forehead throbbed, and his right knee was sore.

His attention turned to the stranger and he was about to inquire about his health, when the person began to spit and cough. He heard muffled sounds and groans, but not until the dust cleared did he notice that the stranger's cloak had flown back over his head. Yeshua started to get up on his knees to help when the stranger swept his hands forward with a violent motion sending the cloak flying and a long thick mop of black hair covered his face. Another violent sweep sent the hair back, and Yeshua, resting on his hands and knees, covered in dust, disheveled and bruised discovered the stranger was a girl. He sat frozen staring at the most beautiful girl he had ever seen, while she sat in the dust, dazed, disheveled, spitting dust, and staring back.

Debborah announced cheerily, "That's her: isn't she beautiful?"

He remained on his hands and knees motionless, mesmerized by her beauty: the blackest eyes, as mysterious as the universe, with sparkles of light like the stars, a round kind face, a small nose and full, luscious lips. Her black hair, though piled on her head was long, thick and wavy. He could have remained admiring her but she shook herself back to her senses and uttered her first words which became etched in his memory, "Why don't you watch where you're going, you blind fool?"

This shook him back to reality, and he tried to speak when she grabbed her shoulder and her face twisted with pain. He reached out to help her but she drew back. "Don't touch me!" she snapped.

All he managed to utter was an incoherent mumble, "I...I..."

"Don't you look where you're going? You almost killed me."

"My fault ...I'm sorry. I..."

"Of course, it is all your fault, you careless fool!"

They looked around in the dust and saw boxes and baskets strewn with perfume bottles half buried, flasks, vials and ivory containers. She gasped and screamed almost in tears, "Mother's entire collection...rarest perfumes, expensive cosmetics...oh, no, look at the oils...rouge..." she tightened her face spitting every word like poisoned darts, "You better pray they're not broken, you careless...creature! Or you will pay...dearly."

He muttered weakly, "Yes...I will pay!"

She started to get up on her knees and asked sardonically, "With what: a miserable starving goat? That's probably all you own! Look at these. "She picked up two miniature bottles, wiped off the dust and pointed at the label, "Persia! Babylon! They're priceless, more valuable than all your miserable possessions." She broke down in tears.

He tried to console her, "Don't cry. I'll work forever to repay. I promise."

"Just help me pick them up," she pleaded in tears.

She took a basket and they proceeded to sift through the dust, picking up small flasks, vials and little containers with elegant shapes and a variety of colors, depositing them into it. When it was full she found another basket and they continued searching.

Suddenly she let out a cry, "Ouch! I cut myself," she dropped the basket and looked at her left thumb, wincing in pain. She saw a deep cut on the tip with blood oozing. He reached for her hand but she pulled back.

"Let me see," he held out his hand. She gave it without arguing and he inspected it. "You have a piece of glass in it," he commented, as he dabbed a clean part of his sleeve to clean away the blood. "I'll remove it."

"Be careful. It stings," she pleaded, looking at him.

Their eyes met and they remained still, looking at each other for a few moments. In that instant he thought he saw a very lonely girl, reaching out in fear. He pulled out the minute piece of glass carefully, and smiled at her. "There, good as new..."

Debborah who was helping ordered them, "Hurry up and find the bottles, before some oafs step on them and crush them."

They returned to sifting for the vials and flasks. The girl found the broken bottle and raised it from the dust. "This bottle had a long neck. It's broken off. Mother will be livid!" She glared at him, her voice trembling, "She will make you pay!"

He felt devastated. How he wished he could turn back the sun dial and fix everything for the girl. He was resigning himself to manufacturing sieves the rest of his life. His head throbbed incessantly.

Debborah was picking up the containers, taking advantage and testing them, sneaking a whiff from one bottle then trying a drop from another. She had never smelled such exotic scents: saffron, balsam, cinnamon, and countless other scents of flowers of spring and rich vapors of summer she could not identify or name.

When all the baskets and boxes were filled, Yeshua picked one up saying, "I will blow off the dust and hand them to you to stack."

He took a deep breath and blew as hard as he could. She took it, looked over the containers and gasped. They were not only free from dust, but all the flasks, vials and jars, were intact. She searched for the broken bottle, but did not find it. Yeshua handed her the second, and again nothing was broken. Moreover, the lids, corks and stoppers were properly set, and the containers were full. At first she thought the broken ones must be in the other baskets, but she did not find any. Perhaps she over reacted, or there were less broken flasks than she thought she had seen. She became confused. She remembered her thumb and looked at it. There was no cut. She touched it then pressed it. It was not sore. Did she imagine everything? She wondered. Then she saw some dry blood on the thumb. A deep fear began to overtake her. She had read books about the Israelis, when her parents said they were moving there. Their history was full of strange stories. They were simple peasants, mostly farmers, deeply religious and very superstitious. They believed their prophets were saintly persons capable of performing miracles and communicating with God. One particular story made a lasting impression on her. It was about an anointed person which their God was going to give the people to lead them to freedom. His title was Messiah! She clearly remembered the fantastic story. One book alleged such a person was born almost twenty years ago…about the age of the young man before her. She had enjoyed it as a romantic fairy tale, but now she was not certain. Perhaps it was all true?

She looked at her unscarred thumb with dry blood on it, and began to back away. She raised her eyes cautiously and looked at him. A brilliant radiance, like two beacons, emanated from his eyes. She wanted to look away but could not. She wanted to bolt and run but her knees seemed paralyzed. She felt she was going to faint, yet remained still, strangely calm. He seemed harmless, indeed kind even handsome. She was confused but felt strangely secure in his presence. He noticed her shrinking back and wondered why she too reacted with fear as if he were some kind of monster?

Her voice cracked as she stuttered, "P-pass me t-the c-containers…I must go…"

He lifted them and carefully handed them to her. The stack was quite high, above her head. When she started to walk she veered towards the fence, so he ran, caught up and guided her through the gate. He rejoined his sister, smiling brightly like a little boy.

Debborah snapped furiously, "What a witch! I'm sorry I dragged you here!"

"She is beautiful," he cooed.

"How can you say that after all the names she called you?"

"She was right. I should have been looking."

"Did you see how she piled up the boxes? She couldn't see you, but it didn't stop her from abusing you!"

He raised his hand, "Calm down, let's analyze this fairly…"

She raised her voice angrily, "Quit thinking like a man, and use your brains. She is no good for you. We don't belong here. Let's go!" She started to leave and he followed a few steps then stopped to look back. She grabbed him impatiently and tugged at him, "I am disappointed in you. You're just like every male; see a pretty face, and out goes all reason!" She pulled him away but he resisted so she admonished him, "She spoke to you three times, and called you a blind moron, careless, and stupid …"

He smiled embarrassed, "I have excellent vision."

"How can you joke about it? Where is your pride?"

Yeshua said, "Look at it her way: she was worried about her mother…"

"Yet she blamed you, when she was equally at fault - maybe more."

"Fear will do that," he defended her.

"So does cowardice!" Debborah retorted.

He began to smell something and came around her sniffing, "What's this rotten scent? It smells like the carcass of a jackal."

She glared as if mortally wounded, "I like this perfume. I tried some of the oils and ointments." She smelled her hands, closed her eyes and seemed to be floating in the clouds. Suddenly she opened them again, "Quit changing the subject! I'm wise to you. Besides, you don't have a chance with her. You're a peasant! She…maybe royalty! That rich, beautiful girl probably has…at least six suitors, all super-rich!!"

That stung him but it did not last long, "You were right. They are foreigners. Didn't she roll her R-r-r's beautifully? I wonder where they're from?"

Debborah spit out, "Some place where they blame everyone but themselves"

Yeshua sighed, "What a lovely voice. She pronounced her words beautifully …"

"How can you say country bumpkin beautifully? Wake up, Yeshua!"

But he was not listening and continued his reverie, "Maybe I cannot have her. But, where is the harm in dreaming?"

Debborah tried to think of the meanest thing to awaken him, "She is probably already married. Girls her age usually are. If not, what's wrong with her?"

That had the desired effect. He did not remember any evidence that she was married or betrothed. But Debborah was right: girls of seventeen, which he guessed to be her age, were married unless there was some drastic problem ...

They walked in silence while he wondered, what was wrong with that beautiful girl?

. . .

When he sat at the work bench Yeshua planned to complete the last of the sieves and get ready for the lyceum. Within a few moments the sieves seemed to be assembling themselves, swiftly and vigorously, and his usual good humor soared for he felt euphoric, that the work order would be finished presently. That was his hope, until he suffered the first strange attack. He froze physically and mentally, suspended in the act of fitting the mesh into the frame. That girl's face appeared in the netting, framed within the circle as if she were alive. His eyes glossed over, his mouth hung open as his memory relived the episode of their meeting; their flight through the air, the baskets and myriad flasks raining on them seemingly from the clouds. He remembered the first moment he beheld her, the most beautiful girl he ever saw. His mind replayed the moment many times, frame by frame, and her every feature became etched permanently in his psyche. Some moments of their encounter struck him as comical and he chuckled, then for no apparent reason he became serious, forlorn, sighed, and his emotions began to gyrate through peaks and valleys out of control.

Suddenly he awoke from this hypnosis, perturbed, for he had never before felt these emotions. Whereas in the past he was able to separate his hands from his intellect, this morning was unlike any others. Not only could he not separate the functions, he could not perform either. It was obvious the collision shook his psyche to the core.

This strange sensation made him cross, not because it interfered with his work, but because he knew nothing could come from it. But, his anger was instantaneous, and, soon all logical rationalization evaporated in the ether, and in the next instant his mind went into a new dimension: the delightful world of daydream where every fantasy and every wish was possible. He looked in the net and saw himself on his hands and knees beside her, sifting, searching for flasks and tubes and restocking the baskets. They worked as a team to salvage her mother's priceless possessions. But, one particular moment replayed in his mind's eyes over and over: the first time he held her hand. He felt the softness of her skin, warm and pleasant, like velvet, unlike the rough skin of peasant girls. What he remembered most was the fact that she was trembling. Yet, it was a hot day. He suspected she was frightened. After removing the glass he held her hand and looked into her eyes. He thought he saw a sad, longing look of someone lonely, searching for something...Closeness? Security? He remembered one such look a year past from a fawn he saw fall into the river. Its mother stood on the bank helpless, as he ran over, jumped in and brought the little fawn to safety. It shivered, though it had been in the water but a moment. And he remembered when he reached for it in the rapids, it looked at him the same way: longing to be held and protected. He remembered that all the while he held the girl's hand she did not pull away, but the trembling ceased. The moment when her eyes swam in his was the climax of the day.

There was another moment he found strange and could not comprehend. After he blew the dust off the containers and handed her the baskets, she inspected the items closely with a surprised look: elation and trepidation all in one. He went over that moment again and again certain that her eyes had a hint of...terror? Why was she so frightened? He sat, warmed by the cloak of pleasant memories, bathing in the radiance of her smile, drinking from the brilliant rays of light from her dark eyes, as Baccus drank wine from the chalice. He was hopelessly infatuated, captured by a mysterious world he did not know existed.

Again he snapped out of the strange dream. Twice more he tackled the sieves and both times the mysterious malady caused his mood to fluctuate between the heights of reverie to myopic lows, now laughing, now sighing for no apparent reason. One time Anna passed his door and heard a roaring laughter from within. Yet she was certain he was alone. She stopped, listened for voices and hearing none, retraced her steps. She was right. He was alone. She shrugged and walked away...as another burst of laughter filled the air. She shook her head and kept walking. Shortly afterwards Debborah appeared at his door, asked him a question, and waited for a response. None came. She repeated the question and watched him, frozen, staring into space. She walked up, moved her hand in front of his eyes, and, failing to revive him, shuffled away mournfully as one leaves at the passing of a dear friend.

By and by he came out of the trance, angry and frustrated, for the total sum of his production that morning netted zero! He wanted to scream and to cry, but, instead marched out of the yard vowing not to return until he was ready to tackle the sieves in earnest.

Miriam appeared at the door and called, "Jude, Sallie, lunch time." She looked around and saw them with her eldest son. "Yeshua, take them to the basin and give them a good scrub, then bring them in for lunch."

He did and they came in. Before they began to eat James ran in excited, "Yeshua, master Quintus is coming with a cart and donkey. It's loaded with wood."

Yeshua got up, "Already? He doesn't waste time."

Joseph quipped, "What did I say? That Roman's word is as good as an Israeli's."

The brothers came out to the gate as Quintus stopped. "Greetings, my dear friend," the Israeli scholar shook hands. "Your word is as dependable as the sunrise."

"Greetings. You should thank your father. His wine softened the legate, so he gave me leave. Your boat crew helped me." He raised a heavy thick plank, "Your first load."

Yeshua laughed, "This may be sufficient."

"It's not half of it", the Roman replied.

Esau came forward, "Master Yeshua, there is enough wood there to build a navy." He turned to the others, "C'mon boys, let's unload."

They carried it to the far corner of the yard. Yeshua inspected it and smiled: it was strong wood, well cured with strong fibres. The planks were too thick and wide but they could be cut and split into thinner manageable planks. It would be good training for them to work and become familiar with wood. When it was all piled, Yeshua brought out a heavy canvas.

"Master Esau, the wood should be covered to protect it from the elements, mainly the sun."

Esau took it and addressed his lead hand, "Master Marcus, give us a hand."

Marcus protested, "Wood does not need protection. Do you see boats under canvas? No! The outer layer weathers protecting the wood."

They stood less than a cubit apart, each a tense mass of energy resolved not to give in to the other, Marcus ready to topple the foreman and take charge. Ahmed and Daniel hoped their hero would quickly crush the outcast. Quintus watched from the side, quietly supporting the foreman, hoping he would let Marcus have it.

But Esau stepped around him, "Alright. I'll do it myself."

Marcus quickly grabbed one end of the canvas, "If you persist with this foolishness I'll be forced to help." However he had no intention of helping, only starting a fight, "These planks are straight, yet the hull is curved. How do you propose to curve them?"

Yeshua interjected, "We will sweat them."

Esau repeated, "Yes, we will be sweating the planks into shape."

Marcus stepped between the two so the scholar could not protect him, "So how will you sweat it?" he asked certain this would finally expose his ignorance.

Esau explained carefully, "Fill a basin with water and boil it to make steam. We'll cover it with a heavy canvas and capture the steam. Put a plank in it, and as the steam penetrates the fibers, the wood will become pliable. We'll bend it carefully until we get the desired shape, and nail it in place. When it dries it will keep the shape."

Marcus stared at him stupefied. Where did he learn that? His supporters looked at him unsure whether to laugh.

Esau asked nonchalantly, "Do you wish me to repeat it?"

Marcus spat out tersely, "My uncle is a fisherman, and he told me. You are right!"

He threw his end of the canvas on the wood violently and marched away. His friends followed.

Quintus marched to Esau angry, "The whole trip from Capernaum he was sparring with you, itching for an argument."

"I know," Esau replied as he spread the canvas.

"Why don't you take his challenge? Delaying will only endanger the project."

The outcast objected, "I don't want to lose the project."

"You have one choice: abandon Marcus, or your leadership," Quintus snapped.

"If he leaves, I'll lose the crew…and the project."

Quintus sympathized, "You have good qualities but it's not enough. Do you know what our generals do? Demand absolute obedience. Your only obligation is to the project and none to the rebel!"

Esau tried to defend his opponent, "He has good qualities."

Quintus gasped, and turned to Yeshua, "Tell him Marcus' insubordination deserved rigorous punishment." He waited for a reply, but was met by his vacant stare. "What's the matter?" He turned to James, "Is your brother ill?"

"Sister Debborah said he was victim of a strange curse."

"Curse? What kind of curse?"

"He saw a beautiful maiden in town and his faculties left him. Ptouf Gone, just like that!"

Quintus smirked knowingly, "He is bewitched by the strongest potion: Paris destroyed Troy over it, and Anthony gave his life for it. It is Venus' currency – LOVE!" He snapped his fingers before his friend's eyes, "Yeshua, wake up."

The young scholar was jolted to reality and took a few moments to regain his focus. "What was your question?" he mumbled embarrassed.

"We have long forgotten. Are you ill? You are as pale as crumbling marble."

"I must be," Yeshua responded awkwardly. "I feel...I have pangs and pains. I cannot concentrate. If I'm standing, I must sit; then I stand up..." He turned to Esau for sympathy, "You're a sensitive soul. Surely you sympathize with my pain?"

"You are asking me about the curse called love? Remember, I'm an outcast. I suffered from love, but soon learned reality. No Israeli girl dares to reciprocate my love for the rabbi would never marry us." He continued bitterly, "An outcast will never find happiness or marriage with an Israeli girl..." He turned and marched out fighting tears.

They stood staring at the ground awkwardly, when the Roman looked up at the sun, "I must go if I hope to reach Capernaum in daylight."

"First you have to join us for lunch," Yeshua led him to the house where he announced, "I brought a hungry soldier who is in a hurry."

Joseph quipped, "Always in a hurry be,

For life is too short;

And death – an eternity!"

They enjoyed a simple lunch of soup and a slice of bread. Quintus entertained them with stories of his travels in Egypt and Ethiopia. James asked many questions for he had just studied about Africa in the lyceum and was intrigued by the ancient civilization. The young siblings listened to the stories of fables and fairylands which excited their imaginations. Joseph asked practical questions about the exotic woods he needed. Only

Yeshua sat quietly, daydreaming, and sighing. He picked up a slice of bread and held it without taking a bite, nor did he touch his soup.

Miriam watched his vacant, look, and finally could not resist a comment, "Eat, Yeshua. Whoever it is she will not run away…" She waited for a reaction, and at length he began to blush, glanced at her furtively, and both exchanged knowing smiles.

When Quintus finished they accompanied him to the gate, leaving Joseph and Miriam alone. Generally the old patriarch was the first to return to work, but today he remained fidgeting with his bowl, picked up a stick and played with the embers in the fire. Miriam knew it was a prelude to something, so she left to clean the dishes.

He started innocently, "Lady Miriam come, sit beside me."

The irresistible invitation reinforced her suspicion, "Why?"

"There is something I wish to discuss …"

"I'm busy. Can't you discuss it from there?"

He muttered under his breath, "I think it is time to tell Yeshua!" Then he sat back waiting for a response. There was none. After a long pause he remarked sarcastically, "I could have sworn I spoke to you!"

"You did."

"Are you going to answer me?"

"Was that a question? I could swear I heard an opinion."

Joseph huffed. He was as wise to her as she was to his body language. When she did not wish to discuss something, he would have better success catching the wind with his hand. "I'll rephrase it as a question: What is your opinion?" He glanced and saw that she was about to concoct one of her convoluted answers, "No more games; just a simple question. Shall we reveal…?"

"No!"

"No - that's it? Don't you have something else to say?"

"No!"

She could be stubborn. He remembered one time they argued for three days, at the end of which he stepped out in the yard, complaining to the heavens: "I could change the orbit of the sun before I change that woman's mind!"

After a few moments she decided to clarify her decision, "Yeshua had the right to know from the first day, but we agreed to protect him until the proper time. Recently events have complicated everything. So, I decided to wait until I get a sign."

"A sign: a sign from where?" He was flabbergasted. The new wrinkle gave him pause.

"Up there," She pointed up.

He looked automatically and a horrible thought struck him.

"Do you expect me to argue with God?"

"When I receive a sign, there won't be arguments."

He got up and walked over purring, "I did not want to say this, but, I'm getting old ... It's my wish, before I'm called," he pointed up to the heavens, "to see my son perform a miracle - just one!"

"My dear, you will see it. Just take time and observe!"

He protested, "Are you intimating I do not observe? Nothing happens in this household that I don't see!" To make his point he emphasized, "I'll tell you something else which has bothered me. When is he going to start showing interest in girls? What's wrong with our boy?"

"My dear Joseph, come sit by the fire, and I will tell you some great news ..."

• • •

Yeshua said good bye to Quintus and returned to work, when he had an idea. It seemed like divine inspiration, for he raised his arms exuberantly, "Eureka! I've got it!"

He searched through a pile of carvings, found a small one of a shepherd boy with a couple of sheep on a grassy knoll. He inspected it closely for damage, and decided to give it a coat of paint: cream for flesh, white for the lambs; and the shepherd's tunic, green for grass, black for the boy's hair. On the bottom he inscribed - "TO A SPECIAL GIRL - YESHUA."

He picked it up daintily and started out to the mansion. What better way to offer her an apology, and introduce himself than a gift, he thought? He went from his hilltop briskly, down the valley and up the hill towards her district. Twice he bobbled the figurine almost dropping it. The first time an exuberant dog snuck up behind him until it was almost at his heels, before barking. Yeshua almost jumped out of his tunic. The second time was his fault, for he failed to see loose pebbles, and almost skidded to a fall.

As he walked he prepared the perfect speech to impress the girl. He settled on a simple sincere statement, "Please accept this carving as my apology and friendship. What is your name?" He decided to present it outside the gate. He was still too afraid to enter the yard.

He was almost at the gate when suddenly the girl appeared, coming out of the house and crossing the yard. His reaction was instantaneous: he turned and walked away. His heart was pounding, his face flushed, his mouth went dry and he perspired through every pore. He marched a fair distance before stopping.

"Whew! That was close," he murmured, congratulating himself for surviving a calamity. By the time he forced himself to glance back, the yard was empty.

He remained a safe distance from the gate, reconsidering his plan. He knew his mind would go blank when he faced her, and would be tongue-tied. So he decided to put the statement to memory.

Thus prepared, he returned to the gate, walked in one direction, turned and retraced his steps, back and forth, watching the doors of the buildings for her. He marched back and forth, like a sentinel guarding the property. Many persons appeared from one building crossing the yard to the other: men, women, servants, slaves, and each time his heart palpitated, his mouth went dry until he verified it was not that girl, before continuing. Still she did not appear. After a long time he admitted he had not conquered his fear, and when he tried to repeat the memorized phrase, he panicked, for not a single syllable could be summoned. Yet he was resolved to make a stand and not retreat. He was going to give her that carving if it was the last thing he did.

He devised a better plan: call a servant and ask her to fetch that girl. He came to the gate and waited for a sympathetic looking servant. Soon he saw her: a young girl, rather fleshy, with a round, kindly face.

"Psst! Psst! Hello, lady ...," he called, but she continued across the yard. He raised his voice, "Psst! Psst! Hey, lady, over here ..." He waved, calling her louder, then louder, until she stopped, looked around every which way but his, and resumed walking. He panicked and almost yelled "Over here, this way, lady!"

She stopped, looked again, and this time saw him. Her hands went to her chest as she mouthed, "Me?" He nodded excitedly, as she let out an exuberant squeal, "Oh!" and rushed towards him.

He raised his hand holding out the carving, "Lady, I would like to ..."

She snatched it out of his hand letting out a shriek of happiness and surprise, and began to chatter, "I saw you pacing back and forth patiently, and I asked myself: 'Who is the lucky girl?' But, never in my wildest dreams did I suspect I was that girl. Oh, I'm so excited, I can hardly speak. Excuse me if I sound like some foolish little school girl, but I cannot explain how happy this makes me ..."

"But lady...what I really want," he tried to interject.

But she would not be stopped, "...Look at the lovely gift you brought me." She looked at the carving, "It's simply...beautiful, and makes me feel -beautiful. Did you carve it yourself? Of course you did! The paint is still wet! Oops! How clumsy of me, to smear it. Well, never mind, I'll wipe it clean. Did you see the inscription under here? Of course you did. You made it." She read it, 'TO A LOVELY GIRL` – That's beautiful. And it is signed ... ISHA?"

"Yeshua," he corrected. "Lady, I'd like to ..."

"Yeshua. What a wonderful name. My name is Hulda ..."

"How do you do. Now, can I ..." he tried to speak.

"Fine, thank you," she prattled ecstatically without stopping for breath. "I'm one of the servants in the family. But, I don't intend to remain a servant forever. No, sirie! As soon as I find a young, strong, gifted fellow ... like yourself, you know what I mean?" She threw two exaggerated blinks his way, "I intend to start a family. I come from a large family and I intend to have at least eight...maybe more...Do you like big families?"

"Me? Well, I don't...look..."

"Of course we could have less. I'm agreeable to any number you want. I believe a man should have a say in all decisions...if he agrees with me. Oh, my, I can't stand here and chat all day. Why don't you come back later, say towards dusk, you know what I mean?" Wink, wink. "We will find some secluded place to get to know each other, you know what I mean?"

Yeshua had long given up hope of stopping the chatterbox, and now gave up on proper etiquette to say farewell. He backed away stammering, "No! No! I must go ... It's a mistake..." shuffling at first, then half running and finally at full flight.

He did not even feel the pain in his knee.

. . .

Yeshua was a few hundred paces from his house, after the dismal encounter, dejected, and ready to give up on that girl. He felt he would climb to the peak of snow capped Mount Hermon barefoot, before he got close to her. He was forbidden, on threat of death to enter the yard, and, even if he dared to enter it, Hulda would intercept further advance. His was a desperate situation.

That was when he saw his sister Debborah coming down the street. He stared at her as a hopeless sailor in storm stares at a beacon: his last hope!

Debborah always had a reputation of being a doer: a tough negotiator or the smooth diplomat, according to the situation. She could bargain with the toughest sun - beaten nomads of the desert. No one could divine her thoughts, yet she read their minds like an open scroll. That was why Miriam always took her when the desert merchants arrived. Many envious merchants offered gold talents, as many as Miriam wanted, to buy the gifted haggler, for they knew they would get their investment back in short order. But, Miriam would sooner part with her life than any of her children.

Yeshua knew if he wished to enlist her support she would demand such an exorbitant price as to make extortion seem a mere gratuity. But he was desperate.

Noticing his sudden energetic pace towards her, she slowed down guarding herself against the expected onslaught.

"Debborah, my dear...did I ever tell you what your name means in Hebrew?" He cooed.

She nodded suspiciouly, "A bee."

"A busy bee," he smiled mistily.

She grinned enjoying his dramatic show as transparent as glass. She asked, "How is the mysterious foreign girl? Did you meet her? Was it fun?"

He sighed, "A disaster! I took a gift but a love-starved servant snatched it..."

She interjected, "And you're coming for my help." She saw his face, a picture of suffering, and rebuked him, "So you want me to do your dirty work: get to know her, win her trust...then, ZAP! You'll nab her. I refuse to be used."

"You're my only hope...I'll give you anything you ask..." he blurted out then quickly corrected the impulsive promise, "within reason!"

She was far from persuaded, "I don't like her...Moreover you don't have anything I desire!"

He knew she was right. He started to shuffle away, his head down.

Debborah sighed sympathetically, "Brother Yeshua, against my better judgment I'll help...However, I will want four things: first, get me some rare perfumes like that girl's mother has..."

"Do you know how dear they are? And, even if I managed to get them mother won't let you use them."

"That's my second wish: you will persuade mother."

"What is the third wish?"

"A majority share in your sailboat."

"Impossible! Master Quintus supplied all the wood and he's not getting more than the others." He stood firm as she turned to leave. "Debborah, I need your help..." He pleaded.

There was a painful tone in his voice which made her stop. He must be truly infatuated for his pining was singularly genuine.

She muttered, "This may ruin my reputation. Forget everything I said. I will help you!"

He embraced her warmly, "I'll be in your debt forever."

"Don't tempt me," she quipped. "Have you made a plan of how to woo the victim ... I mean, the girl? Or, are we just going to hit her over the head and drag her away?"

"Give me credit," he objected. "Come, I'll tell you on the way," he said as they started for the mansion. "You won't have much to do: just go to the house, introduce yourself, welcome her to Nazareth, visit for an appropriate time all the while telling her – most subtly – your fabulous brother's countless excellent qualities ..."

"That won't take long," she quipped.

He glanced at her crossed, "...for instance, his courage, his athleticism, his scholarly qualities, and ..."

"What about his humility? If I'm going to lie..."

"They're not lies...they're...miniscule exaggerations."

"I see it; I sneak into the house, win her confidence, tell fibs about your irresistible qualities..?"

"Ugh- uh!"

"What will you do in the meantime?"

"Wait! ... With open arms ..."

"You are asking for the impossible," she shook her head. "What can I say about your courage?"

"Yesterday I fought off a panther with my bare hands ... and my staff," he replied.

She guffawed, "Yeah! And I made an elephant disappear."

After considering it, he realized it sounded incredible, so he changed it, "Tell her I was the top scholar at the barmitzvah."

"She won't be interested in a scholar. Girls are interested in sports. In what sports do you excel?"

"Tell her I'm the best javelin thrower you know!"

"Do you want me to lie?"

"How many javelin throwers do you know?"

She chuckled, shaking her head.

They were climbing her hill when she uttered with inspiration, "I know! Girls are irresistibly drawn to a young man the others girls want."

He smiled optimistically, "I'm rather popular with the girls in the lyceum." He glanced at her while she stared back dubiously, so he amended, "Most of the girls?" She continued to stare until he confessed, "Some girls?"

She retorted bluntly, "Let's say Drusila will gouge this girl's eyes out to get you!"

They stopped under a tree less than a block from the big mansion. He said, "Let's go over the plans one more time."

"No need to," she interrupted. I'll have her purring like a kitten... she'll want to be petted when I'm done." She pressed her step and left.

He watched her enter the yard without stopping at the gate, meet a servant and be led into the mansion as if she were the guest of honor. "She makes everything seem easy," he murmured with envy. "In a few moments she'll call and I'll be going in..." He held his cupped hands to the sky.

The wonderful expectation of meeting that girl officially caused his heart to palpitate, and he started to fidget preparing for the ecstatic occasion. He ran his fingers through his hair and fluffed it to give it full body, brushed his tunic with his hands to remove excess dust, checked his dusty sandals, tore off some leaves and gave the tired leather some polish. Then he turned his attention to the proper protocol of making acquaintance with a lady of the upper class. He searched his memory for a similar experience in his past only to remember he did not know a lady from the upper class. Fortunately he had read something in one of his school master's books and decided to act it out. He drew a line in the dust with his sandal, crossed to the opposite side, acting Debborah's part as she introduced them: "My lady – blank – I have the honor to present my fabulous brother, master Yeshua, an incomparable athlete, courageous and a great scholar, whose outstanding quality is...humility!"

He quickly stepped beside the imaginary sister, and replied for the beautiful girl, curtsying while chirping, "Enchanted!"

He crossed the line, bowed deeply, and let out a groan, as his knee gave out. But he masked the pain with a valiant smile, "The pleasure is all mine, lady — blank."

Again he stepped across the line, "Are you suffering pain, master Yeshua?"

He crossed back answering, "The expected battle fatigue of a busy athlete: banged up head, pulled knee. Nothing major..."

Once again he crossed the line, "Your little sister tells me you're a skilled athlete."

He crossed back and smiled embarrassed, "Little sisters exaggerate their brothers' prowess...but, I imagine I could hold my own in the Olympiad..."

"Oh!" she exclaimed, properly impressed, "In what sport do you excel?"

"The staff," he responded proudly from his side of the line.

"The staff: is that an Olympic sport?"

Again he crossed and looked stymied, "I don't know!" He blushed, realizing he knew next to nothing about the Olympics. He tried to correct his error, "But, I throw a mean javelin...and I can deliver an arrow as straight...as an arrow!"

He turned to watch the gate for a signal from Debborah. But, there was no sign. He waited, still nothing. To while the time away he decided to practice the introduction once more, without the acting. He searched for lofty phrases, perfect, impressive key words as he strived for a specific impression: of a calm, relaxed gentleman, and a man in control of his destiny. And he kept reminding himself to periodically insert, very subtly, a dash of humility. Most importantly, he wanted to sound very natural.

Having rehearsed it copious times, he relaxed in the shade of the tree waiting for the inviting wave. He waited comfortably for a long time, then leaned against the trunk and waited uncomfortably. Finally he sat on the dusty ground and waited, but still no wave. It was the hottest part of the day when he fell asleep leaning against the tree. When he awoke with a frantic jolt he had no way of knowing whether he dozed for an instant or slept for a long time. The shade had long ago abandoned him and stretched to the opposite side of the road. He decided his sister had probably got involved in some silly girl's game, totally forgetting her mission. He stood up in preparation of abandoning the ill fated plan.

He glanced towards the gate one last time, stopped, and squinted, certain he was seeing someone. He rubbed his eyes and looked carefully. It was Debborah. Only, she was not waving but flailing her arms frantically. Was she in trouble, he wondered? His first thought was of the deep cavernous voice that had threatened him, and his heart pounded, as he rushed to her aid. Debborah continued to wave vigorously although as he got closer he saw that she stood alone. His eyes swept the entire yard but it was empty. Still, he decided to enter, grab her and run to safety.

He was almost at the gate when that girl appeared, seemingly from nowhere, took Debborah's arm and led her to the back yard, under the big tree. He slowed to a walk but kept coming directly for his sister.

The girl raised her hand and ordered, "You've come far enough!" Yeshua froze. "How dare you threaten this innocent little girl?" she demanded accusingly.

"I did what...?" He stepped forward reaching out for her.

"I said don't come any closer or I'll scream for help," she threatened pulling the young girl away from him.

"I won't, I won't," he hurried backwards looking around worried that someone may already be coming. When he was far enough from her he started to ask, "What did you mean I...?"

She interrupted him, "Are you going to try and deny it?"

"Deny what...?"

"Do you deny that you threatened to give your poor little sister a licking if she did not persuade me to come out to meet you?" she demanded accusingly. His jaw unhinged, flapping open without a sound for he could not think of what to say. After some moments she continued, "I am glad to see you don't deny it, as I would not believe you. This innocent girl would not lie to me!"

Yeshua glared at his sister who kept her eyes down on the ground. He wanted to say something but all he could muster was a stutter, "I-I t-threatened you...When?"

The girl scolded him, "It's too late for that. Here I am, to bid your pleasure." She marched at him sticking out her arm. He drew back thinking she was coming at him, only to see her offer her hand, "How do you do. My name is lady Sarah!"

He took her hand and smiled nondescriptly, a mixture of pleasure and disbelief, "Fine. Thank you. My name is ..."

"I know your name, master Yeshua," she rebuked him angrily, pulling back her hand. "You must promise that you will never threaten this innocent little girl again."

"But I...I..."

"No excuses," She interrupted. "I want your unequivocal promise."

"Of course I promise!" He spluttered annoyed, and wished he had not said it as it seemed he was admitting guilt.

Lady Sarah turned to Debborah, "There. You're safe now, assuming we can trust his word." Then she turned to him, "You may leave now, but I warn you never to return here again." She started to leave, then stopped and turned to him, "And don't ever try your sorcery on me again ..."

Yeshua stood absolutely flabbergasted, not comprehending her accusations much less her synnister statement. He began to leave with his sister.

Sarah called after them, "Debborah dear, wait. I will make you a present of the game you enjoyed so much." She called a servant, "Hulda, give her the game as a present from me."

Hulda did as ordered handing the gift, then dug into a pocket of her apron, took out a carving and walked up to him, "Master Yeshua, I don't think we should see each other any more. You can take your carving back!" She thrust the carving into his midsection, knocking the wind out of him.

Lady Sarah called, "Debborah dear, of course, you are welcome to return any time you wish."

The girls waved and they parted.

They walked in silence for a long time, Yeshua limping in pain. He was fuming, too angry and baffled by the accusations, but wisely deciding he would wait to calm down sufficiently, if they were going to have a civil discussion.

However, as his mood was not improving, he demanded without ceremonies, "What happened back there?"

Debborah, ridden with guilt, explained holding back tears, "I went there as you asked and was promptly invited into her room. What a giant place, like a field ..."

"I just want the story" he snapped.

"… Anyway, we started to talk and play this game," she pointed to the box she was given, "and I tried to talk her about you. She was ready for it because she changed topics and talked about Tyre, her city. After a while I tried again, but she told me how she hated our little town, the peasants and everything. As far as she is concerned there is no place in the world like Tyre: it has everything, and we have nothing…" They continued in silence for awhile when she added, "I remembered what you said about fighting the panther and decided to impress her. I told her you fought a full size panther armed only with a staff and defeated it…"

He interjected with a sickly laugh, "I presume she got a good chuckle out of that …"

"No, she listened with great interest. When I finished she reacted strangely, raising her hand and looking at a scar on her left thumb. She asked many strangd questions: Did Yeshua ever perform supernatural feats? Does he have unusual powers? Did our parents ever mention that he was special…like a Messiah? Then she said the strangest thing, 'I believe he could beat a panther, if he were the true Messiah…' What was she talking about?"

Yeshua shrugged his shoulders and screwed up his face, "How should I know?" He thought for a long time shaking his head. Moreover he was quite curious about her accusations, "Why did you tell her I threatened to beat you?"

Debborah replied defensively, "I could not get her to come and meet you, so on impulse I invented the story…" She chuckled quietly, "It certainly worked. What do you think now?"

"I'll tell you what I think. Before, she thought I was a blind fool. Now I'm also an abusive child beater!"

They continued in silence until turning to their street, where Yeshua lamented dejectedly, "Yesterday I fought a panther and came out unscathed. Today I got scratched by a purring kitten…some kitten!"

Debbie did not hear him because she was thinking about something else. Finally she turned to him, "When lady Sarah said you may be the Messiah, she also said there is nothing you could not do…the same words mother used." She looked at him as if for the first time, "Brother Yeshua are you the Messiah?"

CHAPTER IV - RETURN TO THE LYCEUM

The morning Yeshua was returning to the lyceum, there was excitement in the household, like the charge of an electrical storm. When he came down Miriam started to inspect his new tunic, which she and Anna had hurriedly sewed.

His mother nodded approvingly, "Good! How does it feel?"

"Perfect!" he chirped cheerily without realizing he was describing his mental state.

After two months that seemed like two years, he was free. Liberty! He was looking forward to seeing his school chums, and above all enjoying mental exertion after his brain almost atrophied from the mindless labor. Why shouldn't he feel perfect?

Anna who helped with the inspection quipped, "You appear so handsome, master Yeshua, all the girls will find you irresistible."

The mention of girls brought lady Sarah to mind. Will she be there? he wondered. He decided if she came he must find a way to sit beside her. And he vowed before sunset they would become friends. Perhaps more than friends …anything was possible.

The prospect of seeing her made him restless, and he rushed breakfast, picked up his papyrus, stylus, clay tablet, shoved them in a canvas bag and rushed out.

The lyceum was south of town, on the third hill, which meant he would take the road to Sarah's mansion then turn right, to the end of the road. It was a small building with two rooms: the classroom and the teacher's office. Next to it stood the synagogue.

Public education was a fairly recent phenomenon in Israel and quite new in the province of Galilee. Before that, education was in the domain of the parents: a father taught the boys his trade, while the mother taught the girls the wifely duties. And the synagogue taught religion until the boy reached the age of thirteen, went through the ritual of bar mitzvah and officially joined the congregation. Only the very rich and powerful paid private tutors or sent their children to university.

When the Greeks colonized the world, they spread the Hellenistic culture which all countries eagerly adopted. The common language became Greek Koine. Greek tunics became the fashion of young boys and girls. The schools taught classic Greek education: grammar, rhetoric, logic, music, poetry, mathematics, history and physical sciences. When the Romans took over the world, the center of government changed to Rome, otherwise everything remained the same – Greek!

The Israelis saw their culture, tradition, and above all their religion threatened. Hence, the southern province of Judeah introduced public education. Rabbi Simon ben Sketach developed the House of Books which later became the lyceum. Much later it came to the province of Galilee.

The Galileans were more rustic than their bretheren to the south, but they gave more importance to honor and heroism than wealth and riches. All political parties and rebellions were conceived in the northern province: the latest and most important being the Zealots. When Herod died they started an uprising and forced the Romans out of Galilee. Alas, the Judeans failed to join them, and the Romans brought down their legions from Assyria destroying the capital Sepphoris.

The Galileans, tired of being treated as intellectual inferiors, brought in public education. Their children attended school sporadically, often forced to leave, to earn a few pennies to help feed the family. Most only completed a few years of school and gave up. Yeshua's persistence in continuing, at the age of nineteen was remarkable.

Yeshua was not only the scholar, but the most popular student, and was elected class president, a position the school master created to teach them the Greek concept of democracy. The young man did not receive any benefits or special influence, but was expected to help other students with problems, at school or at home.

Master Benjoseph, a scholar from Jerusalem, soon recognized Yeshua's gift. He argued continuously with master Joseph to send his son to the lyceum, and tried to persuade the old patriarch to let the gifted young scholar continue to university.

Yeshua appeared over the knoll of the hill when a boy, playing ball, announced, "Hey, everybody, master Yeshua is coming back!"

They stopped, looked and ran to greet him, "Welcome back, master Yeshua!"

Master Benjoseph, in his office with visitors, stood up and walked to the window. He was a bit over twenty five, with a head full of curly brown hair, brown eyes, of medium height, but a strong physical frame. When he saw the young scholar, he smiled, "I missed him", he said to the visitors. "A rebel and a troublemaker:..He will be a great leader."

The reunion was warm, with handshakes, embraces or mere touches to show happiness at his return. One girl, big boned, with mousy blond hair, named Drusilla came uncomfortably close to him, "Hello, Yeshua. Welcome back!"

He glanced her way uneasily, "Thank you," and walked away with the boys.

He joined a ball game where one boy threw the ball to another while a third boy in the middle tried to intercept the pass. Yeshua, having joined late was put in the middle.

Lady Sarah was close to the school when they noticed the new student. When they saw her they stopped and stared, mesmerized by the most beautiful and glamorous girl they had ever seen. She wore a sky blue silk gown flowing full length, covered by a maroon cape. On her head she wore a tiara which sparkled in the morning sun. Close behind followed a servant carrying a small basket of books. The students stared as she passed them, her eyes fixed directly ahead. She came to the closed door, climbed up the single step, turned around and fixed her big black eyes directly ahead.

Yeshua stood watching her, as if mesmerized. Ahmed standing behind him, whispered, "She is beautiful. I wonder who she is ..."

"I know her he sighed, "Met her yesterday. Her name is lady Sarah."

They started a new ball game to which Yeshua introduced a change. He started to run asking the boy to toss him the ball while he ran in full flight. Each time he ran closer to lady Sarah. He showed off his prowess and dexterity, jumped and caught the ball over his shoulders, or running backwards. He caught it in every position without dropping it. One time he leaped to the sky, stretching every limb to the fullest, while his finger tips reached and grabbed it. He was graceful, agile, and a gifted athlete. After every catch his eyes darted her way to see if she had seen it. Alas, Sarah stared directly ahead.

After tiring of the exhibition he walked up to her, "Good morning, lady Sarah. Welcome to our lyceum," he smiled nervously.

"Good morning," she responded frigidly without glancing his way.

He stood, trying to think of something but Benjoseph opened the classroom door and rang the bell. Sarah walked in, while the servant went to the adjacent office.

The thirty five students sat in groups according to age: oldest in front. Sarah sat on the front bench, and Yeshua rushed to her side. She went tense.

The school master waited for silence, "Good morning everyone." They answered in unison. "Today we have two new students...Of course, master Yeshua is not new...He comes so infrequently that we need to introduce him every time." He let them enjoy a good laugh before continuing, "The lovely lady has just moved to our humble town. Lady Sarah is from Tyre. Can anyone tell us where Tyre is?"

A few little hands went up and he pointed to one, who stood up, "Tyre is to the west, that way, in the kingdom of Phoenicia," a girl said, pointing her hand.

"Very good, but west is that way," he smiled. "Lady Sarah, tell us about Tyre."

She stood up stiffly and uncomfortably, facing forward and spoke nervously, "Tyre is a city kingdom with its own king. It is a port on the coast of the Great Sea. It is one of the most modern cities in the world. It is on the crossroads from Rome to the eastern empire of Persia and Babylon, and between Athens to the north and Egypt to the south.

"Inside our city walls we have the most modern facilities: a gymnasium, an outdoor theatre, a large modern library...none of which exist in Nazareth." She stopped and the students coughed uncomfortably. She continued unperturbed, "We also have public baths and a lovely beach, which cannot be found here...In Tyre only the bigger houses are inside the walls. The mud huts like the houses here are outside."

She sat down as stiffly as she had stood up. The students exchanged glances and shifted far away from her. They had no concept of a gymnasium, a theatre or a library, but they clearly understood her slight about their peasants' huts.

Master Benjoseph seemed uneasy, coughed into his hands nervously and proceeded, "Master Yeshua, take over the class while I work with the youngsters."

Master Benjoseph often turned the class over to a senior student as good training for them to learn to teach, control the class and speak before his peers. Yeshua always did an excellent job, but lady Sarah's presence made him nervous.

He started out shyly, "Today's review is in rhetoric: What was the most important discovery by ancient man that advanced civilization?" He explained the rules carefully avoiding eye contact with Sarah, "You will be examined on your presentation, originality and defence of your proposition. Who wants to go first?"

Esau raised his hand. Seeing this, Marcus thrust his arm up. Yeshua pointed to the first volunteer. Esau stood up, took a big breath and started, "The greatest discovery was – FIRE! Before fire the nomads had to hunt every day, often unsuccessfully. If they killed an animal they had to eat it in one sitting for it soon spoiled. So they lived from feast to famine, hunting and foraging for roots and berries. And they had to follow the animals south to avoid cold seasons. The constant moving used their energy, making them weak and easy prey to predators and enemies. Fire changed that. They cooked the food which lasted longer. And the fire warmed their caves, and was a good defense against predators and enemies. Because they ate better, rested more, they were stronger and better able to survive." Finished, he gave a gigantic sigh and sat down.

Yeshua nodded, "Excellent presentation." He turned to the others, "Any arguments against Esau's proposition?"

Daniel stood up immediately, "Man did not discover fire. It already existed in volcanoes, from lightning and from the sun's rays. Man copied fire by trial and error."

As soon as he finished Ahmed took over, "What greatly detracts from the importance of fire is that man uses it for destructive purposes. Armies burn people's crops and houses and cause famine. Soldiers boil oil to pour over their enemies. So, a discovery that helped them, too often is used for death and destruction."

"Both arguments have merit, "Yeshua ruled. He turned to Marcus, "What in your opinion was the greatest discovery?"

Marcus expounded with great confidence, "THE WHEEL! Before its discovery the ancients traveled slowly and not far. They could only transport what they carried on their backs, so, often they left possessions behind. Heavily ladened, they made slow progress leaving them vulnerable to predators and enemies. The wheel changed everything. Mobility meant survival, enabling them to travel faster and further. The hunted became the hunter. Also they could transport food, and tools to build shelter, roads and bridges. The wheel shrank the world."

Yeshua was clearly impressed, "That is concise and well presented. Who wishes to dispute master Marcus' presentation?"

James stood up, "The wheel was not discovered by man. Nature produced variations of it: a round log rolled down a hill transporting something. Man only utilized a varied form of something which he copied from nature."

Esau rose up next, "The importance of the wheel is minimized because it is often used for destruction. Armies transport gigantic engines of war, and ballistas that can propel rocks the size of houses at their enemies. They transport giant bows to release deadly arrows, and ladders or heavy logs, to climb up fortified walls and destroy everything. Modern man has made the wheel more a curse than a blessing."

"Bravo Esau," Yeshua cheered encouragement, "that is an ingenious argument."

Marcus objected barely able to mask his jealousy, "Well, I think my presentation, and rhetoric was better than his. I should win." His supporters cheered vigorously.

Yeshua realized the competition from the boat was spilling into the classroom. He needed to take control without embarrassing either friend. After some contemplation he smiled, explaining, "Are you not being premature? Perhaps others have submissions?" He smiled asking, "Lady Sarah, do you wish to add to the topic?"

Surprised she was flustered, "Oh, I...not...prepared..."

Debborah asked impulsively, "Brother Yeshua, give us your proposition."

The young scholar frowned and shook his head vigorously to discourage her, but she would not be denied, "How about man's discovery of his Creator?"

Students who had heard him before cheered hoping to persuade him.

Brother James, led by their enthusiasm, chimed in, "Show the foreigner we have better things than circuses and gladiators: we communicate with God."

"Yeshua knew he could not avoid it, so started his presentation, "Until their greatest discovery, men were no different from the beasts around them: eat or be eaten, kill or be killed. One day they looked up to the heavens and became inspired: humans were different. Of all the creatures, they felt pain because of a loss, and joy when they were happy. Only they shed tears and laughed. They could reason and make plans: for a day, or a lifetime. They had dreams and hopes. Why? Why humans of all creatures?

"That day they realized they were created different. To them was given a purpose. By whom, they wondered? An omnipotent Creator Who created everything bestowed all the glory upon them - but why?

"The Creator wanted man to be His representative on earth and care for it. All He asked was to be loved. That was man's purpose: to work, plan, dream, have visions, use his imagination, and use all that was given to him wisely.

"At the moment of the discovery, myriad new concepts germinated: that the Creator made the finite world and the infinite space, and man began to conceptualize the abstract. He could analyze the minutest seed and the endless universe. And he knew time had a beginning at Creation, and an endless continuum into the future.

"All that, man was to learn in time. But the most important discovery sprouting from this was love, forgiveness and charity. Finally he learned that he was given a divine soul and God's strength within him."

Sarah listened to him, curiosly at first, then with interest, and finally with inspiration. His confident composure, the kindness in his eyes and the feeling of security he eminated, warmed her heart. A voice deep inside her whispered that she could trust him. She also discovered he was sensitive and actractive.

Master Benjoseph stopped and listened to his favorite scholar. The proposition seemed to him more than a question of natural history or evolution of man. He felt he was hearing the metaphysical development of man from the cave to a sophisticated, modern creature guided by a divine hand.

When he finished the schoolmaster took over, "That was an inspired discourse. Does anyone wish to argue against master Yeshua's submission?"

The pupils sat in awe by his presentation. Silently they hoped to remember his speech so they could expound it for the exam. "Our next review is history," the schoolmaster continued. "I will name an important leader of history and you tell me what that person achieved. The first name is Nebuchanezzar..."

"A foreign murderer," Yeshua blurted out passionately. "Why waste time on a foreign murderer who invaded and destroyed us?"

"What do you mean?" Benjoseph was surprised by the objection.

"The answer is the same with every foreigner: they invaded Israel; they killed and pillaged; they took us into bondage. Why pay foreigners homage?"

Benjoseph argued. "They were not all the same…"

Yeshua counted on his fingers as he spoke, "The Babylonians enslaved us. Nebuchanezzar held us to ransom. Epiphanes forced us to worship him as a god…"

"The curriculum orders us to study history," the schoolmaster was apologetic.

"Why study foreigners and elevate them?"

"Do you have a better suggestion?"

"The trash bin is where they belong. Ignore the foreigners and perhaps they will learn to be kinder to our people," he persisted.

He did not notice, but every time he denounced foreigners lady Sarah looked at him, at first with curiosity, then with a cold glare and finally fuming, her fists going tight, her body more tense and her jaws locked ready to snap.

"Study our heroes who were good people," Yeshua continued, "Prophets, scholars and philosophers, all excellent leaders."

"Master Yeshua," the schoolmaster interrupted raising his voice as he was becoming impatient. "When you take charge of the curriculum you may change it. Today you will obey present rules!"

Yeshua sat back, crossing his arms. Lady Sarah smirked.

Benjoseph overruled his scholar not because he disagreed with him. But he had to prepare the students for upcoming difficult exams. In his heart he thought it was a breath of fresh air to have him back.

Mid afternoon the students were released. The youngest, full of pent up energy, felt they had been held prisoners for too long, and scrambled out in a rush to freedom. Yeshua was leaving with the boat crew when the schoolmaster waved him back.

He turned to Esau, "Go ahead. We'll start working on the wood tonight."

When they were alone Benjoseph closed the door, walked to his star pupil and spoke in a low, but stern voice, "Did you forget my previous warnings? Measure your words when speaking about foreigners. You do not live in a free country!"

He blushed realizing his error, and tried to minimize it, "They're students...and friends..."

"Herod has spies everywhere. And desperate families know no friends," the teacher admonished him. "Moreover what about the new foreigner?"

Yeshua stared in shock, "Surely, you would not suspect..." he mumbled, looking into the teacher's cold eyes. Then he realized his error, "You're correct..."

When Benjoseph made his point, he softened his tone, "Enough of that. I have someone I want you to meet." He left the room, went to his office and returned with two young men, a tall slender one about his age and by the appearance of his cloth, from the upper class. "This is master Stephanos, a Greek scholar, and a good friend of mine. We were schoolmates at university. This is his slave Germanicus. This is master Yeshua."

The Israeli stuck out his hand but Stephanos bowed instead, "I am honored."

Yeshua pulled back and bowed stiffly, "At your service, sir."

"Master Stephanos is from Corinth, and a graduate of Athens. Presently he is studying at Alexandria, specializing in eastern religions."

"That must keep you busy," Yeshua quipped. "Every Asian tribe has a religion."

The Greek nodded, "That only accounts for the main ones. Many have broken into factions and splinter groups...Some sects worship the sun, sacrifice virgins, and many still pray to rocks or trees."

"Presently master Stephanos is researching Judaism," Benjoseph explained. "However he has run into obstacles. I suggested you might help."

"I cannot help him," Yeshua refused to get into any discussion about Judaism. "He has access to the best library... excellent books."

"I read them all," Stephanos replied.

"Then you know more than I. I am not interested in...any religion..."

The Greek scholar persisted, "Books are very shallow about Judaism. I want to go deep into it and to do that I am told I must live it."

"Correct. So, travel the country and mingle with the people," Yeshua replied curtly.

"Don't you think I tried? But, I'll get more cooperation from an Egyptian mummy. I tried to sneak into a synagogue, and almost got skinned alive. I have books of notes from Persians and Egyptians. But after traveling across your country," the Greek pulled out a notebook and opened it dramatically, "the papyrus is yellowed, without a scribble."

Benjoseph concurred, "Israelis shut themselves up tighter than a tomb with foreigners." He turned to his student, "Master Stephanos is willing to pay for your help."

"Pay to learn our religion? That is insane!"

The school master responded persuasively, "The money will pay your university."

Yeshua remained steadfast, "I cannot help, and I am not interested in his money."

Benjoseph turned to his friend, "Galilean pride!" Then he pleaded with the student, "Why not take master Stephanos to your home, and discuss it? Listen to his proposal." He led the Greek to the door, "Wait outside. I have another matter to discuss with him."

They started to leave when Stephanos stopped at the doorway, "Perhaps this may persuade you: I'm searching for a legendary person, promised by your God!" Yeshua waited but the Greek went out, turned and said, "THE MESSIAH!"

Yeshua stepped back into the room perplexed. There is that name again: the most mysterious person on the planet. He began to ponder, and did not hear the schoolmaster until he asked, "Master Yeshua, did you hear me? I said master Stephanos comes from a very rich banking family. Money is no problem. Put your pride away and consider his proposition."

"I don't need his pity... The order for the thrones will help us through the crisis..."

"How do you think you got that order?"

Yeshua stared at him, then noticed a shadow of a smirk and blurted out, "You?"

"Perhaps fate could have given you a miracle, but I prefer to give fate a nudge..."

Yeshua was totally confused, and began to shuffle to the door absent mindedly.

"Wait! I have not finished," Benjoseph said and quickly walked from window to window to make sure no one was eavesdropping, "Have you ever heard of the Zealots?"

"Everybody has," he whispered. "The rebels were organized two generations ago by Judas of Galilee. They led a successful uprising freeing Galilee…"

"…Until the Roman legions destroyed them," Benjoseph explained.

"I thought the Zealots were exterminated…?" Yeshua wondered.

The schoolmaster responded proudly, "It will take more than two legions to crush us. We're underground, but reorganizing and coming back stronger than ever!"

"We: Are you…?" Yeshua started but checked himself.

Benjoseph nodded, "We have a cell, small but powerful. Every city, town and hamlet in the country has one."

"Why are you telling me?"

"I want you to join!"

"I abhor violence!" Yeshua exclaimed with finality.

"The Zealots are renouncing violence," the teacher replied. "We are forming a political party instead. When we finish, we will apply for recognition. Our plan is to get control of the nation peacefully and introduce democracy, like the Greeks."

Yeshua smiled, finally understanding why Benjoseph introduced elections and democracy in his class. But he had many questions before making a decision.

"If they forswore violence why are they still underground?"

"We are too weak to go public yet," the teacher explained. Seeing the young man's skeptical stare he added, "Does a wounded deer come out of hiding? The Romans would decimate us, and the Judeans would help."

"Why the Judeans?"

"Quid-pro-quo: the Romans help the Judeans and vice-versa. The Romans learned the trick from the Greeks, who learned it from the Egyptians, who learned it from the Persians; buy up the big men of the little country, and, Pouf! You can have the rest for nothing."

The young scholar thought about it for a few moments finally inquiring, "So the Zealots will represent the people without a voice: the commoners?" Benjosef nodded. "If I join, what will be expected of me?"

Benjoseph did not try to hide his enthusiasm, "We need youth: ideas, leadership, and scholars to manage the transition: draft policies and a constitution. Come to a meeting or two, watch and decide…"

"Are you not afraid I may be a spy?"

Benjoseph chuckled. It was the first time he seemed to relax, "You have been checked out thoroughly. The organization has professional investigators, and I am happy to inform you, you come highly recommended. If you are interested, we will be meeting in a fortnight. Come to the five date palms by master Reuben's vineyard at sundown. You will be picked up and taken to the meeting."

Yeshua responded immediately, "I will be there. Have you considered inviting Esau to join? He would be an excellent candidate."

The teacher smiled, "I thought you might suggest him, so we had him checked out as well. You may bring him." The young man picked up his napsack and started for the door. "Before I forget," the schoolmaster added, "Rabbi ben Lebbus wishes to see you. He'll meet you at the synagogue at sunset." Yeshua nodded. When he reached the door the schoolmaster called again, "Are you still friends with that Roman soldier, whose name escapes me...?"

"Master Quintus: yes why?"

"When you join the Zealots you will have to cease your friendship," Benjoseph informed him. When he saw Yeshua's face tightening, he quickly added, "Nobody is accusing or doubting his character. But, if his commander decides to go after Zealots..."

The Young scholar interjected resentfully, "Master Quintus is one of the fairest friends anyone can have. It is the height of cynicism to accuse him..."

"I am not accusing him, or doubting you. But, his duty to Rome will put him in an awkward position." He watched the young man, defiant and angry, so suggested, "Ask Quintus, if his officer ordered him to arrest you, would he do it?"

Yeshua left, irate and confused. Why should he question a friend who just donated cartloads of wood for free? The exchange raised questions about the Zealots. He had nationalistic feelings and wanted Israel free. But, did he have to compromise a friendship? What rights did the Zealots have to ask him to pre-judge a person who was beyond suspicion? If they could force him to end this friendship today, would he have to give up others tomorrow? Perhaps give up members of his family? He began to question the values of the organization. Like all institutions it demanded obedience from the members. But, who would control the Zealots from abusing their powers? Perhaps he ought to join for that very reason: to make sure that they did not abuse their power...

He walked out deeply disturbed not seeing who waited for him: Stephanos with lady Sarah, her servant with the Greek's slave Germanicus. When she saw him, Sarah marched at him resolutely, peppering him with accusations, "Master Yeshua, you are a bigot! For all your inspiring words about a Creator you showed your true character. You are a narrow minded, prejudiced bigot!" As she advanced he retreated, "Who said all foreigners are murderers? I'm a foreigner...and I have not murdered anyone...YET!"

"I did not say all foreigners..."

"Oh! So you're also a liar?" she barked. "Let me quote you: 'All foreign leaders invaded, pillaged and murdered.' Do you deny those words?"

He squirmed, "I may have...I did not..."

"Is that how Israelis see us? I heard this was a closed society. But I never expected it to be bigoted, biased and prejudiced" her voice began to quiver with anger.

"I never meant ...I meant kings and generals..."

Sarah scoffed with disbelief, "You said all foreigners - no exceptions. What about Israelis?" He was about to argue, but she pressed on, "When Abraham arrived, this land was inhabited by Canaanites. How did he get their land? By invasion and wars!"

"It never..." he kept retreating.

She jabbed him in the chest steadily advancing, "And Moses? He stole the land of milk and honey, dividing it with his invaders. Philistines and Canaanites lived here...they stole Jericho and pillaged other cities. Can you defend that?"

"I was not defending Moses," he retreated to the edge of a steep bank.

"You're free with accusations she went on, "Did you not stand in my yard and say, 'I predict the foreigners who will move here probably are murderers?'" His mouth unhinged. Then he remembered his words to brother Simon and sighed guiltily. She continued her onslaught, "I have hardly met you only to learn you run over people, you're a child beater, and hate foreigners! But I'm sure you'll surprise me with baser qualities!" She turned away and called, "Master Stephanos, please escort me home."

Yeshua had never been so thoroughly trounced. He had withstood worse from the congregation but her words pierced his heart. He watched her and the Greek walk away talking and laughing. He remembered his resolve that morning:"Befriend her before sunset"…and quickened his step.

He walked on Sarah's right with the Greek on her left. He noticed she only spoke to the Greek, refusing to turn his way. He decided to apologize and grovel if necessary…if she ever looked his way.

She purred for the Greek, "Why did you leave the enchanted Greek islands for this dark corner of the world?"

"My research," he sighed dramatically as if confessing a crime. "I admit Greece is the cradle of civilization, but Israel is the birthplace of modern religion. The only nation with monotheism: one God! Do you know they have a personal relationship with God? They speak to Him. There are reports of miracles…"

She interjected chuckling, "There is no greater embellishment than superstitious exaggerations by simple peasants explaining a natural event…" Then she caught herself and looked at her thumb, "I was nearly a victim of such sorcery the first day…"

"Really? Tell me about it. This is precisely the type of information I'm seeking."

She almost started, then quickly glanced to her right and changed her mind, "I would rather not. I may be the victim of…black magic…"

"Were you threatened? Who is the scoundrel?" he demanded with bravado.

"I don't know," she lied and tried to gloss it over, "I read that these people practice a curious cult, and blood sacrifices. That may have affected my imagination…"

Yeshua listened hoping to learn about the sorcery she mentioned. Yet he was thankful she decided not to pursue it. He had created enough troubles without having to defend mysteries he did not understand. At the first opportunity he spoke out, "Lady Sarah, I wish to offer my sincerest apologies for all the…"

But she raised her voice over his, "I love Greece: the birthplace of culture and beauty. Father imported statuettes from Athens and I fell in love. They seem so vibrant, I swear they're alive. They're the sole evidence of culture in this barren town."

"Have you ever been to our enchanted islands?"

She shook her head sighing, "It's my dream to sail there someday. Visit the Acropolis in Athens, walk by the Parthenon, sit in the colossal amphitheatre…"

Stephanos added expansively, "To walk among Phidias' sculptures is like promenading the enchanted walks of paradise. Zeus sculpted of ivory and gold at Olympus is one of the modern wonders of the world. Marvel at the majestic figures, the harmony and fluidity of Aphrodite's lines by the great Praxiteles... Ah! There you witness perfection!" he exclaimed to the heavens.

She could barely hide her envy, "You're so blessed to have seen, and touched them. I have only seen books...And there is not even a library in this forsaken town..."

The Greek sang with a reverie, "Blessed are they who heard the greatest philosophers: Xenophanes, Plato, Dyogenes... crystal clear classical reasoning."

"Where has it all gone, master Stephanos?"

His mood swung from sadness to fury, "Barbarians: the Romans invaded, and robbed the best culture in the world. They left nothing but a barren desert in their wake.

She did not seem persuaded, "I understand a Greek not liking a Roman, but are you not exaggerating?"

He countered with venom spewing, "They stole our best philosophers and artists. And in two hundred years they have achieved one invention: the stylus...Unless you include war machines and destruction!"

She decided to drop the topic that upset her companion, and they continued in silence. Yeshua seized the moment and rattled his apology in one breath, "Lady Sarah, I wish to extend my sincerest apologies for my thoughtless behaviour and my insensitive statements..." She started to turn towards him with a tender smile, when he added, "As to our collision yesterday, you must take some of the blame..."

She huffed and turned back to the Greek, continuing as if there had been no interruption, "Romans may be what you say, but I love their theatre - passionate drama."

Stephanos scoffed, "All stolen from us: the style, form, even the messages!"

"Perhaps, but they added passion and romance!"

"Cheap thrills! Superficial slapstick," he retorted. "Take Menander: the mirror of life is unequalled!"

"I prefer Plautus. His play THE MERCHANT where the son, sent on a business trip by the father bought a lovely lady," she started laughing. "Upon returning he tries to hide her from the old man who discovers her and immediately falls in love. The old dottard then persuades a friend to buy her and hide her in his home until he can explain her presence to his son…" she broke out in a loud laughter unable to continue.

Stephanos tried to interject a couple of times but her laughter drowned him out. Yeshua had read the story, and chuckled, shaking his head.

Sarah finally regained control and continued, "The situation of coincidences of the father, son and the girl continuously bumping into each other was hilarious. I admit it strained one's sense of credibility, but he did everything to get a laugh."

"Such brainless humor delights only the senses of those who laugh at the follies of others," Stephanos remarked acidly.

She insisted with enthusiasm, "What about Terence? There is a first class Roman playwright: respects family values, and his stories are filled with love and respect of the young for their elders. And, so full of romance…"

"Utter trash - melodrama!" Stephanos was unforgiving. "He copied everything from the great Aristophanes. There was a Greek who gave great themes to the world."

She countered, "Greek plays are so clinically logical, like a promenade through a proposition of geometry: as frigid as ice - no passion!"

The Greek spat out, "You mean no clever, contrived lessons of shallow morality. No sentimentality. Don't pass concocted mush for good drama. We don't indulge in tears, for ours is an exercise of the mind - pure reason!"

Sarah argued passionately, "Life is not pure reason. Logic! Life is passionate, full of illogical decisions. That's what makes it so beautiful!"

"Overstirred, overcooked mush," Stephanos declared with finality.

"Even Terence's biography is touching. Did you know he was born a slave, and due to his immense talent, his master paid for his education then gave him freedom?"

She was shocked by the Greek's reaction, "Psst! Not so loud! If my slave hears you I'll have no end of problems. He's already demanding more freedom. A slave…!"

Don't you give him any freedom?" she asked somewhat shocked.

"He's a slave!" he replied as if that explained everything. He threw his hands up in the air, "Everybody wants more freedom than they have."

Yeshua soliloquized sardonically, "Slaves are such predatory creatures. He will steal your best pair of sandals when all you've done is stolen his freedom!"

Sarah turned to him with admiration. Stephanos glared. The slave overheard him and took a liking to the Israeli. They continued for a great distance in silence.

Yeshua, who had been left out of the conversation volunteered, "I have never seen live theatre, but read the plays in the schoolmaster's books. The Greeks explain life as if it were simple logic. The Romans are all emotions. Two extremes, neither of them right." They scoffed with an air of superiority as he continued, "Do you want real drama? Watch our peasants. One day of their lives has more drama than all contrived plays."

They continued silently, Sarah resolved not to glance or speak to the Israeli.

Stephanos who refused to let go returned to the attack, "Look how the Roman barbarians skewed the Olympiads. We developed the sport as intellectual development. That was not bloody enough for them. So they dragged prisoners of war, slaves and professional killers, pitting one against the other. Blood is Roman for sport!"

"Do you have a singular dislike for Romans?" Sarah inquired grimly.

"No! I dislike all barbarians equally!"

"Do you think Romans profaned the Olympiad?" She asked with a smirk. "I am told the Israelis invented a new sport: sparring with staffs!"

"A shepherd's staff in the Olympiad...?" Stephanos asked incredulously. "Who are they going to skirmish against - sheep?" They enjoyed a chuckle.

Sarah explained sarcastically, "A peasant youth against a full grown panther!"

"That's suicide," he retorted.

"I was told a young man did not suffer a scratch in one such battle!"

"Incredulous!" The Greek exclaimed. "Hercules would wisely avoid the confrontation." He turned to the Israeli, "Is it true - an Israeli beat a panther?"

Yeshua deadpanned, "Probably an embellishment by exaggerating, superstitious peasants, for which we are famous..."

Stephanos broke into a contagious laughter, enjoying the Israeli's revenge. Sarah blushed and her jaw tightened that her sarcasm had backfired. Yeshua was never more uncomfortable, admitting their differences were irreconcilable. The sharpest saber could not cut the heavy air around them.

After a long silence Sarah sighed dreamily, "Do you know what I will desperately miss about Tyre? The lazy afternoon sails on the Great Sea. Nothing is more blissful than sitting on the gunnel, while the boat skims through the waves serenely, almost dreamily, ghosting along as the sun sinks in the ocean. A cool zephyr blowing through your hair and you daydream…I'll forever cherish those moments, when I felt as free as the seagulls, praying it would never end…"

Yeshua interjected with enthusiasm, "Lady Sarah, you can enjoy those blissful days again! We are building a sailboat. I'll take you sailing as often as you wish…"

Caught off guard she became confused, and reacted impulsively, "Oh! Here is my road. I have to go. Thank you, master Stephanos…" She turned right abruptly almost running over Yeshua who jumped out of the way, as she scurried away with her servant.

The young men were shocked by her reaction, and watched her for a moment before resuming. Yeshua sighed with relief, his confidence shattered. Stephanos had watched Sarah's behavior, suddenly turned to his companion with a broad smirk, walked over and slapped his back, "Congratulations, you cunning fox! The young lady is clearly smitten by you! It's scribed all over her face…and in every action. "

Yeshua almost fell forward, regained his balance and asked stupefied, "Who?"

"Don't tell me you did not notice: Lady Sarah! She's simply mad about you."

The Israeli stared at him skeptically, expecting him to break out into laughter at any moment. When he did not Yeshua sniggered, "You're mad!"

"Never more serious: it was in her every action, every word and every move!"

"She accused me of the basest behaviour, and nearly ran over me to escape," he retorted. "And in between she ignored me. Where was she smitten…?"

"Everywhere - body language," the Greek exclaimed. "I never saw a girl try to avoid looking at someone so hard. She wrestled to not say a word to you. Yes, she was drawn to you like a magnet. It is as clear as the sun in the sky!"

Yeshua let out a sick chuckle at the outrageous proposition. It was so preposterous it did not warrant consideration so he walked away. Stephanos realized he did not believe him, so decided to clarify, "How much experience have you had with girls?" Before he replied he added, "Excluding mothers, sisters, and school friends." Yeshua's face began contorting, "Ten?" The Israeli shook his head. "Seven? Five...? Three?" His question had a hint of incredulity so Yeshua looked down at his sandals. The Greek let out a cheer, "I thought young men like you existed only in books of fiction!" He announced as if he had just discovered a rare gem.

"I have been too busy," the Israeli replied as if begging forgiveness for a sin.

Stephanos put his arm around his innocent companion's shoulders and began as a doting mother, "Three types of women will ignore you: the first will not speak unless forced to. You'll tremble from the frost of her cold breath. The second will look through you as if you were glass. The third will look at you as if you were a pair of worn out sandals."

"Did you not just describe lady Sarah's behavior three times?"

The Greek sniggered, "To the uninitiated eye! In reality none of those are lady Sarah! She refused to look at you, interrupted and changed topics. Why? Because she cares! She wrestled not to speak to you, yet snuck a sideway peek at every chance!" He sighed, "Ah! What rare, clear demonstration of exuberant infatuation!"

"For a logical Greek you speak utter nonsense!"

Stephanos continued unperturbed, "When you found a common topic – sailing – she became so flustered she took the wrong road!" He leaned close pointing with his head, "Don't look now, but she is behind us!"

Yeshua glanced back furtively and saw them following, "You're correct!"

Stephanos was pleased to have earned his trust. Yeshua was shocked by the discovery about the fairer sex, and sought clarification, "Assuming you are correct ...What do you advise I do?"

Stephanos thought a long time, "Give her the same treatment...only double it." He watched his companion but when his eyes did not light up, he added, "When the girl ignores you, you double – ignore her. If she asks a question, don't answer, but ask her a question back! If she answers your question, no matter what, contradict her! I call it a double-reverse psychological extremis. Contradict her, go from hot to cold, love one moment, hate the next. Keep her off guard."

"The cure sounds worse than the illness. Are you certain this will bring her closer?"

"Like iron to a magnet! And, for good measure make her jealous."

He shook his head, "Giving a girl cause to hate, makes her love you…"

"She'll gravitate to you like a moon to the planet!"

Yeshua was far from persuaded, "Have you tried this double-perverse extremis?"

"Reverse," the Greek corrected, "The more bizarre I behaved the more interesting the results. I was successful…sometimes."

Yeshua rebuked him impatiently, "Do you know what I think? You are deranged. If lady Sarah plays your bizarre games I will purge her from memory, and out of my life." He quickened his step leaving the Greek behind.

Stephanos ran after him, "If you're finished with her, can I try my luck?"

That pushed the young scholar over the brink as he screamed, "I don't care! Take her and go to…go to…out of my life!" He swept his arm violently forcing the Greek to duck. He marched away adding bitterly, "Here is my answer; I refuse to teach, or help you in any way…" he turned and retraced a few steps, "or find the Messiah. Good bye!"

The Greek stopped and watched him walk some distance before yelling, "Master Yeshua, where do you live? We passed all the houses…"

Yeshua stopped, looked around and turned back slowly. Retracing his steps he passed them and muttered, "One block back there. But, don't bother to follow."

They retraced their steps and Stephanos tried to joke, "Greece had the greatest philosophers and mathematicians; Pericles, Pythagoras, who solved insurmountable problems. Not one of them tried to explain a woman. Do you know why?"

"I don't care," he snapped curtly.

"Because they cannot be analysed using mathematics, logic or science. Only one – a meteorologist – defined a woman: 'Like the weather – UNPREDICTABLE!'"

· · ·

When Judas and Salome saw their eldest brother arriving with strangers, one of them carrying a spear, they ran to warn their parents, who came out to greet them. The boat crew was busy sawing the planks in the far corner of the yard.

Yeshua introduced his family, "My father, master Joseph, my mother lady Miriam. This is my brother James, and my youngest siblings Judas and Salome. Master Stephanos is a Greek scholar, presently researching eastern religions."

Joseph stuck out his hand, but Stephanos bowed instead. "Welcome to Israel," the patriarch smiled. "Are you here to teach Yeshua?"

"On the contrary, sir, I hope to persuade him to teach me."

Miriam asked as he bowed to her, "Will you join us for a snack? We were waiting for Yeshua to arrive."

"It will be my pleasure."

They started towards the door when Joseph asked, "Is your friend not joining us?"

Stephanos brushed him off, "He is my slave, Germanicus. He is happier outside."   Entering, Stephanos touched a metallic tube, the mezuzah attached to the door frame reciting, "SHEMA ISRAEL, ADONAI ELOHNU, ADONAI EHAD."

The parents, filled with wonder, looked at each other.

"That is the Shema in Hebrew, father," Yeshua explained and said it in their daily Aramaic language, "Hear oh Israel; the Lord our God, the Lord is one."

Everyone touched the mezuzah as always, reciting the shema silently.

Joseph asked very impressed, "Do you speak Hebrew?"

"I picked up a few words while doing my research. This is the only phrase I know."

"It is the only one any Israeli needs to know," the patriarch suggested. "Although I believe in our town no one knows it in Hebrew."

They sat around the fire as Miriam and Anna served soup with a slice of bread. Miriam whispered to the servant girl to also serve the young slave Germanicus outside, and the boat crew. Anna nodded.

Joseph got to the point, "Master Stephanos, why the interest in our religion?"

"All eastern religions intrigue me. As you may know our Greek poets and playwrights invented Zeus, and gave him a family clan. Unfortunately the plays they concocted involve our gods in the most bizarre intrigues, so that today, only the most faithful believe in their divinity. The Roman barbarians fared no better: copied our gods shamelessly, gave them Roman names, and involved them in cheap fiction. Only the easterners, have kept their gods mysterious, none more so than the Israelis.

"One day while researching in Babylon, I met a sultan, a wise old man who told a fantastic story. Almost two score years ago, the Israelis experienced a supernatural event: a bright celestial object stationed itself above the nation. No astronomer could explain the phenomenon. The sultan, out of curiosity, started to travel to investigate. Others followed. By and by he met two elderly patriarchs, a potentate and a wealthy magi, and they traveled together. They arrived at a hamlet and discovered the cause of the commotion: the birth of a special child!"

He stopped, and his experienced eyes of a raconteur, traveled over them seeing their eyes riveted on him. Judas and Salome were biting into the bread eagerly, not missing a word or gesture. Joseph's eyes popped wide as a saucer, and darted to his wife who was ashen white with her hands shaking. Stephanos was pleased to see them so attentive. James nibbled at his bread, half listening, while Yeshua was suffering the agony of the painful promenade from school.

Stephanos continued, "The late king Herod was told that the bright object in the sky announced a special child: destined to be king of Israel."

Joseph went into a coughing frenzy, while Miriam gasped, and the children cheered, "This story is getting good!"

Master Stephanos smiled and continued, "Herod who was already half insane, ordered his soldiers to seek out and murder the usurper. The family disappeared, never to be heard from again."

There was a long silence. The children were clearly disappointed. Only the scraping of the metallic spoon was heard as Miriam's hand shook digging out the soup.

Joseph mustered sufficient courage to ask, "S-so y-you want t-to f-find this family?"

The Greek nodded excitedly, "The more I researched, the oftener I kept hearing the same name…not a name, a title of a legendary person long promised in your tradition. People said this was the anointed one, who I intend to find: the MESSIAH!"

Miriam dropped the big spoon spilling out its contents which splashed in every direction, "Oh! I'm so sorry…" she cried out, handing the pot to Anna and started to wipe off the mats.

Anna was not faring better. The knife trembled as she tried to cut the bread.

Yeshua turned to his mother who had just sat down, "Mother, don't you know the Messiah?"

Miriam who had just taken a bite of bread, gasped, almost choking and went into a coughing fit. Anna jerked and spilled soup almost dropping everything. She glanced furtively to see if anyone saw her reaction.

Stephanos waited for Miriam to stop, but she continued to cough, so he turned to Yeshua, "Did you say she knows a Messiah? Is there more than one?"

"Quite a few. In the past week I heard of three. And the priests in Jerusalem said there were a dozen crisscrossing the country!"

The Greek frowned, troubled by the news, "They cannot all be the real Messiah... can they? Surely your God would only send one...?"

Joseph who thought the question was directed at him nodded, "Y-yes, o-one is e-enough!"

The young scholar concurred, "It will make your research difficult, but more interesting. You'll do investigative work, like a detective. Some are sure to be imposters."

"More complex than you think," Stephanos remarked. "I believe the parents of the real Messiah have not revealed his true identiy..."

"Why would they do such a mean thing?" Yeshua asked visibly perturbed.

Stephanos explained sympathetically, "Don't be rash. Remember that Herod wanted to kill him. The Romans would surely finish him off. What parents would want to expose their child to such danger?"

Joseph and Miriam exchanged glances.

Yeshua studied the Greek with suspicion, and accused him, "Is that why you want to find him? To tell the world and have him killed?"

The Greek demurred defensively, "I resent your accusations. I am a scholar, not a spy. My intentions are honorable. I wish to advance the Judaic religion, I swear!"

James joined the discussion for the first time, "My brother's question is pertinent. Why is a Greek interested in the Judaic Messiah, if not to help our oppressors?"

Stephanos spoke with disarming sincerity, "The potentate said the Messiah was a messenger of God. If so his message belongs to all mankind!"

Anna took the pot and went to feed the boat crew and Germanicus. While Joseph visited with the Greek, Yeshua tried to recall all he had read about the Messiah. He remembered old prophetic scripts. But those were all too general to be any help. Years ago he gave up on the legendary person as a figment of overactive imaginations.

As he sat pondering, he became troubled, because if he existed, the Messiah was about his age. If they persisted they would tear away his only protection, and he would never again know privacy or happiness. That made up his mind and he spoke empathically, "Master Stephanos, I will not help you. I have pressing obligations here…"

The Greek pleaded, "What if I help you with them so you will be free?"

"Well, I still have a few dozen sieves to complete, and I have undertaken to construct a sailboat…"

Joseph guffawed, "James will finish the sieves."

"As to the sailboat, did you not say Esau was in charge?" Miriam reminded him.

"He is having problems, mother…"

"Did you not expect problems?" she countered. "You wanted to give him the opportunity…How will he do it if you won't let go?"

The young scholar realized he could not win, and sighed heavily.

Joseph announced proudly, "Master Stephanos, Yeshua will lead the expedition."

"Let's go on the roof and and check out your plans," the young scholar walked out resolved, and far from pleased.

As they went up Yeshua noticed the slave Germanicus sharing his meal with Anna, seemingly enjoying a good visit. On the roof top he sat down and motioned the Greek to join him. "How long will the expedition take?" he asked.

"I rented a house in town for two weeks. It should be adequately long…?"

Yeshua did not answer, but stared at him, as he computed it in his mind. Suddenly he got up, went to his room, got papyrus, ink and a stylus, handed them to the Greek in a curt manner, ordering, "Start scribing." The Greek got everything ready. The young Israeli started;

'In the beginning God created the heaven and the earth,

'And the earth was without form and void,

'And darkness was upon the face of the deep,

'And the spirit of God moved upon the face of the waters...`Keep writing. Why have you stopped?"

The Greek objected, "What are you doing? I already know this..."

"You cannot learn Judaism in two weeks," Yeshua snapped, "but if you insist you have no time to waste. Keep scribing!"

"How long do you think it will take?"

"You said yourself to learn Judaism you have to live it. First, we have to get the supplies prepared; juice, wine, grain...the journey will be a long one..."

Stephanos was confused, "What are you talking about?"

"It will take months to locate the Messiahs, which means we will need to prepare all supplies: wheat, grain, vegetables, fruit and so on..."

"Prepare? I'll buy them."

"To learn our faith you must live the traditions: harvesting, cleaning, milling, drying. Judaism must be in your veins and permeate your every pore."

Stephanos asked bluntly, "My first lesson: follow your advice if I want your help?"

Yeshua deadpanned, "Very perceptive...for a Greek. I have a meeting with the rabbi. I'll see you again tomorrow. Meantime locate maps of the country. Until tomorrow." As he descended he overheard the slave visiting with Anna.

"How long have you been a slave?" she asked.

"Too long," he grumbled frowning, then added in a low tone, as if sharing a deep secret, "but I have plans...it won't be for much longer..."

"What do you intend to do?"

"Well," he started out then looked around to make sure no one could hear, when he saw Yeshua he answered evasively, "Well, I can't say it right now..."

"Have you tried discussing it with your master? I heard of cases where they let the slave buy his freedom, or let them free after time," she suggested.

Germanicus scoffed, "He won't discuss it. Why should he? He comes from a family of bankers. They don't need money."

Anna saw he was desperate, for his voice was tense, so she touched his hand and murmured tenderly, "Be careful. Don't take unnecessary risks."

"I'll have everything planned to the last detail...I won't be foolish."

She looked directly into his blue eyes, "What will you do?"

"Return to northern Europe, my place of birth."

"Oh, I would love to see Europe," she sighed longingly. "I have never been there…"

"It is truly beautiful, with real changes every season," he explained with a passion in his voice. "Each winter nature goes dormant for a long rest. The cool snow covers everything as if purging the very soul of the land. In the spring there is new life; budding flowers, birds, butterflies…It is as if our gods sang to welcome a new world…"

Yeshua passed by, interrupting them as he went to the back yard to check on the boat crew.

Anna leaned forward and whispered as she pointed to Yeshua, "He is a very special man."

"You mean a politician, or a judge?" Germanicus asked.

"More important than that!"

"Then he must be a priest," the slave ventured. "In our tribe the spiritual man, is very important also."

"He is not really those either. But I cannot tell you…Some day I may be at liberty to…" her voice trailed off.

Yeshua walked towards the boat crew, stopping a dozen paces from them. He could hear Esau and Marcus having an argument.

"The design is quite clear," Esau exclaimed, pointing to the papyrus. "It shows a deep keel right here and that's how we'll build it"

"I don't care what the design shows," Marcus was equally stubborn. "My uncle has fished for thirty years and has never seen such a lopsided boat. That…that appendage makes it looks like a pregnant…whale."

"It's progress," Esau argued, "and it will prove safer than leeboards!"

"My uncle says he's never seen anything like it. It won't work!"

Daniel who had been trying to understand the drawing raised his arms, "Wait a moment. Why argue if we don't know how it works? Explain this."

Esau ran his index finger on the papyrus as he spoke, "The keel will be deep and hollow, but an integral part of the boat. After we complete it we'll put rocks in for ballast. It will keep the boat upright, even with some wind, and it will track better."

Ahmed guffawed sardonically, "Who builds a boat to fill it with rocks?"

Daniel nodded, "I agree. Nobody ever heard of boats with rocks."

"Everybody agrees with me…and my uncle. Why be so stubborn? Let's stay with what the fishermen understand - leeboards. They've been around for generations."

"I thought the same until master Yeshua proved the advantages of a keel," Esau defended his position. "The keel minimizes leeway and will keep the boat upright in storms. And it will not break off."

Marcus interjected with a tone laced with sarcasm "The only use for stones is to fight an enemy attack! I say we build what we know!"

Esau wondered whether Quintus was correct: get rid off the rebel. Instead, he announced with a tired tone, "It's been a long day. We'll discuss it tomorrow."

"Let's put it to a vote right now," Daniel demanded." I'm sure Marcus is right…"

Esau ignored them, and left, passing by Yeshua without a nod. That's when they first noticed him.

Marcus muttered apologetically, "I'm sorry you had to hear my remarks about your drawings. But, the concept is so new…"

"I imagine that's what the boaters said the first time they saw leeboards," Yeshua smiled as he advanced, "What are those ungainly boards? They're too new, they'll break off." He looked at each one, but they avoided eye contact. He said, "I don't wish to discuss design or construction. That you must decide with Esau. I wish to speak to you about him."

"Esau? What's to be said that we don't already know?"

The young scholar started slowly, sadly, measuring every word carefully, "Esau is an outcast…all his life, because he is a bastard."

Daniel spluttered, "Anyone who has lived here one week knows that. What's the problem?"

"The problem is not that everybody knows, but that no one ever forgets," Yeshua replied and let them dwell on the statement for awhile. "A bastard, outcast, outsider… it's a lifetime sentence. It's a cross he bears from birth to his grave." His eyes went from one to the other, as they shuffled uncomfortably. "We were children when the bullies in town punished little Esau, pushing, punching, picking on him for being a bastard as if he were the carrier of a contagious disease. They called him names, belittled him and refused to play with him. Do you remember that master Marcus?"

"I did not make him a bastard," Marcus retorted angrily.

Yeshua continued, "Bigger boys, like you, beat him regularly. Remember?" Marcus looked at his sandals and bit his lower lip. Ahmed and Daniel stared at him. "Bullying only stopped when I warned them if they touched him again they would answer to me. The bullying stopped, but the abuse continued: a subtle, mental abuse. Girls avoided him because no family wanted a bastard. Our synagogue denied him the bar mitzvah. He was the untouchable...discarded and alone."

Marcus interrupted with tension in his voice, "It's not us. Our law says..."

The young scholar interrupted, raising his voice impatiently, "Shall I quote you the law? 'A bastard shall not enter into the congregation of the Lord: even to his tenth generation shall he not enter...'" Yeshua's eyes shone with a radiance they had not seen before as he spoke passionately, "I tell you truly, Esau is more worthy than any of us. He has never abused anyone, and he suffered in silence. His father married a woman already married, but he is punished for the misdeeds of his parents..."

"Why do you blame us?" Daniel pleaded.

Yeshua rebuked him, "We must rebel against unjust laws, or we will be as guilty as the authors of it. Esau wants a chance. He chose you, his friends, to be his judge..."

"He did not. You did," Ahmed snapped.

The young scholar shook his head, "I chose the ultra conservative students. It was Esau who wanted you."

Marcus picked up his belongings grumbling defiantly as he motioned to leave, "We did not make the law, and I refuse to share his burden."

"You already share it," he spoke with a finality in his voice. They looked at him wondering what he meant, so he clarified, "An unjust law needs two people - the victim and the executioner."

They were stung by the rebuke, and stood uneasy. After a few moments they shuffled away into the night.

Yeshua went to the house, peeked in the door and announced to his parents, "Rabbi ben Lebbus wishes to see me. I'm going to the synagogue..."

His parents rushed out with panick on their faces, "Don't agree to any sermons."

The young man stopped at the gate, "Sermons: in Nazareth? Never!"

CHAPTER V - RIOTS IN THE SYNAGOGUE

While Yesua was going to meet the rabbi, Ben Lebbus sat in the small room adjacent to the synagogue where he taught religion to the boys. It was a simple room with a long desk in the middle, his chair on one side, and a long bench for the boys on the opposite side. The ornaments were sparse: the Star of David hanging on the wall, and the menorah, a seven candle candelabra on a small table in the far corner. Whenever the rabbi came in he opened the side door to the synagogue so he could see the Arc of the Covenant which held the Torah.

He looked tired and gaunt. Ever since the biggest crisis of his life, two months ago, he was forced to fight church fanatics, duties for which he had no training. He ran from disgruntled congregants to vengeful church elders, to equally explosive town council, each out-demanding the other to punish the young scholar. Their demands were vicious: death by stoning. The rabbi sat staring at the wall. He had deep circles under his eyes, and his long beard seemed greyer. Where did he go wrong? He wondered.

He was never under the delusion that he was a gifted intellect, or a great scholar. But he was inspired to spend endless hours reading and studying the scriptures, a tedious, thankless task, until he evolved into the religious teacher. He had no training. He received no pay. But, he did not care. His olive grove supported his family. And, his first love, after his family was the Book, and the young children he taught.

To be sure, the children were expected to receive the first religious training from their fathers. They were expected to recite the Sheema by age five, be familiar with the Genesis, the Exodus, the story of the Atonement, and the history and tradition of the nation. At age five they were brought to the rabbi to be taught the Scriptures.

He remembered vividly the first time Yeshua was brought to this room. He was not yet six, and smaller than the average. His most striking features were his vivid dark eyes with such a fixed stare that he seemed to catch one in a vice grip. He placed both elbows on the desk, his chin in his hands, and fixed his dark eyes on the rabbi. Every week he sat, listening, never uttering a sound. Well into the second month the rabbi wondered if the boy was sleeping with his eyes open. One day he decided to test him, asking a question from a lesson he gave two weeks before: "Master Yeshua, why is the Sabbath such an important day?"

The boy lifted his head answering without hesitation, "Because it is the day for worshipping Lord Adonai. We are forbidden to work or go anywhere but the synagogue."

The rabbi chirped most impressed, "Very good my child."

But Yeshua was not finished and asked, "Rabbi, if a child was sick and about to die on the Sabbath, but a doctor could save her if he gave her medicine that very day… would Lord Adonai punish him for doing good work?"

The rabbi's smile froze as he tried to think of a good answer unsuccessfully. Finally he snapped, "Who told you to ask this question: your father? Did he put you up to this?"

Yeshua shook his head responding innocently, "When I asked my father he said he did not know. So I decided to ask you…"

The rabbi tried to carry on, but, every time he looked at Yeshua he felt guilty. So he dismissed them took out the Scriptures, searching for an acceptable answer unsuccessfully. At length he sighed, "The Sabbath is for worship: no exceptions!"

The boy persisted, "God will let her die? But the doctor can come to worship the following day…"

Ben Lebbus sighed wondering why he was being so difficult, "The Lord will come into the congregation when there are ten Israeli adults gathered. If the doctor came next day the Lord would not be present. No exceptions."

Yeshua stared at the rabbi, clearly not persuaded. When the rabbi reconsidered, he realized something was not right but refused to argue with the Book.

A few years passed when they had another confrontation. On that occasion Yeshua asked why Lord Adonai was mean to His people. The rabbi disagreed, so the boy pressed, "Is there a story where Lord Adonai shows appreciation, and gives a reward for good work?"

The rabbi tried to think of such a passage, looked down at the scroll, without recalling one. Instead he retorted not unkindly, "We are expected to perform our duties, work hard and make sacrifices...Good work is its own reward!" he muttered a few unintelligible grunts, finally promising he would research the Torah for examples. Yeshua thanked him and sat down. But the rabbi was not able to continue the lesson, dismissed them early and dug into the books. He researched well into the night without success. Lord Adonai did not congratulate them for good work, yet He was not shy to punish them. The rabbi sat back exhausted and for the second time in his life questioned the writings. Why were there no stories of love from the Creator for His people?"

From that day the rabbi referred to Yeshua as the young scholar.

Within a few months Yeshua posed another question, "Rabbi ben Lebbus, why did we push the Creator out of our lives?"

"We did no such thing. We love Lord Adonai and try to show it everyday."

The young scholar retorted, "Then why do we not call Him by His name? We call Him Adonai when we know it is..."

The rabbi screamed, "Don't say it! It's blasphemy..."

"But the High Priest says it every year." he responded. "Did the Priests from the Temple push themselves between the people and the Creator?"

The rabbi was shocked by the proposition, but did not dare to reply.

The boy's thirteenth year was one filled with crisis. All the deserving students were going to Jerusalem for the bar mitzvah. But the rabbi stubbornly refused to approve Yeshua's application, not because he was not prepared, but, because he argued about the Scriptures, questioned lessons, and said that many lessons in the Book were wrong.

Privately the rabbi respected the young scholar's opinion but he knew the Sanhedrin with their arrongant Priests, would not suffer fools lightly. If he argued or contradicted them, they could refuse him the right of manhood, and throw him out of the Temple, or worse: charge him with blasphemy and have him stoned. He demanded an unequivocal promise from him not to argue, before signing the papers. Yeshua refused to do it, but seeing the disappointment on his parents' faces he relented.

No sooner did the rabbi sign, that Yeshua inadvertently caused another crisis. He refused to go to Jerusalem unless his good friend Esau was also approved. He studied dilligently, but the law forbade a bastard to join the congregation. The rabbi warned him that he was wasting his time, and when the time came he refused to sign.

Yeshua refused to have anything to do with such a mean spirited religion. But Esau pleaded, "Yeshua, you must go. Someday when you become the High Priest, change the law, for all the guys like me..."

Yeshua embraced him, "One day I will build a church...and you will be in it!"

One night as the rabbi walked home after an inspirational talk with his young scholar, he stopped to look up at the universe. It was a special moment with the stars flickering, when the eyes of the imagination knew no bounds, so he allowed himself a rare luxury of wondering: could it be that this young boy has a special quality...a divine quality...Perhaps he, a humble rabbi, may be living in a historical moment, witnessing the development of the child into...a leader of men, the liberator of Israel... the MESSIAH? As quickly as the inspiring flame ignited his mind, he extinguished it, filled with fear. He knew if such tale started, true or fictitious, they would either elevate the child to a pedestal worthy of a God, or just as likely accuse him of consorting with Satan. Either way it would be devastating to Yeshua.

About two years ago the rabbi noticed a radical transformation with the scholar: he began to assert himself. Very often he maintained that the scribe wrote the scripture incorrectly, or the priests misinterpreted it.

Nobody suspected then, but as he moved further from the established faith he sounded like a maverick, clearly on a collision course with the establishment. The events that followed would change the innocence of Nazareth, and ultimately Israel forever. He often said, "Judaism began as a communion between Man and his Creator. But the priests and the rulers changed it to serve their own interests."

The rabbi tried to make light of it, "All religions have problems..."

"Then they are all wrong, and must be changed back to the original principles," he replied. He looked at them announcing, "I propose to leave old Judaism behind: in the trash bin. I will start a new Judaism from the ground up: Make it universal. The people will be at the centre in a personal relationship with God!"

The young men gasped, but were pleased with the new order. But the rabbi's reaction was as expected, "The patriarchs will not stand for their traditions to be dumped in the dust bin."

"They will have to change or get run over by the new popular faith," Yeshua stated matter of factly.

Ben Lebbus protested anxiously, "Israelis have their imperfections but they are not cowards. They'll defend their faith to the last breath." Then he cut off the debate.

The rabbi refused to argue because he knew the country was full of spies: for the Herodians, the Romans and the Priests. He feared exposing the young scholar to danger. Yeshua misconstrued his intention and refused to take part in discussions, and when he did it was for the sole purpose of contradicting the rabbi. That chafed Ben Lebbus and made the students edgy. The two were clearly on a collision course.

Ben Lebbus tried to compromise, "Assuming that we develop the universal religion as you propose. Why must the rest of our history and tradition be tossed in the dust bin? It's inseparable from our faith."

Yeshua knew this was dear to the rabbi, and mellowed his position, "The old scriptures may remain as legends and childrens' stories."

The rabbi looked distressed, "They will not accept that. And I pity anyone who persists in changing their faith. They will be crushed"

"Old patriarchs used the Scriptures to take control, and we will take it back." Then he suggested, "Let me present my ideas to the congregation. I will do a sermon and prove the old teachings irrelevant and incorrect. I already have the perfect title: OUT WITH THE OLD, IN WITH THE NEW UNIVERSAL JUDAISM!"

The rabbi turned white, "They will tear you limb from limb..."

To the young generation a sermon proposing an overhaul of the old faith was a reasonable proposal, so they supported him. The rabbi totally disagreed, but tired and worn out, he relented unenthusiastically, "Alright. Give your sermon...next Sabbath."

The news spread like a brush fire: their promising scholar was going to give his first sermon. No one knew what he was going to say, but all agreed they would never forget it. People dropped in to visit his parents and congratulate them for such a gifted son. Many brought Joseph work orders, and paid him a sizable deposit in advance. They reasoned when the scholar climbed the ladder of success, their deposit, like a seed, would bear fruit.

When Miriam saw all the coins Joseph had amassed, she demanded the greater percentage to purchase new clothes: dresses for the girls and smart Grecian tunics for the boys. She allowed herself the luxury of a new dress, her first new dress since... she could not remember when.

Yeshua went daily to the oak tree and worked on his sermon. It was a daunting task: to persuade simple, unsophisticated peasants, whose faith fit as comfortably as their old robe, to discard it for his new strange concept. He strived to make it a simple, clear message. The last day he worked on it around the sundial.

. . .

Master Joseph's family arrived at the synagogue with the cleanest children in town. Yeshua was already there, helping to take care of last moment preparations. The church elders, eager to be seen with the popular family, saved seats for them on the bench. They pushed the pilgrims out of the way, "Move over, lazy peasant," lady Aquilla, the chair of the church elders struck a pilgrim with her luxurious fan from China.

"Move it!" master Eliphaz, the vice-chair commanded.

The synagogue was packed to overflowing with worshippers to hear the young scholar. Members extended hands to congratulate the patriarch.

Finally the heavy doors 'clanked' shutting out the sun. The first benediction was given, followed by the prayer. After the first reading of the Scripture, the rabbi introduced the young scholar. Yeshua walked up to the bema, the elevated platform, closing the gate behind him. His family admired their handsome oldest boy under the canopy. A tear rolled down Miriam's cheek.

Yeshua took a deep breath and roared like thunder, "WE, THE PEOPLE OF ISRAEL ARE THE MOST ARROGANT PEOPLE IN THE WORLD."

The loud statement remained suspended in the air for a long time without reaction. Then, a few eye lids blinked, some coughed, a few whispered, 'Had they heard him correctly?' Yeshua repeated it louder. This time they heard him and the room went silent: No one coughed. He continued, "Our Scripture says that God created all the people of the world. He created them equal! Then it says He chose the Israelis as His favorite children…His only chosen people! WHAT TRASH!" he barked. There was a collective gasp. His plan was to turf such claptrap, then introduce the new inclusive faith.

"Galilean means in the midst of pagans," he continued. "There are two hundred and forty towns and villages in our province, mostly pagans.

We are a tiny minority. Yet, we dare say God loves us, treating the greater number as outcasts!"

The reaction was instantaneous from every corner of the room:

"PAGAN LOVER!" a raspy voice cried out from the dark.

"YOU WILL BURN IN THE DEPTHS OF HELL!" a woman yelled.

"You'll burn in hell for the blasphemy!" an old man said weakly.

"Suppose an Israeli and a pagan die on the same day," the scholar proceeded. "All his life the Israeli was dishonest, and a liar. But, the pagan was honest and God fearing. Which one will enter paradise first?" He asked and waited, but no one replied. "According to the Book, the Israeli will be first - because he is Israeli! We have a monopoly on paradise. You know in your hearts this is wrong. The Scripture is wrong!"

The pilgrims were dumbfounded, but did not disagree. Still they did not like his criticism of the Book. "I tell you truly, every God fearing pagan will enter paradise before the undeserving Israeli," he pronounced his first principle.

"SATAN LOVER!" a female yelled.

"TRAITOR!" a baritone boomed.

"Get out of this sacred house," an old man wheezed.

Yeshua pressed on, "The scribes violated your rights when they wrote that you were forbidden to utter God's name. Why should only the High Priest communicate with your Creator?"

Ben Lebbus guessed where Yeshua was going, and pleaded, "Yeshua, don't...!"

But it was too late. He raised his arms to the heaven, supplicating, "Heavenly YAHWEH, bless the pilgrims in this synagogue..."

When they heard the sacred name, there was a pandemonium. Old ladies felt faint. Old men ground his name between their teeth, "You have profaned Adonai's name." Some threw whatever they had handy at him: belts, walking sticks and sandals.

The young scholar remained calm, "The problem with the Book is that it was always male dominated. Patriarchal society took control of Yahweh."

The old patriarchs were ready to lynch him. But the younger generation, men and ladies stood up to defend him. But the old men abused him, accusing him of being a pagan lover, an irreligious scoundrel, and a blasphemer.

The false accusations made him lose patience and lash out: "You accuse pagans and gentiles of idolatry, of praying to false gods. Look at you," he pointed to the loudest old man in a far corner. "Master Yacek, show us your anklet of Baal."

"What of it?" the old man barked.

"Do you not pray to Baal to cure the pain on the knee joint?"

The yelling subsided, as they turned and stared at master Yacek. Some quickly covered their own gold bracelets, chains and brooches of pagan gods.

The young scholar continued, "How many of you have permanent altars in dark corners of your rooms, raised to Astarte, El or Jupiter?"

"Throw out this atheist," an old man demanded.

"Stone him," another concurred.

Shouts, threats and abuses reverberated within the small house of prayer, as the old patriarchs wanted him flogged or killed. Equally as loud, Yeshua saw the younger people screaming at the elders, heaving back everything thrown their way. Yeshua tried to explain that Judaism, once a proud and the most advanced religion was turned into a tribal ritual serving the priests and the establishment. He planned to propose a universal Judaism based on love, its cornerstone being, charity, love and forgiveness. But his pleas were drowned out in a torrent of hatred. His message of love was met with an oversized sandal to the face, drawing blood.

Ben Lebbus, afraid they were turning into a lynching mob, pushed his way to the bema. He ordered with a stern voice, "Bow your heads in prayer!" Then he started the longest prayer of his career to allow the hatred to simmer down. He spoke of love, patience, understanding and forgiveness. He was interrupted with outbursts of, "He is Satan incarnate!", and "Blasphemer!" whispered from one side of the room, with replies of, "Old fossils!", and "Dry up and die!" from the opposite side. The rabbi raised his voice impatiently, "Oh Lord, we ask you to punish those whispering hatred: WITHER THEIR TONGUES – FOREVER!" That brought silence at last.

When the rabbi sensed it was safe, he motioned Joseph to run for it. Joseph elbowed his wife, sprang to his feet, pushing James and dragging Debborah. Miriam pushed the youngest as they bounced off the pilgrims on the way out. An old man, bent on revenge, swung his walking stick wildly striking Miriam and ripping her sleeve. When the doorman froze in their way, Joseph tackled him uncerimoniously, flung open the door and exited. The rabbi continued droning until they were sufficiently distant.

After the service he ordered Yeshua to remain within the railings, and went outside to start damage control. As they exited, the congregants abused him fiercely. They accused him of harbouring religious criminals, rebels, and all other problems, from theft to promiscuity. A non-religious patriarch grabbed the rabbi and announced loudly for everyone to hear, "Rabbi that was a sermon from hell!"

"I knew you would recognize it," the rabbi smiled affably.

"I will not come back here for a long, long time," the old man barked.

The rabbi replied just as loudly, "Nothing will change then?"

Most of the congregants were gone when Ben Lebbus peeked inside to check on Yeshua, did not see him and rushed in. The young man was crouched down visiting with master Yacek, the old patriarch with Baal's anklet. The rabbi approached to within a few paces.

Yeshua spoke sympathetically, "I meant no offence about the anklet." He turned the golden figurine between his fingers. "Baal is an impressive figure."

Yacek grunted, "You wouldn't be making fun if you suffered my pains."

The young man saw that his right knee was wrapped in cloth and proceeded to remove it, "Is this the joint bothering you?"

"Don't touch it!" Yacek quivered tensely. "It hurts!"

The young scholar unrolled the cloth, and squeezed the swollen joint. The old man winced, expecting pain, but feeling nothing, relaxed. Yacek was a lonely widower whose children had grown up, moved to the south never returning to visit. Yeshua studied the old patriarch and saw a bulbous nose with red veins criss-crossing it. "I can help cure this knee," he suggested. "But you must follow my advice."

The old man asked cautiosly, "What's that?"

"Drink no more than one goblet of watered down wine, per day..."

"I am not a drunk!" he objected.

"It must be white wine, but only one. And, drink lots of water. I promise by the end of next week you will be dancing with the lasses."

The old man grinned embarrassed, "From your lips to Adonai's ears."

"Let me help you," Yeshua took his arm. "That is truly a handsome anklet."

"Thank you...it is only a talisman," Yacek added when he saw the rabbi. "I swear, I only pray to Lord Adonai".

"I know. Have no fear," the young man smiled. "Your Creator is not jealous, as long as you love Him also."

Master Yacek promised to return next Sabbath. He walked away without a limp, but, being used to pain, a few days would pass before he realized he was cured. A few months later he would remember the date and place where he was cured.

Yeshua joined the rabbi, "A couple of things bothered me today…"

"Only two: I should have your troubles," the rabbi deadpanned.

"I was a little too negative. Next time I will emphasize the positive."

"There will never be a next time!" his tone had an unequivocal finality.

Later that night Ben Lebbus reflected as he walked home. He was impressed by Yeshua's calmness, but he foresaw a life full of conflict for him with the establishment.

As he entered his olive grove, lady Aquilla and master Eliphaz, the two leading church elders, appeared from behind a tree, "Rabbi the board demands a meeting."

The rabbi was about to object when Eliphaz barked, "NOW!"

• • •

Joseph led his family through the fields, avoiding the roads. At the house he placed a heavy timber to close the door. At length James mumbled he was going up to his room and left. The younger children took advantage and requested to play outside.

"As long as you stay in the yard, or the roof top," Joseph instructed, "If you see anyone coming you tell me immediately." As soon as they left he turned to his wife gruffly, "We don't deserve a magician if we won't let him do his magic!"

"He is not a magician. He is just a special boy…who can do miracles…"

"What was he trying to do; start a civil war?" he protested.

Judas and Salome ran into the house and came directly to him. The boy sat on his knees, "Father, who is Yahweh?"

Joseph froze, shocked to hear the forbidden name, and looked at Miriam. He wanted to scold the child but a voice at the door interrupted him.

"Yahweh is the Creator who made everything you see around you."

They could not make out the figure for he stood in the bright light of the doorway making him appear surreal. Only when he walked in did they recognize Yeshua. "He made the heavens, the earth, the sun, the stars and all the people of the world."

"Did he make father?" Judas asked and the older brother nodded. "And mother too?" He nodded again.

"Did Yahweh also make Jude?" Salome queried and Yeshua nodded.

"Then He must be real good," Judas explained.

Joseph interrupted with a gruff tone, "What were you trying to prove there?"

Yeshua could not hide his disappointment. If his kin did not understand could he expect others to do so? He spoke with deep emotion, "Yahweh is the Universal Creator but we made Him a tribal God. He taught peace but we invoke wars in His name; He preaches charity but scribes made Him vengeful; He is kind and we made Him mean."

· · ·

Lady Aquilla started before he sat down, "Rabbi what happened today must not go unpunished."

"Charges must be laid today," Eliphaz ordered. "The town council will approve it this afternoon. Tomorrow morning he'll be stoned!"

"Is this decision unanimous?" Ben Lebbus asked and looked at the six elders, most of whom avoided eye contact. That gave him some hope. "Master Eliphaz, lady Aquilla when did you last read the Scriptures?"

"What do the Scriptures have to do with this?" Eliphaz barked. "We want justice!"

"You want blood!" the rabbi snapped. "I checked the Book and the young man was correct. Charge him, but you will not prove him guilty."

"I sit on the town council," Eliphaz shouted striking the desk with his fist making the oil lamp jump. "They will carve out his eyes if I tell them to!"

Lady Aquilla leaned over, "He spoke the sacred name! He deserves to die!"

The rabbi sneered, "The Scripture says no mortal may utter the sacred name. Yet the High Priest sings it out every year..."

Aquilla snapped savagely. "We must punish him...for something."

The rabbi studied their faces and decided to take the offensive, "I will give you one warning. If you don't leave this room immediately, I will charge you for carrying on business on the Sabbath!" He started to get up and they drew back.

"But...but, it's business of the Lord..."

"It's still business!" Ben Lebbus roared.

· · ·

Next morning the rabbi came to Joseph's house. He recounted the meeting with the elders. Then he offered a compromise, "Next Sabbath you must admit...your errors and apologize...beg forgiveness..."

Yeshua leaned forward to reply, but Joseph raised his hand "Rabbi yesterday we were honored with a historical event, such as Israel has not seen in a thousand years. The first step to return Judaism to the universal faith Yahweh gave us." He felt his face burning when he uttered the sacred name, but seeing the rabbi's face, he added with pride. "We must return it to its roots: a communion between Man and YAHWEH!"

The rabbi was stunned, turning to Miriam, then Yeshua and back to the carpenter, "Where did you hear this?"

"Yesterday's sermon: clear as a bell!" he replied proudly.

The rabbi shook his head. "In all conscience I cannot ask you to apolo..."

"Father, father, three men are here to see you," the young children ran in yelling.

Joseph came out and recognized his customers. He sensed trouble for they were avoiding eye contact. "Master Machpelah, how can I help you?"

The young man mumbled, "I... cancel the work..."

"I understand...if you no longer need it."

Machpelah added nervously, "He also wants to cancel."

Joseph looked at the other man who nodded.

"Me too," the third man added.

Joseph suspected a conspiracy and muttered, "Payback for the sermon?"

Machpelah heard him but continued, "When can we get our deposit back?"

"I don't have it. I spent it purchasing material," Joseph snarled impatiently.

"Pagan lovers!" Machpelah barked.

Joseph grabbed him and shoved him out of the yard, "Get out, and never come back!"

The rabbi and Yeshua came out in time to avert an all out fight. Joseph went out on the street and saw three more men coming down the hill. He saw dozens more standing beside Aquilla and Eliphaz.

"Do you wish to cancel your orders?" he yelled.

"Yes," the three replied continuing down.

"Come no closer," Joseph warned. "Consider all contracts cancelled…You'll get your deposits…when I have money, not a moment sooner!" He turned to the rabbi, "I am doomed! I am bankrupt! The Courts will order the family into slavery…"

The rabbi turned to Yeshua, "Be ready for me tomorrow at sunrise."

· · ·

Before sunrise Yeshua stood by the gate when the rabbi came. They nodded and exchanged grunts and continued, "Rabbi, where are we going?"

"To every pagan town and village: you are their hero only they don't know it."

At the first village, the rabbi went directly into the big general store, and many residents followed them. The rabbi introduced themselves and gave them a synopsis of Yeshua's sermon. They enjoyed hearing that the honest pagan entered paradise before the cheating Israeli. When he referred to a universal Creator, Yeshua referred to Him as El, Baal and Yahweh, telling them the universal religion was for pagans, Romans and Indians alike, in a personal relationship with God. They were speechless when he referred to a new order.

On the whole they found his preaching totally new, and too much to comprehend at once. They were shocked to hear that Israelis mixed religion with commerce.

On the third afternoon, a rich shop owner who had no children offered to adopt him, "I have many properties and shops in neighboring towns," he informed him, itemizing his holdings. "But, you will not have to tend shop. Hire all the help you want. You will be free to travel the country, give sermons and convert people."

Yeshua thanked him but said he could not leave his family.

Every pagan town and hamlet gave him work orders: to manufacture sieves. The merchants did not open their purses to the visitors. Sieves involved much meticulous work which carpenters avoided, and the pay was meager. They realized the Israeli family was desperate and offered a pittance. But, it was more than the Israelis gave.

After five days of trekking and giving speeches, Joseph decided they had enough work. Yeshua left the lyceum and joined the drudgery of manufacturing sieves.

Benjoseph, the schoolmaster, came to the house to get the scholar back and offered to pay for his education, but the patriarch proudly refused charity.

Benjoseph met with the rabbi and told him, "I'll write my wealthy uncle in Jerusalem…not to him directly, for he will not part with a copper penny, but to my aunt." He smiled tenderly thinking about her, "The kindest, gentlest person I know. She'll help."

He wrote about the disaster that befell Joseph's family, careful not to mention the sermon. Within a few days he received a thick scroll and endless questions: about the youth's background, family history, names and ages of everyone…The transparent design was to discourage further communication. Benjoseph burned the midnight oil filling out the docier, and thanked his uncle profusely.

The uncle read it and sent out his own investigators. They were diligent leaving no stone unturned, and returned with copious reports. When he read it one outstanding fact stood out: "Joseph's anscestors go back to the House of David – KING DAVID…"

He passed his bony finger over the sentence savoring the grand news, leaned back on the soft cushions and reached for the silver goblet full of kosher wine. He wheezed and slobbered in the depths of his goblet, weaving an intricate plot.

Within weeks the wealthy nabob held a lavish party inviting the leading families of Jerusalem, and his special guest, Herod Antipas, tetrarch of the province of Galilee and Perea. Antipas, like his late father, Herod the great, suffered from an insurmountable problem: being Idumeans they were foreigners, and they yearned to be loved by Israelis.

At the gala, Herod's chalice was generously replenished, and when he became appropriately lubricated, the nabob slid into a chair beside him whispering, "You are fortunate to have one of Israel's leading families in your jurisdiction." Herod leaned closer to hear more. "Joseph, a carpenter from Nazarth, of royal stock, from the house of David: KING DAVID."

Antipas' unfocussed eyes lit up as if he just discovered King Solomon's mine, "That is precisely the man who can help me. If I can think of something not expensive…"

"It's no time to be cheap," the nabob interrupted, "People will talk. Benevolence will translate into popularity…"

The tetrarch nodded dreamily, "I will grant my kin Joseph a request to build a throne…TWO THRONES! Price shall be no object…!"

· · ·

Before the Roman soldiers left Joseph's house, lady Aquilla and master Eliphaz, demanded an immediate meeting with the rabbi. In the little room Lady Aquilla wasted no time, "Rabbi, you got us into this mess, you get us out!"

"No need to apologize," Eliphaz chimed in. "Just get us a quick resolution."

"What resolution? You have Joseph's family right where you want them."

"Don't play the fool Ben Lebbus," Aquilla rasped grimly. "Herod and the Romans are supporting the family. Pretty soon our people will go crawling to them."

The rabbi chuckled into his beard, "And you two want to be the lead crawler."

Eliphaz shouted, "Rabbi, we're wise to your tricks. Get on with it!"

"Master Eliphaz, I liked you better when you groveled," the rabbi responded and presented his plan. "Joseph's family will demand four concessions: First, an apology which you will give in the synagogue." They tried to object but he raised his voice, "Second, you will order all customers to reinstate their work orders."

"That will put us at his mercy," Aquilla moaned.

"You were willing to crush them into slavery and you seek compassion?" he glared. "Third, after the apology, you two will resign, which I will reluctantly accept."

Aquilla countered arrogantly, "What makes you certain we will resign?"

The rabbi chuckled, "You will when you hear the fourth demand…"

A loud knock on the door interrupted Ben Lebbus' reminiscing…

• • •

Ben Lebbus shook his head trying to regain his bearings, when he heard the knock a second time. "Come in, it's unlocked."

The door opened slowly and Yeshua peeked in then walked in cautiously.

"Don't worry, we are alone," the rabbi said and motioned him to sit down. "I'll come directly to the point. The elders asked me to resolve the problems between your family and the town." The young scholar tried to speak, but the rabbi raised his hand, "I told them you will make four demands. First, the elders must apologize. Second, the customers will reinstate all work orders. Third, master Eliphaz and lady Aquilla will resign…" He stopped and chuckled recollecting the meeting. "They sure argued, but I knew they would resign."

"What is my fourth demand?" the young scholar was impatient.

"You will give another sermon in the Synago…"

Yeshua sprang to his feet causing the table to jump sending the oil lamp flying through the air and landing on the floor. The bench crashed into the back wall.

"I will never give another sermon in Nazareth. NEVER!"

• • •

"YOU - GIVE A SERMON?" Joseph's baritone boomed. "Whose stupid idea was that?"

"Mine," Yeshua replied calmly.

The old patriarch studied him like an old judge about to give a lengthy sentence, "How many congregants contributed in the decision?"

"None - why?"

"Because they will have all the stones and daggers."

"I thought you liked my sermons!"

"I'm your father: I have to like them. But, they will kill you for it."

Yeshua told them as he started to leave, "This time it will be an agreeable subject: Where is the Messiah?" At the door he stopped and turned, "I will be bringing the Greek and his slave into the Synagogue for the service." Then he turned and left.

His parents' reaction was instantaneous, "Did you...did you hear... Infidels in God's house. They will kill them!"

Miriam stuttered, "THE MESSIAH! What was he thinking?"

"Don't worry. They'll stone him before he starts..." the patriarch quipped with a sickly look. "What did I do to deserve this? At age five he withered the schoolmaster's arm; at thirteen got us a lifetime injunction not to return to Jerusalem; at nineteen almost got us killed." He looked up, "Why me? Was there no one You disliked more?"

"Joseph, don't speak to Lord Adonai in that tone," she begged fearfully.

"I am speaking about His son. Maybe He can control him." He turned to her beseechingly, "Miriam, We must tell him..."

• • •

Yeshua forswore lady Sarah every day, only his heart did not hear his resolve. In the school yard he went through the same actions with the same results. He played ball, portraying the appearance of a carefree youth enjoying life, but inside he was a bundle of nerves. He glanced furtively towards the hill, and did not relax until he saw her. Only then a feeling of serenity came over him. He could not explain why he wanted to see her, for he did not rush to her, or speak to her. In fact from the moment he saw her, he was careful not to look her way – too obviously. His glances were furtive peeks, never more so than after one of his spectacular catches. His friends, aware of how much he pined for her, and eager to enjoy a good laugh, continuously threw the ball in her direction.

Yeshua had never seen the Egyptian Sphynx but imagined that formidable goddess must be like lady Sarah: immovable, motionless in space and time, cold and uncaring. It was that mysterious enigma that attracted him so desperately to her.

Every time he forswore her, he remembered the moment they first touched: her hands trembling, with fear in her eyes. What terrible secrets was lady Sarah concealing?

Yeshua was not the only one captivated by the beautiful living statue. All the boys and girls were attracted to her. But with time, her silence and aloofness drove them away from her. Thus without exchanging a word with her, their emotions swung from admiration to a total dislike. Yeshua was always one of the last to come in and had to sit next to her, which meant he sat in the shadow of the Sphynx. He felt like an inert rock counterbalancing his end of the bench.

Because the students were impressed that a "ship" was being constructed in their town, every day they questioned him about sailing. He remembered that lady Sarah enjoyed sailing, so he led them close to her, then told them stories of adventures and survivals he had heard from the shipwright. He hoped to arouse her curiosity and break the barrier of silence.

He noticed her listening, which gave him some confidence. He brought them within a few paces of her, telling a story loud so she would hear it, "Three fishermen took their boat to the Sea of Galilee late in the day. They sailed to a popular fishing hole and threw the net a few times without success. After a while they sailed to two other places, with the same result. It was dark when they sailed to a fourth place, and tried again. This time they dragged in a ton of mush, barely managing to bring it all aboard. The boat sat low in the water, with little free board. They started sailing back, when the winds died.

"It was a moonless night and the stars sparkled like huge diamonds reflected in the calm waters. It was so calm they did not see black clouds gliding stealthily until most of the stars were obliterated. Before they realized a wall of wind and water struck them, causing the ladened boat to lean over, the mast creaking as the sail spilled some of the wind. The vessel slowly veered into the wind, picking up a great amount of water. The sailors quickly lifted the leeboards and dropped all sails, raising only the smallest sail for steerage. The wind howled and giant waves crashed against the vessel splashing them, as the boat lurched and yawed, pounded by the waves. The dark clouds descended, so they could not see their hands in front of their faces, except when lightning cracked. They feared that night was their last.

"What do you think they did?" he asked mysteriously.

He asked the question and watched lady Sarah who was leaning at the edge of the step. He pulled out a small wooden boat and crouched down, lowering his voice. She leaned too far, lurching forward, and almost landed on top of them. He was about to invite her but she quickly returned to the cement step.

The truth was that lady Sarah had a formidable contender - Drusilla. She was a big-boned mousy blond who had coveted Yeshua for years, and interlocked her arms around his as a spider grips a fly. Yeshua welcomed the attention, following master Stephanos' advice. Soon he tired of the game, but was not able to escape from the web he helped weave.

Last night he was preparing for the final exams, and realized school was almost over. He panicked. He was to leave on the expedition, and they may never see each other again. He became depressed, and angry with himself and lady Sarah, for failing to give themselves a chance. He decided to write a poem, his first, and he burnt the midnight oil. When he finished, he folded it twice and wrote on the outside: "FOR YOUR EYES ONLY." He placed it in his notebook, intending to give it to her in class.

This morning when he awoke, he thought about the poem, and his stomach tied up in knots. His courage almost deserted him. In the school yard he looked out for her, but when he saw her, he panicked. He decided he would slip it between the pages of her notebook. When the door opened he ran to sit next to her, then waited the entire morning for the perfect opportunity without success. She did not open her book, and when she did she kept her arms over it, or the schoolmaster stood as if cemented on top of them. Yeshua did not act, or hear a word of the lesson. By afternoon he could not remember a longer day of suffering and was ready to give up.

Suddenly, the perfect opportunity appeared. Sarah opened her notebook, and when she raised her arms, he flicked the folded papyrus on her book. His action made her freeze with her arms up. What he did not realize was that she had been reaching for a handkerchief, as she was about to sneeze. She exploded in a violent sneeze causing the folded papyrus to fly up, higher and higher and further from them, as they watched in horror. It flew and floated like a butterfly, one way then the other, finally descending slowly, and landing on master Benjoseph's sandal. The school master had seen him stealthily deposit the note on her book, and smirked as he picked it up.

"Why did fate deposit this on my foot?" Benjoseph mused with a grin. "It's a secret note master Yeshua covertly gave lady Sarah. It reads: 'FOR YOUR EYES ONLY.' Unfortunately it does not say whose eyes, so I assume it's for me... and I will gladly share it with you!" The students were delighted, and asked him to read it. "Shall I ask the author to read it instead?" They chimed in 'Yes' as a chorus. "Master Yeshua, will you do us the honor?" he teased the young man.

Yeshua's face burnt and he felt perspiration run down his arm pit. He felt like an idiot for embarrassing lady Sarah, and whispered an apology. She sat holding her face in her hands, certain something awful was about to occur.

Suddenly Yeshua's confusion disappeared and he became serenely calm. He stood up, took it, unfolded it and waited for the laughter to subside. Then he spoke directly to lady Sarah, "This poem came to me late last night. When I realized we had few days before going our separate ways, I scribed this…for you:

"Like two shooting stars
Lighting the universe, our paths crossed
And flashed bright for an instant, and burnt
Evaporating into nothingness.
Nary a word passed between us,
Not a nod, a smile, not one touch.
We lived in a vaccum of silence,
For in silence there is no fear
No betrayal and no hurt.
But in silence there is no hope,
And without hope there is no love!

Soon we must part
On a journey through the universe.
Will we ever meet again?
How vast is the endless universe?
Can a burnt star flash again to flame?

But I know we're sure to meet
If not in this life, then next.
What will we dare to celebrate:
Tears of silence, unspoken words,
Memories and dreams that never were?
Will we shed tears over our fears
That stifled hope; and a love we did not dare?"

When he finished, the room was silent. Only Drusilla uttered a guttural noise, "BLAH!" Yeshua returned to his seat. As he was sitting down, Sarah reached out and snatched the poem from his hand and put it in her book.

. . .

Every day after lyceum the boat crew worked on the boat. Ever since the flare up between Marcus and Esau they cooperated and advanced with the project. But it was an uneasy truce, with an athmosphere as tense as a storm cloud laden with electrical charge: one spark and the explosion would wipe out the project. No one wished it yet it seemed unavoidable.

Every day they feared this could be the day. They did not wait long. Esau decided they had split enough wood, and should start construction. He called them together, "I decided we will start building the keel today." He looked at them as if expecting arguments, but was met with blank stares. He placed the designs on a plank and explained, "This is the hull, or the outer shell. The bottom is the keel: this long rectangular box with a fine lead at the front end. So we'll start there."

Marcus reacted immediately "To build the keel first is stupid. Where did you learn to build boats, Yeshua's drawings in the sand?"

"What is your point?" Esau demanded.

"If you build the keel first, its top will have a specific dimension. But when you build the boat, the bottom which will attach to the keel will not match it."

Esau interjected, "Don't you think I thought about that? Many times, and I made up my mind. We will construct the keel first."

Marcus looked to his companions for support, but they did not grasp his argument. It was clear that he would have to fight this battle alone. "For once, forget you are the manager and listen," he pointed to the drawing insisting, "The opening at the top of the keel and the opening at the bottom of the hull will not match. We'll have to build the keel twice."

Esau reconsidered, biting his lower lip. He mumbled shaking his head, "I studied it many times…How could I have missed it?" He looked at the others shaking his head bitterly, "You are correct. How did I…?"

"Because you're wasting time building your ego, not the boat," Marcus sneered dispassionately. "If I were manager I would not concern myself with who's the outcast and who's the manager. It's a waste of time."

"What are you talking about?" Esau was surprised by his outburst.

"That's what Yeshua said: he blamed us for your problems. Said you're the victim and we're your executioner. We're here to build the boat right boys?"

"Leave me out of this," Daniel who was tired of the bickering snapped.

Ahmed concurred angrily, "You'd better stop your tirades Marcus."

"You think I can separate my job from who I am?" Esau countered passionately. "Do you think it's that simple? I live and breathe as an outcast. If I ever forget, people like you remind me daily. Master Yeshua was right: you are the executioner."

"If you can't separate your problems from your job, that's your trouble," Marcus rebuked him. "You have to make a decision…"

"I will to make the decision," the outcast finally lost control. "I have the position and the power. Quintus warned me to get rid of you. Master Yeshua left it up to me." He paced away, his voice quivering. "I have been patient, hoping to prove myself, and be accepted by you. I hoped you would help…But, you will never let go…"

Daniel interjected soberly, "I support Esau."

"Me too," Ahmed concurred.

Marcus looked from one to the other with disbelief.

Esau was equally shocked, but continued tensely, "I did not want this, but…"

"Spare me the drama," Marcus interrupted gruffly. "I know you want to release me. I'll save you the agony. I resign!"

He started to walk away but Esau caught up, grabbed his arm, and turned him around, "I am not finished. I will never be anything other than what I am: an outcast. I am satisfied that I can be project manager. However, I want the boat more than the title. So, I'm resigning. You take over. I'll take your position."

Marcus stood speechless, his eyes darting from Esau to the others and again to his opponent. He coveted the position. But he could see the others did not approve. After a while he said, "You cannot resign," he mumbled. "You deserve a chance."

Daniel and Ahmed put their hands on Esau's shoulder and nodded.

Marcus ordered them gruffly, "You heard the manager. Start cutting…!"

• • •

When Staphanos and Germanicus arrived at Yeshua's house, the slave, seeing Anna in the backyard went to her directly, "Good afternoon, lady Anna" he nodded with a smile.

"Germanicus," she feigned surprise. "What have you been up to?"

"Fawning over my juvenile master," he responded sardonically.

"You should not refer to him with disrespect. Is he mean ? Does he beat you?"

"He can be malicious in subtle ways: by never letting me forget I'm a slave."

"Are you not one?"

"Just once, for one day, I wish our roles were reversed," he mused disagreeably. "He'd find out how cruel I could be..."

"Would you take revenge?"

"I'd be vicious, I swear!"

"Next day your stations would revert and he would be doubly vicious," she chuckled. "Is it not wiser to treat him gently, earning his respect in return?"

"You give him too much credit. He's a Greek!"

"I give you both too much credit: you're both men," she countered with a grin. "Braun over brain every time...and sensitivity is a sign of weakness."

Germanicus drew back astonished by her blunt honesty. He felt the sting of being rebuked, and considered walking away. She saw his awkwardness and softened, "Don't mind my bluntness. Mother always said I mean well, but express it badly." They chuckled at her honesty. "Still planning to run away to Europe?" she asked and he glanced nervously before nodding. "Which direction is your country?"

He thought about it and shrugged, "I don't know..."

"Is it far? A long journey?" she queried and he shrugged again. "How will you travel? Have you money for food?"

"One question at a time," he sputtered at the barrage, "I haven't thought about all that..." He paced back and forth somewhat miffed at her for exposing his weak plan. Then he stopped and demanded, "Besides, what is it to you? Why should you care?"

Anna smiled coyly, "My mother told me if I ever met a dreamer, to take care of him...Those types have a tendency to self destruct." They enjoyed a chuckle as she added teasingly, "I have a soft spot for dreamers."

Germanicus looked at her admiringly for he realized she was a rare young lady.

Meantime on top of the roof, Yeshua and Staphanos sat studying maps the Greek had brought. "So this is Israel...Did you plan out the expedition?" the Israeli asked.

The Greek was still annoyed with his errand and wanted his host to know it,

"I had to go to Augusteana for these maps. Why don't you have a library here?"

"Our peasants don't need one. They cannot afford to travel, and if they could, they cannot read."

The Greek stabbed the map with a finger, "Nazareth! We'll go from Inn to Inn where we will stay and ask questions...Except Germanicus who'll sleep in the court yard. He prefers it that way."

"Did you ask him?" Yeshua queried.

"You don't ask a slave. Anyway, we'll ask about a Messiah. The owners or patrons will know. In a couple of weeks we'll cover the entire nation." He looked at the Israeli, who sat staring into space. "Did you hear me?"

"Of course!" Yeshua snapped. "Why don't you save your drachmas and go on your own? Better still go to Augusteana and read about it." He stood up to leave.

"Wait!" The Greek grabbed his arm, "Why are you angry? Did I offend you?"

Yeshua stopped, embarrassed for his outburst. Stephanos guessed what was annoying him, "You are angry, but for a different reason. Is it because I escort lady Sarah from the lyceum every day?" Yeshua glanced at him furtively without replying. "I asked you, and you renounced her..."

"It's the way you monopolize her," he snapped. "Although it is true, I did renounce her...As far as she is concerned I don't exist..."

"For a fellow who does not exist you exert a strong influence," the Greek chuckled. "The other day when you took off ahead of us she pulled out a poem saying you wrote it. She read it silently, and cried all the way home..."

"Why did you not tell me?" Yeshua scolded him.

"You said you did not care!"

"That's right, I don't care. But you should have told me anyway!"

Stephanos shook his head, deciding to change topics, "Now that you made your final decision – again, to maybe not care… what have you against my plans?"

The Israeli returned and sat down, "First, many towns have no Inns. Second, many Inns don't serve food. Most importantly…" he was interrupted when Quintus walked into the yard. "Hello, master Quintus, come up for a moment."

The Roman saluted enthusiastically, "Good afternoon, I brought the heavy piece of wood for the keelson," he said jumping up the steps.

"Meet master Stephanos, a Greek scholar; Quintus is a Roman soldier, born and raised in Israel." The two sized up each other coolly, and bowed stiffly. "Master Stephanos wants to find the Messiah. He wants to travel the Inns, while I prefer…"

Quintus raised his muscular arm, and addressed the Greek, "Say no more. I have lived here all my life: a most enchanting, but enigmatic country. You will love and curse these people, often in the same breath. They breathe their religion from every pore, from sunrise to dark, from birth to the grave…"

"Then you are an expert on their reli…?" Stephanos started to ask.

Quintus interjected with an exaggerated emphasis, "Their friendship has an invisible curtain beyond which they never let me pass. They're as jealous of their God as He is of them."

"Dangerously fanatic?" Staphanos sounded disturbed.

"They can be most charitable," the Roman added. Then he stood almost on top of the Greek emphasizing, "Don't waste time in the Inns. Follow his advice; doors will open, they will unlock secrets…witness their intimate relations with Lord Adonai."

"You sound like you'd like to join the expedition," Yeshua quipped.

"If my commander approved it…"

Stephanos interrupted curtly, "We've no room. It's a small tent!"

"I would be a guard…"

"My slave shall guard us. The subject is closed," the Greek snapped.

The Roman desisted and changed tactics, "I saw a Messiah in Egypt: Master Rabban they called him. Formidable fellow…Fantastic show…I'd gladly take…"

"We'll find him, I'm sure, especially with master Yeshua guiding us."

Quintus did not disguise his disappointment, but decided he did not wish to travel with such an unpleasant prolop, so turned to the Israeli, "I'll bring that log in." He cleared the steps in two leaps.

. . .

It was the last day of classes and Yeshua made no headway with lady Sarah. He blamed it on his lack of experience with girls, and no confidence. He vacillated between fawning over her and ignoring her every other day until it affected him emotionally. He was not eating properly, and lost his lively sense of humor. He sat daydreaming when discussing the boat with Esau, or explaining Judaism to Stephanos.

Finally he admitted that he wanted her more than anything in the world, and yesterday he devised a plan. Late at night, after working on the sermon, he devised a plot. He went over it again and again, analyzing every word and every move. Then he blew out the oil lamp. Alas, the plot hung around all night like a toothache. His mind went over every phrase, making changes and adding more until a simple idea grew into a novella. In the morning his mind was fuzzy, and he fell asleep over breakfast. Walking to the lyceum the fresh air revived him, and he reviewed the plan with renewed optimism.

Alas, when lady Sarah appeared in the school yard, his confidence evaporated. In class he sat at the back, depressed, fighting off sleep. At recess one of the older girls asked, "Master Yeshua, I would like to learn more about your ship. Can I work on it?"

The question jolted him because it was the cue to his plan. On impulse he went into the plot, "Who else wants to work on the boat?" Most of them answered in a chorus, "We do; we do." He turned towards lady Sarah who seemed to be saying something. "Would you like to help?" he asked.

She replied but he could not hear her over the others. Frustrated, he waved her over. To his surprise she came, just as she did in last night's dream. Once again he saw how lovely she was when she smiled, her big dark eyes sparkling, and her full lips teasing the imagination. Her black wavy hair danced in the breeze. He could feel his heart pounding in his ears, and his mouth was dry.

She stopped in front of him. Drusilla's nails cut into his arm and he winced.

"I have never worked on a ship, but would like to learn," Sarah offered shyly.

His heart leaped, "Have you ever painted?" She shook her head. "Polish wood to a satin finish?" She lowered her head shaking it.

"I know: you will make the sails!"

Drusilla let out a groan, worried over their sudden friendly rapture.

"I have never made sails, but am willing to try if you'll teach me," she purred.

"Of course I'll show you how," he chirped, knowing he knew nothing about making sails. Then he added full of confidence, "We'll use goat's hair! It makes strong canvas for tents, so I'm sure it will make fine sails."

"Goat's hair?" she asked surprised. "Where will I find goat's hair?"

"On a goat, stupid," Drusilla spat out. The students jeered while lady Sarah turned crimson. "Find twenty goats and start sheering them, you snob." She yanked Yeshua's arm dragging him away, and bumping Sarah, who lost her balance, and fell to the ground.

· · ·

The day before the sermon Yeshua met with rabbi Ben Lebbus in the synagogue. The young scholar brought some short wooden sticks nailed to a flat base so they stood up. He also had a long rope and a small board on which he wrote an inscription.

"Do you still intend to bring the gentiles to the service?" the rabbi asked with trepidation. Yeshua nodded with confidence. "Are they proselytes?" The young man shook his head. "Believers…?"

"Not in Judaism…"

"Then I forbid them in the synagogue. They cannot come into Lord Adonai's…"

Yeshua interjected, "Rabbi, you agreed the Creator welcomes everyone…"

"He does! But He keeps Himself invisible, leaving me to deal with His very visible, intolerable congregation…"

"I expected that, so I made these," he placed the stands a couple of paces apart in a rectangular formation and tied the tops together with the rope, "This rope cuts off the area from the congregation. Symbolically my friends will be out of the synagogue. And this sign explains it all."

"'GENTILES' COURT,'" the rabbi read the sign, "What is all this?"

"I saw it in the Temple in Jerusalem. It is the gentiles' court, and…"

"Most of our peasants have never been to Jerusalem or the Temple," the rabbi interrupted exasperated. "They won't understand. Moreover, that Court is completely divided and separated. Here they're inside the synagogue."

Yeshua beamed, "It will be alright. Trust me…"

• • •

When Joseph's family entered the synagogue for Yeshua's second sermon, they were directed to the bench, but Joseph chose the mats close to the exit door.

Yeshua entered at the last moment, followed by master Stephanos and Germanicus, both donning caps, with the Israeli shawl, the tallith, over their heads, effectively hiding their faces. They entered the small area he cordoned off and sat down.

When Joseph realized the two gentiles were being passed for Israelis he motioned frantically to Miriam to run. Alas, the doors began to close.

The holy scroll, the Torah, was removed from the Arc and taken through the synagogue on its weekly journey so every congregant could touch it with the corner of their tallith, then kiss the shawl. Stephanos and the slave copied them.

The rabbi gave the benediction and a prayer, then motioned to the two church elders to approach the bema. Lady Aquilla read her statement stiffly, "As the chairman of the board of the elders we apologize to master Joseph's family."

Master Eliphaz also read his prepared text, "I regret to inform you that lady Aquilla and I resign from the board of elders effectively immediately."

A murmur of discontent rippled through the congregation. The old patriarchs suspected Joseph's powerful family forced the resignation.

Yeshua walked up to the bema and greeted the congregants with a smile, "Shalom." Only the younger congregants returned his greeting. "Have no fear. Today I will discuss the Messiah! Who is the Messiah?"

Joseph and Miriam sat like statues of granite, only the fear in their eyes showing they were alive.

The congregants, not used to giving opinions, sat uneasy. Then some muttered monosyllables and a few disjointed thoughts blurted out:

"He is the anointed one..." one man ventured.

"The greatest prophet Israel has ever seen," another opined.

"Like Elijah, he will lead Israel to glory," an older lady pumped her fist to the sky.

"There is no Messiah," an old patriarch bellowed, and wheezed for breath before continuing. "It is all superstition and sorcery..."

Yeshua turned to another group, "When will the Messiah come?"

"When we purge our sins. We must cleanse our lives..." another old timer passed judgment.

"Adonai will not send him until we prove ourselves worthy," a woman added.

"The great prophet Isaiah said," Yeshua addressed a group who had not joined the discussion, "'There will come from the house of David one Messiah who will free the people of Israel, and rule the world'. What did he mean?"

"He will be a great warrior, the like of which the world has never known."

"Not just a soldier; but a general. Invincible, with the cunning of king David," a woman added from the far corner.

"What do you expect when the Messiah arrives?"

"He will take the throne, and crown himself in glory," an elderly lady announced proudly, "The king of Israel!"

"The king of the world," the old farmer wheezed.

"Repent, ye sinners!" his neighbor opined. "Make way for the Messiah."

"It's all witchcraft, sorcery of the worst kind," the first Sadducee persisted."

Different groups started arguing with each other, their tempers rising, making it difficult for Yeshua to understand them. He raised his arms for quiet but they shook their fists yelling. "Beat the Romans? Did you see their legions?" an old man asked, then answered his own question, "Six thousand men: foot soldiers, archers, javelin throwers, infantry, cavalry and elephants...warriors further than the eye can see..."

"We'll need more than a Messiah to beat the Romans. More than one God!" a woman suggested. "We'll need Adonai, and maybe Zeus!"

"Get Hercules," someone shouted.

"Mars is the god of war," a woman pumped her fist again. "If you want to win, get the pagan god Beelzebub...even Lucifer!"

"Forget pagan gods, forget magic and oracles. Lord Adonai is the only one."

Master Stephanos' eyes were bigger than saucers darting from group to group yelling over each other, like vendors in a bazaar.

Yeshua asked the closest group, "Perhaps the Messiah is here already" If so what do you think he looks like?"

A young lady ventured, "A gigantic monster…To beat the Romans he'd be so big he would not fit through that door!"

"Doors would not stop him," a young man next to her declared. "He has to be a god, a spirit with supernatural powers!"

A young lady who had tried to speak many times only to be drowned out, stood up. The pilgrims, not sure what she intended quieted down, "Why are you searching for supernatural gods of pagans and gentiles?" she admonished them. "Why do you seek destructive forces? You may be looking for all the wrong qualities…and wrong reasons."

"Have you a better suggestion?" an old man snapped back.

"I think the Messiah will be a person like any of us. His strength will not be brute force," she explained somberly. "His strength will be his character…"

Her novel explanation gave them pause. She sat down as quietly as she rose, while they contemplated her statement. They expected their hero to be as powerful as an earthquake, more destructive than raging fire, while she proposed a mere mortal no more impressive than themselves. They guffawed and jeered loudly.

Yeshua was impressed with her and raised his arms for silence, asking her, "If the Messiah walked in this door how would you react?"

"I would probably not recognize him," she replied. "Hopefully he would do something grand to prove himself."

An old patriarch said, "That's the problem. We expect some monster. Yet if he appeared we would likely sacrifice him as an impostor."

The same lady added, "The problem is we're impatient and ignorant. If he did not impress us with extraordinary deeds, we would likely kill him for failing us."

A man at the back yelled out, "My brother who lives in the town of Beth-Hazor said two holy men passed through there recently. One was master Eleazar, the other master Abba Hikiah. The people were so impressed they called them Messiahs!"

Yeshua looked at Stephanos who promptly scribed the names.

"I heard of a master Honi," an old woman offered. "They say he can bring rain from a clear blue sky."

Stephanos scribed that name quickly.

"This proved what I suspected; the Messiah is someone different for every person. Sadly we do not know anything positive about him. But we will soon learn. My friends and I," he pointed to them beyond the ropes, "will be leaving on a mission to find him. Meet master Stephanos, a Greek scholar, and his slave Germanicus."

The two removed the shawls, and stood up to bow, when the congregants exploded, "You brought infidels...into the Lord's house?" an old man wheezed.

"You profaned His sacred home!" a woman screamed.

"Pagan lover," a man heaved a sandal.

"Master Yeshua is there no end to your blasphemous crimes?"

A shower of stones, daggers, sandals and whatever was available flew, striking them. The pandemonium was getting out control, when Joseph and Miriam grabbed the children and dashed out, being liberally struck as they exited. Stephanos froze, uncertain what to do. Yeshua tried to calm the pilgrims without any success.

Stephanos stared in shock as an old man came at him with a dagger. Germanicus grabbed him unceremoniously and shoved towards the door. They barely got out. The rabbi ordered some strong young men to lead Yeshua out.

He ran two blocks before catching up to his friends. Stephanos was cut and bruised, and short of breath, "They are fanatics: like animals. Are all Israelis the same?"

"No," Yeshua replied, dusting himself, "the Judeans would have you killed! It's my fault. I forgot," he apologized.

"What are you talking about?" Stephanos demanded.

"The ropes: I placed ropes and signs, same as in the Temple...only I forgot..."

What did you forget?"

"Our peasants cannot read."

. . .

It was the last day of exams for the senior students at the lyceum.

Those hoping to graduate faced two weeks of rigorous tests: written and oral. The oral examinations consisted of being tested by three stern school masters: Benjoseph and two guest teachers. They had to receive satisfactory grades from all three to graduate.

When Yeshua finished the exams he sat in the school master's office.

"Congratulations; the examiners were most impressed with you."

"I owe it all to you. I shall never forger your help and guidance."

"Have you decided which university you will attend?" Benjoseph queried. "I may be able to help you get accepted…"

"I have not had time. I spend every free moment planning the expedition…"

"Oh, yes…the Messiah. It's good you're leaving for a few months. It will take at least that long for the villagers to forget your last caper," the school master teased him.

"I was not trying to deceive them," the young scholar confessed. "I meant to tell them before the sermon."

"Then they would have stoned you before," he chuckled. "The synagogue belongs to the congregation, and they decide who can come into it."

Yeshua replied with a tone laden with sarcasm, "They say it is God's house, but I tell you truly – the only one not in the synagogue is the Creator!"

Benjoseph smirked, "You will build Him one?"

"When I do, everyone will be welcome to attend."

The schoolmaster did not doubt it, but he had a more pressing topic. He looked around to make certain they were alone, and lowered his voice, "Do you remember the meeting of the Zealots tonight?"

Yeshua nodded, "Esau and I are looking forward to it."

"Do you have any questions …?"

A scream from a girl in the distance interrupted them. They ran to the window and saw a dozen students on the brow of the hill, a hundred paces away throwing stones below. "What was that scream?" Benjoseph wondered.

"Why are they heaving stones…?" Yeshua asked, and in the same instance shouted, "SARAH," and ran out to the brow of the hill, with Benjoseph at his heels. They saw the students armed with stones which they were heaving at a fallen person at the bottom. "SARAH!" Yeshua screamed, leaping down the thirty cubits, his feet barely touching the side of the hill. He landed in front of the fallen girl, raising his arms to protect her from the raining missiles. "Are you alright? Can you stand up?" he yelled, looking at her bloody face caked with mud and dirt.

"I don't know..." she stuttered crying in agony. "They pushed..."

He quickly glanced at her legs. They were scratched and bruised but did not seem to be broken. He grabbed her arm and began to help her stand up, at the same time yelling at the students, "STOP! Stop your stoning right now!" But they continued throwing rocks down viciously, striking both indiscriminately. "Stop this very moment!" he screamed, his face trickling with blood. He recognized all the students, among them his siblings, James and Debborah. "Have you gone insane? What is the meaning of this?"

Drusilla, obviously the leader, barked from a few cubits above him, "We're sick and tired of this Phoenician snob!"

Yeshua saw her lift a heavy boulder which she was raising, ready to crush her victim. "Drop that boulder! You can kill her with that!" he ordered.

"I intend to," she defied him stubbornly, "Get out of my way!"

Yeshua pulled lady Sarah behind him, and started slowly towards the assailant, staring into her eyes. She glared at them with hatred, resolved to kill them. But, as she stared into his radiant eyes, she was captivated, and blinked unable to look away. He took the boulder and heaved it to the side, where it landed with a loud thud.

The young scholar turned to lady Sarah who was trembling and sobbing, and held her until she settled down.

"They...they pushed me...I was tricked...They lured me to the edge, and..."

"You are alright now," he consoled her. "I'll protect you."

She closed her eyes and leaned on him, as he turned to the students, "Throw away the stones." They dropped them. He turned to Drusilla, "What is the meaning of this? Who taught you to kill your neighbor: the synagogue? The lyceum?"

"Ever since she arrived she behaves like a queen, and we're her peasants. Well, she's no royalty! And we're not peasants!"

"Of course you are! We all are. Be proud of it," Yeshua laughed loudly at her feeble explanation. "We are country bumpkins, but we are honest, self supporting and proud. And we open our hearts and our doors to foreigners. But we have failed lady Sarah. None of you offered her friendship. None invited her to your homes, or offered to help her. Sister Debborah, if you moved to her city, would you want a reception like you gave her?"

"No," she muttered, her eyes fixed on the ground.

Yeshua addressed them, "Starting today you will treat lady Sarah as you would like to be treated. Each of you shall bring her into your home and teach her a handicraft. Lady Messalina, you will teach her to sew; lady Safia will teach her to grind flour and bake. Lady Drusilla what will you teach her?" He waited, watching her shuffle from one foot to the other, finally mumbling something inaudible. "Speak up girl!" he ordered.

"To weave!" she blurted out.

He turned to Debborah, "You will explain our customs and traditions. Brother James, you will teach her our religion…"

"I want you to teach me religion," lady Sarah pleaded.

Yeshua smiled, "Debborah take her to our house. Lady Sarah, give us a second chance. Remember the old adage: write all bad experiences in sand, and only the good things in stone." Lady Sarah smiled and nodded. "Debborah, wash her wounds, and ask mother to put some ointment…"

"Do you think I'm helpless?" she rebelled. "I can do as well as mother. Come lady Sarah, let me look after my big sister…"

Yeshua watched them leave, and glanced up to the top of the cliff. Master Benjoseph had watched the entire episode. He nodded approval, turned and left.

Lady Sarah brushed back her hair and turned to look at her savior. She had a premonition her life would never be the same again.

CHAPTER VI - JOINING THE ZEALOTS

Before sunrise Yeshua met Stephanos and his slave outside his gate, "Good morning," the young scholar chirped.

"There ought to be a law against rising before the sun," Stephanos muttered.

They continued along the road to rabbi Ben Lebbus' olive grove. "Israelis rise early and turn in early," Yeshua commented.

"That's why the country is bereft of any artistic beauty," the Greek complained. "For us, sensitive souls, the time for creative work is after sundown. How much further?"

"On top of that hill."

"What hill? All I see is a black hole. I hope harvesting olives will not turn into a fiasco like your sermon," Stephanos complained. "I should have known better when I heard about your first sermon. Did you really say Israelis were the plague of the world?"

"Is that what they told you I had said?"

"How will harvesting olives teach me Judaism?" he demanded, still unhappy with the prospect of hard manual labor. When there was no reply, he turned to his companion, only to discover he was alone. Looking back he saw him disappearing through a gate, and rushed after him.

The rabbi and his sons were already by the trees. "This is my older boy, master Amasiah, and my younger boy Hagar. This is master Stephanos, and Germanicus."

"We saw you in the synagogue. Too bad you left so fast," Amasiah chuckled healthily.

Stephanos nodded, without joining in the humor.

Ben Lebbus handed them long strips of cloth, "Lay these under the trees to prevent the falling drupes from getting damaged. Use that stick to beat the branches to dislodge them. Put them in this basket, and when full, they will be taken to the press." Then he addressed the Greek, "Lord Adonai gave us the trees with this instruction: 'Beat the olive tree but once, and do not go over the boughs again, as those will be left for passing strangers, the orphans and widows. Each year we have more of them. You will harvest and help the needy."

"All my life I passed these trees, and ate countless olives, without giving attention…" the Greek mused staring at the tree. "Look how gnarled and twisted are its branches, like an old tired laborer. How old is this tree?"

"It takes thirty years before the first harvest then, it bears fruit upwards of three hundred years," Yeshua explained walking around it. "After that, with pruning and grafting it continues to give fruit almost indefinitely."

An old peasant woman shuffled through the gate and the Greek walked over to greet her. Before long he filled her sack, and she hugged him, "May Lord Adonai bless you and repay your kindness"

"These are a gift from the rabbi," he told her. "He deserves the blessing and gratitude. May I ask an indiscreet question? Where is your family?"

"My husband died many years ago," she replied sadly. "My two sons joined the Roman army…to become rich. One was killed in Gaul. I have not heard from the other…"

Stephanos watched her shuffling away. Others came keeping the Greek busy the entire time.

Except for a short lunch break they worked until late afternoon, when they went to work in the press. This consisted of a millstone in a basin, fixed to a pole. A donkey, tied to the pole which pulled the stone around crushing the olives, with the oil running through a hole into the jars. "The first press is crushed gently, giving a transparent oil, commonly called virgin oil. It commands the best price. I give ten percent to the Temple," Ben Lebbus said.

"Do all grove owners have to pay?" the Greek inquired.

"All farmers do, whether it's staple, fruit or vegetable," the rabbi replied, then continued, "We lower the stone for the second milling, crushing the rest of the pulp with the pits. It's a brownish oil, but still very fine."

"Aha! Household oil," the Greek guessed.

"No. We sell it also, to support our extended family. After that the pulp is put into those sacks," he pointed to canvas sacks hanging on a post. "Fixed in that wooden frame we put it through the final press to extract the last bit of oil. That's for the household. The pulp we feed to the animals and fowl."

"No waste?"

"Waste is a luxury of the rich," Hagar interjected.

The dinner consisted of soup with a slice of rye bread which they dipped in a bowl of oil and vinegar. Although the work was not heavy, it was steady and they worked up a healthy appetite. Stephanos ate his soup ravenously and held out his bowl for more.

"Did you enjoy it?" The rabbi's wife asked.

"Excellent," he answered whispering, "Can you give me a little more meat this time?"

"There's no meat. It's vegetable soup."

"Oh! In that case it...it was delicious," he managed a weak smile.

After the meal they sat back while the women cleaned up. Stephanos asked the rabbi, "Sir, do you believe the Messiah exists?"

Ben Lebbus stroked his beard carefully before answering, "You are asking two questions: Do I believe in the prophecy? That's like asking does a river flow to the sea? But, I suspect you intended to ask, is the Messiah among us today? That is difficult... although I believe yes, he does exist." He glanced furtively at Yeshua. "The question of the moment is: do you believe in God?"

Stephanos did not expect such a direct probe and replied evasively, "Well...I never thought about it..."

"Therein is your trouble: a scholar afraid to take the leap of faith to meet his Creator." The Greek tried to object but the rabbi continued, "One does not think about God's existance. You know it in your heart."

"What do you mean?" Stephanos seemed confused.

"In ancient times our ancestors saw everything around them as miracles: life, survival, every sunrise, the return of the seasons. They had a close communion with the Creator, and derived their inner strength from that. They did not sit and contemplate. They knew."

"Are you sure their God was not their own inner strength?" The Greek mused.

"Why not? He created them so it is natural He should be within them," Ben Lebbus smiled. "Alas, today people analyze, and rationalise... In the end, unless they can see it, they refuse to believe."

"I did not say I did not believe," Stephanos objected. "I said I did not..."

"You had not thought about it," the rabbi finished his sentence. "It's our modern malady. The youth have the luxury of time. But, do they use it to revere the Creator? No! They use it to reason the Creator out of their lives. Without Him to guide them, they are free to do as they please: no God, no rules; no bounds. Everything goes. Nothing is excess!"

Stephanos countered, "Not I rabbi. I am willing to believe." He looked up to the sky, "If there is a God why does He not appear?"

Yeshua rebuked him, "Who are you to order the Creator? To deny His existence as the Creator is like saying chance made everything. Do you know the odds of that happening? You are more likely to change lead to gold!"

"So you do not believe in evolution?" Stephanos asked.

"Evolution needed matter from which to start. Chance does not create matter. Only a miracle can create matter…something from nothing," Yeshua explained patiently. "After creation evolution took over. But, the universe is orderly and sensible only because it was so from the beginning. Find the beginning, the moment of Creation, and there you will find God."

"That is a tall order," the Greek responded, filled with awe at the young Israeli's explanation. "I believe only one special person can travel back there: a God!"

The rabbi decided to bring the discussion from the esoteric to the practical, "Let me explain it more simply. The Lord created the heavens and the earth and everything in it. Only on the last day He created man. That is so man would never forget even the lowly flea came before him."

They enjoyed a good laugh at the humorous explanation. Stephanos posed another question, "Rabbi, do you believe in miracles?"

Ben Lebbus smiled, "More to the point; do you believe in miracles?"

"No! Every demonstration I have seen was a trick," he responded unequivocally, "hypnotic suggestion, a slight of hand, or downright fraud. I never saw anything I could not explain. Never!"

"Our servant Anna was a leper until she was cured, apparently by a Messiah," Yeshua offered. "Surely that was a major miracle?"

"Did you see the miracle performed?" Stephanos demanded and the Israeli shook his head. "Moreover I dare say she is mistaken, as leprosy is incurable. Remember, a miracle is the creation of something from nothing."

When Germanicus heard this he listened closely. He wanted to hear everything, without arousing suspicion.

"I fear, master Stephanos, your intellect tells you, you have no need of God," Ben Lebbus concluded.

"May be I am wasting my time with the expedition," Stephanos sat back dejected. "Are you saying I may never see the Messiah, or a miracle?"

"You may see both without recognizing either," Yeshua suggested not unkindly.

"Rabbi, should I give up the expedition?" The Greek pleaded for direction.

"No. You need to see Israel, and stop questioning everything. Relax. Above all open your heart. There is no telling who may enter…"

They sat back lost in their own thoughts. Stephanos wondered how he would react if he met the Messiah. Would the great man answer his many questions?

Yeshua was deeply disturbed for arguing with the Greek so forcefully. Was he not being a hypocrite, forcing views on him when he was questioning his own faith? Just as he posed the question he realized he had spoken from the heart. Perhaps master El Sharif was correct: his issues were not with the Creator but with the congregation. Ultimately he decided perhaps the expedition would give him the answer.

• • •

They harvested olives for three days, and in return Yeshua was given olives and oil for his family and the expedition.

Every evening they sat discussing the Messiah and the prophets. But Stephanos ended up frustrated because, instead of getting answers to questions, he got riddles, proverbs, or, most frustrating, the same questions posed back to him. The enigmatic puzzles only served to confuse him.

That was when he began to realize faith was not like logic, where he composed a proposition and the answers led to one specific truth. It was more akin to the timeless olive tree: knowledge, like the gnarled branches took a long time to get from the root, through the twisted branches to make the drupe. Moreover there may be more than one answer, like the branches, pointing to the real truth. Perhaps the answer could not be expressed in words. It was felt within. This religion he decided would need infinite patience and time. Would he have the fortitude and discipline to wait for it to awken in him?

Unlike his master, Germanicus had no problems with the faith. He was enthusiastic about the new religion. In his village in northern Europe, they believed in multiple gods and useless supersticions. Above all he was curious about the Messiah who could perform miracles, like curing Anna's leprosy. Could he help him get his freedom?

· · ·

Yeshua brought the olives and jars of oil, and was putting them in the shed, when he noticed Marcus alone in the far corner of the yard, and walked over, "Master Marcus, still working on the boat? Where is the rest of the crew?"

The young man covered the boat and joined him, "The truth is I was not working...I was waiting for you to have a talk..."

"Is there a problem?" Yeshua felt uneasy, suspecting another crisis.

The young man stood, moving from one foot to the other, looking at his sandals. Finally he started slowly, "If I tell you...will you keep it a secret between us?"

Yeshua was uncomfortable with the request, "I cannot promise, until I know..."

"Well, the truth is, Esau is making the same mistakes. I tried to help, but it always leads to arguments," he tried to explain. "He is suspicious... if I ask something, I am trying to undermine his authority!"

"Are you? Are you trying to undermine his authority, master Marcus?" Yeshua stared at his friend intently.

The youth stepped back, avoiding eye contact. "I was...just trying to show his mistakes."

"What do you wish me to do?"

"Can you intervene?" Marcus urged eagerly. "Tell him I'm just trying to help...tell him he is not ready to manage. Maybe some other project...in the future..."

"What do masters Ahmed and Daniel say about this?"

"They feel sorry for...the bastard," he lamented. "So they overlook his mistakes."

Yeshua put his arm around his shoulders and led him to the street where they sat down. "The truth is that any one of you can build a boat. It only takes perseverance and discipline. Oh, you would make mistakes...so, tear it down and start over." He studied his friend and tried to persuade him, "This is not about a boat. It's about friendship and support. True friendship is for life."

"Is this about his confidence again?" Marcus sprang up annoyed.

"It's about all of us…mostly about you,"

"Me? How did I get into this? I'm not the outcast!"

"There is little purpose in helping Esau's confidence, unless we are willing to share his experience," Yeshua explained patiently. "The term outcast is relative. In Esau's universe we are the outsiders…We must go into his world and experience it. Then we will understand it and help him. And we will be his friend for life."

"I knew it! I knew I was wasting time with you," he replied angrily. "I don't know. You're asking more than I am willing to give. I may quit before I have to give that much." He marched away into the night.

· · ·

Yeshua, the Greek and his slave tramped the entire day, hoping to find work harvesting in return for grain, only to be bitterly disappointed.

Their first stop was at master Shalem's. "Good morning, sir, we are available to help harvest for a share of the crop?" Yeshua offered.

The farmer studied them suspiciouly, before asking, "Are your friends Israelis?"

"A Greek, and his slave," the young scholar replied.

"You are welcome, but not they. We're only doing kosher."

"We are a team…" Yeshua started to say, but the farmer shut the door.

They started for the next farm, when Germanicus caught up to him and asked , "What is kosher?"

"Food prepared solely by Israelis' hands according to Mosaic laws," Yeshua explained, but seeing his blank look he added, "Moses was an Israeli leader who scribed such laws."

"Why is that so important?" Germanicus obviously was still not satisfied.

"Some Israelis only eat that and pay a bonus for kosher food."

"Does Lord Adonai only eat kosher?" the slave could not hold back his sarcasm.

"When God created man there was no problem," the Israeli explained. "The troubles began when men recreated God giving Him their prejudices."

They trekked all day but were refused by many, until the following day when one family accepted them.

Yeshua demonstrated the most important tool for harvesting, "This is a sickle. The blade is semi-circular and extremely sharp. Hold the handle and grab an armful of stalk with the other, cutting with a sweeping motion as if trying to cut off your leg."

He wished he had not said that, for the Greek almost succeeded doing it. First, he barely missed his toes, then almost cut off his foot. Fortunately it only cut the skin.

Before starting, Yeshua explained their tradition, "When cutting, make only one pass. Do not return for the grain you missed or the stalk that falls. Those are left for the widows and orphans." He pointed to the Israeli workers who left patches standing, or left some straw behind.

Before long they realized harvesting olives was a treat compared to this back breaking job. The work entailed permanent bending over, cutting, and straightening up to stook the straw, returning, bending to cut another bunch, and so on. There was no rest from the hot sun which beat down as an anvil. It demanded total concentration, for a careless moment resulted in a grave injury to a limb. Going for lunch they could hardly walk, shuffling painfully for their bowl of vegetable soup and a slice of bread. Afterwards their backs seemed seized up with excruciating pain. They watched the smaller, skinny Israelis with envy. These seemingly weak peasants never seemed to tire, working steadily without ever slowing down. They moved in one fluid continuous motion, like well oiled machines, forged from the most durable steel. They were astonished in the late afternoon when they heard strange wailing noises.

"What's wrong with the Israelis?" Stephanos asked straightening up painfully.

"They're singing." Yeshua responded without looking up.

"Why?"

"They're thanking Adonai for the beautiful day, and are pleading that He slows down the sun so they may finish the harvest today."

Stephanos' tired eyes swam over the golden fields, unable to focus, and those maniacs prayed for more work? He cried to the heavens, "Adonai, don't listen…"

When they finished, the sun was low on the horizon. While the Israelis marched ahead with a spring in their step, singing with euphoria, the three youths shuffled behind sore and stiff, none more so than the

Greek. He dragged his sandals through the dusty road, suffering silently. At the door to his room he looked down longingly at his cot, let himself flop onto it, drifting into deep slumber instantly. He did not move until the following morning.

To their surprise before the end of the week they became resilient, not only able to work hard, but enjoying it. After the wheat fields, they harvested barley, and, although not as fast as the Israelis, they held their own.

Once finished, they hauled the bundles of grain to the threshing floor, spread the straw evenly, ready for the threshing sled. The sled was tied to a couple of donkeys which pulled it around and around breaking up the straw and the grain from the seed heads. Stephanos was the first to lead the animals, going around until they became dizzy and toppled over as drunkards, while the Israelis laughed.

Winnowing truly tested his mettle. They worked only on windy days, throwing the straw and grain high in the air, where the wind blew away the straw and chaff, and the heavier grain fell down. By the end of the day the Greek's hair and tunic were filled with straw, and he itched and suffered miserably.

That evening Yeshua received a letter from master Hariph in Capernaum. He was coming with a donkey and cart to inspect the vases in the cave.

· · ·

The following day they went to meet master Hariph. At the town gate they saw two armed Roman soldiers, coming to Nazareth. But, to avoid being seen, the soldiers rushed and hid in the bushes.

Yeshua wondered, was it a coincidence that soldiers were coming on the day the Zealots were meeting? Zealots were still considered criminals, and the authorities sought to destroy them. He was contemplating all this when he heard his name being called. It was lady Sarah with a younger companion coming towards them.

"Good afternoon, what a pleasant surprise," he greeted them and introduced Sarah's companion. "Lady Tamar this is master Stephanos and Germanicus."

They bowed and Stephanos tried to smile, but could not stand still, as the itch was brutal.

"Why do you keep scratching, master Stephanos?" lady Sarah queried teasingly. "Is it fleas, or an attack of lice?"

"Neither," he frowned still itching. "The infernal straw from winnowing: I hate it."

"You seem tense, master Stephanos," she grinned. "Relax. Enjoy the moment. I have learned much of their customs, and I love every moment. It's been a fabulous experience."

Lady Tamar concurred cheerily, "Master Yeshua should have ordered us to teach you our ways long ago. She does everything we ask, and is curious about everything. Won't stop asking questions." Then she added with a twinkle in her eyes, "Most of the questions are about master Yeshua."

Sarah turned crimson, slapping her companion on the arm. Yeshua blushed.

Sarah reached into a bag and pulled out a small tapestry which she held out, "Lady Tamar is teaching me to weave with straw and palm fronds. It's my first attempt. It's not as even or firm as hers, but I'll learn…"

"I will teach her to weave intricate patterns next," lady Tamar announced proudly.

"What is it for?" Stephanos asked.

"It has many uses: floor mats, baskets, decorations…" Sarah started to explain.

Stephanos interrupted impatiently, "I know that! I meant, why are you doing it? This is work for slaves, and servants…"

"Lady Tamar is neither of those, yet she does it," lady Sarah defended her, then rebuked the Greek's air of superiority. "In fact all the ladies in town do it, and everything else for the household. They don't consider themselves above labor…like we do. Only people like us throw money at problems. They are disciplined and self-sufficient."

"They have to be. They're peasants," the Greek replied matter of factly.

"They know how to enjoy life: work hard and play hard," Sarah continued passionately. "I heard more singing these past few weeks than ever before."

"You will be telling me next you would prefer a peasant's life," Stephanos smirked. "Perhaps even marry one!"

"Maybe I will!" she snapped. "I am certain I'd be happier than with a rich dandy!" She blushed and glanced at Yeshua embarrassed at her impulsive outburst.

"Don't be a fool," the Greek interjected. "You are used to luxury. You could no more marry a peasant than a bird mate with a fish!"

"Do you know what is the problem with us: you and I? Commercialism, opulence and wealth," she argued exuberantly. "We have never longed for anything that money could buy. We know the price of everything, but the value of nothing. Some, like you will try to buy happiness"

"What lofty values have you learned here?" the Greek countered with superioriority.

"To spin wool into yarn; how to work the loom and weave cloth," she replied. "Tomorrow at sunrise I will be going to the market. Can you believe it? Almost eighteen, and I have never been to the agora?" Sarah confessed embarrassed.

"You see one market, you've seen them all," the Greek droned.

"My servant will be teaching me to pick the best products, haggle over prices, everything," she continued enthusiastically.

"I could teach you that…" Yeshua volunteered.

"Really? Perhaps you want to escort me?" she chirped persuasively. "Better still, why don't you both come? I should love that!"

The young men looked at each other jealously, each waiting to hear what the other had to say.

Stephanos answered first, "Unfortunately I will be going to the library," he apologized, and turned to Yeshua, "And you promised to meet with the boat crew."

"Oh yes! I forgot!" Yeshua sighed sadly. "I am sorry…"

"Oh, that is too bad, but, there will be other times," she said leaving. "Good bye."

· · ·

Next morning Yeshua introduced master Hariph, the scribe from Capernaum, to his companions. Master Hariph snapped at the Greek, "Germanicus is your slave? It is wrong for one human being to own another." Then he turned to Yeshua, "Is Nazareth having political problems?"

"Just the usual: no freedom," the Israeli replied. "Why?"

"I was questioned by a centurion accompanied by half a dozen armed soldiers. I fear your town is in for troubles. Let's go see the cave."

They walked while Hariph rode the cart. Yeshua could not put the soldiers out of his mind. He was almost certain the Zealots were sure to have problems. When they arrived he led them to the cave, where to their dismay there were three vases broken and the contents scattered. "Vandals! I was afraid of this," Yeshua snapped angrily.

"Young shepherds," Hariph suggested, "searching for treasures. They don't understand that they are destroying irreplaceable history."

Once the vases were taken out master Hariph read the inscriptions, "Yes, it is ancient Hebrew." He glanced at each one superficially, then stopped to read a special message on one, "Prophecies regarding…the anointed Messiah!"

Stephanos almost tripped rushing over, "Break it open. Read the full message…"

"We cannot do that. Some parchments are of leather or papyrus. They will be as dry as a twig," Yeshua warned him.

"And brittle. The slightest pressure will disintegrate them," master Hariph added. "I will have to humidify them carefully before attempting to unroll…"

"Forgive me," Stephanos sighed with embarrassment. "I got caught up in the enthusiasm and totally forgot…You are correct…!"

"After we return from the expedition we will come to Capernaum, and perhaps master Hariph will have deciphered the message," Yeshua suggested excitedly.

"What expedition?" Hariph asked.

"We will be going in search of the Messiah," the Greek replied.

"I have seen some holy men at work," Hariph nodded as he stroked his long white beard. "I cannot say they are the promised one, but you will not be disappointed." He turned to Yeshua, "Come in a few months and I promise I'll have news. Afterwards you may continue to Jerusalem for Passover. You will see master Theudas, from Jerico, who promises to part the river Jordan as Moses parted the red Sea. And in Jerusalem you will see an expatriate from Egypt. He promises to destroy the Temple…"

"My friend Quintus saw him," Yeshua remembered, "Many say he is the real Messiah."

"It's settled then - my house, then on to Jerusalem," master Hariph smiled, then turned to the Greek, "The downtrodden and oppressed are the children of the Messiah!"

. . .

Yeshua was deeply asleep when suddenly he bolted upright exclaiming, "Master Stephanos…you are a fibber!" He sat, his eyes heavy with sleep, repeating, "Stephanos, you're a fibber!" He lay down again, tossing and turning, waiting for morning. At first light he dressed up and left. When he arrived at the open market he saw the Greek with his camel. "Master Stephanos, why are you here? And why the baskets on the camel?"

Master Stephanos looked shocked and stuttered guiltily, "Master Yeshua, I…did not expect you…"

"You were going to the library, you said. Luckily I remembered we do not have a library. You, sir are a fibber!"

Stephanos went on the offensive, "And you were to be helping the boat crew."

"I came to check on you," Yeshua accused him.

"And I to check on you," Stephanos rejoined.

They stood toe to toe when a female voice interrupted them, "What a pleasant surprise," lady Sarah sang cheerily. "Not one but two beaus to escort me. Good morning gentlemen, perfect morning for shopping, don't you agree?"

They backed off, bowing and feigning a smile. Germanicus stood in the background enjoying the drama. Yeshua bowed to lady Sarah, noticing she was overdressed for the open marker, but chose to compliment her, "You look divine."

"Truly divine," Stephanos echoed.

"I brought my donkey and two baskets, to serve you" the Israeli offered.

"My camel will transport twice as much," the Greek interjected.

"Thank you both, but I plan to learn much and purchase little," she chirped. She took each by an arm announcing, "Gentlemen I put myself in your capable hands."

The merchants were just beginning to set up mats and tables, bringing out the merchandise, vegetables, fruits and wares to display. Soon shoppers began to invade the napping agora. The drama of bargaining, of seller and buyer arguing for the best price, was starting in earnest.

"Be patient with me," Lady Sarah whispered. "I am a child at this."

"Your first impression is most important," the young Israeli explained. "Skim over the goods: the greater the variety the more you will be able to pick and choose. Close your eyes and inhale the scent. The sweet perfume-like smell of ripe fruit: dates, figs mixed with the wholesome smell of grains and vegetables, say the products are mature yet fresh."

Stephanos inhaled and frowned, "I feel like I fell in a barrel of fermented fruit."

Yeshua ignored him and continued "Your olfactory sense tells you that the fresh, pleasant smell promises to be a good day to buy."

Sarah imitated him, inhaling then screwing up her face, "I can't separate the smells. I smell sandals, cosmetics, mangoes...everyting."

"In time you will distinguish them and concentrate on what you want."

Stephanos scoffed, "We must look like three blood hounds, sniffing for a fox."

Yeshua shook his head but continued, "Walk slowly, your eyes roaming over the products. When the merchants wave, wave back, but continue. Never appear too eager. They are experts at deciphering the faintest sparkle in your eyes."

They stopped by a vendor selling grapes, where he pointed out, "Be wary when vendors sprinkle water on the fruit to give it a fresh appearance. Some will coat it with wax...Others will mix in and display..." He stopped when Stephanos picked up a shiny purple grape, slipped it in his mouth and bit it voraciously.

The Greek scowled and spat out, "By Zeus! What in tarnation?"

"As I was saying," Yeshua chuckled, "some mix wax fruit with the real thing. Irresistible right master Stephanos?"

"I confess, I was so impressed I was ready to buy them," lady Sarah remarked.

"Beware - a beautiful exterior covers terrible rot," the Israeli observed. He picked up a bunch of grapes explaining, "First inspect the stem. If it is green it is freshly cut. Brown means it's getting old, in which case you look at the grape where it is attached to the stem. If the fruit starts to discolor at that point, forming pockets of air it is old. If it is fresh and healthy like this bunch, give them a light squeeze. A firm grape is juicy."

"This seems good to me."

Yeshua nodded. They agreed on a price, and purchased three libras.

"I fail to appreciate the drudgery of this exercise," the Greek grumbled. "After haggling and arguing an entire day what do you save: a measly couple of drachmas?"

Yeshua concurred, "At most, but, remember a worker toils from sunrise to sunset for one drachma."

After much walking, inspecting and questioning, Sarah was beginning to wilt, and sighed discouraged, "I will never master this. My mind is already confusing everything: some melons are ripe when they sound hollow, others must sound firm, while another is rotten if it sounds hollow... Some I smell, others squeeze, give it a shake, hold to a light to inspect, or...or, I don't know what. I'm all muddled."

"Take your time; you cannot learn it all in one trip," the Israeli empathized.

"Better still, avoid the blasted business and send a servant," the Greek opined.

"Look, figs!" Sarah exclaimed dragging them to the stall, "You don't have to tell me anything about figs! All figs are delicious!"

Both reached for the same fig, Yeshua grabbing the fruit, while she grabbed his hand. They froze. Slowly they brought up the purplish fruit, but neither looked at it. Instead they looked deeply into each other's eyes. Her black eyes were as beautiful as the first day. But, today he saw no fear. Instead there was a sparkle of happiness and confidence. She saw the same intense radiant light in his eyes, and she thought of them as her beacons.

Stephanos stared from one to the other, and sputtered exasperated, "Are you buying it, or making love to it?"

"Uh...? Yes...you are right..." Yeshua stuttered.

"Four libras, please," lady Sarah mumbled.

The merchant who watched her marching to the figs sneered smugly and prattled expansively, "Excellent choice, madam. FIGS! The nectar of the gods: Aphrodite and Apollo; Venus and Mars, all savored the heavenly fruit, while bathing in the fountain of love..."

Stephanos snarled dispassionately, "They want to buy, not adopt them!"

The vendor stared at the intruder, then cooed, "For my special lady, a special price: five yehud coppers per libra..."

Yeshua coughed and tapped her with the elbow.

The merchant saw it and quickly added, "But, I feel generous. I'll charge you only three ..."

She looked at Yeshua who nodded, and she ordered, "Four libras please."

The vendor deposited some figs in a metallic bowl, reached under the stall and brought out metallic weights with a dab of white paint on one corner. When he was about to give her the fruit, Yeshua placed his hand on the figs, "Why don't you use the same weights now as when you bought them from the farmer?" The merchant was about to argue when Yeshua brought out weights from behind the counter with red paint on the corners. "Use these," he said.

The vendor's face tightened but he did as ordered, adding four more figs. Please come back again, young lady!"

After they walked away she asked, "How did you know he was cheating?"

"Elementary, my dear lady," Stephanos replied pompously. "He is a Jew!"

Yeshua chuckled light heartedly, "I cannot deny our people may cheat. But, that particular merchant is Greek: from Corinth!"

Stephanos looked back and threw a couple of unrepeatable Greek words a him.

Shortly after Yeshua recognized an old man, standing alone by a small table, "There is master Yacek, a good old friend." They made their way to him. "Good morning, master Yacek. May I introduce to you lady Sarah, from Tyre; and master Stephanos, a Greek scholar. This is master Yacek."

"Aha! I recognize master Stephanos from the synagogue. You are brave, but foolish to enter our lion's den," Yacek teased, then bowed deeply to Sarah, "I am honored. Your lovely presence adorns this mundane marketplace."

"You are very kind. Thank you," she blushed.

Yeshua saw that master Yacek appeared much healthier. "How is your knee?" he inquired.

"Why, it is fine," the old man replied looking at the young scholar with surprise and emotion. "Thank you for asking." He turned to the young lady explaining, "Until a few months ago I suffered from inflammation of the joints. No matter what salve I used, or how carefully I wrapped them, still I lived in perpetual agony. The infernal pain traveled from knee to toe. One day after his sermon, he cured me. I swear…like a miracle…"

"I only gave you some advice," he explained. "I'm glad you are recovered."

"Did he give you a potion to drink, or paste to rub?" Sarah asked.

"That's what was so strange," master Yacek shook his head. "He touched it and in an instant the pain was gone." Then he went on a tirade unburdening his emotions. "You are the only one who asked me about my health. I was born and raised in this town. Many pass me without a question. They don't have time for a complaining old man."

"Do you still have the anklet of the pagan god?" Yeshua teased him.

Master Yacek dug into his pocket and pulled out a gold charm, "This? She is a wonderful goddess; Aphrodite, the goddess of love. I have not worn it for months." He smiled at Sarah tenderly, "I should be honored if you would accept it as a gift from me."

She nodded graciously, "She is lovely. I promise to take care of her. Thank you."

Master Yacek turned to a merchant, "Please wash this with some vinegar."

"I will do better. I will use alcohol old man," he responded.

Master Yacek turned to the Greek, "Soon you will be embarking on your mission. I am curious whether you will find the Messiah?"

"One can hardly miss with so many roaming your country."

"I would consider my life blessed, if I could see him once," master Yacek mused.

"Here's your anklet, master Yacek."

He took it and presented the shiny jewel to Sarah, who handed it to Yeshua and held out her foot. He bent over and touched her right ankle, opened the two ends and slipped it on. When he tightened it, he held her leg with both hands and closed his eyes. He felt her smooth, shapely leg. Her skin was warm. He felt his heart pounding in his eardrums. Sarah felt his grip, blushed and felt faint. Her cheeks were aflame. Her eyes were swimming, and she brought her hand up to cover her parted lips.

When Yeshua stood up their eyes met. He thanked master Yacek again. Lady Sarah leaned and kissed the old man on the cheek, and they left. The old man smiled watching them, and wiped two tears welling in his eyes.

· · ·

Back at his house, Yeshua and Stephanos went up to the roof to tend the drying fruit and vegetables. Germanicus quietly slipped away to visit with Anna in the back.

The two young men built multi layers of frames from thin wood, covering each layer with palm fronds on which they placed dates, figs, oranges, grapes, beans, peas and a variety of vegetables. They covered the entire contraption with a fine net, to keep insects away.

"I feel like we're back at the agora," the Greek lamented with a sigh. "I feel nauseated by this cocktail of fermenting fruit and salads. It will never dry!"

"Be patient," the Israeli advised.

"I am patient!" Stephanos barked impatiently. He marched to the opposite side along the edge, almost losing his balance, raising part of the net which had fallen. "Lift up your side while I stand this twig." Yeshua raised it while the Greek replaced it and was about to set it down, when he let out a scream, "By Zeus! There is a bee inside. Get away you infernal creature! Shoo! Shoo!"

Yeshua chuckled, "Don't swat. Leave it be, it is coming my way." He raised the net and stood aside to let the bee out. "Gone. See? No danger at all."

The Greek retorted disagreeably. "Yesterday I tried to persuade one to leave when it stung me."

"These are worker bees. They only become aggressive if threatened."

"I did not threaten it. All I did was shoo it away... with a sandal."

"Did you have a sign: FRIENDLY SHOO. WILL NOT HURT?" Yeshua smirked.

"Did it have a sign: WORKER BEE, WILL NOT STING?"

They sat down, and Stephanos started debating how to say something his companion would find very disagreeable. He bit his lip and started slowly, "I have something unpleasant you will not like to hear, but..." He almost lost his nerve when he saw the Israeli staring at him. "Perhaps I should not...but...I value your friendship..."

"What are you trying to say?"

He thought for a long time before finding courage, "Your infatuation for lady Sarah is hopeless. Look at yourself: a pauper. Have you been in their house? It reeks of wealth, power and influence. Do you think her father will approve you as her mate? He will see her dead first..."

Yeshua felt as if he had been stabbed, and reacted angrily, "Is that why you lied about the library? To spare my pauper's feelings?"

Stephanos turned crimson, and confessed, "Yesterday I lied. I did not realize how much you cared for her. Don't feed that flame. It won't keep you warm; it will consume you...Perhaps lady Sarah as well."

The Israeli tensed up, ready to strike, but deep inside he knew his friend was right. He walked away a few paces, "The dream is impossible... I don't want to see her hurt. I shall give her up." He looked away, lowering his face, choking with desperation. Stephanos took a step towards him when he heard a commotion. Quintus arrived at the gate with a loaded cart.

The Roman entered the yard, saw them on the roof top and ran up, barely touching the steps, "Good afternoon my friends. I brought the last of the wood." He stopped, sizing up the Greek, and smiled, "What good fortune to meet again so soon..."

"That depends on what you have to say," Stephanos spat out frostily.

"Drying fruit, Greek?" he smirked superiorly. "Why do you do woman's work? Ah, but the question answers itself."

"I'd rather do their work than murder them," he rebutted with sarcasm.

Quintus grabbed the hilt of his sword barking, "Curb your tongue before I cut it out and feed it to the jackals!"

"Stop it, both of you," Yeshua warned sternly. "I'm not in the mood to separate two delinquents."

"He started it," the Greek whined.

"You called me a barbarian," Quintus countered.

"The truth is my defense."

Yeshua turned abruptly with a warning, "One more slight by either of you, and you will be exchanging pleasantries on the street!"

Quintus turned his attention to the fruit, "Who built this contraption? The layers are too close: no air will flow through this. The fruit will rot before drying."

"The heat will dry them," Stephanos objected.

"Heat does not dry - air flow does. Let's re-do this properly," the Roman ordered.

They started to remove the fruit and dismantle the frames when Quintus stood up enthusiastically, "Oh, my commander approved my request, so I'll be coming on the expedition." He stood up rigidly and saluted, "Private Quintus, at your service!"

Stephanos was so dumbfounded he huffed with short breaths, "Is there no limit to your brazen impudence? There is no room! Forget it! It's final: N-O! NO!"

Quintus smiled coyly, holding the trump card, "Oh, yes, there is! I'm bringing an officer's army tent: spacious, and guaranteed against storms, sand blasts or snow."

"Snow in this blasted furnace?" Stephanos howled.

The Roman lost his patience, pulled out his sword and marched at the Greek, "I'm an expert swordsman, ready to protect you from bandits in the forests of Galilee."

"I have a guar..." he started, when he had to duck to avoid the Roman's sword. He suspected the barbarian had gone berserk, and had to jump to the right, to save an arm from being lopped off. "Have you gone mad? GERMANICUS! HELP!"

Germanicus ran up the steps, and was about to intervene, when Yeshua intercepted him, "Do not meddle. They're having a discussion."

The slave saw Quintus' sword at his master's throat, "What are you discussing?"

"I am persuading your master that he needs my services!" Quintus replied calmly.

"You nearly skewered me, cut me in twain, then say I need you? You are mad!"

Yeshua winked at the slave who shrugged and returned to Anna. Quintus replaced the sword in the scabbard.

"Mark my words Greek," the Roman warned him, "If you travel further than ten miles from here you will be robbed...likely murdered..."

Stephanos tried to scoff, but glanced at Yeshua who nodded. Left with no option he snarled, "You will bring the tent, and your own supplies. But only come as a guard..."

Quintus shook the Greek's hand so violently, he almost fell off the roof, "Best decision you ever made, Greek. Now, let's build this contraption properly..."

"Don't start giving orders..." Stephanos barked.

"Quit arguing and get moving." Quintus snapped.

• • •

While the young men reconstructed the frames, Germanicus visited with Anna while she washed clothes in the backyard.

"Does master Yeshua's family treat you well?" he inquired.

"Oh yes; they are wonderful...Just like family."

"Are you paid a good salary?" he asked and she shook her head. "No salary? Then you're a slave like me," he sounded offended.

"Oh, no! I am absolutely free."

"Free? To do what?" He scoffed sardonically. "Without wages you can't afford anything. You work hard and deserve to be well paid."

"You're very kind," she answered shyly. "But, I'm happy...I get room and board."

"Ha! They could not feed you enough for what you deserve," he sneered and decided to help her. "They're taking advantage of you...I will speak to them!"

He started towards the house when she became frantic, ran and grabbed him, "No! You must not do that! It will only create trouble. Promise you will not say or do anything!"

"They're taking advantage of you," he argued. "You owe them nothing."

"You are wrong, Germanicus. I owe this family everything. I don't ever want to leave them. They are special to me..."

"Why?"

She looked down at her hands and decided to confess, "When I came, I was suffering...an incurable disease..."

"A leper, I know!"

She glanced at him wondering how he had found out, but decided to continue, "Nobody would hire me... no one dared to speak to me. They feared any contact." She began to cry and he pulled her close until she regained composure. "They fed me, and gave me everything."

"But you do not seem a leper..." he commented.

"I am cured."

"Leprosy is not curable," he replied, then asked with curiosity, "I heard you were cured by a holy man...a Messiah?"

She drew back frightened, "It was a miracle. I don't know...a very special man..."

"They say the Messiah helps the oppressed," he pleaded desperately. "He may help me to become free."

"I don't think he..." Anna started then decided to change topics, "Tell me, what happened that you became a slave?"

He turned gloomy as he explained, "The Romans invaded my land... Killed most of my people. I was one of the few to survive."

"At least you're alive," she tried to sound optimistic.

"Alive? I'm a slave!" He added gruffly, "I'm not happy to just survive!"

She studied him closely and murmured, "You are an unhappy man. It's difficult to accept undeserved punishment, but, you must not let it destroy you."

"I live for only one dream - Freedom!"

"There are many types of freedom," she said tenderly, touching his chest. "The type that will make you happiest comes from within."

• • •

The sun was sinking fast when Yeshua started out to his first meeting of the Zealots. He went south of Nazareth, and turned west. He passed the terraced vineyards saw the five palm trees, where he saw Esau hiding in the woods, "Have you been waiting long?" he asked, his eyes darting through the thick bushes.

"Just arrived," the outcast replied, adding anxiously, "I've been reconsidering this and don't like it. Zealots mean trouble."

"I have also been thinking…Rebellions, and death, follow them everywhere. Master Benjoseph said we should walk to avoid suspicion. They will find us." They started to walk. "Earlier this afternoon I saw Roman soldiers coming to town. Master Hariph saw a half dozen. I wonder why they are coming here?"

"I don't like it," Esau stuttered visibly tense. "Let's turn back."

"We cannot overreact to every event," the young scholar replied. After a moment he whispered, "Besides, it's too late. We're being watched."

"Where?"

"Don't look now, but he's on the right, in the trees…"

At the same moment they heard a man's voice behind them, "Do not turn around. Do not speak. Are you master Yeshua?" to which the young scholar raised his right hand. "Your companion is Esau?" Satisfied, the man whistled and a cart pulled by a donkey came out from the woods. "Do not turn around. Did anyone follow you?" the man did not wait for a reply, but proceeded to blind-fold them, helped them into the cart where they sat deep in straw, and tied their hands behind their backs. "Take them," he ordered the driver. As the cart moved he jumped out and returned to the bushes.

The cart proceeded on a straight country road. Yeshua listened to the "clip-clop" sound of the hoofs on hard packed dirt. He surmised they were in a heavily treed area. When the noise abated he concluded they were in open fields. Later he did not hear the hoofs, and thought it was sandy soil. This was repeated a couple of times. He whispered, "They're taking us in circles along the sand dunes."

Not long afterwards he smelled the raw, pungent smell of muddy waters, wet roots and rotting wood. The cart seemed to be descending a steep grade, for the donkey was being pushed by the heavy cart, making for an uncomfortable ride. "We're going down to the swamp area," he whispered to his friend.

Yeshua recalled a few years before when he was still the shepherd boy, hunting in the area numerous times. He remembered a large cabin tucked deep in the trees, which he had investigated and had found it in perfect state of repairs. He had wondered who used it. He wondered if he was going to find out.

When they arrived they were led into the building and handed over to master Benjoseph. "Are you alright?" the schoolmaster greeted them, removing the blindfolds and untying them. "I apologize for the treatment, but we must be careful." He lowered his voice barely above a whisper, "Be careful what you say, as we suspect we may have a traitor in our cell. Keep your ears open, and if you see or hear anything suspicious let me know. Now, can I get you anything - water or a fruit?"

"Water, as long as it is not from the swamp," the young scholar replied. He looked around and recognized the cabin he had investegated long ago.

The one room building was poorly lit with two small oil lamps. Listening to the voices Yeshua guessed there were over one hundred persons though he could only see those closest to the lamps. While he was looking around the schoolmaster called for silence. "Sit down everybody, and let's start the meeting," he sat and motioned the two youths to join him. "Master Menachem," he addressed an elderly farmer, "Stand guard outside the door. Don't forget: three loud knocks if you see strangers." The guard went out. Benjoseph addressed the group, "Most of you know these young men: master Yeshua, and Esau. They were thoroughly investigated."

A local farmer stood up and addressed the two young men, "I have a warning for you two. You may attend two meetings before deciding to join or not. However, if you ever tell anybody about tonight, or identify us to anyone, the penalty is – DEATH! I warn you because I am the executioner!" He pulled out a dagger and passed it across his throat, then sat down.

The young men's eyes popped and they swallowed hard.

Benjoseph turned to another man beside them, whom Yeshua did not recognize, ordering, "Read the minutes of the last meeting."

While the man read, Yeshua scanned the members, but could only discern those closest to the lights. Most were people from town. Some were older men with whose sons' he played or went to the lyceum. Others left school, got married and had children. They were aged and prematurely grey. There were many non-Israelis from out of town: proselytes, gentiles who converted to the faith, and believers.

His eyes kept returning to one man, not because he recognized him, but he felt the stranger's dark eyes fixed on him. But whenever he looked, the man hid behind another. He managed a glimpse of his head; he had thick black hair and a long scar on the left side of the face, from the temple to the eyebrow, continuing to the cheek and down to the chin. He thought had seen him before, but where?

After the first order of business, Benjoseph proceeded, "We have a busy night, so let's not have interruptions or arguments. We must nominate the executive and finalize policies. And we must decide whether we remain a political party with peaceful objectives." Some raised their fists obviously to support violence. "Most importantly, we have to review our security. We suspect we may have a traitor in our midst..."

There was an immediate uproar with some pulling out their daggers:

"I'll kill the son of scorpion, whoever you are," the farmer waved his weapon.

"As Adonai is my witness I'll carve out your heart!" another screamed.

"I'll crush the serpent!" a bass voice echoed in the dark corner.

"My brother lives in a village to the south, and said Romans marched in and went directly to the Zealots' houses," one member lamented. "How did they know?"

"I saw a couple of soldiers coming into town today," Yeshua informed them. "An aquaintance said he saw a half dozen more."

"Master Benjoseph, have we been discovered? Will we be arrested?" a trembling voice uttered almost in tears. "Should we run? In God's name tell us what to do!"

Benjoseph raised his voice to restore order, "The worst thing is to panic and run. I contacted headquarters in Jerusalem and the siccarrii are on their way."

"SICCARRI? The murderers?" voices quivered at the mere mention of the special unit of the Zealots.

"What choice did I have? Three cells were swarmed by the Romans…" Benjoseph defended his action. "The executioners will flush out the traitor, and we'll be safe again. Let's get on with the business to…"

"That's always been our problem," an elderly man barked. "We talk instead of acting. We yell and curse like chickens clucking in a storm…"

A half dozen members yelled and argued at the same time:

FIRST VOICE – "Enough gabbing! Let's act now: burn the Roman fort in Sepphoris!"

SECOND VOICE – "I agree! We talk while they increase our taxes. We starve while Romans get fat!"

FIRST VOICE – "Kill them, I say! Kill the Romans and the tax collectors!"

THIRD VOICE – "We cannot start another war. We have to negotiate. We're too weak…"

FIRST VOICE – "Start a war and the people will join in. Where is our leadership?"

THIRD VOICE – "It's suicide! We're too weak. Give peace a chance."

SECOND VOICE – "Better we die martyrs than grovel as beggars. We're too weak to negotiate. They won't listen until we beat them!"

FIRST VOICE – "With these taxes we'll never get ahead. I sold grain to Rome and what did I get? I paid tax to use their road, to cross their bridges, to use their port and to transport on their ships! I did not earn enough for seed for next year!"

SECOND VOICE – "It's the tax collector. He adds twenty five per cent to the tax. That's criminal!"

FIRST VOICE – "And Temple priests want their silver shekel tax too… How are we to survive?"

Benjoseph tried to calm them without success, and lost his patience, "QUIET! SILENCE! We go through this every time. I told you before; we cannot start a war because we are too weak. We have no weapons. How will you fight professional soldiers - with pitch forks and sticks? It's suicide…."

FIRST VOICE – (Desperately) "Before next year I will be bankrupt."

SECOND VOICE – "That's what happened to my neighbors: one is bankrupt and the other sold his children into slavery. Why waste time negotiating?"

FIRST VOICE – "We're desperate because we're soft. Our ancestors did not care if they were weak. They attacked. And, Lord Adonai always came to their rescue."

"These are different times," Benjoseph argued realizing he was in danger of losing control of the meeting. "In the past they were tribes fighting tribes, all of equal strength. Today the Romans are professionals with Ethiopian warriors, Hispanic cavalry and German foot- soldiers. We'll be crushed under their boots like bugs!"

FIRST VOICE – "Their boots are squashing my neck every day."

SEOCND VOICE – "We demand justice! Burn their forts. Kill all Romans and Herodians!"

Yeshua and Esau watched the shouting, and were shocked. The Zealots knew it was utter suicide to fight the superior forces, but they were desperate, destitute people living from hand to mouth. They only had their pride and preferred to die than succumb to slavery, or selling their daughters to prostitution. But he noticed one man not screaming or making demands: it was the stranger with the scar. He sat calmly watching the others like a disinterested spectator. Yeshua decided to find out about him before the end of the night.

Benjoseph stood up raising his arms, and shouting over the pandemonium, "QUIET! Listen to me! I met with Judean leaders and they support a war…But, they say it is too early, we are not ready."

FIRST VOICE – Interrupting him, "More talk! When do we act?"

SECOND VOICE – "We cannot trust Judeans. When we defeated the Romans before, they were nowhere to be seen!"

Suddenly like a raging flood everybody talked at once and it was impossible to discern the topics or voices. Years later Yeshua remembered the confusion:

ALL VOICES – "Do not trust Judeans! They can be bought!"

) "They only care for gold!"

) "Their taxes are not as onerous as ours. They help Romans!"

) "They're part of the problem: priests and sadduccees…"

Benjoseph argued, "Their taxes are every bit as onerous as ours."

FIRST VOICE – "Do they pay to use Roman roads?"

Benjoseph replied, "Of course!"

OTHER VOICES – "Bridges? Acquaducts? Palaces? The Roman army? Public baths? Ports?"

Benjoseph shouted, "Yes, yes, yes! And, yes!"

SECOND VOICE – "Why should we listen to you? You are a Judean: from Jerusalem! You'll support them against us!"

Benjoseph's jaw tightened and he tried to identify the speaker. But the noise and turmoil made it impossible to pick him out. He knew these were destitute peasants, not much above paupers and beggars. Taxed by the empire, tetrarchs, priests, cities and palaces they treaded helplessly against a strong current, under constant threat of being pulled under.

THIRD VOICE – "Listen to master Benjoseph. He is our leader and has always had our interests at heart."

Before Benjoseph could react, the confusion took on a life of its own. They shouted complaints from every corner of the room:

SECOND VOICE – "When I used Roman roads, I paid Roman denaris; same with their bridges and ports. They paid me with worthless Syrian coins!"

FIRST VOICE – "They depress our currency until it has no value!"

SECOND VOICE – "The priests of the Temple do the same and only accept silver…"

FIRST VOICE – "Kill the priests and their bankers."

SECOND VOCIE – "Kill all the oppressors!"

THIRD VOICE – "This is our fault," a lamenting voice wailed. "Lord Adonai warned us: 'Mend your ways and I shall deliver unto you the anointed Messiah.'"

ALL VOICES –) "Send the Messiah to set us free!"

) "Give us a warrior to battle our oppressors!"

) "A general to liberate us from Rome!"

Master Benjoseph shouted again, "Quiet! Order! I have the solution! Quiet!" One by one they quieted down and he explained, "Most of you know master Yesuha is going on an expedition to find the Messiah! I propose that when he finds him, he persuades the anointed one to lead us against our oppressors!"

They liked the idea, and for the first time saw some hope. They cheered and begged the young man to bring the hero back to win independence.

"Master Yeshua, will you bring the Messiah to us?" Benjoseph beseeched him.

The young scholar wanted to refuse, but mumbled instead, "I promise."

• • •

The meeting ended late. The promise of the Messiah satisfied the desperate Zealots so they carried on the meeting. As they were leaving Benjoseph approached them, "I expect the siccarrii will arrive any day. When they do, we will hold an urgent meeting. You must come."

"Why me? I am not even a member," Yeshua objected.

"They will need your help," the school master replied. "You're traveling southwest, and they'll have a job for you in Caesarea."

Yeshua started to leave with Esau. As soon as they were alone the outcast confided nervously, "I am uncomfortable with these people. They're...suicidal!" He looked to Yeshua for support, but his friend was busy searching and did not hear him. He grabbed him, "Did you hear me?"

"Yes, yes," he answered, standing on his tip-toes, stretching his neck searching, "They are desperate. We should help. If we don't do it where is the future for Israel?" Yeshua gave up and turned to his friend, "I'm trying to find someone. Can you help?"

"Certainly, what's his name?"

"I don't know. It's a man with thick black hair..."

"That applies to everybody here," he replied.

"He has a scar on the left side of his face. Surely you must have seen him."

"I'm sorry, but I got scared with the shouting." Esau's voice was still shaky.

Yeshua failed to find him, and the stranger got away. He could not explain, but he had an uneasy feeling about him. Walking home they split up, proceeding in singles or doubles. He remembered promising lady Sarah that he was to come to her house: he was not to leave without kissing her. Moreover he had to see her and hold her, for he did not expect to see her for a long time. He turned on her street and started up the hill. He did not go far when he sighted a couple of soldiers coming his way. He slipped behind some bushes and listened.

"Why did the commander send us two at a time instead of the entire unit? That would make a greater impact," the young soldier's voice betrayed fear.

"He wants to set a trap. Surround them, then, zap! Capture all of them at once."

"I can't wait to see the Zealots' faces!" the young soldier laughed nervouly.

CHAPTER VII - THE REVELATION

They finished breakfast when Miriam leaned closer to her husband and whispered, "I have decided to tell our son his true identity…" She had to stop as he almost chocked. When he recovered she continued, "I had a dream and received a message." Before he could object Miriam said, "Anna, go and ask our son to join us. When he comes you may remain. You have a right to hear this."

When Anna left he asked, "What did the dream say?"

"Yeshua was on his expedition surrounded by enemies in every direction: Romans, Herodians, bandits and robbers. When he was attacked, all my dead relatives accused me of letting him down. They were led be my deceased mother, God keep her soul. She led the charge with a vengeance"

Joseph was about to say something when the servant returned with the young man. "Good morning father; mother," he bent over and kissed her on the cheek.

Joseph mumbled a greeting and looked at his son standing with a piece of twine in his hands, and longer pieces draped over his neck, "Sit down and have breakfast. Mother has something to tell you."

"I'm in a hurry, father."

"It will not take longer to hear it sitting. Anna, get him some breakfast," the patriarch ordered.

"I have so much going on," Yeshua complained, still standing. "Tie up bundles, meet with the boat crew, and meet lady Sarah…"

Joseph cut him off with an ominous tone, "When you hear what we have to say, you will be glad to be sitting."

The tone warned him this was serious, and he sat on the mat. Anna handed him a bowl of porridge with goat's milk and honey, and he attacked it ravenously.

Except for smiling to greet him, Miriam avoided his eyes and sat biting her lips. She had rehearsed this for almost nineteen years, the key words and phrases should be imprinted on her psyche, but now decided to tell him the events without editorializing.

"Did you have something to tell me, mother?" he asked without slowing down. She looked at him sadly, realizing this was the last time she would see him as her simple boy with a good sense of humor. Joseph touched her hand.

"I should have told you this years ago," she started, staring at the fire. "Before you were born, I had a strange visitor; the archangel Gabriel." She glanced at him and he had stopped chewing. She continued, "He greeted me and told me, 'You will conceive a boy. He will be the son of the Most High...He will sit on the throne of David...' "

In a fraction of an instant Yeshua seemed transformed: his jaw fell open, his face turned white as cotton, and he sat speechless. He repeated the words, "Son of the Most high...What does it all mean?"

"That you are the son of God," Joseph reinforced it.

Yeshua nodded slowly: Son of the most high...a holy child...that explained why he was different, and the strange events he had authored... He was right, he thought, he was different in some ways...but how and why?

But when his mind returned to the present he panicked. He had no time to worry about this. He had too much to do before the journey, and he snapped, "Why are you telling me now? Why not tell me before? This...This changes everything...my life...my dreams, Sarah..." Suddenly he stood up violently, "I don't have time for this..."

"I was going to tell you..." Joseph started defensively.

"I was afraid. We were both afraid..." Miriam interjected.

"Afraid of what?" the young man demanded testily. "I suffered all those years, wondering if I was crazy...seeing people no one else saw... Do you know how I suffered? It was very unfair," he protested in pain.

"We were going to when you were three, but something happened," the mother said. "You performed your first miracle." His mouth dropped and his face was a question mark. "Master Azbar came with his family. Their daughter, Esther, same age as you, wondered onto the road. A vicious dog was roaming the streets, and it attacked Esther. When she raised her little arm the beast ripped the muscle and crushed the bones in its jaws. You took a stick and ran to fight it. The dog turned on you when a strange vision paralyzed me: a radiant light emanated over your shoulders and around your head. A brilliant light shone from your eyes. The beast growled, but did not dare to come near." She saw her son staring at the fire trying to remember the episode. "You took Esther's limp arm and massaged it gently. Within moments she was cured. By the time her parents and your father came out you were calming her down. Do you remember?"

Yeshua tried to recollect the event, but shook his head. "If you had told me, I could have helped many others," he snapped at her accusingly.

"You did!" Miriam explained. "Every night I asked you to pray for someone who was infirm or ailing. Your prayers cured them."

"Mother, you make it all sound so melodramatic," he protested.

"Your mother speaks the truth, master Yeshua," Anna interjected. "When I was cured, I should have been elated, and grateful. Instead, I was never more frightened. I thought I had been cursed by some satanic powers…"

"Are you saying I cured your leprosy?" Yeshua looked at her strangely. When she nodded, he walked towards her, "Let me see your hands again. They are perfect…no evidence of…You said a Messiah cured you…"

"When you asked me who cured me, I said I could not tell you…"

"When did I do it? I don't remember this…"

"I washed in your basin and the miracle occurred…"

"That frightened you?" Yeshua asked.

"When I was told I had leprosy…incurable, my world crumbled," she murmured. "I lived in terror…even God forgot about me." She looked up continuing in tears, "When I saw the miracle, my mind refused to accept it."

"Are you still afraid?" He inquired.

"Oh, no! I am grateful, and I thank you in my prayers every night."

He turned to his mother, "You should have told me long ago. It was selfish…"

Miriam replied with pain in her voice, "You were too young. You could have hurt someone…"

"I would never do that," he argued.

"You caused the schoolmaster's arm to wither…"

But Yeshua was not in a forgiving mood, "This is the worst time…"

He started for the door and almost ran over Debborah who was walking in.

"Why don't you watch where you're going?" she snapped. As she bounced off him and started to fall, he reached out and caught her.

"What's with the rush?" she asked, but he went around her and ran out. She came out after him. "Where are you going? Lady Sarah is coming... Shall I bring her to the oak tree?" She thought he replied, but he continued on into the bushes and disappeared.

His mind was a maze of confusion with infinite details demanding priority and resolution: Thousands of details demanding his attention were wearing him down. The crisis with the boat crew had to be attended to, and lately the uneasy partnership between the Roman and the Greek almost caused him to give up the adventure. At nights when he hoped to get distance from those pressures, he lied dreaming about lady Sarah, the complications of hope and fear of their impossible romance. A love he could not realize or forget...and, now this...

He felt relief to find out he was not suffering from madness or hallucination. But he could not dwell on the positive, because he sensed that the news hinted of a heavy burden the likes of which he had never known. As he ran, myriad questions came to him, each demanding an answer he could not give: Why me? Why today? I am the Son of the Most High... What does it mean? What are God's plans? What about my own life? What will happen to Sarah and me...? He ran as if trying to get away from the questions, but more kept coming. He tripped and went sprawling on the dusty path, got up and continued to his oak tree. There he leaned heavily against it, out of breath, almost out of control. His mind began to focus on the revelation with renewed vigor. He walked from under the tree to the edge of the cliff, looked up to the cloudless sky and shouted:

"So, I am Your son! Am I supposed to feel fantastic...or special? Well, I don't feel either. My faith in Judaism and You is pretty badly shaken up. So...You came just in time...But I'm pretty busy...the boat...helping Esau...the expedition...You know what I don't understand? Why me? What do You want from me? Why today?" He screamed and stared at the blue sky, but all he heard were distant songs of birds. He began to argue, "Are You certain You want me? Are You certain there is not a mistake?"

He liked the argument and was becoming persuaded with the possibility. His mother saw an angel, not his father. He never saw miracles. He began to smile with relief until he remembered Anna. There was no doubt a miracle cured her: his miracle. There was no mistake; he was the chosen one.

Again he continued to yell: "What is my mission…my destiny? What can I do that You cannot do for Yourself?" He looked to one side then the other, and hearing no answer, continued, "Do you realize how much people have changed You? You are a pawn in their wars. It's Your fault for not coming sooner to tell them they're wrong… that You only want them to love You, and one another… now You're going to have to do something fantastic to get their attention!" His soliloquy began to frighten him, and his eyes darted around the sky fearing he had said too much, so he quickly yelled out, "What about me? My life? Will I have a life…lady Sarah…a family and children?"

He stared into the sky for an answer, a hint, an idea or inspiration to guide him. All he saw was the vast serene sky - a perfect picture of peace. The only turmoil was inside him. Knowing he would not get a response, he returned to the tree and sat down heavily, resting against the sturdy trunk.

He decided to go over the announcement again. He was the son of the Most High: The Son of God…but, what were his powers? Were they infinite or limited; permanent or temporary? He was tempted to test them, but decided against it. Nor would he use them to impress others. He remembered traveling magicians he saw as a child. He was exuberant the first time he saw their tricks, and enjoyed it again the following year. But, when they repeated it the third year, he was disappointed, and refused to go again. He foresaw the same fate if he used his powers as mere tricks. He made a momentous decision: to only do miracles in the most urgent cases. Moreover, at this time it was too dangerous to do anything at all. It would invite questions he could not answer, and accusations he could not defend. Besides, he did not wish his private life to become a public spectacle. He wanted privacy especially with lady Sarah. Prophets got married and had children, and he wanted no less. After more consideration he felt this was premature. Her parents would never approve.

Suddenly questions cropped up of paramount importance: If he was the Son of God, was his nature human, or divine? He decided to test it. He held out an arm turning the palm up and pinched the wrist as hard as he could with the other hand. He winced with pain and a couple of tears came to his eyes. When he looked, the wrist turned red, and began to discolor. "I am human!" he cried out with happiness. Then he remembered there was no necessity for the test. All he had to do was look at the many scars where he got cut and bled during childhood. To emphasize the point, he thought of the strangest sensations he experienced recently which made him laugh and cry at the same time: love for Sarah. "Yes," he repeated, "I am unquestionably human. I came into the world a mortal and will leave it like all my mortal friends." Then he suffered a bout of insecurity, "I have some gifts which I do not comprehend, and a destiny to fulfill, which I do not understand…but I know, that I am human!"

He pressed his fingers against his temples as the tension caused his head to throb. When he closed his eyes he wondered how he would fulfill the prophecy.

Will he be Yeshua, the divine? If he could perform miracles and cure the lame and the sick, the people would accept him as a king because of the special gifts. But, the more he contemplated about a divine king the more he foresaw problems. The conservative Sadducees would accuse him of conspiring with the devil and accuse him of sorcery and witchcraft, and have him stoned. Or the Romans charge him with sedition for being a king and crucify him. He decided no throne - terrestrial or celestial was for him.

Perhaps he could be Yeshua the rebel. Perhaps he should join the Zealots who were desperate for leadership. His destiny may well include becoming a warrior and leading his people against tyranny and oppression. But that would involve wars and killings and he detested any form of violence.

Perhaps he could be Yeshua, the sage? He had heard of wise men from the Far East, China and India, sought out by wealthy nabobs and rulers for advice. But, at his tender age, not yet nineteen, who would seek him for advice? He remembered his sermons and realized people were not yearning to hear his opinions.

Perhaps he could travel as an itinerant teacher as he had done recently through the pagan villages. They called him the "young rabbi" and he liked it. He smiled at the thought of a simple rabbi from a humble nation influencing people and perhaps changing the world? But the reality struck him: this would take centuries and he could not do it alone.

He stood up and marched to the edge of the cliff shouting: "Why? Why did You choose me? There are thousands better…smarter…stronger to do Your work. I am insignificant. What can I tell them about the world? What answers do I give about the Creator and the universe…?"

Suddenly a gust of wind came up throwing dust and dry leaves through the air, and shaking branches of trees. Many years later when he recounted what happened, he could not be certain whether this was a living experience or a dream. But he could describe distant cities he was about to see, which he had never visited, with unerring precision.

He felt himself lifting from the ground and levitating, rising ever higher above the spot where he stood. He was higher than the lower branches of the oak tree, going higher than the highest branch. He continued rising and saw the entire meadow, the swamp area and the cabin where the Zealots met, then the three hills of Nazareth, then Sepphoris in the distance, and Augusteana of the shores of Galilee. He felt the presence of someone beside him, looked and recognized the archangel. "You are Gabriel," he said and the angel nodded. "Do you know who I am?"

"I announced your coming. You are the holy one. Come with me."

They flew higher and saw Damascus to the north, the Greek islands and Athens, then the long boot of Italy and Rome and they flew over the Great Sea, over the Atlantic where he saw continents not discovered or named.

They left earth, speeding away higher and faster, deeper into space. Yeshua followed him into the black universe gathering speed more and more rapidly. He saw the earth change from a giant blue sphere covered with clouds to a tiny round speck smaller than a marble, then it became a tiny white speck indistinguishable from blinking stars. The billions of stars changed from flickering specks to blurring streaks, then warped bright smudges and finally disappeared. They entered a part of the universe into a mantle where they could only distinguish shades of light and dark grey, but when they travelled deeper into the black cave faster than the speed of light all evidence of light disappeared.

The journey through the black cave took only a fraction of an instant, but was an eternity on the sun dial and they arrived on the other side of the cave into a different universe altogether, at a different date, before the beginning of time and space; before the beginning of Creation. Their surroundings and the environment in every direction were totally different, strange, alien, and inhospitable, without stars or planets or any celestial bodies. There was no light. They only saw brightness when gigantic clouds and gases collided causing immense explosions that ripped apart all solids and vapors. But there was no sound.

In the momentary explosions with blinding brightness, the clouds and gases traveled helter-skelter, expanding and contracting like giant bubbles floating through the vast expanse, racing and zooming in all directions. Some clouds floated into and through others like ghosts and continued, others collided and shook the black surroundings with blinding light, more brilliant than the sun. The explosions pulverized some clouds, hurling gases until everything disappeared again into the eternal darkness.

"Chaos!" Yeshua exclaimed but no sound was heard. "It is before Creation." The archangel nodded.

Yeshua sensed the presence of another, and when he turned he recognized Him immediately. He lifed his hand, causing all the elements, clouds, gases, and solids to slow their flight and come to a complete stop. Then He raised the index finger, pressing it forward gently pushing all matter and it began to travel from that central point outward in every direction, in an orderly fashion, in a harmonious journey through the endless universe.

Yeshua remembered it well. It was the birth of the Universe: the beginning of time and space; the instant that defined finity and infinity, beginning and end, before and after. It defined life and death. This was Creation!

"Let's follow it and watch its evolution," the archangel said.

They traveled at the same speed, passing through warps and black caves, coming out an instant later, while hundreds of millions of years passed in the life of the universe. They were surprised to see how much the universe had grown, expanded and evolved. They discerned that some gases began to accumulate into clusters, forming nebulae and constellations. Every time they stopped they saw new and intriguing development: more and more constellations were forming, and thousands upon thousands of individual bodies of dense gases converged to form stars. That marked the creation of light. They did not see the force that created everything, but sensed His presence everywhere.

After many journeys through the warps they arrived at a familiar area of the universe; where a sun of average size had a handful of planets orbiting around it. They approached the third one and watched the volcanic explosions, and melting lava run down to the sea, but its atmosphere was inhospitable with poisonous gases. They left again through the time zone, and on their next visit saw a great transformation; it became hospitable, covered mostly with water, with life forming and evolving. There was life from the peaks of mountains to the deepest craters in the oceans. Yeshua had always marveled at the evolutions of life from the moment of Creation, and nodded with admiration to its Creator.

The archangel warned him, "We must return, for they are coming to the tree."

"Only one more stop," Yeshua replied.

They travelled again and arrived at the most important epoch; when the Creator added the most important addition – man and woman. The ancients always said, "He created them a little lower than the angels, but covered them in glory." These primitive beings experimented, analyzed and shared information, enjoying all they saw in their brave new world. Everything they touched smelled and ate was good. They were filled with curiosity and humor. Above all they were full of love. They were in paradise.

They had just returned from the long journey, and he quickly sat under the oak tree when he heard voices, "We're almost there...just around the corner. There he is," Debborah announced as she appeared from the bushes. "Why did you not answer my calls? You were probably daydreaming, with your mind in the clouds again." She scolded him and turned to Sarah, "He can be most annoying: his mind floats to the clouds, and you can't bring it back!"

Yeshua got up and took lady Sarah's hand. She looked radiant, "So this is your secret hiding place," she chirped looking around the grassed clearing. "It is enchanting, almost awe inspiring. Look at that lovely hibiscus bush, and the beautiful flowers. My favorites!" She gasped when she saw the valley, "What a picturesque view! Now I understand why Debborah said this is really your first home. I hope you don't mind me invading your private world?"

"I'm happy you came," he smiled tenderly. "It gets lonely here sometimes."

She took his hand and squeezed it between hers commenting, "Why are your hands so cold?" She touched his face, "Your face is frigid. Were you in the snow on the peak of Mount Hermon?"

Debborah saw them in each other's arms and rolled her eyes addressing the servant, "Oh, oh! I can see we are extra baggage. Pretty soon they will be coo-cooing each other and smooching. Let's get out of here..."

"Where is your favorite place?" Sarah asked him.

He led her to the foot of the tree, helped her sit and joined her. He touched the trunk, "It's oak, durable, dependable, almost eternal. It has probably sheltered a hundred generations and will watch over a hundred more after I'm gone." He picked up a seed from the ground and held it out, "This small kernel contains the entire oak tree within it: a miracle of eternity."

"This is self evident, yet you say it so poetically," she took the kernel and put it in her pocket. "Someday I will plant it in my own yard."

They leaned back and sat in silence, holding hands and listening to the birds singing. He could not get over how relaxed he felt beside her. The pressures he had felt before evaporated. He closed his eyes to savor this peaceful moment, as this was how he always wanted to remember their first time together alone. She was busy looking around the clearing, the bushes, the flowers and the distant scenery. Her eyes settled on some small wild blue flowers and she searched for the bird she could hear clearly.

"If you hear a perfect tune, but cannot find a bird, you may be hearing an angel playing the flute," he whispered softly.

Her eyes sparkled as she smiled, "There is not a lovelier place in the world."

"Nature covers you with a blanket here, and you become part of everything: the grass, bushes and the flowers. The valley envelopes you and the river meanders through your mind. You become one with the earth," he confided his intimate secrets to her. "When I look up there to the heavens I have a personal communicat..."

She waited for him to continue, but when he did not she encouraged him, "A communication with Lord Adonai?"

"You know about Him?"

"When father announced we were moving to Israel, I read every book in the library about it. Israelis are very special people..."

"Don't say that too loud," he chuckled. "They are already too conceited, and make no secret about it."

They shared a healthy chuckle. Suddenly she changed topics, "Speaking of secrets we have two which we must share with each other."

"What secrets could we have?" he wondered. "We hardly ever spoke a word."

"Nevertheless we do," she persisted. "So, you confess your secret, and I promise to...surprise you with a terrible confession." She waited until he nodded though he did so dubiously, and she asked, "So what happened to the fishermen caught in the storm...?"

At first he could not remember it, then it started coming back, "Oh, yes, the storm on the Sea of Galilee?" She nodded. He proceeded with the story, "The fishermen filled their nets to overflowing and loaded the boat until it sat heavy in the water with little freeboard. In the storm the vessel was sluggish, difficult to maneuver, getting battered by wind and waves. As the waves pounded it, water was coming aboard filling it more and more. The waves were growing bigger with more breakers, and the wind more ferocious. The sailors were tiring and realized they may not see another sunrise. They prayed, 'Lord Adonai, if you spare our lives and help us survive this storm, to see our wives and children, we will release all the fish we caught.'"

She interrupted, "Israelis make deals with their God?"

"All the time. While praying for help they promise to give up something very special to them. This is deep in our tradition," he explained. "The boat was pounded relentlessly to the far corner of the lake. Then one gigantic wave, twice the size of the others, raised the little boat so high they feared they would be pitch-poled, and braced for the end. The big wave carried them over fifty paces at great speed and deposited the boat safely on sand in shallow waters. There they sat, the boat filled with water, until morning when the storm passed."

"Lord Adonai saved them," Sarah screamed with excitement. "They released the fish, bailed the water..."

"And returned safely to their families," he finished the story.

"Your people have a very personal relationship with their God," Sarah said filled with wonder.

"He is everybody's God!" Yeshua replied as if there could be no other way.

"Do you have personal conversations with Him?"

He shook his finger chuckling, "Oh, no, I am wise to these tricks...You owe me a secret remember?"

"Oh, I forgot," she blushed, covering her mouth. When she started she lowered her head embarrassed, "Before I confess...I need you to promise, you will forgive me..."

"My intuition tells me to hold out," he teased with a chuckle, but realized she was anxious, so he added quickly, "Of course I forgive you. Can it be that bad?"

She nodded and started without looking up, "Remember the first day… the collision?" He rolled his eyes. "Remember Hulda coming to you…? She did not go by accident…"

He thought about that day and gasped, "Shame on you…"

"The truth is we drew lots to see who was going out to meet you… Oh, I feel so ashamed," she covered her face in her hands almost crying.

He remembered pacing by the gate yearning to catch a glimpse of her, to speak to her, and give her the carving, and he felt hurt. But, when he considered the event from the ladies' point of view; deciding on impulse to have some fun, he appreciated their imagination and good humor. His lips stretched into a grin, then he began to chuckle, finally breaking into healthy laughter, "Priceless! She acted the part to perfection."

Sarah peeked at him through her fallen hair and her worried look gave way to relief, "I feel awful…"

"Was Hulda the winner of the draw?" he asked hopefully.

She shook her head, "She was sacrificed…"

"There is no redeeming feature to your prank," he laughed.

"Do you still forgive me?" Sarah pleaded adding, "In my defense…I was not the author of the prank."

"Just a willing participant?" he asked and she squirmed. He took her hand affectionately, "An innocent prank, but if it is important to you, I forgive you."

She smiled into his eyes, raised his hand to her lips and kissed it. He watched her action as if in a dream. Suddenly she remembered what they had been discussing, "You did not answer my question: do you have a close relationship with your God?"

He went rigid thinking of the revelation and his argument with Yahweh. He did not wish to lie, yet he was not ready to share that news with anyone, yet. Instead, he sat stiffly, his mind searching for a plausible answer. Sarah interpreted his silence as misunderstanding her question, and rephrased it, "I mean, when you pray do you converse as you would with a friend?"

She did not hear his deep sigh as he tried to sound casual, "Oh yes, of course I do…and often ask for favors…"

She pressed on curiously, "Do you ask for miracles? Does He grant them?"

He felt uneasy with the interrogation and decided to find out what she was after, "Miracles? What kind of miracles?"

"Well, I have been troubled by things I heard…even saw it myself…"

"What did you hear?" he queried perturbed. "What did you see?"

"Nothing bad, so don't you worry," she tried to put him at ease. "I want to know how you beat a full grown panther with a staff. Did you pray for a miracle?"

"I did not beat it. The animal left…"

She stared at him incredulously, "I saw a panther in a circus, in Tyre: a formidable beast, as big as a lion…it tore a muscular gladiator like a rag doll…" she closed her eyes and frowned shaking her head.

"This was not a giant panther," he tried to minimize the episode.

"Nor are you a gladiator. At the crucial moment did you pray to God?"

He concentrated trying to remember, shaking his head slowly. Then he remembered brother Simon's words, "A radiant light shone brightly over your head and shoulders." That was how his mother described it when he chased the mad dog. He must have a special communication with God.

Sarah refused to give up, "Remember master Yacek's words? You did not give him an ointment, you cured him with a touch. He called it a miracle."

"Master Yacek's illness was overindulgence of red wine," he felt embarrassed for accusing the old man. "I advised him to cut back on wine and drink an abundance of water. Every housewife knows that…"

"Master Yeshua, you may evade episodes I did not witness," she was not satisfied he was telling her everything. "There is something you cannot explain away so easily. The day we met, after the collision there were vials and glass bottles broken. Perfume was spilled. I remember because Debborah commented about the lovely scent…After we collected everything, you blew away the dust, handing me the baskets. I inspected them and they were all intact. Nothing was broken, no perfume spilled…"

"Obviously you were mistaken. Nothing broke."

"I would have agreed with you, except for this," she held out her thumb. "I cut it on a vial. I felt the cut and inspected it and the vial. It was broken. A few moments later there was nothing broken. I looked at my thumb and it was cured. How do you explain that?'

He knew he could explain it but not at that moment. Instead he brought her thumb to his lips and kissed it, "Does it still hurt?"

"No. It has been fine since that day," she waited for his explanation.

"If it no longer hurts, I would forget about it," he remarked lamely.

She realized he could explain it, because of his awkward fidgeting, but as he did not wish to do it, she dropped it. She sensed she was in the presence of a special person with ineffable powers. She wondered if he was cognizant of of those powers. She decided she was happy with him and wanted to enjoy these precious moments together.

While he rubbed her fingers he wondered about the special gifts he was discovering. If he had stopped a panther, he had powers over all creatures; if he repaired vials, perhaps he had powers over inanimate objects; and, if he had cured master Yacek, he had power over sickness... Did he have power over life...? And death? Perhaps his powers had no limitations?

Lady Sarah studied him closely realizing he was troubled by their conversation and delicately chose to change topics, "When will your expedition leave?"

"Tomorrow sometime, perhaps in the morning."

"So soon? I don't want you to go. We just started to know each other," she pleaded.

"I don't want to, but I promised."

"Master Stephanos said you were going to search for the Messiah," she exclaimed then started to deliberate, "but do you know where to look? What does he look like? Where will you find him? How long will it take?"

"There are many such holy men," he responded. "If we are fortunate..."

"You'll find him and return right away?" She interrupted excitedly. Then she thought about it and looked forlorn, "I read that they have waited a thousand years for him. You'll be searching for a dew drop in the desert...never come back to me."

"I have to find him. I promised to bring him back."

"For what: to lead you in a rebellion, or exodus from the Romans? Wherever you run there will always be another Rome," she commented.

"Hopefully neither," he demurred. "but to give our people faith."

"Faith can move mountains," she concurred pensively, and smiled at him meaningfully. "It did for me. Like you, I prayed...for someone special. And, here you are." His eyes opened wide as she chirped tenderly, "Your poem said we may go through life without touching, or a lasting memory. But, I think we can be...special...with a lifetime of memories..."

"You are already very special," he murmured.

"How special?" she asked softly.

"When I first saw you I thought that I had strayed into the wrong dream…"

"Am I special enough for…a kiss? To be your betrothed?" Sarah asked. Suddenly he pulled back with a shocked look on his face. She saw his reaction and quivered, asking with an agonized tone, "Did I say something wrong?"

"No, no, it's not your fault…I did not mean…I felt the same…"

"Me too. I was too shy…I prayed and dreamt you would say something," she reached for him.

He drew back, "I must not…I cannot… I don't want to overstep my station."

"What are you talking about? Why did you move away?" Sarah became concerned with his sudden aloofness.

"I-I have no right to compromise you," he stuttered in confusion. "I cannot expect the two of us…I'm sorry."

"I don't understand you master Yeshua. What do you have no right to expect? Was I being too forward?" She asked painfully, her voice breaking. "Or am I just too naïve? Please, be honest."

Yeshua looked down mumbling, "I have no right to expect our relationship…It is I…I mean, you are so much richer…I'm a pauper…"

When she understood him, her face hardened with disappointment, "Who gave you the right to speak for my feelings? And…and why do you think so little of yourself?" She admonished him yet felt sympathy as she watched his lips quiver. "Are you saying we are two articles of merchandize in a bazaar waiting for the highest bidder? What is your price, master Yeshua? What am I worth?" She broke down in tears and he embraced her trying to console her, to say something, but she pulled back and continued, dejectedly, "What I found so precious in this town is that people value one another for what they are, not what they own. Why do you bring crass commercialism into something as sacred as love?"

All he could do was to whimper a weak, "I am sorry."

"I do not own a single piece of jewelry," she held out her hands. "I never wanted them. My parents own everything I have…except for these clothes, I have no need for any of it. We are absolutely equal, you and I - two paupers. My only priceless possession is my love for you."

"I am truly sorry…my feelings are honorable. I dreamt and hoped…" he murmured guilty and confused, yet elated. "I was afraid it could not be."

"I should be the one to apologize," she calmed down. "I over reacted. I promised I would not do it, and then repeated the same mistake."

"No, no it is my fault."

"I should not have reacted as I did," she interjected. "I still get very emotional…" she sighed. He waited for her to continue, but she shook her head, "Someday I will tell you; why we moved…why I over reacted."

He wiped away her tears then kissed her eyes gently.

"Is that it? Are you leaving on a long journey without a kiss?" she asked teasingly and he blushed. "If we continue like this, your poem will be realized." She cooed to him softly, "Please, kiss me…"

She closed her eyes and puckered her lips. Seeing this he copied her actions, and they sat still for a long time. Sarah opened her eyes, "You have to come to me."

"Oh!"

They closed their eyes again, puckered their lips, moving closer, about to touch when they heard voices, "Ok, you two, you've had long enough!" Debborah announced loudly. "You probably have been doing nothing but smooching…"

"I'm sorry," Yeshua whispered.

"You must not leave without a kiss," Sarah commanded in low voice.

Walking back, they held hands and she leaned her head on his shoulders. As they came out of the bushes, she looked up the street and froze, "Father!" she blurted out, quivering and staring at the figure on a donkey coming towards them. She pressed her step and quickly walked to the middle of the road with the servant at her heels.

Yeshua realized he had compromised her reputation, and, worrying she would be punished, started to walk towards the rider. The man kicked the animal to pick up speed, passed Yeshua and rode after the girls. He yelled something at his daughter and struck her with the whip, causing her to run faster. The young man could not see the rider's face as he wore a long shawl wrapped around his head and face, leaving only a narrow slit for his eyes.

"Sir! Sir, let me explain. We were just talking…believe me…I respect your daughter. Sir, please…"

"You will pay for this! I will kill you!" The man raised his arm striking him on the forehead with the butt of the whip, cutting him above the eye. Then he kicked and prodded the animal and gained distance. Yeshua gave up and watched him ride away after the girls. He wiped his hand over his temple and saw the blood. But, he knew his injury could not compare with the ire lady Sarah was sure to suffer at the hands of her father. It was the unfortunate custom that a young maiden was never to be alone with a male, without a family member as chaperone, lest she be judged to be no better than a whore. Her family could punish or kill her with impunity.

Yeshua proceeded to his home with a heavy heart, and went to the basin to wash the wound. When Esau saw him, he left the crew and approached him. "Dare I ask what problems you got into this time?"

"Ran into the butt end of a whip," he responded. Seeing his friend's concern he added, "Entirely my fault. It will mend." He saw the crew nailing the frame and remarked, "You are building a fine vessel, Esau."

The foreman grabbed his arm and led him behind his work shed, "If the boat turns out well, it will be because of the crew…although Marcus tests my patience daily."

"Still having problems?"

"He lives to get under my skin," Esau droned grimly. "He arrives smiling, friendly, and cooperative and I thank the heavens for my most gifted worker. Before the day is over, his halo is tarnished, he argues and rebels and I want to drive the axe…"

They went into the shed and sat down. "Is he that bad?" Yeshua inquired.

"He lives to point out my errors, and cause a crisis. We repair it and continue, but he won't let go. What's keeping the crew together is that the others are wise to him."

"You are the leader…" the young scholar emphasized.

"We need each other, Marcus and I. We bring out the best and the worst in each other," he mused philosophically. "I'll survive the daily burps to build the vessel."

Yeshua smiled, pleased to see his friend gaining confidence.

"Did master Benjoseph find you? He has an urgent message…" Esau announced.

He shook his head, "What is it?"

The outcast went to the door to check, and returned whispering, "The siccarrii arrived. There is a special meeting tonight. You have to come."

"Me? Why?" he looked worried, as he was hoping to go to lady Sarah's. He had to make sure her father had not abused her.

Esau shrugged his shoulders, "They must have a special job for you. Meet you at the palm trees?" He slipped out without waiting for a reply.

Yeshua went to his room troubled. The siccarrii were the Zealots' executioners! He wanted nothing to do them. All he wanted was to see lady Sarah...

• • •

The sun was almost gone when he saw Esau hiding in the trees. Although it was going to be a full moon, it had not yet risen, so early evening would be dark. He was hoping the meeting would be short, so he could see Sarah before the moon came up. He teased his friend, "If you are trying to hide, you're doing a poor job of it."

Esau came out cautiously, "I saw two Roman soldiers..."

"I saw them too, and hid in the bushes. They are all over town." he frowned.

"They've discovered the cell," the outcast looked around nervously. "We're crazy to be going..."

Yeshua motioned and they started walking. Soon the cart overtook them and they jumped on. No one came to blindfold them, but they were ordered as soon as they were in, "Bury yourselves deep. We may have unwanted company."

They burrowed themselves in the straw, careful not to leave any limbs exposed, and lay still as the cart bumped and squeaked along the road.

As soon as he lay, Yeshua's mind returned to the problem of his identity. He had spent the afternoon in his room without resolving anything, and thought about the riddle in the message: The Son of God so he should be doing something...but what? How would he know what to do? Was he going to receive signs? What was he expected to achieve? What was his destiny? When should he start? Would he be told by words, a hint or a dream? Or, had he already started? After an exhausting afternoon he was no closer to the solution and started to feel depressed.

Then his mind quickly jumped to lady Sarah. When she saw her father she gripped his hand tight, almost crushing it. There was obviously a strained relationship between them. He feared she may be in danger, yet he felt helpless.

Suddenly they heard the driver, "Bury yourselves. Don't move - soldiers ahead!"

The cart came to a stop. He heard sandals approaching the back of the cart, and a raspy voice demanding, "Where are you going with the straw?"

To my cabin down below, sir," the driver replied.

"At this hour?"

"Peasants have no option: work the farm all day, and small luxury at night, sir."

There was an interval of silence, the Roman staring at the straw suspiciously. Then he barked, "Get out of here!"

The cart proceeded. They could feel it going down hill to the swamp area by the pungent smell and the rough ride. He agreed: Zealots were a magnet for trouble.

"Oah! Oah, stupid animal," the driver stopped. "You can come out!"

They stood up and jumped to the ground, brushing off the straw as they rushed into the building. "Are we flirting with death?" Esau asked as they got in.

There were less than a dozen members, and the same two oil lamps giving off an anemic light. Benjoseph called them over, "Sit here beside me," he addressed Yeshua, "There will be a special job for you. You should feel honored."

They sat down and Esau leaned over whispering sardonically, "Honored!"

Yeshua informed the schoolmaster, "The Romans are everywhere."

"This is our last meeting until things settle down," he replied, then added passionately, "We have to catch the traitor..." He turned to the doorman and motioned him to shut the door, then announced, "This meeting will be short. Give your attention to the vice-chairman." He motioned to a big, burly farmer sitting next to him.

The man stood up, planted his feet apart in a fighting stance, "Only a dozen of you were invited for a reason. You are our most trustworthy members, and we want you to meet two important visitors from the national headquarters: the siccarrii. You are forbidden, on pain of death, to tell anyone including the other Zealots what you are about to see and hear." He stared at each member, his eyes glaring until the member nodded, before he moved to the next person. Then he continued forlornly, "Two cells in villages to the south have been infiltrated by a traitor. Galilean heroes have been killed…many arrested…some disappeared into the woods…The damage is great everywhere." He raised his voice to a dramatic war-cry, "If I catch the snake I will crush him." He extended his arm, and a man in the corner brought out a man of straw, handing it over. The members' eyes were riveted on him.

Yeshua did not miss a word, but took advantage and studied the men. He recognized some faces from the previous night. He stopped when he saw the mysterious man with the hideous scar again. As with the previous night, when he made eye contact, the face disappeared behind the person in front.

"If the traitor is here tonight, I say, beware! This is what I will do to you!" He held the scare crow in one hand, swiping violently across the neck with his dagger lopping the head off. He lifted it high over his head, yelling, "I will burn your body in the dump and leave it for the buzzards and wild beasts." The Zealots watched in fear, for they knew if the body was not buried, the soul would wonder forever without finding peace. He let out a loud roar heaving the straw head at the members. It rolled beyond them into a dark corner. He glared fiercely, and the room was still for a long time.

Master Benjoseph stood up immediately, "Let's meet the special guests from the holy city." He motioned towards the back door and they heard the rusty hinges creaking. Soon two men, clad in black from head to foot stood beside them. No one heard them come in and now could not see their faces for they covered them with a long black shawl, leaving only a narrow slit for the eyes. The Zealots' eyes were riveted on them because none had ever seen a siccarrii before.

"Good evening fellow Zealots," the taller one spoke, a man with a deep voice, and heavy Judean accent. "From the beginning Zealots decided it was necessary to form a secret arm, to combat Herodian and Roman spies who infiltrated our cells to destroy us. All the terror and violence we learned from them. Now we use their tactics against the enemies to our cause." He pulled out a small golden dagger, in the shape of a saber, and flicked it through the air as he spoke, "One swift slit of an enemy's throat, or a thrust between his ribs and the opposition is removed. We try everything to avoid it, but when we can't, we do it: for a free Israel!"

Yeshua instantly recognized the saber – dagger. He saw a reflection from the flickering light in the siccari's dark eyes under his thick heavy eyebrows. His eyes darted from face to face studying each one intently. After a pause he continued, "Your executive asked us to uncover a traitor among you and bring him to justice." As he said that he passed the saber dagger so fast and close to his own throat that they gasped thinking he sliced it open. But, it only cut the shawl which fell open. He warned them, "We are closing in on him and I promise we will flush him out."

When he said this everybody's eyes searched among their neighbors as if expecting the culprit to stand up and run, or else to break down and beg for mercy.

Yeshua was also watching so intently that he did not hear his name until Esau nudged him, "The siccarri wants you."

He turned and saw the dark eyes with the heavy eye brows fixed on him, "Are you the young man going on an expedition?" Yeshua nodded with a grunt and was ordered sternly, "Stand up and salute when a siccar-rii officer addresses you!"

Yeshua sprang to his feet so quickly he almost toppled over, causing the only laughter of the night. "When will you be leaving?"

"Tomorrow, sir…sometime…"

"You will be traveling to Samaria…"

The young man was not certain how to answer so he stuttered, "W-well, I t-think…y-yes, yes, we may…"

"That was not a question. It was an order!" His thick bushy eyebrows seemed alive as he scowled, and his tone left no room for argument. "Emperor Augustus proclaimed himself a deity. They have placed his statues in every colony, and every assembly house. People are forced to make sacrifices to him. Presently, hundreds of his statues are sailing to Israel, to Caesarea Martima. They plan to put them in our Temples: to profane your sacred houses!" He raised his voice directing the last statement at the Zealots to whip up nationalist fervor which he succeeded beyond his expectations.

Zealots – (Springing up to their feet)

"Kill the sons of scorpions!"

"Out with the oppressors!"

"Death to the Romans and Herodians!"

The siccarrii was pleased with the loud screaming and the pumping of fists, and turned back to the young man, "You will lead your party to Caesarea where we will meet you. We expect hundreds from Judea, Samaria and Galilee. We will organize them and turn the leadership over to you." He leaned over the youth so close, his thick eye brows almost touched him as he barked, "Do not fail!"

Yeshua leaned back stuttering, "W-why me?"

"They will be expecting the siccarrii," he snapped as his shawl puffed up every time he spoke. "But, they will never expect a country bum... peasant to lead the people."

Yeshua wanted to refuse it, but his intuition warned him he would not succeed. Instead he asked, "How will I know...? I never..."

"We will be close. We'll tell you what, and how to do it."

Yeshua objected stubbornly, "I am against violence...sir..."

The siccarrii laughed loudly making his shawl fill like a tent, "We all are, master Yeshua. We all are. Sometimes it is the only persuasion. Just to be safe, take this..." He raised the golden saber before the young man's face.

Zealots: "Take the dagger; do it right!"

"Kill the infidel!"

"Slit their throats, master Yeshua!"

The siccarrii chuckled at the young scholar's confusion, put his heavy hand on his shoulder announcing loudly, "If you should meet tetrarch Valerius Gratus, gift this dagger to him as a souvenir - between his ribs!" Then he shoved the saber dagger under Yeshua's belt. "Take good care of it; it identifies a siccarrii everywhere!"

They cheered for Yeshua, happy at last to see action. "Kill Valerius Gratus!" "Kill a Roman for us!" they screamed with exuberance failing to hear the sound of a horn outside. The shouting was finally interrupted when they heard three loud knocks on the door. Two men stood up immediately and snuffed out the lamps.

"Quiet!" Benjoseph stood up and announced loudly, "We have intruders. Wait while I go and check," he said as he walked out.

The members stood up and panic permeated the room. They started to push and shove nervously. Benjoseph returned presently and ordered loudly, "Quiet! There are Roman soldiers up on the hill and they may come down. We must find a way to escape. Does anyone know the swamp area?"

They waited for an eternity, until Yeshua volunteered, "I do."

"Is there a way out through the swamp?" Benjoseph queried.

"Yes, two ways: One will lead deeper into the valley. Follow the river banks and it will lead back to town."

"Is it the safest route?" the siccarii demanded.

"We will gain distance from the pursuers in the dark. But, it is a narrow path, treacherous and we will have to go slowly. It will be daylight before we reach town. The Roman guards will intercept us in the morning."

They started grumbling unhappily.

"You said there were two ways..." the siccarri reminded him.

"The Romans will be coming down the road we traveled," Yeshua explained. "Twenty paces below there is a narrow path parallel to it. It is dangerously close for we will almost be able to touch their sandals...in places the reeds are sparse..."

"It's a full moon tonight," Benjoseph added with a sigh.

The siccarrii fixed his eyes on the young man, "Master Yeshua, we put out lives in your hands!"

"There cannot be any conversation; not a whisper," the young man spoke sternly. "We will hide in the reeds and crawl on our bellies. Be careful! It is a narrow path. One slip and you will end in the swamp...the rest of us will be doomed!"

"Lead on!" the siccarri ordered.

They went outside and gasped. Although master Benjoseph had warned it was a full moon, they were shocked to see how bright it was.

"You can see for half a mile...How can we hide?" a member's voice trembled.

The siccarri whispered, "Quiet! Move!"

Yeshua ran out of the yard, across the dirt road, jumped over the bushes on the opposite side and disappeared in the heavy brush. One of the siccarrii followed, then Benjoseph and the others. Within a dozen steps he found a narrow path worn by constant treading of hunters. But, it was very narrow and they began to ascend it slowly, carefully. After crawling in the reeds and bramble for some time he looked back and saw the siccarri, followed by the schoolmaster, then the Zealots, and at the rear was the other siccarrii. He smiled realizing the last siccarrii had counted heads before joining to make certain that if the traitor was with them, he was not left behind to alert the Romans.

While they crawled Yeshua wondered what they would say if they knew the Son of God was leading a band of fugitives away from the authorities? He started to feel guilty until he remembered Moses led the Hebrews to freedom. But he could not rationalize risking his life now that he knew that he belonged to the Creator and perhaps bigger missions? He decided he would always defend the victims against the oppressor.

They climbed the narrow path with a steep grade paralleling the road above them. The reeds and bushes became sparser as they proceeded making it easier to advance but also making them more visible. Yeshua bent over as low as he could, almost crawling on his hands and knees. He thought of the scorpions and serpents he had seen, for this was an excellent domain for insects and rodents. The crawling was painful and slow. From time to time he looked up to the road, sometimes standing up gingerly to study the horizon above, without seeing any soldiers. He glanced behind and saw the Zealots hunched over like a family of crabs crawling in search of new territory. Twice he saw the fifth person walking almost erect, and he ordered in a low voice, "Get down!" The third time he saw the man stand up, he ordered them to stop, marched through the bramble, grabbed the culprit by the collar and dragged him up, shoving him between the siccarri and Benjoseph, whispering "Keep this fool down!"

He recognized him as the Zealot with the scar on his face.

Their progress was never faster than a crawl, and the greatest danger of continuing in that manner was the discomfort to the lungs causing some coughing. As a result he slowed down and stopped every dozen paces to allow them to catch their breaths. He still took advantage and inspected the road. They had traveled almost half the distance to the top and he expected to cross paths with the soldiers, if they were coming down, at any moment. When they passed the halfway point without sighting the Romans he feared they may be waiting at the top of the hill. Maybe he was leading these men into an ambush. He slowed down trying to devise an alternative plan, but none came to mind except turning back. However, the next time he started to stand up to check, he got down immediately whispering, "Psh-sh-t" and pointing directly above them. Nobody moved. Some got down lower almost kissing the ground. Even their breathing slowed down. The sparse reeds closed up above their heads.

Yeshua looked up again and not more than a dozen paces above saw the silhouette of fifteen soldiers marching down the road to the house below, armed with spears and shields, and their swords sheathed. They were led by a centurion. The young scholar looked down below and his eyes swept over the swamp from which there was no escape. He thought, they must not get trapped here for they would be doomed. When he looked up again he stared directly into the centurion's face. The officer had left the soldiers, who continued to march, and walked to the edge of the hill, stopping directly above to study the valley. Yeshua wondered if the officer was thinking the same as he: they marched half way down the hill, and this was the most likely place to meet the Zealots. But the centurion did not seem to be searching. He was looking far in the distance, perhaps thinking of a similar valley in Rome.

Suddenly someone coughed. They froze. Yeshua knew it was the man with the scar. He quickly removed his robe, handed it to the siccarrii who threw it over the man, and whispered almost inaudibly, "Next cough will be your last!"

When Yeshua looked up, his eyes met the centurion's. There was no doubt he heard the cough and was looking down, his eyes sweeping over the area. His suspicions were aroused for he turned to the marching soldiers about to call them, changed his mind, pulled out his sword and decided to investigate. He stepped down gingerly trying to avoid the prickly bramble. Yeshua saw the siccarrii pull out his saber-dagger and hold it close to his bushy eyebrows. The Roman was about to take another step when a cloud floated over obscuring the moon. The centurion looked up, tried to retreat but slipped and slid into the prickly bushes. They heard curses and noises of sliding sandals, limbs flailing akimbo a sword clanking on stones as the Roman struggled to get back to the road. They fought to suppress their laughter until they heard his loud curses, and the slapping sandals marching down the road.

When Yeshua thought the officer was gone, he stood up slowly to check, and not seeing him, ordered them to move quickly. They covered the second half of the path faster as they were becoming accustomed to the narrow, uneven terrain. When they reached the top the young scholar decided to crawl up and verify if the centurion had left guards at the entrance to the road. He went up carefully over the bushes on all fours. When he reached the edge of the road, he remained hidden behind a large bush, pushing the leaves apart for a clear view. His eyes skimmed the entrance, and the road both ways, and he started to stand up when he noticed a movement on the far side. He froze. There he saw two soldiers lounging.

He crawled back to report, "Guarded. We must continue, but soon the path will end, and there will not be bushes. We'll continue to an area where the embankment slid down. After a few hundred paces we'll try to get up into the forest."

They continued slowly through sparse bush with less and less cover. After a hundred paces they arrived at the area of loose dirt and stones with no path for proper footing. Yeshua was thankful for the full moon as it helped him find larger rocks on which to test the footing before proceeding. But he knew the clear night also meant they would be visible to the Romans above them.

The progress was at a snail's pace. He tested each rock, putting his weight on it slowly, before taking the step. Even so he distributed his weight between his feet and hands, digging in with his fingers into the dirt, hoping to grasp something if his sandals began to slide. They had gone over a hundred paces when he heard gravel sliding behind him. He turned and saw a member from the middle, sliding down. Everyone looked but did not dare to move. They watched the distraught fellow, frozen like a spider sliding down a smooth wall, his eyes fixed, looking up with terror. He stopped a couple of paces down. Yeshua studied the terrain below him and started to go down when the siccarrii grabbed his wrist with an iron grip.

"Don't be a fool," he whispered. "Better lose one than sacrifice two."

"There are boulders there…I can get to him."

They looked down again and saw the Zealot below them gaining against the slippery terrain, as he dug in his fingernails, then one foot, and the other. After a few more tries he gained half the distance. The two companions on either side of him reached down and offered him a hand. He stretched as far as he could reach, slowly as two hands trembled trying to clutch each other. Everyone stopped breathing, watching the outstretched fingers reaching, reaching…then closing desperately. Not until his other hand clutched his savior did they dare to take a breath.

"Good work," the siccarrii whispered. "Let's go!"

They proceeded for another hundred paces where Yeshua saw some rock outcroppings and decided they would climb up. He turned to the siccarrii, "I'll go up and investigate. If I see soldiers, we may have to return all the way…"

He climbed up listening for footsteps or voices, although he knew if there were soldiers they would be waiting quietly. He was almost at the top when suddenly he stopped. He heard the sound of rustling leaves. Then a dry twig snapped. He lifted his head looking in the direction of the noise, at first not seeing anything. Then he smiled, recognizing the faint outline of a deer. He realized if a deer was foraging undisturbed that meant no soldiers. He returned and announced the good news.

At the top master Benjoseph took over, "Travel in twos. Go about a hundred paces. If safe, give one wave, and the next two will leave. Good luck!"

Yeshua walked close to the trees and hedges, ready to disappear if he came across soldiers. He decided to go to lady Sarah's house, for he yearned to see her. He had to find out if she was safe, and if her father had punished her. However the two roads he tried had soldiers patrolling them. Finally he took a round about way, circling the outskirts of town and coming in from the opposite direction. Alas, there were soldiers there as well.

When he entered his room he was exhausted. As he undressed the saber dagger fell from his belt to the floor. He picked up the golden colored weapon, inspected it, then tossed it into the wooden trunk containing his worldly possessions. As he lay on the cot his mind returned to the events of the day: the revelation, and his experiences of the first day. He was the Son… to build a lasting kingdom. His knowledge of history proved no earthly kingdom lasted forever. So, this new kingdom was not earthly, but of a higher degree. He would build a heavenly kingdom to honor his heavenly father, where all the people of the world would find solace and peace. And, he as the son, would lead the building of it and share the honor. Was he expected to build a building? If so, what kind of building? Where would he build it? And, how? Where would he start? Above all, how could he accomplish his mission when his own faith had been shaken to the core?

CHAPTER VIII - JOURNEY...
MESSIAH ben DOSA

It was still dark when Yeshua heard a knock on his door. He rolled over in his cot wondering if the soldiers followed him. Then he got up quickly and peeked through a crack in the door panels. It was too dark to see.

"Master Yeshua, wake up. It's me, Stephanos."

He donned his tunic and opened the door.

"He's here. He's coming to Nazareth today," the Greek spluttered excitedly.

"Lower your voice, sir. Who's coming?"

"The holy man you mentioned - Hanina ben Dosa. We'll have to go and see him. Some say he is the Messiah."

"Really, then the expedition is off?" he inquired, somewhat sad for he had gotten caught up in the excitement of the journey.

"I doubt he'll be the Messiah..." the Greek replied.

"True. Let's go and I'll wash up." At the basin he splashed some water on his face and they left. On the street he asked, "When did you hear ben Dosa was coming?"

"Yesterday in the market. Some who had seen him work showered him with superlatives," Stephanos explained. "I came to tell you...Where were you last night?"

"Busy," he replied curtly. He did not want him to know about the Zealots. The Greek had glanced at him suspiciously, so he decided to change topics, "Why do you get so excited about the Messiah?"

"Ever since I first heard about him I was captivated," he responded agitated. "But he is a most elusive person: everybody knows of him, but nobody knows him...no one ever saw him...I 'm beginning to think he's an invisible demi-god."

"What makes you think he is a demi-god?"

He shrugged his shoulders, "After hearing and searching for so long I've concluded this is someone special: supernatural."

"I read the prophets," the young Israeli explained matter of factly, "and found nothing outstanding. Perhaps master Hariph will give us something interesting from one of those vases."

Stephanos' enthusiasm was unabated, "I maintain he'll be more powerful than Hercules, wiser than Plato with the divinity of Zeus…"

"Master Stephanos, you are a first class impostor," the Israeli guffawed, slapping his shoulder. "Underneath that cold analytical skin, you are as illogically romantic as our pilgrims."

Stephanos continued with an elated tone, "It stands to reason that godly creatures must have godly auras, and supernatural qualities."

"And perform extraordinary miracles to impress skeptics like you?"

"I told you, I don't believe in miracles, and you won't persuade me otherwise."

The marketplace was already filling with people, and more were arriving. Obviously they were drawn for the same reason as the young men: Hanina ben Dosa. They congregated by the town gate, under the high post with community notices attached. The young men joined in.

A worker was putting up a low square fence one pace wide, and a cubit high. At one end he placed a wooden box abutted against the fence, on the outside. While he was setting up this simple stage, an old grey man with long white hair and beard, wearing a white cloak and robe mingled with the spectators. Many recognized him right away.

"That's the holy man: ben Dosa," they whispered.

He was a simple man with a kindly face, and lively eyes who took interest in everyone. People surrounded him, inundating him with questions. "Master ben Dosa will you be doing THE miracle today?" an elderly man inquired.

"Lord Adonai willing I shall be ready presently," he responded, looking at his helper by the fence. Then he added, "I had better do it successfully."

People joined him with nervous chuckles.

"Sir, you are a holy man of God," a distraught woman grabbed his sleeve. "Will you please come to our house and cure our son?"

The holy man looked at her sympathetically, "Dear lady, I am not a holy healer. What I do is the only gift I possess…I am not the one you seek."

"Are you not the Messiah?" Stephanos blurted out involuntarily, blushing and apologizing profusely, "Forgive me, I did not mean to sound impudent."

"You are not, I assure you," the holy man replied, enjoying the Greek's awkwardness. He stroked his beard measuring his every word, "I have been called the Messiah. Sadly I am not the anointed one. Nobody knows who the Messiah is...But he will perform extraordinary miracles to help those poor mothers..." He pointed to the woman walking away.

The helper interrupted him, "Master ben Dosa, whenever you wish to start, sir?"

The old man apologized and turned away, closed his eyes and began to whisper a prayer.

The helper raised his arms and announced in a quiet voice, "Gentlemen and ladies, presently the holy man will perform an incredible miracle. However, he needs total silence as he is entering into a seance. If you need to speak, please whisper."

Yeshua watched master ben Dosa, and was astonished by how quickly he reached the state of séance. The helper disrobed him and led him into the fenced area where he sat down. Then the helper took a short wand, and opened a couple of doors on the box. The spectators stretched their necks to see inside it unsuccessfully. Presently the helper tapped the sides and the top, and a large serpent, almost two cubits long, slithered out to the collective gasps of the spectators. They recognized it as one of the most poisonous serpents in Israel. It slithered towards the holy man's leg.

Yeshua recognized the serpent immediately. About five years before, the first time he met Quintus, the Roman was bitten by such a serpent. His friends panicked and ran away, leaving the young Israeli alone with the victim. Yeshua always thought some miracle had saved him. Now he wondered – was he the author of that miracle?

His musing was interrupted by people's whispers', "That's suicide," and "He cannot survive. The serpent will surely kill him." They were more shocked when the helper struck the box again, chasing out not one, but two more serpents. A couple of women fainted. They were quickly carried away.

The snakes slithered around the holy man, flicking their tongues, touching his legs while he rocked gently to and fro oblivious to their presence. The helper began to chase them with his wand around and around the small area so everyone could have a clear view. When the serpents tried to return to the box he pushed them back with the wand. This angered the snakes which lunged at the stick. One coiled exposing long fangs, hissing and spitting at the wand. He continued to tease and anger them all the more, threatening to strike them, and striking the fence instead. Before long the snakes began to chase the wand which he slid just ahead of the reptiles, up and over the old man's legs. Before the spectators could react, the serpents struck the holy man, biting his knee, the lower leg and the ankle. The people's jaws fell open. They stared at ben Dosa expecting him to drop dead at any moment.

Satisfied the snakes did their job, the helper let them return to the box, and closed the door. Then he stood back with the spectators.

Yeshua remembered when Quintus was bitten. He went into shock almost immediately. His breathing became erratic and he heaved and gasped for air, his face turned red and he perspired. Soon after he became delirious and went into convulsions. His eyes went up into the sockets, his lips turned bluish and his breathing became shallow. Yeshua held him close trying frantically to suck the venom from the hand that was struck, all the while begging the Roman to remain calm. He prayed and pleaded for the Creator to save him.

He could not think about that now, as the spectators started to whisper, expecting ben Dosa to go into shock or become delirious, perhaps die. He panicked, fearing he may have to intervene to save him. Could he do it? Should he do it? He panicked and froze with fear.

A long time passed before he realized the holy man was not having convulsions and was not delirious. Instead, he sat serenely, rocking to and fro, pale white, hardly breathing, and praying. Yeshua saw the tiny marks where the serpents broke through the skin. There were tiny drops of a clear substance with a bit of blood. But the old man's mouth did not froth, and his eyes did not turn up. He remained steady, chanting, and his breathing almost imperceptible. There was no visible effect on him from the most potent venom known to man.

The helper, as if guessing their thoughts, explained, "It is important for master ben Dosa to remain tranquil. He will fall asleep and we'll move him to a cot."

"Will he not die from the venom?" Yeshua asked astounded.

"For a couple of days he will seem mesmerized," the helper said.

The people stood watching, and when they saw no changes they were certain they witnessed a miracle. The young men shuffled away in silence.

It bothered Yeshua that he did not know whether he would have intervened to save ben Dosa. Clearly he faced a formidable problem: he still harbored hopes for a life with Sarah, and they would need privacy. He did not want his identity to become public.

"I saw something similar in India," Stephanos interrupted his musing. "They train their bodies by taking in small doses of venom, and in time become immune, able to survive a bite from a full grown serpent."

"Can they survive three bites?"

The Greek shook his head, "The volume of the venom would over-power anybody's organs. What we witnessed was a classical case of faith healing. There are two types of this: healing others, and healing oneself."

"I saw cases where the healer cured a multitude at the same time. All the people must have unwavering faith in the powers of the healer; they come to a regulated atmosphere, such as a tent where ethereal lights are displayed; and they converse with others, giving collective suggestions and encouragement that they will be cured. Their faith becomes so overpow-ering that when the healer chants and touches them, they become cured. They go into a state of hypnosis, ready to receive..."

Yeshua interrupted impatiently, "None of that was present here."

"But all the same principles applly with one exception: the faith healer and the client were the same person. What we witnessed was ben Dosa's will over his body. When he began to chant he entered into a state of séance, or hypnosis almost instantaneously. That takes much discipline and training. His mind became detached from his body."

"Yes, he turned white, barely breathing," the Israeli noted.

"His will was so powerful, he slowed his organs especially his heart. If you felt his pulse you would not feel a beat. Animals do that when they go into a state of hibernation to survive long, cold winters of northern Europe. With ben Dosa's organs almost stopped, the venom deposits remain isolated, stationary, not able to travel to the vital organs..."

"I understand," Yeshua interjected with enthusiasm. "If the venom can-not affect his organs, his body has time to break down and neutralize the poison."

"That explains the fantastic feat we just saw. Impressive but explain-able to science..."

"Not a miracle?" Yeshua wondered, quite disappointed.

"As I said before: miracles exist only in the imaginations of romantic dreamers."

· · ·

As soon as they returned to the house they began to load up the camel and donkey preparing to leave on the expedition.

A camel, generally known as a ship of the desert, on terra firma is as uncontrollable as a barge. It can change from a cuddly pet to an ill-tempered, vicious monster quicker than a desert storm and with as little warning. Stephanos' camel chose this moment to demonstrate its neurotic tendencies.

He was loading up the tent, boxes, packages, bags and odd paraphernalia on the animal with no apparent problem. In fact the animal stood blinking his eyelids as placid and pliant as a statue. When he turned to pick up a couple of boxes of dried, salted meat, the pet stretched its long neck and bit its master's buttocks. The Greek jumped, let out a shriek, his face twisting in pain. He cuffed the animal's ears with the back of his hand. The camel stared placidly, impervious to the commotion it had caused. After a healthy dose of Greek profanity master Stephanos returned to loading. When he finished and was tying up tons of supplies, he stood beside the animal admiring his work.

Camels are the only animals capable of kicking with their hind legs outwardly. Seeing the Greek within reach, it released the hoof like a spring loaded weapon, striking Stephanos' squarely in the crotch! He was lifted a half a cubit, then fell down immobilized.

James who saw it all announced, "The camel kicked him, right... there!"

They carried him inside, laid him on the mat and splashed water on his face to revive him. Yeshua and the boat crew unloaded the animal and discovered the problem: a rope pinched the animal's hide causing the irrational behaviour. Retied properly and reloaded the animal reverted to a placid, cuddly pet.

Yeshua took James to his workshop, put his arm around the younger man's shoulder, "Brother James, I have always valued your opinions and respected your judgment...In a few moments we will be leaving on a long journey...fraught with danger...I may not return..."

"What are you saying?" James looked at him shocked. "Of course you will..."

"When I go, you will be the oldest son," the scholar continued. "You will have a heavy responsibility. Be just and kind..."

"You will be back, I know..." the young brother's eyes welled with tears.

"Help your parents. If something happens to father, you must step in... be strong," he said, and when James broke down he embraced him, "Take good care of the family."

Yeshua could not find a way to escape and visit lady Sarah's, even for an instant. He looked down the street, hoping she might sneak out, but alas, she must not have had better luck. He was desperate, but he knew his hopes were in vain. He would be leaving without holding her, or seeing her. Not even one last good bye.

Germanicus took Anna to the far corner of the yard. He wanted to tell her how much he cared. That he would carry fond memories of her in his heart. But when the time came to say it, he stood silent, his lips quivering. He started nervously, "Lady Anna, I...I want to...I wish... Thank you for your kindness...I will...yes...every night..." he fidgeted with his hands wishing to say so much more, but his mind was in a state of confusion.

"I will think of your kindness," she smiled into his blue eyes. "And I will pray for your safety every night that Lord Adonai will bring you back safely."

He stared into her dark eyes to etch her beautiful face in his memory so he could see her every night. "Thank you lady Anna," he whispered.

"I need you to promise me something," she pleaded. "It is most important to me."

"Anything you ask..." he nodded with emphasis.

She grabbed his hand, "Look after master Yeshua. He is a very special man... especially to me. Promise?"

Germanicus stared at her, his face hardening: she pined for him and wanted him to defend her man, he thought. "I will protect him...for you," he muttered, turning and walking away, only stopping out on the street.

Yeshua said good bye to the boat building crew and asked Esau, "Help brother James, and look out for him. He has inherited a heavy responsibility."

To his surprise they answered in unison, "We'll help him, master Yeshua."

When he embraced the two youngest siblings they cried uncontrollably, demanding he take them with him. Anna had to take them away and into the house.

The older siblings reminded him to bring presents from the big city.

The time came to say good bye to his parents, something they all tried to avoid.

Joseph walked up and put on a brave front, "Son, put your trust in Yahweh." But his lower lip began to quiver, "Be true to yourself..."

His mother rushed into his arms, crying. "I am sorry I did not tell you..."

"That's all right, mother..." he muttered without enthusiasm.

"I was only thinking of you...I love you, Yeshua..."

"I know, and I feel blessed. I will miss you, mother," he squeezed her, then pulled away. He wanted to say more, but still felt resentment over the secret.

He went into his workshop and brought out four staffs which he offered to his companions. Stephanos looked at the long stick and pointed to Germanicus, "My slave has a spear to defend me."

Quintus drew out his short sword, "Why would I trade this excellent weapon for a blunt stick? I'm a warrior not a shepherd."

He kept one, handing the others to Esau and left.

As they walked, people handed them letters to deliver to villages in the south.

They weaved through the streets, escorted by hundreds of residents in a long procession. Many blessed them, "Shalom, master Yeshua. May Lord Adonai bless and keep you all safe."

The people were optimistic they would soon find the legendary Messiah, and return in triumph to a heroes' welcome. The truth was that they envied the young men's courage to venture to places they feared to tread.

Thus, at the hottest time of day, when the sun's rays punished them, they commenced the long journey searching for someone they could not describe or identify, nor say with certainty existed. Nonetheless they went with enthusiasm and anticipation, confident they would succeed.

Only master Stephanos whose festive spirit was dampened by the camel, hobbled painfully in the rear.

As soon as they left, Quintus, the ever professional soldier, went ahead of the group. He marched some thirty paces ahead, erect and straight as an arrow, carrying out his duties as guard seriously: his hand never far from the sword, he eyes sweeping the forest.

Quintus' parents were Roman, and he was a Roman citizen born and raised in Israel, the son of a retired centurion. He was curious and eager to get to know the land of his birth, and always ready for adventure. He knew that going with his Israeli friend he would learn and experience more for although he was born here he was considered a foreigner and shunned. The irony was that in school in Rome he spoke Latin with an Aramaic accent and was shunned by the Romans. But he was not sentimental and did not dwell on the fact that he was considered a foreigner by both races.

Yeshua followed the Roman, leading his donkey. He was contemplating the journey with mixed emotions. He was glad to be leaving, to avoid the Roman soldiers and the complication of the Zealots. He was reconsidering his enthusiasm for the organization. He was equally happy to distance himself from his parents, as he still felt slighted for not being told. He needed time to reflect about forgiving them. Moreover this morning he faced a terrifying problem: how could he perform a miracle and remain incognito? Perhaps he should not do miracles until he resolves his problems?

He was desperate to guard his privacy. His dream was that of any young Israeli: marry and have a family and children. But the revelation complicated everything. Now the important questions were: Who was he? What was his destiny? How could he fit that with his dreams?

While he considered these matters, one thought consumed him since yesterday: lady Sarah. He spent all morning searching for her in the bazaar, then among the people who came to say good bye. Alas, she did not come. He did not dare go to the mansion, fearing his presence could endanger her. As they walked out of town he searched for her in a sea of faces, because after today he knew he would not see her for many months: perhaps never. He heaved a sigh, on the verge of tears.

Germanicus leading the camel followed the Israeli. Every so often he turned and studied the animal, for he remembered when they came from Damascus, the camel seemed lame, favoring its front left leg. Thus far it seemed alright.

The slave looked forward to the expedition, because of Anna. Oftentimes when they arrived to Yeshua's house he sought her out. Now he felt like a fool for his silly romantic dreams. He shook his head at his stupidity: Anna was free, pretty, and could have anyone. How could he have been so blind and not see that master Yeshua was right there, at her side and available? He went over her words: "Please take care of master Yeshua; he is a very special man…especially to me." The words were like a knife plunged into his heart.

Yet, he did not blame Anna. He cursed his own stupidity for failing to realize no one wanted a slave. He resolved never to become infatuated again. He resented master Yeshua for his capricious behaviour: frolicking with lady Sarah, while Anna pined for him. He decided to have a serious talk with this man about his arbitrary behaviour. He looked at his spear and promised, before the day was done he would find out his true intentions towards lady Anna.

Most importantly, he decided to revive his plans to regain freedom. This time he vowed he would never again sway from his resolve.

Following far behind, master Stephanos, the organizer of the expedition, wobbled without the least enthusiasm. He was consumed by one desire: to get as far away as possible from a town where religious fanatics were dangerous, and now invaded by Roman soldiers.

As they approached the forest, Yeshua chose to leave the path going into the trees, and proceeded to the east, along the edge of the cliffs. There they would only have trees on one side, and bluffs and the valley on the other. He reasoned it was safer to travel, and they could set camp in the clearings away from the forest. That way they would only have to guard one side of the camp.

· · ·

Back in Nazareth lady Sarah faced a major crisis. Her father accused her of being a charlatan and a prostitute, and struck her on the face. He threatened her with further punishment and she knew from past experience he would be true to his word.

When she passed by his office window, unintentionally she overhead her parents discussing her and stopped. Her father was in the middle of another tirade accusing her of coming out of the bushes in the peasant's arms like a cheap tramp, and a slut, dishonoring the family name. He accused her male peasant friend of being a member of the criminal gang of murderers and rebels called Zealots.

Her mother supported his tirade, "I curse the day Sarah was born. She is the cause of all our troubles, and the reason we are fugitives from Tyre." Her voice was harsh and unforgiving, "Sarah is the devil personified… The antithesis of our dear late Helena, may Baal rest her soul…"

The husband announced his vengeful plan, "I have written to the leading families in Antioch and Damascus, telling them she is available for marriage. Today I will send further scrolls to Babylon…"

"Good riddance", the wife concurred approvingly. "The sooner she goes from our lives, the sooner we'll know peace again!"

Sarah gasped with shock, ran to her room, locked the door and fell into bed crying desperately. She lay sobbing for a long time. After the long bitter cry she began to realize her cause would never get better unless she did something about it. She decided on a plan. She wrote to her friend Debborah. The younger girl had an active imagination and may help. She wrote a short note:

"My dearest little sister Debborah,
I write with a heavy heart, as I have no one to turn to. I need your help desperately.

My parents are accusing me most unjustly of horrendous deeds because I was alone with master Yeshua unchapparoned. Presently they are planning to force me to marry someone as far away as possible from here. Thankfully they dare not approach anyone in Tyre as we are pariahs with the wealthy families. Father plans to send me as far away as Damascus or Antioch

Please do not tell your brother as he cannot save me, and it would only upset his expedition.

I am doomed. Nothing will stop father's resolve. I beg you come over as quickly as your wings can bring you. I need your strength and friendship.

Love, Sarah"

When she finished, she sealed the folded papyrus, and handed it to Hulda with instructions to run with it. The servant left immediately.

Lady Sarah returned to her room, locked herself in and continued to cry.

Hulda was at the gate when a senior servant intercepted her and ordered sternly, "Hand me the letter from lady Sarah. I am sure our master will want to read it."

. . .

As Yeshua's group trekked, he returned to his dilemma: What was he expected to do? Leading the Israelis, or the Arab nations, perhaps leading the people of the world? Lead them where? To do what? As before, he had no idea where to start, or whether he was on the right path.

He looked for inspiration, a hint to guide him: perhaps a message in the clouds, in the trees, or down the valley. To no avail. He wondered how long before an idea came to him? With no help from external sources, he decided to devise his own plans. But, what was the plan…to do what? He was totally exasperated.

Then an idea struck him. He looked at his companions: three gentiles not one of Judaic faith, which was excellent, for they were not indoctrinated with Judaic beliefs and prejudices. They were probably not believers, and likely had no faith in anything. This was ideal, because he could find out what they expected from the Creator, if anything? Perhaps their answers would guide him. Could he help them find faith in the Creator? The possibility of that seemed fantastic. He smiled at the irony, for until this moment he had considered giving up on faith, yet here he was thinking of inspiring gentiles. After much debate, he decided that was precisely what he wanted to do, starting tonight.

He decided to look back and see how far they had gone. The hills of Nazareth were mere bluish lines on the horizon. He thought they had gone seven miles, and decided to start seaching for a campsite if they were to settle before dark, "Master Quintus, slow down," he called. "Let's find a site to set up camp."

Quintus stopped, and when they caught up he objected, "It's too early to set camp. We are barely out of town."

"The sun is sinking fast. By the time we raise the tent, get wood and cook, it will be dark," Yeshua explained. "We have to finish in daylight."

He knew that here daylight was their best ally against bandits.

"There is the ideal place," Stephanos pointed not far from them.

Quintus took a passing glance shaking his head, "The ground is not level. We'll be sleeping on the side of the hill."

"We'll sleep with our feet at the low end," the Greek argued.

But no one listened as they continued searching, "Here is an excellent site," Quintus announced, as he pulled the tent off the camel and dumped it on the ground.

"It's full of mounds and dips," the Greek objected and continued scrutinizing. "It will be like sleeping on the humps of three camels."

"Then put it anywhere you wish. I don't care," the Roman snapped impatiently.

"If we set it at this end of the dip, with the door facing the valley, we'll only have our backs to the forest," the Greek tried to defend his choice. "Bandits can only come from the forest. We'll light a fire here so we cannot possibly be ambushed. Germanicus will guard the door, and you will sit at the back facing the forest…"

Quintus interrupted, "I will not sleep in the open. I'll be inside the tent."

"You came to guard!" Stephanos protested.

"I will guard…from inside," the Roman mocked him.

"We can guard ourselves inside. You stay out!" Stephanos roared.

"It's my tent!" Quintus exclaimed with finality in his voice.

They stood nose to nose, while Yeshua and Germanicus found the perfect site two hundred paces further: it was flat, with a steep bluff on one side so they could not be attacked from the valley and a large clearing on the other side. Yeshua returned and saw them arguing. He led the camel between them commenting, "I hate to be the messenger of good news, but, yonder is our site. So, pick up the tent and follow me."

The two glared at each other, picked up the heavy tent and dragged it.

The Israeli pointed out an area, "Put it here, with the door to the valley. Please, set it up." Then he turned to the slave, "Bring some wood, while I unload the animals and start preparing the food."

Quintus and Stephanos, still cross with each other, continued to argue while raising the tent. One complained the other did not pull the floor taut. Then it was too tight and the floor was not square. The sides sagged, with too many creases, ad nauseum. Yeshua was shaking his head. He could intervene, but decided to let them settle their positions in the social hierarchy of the expedition.

By and by Germanicus returned with the wood and Yeshua directed him to put it down by his feet. The slave, standing some distance away, threw the wood which scattered and ricocheted, striking and cutting Yeshua's legs.

"Ouch! What are you doing?" Yeshua jumped to the side, grabbing the injured leg. "Why don't you watch what…?" He glared at the slave expecting an apology, but instead, saw Germanicus mumble angrily as he turned, and returned to the forest. Yeshua suspected that it was not an accident.

He was lighting the fire when the other two finally finished the tent, and joined him. He gave them another task, "You two have a choice: one will bring the water from the stream below, the other will wash dishes after dinner. You decide who will do which task."

"I'll fetch the water," the Roman grabbed the jug.

"No, I'll bring the water. You do the dishes," Stephanos took a smaller jar.

They argued while descending the hill, each accusing the other of taking the smaller jug, comparing sizes, arguing about the thickness, and the circumference of the containers ad infinitum.

Meanwhile the Israeli prepared the food and started to cook, when the slave brought another load of wood. Yeshua watched him carefully, but the slave avoided eye contact. He put down the wood gently, so Yeshua decided the injury was accidental.

He confided to the slave, "I gave Quintus and your master a choice: one will bring water and the other will do the dishes. Both went for water hoping to avoid dishes. Watch the shock on their faces when I tell them both will have to clean up."

"I will clean the dishes," Germanicus grumbled.

"You were not in the discussion," the Israeli replied. "They will settle this."

"It will only start a fight," the slave sounded concerned. "As the Roman is stronger, I will be forced to intervene."

"They're fighting for a pecking order in the group," Yeshua explained. "Stay out of it and let them settle it."

"You could settle it and forbid them to fight."

"I favor a democratic group where everyone has an equal voice... including you."

Germanicus brought his hand to his chest, surprised as if to ask "Me?", and was clearly pleased when Yeshua nodded . Then he reconsidered, adding, "They will never accept a slave's opinion..."

When the others returned, Yeshua put a big pot on the roaring fire. They sat around finally able to relax.

Stephanos remembered something and asked the Roman, "What is the reason for all the soldiers in town?"

"I have no idea," Quintus shrugged.

The Greek studied him suspiciously, "I don't believe you. You're a Roman and a soldier and so are they. Why don't you tell us the truth?"

The Roman sprang up livid, "Are you calling me a liar?" He glared at the Greek who returned his stare unaffected. "I'm stationed in Augusteana, and they're from Sepphoris..."

"I think they're searching for Zealots," Yeshua interjected.

"Zealots? Who are they?" Stephanos queried.

"Traitors and murderers," the Roman replied. "They're terrorists trying to overturn the lawful government of Israel."

"They are neither of those," the Israeli rebuked him. "They are a political organization demanding a voice in their government. They are freedom-fighters!"

"Propaganda," Quintus sniggered superiorly. "I warn you, if I see Zealots I'll arrest them. They are all criminals."

Stephanos' eyes popped wide and he bolted from his seat pointing an accusing finger at the Roman, "You're a spy! I wondered why you wanted to come. To spy! You hope we will lead you to the Messiah, the liberator of Israel, so you can arrest him... maybe kill him. Is that not the truth barbarian?"

Quintus, already standing, drew his sword and barked savagely, "Take back your accusations or, by Jupiter, I will skewer you!"

Germanicus grabbed his spear and jumped up, so he and the Roman stood facing one another with a shocked Greek in the middle. Yeshua jumped between them so he had the sword against his chest and the spear at his back. "Stop that, both of you. Master Quintus put your sword back. Germanicus put down the spear."

Germanicus stepped back and lowered the weapon.

Quintus snarled without moving, "I demand an apology."

Stephanos drawled, "Not before you answer: Are you a spy?"

The Roman did not respond.

Yeshua stared into his eyes, and asked, "Did you come to spy for the army?"

Quintus was furious, breathing heavily, but as he stared into the radiance emanating from the Israeli, he faltered, and lowered his eyes, "Of course I am not a spy."

The Israeli pushed his sword away gently, "I believe you."

Quintus sheathed the sword and sat down.

Yeshua returned to the pot, lifted the lid which released a superb aroma which permeated the camp. It promised to be good and there was lots of it, boiling noisily. He added more spices and water, took a whiff, closing his eyes with a smile. They were famished and watched his every move impatiently.

After a while Quintus stood up uttering a soliloquy to no one in particular, "The problem with Greeks is that all they do is whine, whine..."

he stopped in mid-sentence, then blurted out inspired, "Speaking of wine, where is it? I am going to enjoy a goblet…"

"We will all get one goblet of watered down wine with the meal," Yeshua demurred as the Roman picked up the jug. "Otherwise it will not last."

"Only one? Watered down?" Quintus asked with a painful look. "That's not how we do it in the army…"

"If wine is your priority, I advise you to return to the army," the Israeli said stiffly.

The Roman stood glaring at him, then at the jug, and once more at him, finally replacing the jug and returning to the fire.

Meanwhile Stephanos who had been inhaling the aroma walked up to the pot, lifted the lid and dug in with the spoon, "Hmm, that's irresistible. I'll bet it tastes better than it smells."

"You're right. Now, put down the spoon," Yeshua ordered with a tone laced with annoyance.

The Greek stopped and looked at the Israeli, shocked and surprised. After a moment he decided to test Yeshua's mettle and reached for the pot. Quintus who had picked up a long stick, struck his wrist causing him to pull back in shock. "You heard master Yeshua," the Roman said. "I suggest you obey."

Germanicus' muscles tensed up ready to defend his master's dignity. Yeshua sensed they were on the brink of a fight. A wrong word, and a battle would erupt which could lead to injury, perhaps death. He decided to avoid that possibility tonight.

"Master Stephanos, if you are famished, you may take some…" he conceded.

The Greek considered the offer but chose to replace the lid and return to his place.

When dinner was served they dug in ravenously returning for second and third helpings. The only sounds were the slurps, spoons scraping on bowls, their teeth tearing the rye bread and the crackling of the fire.

"Truly a heavenly meal," Stephanos mused poetically, his eyes rolling to the heavens. "Which meat did you use?"

"None. Just vegetables: roots, potatoes, barley, grains, legumes, assorted vegetables, and rye bread," Yeshua replied. "We have to ration the meat."

"What? What about the two boxes I brought: one salted and one dried meat?"

"Where did you put them?" Yeshua asked confused. "I did not see them."

The Greek walked over and inspected the bags and boxes of supplies and sighed, "We must have forgotten them, when that stupid camel kicked me."

After some discussion they decided it was too late to go back, too far, and decided to forget it. Quintus and Stephanos cleaned the dishes as Yeshua predicted, but being well fed they cooperated marvelously. Then they sat back enjoying the fire.

Yeshua was wondering how to bring up the topic he wished to discuss when the Roman asked, "How much do we know about this Messiah?"

"Precious, little," the Greek replied. "He's the anointed…"

Quintus interrupted, "I know that! What does he look like?" He watched them shrug their shoulders, "I saw a giant in Egypt perform magnificent feats. Once he caused the foundation of a large edifice to shake as if it were made of papyrus, without laying a hand on the building. He only touched his temples like this," he touched his forhead, "then pointed his hands to the building and the brick and mortar trembled. His name is Rabban, and they said he was the Messiah!"

"A cheap trick," Stephanos scoffed sardonically "Did you inspect the area: outside and inside the building?" The Roman shook his head. "If you had, you would have discovered the true source of the magic: horses or elephants pushing or tugging lines!"

"Is that what the Messiah means to you: a sorcerer authoring tricks and magic for the masses?" Yeshua wondered.

"Don't blame us. Your prophets made him a superman, who will beat the Romans, and liberate Israel," Stephanos defended his position.

"No Messiah, not even a god will defeat our army. When I was in Egypt, I saw the size of our legion for the first time," Quintus explained, his voice filled with awe. "Six thousand soldiers filled a valley so big your eyes could hardly see one end from the other."

"Forget confrontation and wars," Yeshua suggested, wishing to learn his companions' innermost thoughts. "Assume you meet the Messiah who will grant your most ardent wish. What would you request?"

Quintus replied without hesitation, "To become an officer, a centurion like my father."

Yeshua turned to the Greek who was struggling with the question, so he turned to the slave. "My freedom," Germanicus blurted out impulsively.

Stephanos now put up his hand somewhat timidly, "You may think I contradict myself, but my greatest wish is to find faith…in some supreme being."

"So you are secretly yearning for someone…or something?" Yeshua was not surprised.

"It may sound absurd," he replied sheepishly. "I know there must be an explanation for this orderly universe. Those stars did not happen by themselves…And the earth is too logical, its cycles too perfect to be accidental. But, I also know our gods on mount Olympus did not create this. Greek gods are too vicious and insane, to direct human affairs."

"Likewise our Roman gods," Quintus concurred. "While studying in Rome, I counted our deities: Janus, Jupiter, Mars, Minerva, Venus, Diana…a temple in every corner: I counted thirty-three different gods!"

"It points to a colossal sense of failure more than a feeling of accomplishment," Yeshua mused with disbelief.

"Your Romans stole our gods like everything else," Stephanos complained. "Zeus is Jupiter; Aphrodite is now Venus…"

"You can have them," the Roman flicked his hand as if discarding a fly. "Since Julius Caesar it is the fancy of emperors to deify themselves, and be worshipped. Absurd."

"Your father found faith," Yeshua remarked diplomatically. "He contemplated converting to Judaism."

"Your father is fortunate," the Greek sighed wishfully. "It would be comforting to think, especially in an hour of bewilderment that a benevolent power existed for us."

"These are the only powers I invoke," Quintus pulled back his sleeve flexing his thick bicep. "My only gods."

Germanicus asked Yeshua, "What about your gods? What do you wish from your Gods?"

The Israeli did not hear him because he was contemplating his group's replies. He was surprised when he compared them, how similar their statements were to his: they had issues with God, including His existence, yet unashamedly turned to Him in time of crisis. Another common behaviour he recognized: when they ceased to believe in God they did not believe in nothing. Instead they believed in anything.

But, recognizing these problems and persuading them of God's existance, would prove a difficult task. He chuckled silently at his cruel irony: suffering a crisis of faith and identity at the time. Still he concluded his problems were miniscule compared to his companions: lives devoid of any faith.

Then it struck him. How did he arrive at his conclusions if he did not have faith? Maybe he did…Maybe Yahweh was not his problem. Maybe his biggest problem was within himself?

Just as he was mulling over the matter, the slave interrupted him impatiently, "Master Yeshua, I asked you, what is your wish from your Gods?"

"We do not have many Gods. We have only one God…"

The slave interjected suspiciously, "Only one God? Why did the others leave?"

The others stifled a chuckle.

"Do your people have many gods?" Yeshua queried and the slave nodded emphatically, "Do you get comforted praying to them all?"

Germanicus' face soured and his voice filled with agony, "I prayed a lot, a long time ago…but, when I needed them most, they failed me. Now I don't, although I curse them liberally." He stabbed a stick into the fire sending bright sparks weaving up to the stars. "My tribe has many gods; Thor, god of thunder, gods of the forest, the wolf… gods to give us a successful hunt, victory in war… what good were they to me? Now, I believe only in what I see; that valley, the stream below, those stars. I'm like master Quintus: gods are not relevant to my life."

Yeshua saw the pain in his voice, and directed his remark at him, although he looked at the fire, "There is only one Creator who made all people…He made them equal and He loves them all equally. His name is Yahweh."

"Yahweh? He created every person, all equal?" Germanicus repeated, far from being convinced. "Then why did He only make me a slave?"

"He did not make you a slave - people did," the Israeli responded. "When His creatures mistreat one another, make war, or put them in chains, it breaks His heart. He wants them to live in peace…free!"

Germanicus looked at him for a long time with renewed interest, before venturing another question, "Does Yahweh know that I am a slave?"

"Yahweh knows and cares. That is why He is sending a Messiah to liberate the oppressed, and give comfort to those less fortunate."

Germanicus could hardly conceal his enthusiasm, "The Messiah is coming to set me free?"

"Germanicus, I resent your tone," the Greek intervened irate. "You speak as if I were your oppressor. Don't I treat you fairly? Did I ever beat you? You should be happy that I am your master!"

"Master Stephanos speaks the truth," the slave drew back guiltily, with a frightened tone. "I am an ingrate. I am fortunate to have you as my master."

His apology eased the tension and they sat back in silence enjoying the fire. The slave continued to ponder the Israeli's statement: there was a God who cared for him and was sending a Messiah. He could hardly contain himself from shouting.

Yeshua left the fire and walked to the animals to make sure they had eaten and had enough water. He started rubbing them down when the slave approached him.

"Master Yeshua, is it really true that your God made everyone equal?" The slave whispered seeking reassurance.

"Yahweh is not my God. He is everyone's Creator."

"Slaves and freemen are equal?" Germanicus wanted this strange concept clarified beyond doubt." When the Israeli nodded, he persisted, "So, in your eyes I am equal to you?"

"Naturally!"

"Then, why do you have two girls while I have none?"

Yeshua turned and stared at him dumbfounded, "What are you talking about?"

"You already have lady Sarah; why do you also want lady Anna?"

The Israeli blurted out still confused, "Who told you I wanted Anna?"

"She said you were very special to her...so don't try and deny it," he warned him.

Yeshua scratched his head trying to make sense out of the accusations, but was not able to do so, and asked patiently, "Start from the beginning and tell me precisely, what did she say?"

He tried to remember every word, and answered, "When we were saying good bye, her last words were; 'Germanicus, I want you to promise that you will guard and protect master Yeshua. He is a very special person...especially to me.' "

"Aha! That's why you threw the wood..."

The slave lowered his head, "I apologize...I did not injure you...?"

"Just a small cut," Yeshua shrugged it off. Then he explained Anna's statement, "She did not mean special to her...not the way you think...Do you know what I mean?"

The slave thought about his explanation and shook his head, "Why would she say special to her...and mean someone else?"

Yeshua knew he could not say more than he already did. After reflecting he decided to tackle the issue differently. "Are you telling me you don't know you are the special person in Anna's life?" He saw the slave smile, blushing with embarrassment. "Why, you would have to be blind not to see it on her face. YOU ARE THE ONE! I saw it in her eyes every time you came around." He watched the slave's eyes light up, and he had a silly grin he could not hide. "Germanicus, I will share a secret with you. Oftentimes I watched her working half listening to our conversation, hoping your name would come up. Many times I announced in a loud voice that you were coming and saw a transformation in her: she walked with a new spring, her good humor reappeared and she hummed happily...Germanicus, you are a fortunate man: Anna adores you!"

Germanicus could not wipe the grin off his face and had started feeling guilty for suspecting her, and the abrupt way he had left her, sighing, "I wish I had said...more..."

"Let's return to the fire," the Israeli suggested. He brought out some papyrus, a stylus and ink from a leather pouch, announcing, "Each day we will scribe our thoughts and events of the day. It will be the evidence of our expedition."

Quintus wrote first, quickly jotting down a couple of sentences. Stephanos filled an entire page. Yeshua wrote his then turned to Germanicus.

The slave was busy thinking about Anna and the Israeli. When he reconsidered their conversation, he realized how cleverly Yeshua avoided answering the question about himself. That aroused his curiosity all the more. What was so special about the Israeli that made Anna worry about him? He wondered if their leader had something to do with her miraculous cure, when Yeshua interrupted his thoughts, "Germanicus do you wish to scribe your thoughts in the diary?" He saw the slave turn crimson, and realized he was probably illiterate and rephrased his question, "Do you want me to write it for you?"

The slave started to shake his head when his eyes lit up with inspiration, "Will you teach me to write?" When the Israeli nodded, he smiled, "Write - Anna."

Yeshua scribed the letters, pronouncing each one. Germanicus listened then repeated. Finally he took the stylus and scribed it on the papyrus with great care. He held it back smiling, "I can almost see her on the page..." He wrote it a few more times enjoying it every time. He returned the papyrus with disarming innocence, "Write - leprosy."

Yeshua's mouth unhinged and he felt his face burning as he glanced at the slave. He was barely able to whisper, "I am too tired."

Germanicus suspected he had struck a sensitive chord and the hair on the back of his neck stood up. He was certain Yeshua knew more than he admitted: but what?

It had been a long day and they began yawning, then one by one sauntered into the tent. Stephanos teased them. "Will anyone volunteer to return for the meat? You'll be back before dawn, with our eternal gratitude."

"I only eat it twice a year," Yeshua replied. "I will not miss it."

Quintus put down his sword next to his cot and got under the blanket, "I'll worry about it tomorrow. Right now... my interes-s-s...is-s... s-s-sleep." Before his head touched the cot he was asleep.

"In that case I vote we get good rest. Good night," the Greek turned in as well.

Yeshua lay down and immediately his mind went to lady Sarah. He rebuked himself again for not kissing her. He had never kissed a girl but was certain kissing her would be the greatest joy of his life. He sighed deeply, and was certain he could smell the fragrant perfume on her; soft and fresh as the roses in spring. He wished he had told her how much he cared. Perhaps he would write her a long letter confessing everything: his love, his identity and most of all how much he missed her. He would send it to his sister to deliver it. Having made the decision he drifted into a pleasant sleep.

Germanicus, left outside to guard, added wood to the fire, wrapped himself in a blanket, and sat by the door, his spear at his side.

He was pleased that he chose to speak with Yeshua rather than exact revenge. Now he knew Anna cared for him. He chuckled quietly at his unwarranted jealousy. He remembered the numerous times he accompanied his master to Yeshua's house and how warmly she greeted him. Sometimes she brought him food and they ate together, and she sat with him, asking questions about his family and his tribe. She was not shy, asking the most personal questions and enjoyed his awkward replies. His life was no longer dreary. He had reason to wake up, hum and whistle, and search for a patch of blue in a cloudy sky, or pick wild flowers for her.

He was grateful Yeshua had pointed out the obvious; that Anna was as anxious for his arrival as he to see her. For a long time he hoped she felt as he did, but could not master the courage to ask. Now he knew, and he looked up to the stars with a big grin.

There was another reason he was grateful to Yeshua. The Israeli gave him another reason to hope: the God of the Israelis cared for him, a hopeless slave.

"Yahweh cares for me," he mumbled filled with wonder. He guarded his enthusiasm for he feared to get swept up by a God and be let down again. Northern Europe did not lack gods, but, now that he was enslaved, where were they? The fact that he felt betrayed had long ago ceased to bother him. What troubled him was that he felt an emptiness which those gods could not fill.

He sat up thinking of his important discovery: he did not feel betrayed because the gods failed to defend him. The fact was when he needed them most, in the lonely and desperate days, they could not offer him anything: warmth, security and above all hope. One by one they vanished from his life...because they had no essence.

That's what made Yahweh so intriguing: He was not a God of war or intrigue. He offered love! Care! Hope! He loved all his creatures: equally! And all He demanded was to be loved. He made no outrageous promises, only that He would love every subject unequivocally forever. Yeshua said, this Universal God cared for him. What God cared for a slave? Were Gods not the exclusive property of emperors and priests? He could hardly believe he could be so important, especially to a God. Then he began to have doubts. No God cared about a slave. He discarded the idea as absurd, and began to fear he was blinded by false hopes, and decided to forget the entire matter.

No sooner he had made the decision, that he was totally immersed with Yahweh's unequivocal love. It captured his psyche and refused to let go. Why won't this God let go of him? he wondered. And he answered his own question: a God that loves unreservedly, and unequivocally does not leave the person. He captures his heart because He is a benevolent God. He was more powerful than all other gods, yet not a word was said about war or revenge. Only love. This God cared. He filled the void because it was most important to make the person happy and secure in His love.

He smiled when he thought of a parallel between Anna's care and Yahweh's love. They were not the same, yet they had similarities. They cared and expressed their care. He did not feel empty though Anna was far away, and he knew he would not feel empty with Yahweh, because He would always be there. Germanicus realized he would never be alone again.

For the first time in his life Germanicus felt secure. There were still countless questions to be answered, but he felt a confidence that the Creator considered him equal to all men, and loved him equally with all others. He was sending a Messiah to set him free and that was beyond comprehension.

Germanicus began to wonder why did Yeshua know so much about Yahweh and the Messiah? He spoke about them intimately as if they were family. Anna said he was a special person...and he remembered Yeshua saying she had been a leper cured by a miracle. Yet neither would talk about it. Why? Why the secrecy? Why did Yeshua know so much, and why was he so special? Perhaps he knew more than he was admitting. Perhaps he knew the Messiah?

• • •

Yeshua awoke in the middle of the night, and lay in the cot overcome by an overpowering desire: to see lady Sarah. He fought the urge, reasoning that he could not go and return before daylight - or could he? The harder he tried to return to sleep the more awake he became, until he sat up groggy and tired. He glanced over and saw the outline of the others sleeping. Quietly he slipped into his tunic put on the sandals and tiptoed gingerly, almost tripping over Germanicus, sound asleep in the doorway. Some guard, he thought.

The moon was delightfully bright and the fresh air filled his lungs and awoke him. A perfect night for a romantic interlude, he decided. He went quietly to the tree where he had tied the donkey, reaching for the rein, then the animal, coming out empty handed. He looked around the tree and into the shadows, searched around the other trees without seeing the animal. He returned to the tent, retraced his steps carefully to where he remembered tying the donkey, stood by the tree and looked around... It had vanished. There could only be two explanations: it ran away, which was unlikely, or, it was stolen.

Yeshua started for the tent to raise the alarm when he noticed in his peripheral vision a sheet of papyrus impaled on a broken branch at eye level. He ripped it off and read it.

"THANKS FOR THE USE OF YOUR DONKEY. I WILL RETURN IT IN THE MORNING.
STEPHANOS"

He was scandalized! "That pilfering Greek!" he grunted burning with anger. "He went back after my lady Sarah... WITH MY DONKEY!"

He marched the dozen paces resolutely to the camel. It too was gone! He did not bother to check if he had the right tree, searching instead for the note which he easily found, and read:

"SORRY OLD CHAP! I DID NOT HAVE THE HEART TO SEPARATE THE ANIMALS. SEE YOU BRIGHT AND EARLY!
STEPHANOS"

"Those animals are as inseparable as oil and water," he clenched his teeth, muttering to himself, "Gone to steal my girl. Didn't tell me! AND TOOK MY DONKEY!"

He kicked the ground, and threw stones at the fire to vent his frustration, then walked up to the knoll of a hill. He could make out, faintly, the silhouette against the sky of a person mounted on a very small animal followed by a much larger one.

He let out an agonizind moan to the stars, "HE IS SITTING ON MY DONKEY!"

Returning to the tent he caught sight of a large boulder...

· · ·

It was mid morning when they finished breakfast, cleaned up and were ready to break camp. Instead, they sat waiting for the Greek to get up. He did not return until almost day break, and Yeshua sat fuming, waiting impatiently to rebuke him. Quintus, who was tired of pacing, waiting for the ne'er-do-well, started for the tent, intending to drag him out. Suddenly, he heard a groan in the tent and stopped.

When Stephanos appeared at the door they gasped. Nothing could have prepared them for that sight. Scarecrows, weathering many rough winters, and summer thunderstorms were in better shape. "What happened?" Yeshua blurted out.

Even the Roman showed sympathy, "Were you attacked by bandits?"

Stephanos held onto the doorway to stop from crumbling. His thick brown hair was matted down with sweat, and dried blood, his face, arms and legs were the multi-colors of the rainbow, and his crisply white tunic, hung tattered on his beaten body. The exposed skin was crisscrossed with deep scratches. When he stepped out his legs gave out, and the slave ran to support him, and sat him on a log. He gave a long painful sigh, trembling, "Germa...I...cold..."

The slave quickly brought a blanket and covered him up.

Yeshua poured water in a pot and put it on the fire, "We'll give you a wash down and you'll feel better."

"Get your master some breakfast," Quintus told the slave.

"What happened?" Yeshua inquired.

The Greek took a bowl of porridge with goat milk and honey, took a couple of spoonfuls which he inhaled, then took a deep breath and recounted his adventure. "I borrowed the donkey and went to town... the meat...A ride from hell after the kick, right at my..."

"Get on with the story," Quintus interrupted impatiently. "We must get going."

The Greek took another couple of mouthfuls, and seemed to be regaining some strength, "I was numb and dreary when we arrived in town. What I saw almost made me turn back: bonfires at every intersection, the town under siege, lousy with Romans.

"I tied the animals far from town, and started to tread my way to master Joseph's house. But, at every corner I was forced to detour, until they caught me...I ran as fast as I could. I flew over a fence up into the air and into the center of...a giant bramble..." He closed his eyes shaking and shivering. "When I came to I was inside a large army tent... like this... surrounded by soldiers. I was afraid I had died. They interrogated and beat me, until I wished I had died."

"They demanded I tell them where all my Zealot friends were hiding. I denied the accusation and was beaten. I pleaded ignorance and was struck. They bashed me with fists, clubs, sticks, swords and their boots. They accused me of conspiracy, treason, instigating riots, uprisings, and it became useless to defend myself. So I lied. And they pounded me... until my body was numb. I passed out. They splashed cold water on me and the instant I revived the punishment continued. I resigned myself to joining Zeus on mount Olympus that night."

He finished the bowl, sighed and heaved, and returned to the story, "Certain I was facing the end, I decided to tell them the truth: that four of us were camped a few miles south of town on a journey in search of the legendary MESSIAH! They guffawed and were ready to resume the beatings when suddenly they were ordered to stop. Within moments I was freed and told I could go.

"I'll never know how I got back to camp. When I arrived my life hung by the thinnest of threads. I lived for one purpose: to sink my head on the pillow..." Suddenly he grabbed the back of his head wincing, "Who put a boulder in my pillow?"

"I'm sorry...I was angry..." Yeshua's face turned red as he mumbled an apology.

Quintus who had heard enough interjected, "I suppose after the adventure you forgot the meat?"

The Greek did not respond, merely glaring at him, and pointing to the animals. Germanicus ran over and lifted two large boxes still hanging on the camel, announcing, "The meat is here!"

They were filled with admiration and congratulated him for his courage and daring. Even the Roman patted his back - cautiously.

Germanicus prepared the water and washed him down.

"We could stay another day to let you recover," Yeshua suggested.

"Not a moment longer," Stephanos cried out. "I want to leave this cursed place – today!"

• • •

What Stephanos did not tell his companions because he did not know, was that his interrogation was closely watched by two very important persons: the Roman legate from Sepphoris and the Zealot traitor.

They sat in the dark outside the tent watching and listening intently to every word the Greek said.

At one point the legate leaned towards the traitor and inquired, "Is the Greek a Zealot?"

"Not yet," the traitor replied. "But he is a close friend of an Israeli named Yeshua: a most dangerous Zealot!"

The beating continued until Stephanos confessed they were camped south of Nazareth, going to look for the MESSIAH!

The traitor grabbed the legate's shoulder and whispered eagerly, "The Messiah is a legendary hero the Israeli God promised to send to them. The Messiah will lead them to freedom..."

"The Messiah will lead them to war against us?"

"Precisely," the traitor emphasized. "Yeshua will find the rebel and bring him here to start a war..."

"What do you suggest?"

"Release the Greek. Let him return to his companions. Then send some soldiers after them. When they find the rebel leader, order them to murder the Messiah as well as Yeshua." He sniggered evilly, "Just think, with one move you will enjoy three coups."

The legate thought about it, finally asking confused, "What is the third coup?"

"Your promotion!"

"I'm glad you're on our side," the legate drawled with suspicion. He ordered the Greek released.

When Stephanos left, the officer called two soldiers, an older veteran and a youth, giving them orders, "I chose you because you are our best trackers. Start first thing in the morning and follow the Greek and his companions. They are on a mission: to find the Messiah, a mortal enemy of Rome! When they find him, kill him and all his companions, especially the leader Yeshua!"

Next day, about mid-morning, when the young men broke camp, seven miles to the north, two Roman soldiers with a horse ladened with a tent and supplies left on their trail: the army's best trackers, trained professional killers.

CHAPTER IX - BANDITS

Master Stephanos recovered sufficiently by noon, so they broke camp and left to get some miles before dark. Yeshua told them, "We must remain close, as we are entering bandit territory. Listen for strange noises or movements. Be ready to defend at all times."

The advice was good but it made them tense. They traveled exclusively along the upper slopes at the edge of the bluffs, leaving the forest far to the right. To the left was the valley of Jezreel, leading to lower rolling hills down to the Jordan valley in the distance. These were rich, green meadows carpeted with wild flowers, bushes and trees splashed with a riot of colors, from greens to hues of blues in the distance until the hills blended into the sky.

They made slow progress as the narrow path carved by caravans was overgrown. Occasionally they came to a spring forming a pool which overflowed and leaped down the cliffs as water falls. Down the valley, a small stream meandered lazily, cutting across the meadows.

Yeshua felt they had walked into the pages of ancient scriptures, and he felt the spirits of prophets and holy men from the past. As he contemplated his nation's history, he whispered under his breath, "All stories about Israelis are painful…" He sought inspiration from the great historical prophets to guide his future.

He stood at the edge of the bluffs identifying some caves below, likely hide outs of today's bandits.

Although Yeshua warned his companions to stay together, Quintus quickly marched dozens of paces ahead, while Stephanos hobbled a hundred paces to the rear, leaving the Israeli and the slave in the middle. From time to time Yeshua yelled, "Master Quintus, slow down! Master Stephanos, pick up the pace."

Yeshua sensed Germanicus was troubled, mumbling as if debating something with himself. A few times the slave turned to him, about to speak, only to stammer and give up.

"For heaven's sake, what is bothering you?" Yeshua snapped impatiently.

"W-who, m-me? N-nothing," he stuttered defensively.

"I can see you are troubled. Last night you seemed happy...What is the matter?"

"How could you see if you were not looking?" Germanicus retorted.

"Peripheral vision."

"I resent being spied on...especially when I cannot see."

After a long time Germanicus turned to his companion sheepishly, "You were right, something is bothering me...but, I don't know where to start..."

"Start anywhere; sooner or later we'll get to the problem."

"Last night I was falling asleep, secure in the thought of Yahweh, when questions came to mind...endless questions...This powerful Israeli God..."

"He is not Israeli. He is Universal."

"Are you certain He exists?"

"Positive!"

"I once believed in the gods of my forefathers..." Germanicus sighed sadly, "But, when I needed them I was bitterly disappointed..."

"You're afraid to be disappointed again. I understand," Yeshua finished his statement. When he glanced at the slave he saw a troubled look, yearning and fear, as if saying, "I want to believe, but..."

"Last night you said the Universal Creator made everything," the slave remarked. "Recently I heard a Greek scholar, my master's friend say, we are a product of evolution. Who is right?"

"They are not mutually exclusive. Both are right. It is true that everything is evolving; some animals adapt and advance, others fail and become extinct. That's evolution. But the question is – from where did it all start? From matter: but who made matter?"

Germanicus' eyes popped wide, "Alright how did this matter originate?"

"Yahweh created matter from nothing after which the process of evolution took over in an orderly fashion. The Creator started it all by moving matter from a central point at the same instant and at a uniform speed, beginning an expanding universe. That was the beginning. Over time, matter intermixed and changed, creating light, forming water, elements evolved into life, some simple others complex, until we have all this!" He swept his arm over the entire horizon.

The slave followed his hand sweep, "What is all this?"

"Everything: people, animals, trees…"

"Did you see Creation?" he asked a most natural question. Yeshua never knew why, but he nodded, and the slave's mouth unhinged. "What was it like?"

The Israeli concentrated trying to recollect something he could never have explained before, "Before Creation matter flew helter skelter in a chaotic way. It was darker than the blackest night. Everything flew into one another colliding: solids, gases, ripped apart in gigantic explosions! The only light was from these explosions, then it was black again. The Creator stopped everything. When He nudged it, everything flowed in harmony through the vast expanse. Before that, there was no time, no space. Evolution started at that moment. In time, clouds and solids unified, forming constellations…then stars. Light was created, then planets. After much time He created life: and man and woman."

"These were like volcanic explosions?"

"Many times bigger. Gigantic explosions!" Yeshua extended his arms far apart to dramatize it. "Like giant mountains colliding…But you could not hear it."

"Why not?"

"There was no atmosphere. No air. Out there it is a vacuum," he explained, only to see the slave gaze at him blankly. He attempted to clarify, "It's like being under water. You can't speak because there is no air."

"Where did all this happen?" Germanicus was getting confused.

"Up there, in the universe, a very long time ago," he pointed.

The slave thought for a moment, looked up at the sky and exclaimed enthusiastically, "Why did you not say that? Now it all makes sense: rain comes from up there…because the universe is filled with water…When it gets a hole in it, it leaks and we get rain…until someone up there fixes it!"

Yeshua knew he had failed miserably. He had made everything too complicated. He vowed to simplify his explanations and his language.

While he was thinking about it, he noticed something moving far ahead in the distance. It seemed like a person, darting into the forest. Quintus did not react, which meant he did not see it. Yeshua made a mental note to investigate when they arrived there.

Germanicus did not wait to pepper him with questions, "If you saw the Creation, you must have seen the Creator?" When the Israeli nodded he continued, "What does He look like?"

Yeshua did not want to fail again, so he thought before answering, "This is a tougher question than the Creation,"

"I understood Creation. It was simple." he replied proudly.

The Israeli vowed not to repeat the same mistake, so he started slowly, "The Creator is not like anything...but he is everything."

Germanicus stared blankly then asked, "Can I see Him?"

"Naturally; He is everywhere..."

Germanicus looked to his left, then searched to the right, up in the sky, the clouds, and finally back at his companion, "Do you see Him?"

He nodded, "Uh-ugh."

The slave did not know what to make of this, "What does He look like? Is He big? A male? Is He a...giant, a dwarf? Is He bearded?"

"Yes," he answered and when he looked at the slave's screwed up face he knew he was losing him. He tried frantically to think of a magic phrase to explain Him, knowing it was easier to describe the wind. When nothing came he sighed, "Yahweh is not like anybody...or anything...because He is everything and everybody. That's why ancient people said, 'He is that He is'"

"Are you having me on?" Germanicus snapped angrily.

"I am serious," the young scholar apologized. "Yahweh is not a person... but, for you to understand Him, He will appear as a person. He is in every person, in every living creature, in every tree and flower, in everything..."

Germanicus bent over and picked a lovely blue bell and brought it up for inspection. Just then a reddish insect crawled out and he exclaimed surprised, "Look at this - a ladybug."

"He is in that ladybug," Yeshua remarked proudly.

The slave's eyes popped, "Why did you not say Yahweh is a wee-little thing of a God?" Suddenly he became livid, "Are you saying a dwarf, no bigger than the head of a pin created the universe? I may be a slave, but I am not a fool!" He yanked at the rein violently causing the camel to run up and bump into him.

Yeshua grabbed his shoulder desperately, "Wait! Germanicus, I am doing my best. This is a very complex concept. Give me a chance!" He waited until the slave took control of his animal, and tried once more, "Yahweh is bigger than that giant mountain, yet small enough to fit into the tiny flower."

Germanicus considered the statement, looked at the flower as he turned the stem between the index finger and the thumb, inspecting every side. He smiled with renewed inspiration and brought it close to his eye, peeking inside. Alas, he was sorely disappointed. "Yahweh will not appear to a mere slave."

"Nonsense!"

"Then why do I not see Him?" he queried in despair.

"See the flower?" Yeshua asked and he nodded. "You are looking at Him!"

Germanicus reconsidered it, and seeing a stone, turned it over, "Is He under here?"

The Israeli saw a worm, some insects, and an ant and nodded, "He is under every rock. He is in all creatures that walk, crawl, fly or slither."

"But, He is the one and only God?" he asked and the Israeli nodded. "He is big, and He is small…He is one…and He is many…?"

The young scholar smiled confidently, certain the slave had got it. He ventured to phrase it philosophically: "He is that He is. He has always been and always will be…in everything He created."

Germanicus contemplated the statement for a long time, looking around at everything. Finally he pointed, "Is He in that camel?"

"Most Definately!"

"If Yahweh is in that ugly beast, I will have nothing to do with Him!"

He yanked the rein so hard that the camel lunged forward, almost running him over. He marched far ahead pulling the shocked animal, arguing with himself. From time to time he frowned at the camel cursing something inaudible. The mystery of Yaweh was too great to comprehend. He knew he would need time to think it all through.

Yeshua, left behind, felt devastated. He blamed himself for failing to explain God to a person yearning to accept Him. He should have been more patient, explained it with simpler words. His explanations were too obscure, too many symbolisms for a mind not used to thinking in abstract terms. He was so desperate he considered calling the slave and confessing, "Germanicus, I am the son of God," then perform a small miracle to impress him. But, as before, he decided against it. It would impress him for the moment, but not satisfy him for long.

Yeshua realized faith was a very personal experience. Often it came with some deep personal crisis or pain. He knew a family which sold itself into slavery, and another which sent a young daughter into prostitution to survive. Their solace was in the synagogue, where they found strength in time of crisis. Germanicus had suffered fantastic losses: defeat in war, loss of family and the greatest degradation of all - slavery. He needed a beacon for his hopeless darkness. He was depressed because he had failed to guide him to that beacon, and give him hope.

From the failure Yeshua received the greatest inspiration: he discarded forever the scholarly terminology, abstract symbolisms and resorted to age old simplicity. He told simple parables which explained life clearly. Alas, that was to be far in the future.

Presently they arrived to the area where he had seen a person run into the forest. He caught up to Germanicus and handed him the donkey's rein saying, "Wait here. I'll be right back," and dashed into the woods.

Quintus did not realize Yeshua had disappeared, for he was too far ahead while Stephanos too far back. Germanicus had no chance to react until he heard a commotion in the trees. "Don't kill me! I'll come out," a male voice pleaded, and a young man walked out carrying a knap sack, escorted by Yeshua.

The young scholar held his staff by one end, pointing and touching the other end against the stranger's temple.

"Take whatever I have...but, please don't kill me. I have small children..."

Yeshua rebuked him, "Quiet! We are not robbers." When the stranger stopped sobbing, he asked, "How many others are traveling with you?"

"I am traveling alone, sir," he said. Yeshua stared into his eyes intently until the stranger stepped back, "I swear, I am telling the truth, sir..."

"What is your name, and what are you doing in the forest alone?"

"My name is Zebedee, son of Silas, I am from the village of Laish, a couple of days' journey to the south," Zebedee replied nervously. "I am on my way to Sepphoris in search of work."

"What employment are you seeking?" Yeshua tested him.

"I am a mason, sir. But I will do any honest work. I am a married man with two young ones to feed. I'm desperate..."

Yeshua looked at his calloused hands, and put down the staff, "Relax, master Zebedee, we will not harm you." He yelled, "Master Quintus, we have a visitor."

Quintus, seeing the stranger, drew his sword and ran back, "Leave him to me. I'll deal with the scoundrel. Where are your accomplices?"

Yeshua raised his hands, "Slow down. No need to create a crisis. He's Zebedee, a traveler going to Sepphoris. He's travelling alone."

The Roman glared at Yeshua, grabbed the stranger and searched him for hidden weapons, and grabbed his knapsack, then walked to the forest to check for more bandits.

"Will you be passing through Nazareth?" Yeshua inquired.

Zebedee shrugged, "I was told the road goes through there."

"Will you take a letter to my family? We will pay you," he asked.

"Gladly. Where is the letter?"

"I will write it presently. Are you hungry?" he asked and Zebedee nodded eagerly. "Germanicus, get master Zebedee some food, and give him some extra to take."

"I am most grateful, master..."

"Yeshua," he answered as he was taking out papyrus and the stylus. "That is master Quintus. Yonder is master Stephanos, and this is his slave Germanicus."

Yeshua sat down and quickly scribed a letter to Debborah, to go and check on lady Sarah, to take his letter to her and send him news of how she was faring. He named the towns they were going to – Laish and Beth Sheeba where she could write him. Then he scribed a lovely letter to lady Sarah. He had sufficient time to decide what he wanted to say, and confessed everything. He said that from the first time he saw her, she had captured his heart and intellect. Not one day went by when she was not in his mind.He wanted to spend the rest of his life with her. Regardless of how her parents felt he would fight for her. He wanted to have a family with her. He said he had much more to say, and promised to tell her about himself, his identity and his destiny when they would meet again.

When he finished, he turned to the visitor who was eating voraciously, "Are there towns close to your village?" Yeshua asked him.

"Four hamlets with a few families in each, scraping out a living."

"Mostly farmers?"

"Yes, although we have some tradesmen and artisans," he replied.

"We are on an expedition in search of the Messiah. Did you ever hear of him?"

"What Israeli has not heard of the holy man? Most await his arrival impatiently," the traveler exclaimed.

Stephanos who had caught up, and regained his breath joined the interrogation, "Did such a person ever pass through your towns or villages?"

"We had holy men pass through, they performed miracles and went on…but I did not hear anyone call them Messiahs," he replied.

"Did you see these alleged miracles performed?" Stephanos asked suspiciously.

"No, but I heard about them. They were astounding stories: miracles that mortals could not possibly do. They were truly blessed by Lord Adonai."

Yeshua joined in, "What kind of miracles?"

"Exorcism. One holy man cured a boy said to be possessed by the demon. He exorcised him, almost killing the child. One healer, the great Shamai cures any kind of infirmity or illness. They say he charges an enormous price…"

"But, you did not see any of them?" Stephanos persisted with a sardonic tone. "How do you know then that they're true? Maybe they were all tricks: hypnosis, or some sorcery or magic…maybe outright fraud."

The stranger remained steadfast, "I know the people who witnessed those things. Honest people. I don't doubt their statements."

Quintus returned with the knapsack, "No weapons here, just masonry tools."

Yeshua brought the letters and folded them, "They are addressed to my sister Debborah. Take it to my parent's house, master Joseph, the carpenter." He turned to the Greek, "Please pay him a drachma which I promised."

Stephanos grunted but pulled out a coin and handed it to the stranger. They bowed, waved good bye and separated.

Within a few moments Quintus was far ahead again, Stephanos again fell to the rear, leaving the Israeli and the slave together in the middle. Yeshua did not wish to confuse or anger the slave further so they walked in silence.

Germanicus heaved and sighed and started a soliloquy, "Ever since I was sold into slavery, I blamed and cursed everyone: our gods, the Romans, the Greeks… everyone became my enemy." He sniggered bitterly, "It is difficult to catch a ray of light down in this dark tunnel." He glanced at Yeshua who nodded, but did not respond. "Lady Anna brought me back to the light…She said I was too impatient. I was lucky to be alive…most of my friends died…Perhaps she is right…"

"But, you are still a slave," Yeshua completed his statement.

The slave nodded knowing his companion understood his hopeless situation, and his fear of accepting an unproven deity. He muttered, "I want to believe, but I am afraid."

"It's my fault," Yeshua apologized deeply concerned. "I failed to explain Him to you."

"It was not that," he smirked unexpectedly. "Gods have a warped sense of humor; playing hide and seek all the time. Just when I think I found Him, He makes Himself invisible." They chuckled and continued to walk. "I will do as lady Anna suggested: be patient. Perhaps He will come to a slave."

Yeshua was pleased that his companion did not give up. Although he was not ready to take the leap of faith, at least he had not given up. He started thinking how to simplify the concept when the slave interrupted, "I still have one question. Will the Messiah be as difficult to recognize as Yahweh?"

"No! The scripts say he will be a living person, like you and me."

"Phew! That's a relief. I refuse to search for two of them in that ugly camel!" Germanicus exclaimed and they shared a chuckle. "Perhaps if we find the Messiah, through him I will understand Yahweh?"

The Israeli was pleased to see the slave persisting and decided to help again, though uncertain where to start. This was when he saw far ahead four men come out of the forest in front of Quintus and stop him. He motioned to the slave and they pressed their step, waving at the Greek to pick up the pace.

When they caught up, Quintus whispered, "Bandits!"

"Maybe not, maybe beggars," Yeshua replied in a soft tone.

"What is your wish?" Quintus addressed the apparent leader, a tall, well proportioned man of middle age.

"Your supplies and the animals," he replied. "Give them up and we will guarantee you safe passage."

Quintus laughed heartily, not displaying the least concern, as if he were inviting the opportunity for a battle. "We regret to refuse your offer. We put more trust in a mirage than a bandit's word!" His confrontational tone caused the strangers to tense up, and the leader gripped his staff ready to battle. Quintus continued calmly, "We enjoyed safe passage and will continue to do so. Now get out of our way!"

Yeshua hoped to diffuse the situation, "It is obvious you have nothing while we have plenty. We offer half our supplies, but we cannot part with the animals as we have a long journey ahead."

"Witness the weakness of our youth?" a heavy set bandit opined from the rear. "At the first sign of trouble you compromise. Fight for your convictions. We gave you an order not a choice: give up everything or fight!"

"We'll fight!" Quintus growled, nudging the Israeli back, and drawing his sword. "You and me," he pointed the weapon at the leader. "Winner takes all!"

"Spoken like a warrior, Roman. I'll happily teach you the superiority of a shepherd's staff over a toy sword. Prepare to die!"

As he was speaking, he swung his staff at the Roman's head, so quickly that the latter failed to duck and turned away partially, so his shoulder took a direct hit. Taken by surprise, he lost his balance while the staff was coming at his knees.

But Quintus was a well trained soldier and jumped out of the way, launching a counter attack, swinging the sword wildly to carve the bandit in twain. The man twisted and retreated but the second swing cut open a section of this cloak exposing bare skin.

The Roman advanced with great furious strides, certain of a short battle, slashing upwards, downwards and across, using his sword as a meat cleaver trying to chop the opponent into so many dismembered limbs. The bandit saw the young warrior's impatience and defended himself, causing the sword to glance off the hard wood 'clanking' and ringing with no evidence of a dent. Quintus did not know these seemingly harmless sticks were as hard as steel, hard enough to crush a skull, yet so light that a trained fighter could swing it for a long time without tiring.

The bandit retreated, persistently standing on higher ground forcing the Roman to expend energy. Ever so slowly the bandit backed uphill and into the trees where the sword struck branches frustrating his attack. When Quintus was caugnt in the branches, the bandit shoved the end of the staff into his gut, then struck him twice in the face. The bandit swung to crush the soldier's skull, but the same branches prevented him from swinging freely. Quintus, his nose and face cut and bleeding, swiftly stepped around the tree trunk and attacked the bandit from the rear as he struggled to free the staff. The Roman slashed twice about the spine, cutting him, but when he thrust to plunge the sword, the bandit jumped out of the forest and into the clearing. Out in the clearing the Roman hacked at the bandit's feet savagely, causing him to jump back helter-skelter, off balance, unable to mount a counter offensive.

For a long time the battle continued at a furious pace, now the sword taking the offensive, seemingly with the upper hand, pushing and crashing the bandit.

But, the bandit was the ideal match for such brute force. Slightly taller, more slender, not only was he endowed with powerful muscles, but a lifetime of long hard labor, taught him tactics, endurance and survival. Hence, he easily defended the ferocious attacks from the iron blade, while whipping the staff swiftly, punishing every mistake his opponent made.

After long intense attacks Quintus realized he could not succeed in hacking the enemy, so he changed tactics. He varied his offence, alternating attacks, first with blows to the upper body, then slashing at the feet, and vice-versa. This gave him some success for it forced the bandit to retreat and threw him off balance. The bandit instinctively swung the staff catching the soldier's head with full force with a loud 'whoof', like crushing a water-melon. Quintus leaned back, visibly dazed and fell on his back. The bandit plunged one end of the stick into the enemy's face, throwing his whole weight behind the final blow. Quintus continued to roll backwards, pirouet-ting end for end and came up on his feet, as the attacker stabbed the ground. He swung the sword with all his might at the bandit's neck. Sensing the blade gaining, the man lunged forward rolling towards the Roman, kicking him in the gut, causing him to fall. Thus the combatants traded places, each within a hair from inflicting a mortal wound to the opponent, at the same instant miraculously avoiding getting killed.

In one final, desperate effort the bandit attacked fiercely, throwing all caution to the wind, forcing Quintus to scramble in retreat, twisting and turning to avoid the whipping staff. The bandit pushed him to an area of loose gravel, where he swung wildly causing the soldier to bend, twist and duck, until he lost his balance, slipped and fell heavily on his back. He tried to stand up unsuccessfully, slipping, leaving his upper torso exposed. The bandit whacked him across the mouth, cutting and smashing his lips. Then with precision of an artist, he stuck the end of the staff in the hilt of the sword wrenching it out of the Roman's hand, and flung it high in the air. It soared end over end, and as it floated down, the bandit caught it and thrust it into Quintus' chest.

Yeshua, standing a couple of paces away, swung his staff mightily at the bandit's hand. The wood crushed his fingers dislodging the sword which tumbled harmlessly down hill. The man held his aching hand, twisting his face in pain, as Yeshua sent another blow to his head, causing him to fall to his knees.

Yeshua apologized, "Sorry. I had to save my friend."

The bandit barked ferociously, chewing every word between his teeth, "I'm going to kill you! I'll break every bone in your body." As he attacked, froth spewed from his mouth.

He was taller and more muscular than the young scholar, attacking like a maniac possessed, while Yeshua, more slender but a wiry fighter defended himself cautiously. It seemed to those on the sidelines that the battle would be over in a fraction of a moment, and the bandits smirked as their leader pushed ahead. Yeshua backed away steadily, deftly deflecting the blows without mounting a counter attack. The bandits waited for a quick victory while the young men hoped he could survive the brutal attack. Only Yeshua was confident, for he was using the same tactics the bandit did to beat Quintus. He kept to the higher ground, letting his opponent swing as a wild animal, noticing after a lengthy offensive that the man's swings were slower, and his strikes weaker. Meanwhile Yeshua waited patiently for an opening to bring the battle to the end. He chose the spot where the bandit would fall: the same loose gravel.

He was doing precisely that at this moment: letting the bandit spend his energy while he studied his weaknesses. By the time the man realized the young scholar's tactics it was too late. In a desperate change of tactics he tried to save energy, but he was getting exhausted.

Yeshua decided to end the duel. He feigned a blow to the opponent's left side thrice and when he froze defending the flank, the young man struck his right hip bone, at the very top. He knew this was one of the tenderest areas filled with nerve endings but no protection. The bandit's face contorted in agony, and he could not put any weight on the right leg. Yeshua feigned to strike the sore area again and when the bandit covered it to protect it, the young man quickly struck his left hip, and watched him sink to his knees exhausted.

"Quintus get your sword," Yeshua yelled.

The Roman leaped down the hill, recovered it and returned, holding it ready for action.

The young Israeli held the tip of his staff to the bandit's temple, "I will repeat my offer once more; one half of the supplies..."

Quintus pushed his friend aside, and snarled, "No more offers. You had your chance. Now throw down your weapons: your staffs and daggers!"

"Not the daggers," Yeshua interjected. "They will need those for hunting."

"Alright," Quintus gave in. "Your staffs, over here. NOW!"

The bandits muttered under their breaths, glanced at one another, refusing to obey until he raised his sword and took a step towards them. Then they heaved the sticks so violently that one bounced striking Quintus' leg. They sauntered into the forest, glancing back a couple of times before disappearing.

As soon as they left the young men ran and picked up the staffs, twirling them as if these were newly discovered treasures.

Quintus took one, hurled his sword down the valley, and turned to Yeshua, "Starting tonight you will teach us how to use these weapons. Who would ever suspect staffs to be more dangerous than swords?"

"That's why I detest violence," Yeshua rebuked the Roman. "What did all this prove? They left empty handed, we have more than we need, and we'll probably live to fight them again..."

"What a magnificent duel: a joust worthy of the olympics," the Greek complimented them effusively as he balanced his staff proudly. "These Israelis are worthy warriors."

"They are stiff-necks and whiners, but when pushed they are courageous fighters," Quintus was forced to admit.

Germanicus also traded his spear for a staff, and they resumed their journey. However, the Roman slowed down and Stephanos hobbled faster so they traveled as one unit.

Yeshua had studied the bandits' reaction closely when they were ordered to turn in their weapons. He glanced into the forest often and listened carefully in case they decided to ambush again.

Their progress was slow due to the uneven terrain and overgrowth. For a long time, the slightest noise, a screech of a bird or rustling of leaves, caused them to tense up and they turned to the forest expecting the worst. Stories of brigands in the area were legendary and every townsperson told stories of robbery and gory murder. The young men listened with passing interest at first, laughing off the warnings as exaggerations of imaginative peasants. After the battle their imaginations reacted to the slightest noise.

"Let's set up camp here," Quintus stopped by a clearing. "The sooner we learn to use these weapons the better."

"We'll stop before long," Yeshua relented when he saw their knuckles white from holding their staffs too tightly. "However, we must find water first."

The Greek pointed to the meandering stream snaking in the valley, "We'll bring water from down there."

"Come here," Yeshua took them to the edge of the cliff. "See those dark areas in the cliffs below? They're caves. They house brigands, who depend on naïve travelers."

Nobody argued with him. They continued on a couple of miles and came upon a spring with a large pool. Stephanos almost tripped rushing to be first to sate his thirst.

Yeshua grabbed him, pulling him back, "Do not touch that water." The Greek froze. "These water holes may be poisoned or have leaves pinned to the bottom which bring sleep. A sip may be your last." He knelt beside it and inspected it thoroughly, "The water is clear, and colorless, not opaque. I see no powder anywhere on the grass. There are no animals or insects around it dead; in fact those ants, and the beetle on the surface are very much alive. No strange scent..." He scooped a handful, sniffed again, took some in his mouth, swished it and spat it out. "No strange taste or burning sensation. I believe it is safe."

They fell to their knees enjoying a long refreshing drink, while Yeshua stood watching the forest. What a perfect trap this could be, he mused: defenceless travelers on their bellies with bandits coming from the forest.

Stephanos stood up, looked around pointing to a large clearing, "The perfect camp site is right here."

"If we found this pool, brigands for miles know about it...and probably come for water..." Yeshua started to explain.

"On further consideration, we'll continue on," the Greek concurred.

"Let's fill the jugs," the Israeli suggested.

They took all the water they needed, and trekked a few more miles before searching for a spot. When they came upon a big level area, far from the forest, next to an outcrop of big rocks, Yeshua smiled, "Ideal. We will camp here."

"Yesterday you said a clearing next to the bluff was the best," Quintus argued forcefully. "Today you choose a place between rocks and the forest. You're contradicting yourself."

"Trust me we will be safer here," Yeshua replied. "I thought about it."

The Roman shook his head, "You wanted this as soon as you saw it…" He looked to the others who decided all of Yeshua's decisions proved right, and supported him.

They unloaded the animals and set up the tent. With supper on the fire he told them to take their staffs for the first lesson.

He started the lesson by telling them, "You have to understand some important principles to become adept with the staff. First, it is like another limb to you. Second, it demands discipline and practice; every move is planned, not a move is wasted, as it wastes energy. Third, it is strictly for defense. Let the opponent beat himself."

"Only defense?" Quintus argued unimpressed. "If Romans spent time defending, would they be masters of the world? I want to crush the enemy." He stepped forward, took the staff in both hands holding it at eye level ready to do battle.

Yeshua ignored him, "Within three blows you have to determine if the attacker is right or left handed. Most persons favor their strong side."

Yeshua raised his staff and turned to the Roman who attacked him like a wild animal. The Israeli defended himself easily, backing away letting the muscular soldier spend energy. After a few moves the Israeli tried to stop but the Roman persisted.

"Guard yourself as I intend to teach you a lesson," Quintus declared.

"Shall I tell you where you will fall?" Yeshua teased him, "Right where you stand."

"Never," the Roman retorted, springing at him.

Yeshua stepped aside and as the Roman rushed forward, he stuck the staff between his legs tripping him. Quintus sprawled heavily, releasing the staff to cushion his fall. Before he could reach for it, the Israeli stepped on it, touching the fallen comrade's temple with his stick, "When I touch your temple it means I have subjugated you. Give up or I will crush your cranium."

Germanicus showed more discipline. He listened and practiced every move as explained, and refrained from attacking. While jousting with Him Yeshua was able to explain the sport thoroughly. While he explained it, he looked at Quintus, "The moment you pulled the sword, the brigand decided he would guide you to the loose gravel where he intended to finish you off. I saw him glance there, and walked there immediately in case you needed help. He encouraged you to attack by backing off, seemingly retreating, fearing your blows. He encouraged you to fight uphill causing you to waste energy without purpose or gain. He led you into the trees where your sword became entangled, and he plunged his stick in your gut and face. He hardly exerted himself until the very end. You fought valiantly, and courageously. You lacked only two things: discipline, and a staff."

"Enough of your jabber," Stephanos stepped between them, impatient to have a go at him, "Let me try you. I was pretty good at sports in university."

He took the slave's place, raising his staff. He was the least athletic of the group, and his attacks were as awkward as his defenses. At times his attacks resembled jabs with a spear, then he swung the stick as if it were a club and a few times he seemed to be attempting pole-vaulting. Intent on scoring against the coach, he lunged at him. Unfortunately he lost his footing, stepping into a hole falling heavily on his extended arm. There was a sickening 'crack' and he rolled to his left side twisting with excruciating pain.

Quintus diagnosed the problem immediately, "The shoulder is dislocated."

Yeshua concurred, "The arm is out of the socket. Master Stephanos I can pull and place it back but it will hurt. Shall I do it?"

Stephanos nodded crying in agony. They raised him to his feet, and the Israeli pulled his arm with all his might, gently guiding the bone into the socket. When it popped in Stephanos let out a scream, turned ghostly white and fell to his knees perspiring.

In a few moments he managed a weak smile, "It feels better."

"I'll make a sling to keep your arm immobilized for a day," Yeshua said.

"Our second day and you abused ninety percent of your body," Quintus quipped sardonically. "At this rate you won't survive the journey."

That night Yeshua fed the convalescing Greek who was too battered and weak to hold a spoon.

That day Yeshua became the undisputed leader of the expedition.

. . .

Ten miles to the north, two Roman soldiers leading a horse loaded with supplies, arrived to an abandoned campsite which they inspected carefully.

The older soldier knelt beside the ashes, turned a partly burnt log over, and touched the ground, "Still damp. They doused it with water this morning." He walked about the site inspecting, "The grass is still flat. They broke camp around noon. There is donkey droppings here...camel droppings there. They can't be further than seven, ten miles from here."

"Good campsite," the younger companion commented. "Shall we stop here?"

The old soldier shook his head, "We'll go further. I like to be close to the prey for the hunt. Then 'Pow!' for the kill!" He snapped a dry twig, breaking into sadistic laughter.

They went five miles further, and set up camp. Before long a stranger came up from the south: an Israeli with a knap sack. "Good evening gentlemen," he bowed. "I am traveling in search of employment. May I share your fire, and water? I'll leave by dawn."

"A beggar," the old soldier scowled.

"Not a beggar, sir, a stone mason...law abiding, and God fearing."

The old man studied him, smirked and motioned him to sit down. The stranger found a log and started to sit when the soldier raised his hand, "Before you sit a few questions." The stranger stood up slowly, as his host started interrogating, "Where are you coming from?"

"South, from the village of Laish."

"What is your name?"

"Zebedee, son of Silas," he replied, wondering why the questions.

"Zebedee, did you come across four young men with a camel and an ass?"

"I did indeed, sir," the young mason volunteered, then wished he had not admitted it, as he began to suspect his interrogator.

"Did you speak to them?" The soldier pressed, as Zebedee looked around, recognizing the brown army tent, two swords and the horse. Only Romans used those animals. "Look at me when I'm speaking to you," the solider barked. "Did you speak to them?" He demanded as the visitor wiped his sweating hands on his cloak. "Did they say where they were going?"

Zebedee was a bad liar and his eyes darted everywhere when he shook his head, "All they said, sir...they were searching for...the Messiah."

The old soldier stretched his lips with a smirk, "Did they give you a message...a letter to their family?"

"Letter? No sir...no letter," he instinctively put his hand over the belt where he had hid it, his eyes frozen with fear.

The Roman sprang to his feet, and pulled out a folded papyrus, "LIAR!" He unfolded it and leaned over the fire reading it, "Listen to their master plan: they will be going to Laish...then Beth Sheeba. A gold mine of inf..."

The young soldier interjected, "It'is just like a map. What's the thicker papyrus?"

He skimmed over it spitting out, "A love-sick confession..." He flipped it into the fire which consumed it. Then he turned to the visitor who stared back, biting his lip, and began to retreat, realizing his life was in peril.

The old man snarled viciously, "You lie and expect to stay with us? I should kill you! Get out of my sight!"

As Zeabedee turned to flee, the Roman kicked him causing him to fall on his face. He scrambled to his feet and scurried into the night.

· · ·

After supper, Yeshua's group sat back, resting. "Are we out of the bandits' area?" Quintus asked off handedly.

The Israeli shook his head, "In the very center of it. "Tonight we can expect to be tested in earnest."

They remained seated, their eyes now sweeping the area around the camp continuously. They watched the sun sink on the horizon, as the veil of darkness shrank their world: first the furthest hills disappeared, then the closer range and the valley became a black hole, finally their world consisted of the fire and a dozen paces around it. Until the moon rose, theirs was a miniature world. Their eyes swept furtively over the non-existant meadow, the rocks and the invisible forest. The atmosphere was one of uneasy expectation.

"Damn you, Quintus," the Greek snapped angrily.

"What did I do?" the Roman reacted surprised.

"Did you have to mention bandits? I was content until you ruined it," he lamented.

"Were you happier with false secutity?" Quintus queried quite intrigued.

Stephanos glared at the barbarian's audacity refusing to be humored.

"Do not be afraid," Yeshua said with a soothing calmness in his voice. "We will be alright."

They did not know why, but his calm voice reassured them, making them feel secure. Years later they remembered this moment as the first instance they realized he had a special gift when facing danger.

Everywhere they looked they stared into the black night, but now they relaxed enjoying the sounds: crickets, frogs, and cicadas singing somewhere far in the meadows, the crackling of burning wood sending a shower of sparks to the stars. The sights and sounds inspired them to lofty thoughts.

Stephanos said enthusiastically, "As I walked behind you all day, I thought a lot about the Messiah..."

"What did you conclude?" Yeshua was impatiently curious.

Germanicus, ever cognizant of responsibilities stood up to clean the pots and pans, careful not to miss a word. Yeshua started to get up when Quintus motioned him to relax. "You did enough for one day. I'll help him."

"You said the Messiah may be a prophet ..." the Greek continued.

"...Or a gifted teacher," Yeshua added.

"... Greece had a gifted philosopher about four centuries past, during the reign of Alexander." When he noticed their eyes riveted on him, he proceded with the story, "His name was Diogenes of Corinth. He was a wandering teacher, notable for his simplicity of life, who carried a staff on his shoulder, at the end of which was tied a small bag of food."

"Why the food?" Quintus glanced at him as he scrubbed a pot.

"To assert his independence from everybody. He stood in the agoras of the cities teaching everyone about friendship and non-competition. Above all he taught absolute independence of the individual to the point of subverting authority."

"If he lived today, Rome would try him for treason," the Roman said assertively.

"It was passive subversion," the Greek defended the philosopher. "He taught people to remain independent, and not accept domination. He never espoused rebellion."

"Rome makes no distinction," Quintus sighed laconically. "They destroy any form of individualism."

Stephanos smirked superiorly, "Greeks encourage intellect, and development of ideas."

"Alas, materialism is Rome's loftiest god," Quintus lamented. "We only value comfort, conformity and unquestioned patriotism from all colonists."

Stephanos shook hid head and returned to the story, "There is a story about Diogenes meeting young Alexander as he was about to go on his journey to conquer the world. Alexander came upon the philosopher who was sitting, resting against a tree. The great warrior, sitting astride his stallion, looked down on him and announced proudly, 'I am Alexander of Macedonia, leader of an invincible army. On the morrow I go forth to conquer the world.'

"Diogenes listened unimpressed. Alexander leaned forward, 'I can bring you anything you desire. Speak! Ask for anything in the world…and I shall bring it to you.'

"The philosopher looked up at the great general and replied placidly, 'Just now move aside a bit, for you are blocking the sun.'"

The young men broke out into wild laughter enjoying the story, no one more than Germanicus.

"Your slave is enjoying the simple man's revenge against the ruler," the Roman quipped.

At length Stephanos queried them, "Who is the ruler: the man who holds power but craves more? Or, he who has nothing and feels he has everything?" Then he turned to Yeshua, "Is the Messiah going to liberate Israel? If he hopes to do that he'll have to subvert the Romans more actively than Diogenes."

Yeshua contemplated the question for a long time, "Diogenes taught centuries ago, yet, today his followers are no bigger than a few dozen… Why? Because he taught them to remain individualists: islands unto themselves. When people are divided, there is no strength. Their strength multiplies when they are unified for a common goal. I propose to encourage them to unify in the love of Yahweh, and one another."

Quintus guffawed at the tought that a philosopher could beat a general, let alone the mighty Roman army.

Germanicus pointed the obvious, "Together we will stand. How true."

Only Stephanos noticed when Yeshua spoke, he said he would lead the people. Was that an inadvertent slip? He was about to ask when they heard a "crack" in the woods and froze, their attention turning to the invisible forest.

"What was that?" the Greek blurted out nervously.

"P-s-s-t! Someone is in the forest," Quintus whispered, reaching for his sword, which he forgot he had thrown away. He took the staff and stood up to investigate.

"Don't venture there," the Israeli advised. "It's probably a deer."

The Roman stopped. He was no coward, but also not a fool. He was not able to distinguish anything in the black forest, and remembered his first lesson in basic training: separating from your platoon is tantamount to throwing your life away.

Stephanos returned to the topic, addressing the Israeli, "The concept of a Messiah sermonizing about love will not feed hungry stomachs, or pay their taxes. Do you remember the people's demands in the synagogue? The Messiah must be a fighter! They want to beat the Roman legions."

"If this Messiah tries to organize them, Rome will charge him with subversion," Quintus informed them matter of factly. "The punishment for that is – Crucifixion."

"The Messiah will be peacefully spreading the word," the Israeli commented.

"What word?" Germanicus wondered.

"Love!" Yeshua responded.

The others wondered why a leader would confront the strongest nation on earth with something as innocuous as love. As a weapon, it surely was blunt.

Yeshua wanted to change the topic, and reminded them about the diary, "Shall we scribe today's adventures on papyrus?"

"I cannot imagine surviving today's savage battle, without earning eternal fame in the annals of a diary," the Greek agreed wholeheartedly.

"How do you propose to do it?" Quintus smirked. "You can't hold a stylus."

"I'll dictate and master Yeshua will scribe it."

"Then give me the papyrus first," the Roman demanded. "I refuse to suffer while you dictate a book of fiction." True to his word he scribed the shortest entry:

"Walking south along the upper slopes, we dueled with bandits. I was shocked to learn a shepherd's staff to be superior to our sword. I'll investigate and report to my superiors."

Stephanos filled two pages with the most melodramatic duel: a collection of the most outrageous flowery adjectives and adverbs, punctuated with an assortement of superlatives. As he dictated, the Roman and the slave almost burst trying to contain their laughter.

Yeshua's report as always was a balance of thrift with words, and precise description.

Yeshua whispered to Germanicus, "Do you wish to add to the diary? You have the right…" The slave smiled, but shook his head. "Do you want to practice writing 'Anna'?"

"I cleared an area here and have written it many times," he responded, showing the evidence. After a moment's silence he confessed, "Actually, there is one word I would like to learn…"

"What word: Liberty? Freedom?"

"MESSIAH."

• • •

It was the middle of the night and the full moon was up. The campfire was almost out. Except for the odd cricket and some noises from a frog, it was silent. The young men were long asleep. There was not a movement anywhere…but low in the thick underbrush among the trees, thirty paces from their camp, a pair of eyes peered into the dark surroundings. The eyes blinked once. Then twice. They swept the campsite, looked to the north, then south. There was a whisper, "They're asleep," and the foliage parted as another pair of eyes appeared, then a third, and a fourth. Looking carefully, a dark brown smudge could be distinguished around the eyes but nothing else. They studied the area, glanced at one another and nodded. They invaded into the moonlight noiselessly, the eyes darting nervously. They were the bandits the young men had battled earlier that day.

They slid out of the forest almost imperceptibly, crawling on their bellies like lizards, silently, no further than a palm's length at a time. Their strength was the element of surprise. They seemed to float towards the camp, like death hovering over the body biding its time.

Suddenly a dry twig cracked. They froze. The tiny noise reverberated like an explosion in the silent night. Their eyes darted searching for the smallest movement, their ears waiting for the sound of footsteps of a guard. Even the frog and the crickets stopped. They waited as still as statues, their muscles tense, aching, ready to spring on whoever might appear. But, no one showed up. They breathed easier and returned to sliding and slithering, gaining distance towards the tent. Another twig broke, and again they froze. The leader glared back at the culprit over his shoulder and swung his foot kicking the unfortunate fool. They listened a long time without hearing anyone. The bandits realized their victims were more vulnerable than expected, and their lips stretched in a faint smile.

After an interminable time they reached the back of the tent. The leader motioned for them to split, and they continued to crawl, two to the left and two to the right side. They checked carefully before proceeding around the corner. Before turning to the door the leader pulled the scepter dagger from this belt, showed it to his partners and put the blade between his teeth. They copied him. They peeked around the corner and saw a bundle rolled up in the blanket; the guard deeply asleep. At the opposite corner of the tent their cohorts appeared. The leader motioned to one to take care of the guard. They were within reach of the door; a couple of paces and revenge was theirs.

The leader got up on his knees reaching for the door. The others reached for the guard. They clutched the daggers firmly in their fists.

Suddenly the leader froze. He felt something cold touch the side of his temple and knew it could be only one thing - a staff. At the same instant the others were tapped on the temples and froze.

"Don't move," Quintus ordered from behind. "Throw the daggers away from you, and fall on your bellies, slowly." The brigands were slow to react, so he barked savagely, "MOVE!" Daggers flew away as they scurried to fall on their faces. "YOU!" Quintus poked the leader's back, crawl back here, slowly. NOW!" The bandit hurried to the spot. "Bring your arms up behind your back… high… up here," he kicked his arms up to the waist. Quintus quickly tied the arms up with a twine, then tied his feet to his wrists.

The Roman stood guard while Germanicus tied up the other bandits. Then the young men carried them to the fire, sitting them on their knees with their backs to one another, and tying their arms together. Finally they ran a twine between their arms and tied them to the camel which stood over them.

Quintus informed them dispassionately, "A camel is a very jittery animal. If frightened, it'll tear your arms out from the sockets. So, I suggest you remain very quiet. Oh, one more thing: if you see intruders, I strongly advise you to awaken us, before the camel gets spooked… Sleep well!"

They returned to their cots among the rocks.

. . .

Next morning the sky was clear and the sun shone brightly. It promised to be a scorching day. Nevertheless the young men slept late into the morning. The combination of lying awake uneasy, worrying about their safety and the brigands' invasion, made for a long restless night, sleeping in fits and starts. They awoke with puffy eyes, tired and in foul moods.

Stephanos lamented as he yawned, "Let's eat quickly and leave this lawless jungle to the pirates and jackals. Germanicus, get the tent down."

The slave obeyed immediately.

Yeshua stoked the fire intending to prepare a big breakfast. "What are we going to do with the brigands?" he asked the Roman.

Quintus pulled out his dagger and sauntered towards them, "I am going to get some answers, before throwing them over the cliffs."

"Hear them out first," the Israeli grabbed his arm and pleaded.

The Roman pulled away sneering, and walked around the bandits, slapping the blade against the palm of his hand, enjoying the terrified look on their faces.

The leader pleaded, "Do what you wish with me. I don't ask for pity. But, I beg you, let my son go. He had no part in this."

Quintus stopped, "Which is your son?"

The man motioned his head to a youth behind him. The Roman walked around and was surprised as he stared at a young man about his own age. When the youth looked up there were tears streaming down his face.

"How old are you?" Quintus asked.

"Eighteen," he muttered.

Quintus stopped playing with the dagger and studied him. The boy's eyes dropped to the ground. He had a youthful face, with friendly features and kind eyes. The Roman's instincts told him they could easily become friends, rather than the tough Romans he endured, all of them rough army types. But, his experiences as a professional soldier hardened him against sympathy. "Eighteen," he repeated tensely with a tone of sarcasm, "old enough to accept punishment for your deeds..." He walked back to the leader, "Your son chose a life of banditry and murder. Why should I show him mercy?"

"He is not a bandit, or a killer. None of us are. We were forced into this style of life," the leader argued passionately. "We are fugitives... political fugitives."

"From whom are you running?"

"The Romans, and the Herodians," he replied.

"Liar!" Quintus barked. "I am a Roman soldier, and we don't cause anyone to become a fugitive. What's your crime?"

"None," the leader's face hardened. "You speak of Roman law as if it applied to us. Your law protects Roman citizens...in Rome! In this God forsaken place, the centurion's foul mood is the law!" He glared at the young soldier who was stung by the accusations, unable to respond. "We are political fugitives. Our crime is that we joined a political group...God fearing...asking for a free voice..."

Quintus interrupted gruffly, "What do you call yourselves?"

"ZEALOTS!" the leader exclaimed proudly.

Yeshua who was listening while he cooked, almost dropped the pot. He gave Germanicus the pot, and marched towards the group. Stephanos saw his sudden interest and followed him at a distance.

"Zealots!" Quintus chewed the word scowling. "You call yourselves God fearing? Freedom fighters? You are outlaws against your government and the empire. You are terrorists!"

Yeshua interjected walking forward, "Stop this. What do you know about the Zealots? Did you ever meet one? Or speak with one?"

"My superiors told me all I need to know. They conspire to overturn the lawful government," Quintus countered. "I will turn them over to the centurion..."

"You will not!" the young scholar argued. "I value your opinion, but you are wrong. They want a voice, and democracy."

"Master Yeshua, are you a Zealot?" Quintus demanded accusingly.

The bandits' leader was surprised by the turn of events, and followed the exchange with renewed interest.

Yeshua did not answer, pressing his argument, "These are desperate tradesmen, and farmers, trying to survive...But, the taxes, and the tyranny..."

"We have never killed anyone," the leader defended his men.

"I'll prove what you really are," Quintus, shaking with anger, rushed to the rocks and returned with a golden scepter-dagger in the shape of a saber. "Is this not yours?"

"I was forced to take it..." the Zealot stuttered.

"These saber daggers are used by the siccarri to murder opponents," the Roman held the weapon next to the leader's face.

"I did not want it…!"

"You were forced?" Quintus sneered sarcastically. "Why did you not refuse it?"

"I would be killed on the spot!" the leader exclaimed.

The Roman glared at him condescendingly. Yeshua remembered his experience, and sympathyzed, "I believe you." He took the weapon from Quintus and started to cut the prisoners loose. "How did the Romans learn about your cell?"

"I think we have a traitor."

"Come have breakfast with us," Yeshua suggested. "Then we'll talk."

"They're criminals guilty of treason," Quintus argued. "If you harbor them you will be charged."

Stephanos and the slave exchanged glances, ready for trouble.

Yeshua snapped, "For heaven's sake master Quintus, for once forget you're a Roman and a soldier. Walk a mile in their sandals, and you'll begin to understand their desperation!"

"You did not answer my question: Are you a Zealot?" The Roman demanded, his voice getting harsher.

Stephanos warned the slave in a whisper, "Keep your weapon ready. We dare not trust them."

After freeing them Yeshua joined them for breakfast. It was obvious the fugitives had not eaten for awhile, for they devoured everything given without taking time to chew. The young scholar studied them closely and looking at their dark, leathery skin and big calloused hands, surmised they were farmers. After the meal he introduced his group.

The Zealot in turn introduced his members, "I am Ahira from the town of Noor, to the south. This is my son Asher. My neighbor, Mordacai, and a farmer down our valley Hophnl."

All nodded except Quintus who sat apart by himself. He listened carefully hoping to learn more about the terrorists and their plans.

Ahira spoke loudly for the Roman to hear, glancing his way from time to time, "Almost every man in our village and the countryside joined the Zealots. We're desperate for a voice in the government. We have no quarrel with the Romans. Our fight is with the tax collector who is pushing us into destitution. Who can afford them? Or Herod's palaces and his army? Or the Temple tax? That is what we hoped to change…"

Yeshua looked at the Roman who did not change his surly expression.

"Did you abandon your farms?" Yeshua asked them and they nodded. "Who is farming them?"

"Our wives...our sons..." Mordacai sniggered. "But they won't last long..."

"Soon the tax collector will confiscate my land...tax arrears," Ahira concurred, laughing bitterly, shaking his head, "He always coveted it."

Hophnl who listened in silence, spoke directly to Quintus, "We don't want a rebellion. We want to be free to speak without fear...This is an economic struggle, not a war with Rome."

The Roman stood up and walked away without answering. They realized it was useless to argue.

"Where are you heading?" Ahira asked Yeshua.

"In search of the anointed one: the Messiah."

"Israel can use his help in these difficult times," the Zealot nodded.

"A couple of months past, my cousin said a holy man came to his town," Hophnl informed them.

"What's the name of the town? Where is it?" Stephanos queried.

"Beth-Hazor, a half day's journey north of Laish," Hophnl answered. Then he took a twig and drew in the dust. "This is the path going south. In one day you will see a mountain directly ahead far on the horizon. Shortly after, you will come to a fork in the road. There you will find an ancient well. You cannot miss it. Take the road to the left. You will pass two hamlets and the third will be Beth-Hazor."

"Thank you for the information" the young Israeli stood up, going to the tent. "We will give you some supplies. I'm sure it will help..."

"You have been too kind already," Ahira objected.

Yeshua was already digging in the boxes with the slave's help, taking out some staples, "We cannot let you starve. Desperation creates lawlessness."

"What were they yesterday: a welcoming committee?" Quintus scoffed sarcastically from a distance.

The fugitives were moved when they saw how much he gave them. They embraced their new friends, saying good bye to the Roman who did not respond, and returned to the forest. Yeshua's group loaded up the rest, and left.

Quintus, standing off to the side muttered between his teeth, "Master Yeshua, the friend of my enemy is not...You will pay for this."

Stephanos overheard him, and turned to the slave, "I had a premonition the Barbarian would cause trouble. Let's not take our eyes off him."

As the young men disappeared over the hill, two Roman soldiers, leading a horse loaded with supplies came upon the camp.

CHAPTER X - MESSIAH - HONI

It was mid-morning when the young men resumed the journey, in the same order: Quintus leading, Stephanos in the rear the other two in the middle. The Roman hardly spoke, marching more rigidly, staring ahead as if cast in granite. Normally Yeshua would leave him alone until he calmed down, but in the lawless region it was foolhardy to travel separated. Quintus' mutinous behavior meant he was not keeping a proper look-out endangering the group's safety. Yeshua decided to have a talk with the sulking guard.

He yanked at the donkey's rein, speeding up when he heard a noise in the forest. He slowed down staying back with Germanicus, looking ahead, hoping to catch a movement in his peripheral vision. After a long time he yelled at the Greek, "Master Stephanos, pick up the pace," then ahead, "Master Quintus, slow down."

There was no further noise so he decided it was probably an animal, when a flock of birds squawked and fled from the trees. Obviously something had disturbed them. Were they being stalked? As if to answer him, he saw a blur in the corner of his eye, rushing in the forest. Moments later another blur rushed by. He recognized two men.

Germanicus, still deeply troubled, caught up to him, "Something has bothered me: why did choose to camp besides those rocks…Did you know they would come?"

Yeshua nodded, "I sensed it."

"I don't understand…"

"By the spring we were likely to be attacked by brigands, and I did not want that. By the time we arrived at the rocks, I suspected we were being followed, so I set a trap."

"You knew? How? When did you find out?"

"When they threw their weapons, their action told me their intention."

"I watched them but did not hear anything," the slave exclaimed stupefied.

"Lips can lie, but body language never. Their eyes and actions betrayed them."

"Where did you learn this?"

"As a shepherd, I tended the most timid animals hunted by the most astute predators. I learned a beast's intentions: ferocious beasts, or coy thieves." He listened, heard faint rustling of leaves, saw the blurs again and continued, "When I beat a predator, it communicated its intentions while leaving. If it accepted defeat, it shuffled away, its tail between its legs. However, if it planned to return, it growled, moved a few paces, stole glances, and studied me and the flock, planning its next ambush. I moved the flock to a safe area where I could dictate the terms of the next fight."

"Then you killed it!" the slave exclaimed exuberantly.

"I never killed an animal in anger. Hunting for food was its natural instinct."

"What actions of the bandits gave you warning?"

"When the FUGITIVES," he corrected his friend, "gave up their staffs, they did not drop them. They threw them. When I let them keep the daggers, they glanced at one another as if to say: 'Our chance for revenge.' "

"Yet you let them keep the daggers?"

"I hoped they would reconsider later. But, they were desperate. Later that afternoon I sensed they were stalking us."

"You sensed it? In the name of thunder, how can you sense that?"

"In the heat of the day all beasts rest: predators and the prey. I heard birds rushing and animals running and snapping twigs. I knew we had intruders."

"That's why you chose to camp by the boulders…" the slave conceded. "I've hunted all my life. Why did I not see it?"

"Who taught you to hunt?"

"My father, naturally."

"I had the best teachers: animals. They hunt to eat, and run to survive. They're efficient, simple and truthful. No surprises."

Germanicus was perplexed. This Israeli was more than human: he had an extra sense of perception. He seemed to have extra sight and hearing, and feel his environment through every pore. Yet, he did not recognize the enemy under his very eyes: the Roman.

The slave knew Quintus would take revenge against their leader. Should he warn him, he wondered? After considering it he decided against it. People accepted lies from freemen over the naked truth from a slave. He decided to catch the Roman in a compromising plot, and unmask him.

Instead, he wanted to clear something which bothered him, "When I lay in the rocks last night, I did much thinking." He glanced at his companion who merely nodded with a faint smile. "Before the bandi...I mean, fugitives came, I made a pact with your God: if bandits came, and He helped us capture them, I promised to worship Him..."

"He delivered everything you asked for," Yeshua chuckled, then added seriously, "But you are not satisfied?"

"I was at first. Not anymore...and I don't understand why..."

"You wanted proof...magic...But, you're too wise to settle for something that superficial. You want something permanent."

Germanicus deliberated before responding, "I concluded that your God is no different from mine. He may have created everything and be more powerful, but the end result is the same. I became a slave praying to my gods and will remain a slave worshipping Yahweh. Where is the difference?"

"Don't you mean: where is the advantage?" Yeshua corrected him.

"If there is no advantage, why should I choose Him?" he argued with an exasperated voice.

"That you must answer for yourself," Yeshua replied judicially. "Yesterday you knew the answer – FAITH! What changed your mind?"

Germanicus looked over his shoulder to be sure his master could not hear him, "I need someone to help me become free." His quivering voice cried with agony, "Have you ever lost freedom; a hopeless life...because you know you can never have a future?"

"Israelis lost their freedom many generations past," he replied. "Throughout history we have been slaves to many races... We may lose freedom, but never our faith."

"It's not the same," the slave's voice rose as he argued. "You may be destitute... perhaps hungry, but you are not a chattel." After a long pause his voice betrayed tears of desperation, "I want to believe. If only I had a sign...to guide me..."

Yeshua touched his shoulder, his voice filled with sympathy, "Germanicus, I will help you..." when a loud 'crack' in the forest interrupted them.

"Bandits," the slave panicked, and began to tremble, about to call his master.

Yeshua shook his head, "Do not worry. The two men in the forest are our friends: master Ahira and his son. They have been following us, to make certain we are safe."

The slave looked at the Israeli astonished, "You knew it all the time?"

"I sensed it," he replied and left to catch the Roman.

The slave remained behind filled with wonder. Lady Anna begged him to guard him. He did not need guarding. He was totally in tune with his environment; human and animal. What kind of person is this that sees everything without looking, and foretells a person's plans before he acts. His perception seems otherwordly. He does not fear danger and has an eerie calmness, like an aura, which relaxes everyone around him. A simple peasant but Germanicus is certain battalions would follow him anywhere. What impressed him most, and at the same time unnerved him, was the strange radiance emitted from his eyes.

He had no doubts that master Yeshua saw the Creator. In the slave's mind this young leader was an integral part of the eternal celestial family. What intrigued him was, where did he fit in that heavenly scheme?

Yeshua caught up to the Roman who immediately stiffened up, standing more erect, arching his back stiffer than a board. His nostrils flared when he breathed, and his lips tightened into a thin line. Yeshua imagined that was how his friend marched into battle: a caricature, which struck him as absurd and comical. He copied his manners, marching just as stiff if not stiffer. Quintus maintained the eerie appearance for some time, but when he glanced at the pantomime, he broke down in laughter. "You look like a clown," the Roman guffawed.

"A mirror copy of you. If someone carved a statue of you marching, it would crumble to dust," the Israeli deadpanned.

Quintus broke out into uncontrollable laughter, then quickly controlled himself, "I refuse to be humored."

"You're too late. The rules are clear; if you smile you break the spell."

The Roman reverted to a stern business tone, "Master Yeshua I am warning you: harboring criminals can get you charged and arrested."

"They were not criminals. They were not charged, let alone tried or convicted," Yeshua defended his actions. "Moreover Zealots are political…"

"My superiors say they are criminals," he countered. "And they don't lie to me."

"Did I ever lie to you?" Yeshua protested.

The soldier was caught in a dilemma and knew it. Unable to respond he continued marching, only his eyelids blinking nervously hinting at his confusion. Yeshua knew he pushed their friendship into a corner from which Quintus could not escape, but the Israeli decided to keep the pressure on without compromising. "A soldier hoping for promotion must inform himself about the organization he is willing to destroy."

"My superiors make the decision. I only follow orders. Otherwise we won't have a rule of law," the Roman retorted.

"It is easier to hide behind someone else's decision," Yeshua responded sardonically. "It eases the conscience." Then he countered with passion, "Whose rule of law are you referring to; Rome's? You once said Rome has no friends, only interests. Their interest is to keep us under their boot. Have you ever lost your freedom?"

Quintus barked, "Do you think you are the only one to suffer? I have had untold hardship, my friend..."

"A Roman? You're the rulers..."

"Yes, a Roman born here. I'm shunned by Israeli's as a foreigner, and I'm an outsider in Rome because I'm from here. I live in limbo: a ship without a port..."

Yeshua was surprised to hear it but was not in a sympathetic mood to compromise, "It's not the same. You have freedom and protection from Roman law."

They marched side by side in silence, controlling their emotions for they knew they were pushing their friendship to the limit. One unfortunate accusation would push it over the brink beyond repair.

Yeshua remembered what master Benjoseph had told him to ask his friend, and demanded, "I need to know this: if your superior ordered, would you arrest me?"

Quintus was shocked by the question and the directness of the query. His eyes darted from his friend to the ground, trying to avoid the test, finally fixing his eyes directly ahead. He did not have to answer, for Yeshua knew.

They were leaving the Galilean forest, and began to descend to smaller, gentler hills with less growth. When they left the thick forest, the young Israeli turned back and waved to some people back in the trees.

The Roman turned and looked perplexed, "Are they the...?"

"Yes, master Ahira and his son Asher: the Zealots. They escorted us to safety."

Quintus reached for his sword instinctively, then remembered his staff, and bit his lower lip in frustration.

"Don't be too harsh on yourself," Yeshua teased him. "The fugitives guarded us. Wave and show gratitude."

The Roman glared at the Israeli, but relented, and raised his arm.

"We're out of the worst part. Our problem now will be the arid terrain and deserts," Yeshua commented as he turned back to the others.

They found a worn out ancient path, deeply rutted from centuries of use, and continued south, descending the hills. The new terrain had less trees, and these were smaller and twisted, with gnarled branches, proof of the battles they fought to survive the dry months. The topography was also different: sparse grass, mostly sand and rocks. Within a day they expected to reach the border of Judea. The air was hotter and drier, a parching heat from the brilliant sun. The humid air of the lazy rolling hills of the north, the dense green forest, the meadows with flowers and streams were becoming erased from memory. Their concern was to find a water hole or a patch of grass for the night.

Germanicus, who had grown up in the cool forested area of northern Europe, had never seen so many desolate arid regions as in this tiny nation. He wondered why the Romans could not bear to let the poor Israelis own these few acres of weeds and snakes.

By and by they came upon a small rise from which they could see clearly to the south and identify mount Gilboa: rising majestic from the dark hues of the far horizon. They continued to where the road forked, remembering Zebedee's instructions to turn left. Within a few hundred paces they located the ancient well. Once protected by a high cement wall, now broken off, so that it seemed like a blistered water hole. A few steps away a brave little clump of violets drooped with thirst.

They tested the well as before and finding it safe, quenched their thirst, and gave some to the animals. After re-supplying their jugs, they carried on.

By mid afternoon they entered a secluded valley with sparse growth. Yet in this semi-desert was a wealthy village with large detached houses protected by high fences. The narrow streets were deserted. They entered the village and listened for voices, but the place seemed deserted.

They entered a yard, came to the door and knocked. No one answered. They knocked again. When they were about to give up, there was a creaking sound, as the door opened up a crack. An old man and a woman squinted, peering from the black room.

"Shalom," the young man bowed, "We are travelers, in search of news about a legendary holy man...the Messiah?"

The old faces seemed sculpted with a permanent frown. Yeshua shifted from one foot to the other wondering if they heard him.

"We heard you! We are Sadduccees!" he snapped giving a judgment instead of an answer. "We acknowledge Lord Adonai, but abhor superstition!" He tried to close the door but the young man stopped him. At length he added with great pain, "There is a village down that road. They are into sorcery, and frauds...such as the Messiah!"

The door creaked and closed the dark room like the cover of a tomb.

The young men walked in silence for a long time unable to dislodge the mean faces from their minds. Yeshua tried to rationalize their behaviour, but could not reconcile the scriptures with the inhuman behaviour.

Stepahanos was also deeply affected, "So those are Sadduccees?"

Yeshua nodded, "They apply the scripture literally: mean spirited. The minutest deviation from their interpretation will get you stoned."

"Most unfriendly," Quintus added.

"Theirs is a mean God," the Greek concurred.

After passing a couple of hills, they entered another parched, dusty valley where only the sturdiest clumps of grass grew. They were close to the border of Judea. In the distance they saw a small village composed of a dozen mud huts with thatched roofs, in a sad state of repairs and not a fence in sight. They entered a narrow crooked road where young boys were enjoying a ball game and girls skipping rope. As they came, the children interrupted play and followed them at a distance. They came across a couple of young ladies carrying jugs of water on their heads.

"Shalom," Yeshua greeted them.

"Shalom," the darker one smiled. "You are strangers visiting our village?"

"Passing through," the Israeli responded. "We were told that a special person may be visiting these villages...the holy one they call the Messiah?"

The ladies looked at one another and the dark one nodded, "There was talk about such a person...coming to cure the sick..." But she shook her head embarrassed, "I'm sorry I cannot remember when that was..."

The lighter skinned lady interjected, "The saw sharpener will know."

"Of course," the darker maiden broke in with enthusiasm. "He is a traveller, and talks to everybody. He knows everybody and everything about everybody." She turned to the children addressing the biggest boy, "Isa, take these gentlemen to the saw sharpener." The boy frowned, so she raised her voice, "I MEAN NOW!"

The boy snapped to attention and waved for them to follow.

The saw sharpener was a mine of information, directing them to a village to the south. They thanked him, and pressed on to arrive there in daylight.

As they passed the same ladies, the darker asked, "Was he helpful?"

"Indeed. The holy man is about to arrive in the village of Laish, south of here."

"That's just over that hill to the left, in the next valley," the darker lady pointed out. "You will be able to camp by the stream…it's been dry since the drought. Good luck."

"Thank you and good bye," Yeshua waved, and they continued.

. . .

As the young travellers disappeared over the hills, two Roman soldiers entered the village from the north, the trackers leading a horse. They marched directly to the two ladies with water jugs on their heads. As they approached, the older soldier removed his helmet, ran his fingers through his thick black mane, smiling expansively, "Good afternoon lovely maidens. We are looking for four young lads, leading a camel and a donkey. Perhaps you may have seen them?"

The ladies looked at each other, and back again. Their experiences with Romans taught them one thing: be extra cautious. The darker lady smiled innocently, "Are you friends of theirs?"

The old man chirped effusively, "Yes, you could say that."

The lady continued with a friendly teasing mask, thinking, I don't believe a word of it, but saying, "As a matter of fact we did see them. They wanted to find the Messiah, and we helped them." At the mention of the name the soldiers' eyes opened wide. "We directed them along that path, to the west." She pointed to the right. To her dismay the old man showed a shiny coin as he smiled meaningfully.

"How about it? Some fun: just you and me? It's pure silver," he grinned.

She continued smiling, "Don't forget, your friends are getting away…"

"C'mon, let's go," the young man interrupted. "We've no time for that."

The old warrior glared at the companion who started to leave, put the coin away, bowed gracefully and followed.

As soon as they were out of earshot, the darker lady spat on the ground, "I'd rather sleep with a pig."

The lighter girl cautioned her, "You can't stay here. When they return…"

The darker lady turned to her son, "Isa let's go and pack. We'll go to your grandparents' for a few weeks."

· · ·

The young men walked to the far end of the valley and set up camp at the outskirts of the village, on the bank of the dry stream.

Stephanos' arm was still in a sling so all he could do was search for wood. Germanicus set up the tent while Yeshua started preparing the food. Quintus, eager to get on with the practice of jousting, was trying the tricky maneuvers he saw the Israeli do. Every time he tried it, the staff either dropped or rotated out of control striking him in the face. Yeshua knew the Roman's problems: he was impatient for revenge. When the slave finished the tent Yeshua called him, "Take the staff and practice defensive moves with Quintus," he suggested. "I want to see how well you remember it."

The slave took his staff and walked to the Roman who objected, "I want to duel the master." He turned to the Israeli, "I'll show you what I think of Zealot sympathizers!"

Yeshua replied while starting the fire, "I only promised to teach you defence."

"Save the smug words and take the weapon. If you refuse I'll give you a beating," he threatened marching towards him. The slave stepped between them.

"Get out of my way before I give you a trashing," he barked. The slave did not move, and as the Roman tried to side step, he impeded him.

Yeshua knew the Roman would not quit, "Germanicus step aside. If he seeks a duel, he shall have it," the Israeli came forward. "If you persist dueling in anger, I suggest you return to the sword. A staff is an art for the brain, not braun."

"Save your air of superiority for I intend to crush your bones," the Roman sneered attacking like a wild bull.

He rushed forward demonically, swinging, slashing, turning, twisting, jabbing and stabbing like a man possessed. His strikes were powerful and had he made contact, the Israeli would have suffered many broken limbs. Unfortunately for the Roman his attacks were defended, and the strikes glanced off Yeshua's staff harmlessly. The Israeli was content to back off, defending, ducking and jumping to avoid the wild staff which ripped through the air. All the while he studied his opponent carefully, anticipating his next move. At one point they stood face to face, the staffs between them. The Roman's face twisted with anger, his nostrils flaring as he breathed heavily. He glared at the Israeli who teased him with a grin and a wink. Quintus lost total control, growled savagely and pushed him away, then attacked with renewed vigor.

Yeshua could see that the young soldier would make an excellent jouster, if properly trained and disciplined. Alas, to an experienced jouster he was an out of control tornado. Yeshua watched him spend its fury like a tempest in a pond. Soon the fury was spent, and Quintus started to labor, huff and puff, swinging without authority. At the last he stood, stooped, his knees trembling as he heaved for breath, staring at the Israeli.

"You beat yourself, soldier," Yeshua chuckled. "You have no energy left to defend yourself."

"Shut up...and...fight..." he was not able to raise his staff.

Yeshua touched one end of his staff on the Roman's forehead, pressed it lightly, causing him to topple on his back, raising a cloud of dust. He stood above him and lectured, "I warned you yesterday: attack in anger, and you sign your death warrant." Leaving he said, "You're welcome!"

"For what?" Quintus gasped, sitting up.

"Saving your life..."

The Roman accepted his defeat in silence, if not with grace. After he recovered, he joined them, sitting by the fire, subdued and quiet.

Yeshua continued cooking with the slave. Stephanos left for the village to learn about the anticipated holy man. When he returned, the meal was about to be served.

The Greek announced with enthusiasm as he entered camp, "My friends, I have excellent news. By all accounts we will be in for a rare treat: a holy man, HONI, the circle man, will be coming to save the entire region...with a supernatural miracle -RAIN."

Yeshua dished out stew, as Germanicus gave each a slice of rye bread. "I thought you did not believe in miracles," the Israeli remarked. "Why the sudden enthusiasm?"

The Greek took his plate, still beaming with confidence, "I did not say I did not believe. I said I never saw one. Why the enthusiasm? All my adult life I travelled searching for the person who could help mankind. Everywhere I went, I heard the same name: the Messiah! Now in this dusty, flea bitten village…we are on the eve of witnessing a living prophet…"

Quintus interrupted from a distance, "What makes you so positive he'll be the Messiah?"

"Before I finished my questions they said, `master Honi, the Messiah,` " he responded with passion. "There was no doubt…"

"How is he going to save the region?" Yeshua queried.

"Look around you: dry as a bone. They have had no rain for over three years. Many families moved away, and the few left are hanging on by a thread…"

"That's true, I have not seen a cloud for days," the Roman concurred.

"Tinder dry," the slave nodded agreement.

"Honi, the circle man, will bring rain: HERE!" Stephanos pointed to the ground. "If he succeeds, that will be an undeniable miracle."

The group looked up and searched the skies. The Roman pointed to the obvious, "Not a cloud…If he makes it rain I'll… I'll…"

"Carry me piggy-back through the town square?" Stephanos teased.

"You're on," the Roman agreed impulsively.

"Everybody said master Honi performed astonishing feats," the Greek concluded confidently. "The enthusiasm was contagious."

Yeshua swallowed his food and inquired innocently, "Did you ask if they saw him perform the miracles described?"

"I did not think of it," the Greek's face froze as he tried to extricate himself.

"That's how it is with superstition," Quintus laughed sardonically. "The further the story travels, the more fantastic superlatives describe the simple event."

The Greek's exuberance waned and he began to wonder about his oversight. Germanicus was also deflated as he was hoping this holy man could be his deliverer.

Yeshua tried to revive the enthusiasm, "It's natural to be carried away with everyone's exuberance…and they may be correct: master Honi may perform the supernatural." They agreed that they should not judge him prematurely. Yeshua posed another question, "What quality must he possess to be the acknowledged Messiah?"

Stephanos' enthusiasm returned and he was the first with an opinion, "He will be totally different from Diogenes...HONI will communicate with nature."

"How does a man communicate with a cloud?" Quintus oozed cynicism. "To make it rain, he must communicate with a power greater than clouds..."

"With the essence of the universe," Yeshua volunteered with a tone of wonderment. "He'll communicate with the force that controls the universe."

"He'll communicate with spirits and angels?" Stephanos' enthusiasm was overwhelming. "His powers will be truly supernatural." After considering it, he added with awe, "Don't you see what that means? Honi may be the most powerful man on earth, able to defeat any legion...or nation. "

Quintus laughed slapping his knee, "You mean he will cause it to shower on the Roman legion? How will that beat them?"

"No, you moron," the Greek scolded him impatiently, "If he controls the weather, he controls everything. If he brings rain, is he capable of creating tornadoes? Hurricanes? Perhaps he controls more than weather... perhaps all of nature. Can he cause Vesuvius to erupt? Cause earthquakes? If so, Honi, the Messiah, will be invincible!"

"If he is that powerful, Rome will want him in their service," Quintus muttered with anxiety. "I will have to capture and deliver him to the emperor."

The Greek's mouth unhinged as he jumped up pointing at him, "You threatened that before. You are a spy. Don't try to deny it!"

The Roman leaped at the Greek, at the same time reaching for the absent sword, "Withdraw that, or I'll skew...skew..." but not finding it, he pulled out his dagger, "before I cut out your tongue."

Germanicus grabbed his staff and forced his way between them, ready to defend his master. Yeshua also jumped in, "Master Stephanos, sit down," the Israeli ordered forcefully leaning forward and pushing him down. He then turned to the slave and motioned him to step aside which he did. Finally he stepped towards the Roman until the dagger touched his chest, "Master Quintus we will not live with your threats. Promise you will not repeat that again, or leave the expedition."

The Roman stood tense, his nostrils flaring, breathing heavily. Yeshua took the dagger and put it back in its sheath.

Quintus stuttered as he prattled, "Why do you not...tell him...quit accusing...not right..." His voice trailed off into a mumbling sound. Seeing the Israeli waiting, he took a big breath and said, subdued, "I ask forgiveness...I won't do...again."

The confrontation destroyed the festive atmosphere and the sun set on a somber camp. Yeshua tried to revive the happy mood asking Germanics' opinion abut the Messiah, but the slave shrugged his shoulders uttering some indistinct reply.

The Israeli persisted, "I'm positive you have an opinion. After all, I expect the Messiah will put the destitute front and centre of his movement..."

"I have no opinion," the slave replied. "I'll have to see him."

"You're right," the young scholar replied. "Why guess if in the morrow we may all be proven wrong?"

"Besides, every time we discuss him, it creates arguments."

The truth was the slave had opinions about the holy man. However, as his wishes conflicted with his master's, he feared creating further disturbance.

That night Yeshua lay in his cot, his eyes open, wondering if they would indeed meet the anointed one. He was anxious and nervous about the meeting. They had one quality in common: the special gift to perform miracles. It meant both had a special communion with the Creator. But, would they necessarily possess any bond? Would they like each other? Would they share common problems, or understand each other's heavy responsibility? He envied Honi who knew his destiny and was fulfilling it. Could he help him find his own mission, he wondered?

Unable to get satisfactory answers, he started thinking about Nazareth, and his mind went to lady Sarah. Once again he was filled with questions: Did the traveler Zebedee find Debborah and give her his letter? Did she see Sarah? How did she react to his confession, his desires to spend the rest of his life with her? Did she agree to have a family? What did she make of his promise to confess his identity? But more to the point, did her father forgive her? Did she write him a note? His heart ached because he missed her desperately, and was too far away to help if she needed him. Tired and helpless, he drifted to sleep.

Germanicus bundled himself in a blanket and sat outside, his staff beside him. Privy to the conversation about Honi, his mind imagined many things about the Messiah. He saw mount Vesuvius, presently dormant, when they took him in chains to the slave market in Rome. He thought if Honi could control thunder, erupt volcanoes, and cause earthquakes, he must be a powerful giant many times bigger than any god he knew. He felt secure with such a powerful giant as an ally, to rend asunder the chains of slavery.

He smiled, for tomorrow he would see his superhuman hero. Free! How sweet the sound of the word resonated in his mind. Lady Anna told him to be patient. Now, for the first time he dared to allow himself the luxury of dreaming of a free life in northern Europe – maybe with lady Anna...? He checked himself, afraid to dream too much too soon. But he could not stop enjoying the fact that it was the eve of his meeting the liberator of the oppressed. He slept soundly, filled with hope!

• • •

Although the young men arrived in the village square at sunrise, it was already filled with people from the village and the valleys beyond the hills. They gathered in small groups to discuss Honi's miracles from the past, and what he would do here.

The young men overheard an old rabbi supplicating, "I pray he can cure the cripple. My son had his back crushed. If he could help him, I would die in peace."

Close by a woman lamented, "My poor old mother...It's the lung disease. Will the holy man come to see her...?"

Some brought children in chairs and waited. Others lay in their cots.

All had travelled long distances to see the miracle worker. They all hoped Honi could help solve their problems.

The greatest majority simply wanted rain. It had been three years since anything grew in the region. The farmers seeded every season, then watched the brilliant sun beat the soil, sucking out all vestige of moisture, breaking down the dirt to powder which the wind blew away. The rest became hardened like stone. Birds ate most of the seeds and the rest went with the wind. Every season they repeated the heart-breaking ritual. Some seed germinated and stalks broke through the hard cracks, too sparse to harvest.

Elsewhere grape vines, generally thick and laden with large juicy bunches, now were thin, gnarled, almost bereft of leaves, with sparse bunches of miniature grapes. Even olive trees, the hardiest of all, bore few drupes, most of which dried up before ripening. Truly, the valleys needed heaven's help.

The young men came to a place by the market where an area was roped off with a small platform. Soon an older gentleman, probably the chairman of the village council, pushed his way through the spectators and climbed the platform. He was pleased with the great turn out, and raised his arms for silence. Slowly the noise abated, and they waited for his announcement.

He wasted no time proclaiming proudly, "Friends and neighbors I need not remind you that the drought has decimated our farmers and tradesmen, as the worst calamity in history." The audience nodded somberly and he continued, "I promised to find help and I kept that promise. I brought you a very special person: a holy man, a miracle worker...I searched every city and town of Judea, and everywhere they said, `he brought us the gift of life – RAIN! Enough water to drench our parched fields and replenish our dykes, dams and cisterns; and fill our water wells.` They spoke of him with the adulation reserved for a Messiah!"

While the elder described the superhuman qualities of the man, the spectators' curious eyes wandered over the faces of the multitude, trying to guess his identify. They sought a superman, big and strong, with an aura of holiness. Not finding him they turned back to the elder as he announced, "I give you master Honi, the circle man!"

Their eyes darted in every direction and back to the elder again. Not until he touched the shoulder of a man next to him did they see him - and gasped! Honi was a slight little man, as thin as a dry twig, with long graying hair, unkempt and straying every which way, and a long grey beard. His dark face, like his hands and bare feet were dusty and weather beaten and he wore a dirty cloak which long ago may have been white. Obviously he was used to sleeping in the fields and ditches. Beside him stood a woman about the same age, and in every respect as sun beaten as he. There were murmurs of surprise and shock, mostly whispered under their breaths. They were not impressed.

The elder quickly added almost apologetically, "I admit, I too was not overly impressed, but I was guaranteed that he is the rainmaker of national reputation, and HE-WILL-MAKE-IT-RAIN! He exploded every syllable, as if introducing a champion pugilist who would wrestle with

God Himself for water. Then he almost screamed, "AND THE PRICE IS RIGHT! YOU PAY WHAT YOU CAN AFFORD!"

There was a sigh of relief.

The elder gave Honi an order, "Mister circle man, do your job!"

The people waited for the diminutive creature to say something, but he walked with his staff to the center of the square, and pushed back the spectators. With one motion of the staff he drew a large circle in the dust, handed the staff to the woman, and sat down in the center. The people watched him in silence. After standing for some time, they looked up searching for clouds. Instead the hot sun beat down like an anvil.

They searched around the horizon for a vestige of storm clouds, but everywhere it was a bowl of blue. When they looked down, his eyes were closed, and he rocked back and forth mumbling. They walked around him, outside the circle, studying him from every direction. A few whispered, covering their mouths, "That's no miracle man...Look at him..." Others argued just as emphatically, "He will not leave until it rains: AND-IT-WILL-RAIN!" They poked their index finger as if punctuating an exclamation mark.

The sun climbed and hung high, as it had done for a thousand days, and the villagers began to shuffle away. Some returned to work disappointed. Others returned to their houses where they had nothing to do, for they were farmers, forced to wait for water. Finally everyone left except Honi, the woman who accompanied him, Yeshua and his group.

Yeshua sat on a large rock by the village's gate, watching the holy man with intense interest. At midday the others came to him.

"We are returning to camp," Stephanos announced. "Coming?"

He shook his head, "What do you think?" he motioned his head in Honi's direction.

Quintus was the first to reply, "We were fools last night. This scrawny skeleton couldn't bring a pail of water...He a threat to Rome? Pfft!"

The Greek shrugged his shoulders as he left with the Roman.

"Are you also disappointed?" he asked the slave.

Germanicus stood speechless, looking at the lonely figure, petite and almost fragile, sitting on the dirt road like a common beggar. How could he explain that he too expected someone...someone bigger and stronger, ready to kill for his freedom? Instead, he faced a scarecrow in rags. He could not hide his disappointment, or find the courage to put it in words.

"I understand," the Israeli said. "Go ahead I'll remain a awhile longer..."

The slave followed the others, while the young scholar watched the creature and contemplated. He hoped that if he learned about him, he would find answers about himself. He wondered: Am I like him? Would people who saw me for the first time, react the same: full of skepticism? Will I ever instill confidence? When he remembered his sermons, he shuddered. Like Honi he was destined to fight peoples' doubts and anger, because they had preconceived notions about their heroes. Deviate from peoples' prejudices at your peril, he thought.

Yeshua wondered if, aside from giving rain, could he perform other miracles? Did he communicate with the Creator? As if to answer him he heard a man's voice praying. He looked around but saw no one. He glanced at Honi but his lips did not move. The woman sitting at the side of the road was the only other person present. He concentrated on the holy man, and heard the supplication: "Blessed Lord Adonai, one and only God, Creator of heaven and earth; your humble servant Honi asks for help for the people of these villages and the families in the valleys. For years they have suffered without rain...Lived with drought, suffering... But they need Your help, and deserve a better life. Hear my prayers and help Your forgotten children, and bless them. Lord Adonai, hear my pleas and divert the clouds to rain over me, and the dusty fields of these forsaken valleys and bring them a smile and hope. Blessed be Your name..."

Yeshua was astonished to hear Honi's mental prayers, and became inspired to join with a mental prayer, "Dear heavenly Abba, hear the supplications of master Honi. Give these destitute farmers and villagers the gift of life with an abundance of water..."

Suddenly the young man's prayer was interrupted, "Who are you that can hear my communion with God?"

Yeshua saw Honi staring at him aghast. He heard the holy man clearly though his lips did not move. He replied mentally, "I am Yeshua, of Nazareth. I did not mean to eavesdrop, or interrupt..."

"Are you a rainmaker?" Honi queried mentally.

"No sir. I...I...am not. I wanted to help..." the young scholar thought.

"If you must, pray quietly, and don't interrupt," he rebuked him silently.

"I am praying silently," Yeshua explained. He knew of mental communication, but this was the first time he experienced the phenomenon. He sat stunned not knowing what to make of it.

He heard Honi's next supplication, a truly inspirational plea, and again at the end he joined pleading to his dear Abba for help. When he did it a third time the holy man glared at his interruptions and was about to scold him when Yeshua decided he would be wiser to leave. He walked over to the woman, hoping to avoid hearing the holy man's communications.

"May I sit down?" he asked hesitantly.

"Can't stop you," she snapped.

He sat beside her hoping to learn about the holy man, "Do you know him well?"

"Ought to; my husband — for twenty years," she said as if describing a nagging toothache.

"I don't wish to be presumptuous, but will he cause…rain?"

She retorted as gruffly as her previous answers, "He has never failed!" Then she looked at him for the first time emphasizing, "He communicates with Lord Adonai. He'll bring rain!"

"You don't seem happy with his special gifts," he commented, for something in her tone disturbed him.

"Oh, I'm happy for his gift," she replied unhappily. "It's just the fact that the fool never charges for his valuable services!"

"Why does he not charge?" Yeshua inquired naively.

She squinted her eyes as if to say he was being impertinent, but barked instead, "Because he's a fool! He says it is a special gift, so he must share it. Ever heard anything so stupid?" She leaned closer, forcing him to lean away, "He takes donations. Beggars earn more!" He was mortified by her aggressive remarks. "Israelis are tighter than the skin on a drum. They profit while we sleep in open fields and starve!"

Yeshua looked at Honi, busy praying, then turned back to her. For the first time he noticed that she was an attractive lady. Tears began to well in her eyes, and he felt immense pity. He realized that under that tough, dusty, weather beaten face was a lady who long ago was exquisitely beautiful. He whispered under his breath, "She was once as beautiful as lady Sarah…" but, she did not hear for she was crying.

"I curse the day I met him," she sobbed. "I curse the day I married him…"

He sat uncomfortably, unable to alleviate her sorrow. What she needed was her youth back and a different lifestyle.

"When master Honi finishes his work, we will give you some of our supplies," he offered impulsively. She was about to argue but he raised his hand, "We have lots. I'll also ask my friends to pay your husband for his service…"

"You're not from here?" she smiled wiping away the tears.

"Passing through on a journey…searching…We feel blessed to have met him…"

She turned to him pleading, "Don't say anything of what I said. He is a saintly man. It would break his heart. He wants so much to make everybody happy…"

"You must love him deeply," he observed.

"I do!"

They sat side by side, but in different worlds. The woman's mind traveled back to the security of the past and happier times, while Yeshua watched the circle man, whose eyes seemed glazed and his mind in a trance. He heard the holy man's heart wrenching supplications, but was careful not to interfere.

At mid - afternoon Yeshua brought her to their camp for a meal.

The day passed and Honi sat alone in the square, where he seemed even smaller, like an abandoned rag doll discarded by a child. There were no hints of clouds that day or next. Yet he did not leave the circle or object. More amazing still was the fact that people did not lose faith in him. They went about their daily business, walking around the circle, barely slowing down to glance at him, who now seemed like a fixture.

One visitor informed the shop owner and his customers, "Master Honi, known internationally by the Greek name Onias, once sat in the circle for seven days. He only left for personal hygiene, returning to wrestle with God: never slept; never ate. Not until he brought the people what he promised; clear, cool water from the heavens…"

They listened in awe. One lady exclaimed, "He must be the Messiah."

• • •

When Debborah arrived at Sarah's house, the hostess led her to her room and closed the door. She held her close whispering, "Be careful what you say. My walls have ears." Debborah nodded and her friend asked eagerly, "Have you news from Yeshua? How is he? Where is he? Is he alright?"

"Slow down! One question at a time. Yes, he is alright. A young traveler, by the name of Zebedee, I think, stopped by. Strange fellow. Very nervous..." she explained still wondering about the stranger. "He was given two letters from Yeshua...he wanted me to find out if you were alright. He was worried..."

Sarah interjected, taking her hand and squeezing it, "Father was insanely angry when he saw me with Yeshua. He accused me of being a common slut..."

"I am sorry," the younger girl whispered.

"Later, I overheard my parents planning to marry me off to someone as far from here as possible..."

"You mean Tyre?"

Sarah scoffed, "We are as welcome there as lepers. No, much further: Antioch, perhaps Babylon." The younger girl gasped and Sarah pleaded, "You must not tell Yeshua. There is nothing he can do...and, he must not ruin the expedition." They sat in silence, unable to think of a solution. Suddenly Sarah asked, "Did you bring his letters?"

"When I asked the traveler for them, he said soldiers took them. One letter was especially for you, saying how much he cared and all that, but they took it away. They must have terrified him. He kept looking over his shoulder. When he saw the soldiers camped across our street, he flew from the yard like the wind..."

"Why are soldiers camped on your street?" Sarah asked.

"Who knows?" the younger girl shrugged. "But, they never take their eyes off our yard, as if waiting for someone..."

"Yeshua," Sarah blurted out frightened. "They're waiting for Yeshua. Father accused him of being a Zealot."

"Is that bad?"

"Father said they're conspiring to overthrow the government. He said they're criminals..."

"There must be a lot of Zealots in town. Many were arrested...Most managed to run away. Even the schoolmaster disappeared."

"Master Benjoseph?" Sarah gasped with agony. "I cannot imagine him being a criminal."

"I must write Yeshua about all this."

"No. He will want to return, and will be arrested," Sarah begged anxiously.

There was a light knock on the door, and a handsome middle aged man walked in. He had a thick head of jet black hair with a hint of grey, big black eyes, and full lips. The single flaw on the man was a long, hideous scar running on the left side of his face, from the temple down through the cheek to the chin. He smiled at lady Sarah, leaned over and gave her a peck on the cheek.

"My dear, I came to say goodbye. I must leave again immediately," he said.

"Another job, father?"

"Unfortunately," he sighed. Any word from your friend…his whereabouts?"

"None, father," she spluttered too quickly and blushed. Then she regained her composure, "Coincidentally this is his sister lady Debborah."

"Ahh! Lady Debborah," he bowed exaggeratingly low as if greeting royalty. "Master Yeshua's lovely sister?" he wasted no time to start an interrogation, "Whereabouts is master Yeshua these days?"

The young girl was flattered with the display of chivalry, but his direct question quickly sobered her. She stuttered, "I…I don't know, sir. Nobody knows." She looked into his eyes, but he looked away avoiding eye contact.

"Have you not received a letter from him?" he spoke to her but looked at a statuette to the side.

She shook her head slowly, "No sir…If I should receive any news, is there a message you wish me to give him?"

His eyes darted from place to place as he avoided her question, "N-no…no, just tell him…No, better still just tell me his whereabouts…"

"Why?" she pressed, for she did not trust his evasive mannerism.

But, the man ignored her, and turned to his daughter, again pecking her on the cheek, turning around and exiting quickly. Debborah thought she had never before seen such a show of proper motions with less affection.

"What does your father do?"

"He's an architect; one of the best."

"Designs mansions…and palaces?" Debborah inquired and her friend nodded. "Where?"

"Everywhere. I think presently he said he is busy in Sepphoris."

"Where did he get that scar?" Debborah queried pointedly.

Sarah moved back uneasy at the unpleasant topic, and tried to avoid it, "It's a long story." But Debborah refused to be put off. She leaned forward, taking her hand and holding it firmly, partly to give her friend support but also implying she would not let go until she was told everything. Sarah looked into her eyes helplessly, sighed and confessed, "Robbers...he was attacked in Tyre by bandits."

"I'm sorry. It must be painful for you...Were the robbers captured?"

"No, father would not lay charges..." Sarah muttered. "He was afraid the bandits would seek vengeance against the family. He chose to move away for our safety."

Debborah felt empathy for her friend. She had no doubts Sarah told the truth, but her intuition told her, her friend was not told the whole truth.

· · ·

When the two Roman soldiers were sent in a westerly direction by the two peasant ladies, they had no idea how dangerous a countryside they would find.

As soon as they left the village, the narrow road turned into an almost non-existent path, which was rarely used. That should have given the experienced trackers a hint, but, because they had no reason to suspect the attractive maidens with the warm smiles, they proceeded. Almost at once they were forced to ascend and descend almost constantly through narrow passages wide enough for only one person. It was barren dirt with boulders taller than a man. The first time they saw the countryside, they were totally surrounded by steep cliffs, giant boulders and wadis. They chuckled rationalizing this is exactly the type of god-forsaken terrain the Zealots would have chosen; forbidding and unattractive, for no one would suspect a sane person would choose this hell on earth for a hide out. They sniggered smugly for outwitting the Zealot bandits and the rebel Messiah. They vowed nothing could keep them from chasing down the lawless brigands.

They climbed and descended, proceeding at a snail's pace in the hottest region, where not a breath of wind refreshed them. Perspiration flowed freely under their helmets, into the tunics and down to the sandals. They were scratched, bruised and cursing, but proceeded. They did not catch sight of the boys, nor see any evidence of scuffs from the hooves on the hard ground, nor droppings from the animals. There was no hint of camps or ashes from fires. But they reasoned with so many crevices the Zealots could be anywhere in a neighboring area. At the beginning they were too stubborn, and later too embarrassed to admit they were duped. Instead they carefully inspected every scratch on the rocks, rationalizing they were on the right track.

The older Roman went back to ancient history to support his argument, "You can never trust an Israeli. Take Moses; he led his people through the desert for forty years. Why? Too stubborn to admit he got lost."

"Compared to that, two days in these snake infested, scorpion filled rocks, is a picnic," the young man tried to revive the waning enthusiasm.

The second night was approaching and they tried to find a protected area to camp, for as hot as the place was in day time, it was freezing cold at night. The only cozy place away from the cold wind was to get snuggled up in a wadi.

"Under normal circumstances, never set up camp in a wadi," the old soldier warned. "If it rains, these narrow gullies turn into torrential rivers: pushing down boulders, logs and everything in the way down there…"

"Then we cannot consider the wadi. We'll find another…"

The old man raised his hand interrupting, "But, this is the dry season. It never rains here in the dry season…"

The young soldier pointed to a protected nook in the wadi, "We'll camp there. We'll be snug as a bug in a donkey's ear." He turned to his companion, "Never rains in dry season?"

"It would take a miracle…"

They set up camp in the wadi, and settled back comfortably.

It came in the middle of the night: they were awakened by a horrendously loud noise, reverberating in the tent as if they were sitting in the epicenter of an earthquake. They sat up staring into the darkness, listening, horrified.

"WATER! RUN FOR YOUR LIFE!" the old man screamed, and sprang to his feet.

The torrential waters lapped at their sandals as they tripped, slipped and scratched to get out of the wadi, climbing up the bank to reach the top. Giant boulders, heavy tree trunks and debris rushed past them, tearing down the tent, and carrying it downstream into the night. They stood drenched and cold in the heavy downpour, big drops pelting their naked bodies. Their horse stood beside them shaking off the rain. By good fortune they had left their supplies and extra clothes with the animal, on higher ground.

The cold water shook them to reality. The old man roared louder than the thunder, "Tomorrow we will return to that village...I WILL KILL THAT LYING WENCH!!"

. . .

When the rain came it poured continuously for two days. The first morning, Yeshua's group joined the villagers, singing and dancing in the rain. Entire families arrived from the furthest valleys soaking wet, not making the least effort to protect themselves from the gushing water. This was their gift from heaven, and they wanted Lord Adonai to see their appreciation. They sang their lungs out with ecstasy.

Everywhere cisterns were filling, water holes, wells and dykes were being replenished, many filling to overflowing. The dry stream beside the boys' tent was filled to the brim. They debated moving camp, but as the rain remained steady they concluded they would be safe. After partying and dancing in the rain for a long time the people began to shake from exposure and started searching for places to warm up.

The boys returned to their tent and played cards, dice, dominos and every game they knew. Stephanos sent Germanicus to bring master Honi and his wife to dinner and to give them the supplies and payment promised, then they would leave in the morning for dryer places. "As I recall master Quintus promised to carry you on his back through the village, if the rain came," Yeshua teased his friend. "Are you ready?"

Quintus was shocked and stuttered, "Wha...? Me...? I don't think..."

"Honi had to perform a miracle," the Greek observed, and proclaimed unilaterally, "In my studied opinion he failed."

The Israeli retorted with a frown, "Three years of drought, and he gave them rain. Is that not a miracle?"

"Look outside; an overcast sky with rain clouds," Stephanos countered. "A miracle is creating rain with clear skies."

"Put that way, there is no miracle," Yeshua flicked his hands in frustration.

The Greek explained, "Mere coincidence. Master Quintus you owe me nothing!"

"Villagers said the first sprinkles came from a clear sky...seemingly from the stars," Yeshua remained stubbornly steadfast.

"Winds carry droplets of rain miles ahead of clouds, so the rain can appear to come from a clear sky," Stephanos emphasized.

"It was a miracle," the Israeli refused to budge.

"That's not how I see it," the Greek countered.

Surprisingly Quintus agreed with Yeshua, "I cannot argue mystics or meteorology, but I think Honi warrants investigation. If he caused this rain, with or without clouds, he could be invaluable to the empire. I will have to investigate further and report to my superiors."

"What will you say: that he brought rain from the clouds?" Stephanos guffawed superiorly. "They will send you to be analyzed."

"He brought rain after a thousand days," the Roman emphasized.

"Did he do it? Can you prove it?" Stephanos pressed his point.

They were interrupted by voices outside. They looked out and saw Germanicus with the guests and invited them in.

Before sitting Honi announced, "You know me, so allow me to introduce my wife, Mariamme."

"The villagers are grateful and beholden to you," the young Israeli complimented him. "But, you must be used to such gratitude..."

"Their happiness is my repayment," the holy man smiled.

Yeshua glanced at his wife who rolled her eyes to the heavens.

Stephanos and Quintus donned their sandals and left to prepare the supplies they were going to give to the couple. Left alone Honi lowered his voice and leaned towards Yeshua, "You heard my thoughts...Do you possess special powers?"

Yeshua was taken back by his directness, "I did not know I could hear thoughts."

The older man noticed his embarrassment and eased up, "Perhaps you don't understand your powers. I'll explain. Most of my supplications are not audible. I communicate mentally with Adonai. Yet, you heard me, and communicated because I heard you." He saw the young man's shock, and realized he was not aware he possessed these powers. "It's a rare gift. You are only the second person I know who does it."

The young man peppered him with questions, whispering, "When did you find out you had this power? What other powers do you have: curing the sick, help invalids...?"

Honi explained, "I was a boy of, nine or ten, and heard my father lamenting about a drought in our region in its second year. Father said if it did not rain soon, we would have to move to the city. I became incensed, and resolved to have it out with Adonai."

"You were going to fight with the Creator?"

"I was young. That night I walked to the far corner of the field, sat down and told Lord Adonai I would not leave that spot until He gave us rain. I supplicated and argued. I told Him if I died it would be His fault. I prayed, argued, pleaded and harangued Him the whole night and the next day. Of course I did not tell my parents where I was going. When they did not find me, they worried that some wild animal had killed me. Two days later they found me just as the rain started.

"Walking home I told father I made it rain. He paid no attention, until mother pointed to the clear sky. Father stopped, looked up and tears came to his eyes."

"I am shocked to hear you argue with Yahweh. Are you not afraid…?"

"If Adonai got cross with me, what could He do: recall me? I'd argue and harangue Him all the more up there." Then he remembered he wanted to ask him something and spoke with astonishment, but in low breath, "You called Lord Adonai ABBA: FATHER. YOU ARE THE CHOSEN ONE."

Before Yeshua could answer they were interrupted when Stephanos and Quintus re-entered. The Greek asked Honi pointedly, "Are you the Messiah we are seeking?"

Honi answered with a sparkle in his eyes, "I can tell you he lives among us, but I am not the one you seek."

"You say it with such conviction that I think you know him," Stephanos mused with a trace of suspicion in his voice.

"During my supplications I received a clear message, 'I WILL ANSWER YOUR PRAYERS TO PLEASE MY SON, WHO IS AMONG THE PEOPLE…'"

Yeshua remembered hearing the same message, and turned pale.

The Greek smiled and persisted anxiously, "God said those precise words?"

"He does not communicate like we do," Honi responded patiently, "His messages come as symbols and signs…and must be interpreted."

"Like an inspiration or a vision?" Stephanos guessed, and the holy man nodded. "Did you get an impression…like his face?"

Honi glanced at Yeshua and seeing him white, answered ambiguously, "No…not clearly. But, be assured; when he reveals himself he will be revered by all the people."

Stephanos was ecstatic and had many questions, but was interrupted when Germanicus entered with a small basket covered with heavy canvas. He set it down, and pulled out a small wrapped bundle which squirmed and made a sound.

"A baby?" Mariamme exclaimed.

"Where did you get… that?" Stephanos blurted out.

"It's a baby girl," the slave answered. "I found her…lost in the bushes."

Yeshua reached in the basket and pulled out a soggy papyrus which he read and explained, "She was not lost. She was abandoned." Then he read it, "May Lord Adonai bless and keep our girl safe, and forgive us. No signature."

"How can we take her back?" Stephanos queried.

"They don't want her back," the young Israeli sighed. "In a patriarchal society, if it is a baby girl, she is not family until the father holds her."

"He left a baby to die?" Germanicus hugged her closer. "Why would he do that?"

"They may be poor, not able to feed her," Mariamme answered. "Fathers think they're wasting time and money raising a girl, because when she marries she joins the husband's family."

"And you call us barbarians?" the slave asked incredulous. "We care for every baby we get." He lifted her high over his head, announcing proudly, "God gave you to me, so you will be my family."

Quintus reminded him bluntly, "That is not for a slave to decide. You must seek you master's approval."

Germanicus froze and his smile disappeared. He knew the facts: a slave was a chattel, and all decisions concerning him belonged to his master. But, in his elation he forgot. He brought down the baby and his eyes pleaded. He was met with the Greek's cold stare. His face tightened. He clenched his jaw. He hated his lowly position because he was expected to grovel. He stared stubbornly refusing to lose the little dignity he had.

Yeshua felt empathy and stepped forward to plea for him, "Master Stephanos…"

Germanicus interrupted pleading, his voice breaking with emotion, "Master Stephanos, in my enthusiasm, I forgot my first obligation...to you. This is important...Let me keep her. I will bring her up to respect you... and to serve you..."

Everyone waited for the Greek to respond. But he remained silent.

Yeshua supported the slave, "He begs for the baby's life. Her survival is in your hands."

Stephanos glanced at the little bundle for the first time, took her and asked, "What name will you give your daughter?"

"LYGIA, my mother's name."

CHAPTER XI - MESSIAH:
THE GREAT SHAMAI

Master Stephanos did not approve of his slave keeping Lygia, not because he did not like babies, but because he knew this would complicate the journey. As if to prove him right, Lygia started to fuss, "Your baby is hungry," Stephanos scowled. "Feed her!"

Germanicus' heart sank. His first reaction was to panic, fearing he would lose her.

Lady Mariamme showed her sensitivity and the practicality of a woman, "A new born needs a mother's milk. We'll have to hire a surrogate mother."

"Are we expected to search for one every time she cries?" Stephanos grumbled.

"Why do men see a crisis in the tiniest problem?" Mariamme commented. "We can solve your problem. We'll care for Lygia until you return." When their faces lit up, she continued, "Of course she will need shelter...an impermeable tent like this one. And we will need some coins for food, and to pay a surrogate mother..."

Stephanos knew his slave did not have a coin but he said, "Pay the woman."

The slave knew what his master was doing, and glared at him with hatred.

The Greek smirked but softened, "I will buy a tent and pay all expenses provided you promise: you will never make a decision without first obtaining my approval."

Germanicus blurted out impulsively, "I promise, master!"

"We are leaving today, so let's agree on the expenses," Stephanos said as he and Mariamme sat down in a corner to settle the matter.

Quintus was feeling guilty for causing the crisis unwittingly, took out a bag of coins from his belt, handed some to the slave, remarking loud enough for the Greek to hear, "This is my contribution for the expenses... you don't have to make rash promises."

The Greek glared at him but remained silent. When he completed the list, they left to make the purchases. Mariamme told the slave, "You and I are going to find a surrogate mother." He picked up the small basket with the baby and followed her.

"Such a little bundle, causing such complications," Honi remarked to Yeshua, as they began to put the tent back in order.

"You say that because you never had one," he replied. "I have five siblings and I never thought of them as demanding." When they finished they sat down and Yeshua began to fidget nervously.

"You're more restless than a flea on a hot coal," Honi chuckled: "Out with it!"

"Yes, something is bothering me. You were correct; apparently I was sent to fulfill a prophecy. However I was not told what it is." He pressed his forehead in his cupped hands, shaking his head in agony, "What am I? A sage, a warrior, or a teacher...? How can I tell...? When will I know my mission?"

"That's why you asked how I knew," Honi nodded. He saw Yeshua's exasperation and wanted to help. "I am neither a prophet nor a sooth-sayer...But, I have learned from observation that our past often foretells our future. What were your major experiences in the last few months?"

Yeshua told him about the sermons and the riots, going to pagans for work, the confounded sieves and the sailboat. Honi stroked his beard for a long time before venturing an opinion, "Your sermon tells me you will be a great leader; perhaps a teacher. But, it will not be easy, and you will be misunderstood. You will lead Israelis, gentiles and pagans. Like a sieve you will sift the good people from the undeserving. Your teachings will shake the world..."

"Me...? How can I do it alone?"

"You will not be alone," the holy man continued. "You are building a boat; the fisher of men. You will prepare them, and they will spread the word." The old man had a spark in his eyes, "Did you ever perform miracles?"

"My parents said I did, but I have never seen one."

"There will be great expectations from you. Like the pebble you will disturb the waters, and the ripples will envelope the world. Master Yeshua, are you the Messiah?"

Yeshua's mouth unhinged as he brought his hands to his chest as if to ask "Who, me?" causing Honi to chuckle amused.

Before he could answer, they heard voices outside the tent, the door opened a crack and two faces peered in: an old bearded man, and a young girl about nine. He bowed, "Excuse my intrusion, master Honi. My name is rabbi Beoni, religious leader of the four villages in the valley. This is my daughter Jael."

"This is my friend, master Yeshua," Honi answered. "How can I help you?"

"I must thank you for the miracle of the rain," the rabbi bowed. "They will talk about you for generations." He let him enjoy the compliment, before disclosing the purpose of his visit, "I came to plead for a special miracle…"

Honi shifted uncomfortably, but inquired with trepidation, "What is your need rabbi Beoni?"

"My son Jonathan suffered a horrible accident. A horse fell on him crushing his spine, paralyzing him. Six months he lays…" the rabbi broke down. When he regained control he continued, "He is only nineteen…"

"Rabbi Beoni, I'm sorry, but I cannot…"

The rabbi was too desperate to stop, "We have accepted that he will never walk again. But there is a bigger problem: his constant pain. The horse must have fractured his spine, for he lives in constant agony. No position is comfortable, and he cries…Jonathan is deeply depressed…" He broke down again, but forced himself to finish, "My son is suicidal. He has begged me to finish his life…"

"Suicidal?" Honi repeated with pain.

"It's all he talks about," the rabbi cried dejected.

The holy man was deeply perturbed. After a while he turned to Yeshua whispering, "I cannot help him…you can."

"Me? I don't know how," Yeshua whispered with anxiety. "I'm not ready…"

"You performed miracles…" Honi pressed. "You must." He stared at Yeshua who sat quivering. "What are you afraid of?"

"I'm not ready …" Then he protested with a whimper, "I'll never have peace…"

Honi sympathized because he knew the pressures of the limelight, answering their demands, sacrificing his dreams, even love and family for the public. Then he thought of Jonathan's desperation, "His life is in your hands," he whispered, and felt remorseful for pressuring the young man. He offered a compromise, "Let's both go. I'll ask to be left alone. They won't know who performed the miracle…" Before Yeshua could answer, he turned and smiled, "Rabbi Beoni lead us to your son."

. . .

The rabbi lived at the opposite end of the village. His was a small house of stone bricks, plastered with mud and white washed, though most of the paint was faded and some plaster had fallen off. Next to the house was the synagogue.

They were met by the rabbi's wife and friends who came to see the holy man, and witness a miracle. They were disappointed when Beoni told them, "Master Honi wishes to be alone with Jonathan." Then he turned to his wife suggesting, "Lady Shirmrith, lead our friends to the synagogue. A prayer to Lord Adonai is timely."

They left to the assembly house, grumbling, while the rabbi led the two visitors into the house. It reminded Yeshua of his own home: one long rectangular room, dark, with a fire in the centre. Poorly ventilated, it smelled of smoke, and in this case the stench of rotting sores. As they entered they heard groans and looked to the left where they saw the young man laying, propped up by pillows on all sides. Rabbi Beoni fell on his knees, "Jonathan, I brought master Honi, the holy man…He promises to make you well." He hoped to see him smile, but the young man lay uninterested groaning. The rabbi turned to his guests, "Master Honi, in the name of Lord Adonai…help him."

Yeshua was already kneeling by the invalid, staring with fear. He recognized the sickening smell of open wounds and lesions, from Jonathan lying in the same position for extended periods of time. He could not be touched without pain and agony. Just then Jonathan's face twisted with pain, and his jaws clenched. He tried to move his upper body one way, then the other, slowly, only to freeze and grunt with excruciating pain. After a long time and miniscule movements, he relaxed and breathed easier. But, that was temporary, and soon he was going through the same contortions and agony.

"Can I help you find a comfortable position?" Yeshua offered.

The young man lay without a stir, staring at the ceiling. The only evidence that he heard was a small movement of his eyes towards the voice, then away.

"What caused your infirmity?" Yeshua asked with kindness. The invalid blinked and moved his eyes again but ignored him. "Can you describe the pain: is it from one source or from different places?" he persisted with tenderness.

"If you can cure me…do it…otherwise, leave me to die," the young man snarled gruffly, stopping often because it pained to talk.

Yeshua turned to Honi who was disturbed by his rudeness. The young scholar motioned him to sit down, hinting this was going to take a long time. Then he turned to the invalid, "I can help you, Jonathan," he started and saw the young man's eyes move towards him, and turned his head so he could see the speaker's face. Yeshua smiled, "It is better when we see each other's eyes. How did this happen?"

Jonathan's eyes remained fixed watching the radiant light in Yeshua's eyes, and he felt fear, but also a mixture of hope. After a long time he droned, "Yes, I suffer numbing pain…pins and needles…everywhere…my sides and my legs…I cannot sleep…breathe without pain…My spine is crushed…I will not…walk…" tears filled his eyes and ran down his face.

Yeshua took the sheet and wiped away his tears, "How old are you, master Jonathan?"

"Nineteen…almost twenty," he continued to cry for a few moments, then took a deep breath and froze in pain, moved again until he found a little comfort, and continued, "I was in the lyceum, and graduated. Always active in sports - the best! My teachers entered me in competitions…I won. I won regional games…discus, javelin…even wrestling. They sent me to Caesarea…to train. I won the national championship…Antioch. If I won…I would compete in Athens…the Olympiad." He muttered the phrase as if savoring every word, "My dream…"

"What did your father think of this?" Honi queried.

Jonathan glanced his way and spat out, "He hated it. I don't know if you're aware, Greeks practice all sports in the nude. It is the tradition. We Israelis are ashamed of the naked body. I told father I was going to do it…for Israel. For the people…He did not approve of it…" He stopped and seemed to be reliving painful memories of the past. "We argued… did not speak for years… until this!" He sniggered bitterly, "Adonai's revenge!"

"How did it happen?" Yeshua queried.

"There were dozens athletes from every nation…every sport. One day we decided on an impromptu…chariot race…Stupid! None of us knew...the danger...We raced, got tangled up; iron, wood, horses...I was thrown off and mangled. Friends were killed...They were lucky! A horse stepped on my spine...I heard talk the carriages were sabotaged." His face twisted with pain. It took a long time and much slow twisting before he settled in a new position and released the tension of his muscles.

"Do you have a comfortable position? Yeshua asked and he shook his head. "You said you were in athletics for the Israelis," the young scholar prodded with curiosity. "Were you not doing it for your own glory?"

"Some of that, yes," the invalid snapped. "I desired the apex...the Laurel leaf: Olympic champion!" For the first time there was a sparkle in his eyes. "But, my goal was to return a champion...and use my achievement...to inspire...Persuade them that...persistence is what we need." He stopped for a breath as he became tense and the vigorous speech tired him. When he spoke again, his tone was softer, and sadder, "All my life I heard...excuses. Adonai will look after us...send...a Messiah...to make us free..." Suddenly his voice acquired a passion, "We can do it: sacrifice, work...and reach...the podium...Now, I am...broken...cripple..."

Yeshua was impressed with Jonathan, and took the invalid's thin hand, "Do you still want to help the people?"

Jonathan stared at him, and closed his eyes, letting out a deep sigh as if to say, Are you out of your mind? With this broken body?

Yeshua was not perturbed, and turned to his companion, "Help me roll him over slowly." Before the invalid cried out they had him on his belly. Honi covered his nose and mouth from the stench, while Yeshua tore the material off his back, exposing the spine and oozing ulcers. He touched the spine gently, "Does the pain originate here?"

Jonathan waited until he touched and let out a cry. Yeshua closed his eyes and began to pray silently. Honi was astonished when a bright aura emanated about the young scholar's head enveloping it. When he opened his eyes a radiant light shone brightly from them like beacons.

• • •

It was late afternoon when they left the rabbi's house to return to camp. They had visited and talked to Jonathan for a great part of the day, asking questions about his life as an athlete and the drive and ambition to compete and win. Once his pain was gone, they discovered he was a gregarious young man with a great sense of humor and quick wit. Yeshua delved into every aspect of the young man's upbringing, especially the support he received from his family. The young scholar had a special plan for him but wanted to be certain he had the character, and mental attitude to fulfill his plan.

Honi commented with enthusiasm, "Jonathan has a special gift and a contagious inspiration to influence people…"

"More than a gift of oratory," Yeshua corrected him. "He has a genuine interest in others. He rarely spoke about himself."

They continued in silence, going over the experience, when the circle man turned to his companion with a confiding tone, "Did you know a bright light shines over you…and a radiance comes from your eyes when you pray?"

Yeshua was visibly perturbed. His brother Simon saw it when he fought the panther and recently his mother referred to it. But at that moment bigger problems troubled him: he was thinking about Jonathan.

"Why the gloom? After your accomplishment, you should feel ecstatic."

"I envy him," he answered with sadness. "He knows precisely what he wants to do." He thought about what he wanted to say next as he wanted it to be very clear, "I know you tried to decipher my future, but, what is my destiny? Where will I start?"

"You already started," Honi put his arm around his shoulder. "The first time you answered your mother's wishes and prayed to help someone."

"Why do I feel more is expected, but I don't know what? Why is life so complex?"

Honi let out a belly laugh, "Wouldn't life be boring if it were too simple? The Creator has great faith that you will fulfill your mission however you choose."

Yeshua's problem was greater than he let on. His faltering faith was coming to a crisis and he still did not resolve the problem.

They were approaching the camp site when he slowed down to clarify a matter that troubled him from the first day he saw the holy man, "Master Honi, tell me if my question is out of line. Is it proper for messengers of God, like us, to be married?"

The question touched a tender nerve, and the holy man took a long time to answer, "When we were young we could sleep on the edge of a sword, we were so close. Now, there are nights a cot the width of a field is not big enough." He sighed from the depth of his soul, "I failed her. She deserved better…" He spoke as if he were apologizing, "She wanted children and a home…but, destitute farmers cannot afford my services." Then he answered with a tone of finality, "A man and woman should marry and propagate; especially rabbis and priests."

Arriving at camp they saw a new tent beside the young men's camp. They saw Mariamme smiling as she held the baby. Everyone was full of good news: Stephanos and Quintus had bought the supplies, and Mariamme found a surrogate mother for Lygia.

Only Yeshua sat apart, silent and thoughtful. He was thinking about his future and could not shake off his melancholy mood. He missed lady Sarah desperately.

• • •

Next morning at sunrise the young men had breakfast, broke camp and said their good byes. Only Stephanos and Germanicus remained behind. The Greek gave Mariamme ample coins, enough for expenses and their service.

"I wish the Israelis were a fraction as generous," the lady commented.

"They would be, but for the drought," he replied and turned to Honi, "Do you know of other miracle workers in the region?"

Honi thought for a few moments, "The Great Shamai…is due in Beth Sheeba, a day's journey along that road. Another, master Eleazar, an exorcist will be going to the village of Shalem, by the Samaritan border."

"Is either of them the Messiah?" Stephanos ventured to ask.

"People call both by that name," he replied, then mused as he returned to camp, "But, often we admire the crop on the other side of the hill, failing to appreciate our own."

Stephanos missed his remark for he was giving an order to the slave, "Don't take too long. We have already lost a day."

"I'll catch up presently, master," he replied as he held Lygia and tickled her chin.

Honi and Germanicus sat by the tent, and Mariamme was inside admiring the only home she ever had, and rearranging their few worldly possessions.

Germanicus leaned toward the holy man and whispered, "Alone at last. Now I can speak freely."

"You can always speak freely with me Germanicus. Why are you whispering?"

The slave knew Honi would not understand the need for secrecy, so ignored the question and proceeded, "I am happy you are my Messiah, sent here to make me free."

"Do you think I am the Messiah? Is freedom your main objective in life?"

"Should it not be?" Germanicus was shocked to hear his lifetime dream being questioned. "In northern Europe, I was free! My only hope is to return home free."

"Every man deserves freedom. I will pray for you every night," the holy man touched him with empathy. "But, I tell you sincerely, there is something greater than freedom: in the heart, and the soul. It is peace with oneself. I learned that today from a young man, Jonathan. Someday you will have to meet him."

"Internal freedom?" he asked confused. "Not real freedom?"

"Some call it peace within the soul…"

Germanicus interrupted, "Master Yeshua said the Messiah will set me free."

"I believe he meant a different freedom: from hatred and prejudices… open your heart and clear it from mean thoughts," he explained, but seeing the disappointment on the slave's face he quickly added, "But, I must confess, I am not the Messiah."

Germanicus sat back flabbergasted. How could a holy man who brought rain from the stars not be the Messiah? Why would Yeshua talk about freedom, but not freedom from slavery? Then he remembered Anna's words: his problem was deep inside. He needed to find peace in his soul.

He stood up to leave when the holy man grabbed his arm, "Germanicus, I have something special to ask you. Stay close to master Yeshua. Guard him. He is a very important person. Promise you will do it…"

"I made that promise to lady Anna already," the slave interjected, astounded to hear a similar request. "Of course I will…"

He handed Lygia to Mariamme, and rushed to catch up to the group. After a dozen steps he slowed down, trying to make sense of it all. Why did everyone speak of freedom differently from him? All he desired was to be free as a bird, and go anywhere he wished. Why did the holy man refer to master Yeshua as greater than he? Was that not what lady Anna said? What was so special about master Yeshua? What about the elusive Messiah? He suspected that when he solved the question about master Yeshua, he may solve the riddle of the Messiah.

. . .

The two Roman soldiers watched helplessly as their tent and belongings were washed down the wadi. They stood shocked, drenched and whipped by a cold wind. When they started to shiver, the old man realized they must take control, or they would be dead before morning. He yelled to his young companion over the roar of the storm and raging stream, "Let's huddle with the horse to keep warm." They moved the horse to the protected side of large boulders, and huddled up to it. "Pull your cloak over your head. Keep your head covered to stay warm!"

After a long time in that position they still felt very uncomfortable.

"How long do you think it will rain?" The young soldier yelled, his teeth chattering.

The old man glared at him through the opening of his cloak, tired, miserable and fuming at the stupid question. He wanted to pulverize his young companion with a sarcastic answer, but after consideration, he sighed. They had served in the army for a couple of years, and he had taken the youth under his wing, deciding to train him to become a professional Roman soldier: a killer in war, but primarily, a survivor. The youth responded enthusiastically, eagerly learning everything, proving to be one of the best trackers in the empire. The centurion had paid the youth the highest compliment once, saying, 'Young man, you could track a hawk in the sky by the disturbances in the wind drafts.' Once he calmed down, the old man replied, "We can't wait until it stops. At first light we'll go downstream to find the tent and salvage whatever we can..."

"Can we not just go back?"

The old man screamed over the thunder claps, "Turn tail? Defeated? We are Roman soldiers. We don't know defeat. Understand? We have orders, and we'll do it!"

The youth did not see the fire in his companion's eyes, but the tone and resolution of his voice left no doubt: they would forge ahead or perish trying.

True to his word, at the first hint of light, they descended the rocky hill to search for their belongings. It still rained heavily but the wind subsided and there was no more thunder or lightning. It was a slow, risky undertaking, going down, because if they slipped they could injure themselves or fall into the torrential waters and certain death. They pushed forward slowly, deliberately, searching for solid footing, progressing at a sloth's pace, trembling from the cold and wet to the marrow of the bones.

Less than a thousand paces down the old man squinted, wiped his eyes, letting out a scream of ecstasy, "LOOK! Down there: OUR TENT! WE'RE SAVED!"

The youth tried to scream, his teeth chattering, "Our...ten'...Le's... ge' it."

The old warrior grabbed him and pulled him back roughly, "Don't move! It's in the water: One slip in that current and – CIAU BAMBINO!" He looked deep into the youth's eyes to be sure his words registered, then explained patiently, "We will study every step carefully. Analyze, discuss and rehearse before we attempt the salvage. Understand?"

The young man nodded nervously, shivering from the cold.

After an inordinate time they tied one end of the tent to a big boulder so the current could not rip it from their grasp, and only then removed rocks and debris from the top of it. When they pulled it out they were of mixed emotions: it was badly torn, filthy and muddy, but it could be washed and repaired. Their good fortune was that their uniforms and extra tunics, swords and helmets were still in it.

The old man barked, "We'll wash the worst of it, and..." but, when he looked at the young soldier he saw him shaking uncontrollably from hypothermia. Quickly, the old man wrapped cloth around his head and feet and leaned him against the horse with an order, "Stick to the animal like glue. I'll finish up." And he returned to salvage everything.

Years later the young soldier admitted the only reason they survived the ordeal, was a most fortunate discovery. Going back they found a cave large enough for them and the horse, with some dry wood. They started a fire. After devouring a hot meal, they slept on the ground that day and the following night.

Two days later they arrived in the small village and searched for the olive skinned lady. Every Israeli answered their inquiries with a shrug. Unfortunately some young boys unwittingly took them to the house where the light skinned lady lived. When she saw them she gasped and her whole body began to tremble.

Seeing the terrified look on her face the older soldier smirked, "So, we meet again. You remember us. You and your friend sent us to those infernal hills…to our death." He grabbed her jaw in his huge hand and squeezed it. "Why did you lie to us? Why?" He spat out the words like venom.

Her two young boys stood, frozen in the dark corner, pressed against the wall and started moving stealthily towards the door. The young soldier saw them coming, considered stopping them, but, instead moved from the doorway.

"Why did you lie to us? Answer me," the old man shouted.

She tried to answer, but unable to move her jaw she sounded incoherent, "I didn…see di'…"

"You stood by and let her lie. You're just as guilty…Where is the wench?"

"I do – know… ran way …"

"Ran? Where to?"

"I do – know – fambly…do-kno…"

The old warrior pulled out his sword and pressed the blade against her nose and forehead, "I should kill you…But, first I have work for you." He turned to his companion. "Bring the tent. This Israeli slut will repair it." He turned to her and told her impetuously, "You will mend it…then we'll have some fun…Then, I will kill you!"

The young soldier shivered uncomfortably as he went for the tent. He stood by the horse a long time wavering. Sometimes he hated the old man…but, what could he do? He was powerless. He took the tent and came in.

Inside they opened the tent and she was ordered to start sewing. She worked between uncontrollable sobs and tears, trying to apologize, begging forgiveness, explaining she had children to bring up. The young soldier sat silently, and demurred to his senior, who got tired of her whining. "Shut up, before I make you…" he shouted. "Where is your food? Don't you have wine in this lousy place?" he demanded and she pointed to the corners. They ate her food and drank the jug dry. By the time she completed the repairs they were fairly drunk.

The older soldier inspected it exclaiming, "Very professional! You sew as good as my old lady…" then he looked at her with lust in his eyes, "Only you are younger and prettier…and, I'll bet more fun!" He turned to his companion, "Help me fold it and you take and tie it on the horse, then come back for some fun…"

While they were busy folding it, she took advantage and bolted for the door. The old codger expected this, extended his thick arm and caught her by the waist.

"Where do you think you're going, my love?" he sneered as he squeezed her against him. She tried to free herself by punching and kicking, but in one move he lifted her in the air, threw her to the ground, then pounced on her.

The young soldier took the tent outside, but froze and retreated into the doorway, his face ashen white, his eyes bigger than saucers, "Sir… sir…You should come out…"

The old man barked,"Can't you see I'm busy? Ouch! "he screamed as she kicked him in the crotch.

The young man yelled terrified, "SIR! THERE IS A LYNCH MOB HERE!"

The old codger fell on the lady, fighting for breath and holding his injured organs. When he heard his partner yell, he sprang up, ran to the door, and froze. His eyes traveled the length of the yard from face to face, counting a dozen young, burly Israeli men, standing shoulder to shoulder, armed with pitch forks, daggers and scythes.

The old man had faced death in many battles, and was not easily frightened. Instead, he stood tall, sneering and decided to bluff,"You bring a dozen Israelis against two Roman soldiers? What is your plan: to kill us? If you do, a battalion will come looking for us. They will avenge our deaths…"

A young, muscular tradesman in his prime, smirked, responding just as coldly,"There will be nothing to avenge. They will find your bleached bones in the wadi miles from here. You camped carelessly, got washed down…rolling stones crushed your skulls. A sad, accidental death…"

The old codger knew they were beat. It was insanity to fight, and he could not bluff them. They had only one hope: Israeli fair play. He pleaded, "If we leave this moment, never to return…?"

The Israeli looked at the lady,"Did they violate you?"

She shook her head. The young man pointed a muscular arm to the gate, and the Romans grabbed the horse and tent and ran.

Before evening they crossed the valley arriving by a small stream filled to the brim, crossed it and walked directly to a solitary tent. They saw a small, thin man, his skin dark from the sun, and an equally sun burnt lady holding a small baby. The old Roman bowed low, "Good afternoon and god's blessing be with you. We seek information, and will be on our way...Have you seen four young men with a camel and a donkey?"

The couple looked at each other surprised. Why are Roman soldiers looking for them? Mariamme wondered suspiciously.

The soldier pulled out an old, yellowish papyrus he took from Zebedee and explained, "We have a letter for Master Yeshua from his family."

Honi was satisfied they were friends and pointed, "They left for Beth Sheeba this morning by this road, but you will catch up easily. It's a day's journey. They'll be staying a few days...waiting for the Great Shamai. He performs miracles; says he is the Messiah!"

The Romans gasped at their good fortune. They thanked the family and pressed on. By morning they camped within striking distance of Yeshua's group, by the town well. With a bit of luck they would capture the Zealots and their leader – the Messiah.

· · ·

That morning Yeshua was about to start preparing breakfast when his companions stopped him, "Master Yeshua, you have cooked every day since we left. Today we will cook and after breakfast, go to town to gather information about the Great Shamai."

Yeshua tried to object but they would not hear of it. Germanicus explained, "I will be tending to the camel's leg. He's limping again. But, it's only one leg, and I can do it."

After eating he left. A few hundred paces, past the water well, deep in the bushes he noticed two Roman soldiers setting up camp: an older man and a youth. Why were they setting up camp in the morning, he wondered? He glanced at their horse which was sweating, which meant they traveled the whole night. Would Romans travel the whole night to see the Great Shamai? They came on pressing business, which could only mean trouble. His curiosity was aroused and he decided he would watch them closely, and proceeded.

The town was a bustling place with a large square and many two storey buildings. As he came to the town gate, workers were busily preparing for a big occasion. The gate was newly painted, large ceramic pots were scrubbed and given a coat of white paint, and blossoming flowers were quickly potted. All buildings were repaired and whitewashed. Even the dirt streets were being swept clean. The town was given a handsome façade, clean and pristine as if preparing for a royal visit. As he entered the gate, workers were covering it with ornamental garlands of green vine interspersed with a variety of attractive flowers blossoming everywhere, so when the colorful gate opened the Great Shamai would feel he was entering the portals of paradise.

The town was filled with strangers, newcomers and tourists, and Yeshua was certain he recognized some people from Laish. "What is the occasion?" he asked.

"The Great Shamai is coming to cure master Hegesippus," the worker responded.

"When is he arriving?" Yeshua asked, but the worker was gone.

He went to the Inn, a great source of information, but the workers marched every which way with tools, paint brushes or a broom in hand. He walked to the backyard where guests camped. A man walked up immediately, "My name is Isaac. I'm the owner of the hotel," he introduced himself and leaned over lowering his voice, "The Great Shamai will be staying here. He is a couple of days late, but, his excellency is in great demand. He will be curing master Hegesippus, our wealthy merchant."

"What is master Hegesippus' illness?"

Master Isaac looked around both ways to satisfy himself no one was within ear shot, and whispered, "CONSUMPTION! His days are numbered."

"The disease of the lungs...not curable," Yeshua sighed. "Very contagious?"

"Extremely! His family and the servants moved out...abandoned him...His only hope is a miracle. The Great Shamai costs a fortune, you know?" he volunteered.

"Do you know the Great Shamai?" he asked.

"Everybody does...or knows of him. He guarantees to cure old Hegesippus."

"You speak of him as if you know him well," Yeshua smiled.

"Everybody knows he is excellent," Isaac reacted indignantly. "They say he is the best since the ancient prophets." With that he turned and went into the Inn.

Yeshua wandered the streets admiring Beth Sheeba. He noticed people coming from every direction, loaded with baskets of food or flowers, proceeding to the same destination. He stopped a sojourner, "Pardon my curiosity, sir, but are all these people going to the same place?"

The stranger nodded, "To pay respects to master Hegesippus, the living – dead." He shook his head, "I doubt the great miracle man will save him...Come with me, I'm going there."

Yeshua had to walk fast as his companion was obviously on a tight schedule. His speech matched his quick march, "Master Hegesippus is the richest, most influential merchant in town, probably in the whole region. But, since this sickness, he was abandoned...and vulnerable. Look there," he pointed ahead and a little to the left, "You can see his big mansion."

Even from the distance of three blocks he could see an expansive edifice that dwarfed the trees surrounding it. It resembled an ancient castle owned by sultans and potentates: a two story magnificent structure topped with turrets and spires on every corner. The living quarters were constructed in three joining rectangles surrounding an exotic garden in the inner yard. One critic compared it favorably with the famous hanging gardens of Babylon, one of the seven wonders of the ancient world.

The epicenter of the garden was a rare sight in arid Israel: a natural water fountain. Springing from underground, under natural pressure, the water rose through pipes inside a pink marble statue of a Greek maiden, and poured out of a jug in her arms, into a large pool. From there it flowed along intricate streams and channels, so gravity caused an uninterrupted flow through dozens of verdant islets and flower gardens throughout the yard. The palms, trees, shrubs, ferns and flowers were imported from the furthest corners of the world. Not one drop of water was wasted, for whatever the thirsty tropical vegetation did not use, went into the mansion.

Yeshua stood beside the statue in the fountain. His companion sighed, "Almost too perfect for this world...and master Hegesippus cannot take it to the next."

"You said he is alone in this...castle?"

"Abandoned...awaiting death," he replied grimly. "This is the first time anyone has entered his garden. He is a very private man."

Yeshua saw many baskets of food, fruit and flowers set on the islets and paths. His companion put his basket beside the others then quickly returned.

"Will he come to take these baskets?"

The stranger shook his head, "There is no one else here..."

"I was told he is dying of consumption?"

The man nodded. As if to support the prognosis, a dry cavernous cough exploded from a room echoing out of the open window, and over the yard. "The disease is like worms," he explained in a low breath. "They eat at his lungs."

The man turned to leave, but Yeshua grabbed his arm, "Just one more question, please. Seeing these gifts, he must be dearly loved by the people...?"

The man turned back to face Yeshua. His mood changed from the amiable disposition as he scowled, "He was the most hated man in Beth Sheeba. Miserable! Greedy! Selfish! He was cruel to his family and abused his servants. He would sell his own mother for one Yehuda." He glared with hatred at the open window, "He was a ruthless man!" He swept his hand over the estate, "This was once the town water well, until he decided he wanted it. From that day on it was all out war. He fought the people, the town council, the rabbi, and when he could not beat or bribe them, he went to Herod Antipas and the Romans. They threatened us... What could we do?"

"He left the people without water?" Yeshua looked astonished.

"Did he care? He got what he wanted. We searched and found water at the far side of town."

Yeshua knew the well, as they camped close to it. He looked perplexed seeing more baskets arriving, "I cannot understand...Then why do you bring gifts?"

The stranger replied philosophically, "Why not? He is alone in the world...And, Lord Adonai would want us to forgive him."

They walked out to the street and again heard the dry cavernous cough in the distance.

•   •   •

Back at the camp the young men had long ago completed their work, and sat waiting for Yeshua. When he did not return, Quintus decided to go and find him. He had barely passed the water well when he was brutally assaulted from behind, his right arm twisted behind his back, and he felt a cold blade against his throat.

"Don't fight. Don't make a sound. Do as you're told and you may live," a hoarse voice behind him whispered. The assailant pushed him through the bushes into a brown army tent, and threw him to the floor. When he dared to look up, he was shocked to see two Roman soldiers. The old man waved a dagger in his face threateningly, "If you cooperate, you may live to see the sunset, Zealot!"

"I'm not a Zealot," Quintus responded gruffly. "I'm a Roman soldier."

They froze, glanced at each other stunned and demanded, "Prove it!"

"I'm stationed with the garrison at Augusteana by the Sea of Galilee. My commander is legate Vinicius." When their jaws dropped, he went on the offensive, "What's your unit? What are you doing here?"

"We're from the fort in Sepphoris," the old man replied defensively. "Our spy infiltrated a Zealot cell in Nazareth. We were ordered to follow four Zealot criminals with a camel and donkey, to meet their rebel leader named Messiah!"

"Messiah is not a name, it's a title," Quintus corrected him. "The superstitious Israelis believe he can perform miracles." When he mentioned this, the two soldiers guffawed which angered him, "Don't laugh! I did not believe it until the little man Honi, back in the last village brought rain. He did it during dry season after years of drought."

"How did he do that?" the young soldier queried with curiosity.

"Drew a circle on the ground and sat in it praying and chanting to his God, until it rained. Torrential rain!"

"Was he camped by the stream with a woman as sunbaked as he, with a baby?" The old man asked and Quintus nodded. "That storm almost killed us. I knew I should have skewered him," the old man snarled.

"How did he bring rain?" The young soldier persisted.

"From clouds, how else?"

They stared at him, then at each other and burst out laughing, "It rained from the clouds, and you call that a miracle?"

Quintus knew what they were thinking, and became furious trying to explain, "I wondered about it myself, but they got into some esoteric discussion..." then he quickly changed topics, "But, they say the real Messiah is coming here..."

"Shamai the Great?" The old man inquired. "What makes you say that?"

"I overhead talk at the water well. Shamai is coming to cure a rich merchant Hegesippus who is dying from CON-SUM-PTION!" Quintus emphasized each syllable.

The two soldiers drew back as if the very word would contaminate them.

Quintus regained his wits and became curious about his "hosts, "What are your orders when you capture these Zealots?"

"You get them to admit they're Zealots, we'll do the rest," the old man replied evasively.

"If they don't confess?"

"Get incriminating admissions –anything, " the old codger continued gruffly. "We'll do the rest - especially the leader - Yeshua."

Quintus felt dizzy, recalling Yeshua's statement, "Quintus, if ordered, will you arrest me?"

The young soldier shook him, "Are you alright? You look pale."

Quintus tried to regain his composure, "I have to know your intentions."

"Turn them over, and they'll be our concern," the old man barked and started pushing him out to stop the offensive questions.

When Quintus was pushed out he looked up and saw Yeshua returning from town. He panicked and started pushing back in before being recognized.

As he approached the Roman camp, Yeshua remembered it and slowed down. He saw an unusual episode: someone scrambling out of the tent, then scrambling back into it just as panick-striken. Why the bizzarre behavior, he wondered…?

That afternoon, and during dinner Quintus sat unusually quiet. He went over the episode time and again, wondering if Yeshua recognized him. He glanced at the young Israeli furtively, unable to make eye contact. By evening he was certain Yeshua knew, for he seemed to be avoiding him, and had not spoken to the Roman once. Quintus was getting tired of his game, and was quickly losing his humor. Why did Yeshua not admit he saw him with the soldiers and be done? Moreover, he was thoroughly dissatisfied with those soldiers' evasive answers. He sat apart, getting angrier with all their games: Yeshua playing cat and mouse, and the soldiers' deceitfulness…

Stephanos watched the sullen Roman, and decided to tease him, "Master Quintus, you're not sulking because you failed to find master Yeshua in such a small town?"

"Did you go to town to look for me?" Yeshua's curiosity was aroused. When the Roman nodded, he queried, "Which road did you take?"

"The road by the water well," he mumbled moodily.

Yeshua wondered how they could miss each other, when he remembered the mad scramble at the Roman camp. He rubbed his chin, staring at his friend who fidgeted nervously. He smiled and asked disarmingly, "What did you think of the big sun dial in the town square?"

"S-sundial?…T-town s-square?" Quintus stuttered in confusion.

"You could not miss it; such a gigantic display."

"Oh yes, of course…the sundial," the Roman grinned nervously, perspiration running down his forehead. "How could I forget?"

Yeshua's radiant eyes fixed on him as he demanded, "What were you doing at the Roman soldiers' camp?"

Quintus let out a deep sigh, relieved the truth was out and confessed, "They want me to obtain confessions that you are Zealots."

Stephanos jumped to his feet accusing, "I heard you muttering threats back in the forest. You want confessions from us? Until recently I did not know what a Zealot was. Today I'd gladly join them just to get rid of you."

"I would also," Germanicus rejoined. "They escorted us safely from the forest. But you, nothing but problems."

"Why don't you go to your friends?" Stephanos was revolted.

"I did not know they were following us till this afternoon," Quintus explained lamely. "They grabbed me thinking I was a Zealot…"

But the Greek and his slave left the fire, to get further away from him.

"What are they planning?" Yeshua asked him.

"They wouldn't tell me," he shrugged his shoulders.

That night Germanicus slept lightly. Yeshua allowed Quintus to remain against the wishes of the others. He believed Quintus' explanation and that he had not betrayed them. But the Greek demanded that he leave his staff and dagger outside the tent.

Germanicus sat outside the tent trying to understand their complex leader. He had a supernatural sense about everything, and knew precisely everybody's movements. But, he was exasperatingly frustrating.

How was he to guard someone oblivious to danger?

· · ·

At sunrise the town square was quickly filling with people: pilgrims, tourists and town folk, in anticipation of the imminent arrival of the great curer. They listened to stories by those who had seen Shamai, or knew of his feats.

When the young men were going to town, Germanicus said they were being followed. Yeshua refuted it as mere coincidence, but at the slave's insistence they turned at the next intersection, then once more. The two soldiers not far behind did the same. After that the group remained close together for safety.

In the town square they mingled with the crowd, waiting for the holy man to arrive. Mid morning the mayor sent out a scout on a donkey to the highest hill to see if the entourage was visible. Returning he announced gleefully, "They're only a few miles away...what a spectacle!"

The show was worth the wait. Led by a small orchestra, with blaring trumpets, rattling tambourines, and booming drums, the long procession of hundreds of people leading the main attraction and spectacular highlight arrived: the great Shamai's carriage. A large, heavy, totally enclosed wagon brightly splashed in a rainbow of colors; reds, greens, blues, whites, oranges and yellows, it was pulled by four white stallions from Hispania. The coach driver sat high on the cart maneuvering the horses which pranced proudly through the ornamental gate. As they entered the square, the spectators scurried out of the way. The carriage had doors and windows on either side, covered with silk curtains which were pulled open by the passengers to peer at the gawking masses. The driver took the carriage into the square, stopping by the steps of the Inn.

The driver descended and opened the carriage door. A heavy matron came out and joined the town elders, followed by a pretty young maiden, then a couple of young men and finally two middle aged ladies. After an appropriate pause the special guest came out. At first a large white turban, with two long pink plumes followed by a brilliant blue silk cape with thousands of gems sparkling in the sun. When he stood to full height, one saw under the cape a full burgundy robe under a green cloak. He climbed the steps regally, turned to the left and to the right so the sun would reflect the luxuriant precious gems. He was a full head taller than the others, an imposing giant and quite handsome. In his late thirties, healthy and tanned, with a rectangular face, thick eyebrows over vivid black eyes, he had a long thin mustache and well proportioned goatee.

With one sweep of his darting black eyes, he uncannily computed the size of the crowd – over five thousand – and the wealth of the community – Rich.

Yeshua's eyes also swept over the spectators and he saw the two Roman soldiers among them, their eyes going from Shamai to Quintus. He avoided looking their way or acknowledging he saw them.

The mayor stepped forward, announcing in a loud voice, "Your excellency, the great Shamai, allow me to welcome you to Beth Sheeba on behalf of our town council." He bowed deeply, "As I told my wife earlier, we are living in the pages of history, honored to be witnesses to the miracle man, who will be known as one of the greatest prophets..."

Shamai's eyes looked horrified at the prospect of suffering through this prattle. He leaned over the diminutive mayor and without bothering to lower his voice demanded, "Save the speech...Is this the Inn?"

The mayor was stunned by the rude interruption, tried to regain his wits, and stammered. "Ahem! y-yes, y-your excellency, y-yes, a room was reserved for you..."

"One room?" Shamai blasted the question. "What about my entourage? How many rooms do you have? I want them all!" The owner began to stutter objections, which the holy man overruled, "All the rooms!"

The mayor tried to avoid a scene and replied diplomatically, "And you shall have them. Master Isaac you heard his excellency's wishes: give him the hotel!"

"But...but...my guests...?" master Isaac sputtered.

"Put them in your house...or, out in the street," the mayor replied off handedly.

Shamai grabbed the mayor by the shoulder and pulled him roughly, "Did you secure my fees? Two hundred gold talents..."

The mayor was terrified, "Master Hegesippus has been sick, your..." but seeing Shamai turn away in disgust, added, "I'll have it this afternoon...I promise!"

Shamai blurted out going in, "Then I'll do the miracle tomorrow..."

The mayor wiped the perspiration from his face, "Tomorrow...for the great specta...I mean, miracle. Fine!"

• • •

Word spread about the fantastic visitor so that before sunrise the following morning the square was packed to overflowing. They waited. And they waited. The sun rose, and kissed the bottom branches with no sign of the miracle man. The sun leaped above the trees, then past the meridian, and still no sign of him. No one knew what was the problem, or whether there was a problem, and no one dared utter a word of criticism for fear of offending the great man. When the shadows were stretching out, four white stallions pulling the carriage rode to the steps. After a short wait the entourage came out and proceeded into the wagon, followed by the Great Shamai.

The stallions pranced their load the few hundred paces to the magnificent mansion where the entourage descended and marched in single file into the yard.

Shamai came to the exotic fountain with the pink marble, his eyes sweeping the tropical gardens and the wealthy estate, mentally wishing he had charged twice the fees.

He climbed up onto the fountain where the two young men held him, and looked down on the spectators, waiting patiently while the mob pushed and prodded to enter. Late comers climbed the fences and higher trees. When the place was overflowing with people, he closed his eyes and began rocking back and forth, putting himself in a trance.

Yeshua's group was fortunate to find a small space by an islet, and held onto each other precariously. The two soldiers stood in a far corner of the yard and watched the young men and Shamai simultaneously.

After a long time Shamai raised his head and seemed a transformed man: no longer the showman, he had a sympathetic face, intent on helping the distressed, "Dear pilgrims of Beth Sheeba, I have been blessed with a special gift, by Lord Adonai to help and cure the sick. You will witness the Great Shamai enter this house, into that room where master Hegesippus awaits death and perform the miracle of life."

The people looked at one another shocked that he was going in, and began whispering, "Does he not know...? Is he out of his mind? That's certain death!"

Shamai heard some comments and smirked that only he had the courage to enter the house. He raised his arms, and waited for complete silence before continuing, "I call upon the Most High Lord Adonai, to thank Him for the gift of curing. I call upon His supernatural powers, to use me for the miraculous forces of life unto the dying man, and to rend asunder the demons of death...And save our suffering master Hegesippus..." Alas, his inspired words were interrupted by loud fits of coughing from the dark window, which echoed through the yard and over the spectators. Shamai stopped and stared at the window, waiting. As soon as it stopped he continued, "Within a few moments I shall promenade into that room, with the supernatural forces traveling through me...to arrest death...AND...DEFEAT DEATH...!"

Suddenly the cough interrupted him louder and more prolonged. Shamai glared at the window, visibly annoyed, and turned to the mayor, "Who dares to interrupt...?"

"Master Hegesippus," he responded on this tiptoes.

"What is the illness?" he asked suspiciously.

"CON-SUM-PTION!"

He froze staring at the mayor, bent over and stuttered, "C-contagious?"

"DEADLY!" The mayor responded grimly.

The Great Shamai straightened up slowly. His eyes lost their brilliance, indeed their focus, as he stared into space visibly shaken, considering the full ramification of the situation. His trance was broken and he could not regain his composure. He looked one way and the other, clearly searching for an escape. Finally he turned and stared through the open gate at the stallions and the carriage waiting on the street.

He returned to his speech without inspiration or enthusiasm, "It is not necessary for the Great Shamai to enter the ...the room...or the house. The celestial energy is powerful...and will travel to the old man..."

Shamai gave the service, mixing chanting prayers, some aloud, some silently, mixing ancient Hebrew with Aramaic, much of it incomprehensible to the listeners. The only blemishes, which were not his fault, were the interruptions by the cavernous cough punctuating his chants, as if taunting his pleas and reminding him death ruled this mansion. His composure faltered with each interruption, and with perspiration running down his face, he brought the service to a halt and turned to exit.

Later they learned that Shamai dropped off those in the carriage at the Inn, with an order to make arrangements to bring his possessions, while he yelled to the driver to whip the stallions and fly from the infernal town.

Back at the mansion the pilgrims discussed the man's strange behavior. Many said miracle workers were in high demand, forced to travel continually. After that they shuffled back to town.

Only Yeshua had a nagging suspicion that master Hegesippus was still doomed. He followed the crowd deeply troubled, debating whether to return and try to help the old man. However he was filled with doubts: Could he defeat death? Was he being presumptuous to think he could change nature to that extent? But, his biggest fear was being discovered, and losing his privacy forever. He did not want an itinerant's life such as Honi, traveling, without roots or family, sleeping in the fields. He wanted a life with lady Sarah, a home and children to dote on and to love. Above all he abhorred Shamai's extravagant theatrical life. While he debated this, he did not notice Germanicus beside him or the two Roman soldiers a couple of paces behind. After a long debate he decided Hegesippus had been greedy, and deserved his fate, and pressed his steps ahead.

Yeshua was never able to explain what made him suddenly turn right, take one step into the tall bushes and disappear. Once out of sight he started to run as fast as he could maneuver in the thick vegetation, in the direction of the mansion. Germanicus quickly followed, with the two Roman soldiers not far behind. A few pilgrims became curious, and ran after them.

Yeshua arrived at the mansion, found a side door and entered the house. No one dared follow inside. Germanicus ran around to the front through the garden and to the open window. There he had to jump up a couple of times to grab and pull himself up to the window sill and hang on precariously.

At first he could not see anything in the dark room, until he squinted and started to identify objects: a massive bed, and in it a skeletal, pale old man in a cloak far too big for his bony frame. His thin face in the pillows seemed like a scaffolding of bulging bones thinly covered by a transparent parchment, with blue veins parting his forehead. His breathing was shallow and erratic. Obviously death hovered over him.

When the door opened Germanicus froze, until he recognized Yeshua. The old man's big bulging eyes opened and fixed on the visitor as he approached the bed.

"Are you...the Great...Shamai?" the skeletal face wheezed.

Yeshua shook his head explaining, "He is gone...but he prayed..."

Hegesippus, wheezing louder and breathing heavier, called out, "Thief...Fraud..." His guttural words seemed to originate from the depths of a sepulcher, as he poked a bony finger at the young man's chest. His mouth began to foam and saliva drooled, "Scoundrels all of you... Vultures!.. Have you come...for the rest...of my money?"

Yeshua sympathized with the old man's helplessness, as his life slipped through his bony fingers, like fine sand through the hour glass. He took the frail hand and looked at the veins like spider webs beneath the transparent skin. He pressed it caressingly, "I have come to pray with you."

The tender touch calmed the old man. He looked into Yeshua's radiant eyes and felt a warm glow, "Have you come to take me away?"

"I came to help," he responded. "You need a friend."

The ancient man complained in monosyllables, "My wife...my children...I did it...all for them...They left me..."

"You did it for yourself," Yeshua contradicted him, "to satisfy your greed!"

Never before did anyone speak the naked truth so bluntly. But, it no longer mattered. He gazed into the young man's brilliant eyes and knew he had little time. Now, only the truth mattered. Hot tears gathered in his eyes and overflowed, as he confessed, "True...I was greedy...I beg forgiveness."

Yeshua leaned closer, "Master Hegesippus, do you repent for your evil life?"

"Yes, yes!" he cried out. "My wife...family...I don't deserve them. Ask...they forgive, I love them..."

"Do you believe in the one and only creator Yahweh?"

The sobbing man stopped and his eyes opened with fear, "You spoke His name...Who are you?"

Yeshua did not answer him but ordered sternly, "You must return the water well to the people."

"I should never have taken it," he cried out. "The water belongs to them...I shall return it..."

The young scholar held Hegesippus' frail hand placing his left on his sunken chest and prayed. A bright aura appeared over him and enveloped his head. A bright ball of fire seemed to travel along his arms covering the old body as if he were on fire.

Germanicus was flabbergasted by everything. He got a strange sensation that he was not alone, turned his head and saw persons perched on trees and fences peering. When he looked back in the room Yeshua was gone.

He looked at the old man and saw the strangest sight: Hegesippus' cheeks had acquired a rosy, healthy color. He seemed at least a decade younger. Slowly, he sat up in bed, reached for a bowl of fruit, took one and bit into it. When he coughed it was a normal cough. Germanicus felt goose pimples all over his body. Something tugged at his ankle, he jerked, losing his grip and fell into the bushes.

Years later when he tried to recount his escape, it was still a blur. He could not remember getting out of the prickly bushes, but recalled seeing a helmet as he was falling, probably one of the Roman soldiers. He did not remember running, whether he ran over or through the islets, or if the gate was open. He did not know which direction he took or how far he ran only that it was dark before he stopped.

That night he coaxed his master away from the campfire and explained, what he had seen; after Master Yeshua prayed, old Hegesippus was miraculously cured.

Stephanos listened attentively, commenting superiorly, "I am glad you came to with this fantastic story. You were a victim of Shamai's hypnotic powers; all the pilgrims were. He planted a seed suggesting Hegesippus was getting cured. Being a slave you easily fell prey to his tricks. Naturally when you saw the old man, you thought he was cured." He started to leave, stopped and advised him, "Don't repeat this to anyone, or they'll think you lost your mind..."

Germanicus remained alone reconsidering the episode. Was he an unwitting victim of hypnosis? He remembered Anna's words: master Yeshua is a very special man. The holy man Honi concurred. He had no doubts he had witnessed a supernatural miracle. He began to wonder, was master Yeshua superhuman?

· · ·

After they returned back to camp, Quintus noticed the two Romans spying on them all afternoon and into the night. Tired of this he decided to pay them a visit and resolve the problems. As he approached their camp they grabbed and pushed him into the tent, "Did you get the confessions?" the old soldier barked.

"They are not Zealots," he snapped back. "They sympathize with the cause, but, no more."

"That's as good as being one," the old man persisted.

"Like you said, we will do the rest," the young soldier tried to appease his senior companion.

"No! Give me time," Quintus tried to defuse the tension.

"So they can escape like that conspirator Shamai? He should be in prison − or dead," the old warrior shouted angrily.

"Should we arrest the Zealots, and kill...?" the young soldier joined in with impulsive enthusiasm.

Quintus panicked, "Is that what you're planning? What do you intend to do?"

The old codger realized his young partner had revealed too much and tried to control the damage, "No! Nothing…Go back. Tomorrow we'll…chat." He urged Quintus out the door brusquely, "Go back, and don't mention anything."

Quintus walked away uneasy. Part way he reconsidered, and turned back to get some clear answers. After a few paces he stopped, reconsidered it, and returned to camp.

Meanwhile the two soldiers began undressing in their tent. T h e young soldier suddenly turned to his senior, "Sir, are we wise to wait until morning? By then Shamai will be long go…"

The old soldier sniggered, "Don't you think I know? We'll get a nap until they're all asleep. Then we'll act,,,"

"…AND KILL THEM ALL?" he could hardly contain his enthusiasm.

CHAPTER XII - MESSIAH ELEAZAR

In the black of the night the two Roman soldiers got out of their cots, donned their tunics, grabbed their swords and went out. They walked silently, stealthily, from bush to bush, swords drawn, towards the young men's camp. They were trained silent killers, intending to invade and kill: quickly and swiftly. They approached their destination without seeing or hearing anyone, as all campers were asleep and the fires burned out. At the destination they separated to attack from opposite sides. They went around a large bush and continued right through the camp, without seeing a tent. They met at the other side, "Did you see the camel or the donkey?"

"No. Maybe we missed them?" They searched a larger area, and returned empty handed. "Quintus warned them," the young soldier stated the obvious.

"Mark my words; private Quintus will pay dearly," the senior soldier ground his teeth. "Which direction do you suppose they went?"

"South," the young man guessed, "to join their leader Shamai."

The old soldier considered it, and when he spoke, it sounded more like a soliloquy than a speech, "I lay in the tent thinking. Shamai and the Zealots made no eye contact. When Shamai left, they did not follow. Why? They don't know this Messiah any more than we do…"

"How can they not know their leader?" The young man found it preposterous.

"If emperor Augustus walked by, would you recognize him?" He asked and answered himself, "Of course not: nabobs don't want to be recognized by rank and file."

"Well, I did some thinking too. Why did master Yeshua run back into the mansion?"

"To rob it!" the old codger snapped. "What does that have to do with the Messiah?"

"I heard people talking," the youngster continued. "They said Hegesippus has been cured. Shamai ran away, and Yeshua went in. What does it tell you?"

"That you're out of your mind. You're as superstitious as the peasants!" He was losing patience with his protégé. "I think Shamai is a fraud…"

"At the well people were talking about someone named Eleazar. They said he is the real Messiah. And he will be doing a miracle in Shalem to the west…"

The old man exclaimed with enthusiasm, "I'll bet our legion's eagle the Zealots will be heading there. And so are we!"

"We've no time to waste: break camp and go after them," the younger man was excited. "Catch them by surprise."

"No rush. Their first impulse was to run, until they realized that's what we'd do, because we thought that's what they did, so they decided not to run, and that's what we're going to do. Do you know what they're doing?"

"I don't even know what you just said…"

The old man shook his head, "Hiding…somewhere. We'll get a good sleep, and at sunrise start for Shalem to catch Eleazar – and the Zealots!"

• • •

Before sunrise, at the Inn, a traveler entered the reception area, and greeted the owner, master Isaac, "Kind sir, I'm on my way to Jerusalem. I'm looking for four young men traveling with a camel and a donkey…"

Before he could finish, the owner grabbed him by the throat with one hand, "Did those soldiers send you? Confess before I break your neck."

"N-n-no! No sir," the traveler quivered, fighting for breath as his wind pipe was being crushed. "P-please, s-sir, you're choking…I'll explain."

The hotelman eased his grip barking, "Speak! Fast and clear. Persuade me why I should not break the neck of a traitor."

"I'm no traitor," he squealed a protest, pulling out a sheet of papyrus. "I have… a letter, for master Yeshua…from Naza…"

Master Isaac ripped it from his hand, holding him captive still, glanced at the message, saw Yeshua's name, and finally released him. "Go get master Yeshua," he ordered a servant girl who ran. "Tell him he has news from Nazareth."

Yeshua and the boys arrived instantaneously, and took the letter, "Thank you, it's from my sister Debborah." He turned to Stephanos. "Pay the good man."

The Greek dug out a coin while Yeshua opened and read it:

"Dear brother Yeshua,

"I hope you're fine. We have a crisis here. Roman soldiers invaded, and are arresting people, accusing them of being Zealots. Many were taken away. Others ran to the hills and forests. Master Benjoseph disappeared without a trace.

"A couple of soldiers have set up camp across our street and father says we are being watched. They suspect you are a Zealot and want to arrest you.

"Father says you must not return or communicate with us, because you will be at risk, and put us in danger too. So, for once in your life, listen and stay away. And don't write.

"Everybody sends their love. I was also told to say lady Sarah is fine, and there is no trouble. She misses you terribly, but cannot write.

"Your loving sister

"Debborah (busy bee)"

Postscriptum – Esau says the boat is coming along fine. Marcus is shockingly cooperative. Can you believe it?``

The letter had the opposite effect for he announced immediately, "I'm sorry, but I have to return to Nazareth. My family needs me."

Stephanos glanced at it arguing, "Your presence will only complicate matters."

Quintus was more forceful, "They will arrest you before you set foot in your yard."

"Did you not say once: trust Roman justice?" Yeshua countered sardonically.

"I did. But, I know my commanders: they arrest everybody and let the magistrates decide. You'll rot in prison for years before a hearing."

Stephanos thought of one person who could stop him, so he confided, "Think of lady Sarah. If you're arrested, it will break her heart."

"You're correct," he sighed adding, "I will write them instead."

Stephanos interrupted stunned, "If the letter is intercepted they will learn your whereabouts."

The Israeli reconsidered; to whom could he write safely? His family and closest friends were out of the question. He did not want to compromise lady Sarah. Suddenly he blurted out enthusiastically, "Master Yacek! Why did I not think of him before?"

"Is he a trusted friend?" Quintus demanded with skepticism.

"Not exactly: he led the opposition to my sermon," he replied lamely. "A lonely widower...but he is honest"

"Don't do it," the Greek warned him. "Old men never forgive or forget. He'll carve your heart out and hand it to the Romans."

Quintus concurred. "A lonely man will seek sympathy from strange quarters."

Yeshua persisted and wrote, not one but two letters: one to master Yacek requesting he take the second letter to Debborah. He handed it to master Isaac to give it to a traveler going north. "Thank you for taking us in last night," Yeshua embraced the owner. "Are you certain you don't want to be paid?"

"You should thank Shamai," master Isaac laughed. "He paid for the week."

"I had forgotten the luxury of a good bed," Stephanos chirped.

Master Isaac directed them to Shalem, "Take the main road to the west until you arrive at the synagogue where you turn right. That will take you to the village."

As they left the square, two blocks to the south, two Romans leading a horse were entering the gate. When the old soldier saw the young men, he stopped, "By the most sacred Jove, patron god of Rome...Do I see an illusion?"

"That's no mirage, sir. The Zealots and the traitor Quintus, are going our way. We only need the Messiah and we'll have all the terrorists."

"Let's stay back out of sight. In Shalem we'll pounce, and, phtt! Slaughter the lambs," he enjoyed the expectation of sweet revenge long overdue.

The young men turned at the synagogue with the pursuers well behind blending with the crowd.

They walked abreast except Germanicus, who gave wide berth from Yeshua. He could not get the transformation of Hegesippus from his mind and could not stop shaking. His tribal priest in Europe said that evil spirits caused all supernatural occurrences, including sickness and death. Hence he concluded, since he discovered Yeshua's secret he would be the evil spirit's next victim.

Last night Germanicus refused to sleep in the hotel room as he feared Yeshua. Alas, even in the hallway he suffered terrible nightmares. He dreamt that as he was hanging onto Hegsippus' window sill, Yeshua transformed himself into a giant snake which hypnotized the dying man. Then it entered inside his body through his mouth, into the chest cavity, and proceeded to devour all the worms and maggots. Coming out, it saw the slave, hypnotizing him. It started slithering towards him. He fell into the bushes and ran as fast as he could. Alas, every time he looked back the snake was at his heels, and he was not able to get away. He ran through the streets and fields, jumping over fences but the snake was on top of him ready to pounce. He awoke in panic, perspiring, and out of breath. Every time he closed his eyes the chase resumed, and as much as he tried to flee he failed for his feet seemed stuck to the ground.

Yeshua walked oblivious to the slave's problems. He worried for his family's safety, blaming himself for the problem he had caused. He remembered one sentence in Debborah's letter: "I was told to tell you lady Sarah is fine…" Why did she not write: "Lady Sarah is fine?" He suspected that lady Sarah, not wishing to worry him, told her to write she is fine. His fear that her father would take revenge was being realized.

In a patriarch society appearance was everything.

Master Stephanos watched his friend's somber mood, and feared that unless he was distracted he would continue to worry, until he decided he must turn back and no one would be able to stop him. So he decided to try and brighten his spirits.

He began with a general remark, "So far we witnessed two so called Messiahs. After considering them I say both are shams. Unless Eleazar proves otherwise, I'll pronounce them all to be frauds." He glanced at the Israeli who did not react, "Are you sleepwalking? I disparaged your holy men without getting any argument?"

"They're all right," Yeshua muttered uninterested.

Quintus joined the debate. "Master Stephanos is right. They were all glitter and show. Shamai was a circus, and Honi what a sham."

"The title of Messiah was wasted on them," the Greek continued. "Religion is fodder for the masses. It keeps the population sedated, praying to God to take them out of desperate straits." He sniggered cynically, "Emperors should pay these Messiahs handsomely for keeping the masses preoccupied." There still was no reaction from the Israeli, so the Greek tried again, "The best of the lot was Hanina ben Dosa. He survived bites from three poisonous serpents...a most amazing accomplishment."

"I had an experience like that," the Roman interjected. "I was bit by one of the most poisonous serpents in Israel. I swear a miracle saved me. Master Yeshua was there."

Yeshua did not hear him as he was still fuming at the Greek's previous sarcastic remark. Unable to hold back any longer he protested, "Master Honi's prayers brought that rain. All the people who were there agreed..."

"But he admitted he was not the Messiah," Stephanos retorted, adding sardonically, "That leaves Hegesippus. Can you prove Shamai cured him?"

Germanicus who had waited impatiently for the subject interjected impulsively, "I saw the old man cured...It was not Shamai."

"Who else could it be? We all saw Shamai pray for him," the Israeli insisted, trying to discourage any discussion which may hint of his involvement.

"The one who changes into a snake did it," the slave exclaimed. "Yesterday I went back to the mansion. I hung onto the window sill and saw the old man change from a skeleton to a robust man..."

Yeshua tensed up, feeling the small hairs on his neck stand, but tried not to betray his emotions. How did he miss seeing the slave, he wondered? He decided never to do another miracle unless he was positively alone...better still - never again!

Stephanos let out a roaring laughter, "Are you still persisting with that? Did I not say Shamai hypnotized the masses? You innocent fool!"

"Don't let it get you down," Quintus tried to help him. "Those showmen are excellent tricksters."

The Greek and the Roman shook their heads, as if to say, "What can you expect from a mere slave?"

Germanicus' jaws tightened at their derision.

They continued the trek arguing, discussing and bantering. Stephanos' plan succeeded, when Yeshua admitted that turning back was not the solution. Only Germanicus felt slighted, by their arrogance, and frightened by the snake man.

Late in the afternoon they set up camp in Shalem. After making inquiries they learned that master Eleazar had performed a miracle three days ago, but left to a small village a couple of hills yonder to the west, well inside Samaria. The two Roman soldiers camped in the woods, from where they could easily spy on them.

With dinner cooking, they jousted with the staffs, which became a daily routine, holding friendly bouts, with Yeshua overseeing and advising. Privately he thought Quintus was the strongest fighter, stubbornly aggressive, always on the offensive but tardy to defend. Stephanos was the extreme opposite; excellent beyond reproach on the defensive, but failing to take advantage of openings presented by an opponent. The pleasant surprise was the slave for he proved to be exceptional with every facet of the sport. He was patient, defended himself carefully, analytical as he tested the opponent, and ready to strike when a weakness appeared.

After dinner Yeshua, who had noticed Germanicus' aloofness, decided to find out what was the problem. Normally he let the slave resolve whatever bothered him, but he wanted to know precisely what he had seen in Hegsippus' mansion. He picked up some papyrus and a stylus, mixed some ink, and approached the slave. He was still a few paces away when Germanicus tensed up, so he asked innocently, "Have you thought about your daughter Lygia?"

The slave relaxed and sighed longingly, "All the time, master Yeshua. I see her smile in everything…How can I miss someone so much, when I hardly know her?"

"Would you like to write her a letter?" he asked.

He nodded emphatically then checked himself, "You know I cannot write."

"Tonight you can. You dictate, and I'll write."

"You would do that for me?" his eyes beamed.

Yeshua motioned for him to sit closer, and they wrote a letter which the girl cherished and guarded until she grew up into a young lady, and the papyrus yellowed.

"My dearest daughter Lygia,

"You are too young to read or comprehend these words, but I must write to explain my thoughts and feelings, lest fate deal me a blow and we never meet again. If this should happen I want you to know that I will always bless the day God gave me you.

"I had to leave you because I must help my master search for a holy person: the Messiah. We have had many strange adventures fraught with danger. In this strange land, outsiders always live in danger and give thanks for surviving each day. Someday when you are old enough to understand the divine, the Creation and destiny of man, I will explain this journey and the need to search. For me the Messiah is my quest for freedom. But, every person has his reason to search for him.

"Tomorrow we will be traveling west into Samaria. I am told they despise Israelis, so the dangers will be greater still.

"If my premonition comes true and I fail to return, think kindly of your father whom you barely knew. Remember me as the enemy of tyranny, and defender of the disadvantaged. Never forget I love you.

Your loving father
(signature mark) X

Yeshua folded and addressed it to master Honi's tent at the outskirts of Laish, "Tomorrow we'll give it to a traveler going east."

"Thank you master Yeshua," the slave mumbled. "You are too kind."

"Tell me precisely what happened with master Hegesippus?" he whispered.

The slave stared at him disbelieving he did not know. Then he suspected this was a trick to find out how much he saw before crushing him. A cold perspiration ran down his spine, and he drew back. Yeshua saw him flinching, and leaned closer, "You see, Germanicus, I was recently told I could do some extraordinary things, but I never saw any of it..." He admitted being told on the eve of the expedition that he performed miracles, but did not know the extent of his powers, or what he was to do with them. The slave listened to the extraordinary story and believed him. In turn he described the fantastic transformation of Hegesippus. He told him how he became frightened and fled.

"Why were you afraid?"

"My tribal priest said all supernatural events were the work of some evil gods. Last night I dreamt you changed into a snake."

Yeshua wanted to laugh but seeing the slave utterly serious, he explained, "You have no reason to fear. I only want to help." When the slave nodded, he added, "You must never repeat to anyone what I confided. You must promise."

"Does lady Anna know?" Germanicus asked and he nodded. "Did you cure her?" He nodded again. He felt sufficiently inspired to ask, "Are you the Messiah?"

He tried to remember the words his parents used when they told him, before answering, "That word was not used." He smiled then added coyly. "Perhaps when we finish the expedition I will ask you: Germanicus who do you think I am?"

Next morning they started for the village before sunrise, and were surprised to see more and more travelers – singles, couples, and extended families – trekking west. Master Eleazar must be very popular, they thought. Finally Yeshua asked one group why they were interested in the holy man.

"We will not be stopping at the village," their leader informed them. "We must proceed to Caesarea. The emperor's busts arrived in port. They will put them in the Temples and every synagogue. We must stop them from profaning our prayer houses."

Yeshua remembered his orders from the siccarrii and turned to his companions, "I cannot go with you. I must go to Caesarea. I have to help..."

"What about Eleazar?" Stephanos was surprised by the sudden change in plans.

"If they are not stopped, Eleazar and everything else will become irrelevant."

"Your friend is correct," the stranger agreed.

"Why not compromise? We`ll go to the village for a day..." Quintus suggested.

"Today," the Israeli was adamant. "If master Eleazar is not ready, I will not wait."

At the village they were directed to an empty field away from the houses. A large canopy was raised and bleachers were being constructed on three sides of the covered area. An old worker pointed out Eleazar. The young scholar liked the old, bearded patriarch, with long white hair, the moment he saw him. He explained their dilemma, "We want to see your work, but are pressed to continue to Caesarea..."

"I understand," the old man nodded. "The statues must be stopped... a dangerous undertaking, but crucial to Israelis' very existence."

"If you can do the work today, we will..." Yeshua started to say.

"Say no more," Eleazar assented. "Join in and help us, and I will do it tonight."

The boys turned to start working when the patriarch stopped them, "Before you jump into it, I must warn you, your work tonight will be extremely dangerous." He looked at them, and explained their responsibilities, "Each of you will be stationed at each side of the canopy, to protect the audience. I expect a terrible battle…"

"Battle? I understood this to be a miracle, not a duel," Stephanos retorted.

"Exorcism: a battle of God versus Satan is a combat to repossess a person from the devil. Tonight I will attempt to expel demons from a fine lady. The demon took over her mind and soul." He pointed to a wagon parked nearby, totally enclosed except for a small window with iron bars. They went and inspected it as he continued, "It will be a war of wills for her spirit."

"Why is she chained?" Yeshua inquired.

"Demons don't relinquish control without a desperate fight: a combat to the finish. That is why it is dangerous. Still interested?"

"Is it not dangerous to you?" Quintus asked.

"I am willing to risk it. But spectators become mesmerized, and fail to defend themselves when the possessed person lashes out…or if the demon attacks…" He rolled his eyes to the heavens shaking his head, "I have seen innocent people killed…"

"Are we…the first line…of defense?" Stephanos stammered when he guessed their responsibilities.

The old man nodded. They looked at one another, shrugged and joined him.

• • •

When the traveler arrived in Nazareth with Yeshua's letter, two boys escorted him to master Yacek's home. They knocked on the door and left. The traveler told the old man he was bringing a letter, holding it out, but master Yacek stood in the doorway making no move to take it. Many thoughts raced through his mind: first, he thought it was a mistake for no one ever wrote to him; second, he suspected this was a message of sorrow, about the death or terminal illness of one of his children. He looked at the traveler's eyes with fear, but drew a blank. He reached out with a trembling hand, took it, and did not see the traveler leave, and forgot to thank him. He closed the door and shuffled back in for the bad news. He fought to break the seal, finally opening it:

"Dear master Yacek,

"Shalom. May the Creator bless you and keep you. Enclosed is a short scroll addressed to my family. Our house is under surveillance by Romans making it dangerous to write to them directly. I ask you as a friend to deliver the scroll to my sister Debborah. Please be careful, and make up some plausible excuse for going there, as the soldiers may question you.

"Yeshua"

Intead of relief, he sneered complaining, "Does he think I'm a fool? I know I need a pretext to go there; If I decide to go there."

Going to the carpenter's was the furthest thing on his mind. His memory rushed back to the Sabbath, and Yeshua's first sermon. The events of that day rushed through his mind infuriating him. He remembered the young arrogant pup accusing him, a God fearing Israeli, of wearing an anklet of a pagan god. His imagination took over his memory, distorting the events of the past. He saw Yeshua's accusing finger, "That's him: Yacek, the blasphemer! Idolater! Stone him!" He remembered the entire congregation glaring, while he covered his face, suffering their accusations. He felt frightened, vulnerable, humiliated. Now the deep lines on his face darkened, "Well, self righteous, arrogant Yeshua. You thought you were above everyone…better than old man Yacek. Now who is crawling, begging for favors? Now it`s time for revenge!"

He hid the letter inside his robe, wrapped a shawl around his neck, though it was hot outside, took his walking stick and started for the door. He stopped outside, arguing with the imaginary Yeshua, "So, you came crawling like a crab, begging for help. Oh, I will help…I'll turn you over to the Romans, ha, ha, ha…"

As his subconscious struggled with his memory, he walked, excited at the expectation of exacting revenge. He saw two Roman soldiers, and started towards them. Soon he recognized an officer, "Ho! Master centurion," he called from a distance.

The centurion half turned with a frown, "What do you want old man?"

He tried to rush calling repeatedly, but kept tripping on the uneven dirt road. The soldier standing with the centurion begged off and left. The old man was so excited that he exhausted himself, arriving out of breath. In the short moment he stood catching his breath, his subconscious replayed the events of the Sabbath long ago. He remembered how

Yeshua came to him after the sermon, and before Yacek could warn him not to touch the sore knee, the young man unwrapped and held it. He cringed expecting horrible pain, only to be surprised. It never pained again. Was that the moment he was cured?

Yacek next remembered the marketplace when Yeshua brought the beautiful young lady Sarah to meet him. Ever since his wife passed away, no one cared or visited him. But the young scholar cared. And his lady friend cared. They stopped, visited and listened. He smiled, remembering her gracious reaction when he presented her with his gold anklet. Her smile was a beam from the sun, reminding him of a time almost fifty years before, when he presented a pair of earrings to a beautiful young lady, who later became his wife. She was not as beautiful as lady Sarah, but he loved her without reserve. What she gave him in return was priceless: her love. And she taught him to listen to the birds singing.

He wondered if lady Sarah would give young Yeshua something as important. He remembered how she touched his face softly, kissing his cheek saying, "Thank you for the anklet," and tears rolled down his cheeks.

The centurion barked impatiently, "Hurry up old man. I haven't got all day."

Master Yacek looked deeply into his eyes, "You should have a whole day, sir: to listen to the birds singing." He pointed to a tree, "There, do you hear them?"

The officer grumbled angrily, turned and marched away furiously.

Master Yacek continued to master Joseph's house. As he descended the hill he saw two soldiers camped in the field across from the carpenter's. He placed his walking stick's end on a rock, the other end on the ground and stepped in the middle breaking it. He picked up the broken halves, happy with the pretext to visit his carpenter.

"Yeshua has always been special," he replied to their warm welcome. "He is like a son to me!"

They gathered around the fire while James and Debborah explained Yeshua's message: they were on the way to Caesarea to negotiate with the tetrarch over the emperor's statues. Joseph and Miriam exchanged worried glances knowing that Samaria was dangerous for Israelis. Many locals left, on impulse, to Caesarea to stop the Romans. There was much talk about a confrontation, perhaps a battle with the oppressors. Why was their son risking his life, they wondered? Debborah read about a traitor who had caused many deaths, and who had to be stopped.

James sent Debborah up to the roof saying, "I'll get Esau and Marcus and we'll send them on a special errand…" When they got there he came to the point, "We want you to investigate master Nehemiah's past." They looked at one another wondering what was going on. "Master Esau you will go to Tyre, master Marcus you will search in Sepphoris. Find out everything about him: his reputation, what architectural work he has done and most importantly, find out if he ever collaborated with the Romans." Then he added some timely advice, "Ask only the commoners and servants. Their ears are close to the ground, and they will tell the truth. Avoid royalty and the rich as they have agendas, and cannot be trusted." He handed them a few coins.

The two young men left immediately. He smiled at his sister, "I wonder what evil secrets lurk in that man's heart?"

· · ·

The sun was setting and the first stars appeared, as the people arrived anxious to see master Eleazar at work. At first they trickled in singles and couples, then larger groups and finally entire families. Soon the bleachers were full yet more people continued to come, sitting on the ground in front of the bleachers.

Eleazar's young helpers brought out oil lamps and lit up torches which they set up around the canopy making the area as bright as midday. Straw mats were laid under the canopy and they brought out holy water, burning incense, a large jug of water and a basin. While the props were coming, a feeling of drama and expectation rose in the crowd. Spectators exchanged fantastic stories about the holy man's past successes, for his miracles were legendary in Samaria.

When the atmosphere reached fever pitch, workers donning colorful tunics came out with tambourines pounding and horns blaring, announcing the beginning of the night's event. Finally, from the depths of the black night came out the old man, wearing a common but handsome brown robe and sandals. There was nothing glaring or loud about Eleazar, as he walked to the center of the straw mats, looking around, clearly pleased to see a large crowd. He stood erect and proud, as a stately holy man. He raised his arms for silence and began his announcement.

"Good evening friends and visitors. My name is Eleazar. Tonight with Lord Adonai's help, and your prayers, I will liberate a lady who many of you know, a widow, and mother of six children, from the controlling grips of the demon. Most of you know lady Priscilla's story. Allow me to tell the visitors. She is twenty seven years of age, recently widowed, with little children. A year ago neighbors began to notice her behaving strangely: talking to herself, sitting and staring vacantly, arguing with herself using multiple strange voices. They reported a man's voice, a woman's voice, even a child crying and a baby wailing, all apparently speaking at the same time out of her mouth. There seemed to be multiple persons within her, fighting to take control. Make no mistake those are different personas of Satan within her. Neighbors said she started leaving her children, more and more often and for longer periods of time. The past six months she has hardly been around to feed or cloth them.

"Why did she become Satan's prisoner? Opinions vary. Perhaps pressures since her husband died, constant demands to care and feed so many mouths, or pressures from creditors and tax collectors. People pointed to her irreligious upbringing as the fatal flaw in a weak character, too easy for Satan to overpower and control. Some openly accused her of weak morals and living the life of a harlot. But, we are not here to judge, but to help." He raised his voice in a crescendo, speaking louder and louder exploding every syllable as he announced, with his eyes riveted on the audience, "AND-LORD-ADONAI-WILL-DELIVER-THIS-SINNER-FROM-SATAN!"

He glared directly at the spectators as he spoke, and the sparking fire from the torches reflected in his eyes. They seemed mesmerized. He lowered his voice and spoke softly, forcing them to lean forward, straining to hear, "I do not exaggerate that this is the worst case I have seen. Do not be disappointed or angry if I don't succeed liberating her tonight, for I dare not push her too far. That may kill her. But, if I fail, I will return, again and again until I defeat Satan. You can help by praying to Lord Adonai to help me liberate her soul."

Then he addressed the pilgrims at the front, closest to the canopy, "I must warn you that lady Priscilla, like all the possessed, has almost supernatural strength. She is chained for her safety as well as yours. If she should break loose, those of you at the front will be in danger. So, move back beyond the bleachers." He motioned them but they barely shifted back one cubit. He raised his voice, "go back at least twenty cubits."

The pilgrims grudgingly shuffled back another cubit.

When he looked back at the unhappy spectators, Yeshua recognized the two Roman soldiers sitting no further than a couple of paces behind him. He glanced over to Germanicus who nodded. The others winked that they also recognized them.

Eleazar continued, "When I drag the demon out, you will not see him, for he is invisible…" Some spectators guffawed sarcastically, "Yeah, yeah!" but the old man ignored them and continued, "The truth is no living person, including myself, has ever seen him…Perhaps a special person, with divine qualities may see him, but, I am positive none of you are he." They laughed at the witty remark, as he picked up the jug of water explaining, "However, if you pay close attention you will witness Satan's presence though you will not see him. I will pour some water into this basin and leave it here. When I dispossess Satan, I will order him to step through the basin as he exits. Watch closely and you will see the water disturbed, and boiling steam appear from it." The people who jeered now sat silently. The old man filled two cups which he gave to his helpers, saying, "Take a sip from it and verify it is indeed cool water, and fresh, from the cistern. After the demon steps in the basin, if you touch it, you will find it boiling hot."

Germanicus and Quintus tasted it and agreed it was cool water. The basin was placed a couple of paces to the right of Yeshua.

Eleazar pointed offstage, and two muscular youths approached, escorting a small thin person, robed and chained, to the center under the canopy. It was lady Priscilla, though many who knew her did not recognize her. She looked like a wild creature from the deep jungle, with long, frizzy, disheveled hair, filthy with caked mud. Her face was multi-colored, swollen and bruised, her robe in tatters, and her feet bare and dirty. The chain tying her upper arms and wrists bound them behind her back. It was a thick chain strong enough to tether a good size bull. Her escorts turned her around, so everyone could see her clearly. She gazed, but did not see them as her eyes seemed out of focus. She let out a growl and puffs of smoke spewed from her nostrils and mouth. Children shrieked and women gasped nervously, as tension mounted with fear. Some spectators in front stood up and ran back behind the bleachers.

Eleazar motioned the two escorting men to sit Priscilla down. One of them whispered to her and they tried to force her to sit, but she lunged for their throats, hissing and snapping her jaw trying to tear into their jugular. They scrambled tripping over each other, and ran away into the dark. The crowd roared enjoying the mishap. Priscilla turned to the source of the noise, realizing there were people present, but when she stared her eyes had a vacant look as a cow looks, glassy-eyed without emotions.

Eleazar approached her slowly, carefully, making no sudden moves, speaking softly, soothingly, to keep her calm. He took her arms and coaxed her to kneel down with him. Then he got her to sit down. He began to chant prayers. The words and the tune were strange to the audience for they never heard the song, or recognize that it was ancient Hebrew. But, the chant caught Priscilla's attention and for the first time her face relaxed and she appeared serene. He repeated the phrase many times until her lips began to move mouthing the words. She began to utter a tuneless sound. Then he spoke to her, in a soft tone, almost a monotone, staring intently into her eyes. Some thought he was trying to reach inside Priscilla's head where he could grab satan and rip him out. Their hands tightened as they willed him to bring out the demon. But, Priscilla stared back like an emotionless rock. He spoke for a long time, pleading, then ordering, whispering persuasively, then yelling, and finally he started to pray. The audience, hearing the familiar supplication, joined in and the powerful invocation of thousands of voices resonated and traveled towards the stars. Many said afterwards they felt a mantle of tranquility come over them as if a powerful spirit descended and hovered above them.

His helpers handed him a container of burning incense. He swung it at the end of the chain, sending perfumed smoke at her, all the while chanting benedictions. He went around her twice and the aromatic fumes totally enveloped her. He returned the incense and was given an urn filled with holy water. From it he took out a sprinkling silver tool, showering her as he prayed. As the droplets fell on her there was a loud sizzle and the liquid instantly evaporated forming large white clouds. She shrieked and cowered trying to defend herself from the liquid as if the droplets were sharp needles, piercing her. The old man went around her, bathing her with the holy water, singing incantations until most of the area beneath the canopy turned into one gigantic cloud. Some people surmised that if the liquid evaporated on contact she must be as hot as molten steel. Eleazar handed back the urn and walked into the vapor clouds totally disappearing. All they heard were his shouts to the demon:

"SATAN! In the name of Lord Adonai, I order you to free this woman and return to your eternal fires! Satan of the dark, leave Priscilla's body now!"

He held her by the shoulders shaking her and shouting until his voice became hoarse. His face and hair were dripping wet. Suddenly a blood curdling scream exploded somewhere within the cloud, and cut the night. Multiple voices of men, women and children started a clatter of arguments together with animal growls which came simultaneously from the possessed woman. Suddenly a baby's screeching cry drowned out all the voices and growls. The high pitch hurt the people's ears and they cupped their hands to cover them. It seemed dozens of persons were trapped inside her, arguing and fighting, but when the clouds dissipated they saw only the holy man standing over Priscilla. Her face was contorting and the strange voices came from the depths of her bowels. Her body started going through convulsions, her muscles writhing, flexing and her arms and wrists bleeding from the chain which cut into her flesh, as she struggled to break free. The pilgrims saw the thick chain and sympathized with her, screaming and demanding she be freed. Eleazar continued shaking her and arguing for Satan to let her free. Suddenly there was an explosion, and pieces of disintegrated chain flew like missiles in every direction. There was a collective gasp. Chunks of iron, short and long, struck the surprised spectators cutting some and leaving welts and blood. One sizable piece crashed into a pilgrim's temple, not far from Germanicus, and he watched in awe as the man stiffened up as if frozen, a shocked look on his face, blood oozing down over his eyes and cheeks, as he toppled in a heap, dead. People cried out from injury and shock and hurdled over each other rushing to escape. Women fainted, children screamed and bellowed, terrorized, while parents tried to cart them away. Some lost control and screamed uncontrollably, frozen with fright, unable to run or comprehend orders. It was a general pandemonium.

Eleazar shouted orders at Satan and prayed frantically, for he knew if he stopped now it could prove fatal to them as well as himself.

Yeshua's group, stationed at the edge of the mats, stood shocked and perplexed. If Priscilla made a dash for the spectators, they were expected to stop her. Germanicus, who had suffered from nightmares the previous night, felt this was a continuation of his battle with Satan. He stood trembling, his body clammy from perspiration and his face ashen white. He felt exhausted and on the verge of passing out. Quintus, though born and raised in Israel, learned more about the spiritual life of the country this night than in his entire life. Stephanos who had studied and witnessed every aspect of religion from the pagan plains of Lusitania to the mystic mountains of northern India, had never seen a more surreal clash for control of the soul and the person.

Yeshua suffered Priscilla's pain, as prisoner of the demon's work, and had a premonition his destiny would be to wage eternal war against this evil.

When Priscilla snapped the heavy chain she stood up, raising her arms and grabbing Eleazar by the scruff of the neck, growling and squeezing her hands to crush his wind pipe. He felt as if all the persons inside her grabbed him, and did not fight her, lowering his voice instead, chanting softly, lyrically, the same chants that initially put her in a trance. He knew his life hung by a thread, and the next few moments were precious. She squeezed while he chanted, his face turning red and the veins swelling, but his eyes remained riveted on hers, oblivious to danger. He was about to pass out when she eased the pressure, her tense body relaxing, and her fingers finally releasing the death grip. He took her hands gently in his and sat her down again. He whispered chants and his intense steely eyes mesmerized her until her eyelids began to droop in slumber.

At that moment the old Roman soldier leaned to his companion, "When the holy man starts yelling again, kill those two. I'll get Yeshua and the other."

Yeshua overheard him and saw them pointing at him. He tried to warn his companions, but before he could react, Eleazar commanded Satan to free the woman. Priscilla was deeply asleep, yet her body started to shake and convulse as if inside her a volcanic turmoil boiled ready to erupt. Her body levitated and floated above the mat. She started to heave and breathe heavily, puffs of smoke gushing from her flared nostrils. Eleazar raised his voice, prayed, took the urn, showering holy water over her, filling the area with white clouds. He shouted hoarsely, "IN THE NAME OF LORD ADONAI, I ORDER YOU TO GET OUT!"

As the clouds drifted away they saw her open her jaw exposing fangs while myriad voices screamed and swore at the holy man. She began to stand up. The spectators, fearing the battle would spill onto the bleachers, started to push to get out, tripping and falling over each other, spilling oil lamps and knocking over torches on the ground. Some caught fire. Panic ensued. The two Romans unsheathed their swords but were knocked over by the frantic mob.

Eleazar was locked in a battle to the finish. He knew if he failed she would tear him to pieces. He ordered and prayed, Priscilla growled and rebelled. Then something supernatural happened: puffs of smoke spewed from her nostrils which grew larger. It seemed Priscilla was spewing smoke from the depths of hell. The clouds grew larger as she screamed terrorized, flung herself in the air like a discarded rag landing on the mats heavily, and passing out.

Only Yeshua saw exactly what happened next. He watched a hairy creature coming out of her nostrils. At first a large hoof appeared, then an entire hind leg followed by the other, then the lower body of the animal came out which looked like a giant goat. But, the upper body was an evil looking man with a goatee. He recognized one of the many disguises of Satan. Seeing Yeshua it turned to run away.

At that moment the two Romans attacked them. Yeshua grabbed the invisible Satan and wrestled him back to the basin, where he forced him to step into the water. When the demon touched it, it sizzled and puffed forming giant white clouds engulfing them. Watching the surreal scene, the spectators knew Satan was loose they panicked and ran helter - skelter. Yeshua pushed the billowing ball of clouds at the two soldiers, who, backed away terrified, then took off into the night.

A few spectators remained in the bleachers trembling with fear. Dozens were injured. Four were killed. For generations historians described this as a terrifying battle when good won over evil.

Yeshua watched the two Romans disappear into the night. Stephanos and Quintus went to Eleazar who was kneeling over the unconscious woman. Only Germanicus took an oil lamp and walked over to inspect the ground where Yeshua had struggled with an invisible force. He recognized the imprints of Yeshua's sandals, and beside them saw something out of this world: deep imprints of something resembling large hoofs of a beast. They led to the basin, and from there wet prints continued towards the bleachers. He touched the water in the basin and it was boiling hot. Yet he remembered drinking it before and it was cool. He looked at Yeshua and marveled, "What man is this...who fights invisible monsters?"

Master Stephanos asked Eleazar, "Is she freed from Satan?"

The holy man nodded all the while staring at Yeshua, for he too had seen the young man wrestle the invisible demon. He turned to the Greek, "She will not remember any of this. She'll need a long quiet rest."

"There were times I swore you were breathing your last," Quintus commented enthusiastically, still worked up from the battle. "Were you not afraid?"

"I was too busy to be afraid," the holy man chuckled as he stood up. "I was an instrument in the hands of Lord Adonai. I knew I would be spared."

Yeshua and Germanicus joined them. "Those two soldiers were here."

"There is no time to waste," Quintus urged them. "Let's be gone before they find us again."

They quickly said good bye to the holy man and took their animals. Eleazar detained Yeshua, "You wrestled the invisible Satan. Only one person is capable of seeing him. Tonight I was blessed, for I beheld the anointed one. Go, master Yeshua, and may you always travel under the protective wings of the Creator. Shalom."

They traveled under the glow of the stars, for the moon was long gone. The uneven road was filled with ruts, and they kept tripping on clumps of dirt or slipping on loose stones. But they pushed ahead knowing each step increased the distance from their pursuers. They trekked for a long time and were the only ones on the road for miles when tiredness began to overpower them. Stephanos noticed this and decided to shake them awake, "After much consideration I concluded master Eleazar was the greatest hoax of all: a bigger fraud than Shamai..."

That started them arguing and yelling instantly.

Quintus objected the loudest, "I was most impressed. That skinny woman, little more than a pile of bones snapping a heavy chain that two full grown horses couldn't...it was shocking. Did you see those two men struck by the chain crumple over dead?"

"Explain how the holy water sizzled and boild as it touched her? And the smoke that spewed from her nostrils?" Yeshua yelled forcefully.

The Greek scoffed superiorly, "The chain links could have been pre-cut leaving a thin strand of steel holding it together. One pull and – BOOM! It snapped. The water evaporating, it's a chemical reaction. I suspect her rags were bathed in some secret chemical which when mixed with the other liquid sizzled instantly. As to her spewing smoke, that is elementary. She ingested something or held it under her tongue which at the appropriate moment she bit into it, causing smoke and clouds to exhale."

"And the multiple voices we heard? There were men, women, grown ups, children, even animals within her," Quintus countered stubbornly.

"Ventriloquists train to emit any sound they wish," the Greek shrugged it off.

Yeshua shook his head exasperated, "Rabbi ben Lebbus was correct. You accept skepticism so enthusiastically, that the flimsiest argument against the supernatural will always win with you. You would not accept God, if He stared you in the face."

"I am not faithless," the Greek sounded injured. "Prove God or Satan exists and I'll embrace Him willingly."

"What about me wrestling Satan?" Yeshua asked something he knew the Greek could not refute.

"WHAT SATAN?" Stephanos and Quintus asked in unison.

Yeshua suddenly remembered Eleazar's statement that Satan was invisible to all but the rarest person. They probably did not see him, and he was not able to explain it.

Luckily Germanicus came to his rescue, "After the exorcism I inspected the ground where they wrestled and saw hoof prints of some big animal, probably a giant goat in the dust..."

"So Satan has the shape of a goat?" Stephanos guffawed sardonically, "The most common animal in Israel? Germanicus, you suffer from an overactive imagination. "

"When I touched the water in the basin, it was boiling hot after the evil spirit disturbed it," the slave insisted.

"I admit old Eleazar was a master, leaving no trick unused," the Greek smirked. He was a show to behold, but no miracle, I assure you."

Stephanos marched smugly, for he had succeeded awakening his companions. Secretly however his own resolution had been shaken. Though outwardly he sounded confident, deep inside he wondered if he did not witness more of the supernatural than he was willing to admit. When he analyzed everything, tiny lady Priscilla seemed possessed; how else could one explain the flying piece of chain killing the spectators? How to explain dozens of voices and animals screaming all at once? No ventriloquist he knew could match that. He could not explain the boiling water, or Yeshua wrestling Satan, because he and the Roman were giving all their attention to the soldiers, missing Yeshua's battle altogether.

Quintus also felt an aura of the supernatural that night, admitting it contained surreal moments. He hoped all Messiahs would prove as entertaining.

Germanicus kept touching the tips of his fingers which were still numb from the boiling water, and was certain their leader had wrestled an invisible spirit.

Yeshua was deeply troubled, not so much because he was the only one to see Satan, but because nobody else saw him. He remembered throughout his life, when he clearly saw a being which nobody else did. Why was this happening to him? Was he suffering illusions? Or was he insane? Did he live in more than one dimension at the time, the present and the world of angels and spirits? So, far from finding the answer, he only fortified his suspicions that his problem was real, but no hint of a solution.

Before sunrise they were well into the hills of Samaria. Pilgrims, who camped for the night, started to come out and join the march. Yeshua took his group aside to warn them, "Be careful of what you say, and under no circumstances get involved in arguments about Samaritans versus Israelis."

"Why? Don't you get along?" Stephanos queried.

"Like oil and water," he replied.

"I always suspected there was deep animosity between them", the Roman remarked, "but every time I asked, they responded curtly, `We're the same people.'"

"We are the same," Yeshua explained. "But, many centuries ago when the Babylonians conquered Israel and exiled the people to Babylonia, they transplanted Asyrians here. The Israelis who remained in Samaria inter-married with the Syrians, who were not people of the book. When the exiled Israelis returned centuries later, they refused to accept the Samari-tans accusing them of being impure. It tore them apart to this day. Both pray to Yahweh, but Judeans worship in the Temple at Jerusalem, while the Sumaritans go to mount Gerezim."

The crisis unified both peoples against the Romans. They marched shoulder to shoulder on the long road to Caesarea, with nary a word being exchanged. But, they had made hard decisions many times in the course of history, so danger and death were a part of life. Most trekkers were males: brothers, neighbors, in laws, fathers and sons, but, there were a few married couples. The young men were quite surprised when they caught up to a family with small children. The men bowed, and continued side by side in silence. Soon the children 'adopted' Yeshua's group, taking their hands, marching with them and jabbering child talk. The youngest child, a cute little girl, walked with Germanicus carrying on an animated conversation. Memories of Lygia rushed through the slave's mind.

"Children," the father rebuked them harshly, "leave the gentlemen alone."

"It's no bother," Yeshua smiled. "Rather nice..."

The stranger extended his hand, "My name is Jacob. This is my wife Metella. These are some of our children, Onan, Ali, Uzziah, and our youngest, the chatterbox Paulina."

Yeshua introduced his group.

"You are Galilean?" Jacob asked and the young scholar nodded. "Perhaps you are wondering why we are bringing our children on such a dangerous mission. I argued with Metella, but she presented an iron clad case..."

Metella interjected and happily explained, "I told my husband when we married, he must not go anywhere without me, and I swore I will never go anywhere without my children, so here we are..."

"Did you say these were only some of your children?" Stephanos inquired.

"Our oldest boy stayed behind to care for my aging parents," Jacob explained, and posed his own question, "I can understand an Israeli going, but why a Greek and a Roman?"

"We are on an expedition searching for the Messiah, and this is a diversionary trip," Stephanos quipped. In turn he countered, "Why are Samaritans interested in Caesarea?"

"If they put the emperor's statue in Jerusalem, how long before they defile our Temple? In this crisis we must face the oppressors together."

Quintus was tired of the continuous criticism of Rome and lashed out, "Why must you exaggerate everything? You are marching by choice, planning a confrontation with the army, and blaming us. Why not compromise? Everybody knows Augustus is not a god, and won't live long. Let the statues in, and when he dies trash them."

"We compromised with the Greek emperor Antipas," Jacob responded firmly, "He made small demands, and when we gave in, he made bigger demands. By the end, we were sacrificing pigs on the altar of the Temple. After that we swore, never again!"

"I am a Roman. I swear, we won't harm your people," he responded with sincerity.

"I trust the soldiers. My troubles are with the generals," Jacob laughed, and added with a twinkle in his eyes, "If you trust your leaders why not join us?"

"Who...me?" he stammered confused. He wanted to argue, but remembered the two soldiers chasing them. He was sure they wanted him for helping the alleged Zealots. Moreover he knew Roman law was clear on that: soldiers commiserating with rebels will be executed summarily. He shook his head nervously.

Jacob turned to Yeshua, "You say you are searching for the Messiah? After Caesarea, come to our village. The Taheb, our holy man, Simon Magus will be locating Moses' original vessel. If he succeeds he will be pronounced the undisputed Messiah."

The roads through the mountains were rough and uneven and they made slow progress. Germanicus watched their camel closely and saw that it was limping worse than before. He suggested they stop to give the animal a rest.

The day's rest helped the camel, but revived an ongoing problem: the Roman soldiers. Germanicus was the first to recognize them following at close quarters.

"I refuse to live in fear," Yeshua protested. "Tonight I will pay them a visit."

"You will start a crisis we cannot win," Quintus argued. "Your first responsibility is Caesarea."

"Master Quintus is correct," the Greek concurred. "While we are surrounded by Israelis and Samaritans they won't attack. The pilgrims would tear them to pieces."

The Israeli wanted to argue, but after reconsidering he realized they were right.

Next morning they rejoined the trek making slow progress, to avoid re-injuring the camel. Two days later they arrived at a small village only a few miles from Caesarea. They were directed to an area where hundreds of tents were set up, around a large central clearing with a giant pile of wood. Late that afternoon, announcers dressed in black from head to toe visited all camps, telling them to attend a general meeting that night by the big pile of wood.

Two men dressed in black with most of their faces covered watched all new arrivals, and when they saw Yeshua, followed him from a distance. After they set up tent, the men came directly to him. "Shalom, master Yeshua," the leader greeted him. Yeshua remembered the heavy Judean accent and recognized the siccarii with the heavy eyebrows. "We were waiting for you…we have work…You should be commended for saving the Zealots that night in Nazareth." Yeshua started to say he did not want the job, but the man insisted, "Be at the meeting tonight, and sit at the front where you can be seen easily. We have a special task…" Before he could object they started to leave, then stopped and turned, "Oh, and find a Samaritan who will be your co-leader."

Yeshua asked why, but they disappeared beyond the tents.

A short time after, the young men noticed the two Roman soldiers in the distance. When they saw the large congregation of Israelis, they wisely decide to proceed to Caesarea, and warn the tetrarch Valerius Gratus to get his army ready.

After dinner the young men were among the first to arrive to the meeting and sat at the front as instructed, accompanied by Jacob's family. Before long a big fire was lit and the siccarii started the meeting.

The Judean announced, "Fellow Israelis and Samaritans, Lord Adonai willing, tomorrow we will be at the gates of Caesarea. I will not lie, or pretend we are not heading into danger…probably death! It is reckless to proceed further without a leader who can negotiate…or lead you in battle." He stopped to allow the statement to take full effect before continuing, "Is there a man among you with the courage to lead you?" He walked around the fire as he spoke, his dark eyes sparkling, "I want a man with the qualities of a Messiah: a leader, fearless, decisive - a man of destiny!" He barked the last word to emphasize, "You are living in a historical moment, so unite your destiny with your leader. I have such a man, sitting here: master Yeshua is a young Israeli scholar." He motioned, "Come forward young man!" Yeshua's friends pushed him ahead and he found himself beside the siccarii. "A few weeks past this youth risked his life to lead dozens of us through a swamp to safety, from certain death at the hands of the Romans. I endorse and support master Yeshua to be your leader." The people accepted and cheered him loudly. The siccarii motioned for quiet and asked, "Master Yeshua do you have a Samaritan willing to work as your lieutenant?"

"I choose master Jacob," Yeshua pointed to his new friend.

The Samaritans, pleased to be represented cheered even louder.

"I now turn the meeting over to your leaders," the siccarii said concluding, "If you need weapons, we will supply you with these sabre-daggers." He pulled out a golden dagger shaped as a saber and held it up. Before leaving he informed Yeshua, "We will remain close by to enforce your decisions. Lead us to battle, that we die proudly."

Yeshua stood facing the pilgrims, wondering what to do next. He decided to speak to them, and started slowly, nervously, "My countrymen, you were advised to arm yourselves...with daggers...Advice that will guarantee your deaths as martyrs...and the bitter failure of your objective." They listened silently, as he began to assert himself. "I say let us go to the Romans without arms. Open our robes and prove we come in peace." He opened his robe to prove he had no weapons. The reaction was immediate and boisterous. Some laughed, others swore, but everyone concluded this young man was both naïve and a lunatic. The siccarii looked at each other, but did not interrupt. Yeshua raised his voice, "Soldiers are trained to kill. They fight armed resistance. Forget arms. Forget war. Refuse violence. We want to communicate; converse in peace. Will they murder us? Cowards murder, not professional soldiers." He watched them and they stared back baffled, and waffling. Most still objected, but many nodded approvingly, some expressing it vocally. Jacob, who initially objected, smiled. Yeshua pressed on, "Arm yourselves and go to certain death: Go unarmed and give peace a chance."

"What if they kill us though we go without arms?" a Samaritan queried.

"They will have blood on their hands. The nations will turn against them. In death we will win," he spoke emphatically.

There was a long silence, while people, used to meeting force with force, tried to rationalize. Could unarmed peasants match soldiers with swords? They started arguing when Metella came forward, "Fellow Samaritans, and Israelis, listen to master Yeshua," she pleaded. "I am Jacob's wife. These are our children," she motioned and they joined her. "Master Yeshua is correct. Our family will go and converse with the Romans without arms."

Her courageous decision silenced the loudest critics. Before they could object, Quintus stood up impulsively joining Yeshua, "My name is Quintus. I am a Roman soldier born in Galilee. Master Yeshua is right: unarmed you will be successful..."

"Private Quintus, if you're so positive why don't you join us?" an old woman dared him. "Words are hollow. If you join we'll be persuaded!"

Quintus' eyes swam over the crowd as they dared him to prove his mettle. He had backed down when Jacob asked, but this time he was resolved, "All right, I will! I'll join!"

The pilgrims cheered, as he smiled nervously, deciding to worry about the decision tomorrow.

While they cheered, Germanicus came beside Yeshua, "I am Germanicus from northern Europe. I trust master Yeshua's leadership. I too will join."

"Germanicus, go back," Yeshua ordered, but was drowned out by the cheers.

Stephanos marched to his slave screaming angrily, "Are you out of your mind? What about me?"

"Buy another slave," he shrugged. "And take good are of Lygia, if I don't..."

Stephanos looked at the slave and the Roman, certain they had lost their minds.

Quintus yelled at the Greek, "Come with us. Together we're an invincible team."

The Greek vacillated while the the crowd screamed for him to join also. Thus he found himself with the Isralis when he nodded and stood beside Yeshua.

Some pilgrims began to discard their weapons. It was too much to expect people who grew up believing might was right, to embrace non-violence in one instant. But in their long history they always put their lives in Yahweh's hands, and did it once more.

• • •

At mid-morning of the following day they were within a couple of miles from the modern harbor of Caesarea Maritima. They could clearly see the high robust walls protecting the port city.

The late king Herod, the great, always wanted to construct a state of the art harbor along the Israeli coast. When it was finished the king had achieved a miracle of modern engineering that rivaled the port of Alexandria, and was considered one of the great marvels of the world.

Because the Israeli coast did not have a natural deep bay or coral reefs to act as barriers, his engineers, stone workers and divers, constructed, cut and shipped gigantic stones then lowered them in the Great Sea to create twin breakers. They also poured concrete into floating prefabricated forms, which when lowered formed foundations upon which robust walls were constructed.

At high noon the pilgrims stood in the shadows of the giant gates of the city. Yeshua looked back at the road to Jerusalem, and estimated there were close to one thousand pilgrims, waiting for the dramatic confrontation. He looked at the road from whence they came, and saw at least as many arriving.

Before they settled down there was a loud creaking noise of chains. He turned and saw through the cracks in the gate, giant wheels rotating, pulling heavy chains taut, causing the gigantic gates to creak open. Within moments they saw hundreds of Roman soldiers, fully dressed for battle marching steadily towards them. Behind them were the giant statues of the emperor towering over the warriors, seemingly floating through the air, approaching steadily for a confrontation of two peoples: for the religious life of the Israeli nation.

CHAPTER XIII - CONFRONTATION AT CAESAREA MARITIMA

As they approached Caesarea, Yeshua planned a meeting to prepare the pilgrims for the ordeal. But, when the city gates opened and he saw soldiers marching towards them, all discussions seemed superfluous. Instead, he joined the pilgrims to block their exit. He quickly studied his most unlikely heroes: a mixture of farmers, laborers, peasants and homeless beggars, untrained and unimpressive but ready to be martyrs.

Yeshua and Jacob exchanged glances, careful not to show fear. They turned to study the young Roman officer in the chariot leading them. Beside him, sitting on a small donkey, sat a large man, who, by his colorful robe, probably was an important Israeli.

Quintus, donning a shawl he had borrowed to hide his occidental features, watched the army with detached interest. But now that he realized he was in the center of a life and death drama. He came to Yeshua's side and whispered, "That officer is tribune Cornelius, son of a rich Roman senator."

"Will you speak to him?" Yeshua suggested.

"If he recognizes me as a Roman, I'll be arrested for treason...and killed."

Yeshua nodded and motioned him to the back. The tribune stopped the chariot in front of the Israeli. He looked at the long line of pilgrims, but was not able to see the end. His eyes fell on Yeshua and Jacob, then on the first row, stopping on Metella and her children. He was probably wondering why the children were there. When Paulina the youngest girl smiled, his lips stretched. He turned to Yeshua, "Are you the leader?"

"I am one of them. I am Yeshua of Nazareth. This is master Jacob from Samaria."

The tribune raised two fingers to his temple in a symbolic salute.

The large Israeli on the donkey sneered, "From Galilee?" His laughter made his body shake. "A Galilean with a Godless Samaritan: How disgusting..."

The tribune glared at his interruption unimpressed. Yeshua hoped the tribune's privileged upbringing made him sensitive to their plight. But Roman officers were trained to hold strict discipline, like their battle-hardened generals. "Master Yeshua, why are you camped on the road?" the tribune asked.

"To stop those statues from being placed in our Temples," he replied firmly.

The officer admired his honest explanation and countered with equal firmness, "I have orders to transport and distribute them through Israel and Samaria. Are you seeking a confrontation?"

"We come in peace, tribune. I ask you to delay. I will get an audience with tetrarch Valerius Gratus to..."

"To disobey an order from Rome?" the legate interjected with disbelief.

The corpulent Israeli moved the donkey closer to the chariot and whispered to the tribune, who shrugged his shoulders. The big man addressed the pilgrims with an air of superiority, "Israelis, I am Joseph Caiphas, son in law of the High Priest, Ananus." He stopped to let them be appropriately impressed, then continued, "I order you to return to your jobs, and your fields. Your presence will inflame a delicate situation. I am negotiating with the tetrarch to resolve..."

"While the statutes are transported?" a burly peasant scoffed.

"Are you selling Samaria to save Judea?" an old lady demanded accusingly.

"Don't be fools," Caiphas screamed, his face turning beet red. "These young fools will lead you to certain death."

"Death with honor before compromising with godless pagans," an old man barked.

The tribune listened, then turned to the leaders, "Your priest speaks the truth. Where is honor in senseless deaths?" Looking at their faces, he realized they would not give in. He turned to Metella, "Mother, will you lead your children to a slaughter?"

She stepped forward pulling the children, "Will you kill innocent children, sir?"

The young officer was visibly perturbed, and his face darkened.

Yeshua raised his hands pleading, "Tribune, we ask for one day..."

But the tribune yelled over his head, "Israelis! Your stubbornness is legendary, but infinitely foolish! For the last time, I order you: move off the road!"

Yeshua walked in front of his stallions, pulling his robe open, "Tribune, we have no weapons." The Roman was surprised, then astounded to see them copy him showing no one was armed. Yeshua said, "We came in peace, to speak to reasonable people."

The tribune's eyes went from the peasants to Yeshua, to his soldiers, and again on Metella's children. He stared longingly at the youngest one, perhaps thinking of his own daughter. "Master Yeshua, I bow to your courage...but I curse your foolhardy act. I have orders to take the statues, of a self-proclaimed god. But I refuse to kill women...One day." He spat out and yanked at the reins, and stopped to warn them, "Tomorrow you will meet general Fulvius. He will not hesitate to kill your children, madam"

He ordered the centurion to take over, whipped the stallions and fled.

Yeshua spoke to the pilgrims as he was leaving for the city, "Get ready for the next meeting, if I don't succeed with the Tetrach."

As he entered the gates, his eyes feasted on modern buildings unlike any others in Israel, and he felt he was entering a different world. Everywhere he saw heavy pillars of imported marble rising from the steps to the high roofs, and heavy bronze doors, keeping the world shut out. The streets were spacious and clean, paved with cobble stones. As his eyes panned the scenery from one building to a more impressive one, he imagined that was how marvelous Athens and Rome must appear. Yet he realized that like them, Caesarea Maritima would always be a foreign city within Israel. It celebrated the most modern architecture, the finest contemporary art and flawless engineering of the Hellenistic culture, but it would never touch the Israeli soul. It was the wonder of the world, a pride of contemporary art and engineering. But it was overpowering and cold. It was Jerusalem, with its crooked narrow overcrowded streets, and stuffy bazaars that had the flavor, tradition and spirit of the east. It was the center of their universe, capturing their soul and would forever be their Holy City.

He walked the length of the boulevard, unable to decipher which was the government building. His only option was to make inquiries. The first person he asked shrugged his shoulders and walked away without answering. The next few replied curtly that they did not know. He sensed an air of fear at the mention of Valerius Gratus. He decided to try the largest building. Just as he approached the giant edifice, he felt a sharp point poking him in the ribs from behind, and a male voice whispered nervously, "Don't turn around. Follow instructions and you may live to see the sunset."

The stranger led him away from the center, holding one hand on his shoulder and a sharp object against his ribs, carefully avoiding the area of the bazaar, until they reached a dark alley. As soon as they entered the shadows, Yeshua knew he must get free or chance being killed. He quickly turned around raising his staff and faced his assailant. "If it is coins or jewellery you're after, you will be disappointed."

"Neither, but a friend's helping hand," the bearded stranger replied.

Yeshua thought he recognized the voice, but could not place the bearded face. He replied, "My hand I will gladly lend. But, pray who are…?"

The man removed his false beard and even in the dark shadows Yeshua recognized the schoolmaster Benjoseph. He opened his mouth, but his friend quickly covered it.

"In the name of Adonai, don't utter my name," he whispered with desperation. "If I am discovered, I am doomed. The city is lousy with undercover police."

"That explains why it is so unfriendly…"

The schoolmaster led him to the empty circus, where they sat alone high in the bleachers for safety in case anyone approached.

Benjoseph brought him up to date about Nazareth, "We were infiltrated by a Roman spy. No Zealot is safe while the traitor is free."

"Who do you suspect?"

Benjoseph sighed, "Anyone: a desperate farmer in arrears with the tax collector… someone pressed by creditors or on the verge of bankruptcy…or slavery…"

The young scholar nodded, "Hardly excludes anyone…what are your plans?"

"I tried to board a ship, but I need written authority from the tetrarch. They check everyone…" His voice trailed into a whisper. "I'm doomed."

Yeshua sympathized with his friend and tried to sound optimistic, "We will hide you in a little town, in a different province."

"They have spies everywhere. How long before I'm sold out?"

"I know," he tried to sound cheerful, "My co-leader will get you into Samaria."

Benjoseph was confused, "Co-leader? What are you talking about?"

Yeshua chirped full of enthusiasm, "He is a Samaritan. We are leading the Israelis to stop the emperor's statues…"

"I remember, the cursed statues," Benjoseph interjected. "Are they here already? I've been a fugitive for so long, I lost track of time."

"Has it been that bad?"

Benjoseph was deeply affected, "I spend my waking hours trying to avoid capture."

Yeshua refused to wallow in pessimism, "I'm positive master Jacob will help, as soon as we finish with the Romans."

The schoolmaster grabbed him pleading, "That saber-dagger the siccarii gave you: don't use it. I'll never forgive myself if something happened to you."

The desperation in his voice shook the young scholar. He tried to reassure him, "Master Jacob is from a little village, Tirathana, where you will be safe."

"There is a better person right here," Benjoseph interrupted. "The Persian merchant with the caravan…"

"Master El Sharif is here?"

"That's his name. If you speak to him, perhaps he can get me to Persia."

"Where is he?" Yeshua sounded elated. "Of course he'll help you.."

For the first time since they met, Benjoseph's eyes lit up with hope. He led Yeshua carefully avoiding the busy areas. As they passed a large building which Yeshua intended to enter, the schoolmaster explained, "That's the tetrarch's mansion. The left side is his residence, and his court is on the right. They say his private rooms are filled with rare gems, gold and bribes he extorted from the people."

"Are you saying I may not get an audience?"

"Did you bring rubies or gold?" Benjoseph smirked, then added, "You have a better chance of becoming the High Priest…"

They continued a couple more blocks, to a section filled with merchants under canopies and tents. They had all types of exotic wares from every corner of the empire.

"Your friend has the most enviable piece of real estate: at the foot of the steps of the Temples of Aphrodite and Venus," Benjoseph pointed out. "The wealthy wives of the powerful pass by the exotic silks and rare perfumes and keep his shop full."

Yeshua smiled, for that was how he envisioned his Persian friend: controlling everyone no matter where he went.

Benjoseph declined to enter the area, fearing spies and undercover police, and returned into the shadows. Yeshua continued on and soon recognized the colorful tents with tables heaped high with exquisite cloths. He was still some distance away when the fragrant perfumes teased his nostrils.

Master El Sharif was ecstatic to see him. They embraced and danced around speaking and laughing boisterously, both asking questions simultaneously. The old man invited him in for some watered down wine and cakes. They exchanged stories about their adventures. Yeshua told him about the expedition to find the Messiah.

"What brings you to Caesarea?" he asked. "I have not heard of a Messiah here."

"We came to stop the Romans from taking the statues into the sacred Temples," he replied proudly. "I am one of the leaders."

The old man's jaw unhinged and he stammered, "T-That's s-suicide. Why are you doing that? You m-must not..."

"I'm in no greater danger than hundreds of others," he downplayed the risk. "Moreover, we're not even armed..."

"You don't have weapons?" his lips began to quiver. "And you're facing armed soldiers? W-Who is s-so naïve...?" The Persian started when he saw the young scholar pointing the finger at himself with a proud smile. He sighed heavily. He wondered whether to reveal his identity, and tell him there were great expectations. But he only managed to mumble, "You c-cannot...You have...Don't...your m-mission..."

Yeshua had never seen this paragon of self control, totally lost for words, and it confused him, "What are you trying to say? What about my mission?" He became suspicious when the old man stared without replying. "Master El Sharif what do you know about me? My birth? My destiny?"

The Persian sighed, "So your parents finally told you? That's why you can't go. It's too dangerous."

But Yeshua was more interested about his birth and destiny and questioned him, "What do you know about me...and my mission?"

The old merchant was only too eager to tell the story. His eyes glazed as he smiled reliving it, "I was traveling with two caravans, a magi and a wealthy lord, when we saw the brightest star. We knew it was an omen. We followed it to a little hamlet...There were festivities everywhere...Everybody talked about the arrival of a special person..."

"Who? Who talked? What did they say? I want to hear everything."

"How do all easterners describe extraordinary events? With superlatives, making it sound many times bigger than it warrants. Everybody talked, and it was difficult to distinguish fact from fiction. But, who could blame them? They were simple peasants who had waited a thousand years...Now, the promised one came, and a star pointed out the place. They celebrated the arrival of the new leader of mankind. He embodied the hope of the people..." El Sharif shook his head chuckling, "That's why Herod was furious: the new king came to take his rightful throne!"

"That's what I feared," Yeshua murmured disappointed, "It was exaggerated enthusiasm of peasants: false expectations, mixed with wild dreams."

"You must not say that," the old man interjected forcefully. "Don't discard it as fiction because of the atmosphere of carnival. There were kernels of truth in it. A special person, was given unto them, someone who would change the world."

Yeshua's interest perked up and he listened for the Persian to continue, but he had finished. He asked timidly, "Did they say...the Messiah?"

"Oh, yes!" El Sharif responded. "They called him the Messiah, a modern Elijah, he was the Emmanuel, the new reincarnated Moses...He was something to everyone."

"Did anyone say...the son of God?"

The phrase awakened a special recollection, for the old man's eyes lit up and he smiled, "Master Joseph said an angel delivered the news to lady Miriam before conception." He smiled warmly adding, "What loving parents don't see the universe in their expected offspring: the best physician, world leader, ruler...?"

"If I am supposed to be all those, I have failed miserably," the young scholar mumbled dejectedly. "A generation has passed, and what have I achieved? Nothing!"

"Why is youth so impatient? What is a generation in the timeless history of the world?" El Sharif put his arm around his shoulder to share an important secret, "Your parents described the most wonderful miracles you have already performed."

"But, I have never seen them..."

"Patience. You will see them. Who knows your potential?"

They sat in silence pondering the full meaning of his statement. The old man wished he could give his young friend comfort, while another part told him to let him discover his destiny on his own, "Has this bothered you? You seem unusually perturbed."

"That's all I have thought about," he complained. "I haven't had a moment's rest; day and night. It grips me first thing in the morning, and the whole day, and I lay awake at the end of the day more confused than ever. Worst of all, I fear my secret will be discovered, and I will never have peace..."

"What's causing all this trouble?"

"Everything," he lamented. "I don't know who am I: a warrior? a rebel or a prophet...? What is expected? What am expected to do? Where do I start? Why me? I go over and over the same riddle..."

"Why waste time on riddles? They're of no import. Devise a plan and forge ahead. Sometimes you may give conflicting lessons. Don't worry unduly. The seeds you plant will germinate and grow. After you're gone, others will tend your garden and help it grow until it covers the world."

But the young man had not told him everything and sighed, "I have a lovely lady who I love and hoped to start a life..."

The old potentate smiled, "Don't worry about it. It will sort itself out as it should. Never underestimate your intellect not to resolve matters of love. The important matter is to avoid confrontation with the Romans."

The warning jolted him back to the present, and he gasped, "Oh! I almost forgot! Master Benjoseph is in trouble," he blurted out. "He is our schoolmaster, being pursued by the Romans...for leading a political org..."

"The Zealots!"

"Do you know about the Zealots?"

"Romans love to talk...I love to listen," El Sharif chuckled. "Let me guess; your friend needs to get out of the country. Is he nearby? Why don't you bring him here?"

Yeshua left and within a few moments returned and introduced them. El Sharif clapped his hands and a young servant came with wine, another goblet and more food which Benjoseph attacked savagely. "You may remove your beard," El Sharif said.

"Is it that obvious?" Benjoseph was clearly disappointed.

"A grey beard on a young face," the Persian clicked his tongue unimpressed. "It can only fool the Romans."

"Fortunately that is who I am trying to fool."

"The Romans don't know you, so your disguise must pass the trained eye of the traitor," the Persian observed. "Unfortunately they are very cunning."

"How did you know we had a traitor?" Yeshua was astounded that the merchant seemed to know everything.

El Sharif explained philosophically, "The Romans control Israel with the help of your people: the rich conspire with them, and in return keep their lofty position secure. And the poor sell you for money. These lessons are as old as the world." He turned to Benjoseph, "So you want to escape from Israel?"

"Not if it endangers your caravan."

"Nonsense," the old man assured him. "We must help one another. Moreover, our lives have become too predictable. It's time we spiced it up: put some excitement, and adventure back." They clinked goblets and took a long sip of wine while the Persian concocted his plan, "I will hire you to be my business manager, and pay you a salary." The schoolmaster tried to object but the old man raised his hand, "It must be a business relationship to the smallest detail. Speak to me only to answer questions, and never to the other servants, especially about personal matters. Soon we will travel north by east via Nazareth..."

"Must we go there?" Benjoseph stammered knowing the danger.

"It has been my route for over twenty years. If I change now people will talk," El Sharif saw that the schoolmaster was worried and tried to reassure him, "I will teach you to disguise yourself so your birth mother will not recognize you."

The statement accomplished its purpose, for Benjoseph relaxed and smiled luxuriously, as if the weight of the world was taken off his shoulders.

El Sharif turned to Yeshua, "And you, young man, must cease your rebellious confrontation."

"You said we must help one another," he retorted. "However, if I get an audience with the tetrarch I'll try to persuade him to desist."

"Valerius Gratus will see you if you can do one of two things for him," the Persian rasped ominously. "Help his ambition, or fill his vault."

Yeshua contemplated the desperate situation and countered optimistically, "I may be able to help his career..."

"Tell his guards you can divine his future..." the Persian started.

"But that's not true," Yeshua interjected.

"Romans are most superstitious," El Sharif emphasized. "Logical explanations will fall short, but as a fortunate teller you'll bend his ear."

Yeshua thanked him, and left for the gigantic building with the bronze doors. He told the outer guard as instructed, and in a few moments was whisked inside to the inner guard who led him to his superior, sitting at a desk in the spacious hallway. Yeshua congratulated himself for the ingenious idea when the officer brusquely questioned him about his wishes, the urgency of it and the time he needed.

The young scholar leaned over the officer's desk with new-found confidence, "You don't understand, I am not requesting a favor. I am here to help him."

The officer drawled, "How many gold talents will you pay for the privilege?"

The young man stood up and leaned over his desk, "You don't understand. I..."

Before he started, he was half escorted, half dragged out the bronze doors and dumped unceremoniously down the marble steps.

As they dragged him out he saw two Roman soldiers who seemed vaguely familiar; an old codger with a youth. Fortunately they were busy and did not recognize him.

Disillusioned and dejected, he shuffled back to the Israeli camp, arriving in the evening with the disappointing news.

Soon he discovered some pilgrims had demanded their weapons back. Some obtained daggers and others weapons from the siccarriis, or found clubs or whatever weapons they could, arguing they wanted to go down fighting.

Yeshua repeated his argument that their only hope was to go unarmed, for their strength was a moral victory. He argued with fervor and passion, when, unexpectedly a young man yelled out, "MORAL RIGHT IS OUR MIGHT!" Another person took up the chant, then a few more, and soon everybody was chanting it with fervor and zeal.

Yeshua closed his argument with a courageous statement, "The majority support non-violence. Therefore, those who wish to remain must discard their weapons, or else."

Hundreds discarded their weapons. Not one pilgrim left. Yeshua noticed in the dark a dozen siccarii dressed totally in black. He saw the leader with the bushy eyebrows, shaking his head, obviously disappointed. The young leader debated checking them, but they opened their robes to prove they too had no weapons.

That evening the pilgrims started a big bonfire and after dinner began singing, dancing and telling stories. They joked and played games, occasionally interrupting the festivities to chant, "MORAL RIGHT IS OUR MIGHT!"

Hundreds of residents from the city came out for a stroll in the warm evening, and watched the peasants enjoying themselves. They celebrated life, for the moment was eternal. Tomorrow they may journey into history books and peoples' memories.

The strollers envied them, commenting these peasants knew how to celebrate life.

· · ·

Early next morning Yeshua discussed the plans with Jacob. At sunrise the reality of their fate made them think of their lives, homes and loved ones left behind. From time to time someone chuckled over some inconsequential event from long ago about which they never found time to think. Some cried in silence, not because they feared death, but, about the absurdity of life. Most sat in silence mesmerized, their minds replaying highlights from the past, from which they drew courage.

Yeshua felt their sadness and suggested to his co-leader that he should speak thanking them for coming, and tell those who did not wish to proceed they would be free to return. The co-leader approved the message.

He stood up to speak, when an old timer rushed up, coughing and wheezing. He explained privately in a weak, raspy voice, "Master Yeshua, I overheard your conversation…and what you wish to say…We like you as a leader, but, that speech will…alienate them." The ancient patriarch stopped for breath and almost lost the courage to continue. At length he resumed his message, "Every person here already suffered soul searching agony, and painful thoughts for days, perhaps weeks, before deciding to come…It was not impulse that brought us…Many argued with families…broke hearts of loved ones when they left…" He coughed trying to get control of his emotions, for he was becoming overwhelmed. "We knew…we were going to our deaths…Why make us suffer the same agonies…again?"

Yeshua realized that until that moment he did not fully appreciate the pilgrims' sacrifices, "You speak wisely, ancient one. I confess, I failed to appreciate the pain and agony you have already suffered."

"Go, speak to them," the old man encouraged. "Give us inspiration."

"Right, old man," he touched him, and got a warm toothless smile in return.

Yeshua mingled with them as he spoke, "Friends, you left behind everybody and everything dear to you, to defend your faith. Your courage will be remembered for generations…" He strolled along the road, picking up little ones, repeating the phrases so everyone heard the message. "A thousand years from now they will write about you… forsaking weapons, and opening your hearts to reach a peaceful solution…" Suddenly his speech changed dramatically as he said, "Before sunset today we may all die as martyrs and travel to a distant place…for eternal rest. When your spirit arrives, you will see me at the right hand of my heavenly Abba, where you will find peace. I tell you truly, those who die with love in their hearts, will receive the highest honor from my heavenly Abba."

That morning in the shadow of the gates of Caesarea, Yeshua spoke about his Abba, his heavenly father, a theme he would use frequently. His words comforted the peasants and gave them courage. But it did more: it promised eternal bliss, offering hope and reward none would ever know in this life. They felt an inner peace as if mesmerized.

During his speech they heard a loud squeaking noise. It was the rattling of heavy chains and the squealing of iron wheels as the giant gates began to part lethargically. They turned and saw a thousand soldiers marching in the distance, followed by the large statues. Yeshua searched but did not see the tribune. Instead, the soldiers were led by a professional soldier astride a restless black stallion. Yeshua's first impression was that this warrior with a rugged face, with deep lines and battle scars, evidenced a fighter who had faced and inflicted death many times. The horseman rode until he was almost on top of the people, looking down on them with the arrogance of one who loved power.

"I am general Fulvius," he barked imperiously, "I order you to move out of my way, and give my soldiers unimpeded passage."

"General Fulvius," Yeshua addressed him from under the neck of the horse, so that the general did not see him at first, "my name is Yeshua. We come in peace. We are not armed and do not wish to cause trouble."

"You are wrong on both counts," the general growled sardonically. "You are obstructing my army thereby breaching the peace, and your insubordination creates a confrontational condition for combat. Get out of my way!"

"I plead that you forgo the mission and get us an audience with his excellen…"

"I don't run errands for colonials," Fulvius' jaws clenched. "Get off the road…"

Yeshua interjected supplicating, "General, we are not armed. Look" He raised his arms and they could see he had no weapons. The pilgrims opened their robes and the Romans were astounded to see them unarmed. Yeshua explained, "We are defenseless. If you attack, it will be murder…"

"Then prevent it. Get your plebeians off my road," the general screamed with fury, his eyes gazing fiercely at the pilgrims. He realized he could not reason with the young fool, and decided to address the masses. He was fond of an old trick he had used successfully many times to unnerve opponents, causing the bravest men to squirm. He started, "Israelis, I will count to four, at which point those still in my way will be cut to pieces…" He stopped for a moment to let his message sink in. Then he counted in rapid succession, 'ONE-TWO-THREE…" He stopped and his thin lips stretched in a sneer, expecting them to scurry in panic like rats abandoning a sinking ship.

But the old trick failed. He sat on his stallion astonished that not only did they not run, they broke into a popular song of redemption. His smirk turned to a scowl, then a blank stare of disbelief. After a while he tried to interrupt them, only to be drowned out as they continued the song with passionate energy. Fortunately for the soldiers, he did not see them grinning as they watched unarmed peasants stand up to their general.

Defeated, he sat rigidly in the saddle, the muscles of his jaw tightening, and a glare of murder in his eyes. The peasants continued their ancient song, praising God, for a glorious day.

As soon as they finished he sat up rigidly in the saddle, "You will pay dearly for... this unprovoked assault." He turned to his subordinate, "Centurion, lead your soldiers and surround the enemy. Prepare for combat!"

The centurion stepped back, mumbling with disbelief, "But sir, they're not armed!"

The general screamed so loud his voice cracked, "Centurion, obey immediately, or I will have you arrested."

The officer stared at his superior, his face turning pale, and at length gave an anemic order. They surrounded the pilgrims and stood rigidly looking from the centurion to the general.

"Your theatrics are over," the general snarled at Yeshua. "Admit defeat and order your rif-raf off my road!"

The young Israeli replied with a calm voice without a trace of animosity, "We cannot allow our Temples to be profaned. I ask you to reconsider..."

General Fulvius lost control and his body shook with anger at the young pup's impertinence, "Israelis, you are fools. You don't deserve to live. Centurion, I will raise my sword. When I drop my arm you will give the order to destroy the enemy." He glared at the subordinate officer watching his bottom lip quiver.

The general unsheathed his sword and slowly began to raise his arm, his eyes riveted on the pilgrims, expecting them to break rank and retreat. To his surprise he saw them begin to lay prostrate, pulling back their tunics, robes, or shawls, offering bare necks to facilitate their beheading. The general's arm froze part way and he sat motionless staring at a scene of total submission, with utter disregard for their lives. The soldiers shuffled back, their mouths dropped, their minds not believing their eyes. The Israelis began to sing a sad song from ancient times when they were being taken into slavery in Bablyon. Fulvius who had interpreted the confrontation as war, was forced to admit this was mass suicide, and he was about to order the murder of foolish, but courageous people. At that moment he hated his job and wavered, considering stopping the farce. But he was a career soldier, trained to kill, and expected to be obeyed. Now it was too late, for the matter had gone too far. A retreat now would be seen as defeat. Moreover they caused the provocation, so he continued to raise the sword.

Quintus was angry blaming his impulsive decision. Why was he defending a religion he did not believe in? And he was shocked beyond belief that the Romans were going to murder defenseless peasants. His orderly life and beliefs were shattered.

As Stephanos pulled back his tunic exposing his neck, he felt strangely at peace. Now he understood Aristotle's last moments when he willingly drank the hemlock which killed him, rather than betray his ideals. Like his hero he awaited death impatiently.

Germanicus was sad that he would never know Lygia growing up, or be able to help her through her formative years. He hoped someday she would learn about him and be proud that he chose to die for a leader and a faith he had just begun to understand.

Yeshua suffered bitterly, because he had failed his Abba. He reasoned the special gifts and powers he was given should have been bestowed upon a wiser, more capable person to fulfill the prophecy. He whispered a prayer apologizing. And tears ran down his face, for his family, and the people of the world.

General Fulvius raised the sword high, ready to bring it down like a chopping axe.

• • •

Marcus completed his investigation in Sepphoris and was returning, eager to report his findings about master Nehemiah. As soon as he entered the yard James and Debborah led him to the roof top. His report was like a bursting dam raging wild, "I found out everything you asked…You will be astounded to hear…This man is full of secrets."

"Not so loud, master Marcus," Debborah tugged at his sleeve.

"Take your time," James rejoined. "Start from the beginning and tell us everything."

Marcus took a deep breath and started over, "You know Sepphoris was completely destroyed in the last uprising. From the moment I entered the gates to the city I was surrounded by construction: renovations here, brand new buildings there, one and two story edifices, private homes springing up like weeds in an oasis. Signs advertised the architects or general contractors. Nowhere did I see master Nehemiah's name. I asked workers and overseers: Did he design the building? Was he project manager? Did they ever hear of him? They shook their heads as one."

"Tsk, tsk, tsk, just as I suspected," Debborah shook her head smacking her lips.

James considered everything before speaking out, "Master Nehemiah is new in the area...It is difficult to win important contracts if you're not known."

"I thought you would say that. There were foreigners from every corner of the empire working," Marcus explained. "They came from as far west as Hispania, and as far east as India."

At that moment they saw Esau entering the yard and called him up.

"Esau, master Marcus is giving a report, and says master Nehemiah is not doing any construction work in Sepphoris," James told him.

"Are you finished with your report?" Debborah queried.

Marcus had the smile of a Cheshire cat, "I left the best for last."

"Go on man; what are you holding back?" James demanded.

Marcus spoke deliberately savoring every word, "While I was making inquiries on the roof of an edifice, who did I see passing by on his donkey? Master Nehemiah. I followed him...into the Roman fort!" Their jaws fell, which pleased him immensely. After a pause he hinted, "There is more..."

"I can hardly stand the suspense," Debborah protested exasperated. "What did you see?"

"He met with a Roman officer, obviously a long time friend, for they shook hands warmly and talked for a long time. He spoke while the officer scribed."

"Did you...?" James started to ask.

"... Hear them?" Marcus interjected, and replied, "No. I was too far away to hear them. But what I saw, told me everything as clear as a signed confession." He thoroughly enjoyed watching them hanging on his every word. Before they could object, he continued, "As they were about to separate, the officer handed him a small purse filled with coins. Master Nehemiah took it, hid it in his belt and left."

"That was his pay off," she concluded. "I didn't like him the first time I saw him."

James turned to Esau, "What information do you bring from Tyre? Is master Nehemiah an architect or a traitor?"

"He once was an architect of great repute, but that was a long time ago. Today in his city of birth he is a pariah. The first person I asked, cursed him as a traitor and murderer from hell. According to him master Nehemiah is the blight of Phoenicia. Every time he uttered the name, he spat on the ground. He introduced me to many others who corroborated the accusations, with further evidence of atrocities he perpetrated against his people. They recounted stories of people arrested, tortured, and slaughtered, for a handful of silver coins he received. Some said master Nehemiah was responsible for more deaths of Phoenicians than entire wars they suffered."

James mulled over the statement and queried rhetorically, "Have you any doubts master Nehemiah is the mole within the Zealots?"

"None," Esau stated positively. "However we have to be careful. They said he is as slippery as a serpent, and many times more deadly. When the people discovered he was selling them, they hired three professional assassins who cornered him in a dark alley. The locals waited at the far exit to celebrate the pariah's death. They heard the loud clicking of steel against steel, and thuds of heavy punches, thrusting of daggers, and desperate wrestling, as they waited nervously. When all was quiet they were about to go in, when a bloody man came out. At first they did not recognize him, for he had a long vertical cut from the forehead down to the chin. When Nehemiah shuffled past them, they ran into the alley where two bandits lay dead, their throats slashed, and the third in the throes of death. Shortly after master Nehemiah left Tyre."

James rubbed his chin for some time before questioning Esau, "Did the people say the events happened to them, or were they relaying information from third parties?"

"None were personally involved," Esau explained. "It involved other people."

"Hearsay," James concluded judicially.

"I have no doubts we could easily locate the witnesses," Esau defended his findings. "The wealthiest family in Tyre is still searching for him. They said lady Sarah belongs to their family…"

"Lady Sarah? Why?" Debborah wondered the meaning of the allegations.

"I did not stay long enough to find out. They were pressuring me to divulge the traitor's hideout, so I decided to leave."

"Getting back to master Marcus," James decided to test the first report, "you said that you did not hear the conversation between the Roman and master Nehemiah…?" he asked and Marcus nodded. "Did you see any coins or hear the sound of coins in the bag you allege to be a purse?" Marcus shook his head, and James continued the inquiry with a studied deliberation, "The Israelis destroyed the Roman fort during the uprising. Only now it is being reconstructed..."

"You don't believe master Nehemiah is the architect rebuilding the Roman fort?"

"Why not?" James countered. "The explanation is as plausible as any."

"Brother James, I cannot believe you are defending him," Debborah protested vehemently. "You don't believe he's innocent anymore than I..."

"I'm asking questions brother Yeshua will pose," James explained unflinching. "You know our brother will leave no stone unturned..."

"Yeah! He's always giving the benefit of doubt to everybody..." she lamented.

Marcus and Esau nodded sadly at the prospect that the traitor may go free while their townspeople died or rotted in prison.

Suddenly they saw lady Sarah come in the yard. When she saw them she ran up, stopping at the top with an ecstatic smile, "I bring good news. Father knows where Yeshua is, and he is presently leaving to meet with him. Isn't that great news?"

• • •

General Fulvius remained holding the sword up for a long time, not because he was vacillating, but because there was no immediate rush to execute unarmed pilgrims. For an instant he debated dropping it when he heard a commotion in the distance and turned to check. He saw a cloud of dust in the distance, as if someone was racing towards them. He watched the cloud growing bigger, getting closer, until he identified a chariot, and close behind two camels, one with a rider. From the tumultuous noise of hoofs and wheels, he heard a frantic voice yelling, "STOP! STOP!"

As they approached, the tribune, riding the chariot yelled, "Stop everything, general. The governor has ordered the statues not be moved."

"What? Why?" the general barked, somewhat relieved to end the infernal farce.

Master El Sharif, the rider on the camel replied, "His excellency has ordered the leader, master Yeshua and his party to attend court immediately."

Hearing the news the pilgrims stood up and exploded with cheers. Lost in the noise were the cheers of the soldiers, the loudest one by the centurion.

"General, why are you holding up your sword?" tribune Cornelius smirked.

Too embarrassed to explain, the general turned to his officer barking an order, "Centurion, disregard the previous order."

That was unnecessary for the soldiers and pilgrims were too busy celebrating to hear him. The general tried to bring some semblance of order to the chaos, finally yelling to the tribune to take over. He pointed to Yeshua to move without delay, kicked his horse and galloped back to the city. The tribune motioned to the centurion to take charge, took Stephanos in the chariot and followed the general. Yeshua jumped on the camel behind El Sharif, while Quintus and Germanicus mounted the other and followed them.

Yeshua hung onto the Persian and bounced precariously as he tried to find out what happened.

"There is an old Persian saying: To get the king's attention, speak to the queen. When I saw Valerius' wife going to the temple of Aphrodite, I invited her to try my exotic perfumes. Subtly I hinted a world famous astrologer confided that her husband's career was directly connected to the statutes. She was curious but I said only the astrologer could answer. Before sunrise a small garrison dragged me to the governor."

"Me, a world renown astrologer?" he repeated with trepidation. "What shall I say?"

"Make up something...fast. Make it big, for, that is what he expects."

"I'm terrible with lies," the young scholar protested.

"Start practicing, because we're almost there," El Sharif warned him.

They rode into the large courtyard. The guards whisked them inside, and the impenetrable fortress of the previous day could not swallow them fast enough.

Valerius Gratus held court in a gigantic room with a vaulted ceiling, marble columns and floors. There were busts of Roman emperors and senators standing on pillars throughout the room. Court was already in session when they were brought in, and they stood by the big door with dozens of citizens waiting their turn. On both sides of the long room, were rows of benches and chairs, filled with ambassadors, heads of state the wealthy and influential currying favors. At the far end of the room, up three steps stood a big throne where the tetrarch sat. When they walked in, general Fulvius walked to the tetrarch, leaned over and whispered, pointing to the visitors.

Quintus leaned to Yeshua whispering, "When you go forward, measure your words carefully. Avoid sudden moves, and say nothing to berate the tetrarch or Rome. And, watch these civilians around us; most are disguised spies."

Yeshua's eyes went from face to face trying to guess which were the secret police. He thought of the saber dagger the siccarii gave him. While he mused, he did not hear his name called until Quintus pushed him ahead. He advanced too far and an armed guard motioned him to stop. He bowed and blushed in confusion.

The tetrarch studied him carefully and addressed him deliberately, not missing a single gesture, "I am told you led a band of defenseless Israelis against my army...?"

"Your excellency, I was only trying..."

The tetrarch raised his voice for he was not finished, "...And faced certain death singing and laying prostrate, and baring your necks? Is that true?"

Yeshua bowed deeply, "The report is correct, your Excellency."

Valerius Gratus slid forward, his eyes riveted on him with a mixture of admiration and astonishment. At last he spoke rhetorically, "Yours is a classic example of dying for a principle." He looked around the room while the audience nodded and concurred. He returned to his special guest, "But, you are still young...When you reach my age, you will learn - all principles have a price."

"Is your Excellency intimating, as one matures principles disappear and price tags appear?" Yeshua immediately wished he had not said it.

Ambassadors and sultans burst out chuckling, but when the tetrarch glared their way, they quickly stifled it, and covered their mouths. He drew back in his throne, his face hardening. His frosty glare kept the court in suspended animation. No one coughed. No one shuffled a sandal. Yeshua stared back at the tetrarch who looked into the young man's radiant eyes, wondering if his remark was meant to offend. Instead, he took a liking to the young Israeli's honesty. He decided he could trust such a sincere speaker, and his lips stretched into a faint smile. The audience sighed relieved, and the court returned to life.

"I congratulate you for the honesty of your remark, the rarest commodity in this office," the tetrarch declared and saw many of his guests nod approval. Then he returned to the business at hand, "Why do you object to the statues in Israelis' Temples?"

"We don't object to them in the parks or streets. We refuse to bow to him as a god."

The tetrarch did not like the blunt statement, but refused to be drawn into a discussion about faith. He decided to take a different tactic, "Is it true you have only one God?"

"There is only one Creator. And we are all equal in His eyes."

"Is He also my God?" Valerius queried surprised, to which the young scholar nodded. "Why have I not heard of Him?"

"He knows you. When you need Him, pray and He will be there."

"I don't know Him, but He knows of me?" the tetrarch was curious but also suspicious of such a dangerous deity.

"He cares for you, and loves you, as He loves all the people here," Yeshua announced and saw the visitors and soldiers react with astonishment.

The tetrarch contemplated it, finally dismissing it, "Your God is too subtle for my simple intellect." Then he came to the real purpose of his presence, "I am told you bring sage advice concerning my future…career. Are you a sorcerer or soothsayer?"

"I do have timely advice…" he replied enigmatically.

"Speak," Valerius Gratus ordered.

"My counsel is for the tetrarch's ears only," he confided in low breath.

The tetrarch frowned. Only his most intimate ministers and trusted advisors had his private ear. His first suspicion was an attempt to assassinate him, which had been tried before. He studied the young man and something about his radiant eyes calmed him. Moreover, he remembered they were not armed. Surely this young man was no exception, or could he have a hidden dagger? He turned to his advisors who unanimously shook their heads.

He motioned, "Come forward. I want hear your counsel. But, this better be good."

As Yeshua approached, the big corpulent priest, Joseph Caiphas, sitting on the sideline, stood up, "Your excellency? I have a matter of great urgency to relay privately."

"Wait until I finish, master Caiphas," the tetrarch rebuked him.

Yeshua walked up a couple of steps and leaned over speaking so low as to be almost inaudible, "Your excellency, there are over one thousand pilgrims at the gate of your city: an impressive force… invincible…"

"Without arms? I can crush them like so many flies," he flicked his hand.

"The fact they are not armed makes them invincible. If the statues move, they go through a sea of Jewish blood. Before Jerusalem thousands more will be sacrificed – more blood."

"Is this what you came to tell me?" Valerius sneered, visibly annoyed.

"The foreign entourages present here today will report our murders to the world. Nations will be horrified, and demand explanations from Rome. Emperor Augustus is old and feeble. How long will he defend you, before sacrificing you on the altar of political expediency?"

"I have a written order signed by the emperor," he shrugged defiantly.

"To murder defenseless civilians? Did he promise to defend you at all cost?" he phrased the question so it answered itself.

Valerius sat frozen, his eyes blinking as he considered the scenario. Finally, he began to show interest in the young man's counsel, and leaned forward. Yeshua climbed the last step to whisper when two guards drew their swords and started forward to intervene. The tetrarch waved them back.

"Augustus and you are bound to each other by reciprocal principles: you obey him, and he defends you," Yeshua said. "But as you said, all principles have a price. How much pressure will he withstand before sacrificing you to buy peace?"

After much contemplation, the tetrarch muttered weakly, "If it comes to survival, I'll be sacrificed. You speak the truth, master Yeshua." He stared into the radiant eyes pleased. "I have need of an honest, perceptive advisor. I am surrounded by mediocrity and corruption. Will you accept the position? It pays well..."

"I am grateful, your Excellency, but I have aging parents..." the young man bowed deeply.

"...And your family needs you," Valerius sighed, smiling sadly. He looked at the audience as he addressed the scribe, "Let the record show, and all present witness my order: master Yeshua of Nazareth shall be a free citizen of my provinces of Samaria and Judea during my tenure. I shall guarantee his freedom."

Yeshua descended the steps and began to shuffle back when Joseph Caiphas rushed up the steps.

"What can you add to what has already been said?"

Although Yeshua did not intend to eavesdrop, he overhead Caiphas, "The Samaritans are about to have a big gathering at mount Gerezim. Simon Magnus, their holy man, will lead a procession to Gerezim to locate…"

Valerius interrupted, "I don't need minute descriptions. Get to the point."

"The Taheb will proclaim himself the Messiah…to liberate them from Rome," the priest spluttered.

"Lead a rebellion?" he asked dumbfounded. "That's sedition. Punishable by death."

"I thought your excellency should know," Caiphas smirked with a sneer.

The tetrarch turned to the general, "Prepare two hundred of our best soldiers, cavalry and infantry. At sunrise we will leave for mount Gerezim."

The young Israeli could not believe Caiphas' audacity. He realized immediately that the Samaritans were in danger and had to be warned without delay.

As they were leaving the building two soldiers, an old warrior and his young companion recognized Yeshua's group, and intercepted them. The old man sniggered, "Are you Yeshua of Nazareth?"

"I am. Who wishes to know?"

"You are a criminal Zealot, as are the rest of you. You are under arrest. Come with me," the old man grabbed and started pushing them.

Quintus grabbed the soldier's wrist, "Take your filthy hands off him. He is a friend of the governor, who guaranteed his freedom." The soldier released him.

The old warrior shouted defiantly, "Private Quintus, before I'm finished I'll have your head."

Yeshua was stunned by the threat, "I don't like his tone. You may well be in danger. He'll stop at nothing to get you."

"Just a mad dog barking," Quintus scoffed lightly.

When they reported the news to the pilgrims, they were greeted with loud cheers. Everyone wanted to hear the full story, and Yeshua had to repeat it until his voice became hoarse. The leader of the siccarii came next to him whispering, "Why did you not use the saber-dagger?"

The young man replied sheepishly, "Oh! I forgot it back in Nazareth."

Yeshua joined the pilgrims' celebration. They partied in earnest, drinking watered down wine, celebrating a renewal of life. Yeshua confided to Jacob what Caiphas' said, emphasizing they leave immediately, but they wanted to celebrate first.

They started for Gerezim in the middle of the night. It was pitch black with no moon, and they proceeded at a snail's pace. Master Jacob's children had to be awakened for the long trek. At first they dragged the little ones, but discovered that to keep a faster pace, they had to carry the younger ones, and tie the older two on the animals.

They knew that at sunrise the soldiers would catch and pass them and a feeling of panic began to take hold. They continued relentlessly hoping to leave Caesarea far behind. Alas, when the horizon appeared, the city walls were only a few miles behind. They imagined the soldiers fortifying themselves, and marching like well oiled machines.

Yeshua knew they would be losing ground and tried to think of a strategy to travel faster, to no avail. About mid-morning when they stopped for a quick meal, he told Jacob they would have to leave them behind. To his surprise everybody argued against him. "I have family in Gerezim," Jacob's said with a tone of desperation. "I must warn them."

Stephanos and Quintus sympathized with them. Yeshua argued that at their pace there would be no one to save. But Quintus countered, "Soldiers only march in daylight and camp for the night. If we walk day and night, we will arrive first."

Yeshua was not convinced. But faced with a general mutiny, he chose to compromise, "If master Jacob wants to arrive first, why not take the camel?"

"Master Yeshua, this camel can't travel day and night at a fast pace," Germanicus shook his head. "He may not go much longer at any pace. His limp is worse."

"I agree," Jacob nodded.

Nevertheless they concurred with Quintus, they may walk slower yet win the race.

Only Yeshua had grave doubts.

• • •

Two days after Yeshua's group left, a traveler from Nazareth arrived in the port city inquiring for him. The Israeli had become a folk hero, so everyone knew that to get to him they should speak to master El Sharif. The traveler told him, "I was paid handsomely to travel non stop to deliver this letter to master Yeshua." He looked around searching for something, "Is there a place where I can sit? I have hardly slept since Nazareth."

"Of course my good man," El Sharif put his arm around his shoulder. "Please come, sit and rest in my tent." As soon as they entered he clapped and when the servant girl appeared he ordered, "Our best wine and a warm meal for my special guest."

When the food arrived the Persian excused himself, went to his new business manager, master Benjoseph, whose new disguise made him unrecognizable, and told him about the traveler with the letter.

They joined him, and Benjoseph explained, "Unfortunately the person you seek left Caesarea two days past, heading for mount Gerezim." When he saw the man's look of disappointment, he quickly added, "However Yeshua is our best friend and if you give us the letter, we will guarantee he gets it." He held out his hand.

Instead, the traveler drew back anxiously, "Master Yacek paid me very well to guarantee I fly non-stop, and hand it to him personally..."

Benjoseph decided on a different approach, and smiled expansively, "It is obvious they chose a trustworthy messenger." He refilled the stranger's goblet which he emptied eagerly. "We also came from Nazareth recently. Is it still lousy with Romans?"

"You would swear they had a coup d'etat," the stranger volunteered. "Soldiers on every corner, searching houses and dragging men off to prison. I was stopped three times before getting through town. Why are they interested in such inconseque... inconseque."

"Humble," the schoolmaster helped.

"...humble town?"

"They suspect a Zealot in every hut," Benjoseph volunteered, noticing the stranger was slowly succumbing to the wine, and promptly refilled his goblet.

"What if there were? Can the poor Israelis, not be masters of their own destiny?" the traveler asked with an air of defiance.

"Psst! Not so loud," the schoolmaster put his index finger across his lips speaking in low breath. "You can say it to us: we're friends. But, be careful outside the walls..." The traveler nodded exaggeratedly, and Benjoseph saw that his eyelids were heavy. He handed him the full goblet,

"Did master Yacek pay you to come to Caesarea, or search for master Yeshua around the world?" he asked casually.

"Only as far as Caesarea," he blurted out with a slur.

"Then, my good man, your job is done," the schoolmaster roared with exuberance. "It's not your fault he left. But, you're very fortunate, for we can help you. We will fulfill your guarantee and take personal responsibility to communicate the news immediately." Benjoseph purred persuasively as he stuck out his hand for the letter. Seeing the traveler hesitate he pressed, "These news are most important: either his family is warning Yeshua to stay away to avoid arrest, or to get back immediately to help the family. Should he not be told the urgency of the situation?"

The traveler, handed the papyrus obediently, yawning, "Will...you do...for me?"

"Anything for a friend," Benjoseph grabbed it and started to leave saying, "When you finish eating, sleep in that corner without fear. We'll look after this for you."

Outside Benjoseph and the Persian found a quiet corner, broke the seal and read the news. The schoolmaster's eyes went as cold as steel and his muscles tightened.

"Bad news?" El Sharif asked anxiously.

Benjoseph responded with hatred dripping with every word, "The mole is master Nehemiah, a Phoenician architect, recently from Tyre."

"Is he the one who constructed the monstrosity on the hill?"

"The one whose smile melts ice," the schoolmaster described bitterly. "I don't understand how he fooled me and everyone? We double checked every one of his references...."

"The Romans are expert at covering their trails: falsifying documentation, and paying references handsomely to lie. They are professional, and don't lack for greedy scums willing to sell their services."

Benjoseph re-read the letter, "Nehemiah is leaving for Caesarea immediately to look for Yeshua..."

"If they cross paths, our young friend will be doomed," El Sharif's voice trembled with anxiety. "Yeshua will be in chains...maybe killed."

"Nehemiah threatened to kill him recently," the schoolmaster's voice was tense.

"We have to leave...NOW!" El Sharif started to give the servants orders.

• • •

About mid afternoon of the second day the youngest child, Paulina, announced, "Look daddy, all those people are following us."

Jacob turned around and blurted out, "Romans - less than a mile back."

Yeshua knew they were losing ground, for the exhausted children refused to cooperate, and the camel again favored its leg.

"We cannot continue on this road," Yeshua suggested. "They will overtake us before evening. Is there another path to Gerezim?"

"This is the shortest route," Jacob replied. "If we take another they'll overtake us."

"They'll overtake us in any event. And if they learn we intend to warn them, we will be the first to be killed," the Israeli decided to speak bluntly.

"Let them," Jacob screamed, losing self control from the pressures and exaustion. "Before they kill me, I'll take as many as I can with me."

"They will kill your wife and children. Is that what you want?"

"I don't care," he broke down sobbing.

Metella embraced and held him while he cried as a child. She spoke with love and kindness, "Before, we had a good reason to die, but now we would be wasting our lives." She pointed to the hills, "Over there is a narrow path. We'll travel beyond those hills."

They took the path and after a couple of knolls were out of sight. They continued sadly, certain that the Romans would soon be far ahead. Only Yeshua hoped, watching the setting sun, praying that the army did not reach Gerezim in daylight, and would have to camp for the night.

He prayed silently, "Hurry up sun: go down…Quickly…"

CHAPTER XIV - MASSACRE AT MOUNT GEREZIM

After trekking two days and a night without sleep, Yeshua's group slowed to a crawl. The children were exhausted, the animals worn out and the adults at the end of their wits. Although they could not see the Romans, they were certain they had been by passed them and were closing in on Mount Gerezim.

To avoid the soldiers they took a path through wadis and ravines to the town. They forded small streams, and climbed over rolling hills, hoping at the next crest to see the silhouette of the Temple against the stars. Alas, all they saw were more hills ahead.

When they descended into a deep valley they thought they heard screams, stopped and listened. It was a faint noise, easily confused with wind or animal noises. They rationalized they were over reacting and resumed walking. They barely started, when loud screams cut into the night. There was no mistake: the blood curdling cries were from terrified people.

Yeshua's heart sank for he knew the Romans were slaughtering the villagers.

"Let's hurry," he yelled and began to run. "They need help!"

They ran down the hill only to find a large stream and a pool of water in their way. Yeshua told lady Metella to remain with the children and the animals, while they crossed the pool, which was chest deep, and ran up the opposite side. They ran the last three hundred paces through high, thick bushes, and at the top saw a gigantic bonfire in the town square. The Romans had surrounded the pilgrims, and proceeded to slaughter them. The young men assessed the situation: the soldiers were hacking and piercing the victims, as they ran helter-skelter like dazed animals, often into the soldiers' paths, only to be cut down. Some escaped then turned back for their children left behind, only to be massacred.

"Let's go help," Yeshua yelled, as he ran into the melee. They grabbed the closest persons and dragged them from the fracas, rushing them back into the bushes. On their first run they saved five people, then six, four, and another five. At that point Yeshua called Stephanos. "Take them down to lady Metella and come back for more."

The Greek grabbed the closest person and ran downhill yelling, "Follow me."

Like stricken animals they ran, tripping and falling, terrified to the point of paralysis, unable to comprehend the simplest directions. At the bottom Stephanos had to push them across the pool as they feared drowning, though they had swum in it since childhood.

Meanwhile Yeshua and the others returned to the square, grabbing the next person, man, woman or child, dragging him to safety. Some were so terrified they scratched, bit or punched their saviors. Yelling above the screams and cries, they tried to explain they were friends, while the victims stared, their eyes fixed with terror. Sometimes they were forced to knock the person out, and drag him to the bushes. At first they could infiltrate among the soldiers without being detected, for they were too busy hacking at the pilgrims, to notice a handful of intruders. They had saved dozens more when Yeshua stopped the Greek, "After taking them down, bring one back to take over. We need you here."

The Greek grabbed the closest person yelling, "Follow me," as they ran down, tripping over roots or each other, running for their lives. In their rush they nearly ran over Stephanos. He stopped by the pool and waited for the stragglers, frozen with fright, who had to be dragged down. The Greek put his arm gently around a youth and consoled him, "Have no fear. You are safe now. They will not find you."

Stephanos chose a strong young man, "Come, you'll bring the next groups down."

He was shocked when the young man broke down sobbing uncontrollably, "I can't...I cannot do it," he cried out. "They'll kill me...I don't want to die..."

The Greek was flabbergasted, with a feeling of pity and repulsion. He wanted to smash the oaf's face, but held back realizing under different circumstances he might be a hero. Before he could find another, a young lady of seventeen grabbed his sleeve, "Mister, I'll come. I'll help you"

Stephanos motioned to her, and they ran up. There were already a dozen persons waiting. He told her to wait, rejoining his group. This time he had to jump over dead and dying pilgrims. The Romans realized there were intruders saving the Samaritans, and fearing that survivors could be witnesses against them, intensified their attack.

The Greek was dragging out a mother with a small boy when a soldier ordered him to stop, and swung his sword at Stephanos' head. He raised his staff instinctively, deflecting the blow, then swung the stick with all his might full in his face. Before the soldier regained his wits, Stephanos swung the staff like an axe crushing his head, and watched him crumple down. He dragged the woman and her boy to safety.

Quintus, only a couple of paces away was dragging a man who was pulling his wife by one arm as she carried a baby in the other. He was almost out of the square when a soldier sent his horse at him. He pushed the family out of the way, but was run over. He got back to his feet, only to see the soldier returning to finish him off. He stepped aside swinging his staff upwards knocking him off his mount. As he fell Quintus raised his staff to finish him off, but the attacker lay immobile, his neck broken. Quintus glanced at Yeshua and mentally thanked him for teaching them to defend themselves.

Yeshua reached to save a woman, when he saw a Roman holding up a baby by one leg, ready to swing his sword and cut him in twain. The Israeli swung his staff deflecting the sword, then brought the end of the stick into the Roman's gut folding him over. He grabbed the baby, handed him to the woman and led them to safety.

After many trips Yeshua guessed they had saved over two hundred Samaritans, when he stopped surprised: some villagers they had taken down were returning. They had regained their composure and came to help. They grabbed sticks, branches, or swords and spears from fallen soldiers and fought valiantly beside the young men.

"Germanicus, get your master and go to those houses," he yelled. "The Romans are looting and burning everything."

The slave looked at the area and saw soldiers running in the shadows, some with torches, others with sacks filled with booty. He found his master and they ran up to help.

Yeshua ran into the dark rooms but the place seemed empty. He cupped his hands and yelled, "We are friends here to help. Come out, you are safe." An old patriarch came out, and called out his family. Soon a dozen persons came seemingly out of the woodwork. Yeshua ordered them out. "Go up on the roof." They ran up the steps with other families, and Stephanos led them from roof to roof, to the end and down into the bushes. Soon he found volunteers to lead the families in a steady stream down to Metella.

Sometimes they arrived too late, and tripped over the bodies. They could not stop for they had to run to other homes to save those families before the Romans attacked. Many times Yeshua was literally one step ahead of the soldiers.

Germanicus rushed into one house, almost colliding with a soldier running out, loaded with a sack of silverware, "Please accept my apologies," he bowed and stepped out of the Roman's way. As the soldier ran, the slave nimbly stuck his staff between his legs tripping him. As he was falling, Germanicus, swung his staff across his neck, and heard a horrible crunch. He saved the terrified family and led tem to safety.

"In case I did not say so before, I'm grateful you taught us how to use this stick," Germanicus saluted him.

Yeshua yelled, "Master Stephanos, take my place. I see Romans entering the Temple."

When he left they followed him. Quintus caught up and joined them. Inside the Temple, in the praying courts they found soldiers attacking the trapped pilgrims. Some were ripping down gold and silver ornaments from the windows, walls and the altars. The young men fought the invaders fiercely, and the Romans, shocked by the vicious counter attack, retreated, happy to continue looting elsewhere. The remaining Samaritans picked up abandoned swords and spears, and joined the counter attack to liberate the Temple.

Yeshua told Stephanos and Quintus to take the survivors to the roof tops where others waited to guide them to the valley. Meanwhile the young scholar searched the other rooms. When he entered the innermost sacred room, the holy of holies, he stopped at the door. Should he, a Galilean, enter the sanctum sanctorum of the Samaritans? The probability of finding survivors persuaded him to open the door. There were dozens of women and children wailing terrorized. He explained that he came to take them to safety, but they refused to move, pointing to the ground in the center of the room.

"Our holy Taheb...save him," the women cried out. Yeshua went around the altar and made out the figure of a man in the dark, half sitting, leaning against the Ark of the Covenant. He bent down and saw an old man in a very colorful robe: the High Priest. He was gasping for breath, holding one hand tightly against his diaphragm. Yeshua saw Quintus entering. "Take the people out. The Taheb needs air. He is badly wounded."

The Roman started to push them out and to the roof tops.

Meanwhile Germanicus entered, and seeing Yeshua, approached the altar.

Yeshua sat beside the holy man and stretched him out on the floor, resting his head on his lap. The combination of more air and comfort helped him breathe more freely. He opened his eyes and stared fixedly into Yeshua's radiant eyes for a long time. At last he whispered almost inaudibly, "Friend...?"

"I am Yeshua, from Galilee. Yes, a friend."

The old man's lips stretched in a weak smile, "Galilean...good friend..."

Germanicus advanced and stood about a pace from them. He did not know he was in the sanctum sanctorum, the place where Yahweh resided, forbidden to them. When he saw the Ark of the Covenant, he sensed this must be a very sacred place. When he saw the old man wheezing, he was certain the ancient one was doomed.

"If you wish, we will move you to safety and a comfortable cot," Yeshua whispered.

"I will not survive... I am... pierced," he replied, moving his hand from the torn and bloody robe. He coughed and pleaded, "Master Yeshua, pray for me..."

Yeshua placed his hand on the wound, closed his eyes and whispered, "Dear Yahweh if it is Your will, for the sake of the villagers and the Samaritans, save this holy man...They will need his wisdom to guide and give them courage...However, Dear Abba if it is Your will that his spirit comes to you, give him peace at Your side forever."

Yeshua remained with his eyes closed. A bright radiance enveloped his head, and a small ray of light moved like a spark along the length of his arm, dissipating over him and the Taheb. Germanicus saw the strange phenomenon, ran back and shrank in the far corner, trembling with fright. Again he feared that demonic spirits were being released.

The Taheb opened his eyes, breathing weakly but more regular, and whispered, "You called the Lord your Abba..." He stared into Yeshua's eyes, "Who are you?"

"Do not get agitated," Yeshua tried to reassure him.

But the Taheb, wishing to say more, grabbed the young man's tunic and pulled him closer, "I had a dream...a vision...not long ago..." He stopped for breath, then continued "I was told, I would see the promised one...Are you the Messiah...?"

Yeshua pleaded, "You must rest." He began to help the Taheb to lie down again. "I will get help to get you out of here and into safety."

As he stood up two Roman soldiers rushed in with swords drawn, "By the most holy Jupiter," the first one commented, "This room is as black as the bowels of hell."

"It's in places like these they hide their biggest treasures," the other responded.

They came forward until they were almost on top of Yeshua, before seeing him. "Who are you?" the Roman demanded, unsure he was not seeing an apparition. When Yeshua came forward, the soldier raised his sword yelling, "Where is the treasure?"

"Down there," Yeshua pointed to the Taheb.

The Romans leaned forward when Germanicus, came up swinging his staff, "Come get it, you miserable murderers." One of the soldiers folded like a broken twig. The other flew from the room as if possessed by ghosts.

Yeshua located some villagers and told them to find a cot to move the Taheb. The Samaritans rushed into the sacred room, as the young men went out on the street.

"Did you cure him?" Germanicus asked. "Did you perform another...?"

But Yeshua was already out in the street where the screams and clashing swords drowned his answer – if any. They stood side by side analyzing the situation. "The bonfire hinders the villagers," Yeshua yelled. "We must put it out." He pointed to a couple of chariots stationed not far from them, with the tetrarch Valerius Gratus standing in one and general Fulvius in the other, watching the slaughter.

"The chariots," Yeshua pointed and ran into a commercial building a few doors away, "Come with me." Inside they saw a merchandise shop with everything from carpenters' tools to farm equipment. Yeshua took two lengths of chain and a heavy fence post. "Help me with these," he demanded.

They tied each end of the post to a piece of chain, crawled stealthily under the chariots where they tied one chain to each axle of the chariots. On a signal from Yeshua they jumped into the chariots, pushing the Romans out, and whipped the stallions at full gallop towards the bonfire. At the last moment they steered the horses around it, pulling the chains taut which acted as a dragnet crashing into the burning wood, scattering everything in the air. In the next instant the town square was dark. The chariots continued on and the young men jumped out a moment before the horses and chariots ran off the road. When they looked back the Samaritans had gained the advantage because they knew the square area better in the dark.

The battle raged past midnight when the tetrarch called off the massacre. They gathered the prisoners to help with their wounded soldiers and bury their dead. Before sunrise, they started back to Caesarea. Their prisoners were destined to be sold into slavery. There were dozens of Romans killed, and hundreds of Samaritans slaughtered. Israelis had suffered greater losses in wars, but none as absurd as this night.

After the Romans left, the villagers began to return. Many ran into the square searching for loved ones, walking among the dead, bending over twisted bodies, and praying they would not find them dead. Yeshua could not hold back tears, when a mother froze with horror recognizing her little child. She let out a piercing cry that rang through the air, and fell on the lifeless bundle.

According to Mosaic law the dead had to be interred before sunset. Yeshua pleaded with the survivors to turn their energy to tend to the wounded. He persuaded dozens to start digging mass graves. It was difficult to dig in the hard ground for their energy was sapped from the terrifying battle. But, they labored without complaints.

Yeshua's group and Jacob's family were beyond the point of exhaustion, their minds numb. They worked with the villagers, too outraged to try to make sense of the absurdity. But they too were affected. At one point Quintus dropped his pick and walked from cadaver to cadaver, turning some over, searching others as if looking for something, all the while mumbling. After a while he started to run among them, like a madman.

Stephanos suspected his friend was suffering a mental crisis, and ran after him, "Are you searching for someone you know? Can we help...?"

Quintus stopped and stared at him, "Not one...was armed...They... could not defend." He looked into Stephanos' eyes, and tears rolled down, "They...murdered..."

Late in the afternoon with three big holes dug up, they picked up corpses, and laid one on top of another in a heap. Quintus worked with a Samaritan who kept staring at him. After many trips he could no longer remain silent.

"Are you Samaritan?" he asked suspiciouly.

Quintus shook his head, "From Cappernaum."

"You don't look Galilean," he replied, then said a few phrases in Aramaic which the Roman barely understood. "You're not Galilean. You are a foreigner. Who are you?" he demanded with fire in his eyes. When Quintus did not reply he accused him, "Are you a filthy Roman? CONFESS." When Quintus did not deny it, he screamed, "HE IS A ROMAN; A FILTHY MURDERER!" All the others stopped and looked at them. The accuser picked up a boulder and marched at Quintus, while he stood, dazed and dejected. His world, his sense of order had come crashing, and there was no reason to defend or fight. It was not that he sought death. Worse than that: he did not care.

Germanicus ran at the assailant knocking the boulder away.

Yeshua put his arms around Quintus' shoulders, "This Roman is a hero. He stood beside us in Caesarea ready to die for our faith and the nation."

"He is still a Roman dog," the assailant screamed. "Let's kill the dog!"

"Kill the Roman," the others joined him.

"Butcher him, like they butchered my family," another cried out.

"Listen to me," master Jacob stepped forward. "This is a courageous man. He was ready to die; he fought the army last night. He is..."

The seventeen year old girl who led the villagers the previous night stood beside Yeshua, "Revenge! Is that all you ever want is revenge? You don't care whether he is kind, only that he is a Roman. Well, I don't care if he is a Roman. He is a saint!" She walked up to the assailant, yelling into his face, "Last night he ripped me from the arms of a soldier...I'm alive because he killed that soldier." She looked at the mob and spoke to each of them, "If you kill him you may as well kill me."

Her pleas stopped the mob. But the assailant, insane with hatred, shouted, "Get out of my way: I want to finish him off."

"You'll have to kill me first," she retorted.

Quintus stepped around her and walked up to the assailant, "Stop it. There have been enough senseless deaths." He stared at his accuser, "You're right. My ancestors are Romans...I was born in Capernaum. Until recently I was proud of...Roman fairness...justice..." he scoffed half sobbing. When he continued, tears welled in his eyes as he continued with deep pain, "After what happened, I am ashamed...I disown...my ancestors. As long as I live, I will do everything in my power to tell the emperor in Rome about...this massacre. I will defend my people against the oppressors." He spoke with passion, tears rolling, "In my heart I will always be an Israeli."

The Samaritans listened, surprised and impressed. When he finished, to a man they nodded and muttered approval. Some stepped back unwilling to attack him.

Quintus picked up a discarded sword, and handed it to the assailant, "You lost your family because of the Romans. Take the sword. Have your revenge."

The man took the sword, stared at him for a long time, and threw it away. He walked up to Quintus embracing him, "You are not like them... You are my brother."

The villagers mumbled, some of them crying. Others touched and thanked him.

By late afternoon the burials were complete. Yeshua's group gathered by the pool for their meal and a well deserved sleep. Jacob joined them for their last supper together, as they were leaving for Laish in the morning. After the meal they sat around the fire, subdued, contemplating the events they would never forget, or comprehend.

Germanicus asked his master to join him by the pool, where they sat talking and tossing pebbles in the water. He described what he saw when master Yeshua held the mortally wounded Taheb's head on his lap, and the holy man's statement.

"What were the Taheb's precise words?" Stephanos queried with curiosity.

"He said: 'I had a dream, and a messenger of God said I will see the saviour of Israel, before I die...Are you the Messiah?'"

"What was his answer?"

"Nothing. He performed a...a superhuman miracle," the slave shuddered recollecting it. "A light as bright as the sun appeared around his head as he prayed, then a bolt of fire, rushed down covering the Taheb. I was terrified..."

"Then what happened? Did the Taheb survive?"

Germanicus tried to remember for a long time before responding, "I don't know...he was very weak...I don't know."

"I am not surprised by what you think you saw," Stephanos replied rhetorically. "It's been an exhausting journey: almost getting killed in Caesarea; and a horrible battle last night. Under such conditions any of us could imagine, or see illusions…"

The slave interrupted resentful, "Are you saying…you don't believe me?"

Stephanos raised his hands, "These visions were like old Hegesippus': Illusions."

The slave was barely able to utter the question. "You think I'm seeing things?"

The Greek knew this was a sensitive topic, and treaded carefully, "We buried hundreds of Samaritans yet the Taheb was not there for the service. He probably did not survive…" He spoke kindly, "I believe you honestly thought you saw…"

"Save the scholarly double-talk for your intellectual friends," the slave stood up abruptly, heaved the pebbles into the water, and snapped at his master bitterly. "I know what I saw and no amount of glib verbiage will change it!"

He turned away and marched to the fire deeply hurt.

Stephanos shook his head. He would never cease to be amazed, how these innocent creatures of the uncivilized frontiers of Europe, were easy prey to superstition and religious cults. He wondered how to persuade his slave to recognize such tricks?

They turned in before the first star appeared, and were fast asleep. Only Germanicus sat outside, tired and angry. His master did not believe him because he was a slave; mere property, no different from the camel, and who would believe a camel? His exhausted mind took all arguments to the absurd extreme, until he gave in to sleep.

. . .

It was noon when they awoke, and only because the villagers came to say good bye. They hurried breakfast and broke camp. It was a sad parting. Jacob and Metella cried unabashed, talking and laughing all at the same time. Jacob took Yeshua aside, "The Taheb apologies for not coming down, but he is still too weak to move."

"Will he be alright?" the young scholar asked.

Jacob nodded, "He bled profusely, but he is a stubborn Samaritan... They always survive. He thanks you for your prayer. He asked that I deliver a message verbatim: 'Master Yeshua, you are the one promised to us. I will pray that you make His word come true.' Do you understand that?"

Yeshua smiled, "Your holy man is kind. Tell him I will pray for his recovery."

They trekked the rest of the day towards Beth-Sheeba. Their minds were overwhelmed by the experiences: from the sacrifice by the rain-man, to the barbarous massacre. After the evening meal Yeshua and Germanicus were cleaning the dishes, and the Israeli noticed him unusually solemn, "Are you not excited about seeing Lygia?"

"Yeah," the slave mumbled.

Yeshua thought he seemed depressed, "Do you wish to talk about it?"

"About what?" Germanicus droned uninterested.

"Your bottom lip is drooping on your sandals. What's the matter?"

Germanicus debated whether he should bother, but when he started it was like a broken dam, "My master will never see me as a human. If that camel could speak he would accept its word over mine." His voice was shaking with anger and disappointment. "When we return, I'll take Lygia, and lady Anna, and run for freedom."

Yeshua knew Germanicus resented his hopeless position, but the threat stunned him, "Bounty hunters will track you down and kill you... Perhaps Anna and Lygia too..."

"I don't care," the slave snapped.

"What makes you so angry?" Yeshua queried.

"Everything; according to him I suffer from illusions. Am I an imbecile?"

"Precisely what did you tell him, and what did he say?"

"Last night I explained the miracle you performed in the Temple, and he scoffed!"

"What exactly did you see?" Yeshua was barely able to control his inner turmoil.

"That bright aura around your head; it covered the Taheb like a sparkling blanket," the slave explained, "Why are you asking? Don't tell me you did not see it!"

Yeshua shook his head, "I close my eyes when I pray."

"When I told him, he called it sorcery, and hocus-pocus. He thinks I'm crazy..." He glanced at the Israeli and seeing him staring back worried, covered his mouth, "Oh, I promised not to...and I told him..."

Yeshua sighed, but decided not to argue, replying philosophically, "Luckily your master did not believe it..."

"Luckily?" he retorted bitterly. "You agree with him? I hoped you'd sympathize."

"I do sym..." he started apologetically.

"I'll never get fairness from any of you. I won't find happiness until I'm free."

"When we arrive in Laish, I'll take you to see a very special young man. His name is Jonathan..."

"Why? What will do for me?" he demanded rebelliously.

"You two have much in common," Yeshua responded enigmatically.

"Then come with me and tell my master that I'm not crazy."

"He doesn't believe miracles," Yeshua tried to avoid a confrontation.

"You mean you won't support a slave," he grumbled frostily, and marched away.

. . .

The following night they camped in the backyard of the hotel in Beth-Sheeba, and shared supper with master Isaac. "Master Hegesippus has been the talk of the town since you left," he reported. "He seems a decade younger...and completely reformed."

"Is he cured?" Stephanos queried with surprise and suspicion. When master Isaac nodded, the Greek stared speechless.

Master Isaac continued, "Many people report that they followed a young peasant back to the mansion and saw him cured the old man. Did you see anything?" he asked Yeshua who shook his head nervously. "But, his total reformation is the biggest miracle: he has turned the mansion into an orphanage, and returned the water to the town."

"I knew he would. He promised it before the miracle," Germanicus blurted out. When they looked at him, he blushed, stood up and started to clear up the dishes.

. . .

Before sunrise they left for Laish to rejoin Honi and Mariamme. By mid afternoon they were approaching it, and saw an amazing change with the countryside which now was a green carpet, with every bush and tree full of leaves. The fields were splashed liberally with yellows, blue and red flowers. Nature came alive with the rain, and the fields, recently plowed and seeded, were filled with grain stalks promising a healthy harvest. As if to prove the rain was not an accident, a light drizzle started.

Throughout the day, Germanicus who had been somber and sullen since Gerezim, was becoming excited. He talked about Lygia and singing lullabies, and about her growing up. He decided she would receive religious instruction from master Yeshua. Then he spoke of registering her in a fine lyceum in Greece, after which she would attend university in Athens. To complete her studies he would take her to northern Europe to visit his village and learn the customs and traditions.

The others smiled furtively, touched by his affection for the girl. As he dreamt the tender dreams of a father, he forgot he could not afford a fraction of those dreams.

When they saw the tent by the stream, they rushed up only to discover no one was there. On closer inspection they saw smoking embers in the fire and the pot was ready to put on to cook, and concluded they had left recently and would return shortly.

They set up their tent next to them, and while the slave went to find firewood, Yeshua walked to the community water well to fetch water. As he turned to leave a stranger approached him. "Are you master Yeshua of Nazareth?" he queried. When he nodded, the man came closer and whispered, "You are one of us. The Zealots are meeting tonight at the school house. Be there." He stopped, checked that no one was listening, and continued, "Go down that road to the oak tree, where you will be picked up..."

Yeshua looked where he pointed, but seeing only bushes, he walked up to the road and saw a lone tree. He turned back to verify, but the stranger had disappeared. He returned to the water well, looked around again without success. Then he saw a movement in the shadows, a man's face for an instant; a head with thick black hair, very dark eyes and a long scar on the left side of his face, from the temple down to the chin.

As he carried the water he wondered about the stranger with the message. He wondered if this was an entrapment, and chuckled. The recent events made him too cynical. After some consideration, he decided he would go to the meeting. He wished to tell them about the non-violent confrontation, and to warn them to be cautious of traitors.

Back at camp he heard loud cheerful voices and laughter and recognized Honi's distinct voice. He saw Germanicus swinging the little bundle, laughing and talking like a child with his first toy.

Honi greeted him warmly, "Were you involved in the massacre at mount Gerezim?"

"You heard about it already?" he asked surprised. "Yes, we were there."

The holy man was visibly upset, and wanted to give him a stern warning, but with all the others present merely suggested, "Master Yeshua, you must be more careful ..."

The young scholar saw his stern look, and nodded guiltily, "I will, I promise..."

They explained the absurdity of the massacre, but the real discussion started when they described the Messiahs: the Great Shamai and master Eleazar.

"They say Shamai is quite impressive," Honi remarked.

"There is talk that Shamai did not perform the miracle," Stephanos interjected. "They say a young peasant entered the mansion furtively and..."

Honi's eyes darted to Yeshua, and back to the Greek, who noticed it, but did not make a comment. The circle man wisely changed topics, "I have a few names of holy men you may want to check: Ben Stada is truly a good man; then there is Hanina ben Dosa, in Sepphoris, who survives bites from deadly serpents."

"We saw him already," Stephanos replied. "Truly impressive but..."

"Of course there is Messiah Abba Hikiah. And two others you dare not miss," the circle man said enthusiastically, "Master Theudas, from Jericho, who promises to part the river Jordan as Moses parted the Red Sea. And a giant from Egypt an expatriate..."

Quintus interrupted, "That's Rabban, the man who performs impossible feats."

"We will be going to Jerusalem via Capernaum," the young Israeli explained. "We'll visit master Hariph about the parchments from the vases in the cave, and see masters Theudas, and Rabban before going to Jerusalem."

Mariamme who had been listening directed a caustic remark at her husband, "I'll bet none of those Messiahs have to beg for a meal. Why don't you copy them and get a fortune for your rain?"

"Mariamme, please..." Honi was mortified with the unprovoked attack.

"Do you know what the villagers paid him?" she continued unabated, "Ten lousy drachmas! I begged rabbi Beoni to help, and he shamed them into parting with a few coins. But they moaned and groaned as if we were robbing them..."

"Keep your voice down, dear," he pleaded with her.

"I'm sick and tired of cheap Israelis. The grapevines are loaded, the olive trees laden, and the fields promise rich harvest," she refused to be silenced. "Why should we have to beg for our meals?"

Stephanos, eager to avoid a confrontation took a purse with coins and handed it to her, "Take these, for caring for Lygia..."

She grabbed the purse like a desperate beggar. Honi led her to a corner and sat her down, putting his arm around her to console her.

After an early dinner Yeshua asked Germanicus in a whisper, "Now that you're back with Lygia, have you changed your mind...?"

The slave replied with a definite tone, "Never! I'll get free...or, I'll die trying."

"Come, we will go to the village," Yeshua suggested. "Young Jonathan is giving a speech." When the slave pointed to Lygia, he added, "Your master can look after her."

Germanicus smiled, "Right, it's time he took on some responsibility."

When they arrived at rabbi Beoni's house there were almost a hundred people, most of whom brought a sitting stool or blanket, and sat in the yard waiting for the speaker. They found a grassy area and joined them.

Germanicus saw a young man sitting on a stool with a backing, surrounded by people. "Is that the speaker?" he asked. When Yeshua nodded, he commented, "He's young." He watched him with interest, wondering what the young man could talk about. But he certainly was popular and in great demand. He noticed that when Jonathan wanted to move his legs from one side to the other, he picked them up to do it. He turned to his friend, "Is he crippled?"

Yeshua nodded, "Physically."

From that moment Germanicus could not take his eyes off him. Myriad questions rushed through his mind: Was he born a cripple? If not, what happened? What could a young cripple know about life, or slavery? He became curious and impatient to hear him.

While the slave mused, rabbi Beoni stood up to make the announcement. He introduced one section in the audience; students and the school master of the lyceum in Beth-Sheba. They comprised of about sixty people, and had traveled the entire day to hear the speaker. He introduced his son and turned the meeting over to him.

Jonathan was a natural speaker. He started with a short anecdote, then directly into the speech. He looked at the people and spoke as if he were discussing the topic with each person, making a point, moving to the next listener, holding everyone's attention as he developed the theme. His presentation was interesting because it seemed like a debate: asking a question then answering it, often giving an example to emphasize a point. He spoke slowly, clearly, and above all with enthusiasm. And the fluctuation of his voice, raising it, stopping at the peak to allow the point to become fixed in their minds before proceeding, were perfect. Then he lowered his voice almost to a whisper so they strained not to miss a word. And he varied his phrases: now short and staccato, or lengthier and more complex. Most importantly the presentation was done with fervor and inspiration: and just as importantly he kept it short. He learned early how to make a point, develop the message, perhaps tell a story or two relevant to the topic, bring it to a climax and stop. His favorite saying was, "A good speaker quits leaving his listeners asking for more."

Master Yeshua had the foresight to write a synopsis of his speech in the diary they kept. He often referred to Jonathan as one of his most inspired miracles, when giving sermons in his synagogue later in Jerusalem:

"People spend their lives praying for divine intervention to guide them. Israelis have waited a thousand years for the Messiah to come and inspire them. It is sad to see them search for the miracle, when it is within them. They need to reach within and get it done. How? Easy! Be your own source of inspiration. Find a dream and strive to fulfill it. Any size dream will do: easy, or as outlandish as your imagination. What is important is to decide on the dream and start work immediately. You may fail: once, twice, many times, but never lose sight of your destiny.

"Do not waste another millennium waiting for the Messiah. He is as different for each person as the questioner. As my friend master Yeshua often says, 'The Messiah is within you – the divine spark of your Creator.' You all dream of a free Israel. If you want a liberated nation, first liberate yourself. How? Start with a dream, collectively; within a generation you'll make Israel a leading nation. And you'll enjoy the power to lead other nations to moral freedom."

When he finished, the audience sat in stunned silence. What he said was simple and obvious. Then as one they stood up and mobbed him, to discuss and congratulate him, promising to start on their dream. Yeshua and Germanicus had to wait a long time before approaching him.

As soon as Jonathan saw the young Israeli, he beamed a cheerful smile and opened his arms, "Master Yeshua, I am so happy you came. Did you enjoy it?"

"I always do, but it's too short. I brought a friend, Germanicus, to hear it too."

"You are too kind," he chuckled, and turned to the slave, "You are not Israeli?"

"From northern Europe," he replied. "But, your speech would inspire anyone."

"Mark my word, before long, he will be in Europe with inspiring speeches," Yeshua quipped, "I'll leave you two, while I go to say hello to your father."

Left with the young man Germanicus did not hide his enthusiasm. "I was very inspired. If you forgive me being forward, how can so much optimism flow from…"

"…A cripple?" he finished the statement, enjoying the slave's uneasiness. "I'm sorry, but I forget and get carried away…"

"Were you born…like that?"

"Until almost a year ago, I was an athlete, a champion discus and javelin thrower, training for the Olympiad. Alas, an accident left me paralyzed. But, a miracle…"

"Master Yeshua?" Germanicus interrupted filled with wonderment.

Jonathan blushed awkwardly and motioned the slave closer, whispering, "Everybody thinks it was master Honi…."

"So you're no longer crippled?" Germanicus pressed, trying to understand.

Jonathan enjoyed the enigmatic conversation and chuckled broadly, "Before I met master Yeshua, I existed in constant, excruciating pain. I could not find comfort. The only sleep I knew was when I passed out from exhaustion." He stopped, as the painful memory was still fresh in his mind. "After some months I must have gone insane. I drove everyone away...In a fit of depression, I begged father to help me commit suicide." He looked at the slave's forlorn face, and brightened up, "That's when I met master Yeshua. He asked what I most desired to do. I told him, to inspire people. We discussed it and, as you see, I am fulfilling my dream."

"You are happy as a...?" he asked with disbelief.

"I bless my benefactor every day."

"I fail to understand..."

"If a wealthy man said to you, 'Money does not buy happiness,' would you believe him? Would he say the same if he were poor?" He saw the slave's puzzled look, "My success is that I was near the summit and glory. Now I am not, but my message is the same. At the outset people came from curiosity. They reacted as you did; they were confused. How can a cripple speak of optimism, and inspiration? After a long time they changed. They said, if he can be positive and inspirational, I want to be like him!"

"But, but... How can you be so happy?" Germanicus stammered confused.

"I am alive! I have my parents, a wonderful little sister, and my betrothed...We are soon to be married, you know. I am fulfilling my dream. I am truly blessed!" He beamed watching Germanicus staring. "But enough about me; what is your dream?"

"Me? Well, I...I don't..." the slave did not expect such a direct question and was not ready to share personal secrets. His eyes were darting for an escape.

Jonathan knew he was not forthcoming and persisted, "You are intelligent. Perceptive. You are fibbing? Can you share your secret with a friend?"

Germanicus looked down on his sandals, fussing, before finally relenting, "I...I'm a slave. My freedom..."

"Don't feel ashamed. It's an honorable dream. Did you know one of the greatest Roman playwrights started out as a slave?" Jonathan asked and promptly responded his own question. "He developed his talent until his master gave him freedom."

"Master will never give me freedom...and, I can't see how I can persuade him," the slave's face hardened thinking about his desperate dilemma.

"What I did not mention tonight," the young man confided, "was that reaching the dream is secondary. The important point is to find and work towards it." He saw the slave's puzzled look, so he expounded, "When I trained for competition, I remember the daily hard work to reach perfection of the body and mind. When I won and stood on the podium, the moment seemed anti-climatic in comparison to the work, preparation, and the dream. The magical time was the journey."

Germanicus stared unable to accept that he would not enjoy freedom, but was unwilling to argue. He was relieved to see Yeshua return ready to leave. They embraced with a sad farewell and Jonathan fixed his eyes on the slaves' with parting words, "Remember me with kindness. Find a dream, and lead your people."

They were returning to the village, when Yeshua turned to him, "What did you think of master Jonathan?"

"I don't know…I am overwhelmed with his speech, but it's too complex," he responded meditatively. Suddenly he snapped, "How could you do that to him? You had the power to cure him; but you left him a…a half a man…"

Yeshua did not try to defend or explain. Nor did he tell him the decision was Jonathan's. But he knew the slave would have to think about it for a long time.

They were back at the village when Germanicus wondered, "You said he and I have a lot in common…How? I fail to see anything."

"You are prisoners: Jonathan to his bed, you to your master," the Israeli replied, then added winsomely, "Only, he has found freedom."

Germanicus did not understand, and did not wish to continue the conversation. He was confused with the conflicting messages that spoke in riddles and was too tired to try to resolve, or think about it tonight. Yeshua hoped he would grasp the message before running away only to be chased by bounty hunters, which could cost him his life.

When they passed the water well in the town square Yeshua suddenly stopped, "Oh no! I forgot it…" The slave looked at him puzzled, which made him explain, "The Zealots meeting. I forgot…"

They continued in silence, Yeshua feeling a bitter disappointment, because he wanted to warn them about the traitor.

• • •

Because of the baby, Germanicus was given one corner of the tent, although he still slept outside guarding them. Exhausted from the adventures they slept so soundly, no one heard Lygia crying or Germanicus rummaging about to feed her.

Next morning they were enjoying a leisurely breakfast, when villagers rushed by on the way to the village. They quickly finished and followed to discover the cause of the excitement. They arrived in the square in time to see six Roman soldiers marching in their direction, two abreast, leading two prisoners in chains. As they approached Yeshua saw that the prisoners were young men, of about seventeen or eighteen years of age, who by their facial features and dark auburn hair appeared to be related. The young men pushed to the front, for a clear view. Yeshua asked a villager standing beside him, "Are they local boys?" When the stranger nodded, he asked, "Who are they? What happened?"

The man looked about nervously and responded in low voice, "The Romans broke into a meeting of the Zealots last night...in the school house..." Then he muttered grimly, "They are brothers, Simon and James, grandsons of the founder of the Zealots."

Yeshua felt the small hairs on his neck stand up. The stranger he saw the previous day had tried to trap him. Why? Who was he? Yeshua wondered. When he looked at the prisoners he saw a man vaguely familiar walking with the Romans. Dressed in the eastern style, his head had thick black hair, and a long hideous scar running on the left side of his face from the temple to the chin. The man raised a hand and waived in Yeshua's direction, but when they made eye contact, he quickly slipped behind the soldiers.

Yeshua turned and saw Stephanos still waiving at the man. "Do you know him; the man with the scar?" When the Greek nodded he queried, "Who is he?"

Stephanos replied surprised, "Don't you recognize master Nehemiah? He is lady Sarah's father."

Yeshua was flabbergasted. In a flash he remembered the scarred face, and recalled all the instances he had seen him: the first time was at the mansion where he threatened to kill him and his brother Simon. Next he saw him at the Zealots' meetings, and when they were escaping through the reeds he was the one who had coughed. He was probably trying to signal the Romans. Finally, he remembered seeing him yesterday in the shadows by the water well. "Nehemiah is the traitor," he blurted out. His companions wondered what he said, so he repeated, "He is the mole. He sold out the Zealots..."

Quintus pulled out his dagger and started after them instinctively, "Let's get him...I'll plunge this dagger into his ribs."

Yeshua ran and stopped him, "No...We will see him again soon in Nazareth."

They returned and started to break camp and start for Nazareth. After quick good byes to Honi and Mariamme they pressed north to the forest of Galilee.

They passed the time with an animated discussion about the punishment to be meted out to the traitor. Quintus demanded to be the prosecutor, judge and jury, as well as the executioner. He decided on beheading him. He said he'd stick his head on top of the pole at the gate to Nazareth as a deterrent. He'd cut up the body into cubes and salt it so not even beasts or fowl would touch it. Stephanos felt the punishment was too harsh. He would bury at least one of his little fingers, rationalizing that way his soul could get proper rest. Yeshua cut off the discussion curtly, saying that the sentencing was premature, as Nehemiah had not been proven guilty of any crimes. Meanwhile Germanicus was totally engrossed with Lygia who was giggling and blowing bubbles.

Two days later at high noon they arrived at the entrance to the forest and started the long ascent. They felt they were entering a tropical jungle compared to the sparse growth to the south. The thick forest and underbrush with vibrant tones of green was soothing to the eyes. But it was the spacious meadows with a green carpet and a wide variety of flowers, cut by the meandering stream that touched their souls. They were enjoying the forest teeming with life, and failed to notice a camp directly ahead until they were almost upon it. Quintus was the first to spot it, sticking out his arms to stop them, and quickly pushed them back into the bushes and out of sight.

They walked through the thick underbrush deep into the forest for almost a mile, then turned in a northerly direction following a worn out path. After another half mile they took another path to the west for half a mile. Only then they dared to stop.

"Did you see anyone in the camp?" Stephanos asked and the Roman nodded. "Did they see us?"

"Hard to tell," Quintus shrugged. "They made no move which is a good indication."

"Do spiders move before the fly is completely entangled?" Yeshua mused.

"How many bandits did you count?" Germanicus asked.

The Roman closed his eyes concentrating, then pointed his index finger to imaginary parts of the camp, replying, "Definitely three, maybe four."

Yeshua suggested they go further west again, until they come across the next path going north, giving that camp a wide berth. They continued along the sandy narrow path which meandered and twisted around trees and heavy bushes, generally in a westerly direction. The trees were high, and above them the branches interlocked, forming a dark tunnel with intermittent openings where shafts of light stabbed the darkness. The underbrush had thick vegetation where tall grass, ferns and crawling bushes competed for space, oftentimes pushing into the path. The darkness of the tunnel gave a sensation of coolness, but in reality the enclosed area kept out any breeze and the still air proved to be hot and humid. Moreover, the scent of rotting fallen trees and roots gave the air a pungent smell of stale mold. Myriad bugs, insects and voracious mosquitoes thrived in that dark tomb. About every five hundred paces, paths crossed at right angles. Yeshua realized that bandits who had habituated this region cut the paths for ease of travel. They also knew the general formation of the paths and could ambush them at will. Hence they decided to change directions often, continuing generally in a north- by-west direction. He made mental notes of the directions and distances traveled. And, they spoke in low voices and kept constant watch, careful not to walk into another camp. After zigzagging north and west numerous times they stopped.

"We have traveled mostly north, paralleling the path along the brow of the hills. Now we will continue north until the next crossing, then start returning to the right. Go ahead and I'll stay behind to see if we are being followed. If I fail to catch up, continue east until you come out at the brow of the hills. You will be a safe distance north of the bandits' camp. Only then proceed to Nazareth."

They objected, but none stronger than Quintus, "I'll stay with you and fight."

"I'm not staying to fight, only to find out if we are being followed," the Israeli retorted. "Go with them; they'll need you more."

They proceeded with the animals while he hid deep in the bushes. He did not wait long before he heard voices and the scraping of sandals on the sand. As soon as he made out the outline of men advancing in the dark tunnel, he fled. When he caught up to his group they had already turned east. "They're not far behind," he reported. "We have to go faster."

"Did you count how many?" Quintus asked.

"No, they were too far, and I did not want to be seen."

They continued on until they came upon a hill, a few hundred cupits high. At its base the path forked around it in both directions.

"Take the path to the left," Yeshua ordered. "I'm certain it circles the hill. I'll go to the top to find out their number and identity. Go on."

"I'm coming with you," Quintus said stubbornly. "We may get an opportunity and ambush them."

The Israeli looked at him doubtfully, but did not argue. "Let's hurry," he ordered and jumped into the thick underbrush. He pushed through it, crawling under or climbing over the thick growth. The climb proved difficult because they could not get good footing, and had no machete to cut through. They started to have second thoughts when they found a channel carved out by heavy rains, where they made better progress. As they ascended, a horrible thought went through his mind: what if the bandits took the path to the right, to circle the hill and ambush their friends? The fear made him rush, snapping at Quintus below, "Hurry up! You're too slow."

"Then move or I'll run you over," Quintus barked at his heels.

They climbed the channel, with the hot sun beating down heavily. The grade proved steeper than it appeared from below, and they were slowing down visibly. The heat, humidity, and lack of proper rest were taking their toll. They were soaking and their tunics sopping wet. And it seemed they were inhaling the same hot breath they exhaled. Finally they reached the summit and fell on their backs, panting and out of breath.

"Do I feel...a fresh...breeze?" Yeshua heaved a sigh.

"Uh-gh... no mos...quitoes," Quintus snorted.

Suddenly they remembered their friends, stood up and ran around the top of the summit. It consisted of a few hectares of flat rocky terrain almost bare of trees. They walked along the edge searching for a clearing where they could see the path below. At the moment they found it, they saw their pursuers walking through it. When they identified them, their mouths unhinged. "The R-Roman trekkers?" Yeshua stuttered. "Was that not master Nehemiah?" he pointed at the thick black hair.

"They set a trap," Quintus sighed, "How many did you count?"

"Four."

Quintus ran ahead, picked up a large bolder, lifting it over his head.

Yeshua caught him just as he was ready to toss it, "Don't do that."

"What do you mean? They'll come up and we'll crush them."

"When they discover two of us are here, they'll attack the others, knowing it's four against two," Yeshua explained. "Then they'll come for us. We have the advantage now: they don't realize we know we are being followed. We'll set up an ambush…"

Quintus eyebrows furrowed trying to understand how fugitives could have an advantage over their pursuers.

They ran to the north side, and saw their friends proceedings east. They waited a few moments and saw the pursuers take the same path. The young men ran along the edge to the south-east side, found an open clearing and started to descend. Fortunately this side was not as steep, allowing them to run part way, and slide on their sandals on the sand and loose stones, until the muscles of their legs tired and began to tremble. They arrived at the bottom at the same moment as their companions.

"They are gaining. We'll have to walk faster," Yeshua said between breaths.

"Roman soldiers who tried to kill us, with the traitor," Quintus informed them.

"Master Nehemiah?" Stephanos was flabbergasted.

Yeshua nodded, "I am certain they intend to capture us and finish the job…"

"Hurry, we're wasting time," Germanicus started to push ahead. "Let's go!"

They picked up their pace. Lygia who had been angelically cooperative began to fuss. The slave tried to calm her, but the oppressive heat and the mosquitoes, as well as hunger made her uncomfortable and unhappy. Germanicus realized his baby needed attention which he could not give, and he feared her fussing would give them away. He stopped and offered the basket to his master, "Take her and go ahead. I'll stay back and ambush them. I'll hold them back long enough for you to get away."

"Nonsense," Quintus objected. "If you stay so will I, and fight."

"Nobody is staying," Yeshua commanded firmly. "We survived as a team and will do so…to the end." Then he noticed hoof prints behind them, "Our animals are giving us away. We have to find hard sandstone, or rock if we hope to get away."

They continued at a hectic pace. Germanicus took the baby out of the basket so she could cool off. Stephanos kept looking back as if expecting them at any moment, "Why have they not attacked us? Surely they must be aware they can catch us…"

"They know they don't outnumber us," the Roman surmised, "and don't wish to gamble. Why should they? They'll wait until dark then finish us off."

At the south end of the hill they turned east. At the next intersection they went north again, then west, then north. Yeshua searched for sandstone to no avail. It was all the same sandy soil. At the next crossing they turned west, proceeded to the next intersection and stopped. "It's no use. The ground is the same everywhere. Master Stephanos take Germanicus and turn north, proceeding as fast as you can to the next intersection. There you turn east and go to the brow of the hill. But, don't get out of the forest. You will be in the vicinity of our campsite by the rock outcrop. We will take the animals and lead the pursuers deeper into the forest. At nightfall we will join you. Take all the supplies you need and go."

Germanicus took a small container of food Mariamme prepared for Lygia, some water, and they left. Yeshua and Quintus waited for the pursuers. "When we hear them we'll start talking loud to entice them to follow us," the young scholar suggested.

They were surprised how close the pursuers were, for they heard them huffing almost momentarily. As planned they talked loud, singing and joking going at a slower pace for another Roman mile, when they stopped to listen. "It worked," Quintus sounded excited." They're following us."

They started again, this time at a faster pace in total silence, changing direction at every intersection: north, west, north, east, and so on. But, whichever direction they took the soil conspired against them. They resigned to the reality that they would be in sandy soil until dark, before rejoining their friends. However, late in the afternoon they found a different terrain: hard sandstone which turned to outcroppings of rock. They made a couple of turns and looked back to be certain there were no imprints. They broke into a glorious smile daring to think of victory for the first time: for there were no visible prints. "Just in time," Yeshua sighed, tired but cheerful. "If this terrain continues, we'll take two more turns, and fly to our glorious rendezvous for a well deserved rest."

Quintus concurred with exuberance, "Not even professional trackers will be able to follow us."

They continued, allowing themselves the luxury of a slower pace. They went as planned, turned east, heading towards the brow of the hills and out of the forest. They picked up their pace as the sun was sinking fast.

Quintus was the first to look south when they got out of the forest, and seeing the outcrop of rocks, nudged his friend, whispering, "You must possess a sixth sense. There is the place where we camped on our way south."

"We will continue south half a mile and turn into the forest," Yeshua responded. "Our friends will be close by."

They paced leisurely, listening carefully for their companions. They were about to turn into the trees when they heard Lygia cry, not more than a dozen paces from them. A cold shock crept up their spines: if they heard her, could the pursuers be far behind?

A few moments later they were reunited. Germanicus paced back and forth frantically in the small clearing, whispering and singing a lullaby in low voice to settle his baby. Every few moments he whispered, "I'm sorry, fellows…"

Yeshua touched his shoulders encouraging support, "She cannot help it…She is telling us she too is not comfortable…or happy. We must prepare a plan…to turn this situation against our pursuers."

They gulped a quick meal, swatting mosquitoes steadily. Only Germanicus continued pacing, for as soon as he stopped she fussed and resumed crying.

Alas, they did not see the leaves gently opening and four pairs of eyes peering at them. The pursuers were ready to finish them off…

CHAPTER XV - RETURNING HOME

When master Nehemiah saw Yeshua in the village of Laish, by the water well, he could hardly believe his luck. It would save him a trip to Caesarea. He bribed the villager to persuade the young scholar into going to the Zealots' meeting. He was furious when the Romans broke into the meeting, and Yeshua was not there.

He persuaded the trackers to join him to capture and murder the Zealots, and they impressed him with their abilities. "You could track the devil through the fires of hell," Nehemiah exclaimed impressed. They were less than a hundred paces from Yeshua's group when they lost all contact. But Lygia's cries gave them away.

They knocked out Quintus and Stephanos and yelled out, "Don't make a move. You're surrounded."

Yeshua grabbed Germanicus, pulled him down, and got his staff ready to defend.

The Romans began to mock them, "You thought you were smart. Well, we caught you, and now we'll exterminate...ugh!"

There was a sickening "thud" of a body falling heavily on the ground; a great burst and commotion with loud cracking sounds of breaking branches, clubs smashing hard objects, and more bodies falling. Then all was silent. Yeshua grabbed the slave and started to run.

"Master Yeshua, have no fear," a voice called in the dark. "It is I Ahira with my son Asher, and our neighbors Mordacai and Hophnl."

"The Zealots; our fugitive friends?" Yeshua asked stupefied.

"Precisely," Ahira responded. "Help us tie up these scoundrels."

They did it quickly, brought their friends to consciousness and moved out of the forest, setting up camp by the rock outcropping. Then they started a fire and cooked a hearty meal. As soon as Germanicus fed Lygia she fell asleep.

They put the tied up prisoners far from the camp so they could not identify them in the future. With the work done they sat down for a good visit. "Life is full of ironies," Ahira laughed. "Not long ago we were prisoners here. Today we saved your lives."

"Had you not showed up," Yeshua started then stopped. "How did you happen to arrive at the precise moment...?"

"It was no coincidence," Mordacai explained. "In the afternoon, from our camp, we saw two persons up on top of the hill. We recognized you and master Quintus. Suspecting you were lost we came to help and almost collided with your pursuers. So we followed."

Asher added relieved, "We lost them in the dark, but Lygia's cry led us to them."

Yeshua queried, "Did you ever meet a Zealot, a foreigner from Tyre, with a scar running down the left side of his face?"

"Master Nehemiah," Hophnl replied immediately. "Strange man that one."

"I never trusted him," Ahira interjected. "He said he was from Antioch...an architect."

"From Tyre, recently moved to Nazareth," Yeshua corrected him. "He is the traitor who sold us to the Romans."

Mordacai's voice hardened. "Are you certain of what you say?"

"Two days ago he led the Romans into a meeting of Zealots in Laish," Yeshua informed them. "They took young Simon and James in chains."

"I pray our paths cross," Ahira exclaimed. "I swear that will be his last day."

"You will feast your eyes on the culprit in the morning," Stephanos pointed in the dark. "He is one of your captives."

Quintus interjected gruffly, "When I finish with him there won't be enough to fill a dust pan."

"Are my ears deceiving me?" Ahira queried perplexed. "Is master Quintus sympathizing with the Zealots?"

"Yes," he responded proudly. "I listened to master Yeshua and walked a mile in Israeli sandals. I am ashamed of what I saw. I curse my race..."

His listeners saw the pain in his eyes and empathized with the conflict he was suffering. Only Yeshua knew the extent of his inner turmoil. Quintus was more than a Roman sympathizing with the Israeli; he was an Israeli in a Roman skin.

That night, lying in his cot, Yeshua was thinking about lady Sarah. Alas, her face faded, only to be replaced by another: master Nehemiah. What will he say to her? If he said he was a traitor, would she believe him? How will she react that her father is his prisoner? If they execute him will she blame him – and forgive him? All night he had nightmares that he would lose her.

They slept late into the morning, awakening to a loud commotion outside the tent. At first they thought the prisoners escaped, when they heard Aramaic spoken. Suddenly the tent door was flung open and a bearded Persian invaded. He jumped on Yeshua waiving a golden saber-dagger menacingly, "Are you the Israeli dog, leader of the criminal Zealots? Don't deny it or I'll cut off your head."

Yeshua lay staring helplessly, certain they were invaded by bandits. Yet, the voice with a Judean accent was familiar. After a moment he asked astonished, "Master Benjoseph, is that you?"

The stranger backed off clearly disappointed, "Master El Sharif promised my own mother would not recognize me..."

"She won't if you don't speak," he replied.

It was a happy reunion. El Sharif explained the letter which had caused them to rush after him. Seeing the traitor tied up relieved them immensely. "Master Nehemiah breached his oath as a Zealot and will be my prisoner," Benjoseph insisted.

"I want your assurance of a fair trial," Yeshua demanded.

Master Benjoseph did not answer, but walked away. El Sharif had a twinkle in his eyes when he advised Ahira what to do with the soldiers, "Release them in the heart of the forest, without weapons, food or water, to find their way to their garrison."

• • •

Two days later they arrived in Nazareth. Everybody wanted to hear stories about the dangerous forests of Galilee and the far places beyond, about which they knew very little. A multitude followed them to master's Joseph's house. He was shocked and elated by the invasion. He bellowed in his rich baritone, "James, run to the shop and bring five of their largest flasks of the finest wine. Hurry!" Then he turned to the other children, "Joses, bring jugs of water from the well. Take Simon and Debborah with you."

When the wine arrived he mixed it with water and filled the goblets, while Miriam and Anna took them around. Yeshua gave out toys and lollies to his youngest siblings who ran into the safety of the house to enjoy them.

As soon as Anna finished serving the wine she sought out Germanicus who immediately handed her the basket. She took out the baby and held her close, showering her with kisses. "She is beautiful. How did you get her?"

"I found her in the bushes, abandoned…I named her Lygia after my mother. "

Anna knew the circumstances of such a birth, "Lygia: such a pretty name." She tickled her chin. The baby smiled, making gurgling noises. "Come, we must bathe and change her if she is to grow big and healthy."

Germanicus followed her. He thought she was more beautiful than he remembered, and realized how much he had missed her.

The people, happy to see them safe, asked for stories of their adventures, "Master Yeshua, are the hills of Galilee really full of bandits and murderers? Do they really live in caves? Is it true what they say about the Samaritans?"

"What do they say?" Yeshua countered, expecting to hear age-old prejudice.

An old man volunteered, "That they are not trustworthy, very dangerous and Godless people…"

Yeshua was shocked and enraged. However, others asked more pressing queries, so he turned to them.

"As you know the Romans invaded us," one man complained. "Many people were arrested, and residents tortured…"

"It's only the last couple of days that the soldiers started to leave. I guess their work is finished here," a young man opined.

"Not if you look across the street," a woman pointed to a tent. "They have been there…since you left."

Yeshua saw a big brown army tent just like the one Quintus brought. There were a couple of soldiers sitting, watching the celebration. The young scholar started for the street when his father stopped him, "They'll be here soon enough. Leave them be."

Yeshua reconsidered it and returned. Instead, he started searching for lady Sarah.

The visitors formed into smaller groups, each surrounding one of the young heroes, asking about their adventurers. Lady Miriam wanted to hear about Caesarea, and moved around. However no one touched on it, so she suspected a conspiracy of silence. She listened to master Stephanos, a natural raconteur of witty anecdotes, but he stoically avoided Caesarea. Quintus' stories were shorter. But she noticed he was learning to copy the art of story-telling from the Greek, but he too avoided the topic. She did not bother with Germanicus' group, for he was greatly influenced by her son, and would never reveal his secrets. She had no option but to go and ask her son, "Yeshua! Son." She yelled from the rear, interrupting another inquisitor. "What about Caesarea? Did you have a confrontation with the Romans?"

Everybody heard her, and deferred to her. Yeshua, caught by surprise, looked around stunned, hoping his friends would help, but they refused to get involved. He cleared his throat, coughed and stuttered, "Oh! That was no...Not in the strict sense..." He looked around helplessly, and continued, "General Fulvius...wanted the Statues, but after a conf...gave up" He quickly turned to another inquisitor.

Miriam knew his tricks and persisted, "Did unarmed Israelis confront the Romans?"

Yeshua pleaded, "Master Quintus...please answer mother..."

Quintus was about to start until he looked into her stern eyes, "I would love to but...I need to replenish my goblet." He apologized and quickly left.

Rabbi Ben Lebbus realized they were as intent on avoiding the truth as she was on uncovering it. He stepped forward, "Friends, we are thankful our heroes returned safely, and I ask each to tell their most impressive experience?"

The people heartily approved the request, as the rabbi pointed to Germanicus.

"I...I confess I saw...many miracles," he started slowly and nervously. "In this enchanted land, God...speaks to us...The rain of master Honi... saving the Taheb's life...But my greatest miracle...the Lord's guiding hand to find my little baby, Lygia..."

Yeshua's speech gripped their attention, "All his life old man Hegesippus was selfish and greedy; his only drive was for money and power. He dispossessed the people from the water well for his luxurious garden. When a terminal disease got him he was left to die alone. But the people who he abused and cheated, brought food and love. They forgave him. A miracle cured him, he was touched by their love, and turned his mansion into an orphanage and returned the water well to them."

Miriam was surprised how much her son had matured. She learned the extent when Stephanos said, "Master Yeshua led hundreds of pilgrims from Galilee, Judea and Samaria to face the Roman army. He inspired us to confront them unarmed." The Greek was so involved int the story he did not see Yeshua frantically signaling him, or lady Miriam turning white. "The soldiers stood with swords drawn, when we sat prostrate and bared our necks thus." When he pulled back his tunic, lady Miriam fainted. Only then he saw his friend's frantic signals.

Quintus, not given to hyperboles spoke to the point, "I was most impressed by the simple shepherd's staff. Twice it proved to be superior to the sword: in a duel, and later when I fought a cavalry man. I intend to so advise my superiors."

They were pleased and cheered him. Their enthusiasm and the wine he imbibed led him to say impulsively, "After the injustices I saw, I decided that because I was born here, I want to become Israeli – just like you."

Hearing this, the Rabbi said with a smirk, "I will help you become an Israeli."

"Really? I would be most grateful."

"When our people were nomads, the Lord made a covenant," he explained with a twinkle in his eye, unsheathing a blade, sharp enough to cut through steel. "Every male Israeli must be circumcised." He held up the blade, "Still want to become an Israeli?"

Quintus' jaw unhinged, and his eyes fixed on the weapon, "But… do…I have to?"

An older guest interjected, "Rabbi, why did you bring the big blade? He is a Roman. The little-wee knife will suffice."

The audience exploded with laughter. The rabbi sheathed the blade and embraced the Roman, who made a mental note – again – to curb his impulsive tongue.

Yeshua saw master Yacek in the corner of the yard and walked over, "Shalom dear friend. Thank you for helping establish communications with my family."

"At my age it is an honor to be useful." the old man's eyes became misty.

"You seem younger than the last time I saw you," the young scholar commented. "How is that knee; no more troubles, I trust?"

"None. I thought about it the other day…my knee did not get better because of the remedy you prescribed," he looked strangely at the young man as he spoke, "It was cured when you touched it...How could that be?"

"Clearly, your faith is very strong. I saw faith bring rain...What's a mere knee in comparison?"

The old man fixed his eyes on him persisting, "Tell me, did you cure my knee?"

But he did not hear the reply, for the young man saw lady Sarah at the gate. He excused himself and pushed his way toward her. "Lady Sarah! Over here...lady Sarah."

Yeshua stopped before her, admiring her. She was lovelier than in his dreams, he thought. Their eyes met, she blushed and smiled nervously. His impulse was to grab and crush her in his arms, but they became aware of a strange silence around them. Everyone stopped talking and watched them, as they embraced self consciously.

"I am so happy you are safe," she murmured. "I came as soon as I heard..."

"Now that you're here, my life is complete," he whispered. "Come inside." He took her hand and led her into the yard.

"I can't stay long," she replied. "I expect father...He is long overdue."

Yeshua was about to say something, but froze and his mind went blank.

"Did you see my father?" she asked. "He went out to find you."

But he did not hear her and continued pushing through the crowd. Finally he brought her to his parents. Miriam was up again though pale and shaken. She saw the people watching the young couple, eager to see any special display of affection so they could start a rumor. She took Sarah's hand, "Come, young lady. Anna baked biscuits and you can help serve them."

"Mother, she just arrived," Yeshua objected, holding her other hand.

"I'm happy to help," Sarah smiled shyly. "We'll have ample time later."

"When? You said your father..." he started, but checked himself.

Master Esau who had been watching approached him, "Welcome back, master Yeshua. Thank the Lord you are safe." They embraced warmly.

"It is a blessing to be back," he said. "How is the sailboat progressing?"

'Almost completed waiting for your inspection. Do you wish to see it?"

"Tomorrow: too much commotion now. I chose the best man for the project."

Esau smiled pleased but embarrassed. Then he began fidgeting. Yeshua watched him making designs in the dust with his sandal. "Do you wish to say something, Esau?"

He glanced furtively and spoke under his breath, "Just want to warn you...don't get too close to her..."

"Why? What's the matter with her?" he frowned in confusion.

"You don't know this, but her father is the traitor...sold the Zealots to the Romans."

Yeshua wondered how he knew, but that seemed unimportant. He demanded curtly, "Has he been tried and declared guilty, or is it all suspicions?"

"You wouldn't call it suspicion if you heard the people of Tyre," Esau defended his position. "They accused him of murder and torture..."

"Did they also accuse lady Sarah of atrocities?" his eyes were as cold as steel.

"No, but it looks bad," his friend explained lamely. "Displaying affection for a traitor's daughter..."

"Have I not defended you when others prejudged you for the misdeeds of your parents?" Yeshua scolded his friend who shrank back. "Who are you to judge her? I expected compassion..."

Esau froze with the vehement attack, and backed off as people around them stared.

"I...It never occurred...I'm sorry," he mumbled in confusion, turned away pushing frantically out of the yard, and disappearing down the street.

Yeshua walked away to the far corner of the yard to be left alone and to calm down.

Germanicus was the only one who avoided the peoples' incessant questions. After replying to the rabbi, he rejoined Anna who tended to Lygia and baked biscuits. "I observed master Yeshua and learned how special he is," he confessed. "But, I find some of his teachings too complex and unclear...."

"What special things did you see?"

He debated how much he dared tell her, fearing she may scoff at him as his master did. She saw this and encouraged him, "Have no fear. You can tell me everything."

Encouraged by her genuine interest, the words rolled off his tongue. He told her about master Hegesippus, a pile of bones until Yeshua arrived.

She asked if the man repented and he replied yes, after which he was cured...

"Then what happened?" she inquired impatiently.

"I was too frightened to stay. I was afraid of the demons he released."

She looked at him strangely but did not pursue it. He described a young woman exorcised, and how Yeshua wrestled the invisible demon, forcing him to walk through the basin of water. Anna's eyes were riveted on his every word. He explained how he inspected and found hoof prints, and the water, hitherto cool, was boiling hot.

"Germanicus, I am most disappointed in you," she interjected, criticizing him.

"I'm sorry. I thought you'd find the story too fantastic."

"On the contrary, I believe what you say," she broke in. "I am disappointed you found it necessary to investigate master Yeshua's work."

Encouraged by her sympathetic ear, he explained how Yeshua saved the Taheb and the brilliant light emanating from him covering the old man in a shower of sparks.

Anna called it, "The energy of life." She explained how she washed in the same water Yeshua had used, and watched irreversible leprosy dissipating. "I stood astonished, refusing to believe my eyes. I was cured!" Then she turned to him, "Why can you not understand his teachings?"

Germanicus sighed, thinking of the many times he had ended up confused, "He once said, 'Do not try to define God as you will be trying to set limits, and you cannot capture Him so. He is beyond comprehension, He is so big. Next, he tells me God can be found in a little lady bug.' Which is it?" He shook his head exasperated, and proceeded with another story, "He went to cure a young cripple Jonathan, but instead of doing it, they talked and he only alleviated his pain and left. Why?"

"Was Jonathan unhappy with that?"

"No, he felt blessed, and I'll never understand why!" the slave shook his head.

"There are many things which you will have to contemplate until you resolve," she murmured tenderly. Then she added a warning, "We must keep these matters to ourselves. I'm sure master Yeshua does not want anyone to know..."

Germanicus did not need to be reminded, for his experiences with his master made him realize most people would call his stories illusions of a deranged slave.

Lygia sneezed a couple of times and they turned to her. He wiped the baby's mouth and nose, while Anna held her. "She is such a pretty baby. Are you planning to keep her?" she queried.

"Of course! Why?" he was stupefied by the strange question.

"I wondered the strange life she will have, with two resolved bachelors."

He nodded with a grunt, "I thought about that and foresaw many complications."

"So what are you going to do about it?" she chirped softly.

"What can I do?" his voice betrayed a hint of desperation.

"Give her a family," she purred affectionately, and pressed closer.

"Who...? Whose family?"

"Your family," she cooed mistily.

"I'd love to," he responded exasperated, "But, I don't know where they are..."

Anna sighed with despair. She wondered how an otherwise bright man could be so obtuse. She decided to light the wick behind his eyes, "I mean give her your family."

"How can I? I'm the only one," he whimpered.

She rolled her eyes to the heavens and shut them firmly for some moments. It was obvious she would have to take matters into her own hands. She took his arm, put it around her shoulders and posed a question in a very business-like tone, "Germanicus, will you do me the honor and marry me...so we can give Lygia a family?"

He stopped in mid-breath with a gasp. His mouth dropped and his eyes popped. "Oh!" He uttered, wanting to say something, something profound, but his mind went blank. So he stuttered, "Oh, is that wha...? Well, I'll be...Should I not prop...? Well, I wanted to, but..." he prattled aimlessly.

"You're not already married, are you?" Anna decided to clarify his availability.

"Who...me? For heaven's sake no!" he responded emphatically, trying to recover his wits. "I did not think...You know, me being a..."

"A slave?" she chuckled teasingly. "Mother always said being a married woman was like slavery, so, we'll make a perfect couple."

He grinned, embarrassed but radiant and happy, "Well, who would ever? In my wildest dreams..."

She interrupted impatiently, "For heaven's sake, will you give me your answer? Or do you want me to go down on my knees?"

"No! – I mean, Yes!" Germanicus looked shocked. Then he added tenderly, "Of course I will marry you…for Lygia…for me…for all the future children we will have."

They embraced tenderly. As soon as they agreed, they decided to make the announcement public, and came to the center of the yard. "Can I have your…?" he started, but the chatter and laughter drowned him out. He tried again without success.

Master Joseph saw this, walked over, took a deep breath, and bellowed, "QUIET!" Everything stopped in suspended animation. "Germanicus has an announcement."

The slave stood with Anna at his side, and started shyly, "Thank you… master Joseph. I wish to tell you…I just proposed….No, she prop…." He stopped tongue-tied, took a deep breath and blurted out, "We are getting married!"

The people cheered and applauded, yelling out "Congratulations," and "May you live a hundred years." Yeshua looked at Stephanos who was scowling, beside Miriam.

Miriam also saw the Greek frown, sensed a problem and stepped forward announcing, "Master Joseph's household will be happy to host the wedding ceremony." She raised her goblet and everyone joined in a toast. Joseph, caught by surprise, looked stunned, then wisely decided to make the best of it, and raised his goblet with a smile.

Stephanos raised his arms stiffly. They saw his somber face and realized there was going to be trouble. He glared at his slave, clearing his throat. As soon as Germanicus saw this he realized his happy decision was another transgression against his master's authority. The muscles of his jaw tensed, and he bowed deeply with a forced smile. "Of course I acknowledge that our bliss depends on my master's blessing," he conceded in agony, adding weakly, "I beg master Stephanos…?"

The people looked to the Greek for approval or a nod, but he stood unmoved. He desired to teach him a lesson, to stop him from taking his absolute right of ownership for granted. And this forum was the ideal place to do it, "When I allowed you to keep Lygia, I took on a burden I did not want. I did it to please you." He glanced at the people, seeking approval, but was met with a cold stare. "You promised never to make major decisions without my approval. Now you want to add a woman to my responsibilities?"

Germanicus' face turned crimson. He glared at him with hatred but did not argue. Stephanos saw the ladies around him shuffling away.

Yeshua put his arm around the Greek's shoulder and whispered, "Germanicus is an excellent slave. But, the baby needs a mother, and neither of you fit that category." He looked at the Greek who listened with interest, "Lady Anna will be good for her, and you will gain, for she also will serve you."

Stephanos waivered and his face softened as he looked at Yeshua. He turned to the couple smiling, "I will give my blessing provided that you name your first born after me."

"Congratulations, master Stephanos," Yeshua shook his hand heartily.

The people surrounded the happy couple, laughing and embracing them. Many others, mostly ladies, congratulated the Greek.

One man proposed a toast, "Let's drink to the kindest Greek we know!"

"The only kind Greek we know," another added with a wink.

Germanicus and Anna came over and she embraced him, thanking him. He blushed when she kissed him on the cheek.

Yeshua saw lady Sarah standing with the tray, now empty, her eyes filled with tears. He was about to go to her when Debborah, grabbed him by the tunic.

"Did you hear about master Nehemiah?" Debborah asked excitedly.

"What are you referring to?" he asked.

"Oh, you haven't heard. He is the traitor. I was the first to suspect him, and James and I led the investigation," she said proudly. He knew she was going to tell him every sordid detail and searched for an exit. "Do you know what made me suspicious? His evasiveness. He kept asking your whereabouts refusing to explain why he wanted to know. One day he told Sarah he was going to a town to the south. Later when I asked he said he was going north." She chuckled shaking her head, "People who lie are so careless with details. Master Marcus and Esau investigated, and found out he is the traitor!"

"That's why Esau knew," he muttered to himself. "Remind me never to cross you."

Debborah saw Sarah coming and whispered urgently, "Oh, oh! I had better slip away...I can't lie to her..."

Sarah leaned on his arm sighing, "Your mother heaped this tray hoping to keep me away from you til midnight..." She watched the young girl rushing away, "I get the feeling Debborah is avoiding me. Is there something I should know?" Se turned and saw him gasp. "Have you been avoiding me? You hardly said a word..." she said.

"So many people...everything happening at once," he tried to sound normal.

"And they're all making demands on you," her tone betrayed a hint of jealousy. "I don't like to share my hero with the public."

"Tomorrow, early in the morning, let's meet under the oak tree," he held her hand affectionately and his eyes swam in hers. "Just the two of us...talking and dreaming..."

"I won't sleep all night," she whispered affectionately. "There is so much I want to tell you." She smiled affectionately, "And you owe me a kiss, remember?" That triggered something she wished to ask him, "I also need a special favor...to locate father who is long overdue. Could something have happened to him?"

His eyes froze, and his lower lip quivered. He could not think of anything to say. But she saw Miriam coming, "I have to go. Your mother is going to put me to work." She pecked his cheek handing lady Miriam the tray, bowing with apologies and left.

Miriam came to her son with master Joseph in tow, "You must be more discreet in public," she advised him in a low voice. When his face tightened she added, "I'm not worried about you, but about an innocent girl like lady Sarah; people talk."

Yeshua knew she was correct, and relaxed, "I will be more discreet, I promise."

Miriam admired her oldest son, took his arm and brought him closer, "It's wonderful to have you back. We were worried for your safety..."

"We were always safe, mother," he protested.

"Even in Caesarea?" she pressed.

Yeshua looked to his father for help, but the patriarch shrugged his shoulders.

"You were sent to fulfill a special purpose," she reminded him. "You must not take unnecessary risks."

"I will not live in fear," he objected. Then he toned down his statement, "Although I admit, in Caesarea I felt guilty, for I failed my heavenly Abba."

Joseph and Miriam exchanged glances, surprised to hear such familiarity with the Creator. They stood silent for a few moments, and when they spoke, the mother and son started simultaneously. "I was thinking..." they started and stopped. Then, they started together again, "...about the revelation..." They enjoyed a good chuckle and he deferred to his mother who continued, "You were correct. I should have told you the truth earlier. It was not fair to you to withhold it for so long," she apologized.

He interjected, "I thought bout it too...there was no 'right time' for that. After all this time I am no closer to divining my mission. Sometimes I feel I will never know..."

Joseph spluttered matter of factly, "Your destiny is to lead the world. Lead it!"

"How? Where? In what way? " He rattled off the questions he wrestled with, and when the patriarch stared astonished, he tossed a few more, "Where do I take them? What will I say? What will I do once there? Do I take all the people? If not, which are to stay?"

"Oh! It is more complicated than I..." Joseph's voice trailed off.

"I have a confession; I do not think I am right for the job," he started, but when he saw them staring dumbstruck he tried to clarify, "Can I be a warrior? I abhor weapons. I fail as a sage because they will not listen. As a rabbi I muddle up the simplest question."

"But you are a scholar," Miriam argued as if that solved everything.

"When Germanicus inquired about the Creator, I confused him thoroughly," he muttered as if confessing a crime. "And I keep seeing people that are not there."

"What people?" Miriam asked curiously, although she already suspected it.

"Angels, Satans."

"Oh, so that's what they were," Joseph confessed relieved.

"That's not all. After an exorcism I wrestled the demon. Imagine how I felt when I found out nobody else saw it. It troubled me for weeks!"

"Why, because you saw the demon?" Joseph asked surprised.

"No, because nobody else saw it!" he responded impatiently. "Was I seeing or imagining? Was I going insane? For weeks I refused to acknowledge ordinary things until someone identified them first." They did not understand the extent of his problem, but appreciated his suffering. "Moreover, I dread the nightmare of doing endless miracles," he lamented desperately. "What about my life, my privacy? Do I not have a right to happiness?" But he did not dare to mention his faltering faith, or that master Nehemiah was their prisoner, not wishing to burden them further.

. . .

The sun was setting when the last visitors left. Yeshua devised a plan to leave the yard without being detected by the soldiers, to go and check on their prisoner. They climbed to the rooftop, across the neighbors' roofs to the end of the block, jumped down and went to the Zealots' cabin by a back road.

On the way he enjoyed watching the valley teeming with life. He felt the wonderful grandeur of a spot pure and untouched, except by the hand of God. How much smaller and insignificant were the pillars and edifices in Caesarea, contrived to impress man, he thought. The giant city humbled him, but here his heavenly Abba welcomed him, and invited him to share everything He had created. Here he felt no fear.

When they arrived they proceeded along the narrow path to the cabin, and reached for the door, when a voice called, "Stop! Identify yourself. Give the password."

He recognized the voice, and replied, "Esau, it is I, Yeshua."

"Sorry, I did not recognize you in the dark."

Yeshua turned around, "It is I who should apologize. I realize now you were only trying to protect me. What I said was unfair…Please, forgive me."

"On the contrary," Esau responded. "Lady Sarah should not pay for her father's crimes…I was insensitive,"

"Friends again?" Yeshua opened his arms and they embraced warmly.

Esau gave the password and master Benjoseph, still with the elaborate disguise, opened the door. Inside were a couple of oil lamps throwing an anemic light. Nehemiah sat with his hands tied behind his back, in the far corner under a window.

"Master El Sharif and I will come to visit you in the morning," Benjoseph informed Yeshua. "I'm told your place was a madhouse today?"

"Be warned, there are soldiers camped across the street," the young scholar informed him. "I'm certain they did not arrest me today because of all the visitors."

"With him out of circulation we will be safe," Benjoseph pointed to Nehemiah.

Yeshua glanced at the corner, and saw Quintus approaching the prisoner. The Roman paced back and forth before him, his breathing becoming louder and heavier working himself into a frenzy, "Do you know the lowest form of life?" he demanded loudly, bent over the prisoner. "A traitor…Feigning friendship while sending them to their deaths. You are lower than a lizard. Your mother mated with a scorpion!" he spat on the ground. "I want to take you into the desert and watch you crawl aimlessly in the sun, on your belly. I want to see your mouth parched, you tongue swollen…." He leaned over him whispering, "Water! I pray you see the faces of all your victims before you die."

Suddenly the Roman pulled out a dagger and lunged at him. Yeshua jumped and grabbed him, "Don't! Master Quintus, stop."

"Let me go. I'm going to kill him."

Benjoseph grabbed Yeshua's arm, "He's correct. He murdered dozens maybe a hundred…"

"The people of Tyre cursed his name," Esau added. "They want him dead."

Quintus grabbed Nehemiah's hair with his free hand twisting his head. Then he spat out, "Look at me. I am the one who is going to kill you. I'll cut your head off and plant it on the post at the town gate."

"Let him go," Yeshua pulled him back. "He has rights… to defend himself."

"What rights did he give the brothers, Simon and James?" Quintus barked.

"What about my rights?" Benjoseph demanded. "Why worry about this monster?"

"Did you see him kill anyone?" Yeshua demanded, and they stood stunned. Yeshua pressed again, "Well, did you?"

"You know the answer," Benjoseph's nostrils flared and at that moment he hated him. "No, I did not!"

"Did you see it?" Yeshua turned to Quintus.

"No!" The Roman snapped. "But explain this; what was he doing beside the soldiers with the brothers in chains?"

"The evidence shall be presented to a judge," Yeshua responded. "Impartially."

"All the Phoenicians want him dead. Why did he move here?" Esau persisted.

"I hate to interrupt a good argument," Stephanos cut in, "But while we're debating his future, who is guarding the building?"

They looked at each other guiltily. Benjoseph motioned to Esau, who ran from window to window peering out into darkness, then went out.

Germanicus smirked because he had already inspected the yard, and the road then returned. He was trying to check the prisoner to see if he was properly tied, but Nehemiah turned and faced him, not letting him see his arms and back. Germanicus walked away slowly, picked up a length of twine and joined Esau outside, "The prisoner is planning to break free. Go in, stand beside him and wait for my signal."

Esau re-entered while the slave proceeded outside stealthily to the window behind the prisoner and peeked inside, while he tied a noose. He noticed Nehemiah busily moving his hand up and down in a sawing motion. Esau arrived and stood facing him. Germanicus opened the noose slowly, reached in and tossed it over the prisoner's head. As the twine fell over his shoulders the slave yanked it with all his might, tightening it around his neck, yelling, "Grab him, Esau."

Esau jumped on him but at that moment Nehemiah broke free. He grabbed Staphanos with one arm, raising the other high in a stabbing motion.

Germanicus screamed, "Master, watch out!" He pulled Nehemiah to the window and in a superhuman effort leaped into the room and onto the prisoner, sending the Greek to the floor. Germanicus felt a sharp painful sting in his chest. The others overpowered the prisoner. Quintus took away the knife, and struck him on the forehead, almost knocking him out. They retied his hands behind his back, and for security, tied his arms above the elbows. Then they dragged him to the center of the room, and ran the twine from his hands up and over the beam, then down around his neck. Quintus searched the prisoner's tunic and discovered two false pockets, each with a concealed blade.

Yeshua warned the traitor, "Your survival hangs by a thread..." He turned to the others, "Start preparing his trial: witnesses, prosecution and a judge...an impartial judge."

"Give him to me, and I'll you save you the trouble," Quintus spewed his venom.

"Senseless violence," Yeshua pushed the Roman away. "The solution is to banish him to the furthest corner of the empire where he could not harm anyone…"

The prisoner perked up, "Banishment. I will go anywhere…I don't want to die!"

Quintus brought up his arm up to back hand him, when Germanicus fell in a heap. They rushed over, turned him over and brought an oil lamp. He was stabbed in the chest.

Stephanos turned pale and began to prattle, "Blessed mother of Zeus! He is wounded. Fetch me clean water. I have to wash it…Hurry!" he ordered and ripped off one of his sleeves folding and placing it over the wound, "Press it down to stop the blood. …You saved my life. What valiant courage! I pray to all the gods on mount Olympus you will be alright. I'll sacrifice in every temple…a big healthy bull." He looked at Yeshua worried, "He'll be alright, won't he? Tell me so, but, if he is not…Forgive me Germanicus, I am being tactless…Of course you will be fine…You know I love you like a brother…nay, more…I don't know what I'll do if…"

Germanicus, pale and weak, grabbed him and brought him close, "Master, I will survive…But, I'll surely die, if you don't stop…"

Yeshua touched the Greek's shoulder, "It's a shallow wound. If he is properly cared for, he'll recover." He debated whether to pray for a cure.

Germanicus saw him, and whispered, "Don't…no miracles…"

"Afraid of demons?" Yeshua smiled.

They made a stretcher and Esau joined them to take him to master Joseph's. Quintus involved the soldiers on the street in a conversation, while they snuck him in. Anna gave him some warm soup and remained at his side the entire night.

• • •

The sun had not come up when the boat crew arrived at master Joseph's house. Esau awoke Yeshua who had spent a restless night with Germanicus. He could not get over the irony; the slave was the only one to accept Yahweh, yet when he could use help he refused it. Obviously his pagan beliefs were deeply entrenched.

When Yeshua came down to inspect the sailboat, Esau removed the canvas announcing, "Master Yeshua, behold the most modern boat of the modern era."

The boat sat high and proud on its keel, supported by wood props. Yeshua stood staring without changing expression. Only his eyes traveled along the sheer from the stern to the bow, then back. They smiled nervously, waiting for approval, but when he did not react they became serious and somber. Had he discovered unseen flaws? Was that a twitch of disappointment? They remembered when he inspected their work before pointing out flaws and making them take it apart and reconstruct it. They hoped this would not be so drastic, as they could not bear tearing apart the complete boat, and starting over.

The corners of his mouth stretched, imperceptibly at first, then broke into a broad grin, "Beautiful," he purred as if referring to a lovely lady. "I forgot how pure her lines were. She sits proud, ready to conquer the waves, like the queen of the seas..."

There was a collective sigh of relief as they slapped each other's shoulders, and nudged with the elbows. The sun began to rise, changing the yard into a checkerboard; long dark shadows interspersed with shafts of light. A flood of light highlighted her, and she sat like a goddess ready to leap through the Sea of Galilee.

Yeshua ran his fingers along the sheer enjoying the feel as if it were soft velvet. He got down on his knees to inspect her hull and every plank closely. They went down with him, watching his every move. He tapped a plank with his knuckles listening for the sound of solid wood. Then he put his hand inside the boat and ran his fingers on both sides of the ribs to make sure not a single nail missed a rib. The minutest weakness would be magnified in a storm and expose her weakness, with a disastrous loss of lives. There could be no compromise with safety.

When he tapped they listened; when he dug at a plank with a fingernail, they wanted to know what he searched for. He studied the length and breadth of every plank, every nail hole, every space between planks, all joints from topside to the keel. He grabbed the transom, heaved and pushed, and she moved one way and the other.

Finally, he stood up to give judgment. He spoke judicially, "Some planks are nailed too close to each other. Planks of that width need at least this much space," he held his thumb and index finger apart about half thickness of his little finger.

"We left a little space between most planks," Esau argued, his face hardening.

"The shipwright told me to beware nailing planks too close. With water they'll widen pushing against each other and away from the ribs. If you err, leave a wider space. You can seal the spaces with cotton rope soaked with bitumen to make it impermeable."

"I must take blame for that," Marcus stepped forward with a confession. "Esau told us to leave wider spaces, but I told him my fisherman uncle argued against it."

"Does that mean we have to tear everything apart and start again?" Daniel sounded dejected.

"Will we have to steam the planks to shape again?" Ahmed's voice was desperate.

"Most planks will keep their shape," he replied. "But, every plank has to come off and be nailed giving more space."

"I'm beginning to think we'll never complete her," Esau rolled his eyes to the sky.

"It will go faster next time," Yeshua explained. He walked to the bow sighing, "She is beautiful, with lovely curves…"

At that moment lady Sarah was entering the bushes with a lady servant on the way to the oak tree. The boys saw her and bantered, "Whose curves: the boat's or lady Sarah's curves?"

He blushed and started to leave, "I…I have to go."

But he was met at the gate by master El Sharif with his "business manager" master Benjoseph. He announced them to his parents, as they proceeded into the house.

His next attempt to leave was foiled when half dozen soldiers entered the yard. He turned and announced, "Father, the Romans from across the street are here."

Master Joseph came out and met them. "Are you master Joseph?" the centurion asked. "And you are master Yeshua? We are informed you are a member of the Zealots."

"Who makes the accusation?" Yeshua demanded.

"I'm not at liberty to disclose…"

"Do I not have the right to confront my accuser?"

"You will; at your trial," the centurion sneered condescendingly. He motioned his arm and the soldiers dispersed, some to the rooms on the roof, others in the house and the work sheds, and began a thorough search. The centurion looked at Joseph and drawled arrogantly, "I have orders to search your property. Do I have your permission?"

"Your request comes a bit tardy, don't you think?" Joseph smirked sardonically.

The centurion stared at Joseph as he yelled, "Men, search through every room and every corner. If a box or trunk is locked break it open!"

The old patriarch did not flinch, but countered in a calm voice, "Centurion, do you know legate Vinicius?"

"Of course: the commander at the fort in Augusteana. Why?"

"Good friend of mine," he continued with the same placid tone. "He told me if I ever had troubles, to come to him…" The patriarch studied the Roman's face, and saw the precise instant a light came on, and his eyes opened as wide as saucers.

He turned on his heels like a man possessed, screaming, "SOLDIERS, HALT! DO NOT BREAK ANYTHING. I REPEAT – ANYTHING! If you break ANYTHING, its value will be deducted from YOUR pay!"

"Sir, if a box or a trunk…" a voice in the house started to ask.

'NOTHING IS TO BE BROKEN! IS THAT CLEAR?" he bellowed.

Voices echoed from every corner of the buildings, "Aye, aye, sir."

The boat crew standing a few paces away stifled a chuckle.

The soldiers investigated every corner, under everything, spying into trunks and boxes with the greatest care to replace them as found. It was not uncommon for a soldier to slip a loose coin or item of jewellery into his tunic, but today they did not dare, for their meager pay would take weeks to repay a missing brooch.

Yeshua paced impatiently, worrying about lady Sarah, and wanted to ask if he could leave, but did not want to abandon the family. Suddenly a soldier yelled from the roof, "Centurion, sir, I found it," the soldier came to the edge holding something shiny high above his head like a prize.

"What is it? Bring it down here," the officer barked.

The soldier rushed down and presented a shiny bronze saber-dagger, "It's a knife, sir…no, a scepter…dagger…"

"Where did you find it?" the centurion demanded.

"In the first room up there," he pointed.

"Whose room is that?" the officer asked.

"Mine, sir," Yeshua recognized the scepter the siccarii shoved in his belt.

The centurion's thin lips stretched into a sadistic smirk. He held the point of the saber against the tip of one index finger, the handle against the other, at eye level. He rotated it with his thumb sending brilliant flashes at the Israelis like poisoned darts. He stared at Yeshua and spoke as if reciting a lesson memorized, "A bronze scepter dagger... the preferred weapon of the siccarii..." His voice hissed when he asked, "Master Yeshua are you a member of the terrorists?"

"I have not joined," he replied, his eyes fixed on the officer.

His radiant eyes disturbed the centurion who looked away. He was sure the young man was telling the truth, but he had orders from his superiors. "The evidence is damning, and was discovered in your room. You are under arrest..." he said.

Master El Sharif who was listening in the doorway stepped forward, "Arrest him for possessing a common household knife? Is this what the empire is coming to?"

"This is not a common household utensil," the centurion reacted defensively.

"Of course it is," the old potentate interjected. "If you arrest him, you'll have to arrest me," he pulled out an exact duplicate of the scepter.

"Me too," Benjoseph pulled out a similar item from his belt.

The centurion tried to argue, but in his confusion only managed to stutter, "But, how could this...?"

El Sharif explained in a fatherly manner, "My dear centurion, I gave that scepter to master Yeshua. In my caravan I have dozens more. All my servants and cooks have them." He teased the Roman with a wink, "In my city, in Persia, I own a foundry which manufactures tools, swords, sabers, and common household scepters...If your unit is interested in some give me an order...A dozen? One hundred? Five hundred? Delivery is guaranteed within six months..."

The centurion, raised his arms dumbfounded, "I've heard enough." He turned to Yeshua handing him the scepter, "Master Yeshua, I have no option; I'm persuaded to let you go." He turned to his soldiers, "Men, fall in formation outside the gate..." He smiled at Yeshua, "Private Quintus will be happy to hear you're free. He argued half the night defending your innocence." He started to leave stopping at the gate and turning, "Master Joseph, when you next see the legate, tell him you were treated fairly."

"I'll tell him I was visited by a professional..." the patriarch saluted.

Before they crossed the street, Yeshua ran by for an important rendezvous.

. . .

Sarah was standing by the cliff admiring the expansive valley, her long wavy hair fluttering in the breeze. He stopped to enjoy the perfect picture as he would always remember her. She turned and smiled radiantly. They rushed into each other's arms, while the lady servant wisely walked out of sight. "I could not sleep all night," she cooed. "I prayed for the sun…it took so long…"

"I swear it plays with our feelings; stopping when it should rush," he whispered.

"I missed you terribly, Yeshua."

"I thought about you everyday," he chirped softly, then sighed, "I waited for your letters, but they never came."

"I wrote, but father intercepted it," she explained. "I could not chance writing again. Then Debborah warned me not to write…it would put you in danger…"

Yeshua suspected he knew the reason but chose not to pursue it. He took her hand and led her to the oak tree where they sat down.

"Are you finished with the expedition? Was it successful?" she asked.

He shook his head, "Far from it. Soon we'll start for Jerusalem."

"Why? I'll hardly get to see you…" her voice was filled with a pain.

"Passover, and a couple more Messiahs," he responded apologetically. "And I must go to the Temple to purify myself…"

"Why, were you adulterated?" she asked, not understanding what he meant.

He chuckled at her mistaken description, "I handled dead corpses, which our religion forbids. I will have to go through a cleansing ritual…"

She shook her head wondering about the tribal religion. "I want to hear everything about your journey. Was it exciting?" she asked.

"Second day out we fought a terrible duel. We thought they were bandits, but they turned out to be friendly Zealots."

"Friendly Zealots?" she looked anxiously. "Father said they're terrorists…and murderers. He also said…are you a Zealot?" she drew back frightened.

He was taken back by her accusatory tone, but masked it, lowering his eyes. She noticed he was uncomfortable, and quickly changed topics, "Did you find the Messiah?"

"Anyone of them fit the description," he replied pensively. When she looked blankly he explained, "Unfortunately our prophets spoke in generalities and riddles, so it is impossible to know. We may not identify him until after his death…"

She had long suspected he could be that person, but decided not to say it. She was just happy to be with him and wanted to enjoy their time together. She moved into his arms and admired him in silence, enjoying the security of his embrace.

Yeshua enjoyed the warmth of her body against him, and the feeling of peace with her made him feel complete. "Last time we were together you promised to tell me everything about yourself. Why did you leave Tyre?"

She sighed before going into what was obviously a sad memory, "Until two years ago I had an older sister. She was as beautiful as an angel, and as warm as the dawn. Her name was Helena." She spoke in a quiet whisper as if communicating with her spirit. "An aristocratic family, the richest and most powerful in Tyre persuaded father to betroth her to their oldest son. Father's ambition and vanity blinded his reason. Helena did not love the boy but agreed. They were married within the year.

"Helena's worst fears were realized. Once she was her husband's possession, he treated her worse than a slave. He abused her and beat her without cause. He brought concubines into their house, and took them to their bed. Within months her eyes sank deep, and in a year she aged twenty. She suffered depression, and broke down. Both families saw it but neither intervened: his family did not care, and father did not dare."

She stopped visibly angry remembering the injustice. Yeshua held her hand until she calmed down, "Yet, that boy's family persuaded father to betroth me to their younger son. Father, ever ambitious signed the betrothal contract, then asked me. I refused. Father said he had already agreed. I replied, `Then you go live with the scoundrel.`"

"The gods warned us when Helena died. Yet father threatened me. I told him if he forced me, I would take my life. I had already obtained the poison."

"You were a brave girl," Yeshua commented in shock.

"Desperation was my courage," she began to cry. "What were my choices? Death: slow miserable death with the scoundrel or quick death by my own hands…"

"You do not have to continue," he pleaded. "It is too painful for you."

She shook her head, "My courage destroyed our family. Mother knew I would carry out the threat. Father tried to buy out the contract, offering money, and begging them to release me. But their arrogance knew no bounds. They sued and the judges, close friends of the aristocrats, awarded them a sizable judgment. My parents went bankrupt. They took everything we owned. But they wanted more - to destroy us. They persuaded the leading families not to award father any architectural contracts. Then they told the merchants not to sell us foodstuff. Soon father was forced to travel to the farms to purchase basic food."

"I don't understand," Yeshua interrupted," If you were bankrupt, how did your father pay for the opulent mansion?"

"I think he started getting work outside of Tyre…in the countryside," she was obviously guessing. "He was gone for long periods of time…"

"That's why you said you only wanted a relationship with love," he murmured.

"After what happened to Helena, I swore life without love was not worth living," she said. Then she added resolutely, "But, enough about me. I want to learn about you. If my intuition is correct, your past is more intriguing and your future far more interesting than mine." She saw him smile, but did not realize his mind was warning him to prepare for an invasive probe. She remarked disarmingly, "It must be a national pastime of Israelis to speak in riddles. I worked on the sails at your home with your mother, and she always spoke in riddles and enigmas which I never understood…"

"What did she say?"

"One time an angel appeared, announcing a supernatural conception, and an important birth…Another time she described a birth with fanfare, and great expectation for the whole world…His destiny was to fulfill God's word…Was she talking about your future?"

He sat agonizing, uncertain how much to tell her. Returning to Nazareth he had decided to tell her everything, but the Nehemiah episode complicated everything.

"Yeshua, don't you trust me?" she pleaded, suspecting he was being evasive. The truth was that he did not know how to reply. She misunderstood his silence, expecting to hear another riddle, and decided to prove she knew more about him than he realized. "Yesterday I overhead Germanicus tell Anna he saw you perform a miracle that saved the Taheb's life. He saw a brilliant light emanate from you and cover the dying man. The holy man then asked if you were the anointed one." She watched him fidget nervously and continued, "Anna told him she suffered incurable leprosy...and you cured her. Why won't you tell me about yourself? Why do you keep secrets from me?"

"Not now...not today," he mumbled, shaking his head. "I wanted to talk about us."

Sarah was not going to be denied, and persisted, "I already know some of the stories: your duel with a panther, curing master Yacek's knee all proves you have a supernatural gift...That's how you mended the broken vials and cured my thumb. When I looked into your eyes I sensed a special quality: a raging superhuman power, yet a tranquil serenity that could calm the fiercest storm." She took his hands and gently turned him to her, "Yeshua, tell me, are you the Messiah?"

"What do you want me to say? he lamented exasperated. He looked at her pleadingly, "Don't ask me to explain what I do not comprehend... Someday, maybe..."

She noticed a hint of anger rising from his desperate situation, and placed her finger across his lips interrupting, "You don't have to explain... I thought if I understood I could help." He tried to say something, but she embraced him warmly apologizing, "We are both tired, and I was unfair... Let's just lie down and rest."

He stood up and walked to the hibiscus bush, chose the brightest red flower, picked it and brought it to her. He lay down beside her and put the hibiscus in her hair, "I want this flower to be the symbol of our love. Treasure it as I treasure you."

"I'll save it between the pages of my diary...with your poem," her eyes became misty as she smiled softly. "It is a precious treasure. I have never seen such brilliant red...Like the red of blood!" She reached, brought him close to her and they kissed.

He held her tight and murmured, "I want to spend the rest of my life with you. Let's go away, far away, where we can marry and start a family.

There we will enjoy our lives together far away from the demands of the world. That is all I wish in life."

She smiled radiantly, about to agree, when something came to mind and she turned somber, "I can't, not at this time. My father has not returned, and I can't leave mother until he gets back. Then I promise we'll run away and be happy together forever." They lay in each other's arms, kissing and enjoying their moments alone, to love and to dream.

. . .

The long shadows of the afternoon hovered over the valley, when he awoke with a jolt, for he felt her moving restlessly in his arms, and heard her moaning, "No! Don't kill him. Please..."

"Lady Sarah, wake up. Wake up," he called and shook her gently. She continued moaning. "Wake up, lady Sarah." She opened her eyes staring at the surroundings then at him dazed. "Lady Sarah, you were having a nightmare."

She sat up, looked at him vacantly and began to cry, "My father. I saw my father. They have him tied up...he's a prisoner...crying to me for help." She grabbed him by the shoulders and cried out, " 'HELP ME! THEY'RE GOING TO KILL ME`, he cried out. Yeshua, save my father..." she sobbed desperately, "Don't let them kill my father..."

CHAPTER XVI - THE CRUCIFIXION

Master Joseph's household was buzzing with everyone helping to prepare the wedding of Anna to Germanicus. There was much to do as Master Joseph wanted the wedding to be a big feast, and was sparing no expenses. He remembered his wedding to Miriam as a puny little affair: grudgingly given by her frugal relatives, short of food, and the watered down wine did not last for the toasts. He made a vow that his children's wedding would be grand feasts, and the small fortune he received for Herod's thrones gave him the opportunity to fulfill his fantasy.

Miriam and Anna directed the work, designing, measuring and sewing the wedding dress, her veil, the ornamental flowers and borders, and the clothes for the entire household, all of whom the servant wanted in the wedding party.

All hands, girls and boys, were given needle and thread and shown how to sew, embroider and attach borders, while Miriam went from one to the other checking the progress and quality of work. Every square cubit of floor space in the house was taken up with assorted materials, ribbons, ornamental flowers and fruits destined for the finished dresses.

Because they invited many families, they purchased large slabs of beef, mutton, and goat as well as a variety of fish which the men together with the boat crew began to season, salt, dry in the sun or smoke as the best way to cure and preserve everything until it was to be cooked. They also brought cart loads of fruit and vegetables which they proceeded to dry, although much of it was going to be cooked as sauces, and cakes. Miriam knew that soon they would have to start baking a variety of breads, buns, cakes and biscuits, so they purchased sacks of grains and corn.

Germanicus' only tunic was ripped and bloodied when he was stabbed, so they decided to sew him a new one, saying it was bad luck to marry in the old tunic.

Germanicus wanted the wedding to be in the Israeli tradition, and Yeshua to teach him everything: the betrothal, the ceremony and the obligations. "Traditionally the parents choose the partner, propose and negotiate the terms", Yeshua explained. "Marriages are held on Wednesdays to give the groom a chance to prove his bride's chastity. If she is not a virgin, he presses charges on Thursday when the local Sanhedrim convenes. The marriage is dissolved by Friday."

Germanicus was astounded, "How does she prove her husband's chastity?"

The young tutor was stumped, "She cannot." Then he carried on, "The wife has four obligations, and the husband has ten. He must provide medical treatment, support her daughters until marriage, pay for a respectable funeral, and so on..."

"Does he have any rights?"

"Many: he can have more than one wife, even concubines; and he can divorce her with a simple document, just like that," he snapped his fingers.

"Can she take a lover?" Germanicus asked and the tutor shook his head emphatically. "Then why would she want to be married?"

"In a patriarchal society a woman suffers a worse stigma if she is not married. So she competes very hard to be betrothed as early as possible."

"Is that why you are so strong against patriarchs? Aside from stigmas, penalties and punishment, does love come into the marriage?"

Yeshua replied lamely, "Love is a luxury no one considered..."

When Yeshua took the slave to the Rabbi, he expected an argument when he asked, "Rabbi, Anna and Germanicus wish to be married in the Judaic tradition."

"Impossible", the rabbi snarled resolutely. "He must be fully converted, including the covenant, before I can do it."

"He intends to become a proselyte...he has not had time..." the young Israeli explained with a plea in his voice.

"Wishing to be one does not make him one."

The young scholar expected the rebuff and replied with equal resolve, "Three priests from nearby villages offered to perform the wedding without compromises."

Ben Lebbus sighed. He knew their strict, uncompromising religion was sending many fine couples elsewhere when refused. He did not wish to lose Anna, Lygia and all their future offspring, so decided to take matters into his own hands, "Germanicus, will you allow Anna to practice the Judaic faith unimpeded?"

"I will encourage her to do so," he responded with sincerity.

"Will you bring up Lygia in the Judaic faith?"

"Of course,' the slave replied emphatically, adding, "as well as our offsprings."

The rabbi smiled at his firm tone. He decided to extract one more promise, "Do you promise to convert to our faith?"

"I already follow master Yeshua's teachings", he nodded proudly.

"That's not saying much," the rabbi mused, enjoying a chuckle. Then he announced cheerily, "Germanicus, I will be happy to perform the marriage ceremony. I cannot do it in the synagogue but I'll do it in master Joseph's house, not to offend the Sanhedrin."

Yeshua visited master Nehemiah daily, to be sure the Zealots were not mistreating the prisoner. He pressed for a fair trial as soon as possible, as his presence was creating tensions within the cell. Meantime he avoided lady Sarah for he knew he could not lie to her. As a result she accused him of losing interest in her.

Every day he pressed the prisoner for names of witnesses to mount a defense, but Nehemiah fell into a deep depression. His eyes began to sink deep into the sockets and he became unfocused. Yeshua feared he was giving up, perhaps accepting his inevitable fate; a finding of guilt and a summary execution. This morning Yeshua barely acknowledged Esau guarding, flung the door open violently, and marched directly to the prisoner, "Today I will not leave until you give me names," he ordered sharply. "The prosecutors have dozens of witnesses, and hundreds of pieces of evidence. And you? Nothing: no answer, no alibi, no witnesses." He stood almost on top of the prisoner who leaned back. But the result was the same: not one muscle on Nehemiah's face flinched. Yeshua marched furiously around him, barking loudly, and making demands, only to be met with the same vacant look.

As a last resort, he leaned over speaking almost in a whisper, "Lady Sarah told me...you betrothed your older daughter Helena to that aristocratic family, and she died of depression..." For the first time Nehemiah's dark eyes focused on him. He continued, "You contracted lady Sarah to the same family, breached the betrothal, was sued and they forced you into bankruptcy. Is that why you turned to the Romans: out of desperation?" He waited anxiously for a confession, a nod, a word, only to see his dark eyes sink into oblivion. "Say something!" Yeshua screamed. "If you don't, you will die. Don't you care?"

"Give up, master Yeshua," Esau, entered the room, and joined them. "I think he has given up hope. He even refuses to eat."

"When did that happen?" Yeshua turned to him surprised.

"Last night. I begged him to eat…then threatened to force-feed him, but he turned away."

"Bring me his food," the young scholar ordered. Esau brought the plate, and he sat before the prisoner, holding out the broth, but he turned his face away. "Don't you want to live? You are unbelievably selfish. You sent one daughter to her death, then tried to send the other to the same fate. Now, under pressure, you seek freedom in your own death. What about your family: wife and children? Lady Sarah? Don't you wish to see them?"

"Master Yeshua, they won't allow visitors…" Esau informed him.

Yeshua hung his head, muttering, "You have a saintly daughter…after all you did, she worries…and wants you to live…"

"Lady Sarah," the prisoner mumbled looking into space, his eyes filling with tears, "I am sorry…sorry for lady Sarah…and Helena…"

Yeshua tried to prod him to continue and say something about his girls, his boy, or his wife, but his eyes drifted into the world of depression, not to be dislodged.

Yeshua went to the door, stopped, and turned back to Nehemiah, "With your death, you will have your victory…lady Sarah will forsake me…"

He left and walked directly to the oak tree, mentally going over the questions he intended to ask lady Sarah about her father. He needed the names of his business associates, places and dates where he had been in the past two years. How could he ask that without arousing suspicion? Should he admit he knew her father's whereabouts? He wrestled with the questions when he was startled from behind, "Did I frighten you?" Sarah chuckled with guilt. "I'm sorry…" She was relieved to see him smile. She sat beside him taking his hand. He pulled her next to him, and his eyes brightened up. She whispered tenderly, "I am so happy to meet with you after so long. I worried that I offended you…"

"No, no," he replied affectionately. "I…have been busy…"

"I know, the wedding…Debborah said you wanted to see me urgently?"

When he saw her anxious look, he wished he had not used the word, "It's not all that urgent…Actually, I did want to see you…To invite you to the wedding…as my escort." He blushed, for he made that up on the spur o the moment.

She recognized his fib when she saw his face turning red, but the excitement of being with him, and not sharing him with everybody cheered her spirits. A permanent grin sparkled her face as they held each other affectionately. She caressed his face murmuring, "Anna and Germanicus are the happiest couple I have seen: it's in their eyes, their faces…when they touch…everything they do."

"Blessed are they who live in the bosom of love," he mused wistfully.

Sarah purred longingly, "That's how blessed I feel…with you." Suddenly she sat up and asked shyly, "Are mixed marriages like theirs encouraged by your church?"

"Our religion has become too rigid and inflexible with the most irrelevant matters, forcing many devout people to leave," he confessed sadly. "Instead of welcoming them, they make unrealistic demands that they convert first…"

"I'll convert," she interrupted eagerly, then looked down embarrassed, adding, "…if asked."

He smiled tenderly watching her blushing, "When we were returning from the expedition, I lay awake at nights contemplating how I was going to ask you…"

She gasped involuntarily, grabbed his arm and squeezed it against her bosom, overjoyed, "I'll go and see rabbi ben Lebbus, and ask him to start giving me lessons…"

He smiled and nodded, but his expression changed when he remembered the questions he had to ask about her father. She misconstrued his change of moods, and decided to disclose how grave her situation was becoming, "I have an offer to teach in a small town outside Jerusalem. With father gone so long, we fear the worst…bandits, or murder. There is no income…I may be forced to take that job…"

He wanted to grab her and plead, don't go. I don't want you to move. Don't give up hope. But, he knew that he could not promise her anything, and suffered in agony.

When she saw his somber look she quickly added, "I thought about what you said…about running away…I changed my mind. I want to go away with you, wherever you want to go. I want a family…and a home with you."

"What about your father?" he stammered, clearly stunned.

She sighed deeply troubled, but when she spoke it was clear she had considered the matter thoroughly, "Too much time has passed without word...I'm certain bandits or robbers have murdered..." She stopped for a moment, then looked at him pleadingly, "I want a new life with you, wherever you go...You still want me, don't you?"

He stared back at her wanting to cry out — Yes, yes, I want you more than life. But, he realized he was master Nehemiah's only hope, and droned stiffly, "Lady Sarah, you asked me to help you with your father. I want to, but I need many answers; did you ever see any edifices your father designed or constructed in Tyre?"

"Yes, many," she answered enthusiastically happy that he was going to help find him. "Is that why you seemed so preoccupied?"

"Did he construct them after his fight with the aristocratic family?" Yeshua continued. She thought about it for a long time and shook her head. "Did he construct any buildings after his bankruptcy in Tyre?"

"I don't think so. He did not talk about his business after the fight started."

"What about here? Sepphoris is being totally reconstructed...?" She shook her head. "A road? A library? Anything...?"

"...I already told you: I don't know," she retorted defensively, feeling pressured by his persistent questions.

"Do you remember a town or a village he traveled to? Did customers call on him?" Yeshua pressed, and she shook her head each time. "Will you search his office for names or address...anything that I can use as evidence...?"

"Evidence? Evidence for what?" She interrupted suspiciously. "Why all these questions? This is not to discover his whereabouts. Why, then? Master Yeshua, do you know where my father is...?"

He sighed with overwhelming pity, "Master Nehemiah is accused of infiltrating the Zealots as a traitor, and selling them out to the Romans..."

"Father, a traitor?" Sarah asked horrified. "Where is my father? Master Yeshua do you know where my father is held? What will they do to him?"

He held her arms to calm her down, "He is alive...But he refuses to eat...I know where he is being held."

"Take me to him," she begged with tears in her voice. "I want to see my father!"

He shook her, "Listen to me: your father is a prisoner, about to be tried. They appointed prosecutors...and have a judge. I cannot tell you for his own safety."

She started to cry, "They will kill him. The aristocrats swore to kill him…"

He held her close, while she cried. When she slowed down and regained some control he explained, "I am trying to help him…to defend…"

She pulled away from him demanding, "He has been charged? As a traitor?" When he nodded she uttered with horror, "The sentence for treason is…death!" She stared at him in disbelief, "He is a traitor against who…the Zealots? Are they not outlaws? Murderers? Father said so himself…He said you were one of them. He was right…" He tried to take her hand but she drew away from him, "Master Yeshua, the government is not charging him…are the Zealots charging him? Are you one of them?"

"I see him every day. I plead and beg him to let me help him. But, he refuses to cooperate," Yeshua lamented. "He will not give names of witnesses…here or in Tyre."

"Witnesses? How can he get witnesses? The Zealots kidnapped him and are fabricating charges. They are all Israelis: prosecutors, judges, witnesses…bandits and kidnappers," she lashed out in desperation. "What witnesses can he get: Israelis to go against their own? And the aristocrats will buy as many witnesses as they need…because they want him dead." She placed her face in her hands crying inconsolably. "They will kill him… It's all my fault."

"No, it's not. You must not blame yourself," he reached out for her.

Suddenly she stopped crying, looked at him through her tears, "My father is doomed. He will not survive. The aristocrats killed Helena and they will kill father." She looked at him horrified, "Yeshua, if you get in their way, they will kill you also. They will stop at nothing." She grabbed and pulled him close, "You can't save father…and I can't bear losing you. Please, let's run away…now, today." She was clearly terrified.

He took her hands trying to reassure her, "I will be fine. I am fighting for a fair trial."

She raised her voice with passion, "You innocent fool, can't you understand? Your life means nothing to the aristocrats or the Zealots; only to me. They will snuff you out like they did Helena." Tears ran down her cheeks as she gave him an ultimatum, "Master Yeshua, if you remain with the Zealots when they kill father, I swear, it will kill my love for you. I won't have the strength to forgive you…or continue to love you. "

Her bluntness had the desired effect, and he made a decision, "I...I do not dare lose your love."

"Then it's decided. We'll move to some place in the furthest corner of the nation where our love will be safe."

He pulled her close and they lay on the grass, under the oak tree, "The day after the wedding we will start a new life...of happiness." They held each other and kissed passionately with abandon.

· · ·

A couple of days later, in the morning of an unseasonably cool and foggy day, a small contingent of Roman soldiers arrived in Nazareth. The centurion galloped the two white stallions pulling a chariot out of the fog, through the town gate and into the centre of the agora. He stopped and waited for his foot soldiers, armed with spears and shields. Then he pulled out a scroll from his belt, unfurled it and read it:

"Hear Ye! Hear Ye! Hear Ye!

"Be ye advised that I, Herod Antipas, tetrarch of the provinces of Galilee and Perea, by the grace of Emperor Augustus Caesar,

"Order every Israeli man, woman and child within my jurisdiction to attend to the city of Augusteana, at the hour of high noon, on Thursday next, there to witness the just punishment to be meted out to two criminals, brothers by blood, to wit, masters Simon and James, confessed members of the outlawed terrorists known as Zealots.

"No person may be excused from attending without the authority of the tetrarch. Anyone breaching this order will be charged and punished to the full extent of the law.

"Herod Antipas, tetrarch."

He handed the parchment to a soldier who nailed it on the high post next to the town gate.

As soon as they left, the people congregated at the foot of the pole to read and discuss it. The first unequivocal fact was that in three days every Israeli had to trek on a day long journey to a city all Galileans despised and avoided - Augusteana. Every Israeli had to go or be severely punished: no exceptions. They concluded the punishment to the teenagers was likely to be severe. They remembered some terrible punishments: flogging, stoning, or cutting off a limb of the criminal. One peasant remembered a man being beheaded, but they doubted such drastic penalty would be meted to mere youths.

That germinated the wildest gossip that spread through the countryside by noon.

The tetrarch's order also caused an immense crisis in master Joseph's household; Thursday was the day of the wedding. They held an urgent meeting to deal with the issue.

"We cannot postpone the ceremony until after the journey," Yeshua opined. "What if it is a horrible punishment? Who would be in a mood to celebrate?"

"Trust me, the punishment will be horrible," Joseph grumbled.

"We have no option but to advance the wedding..." Yeshua said the obvious.

They looked at the young couple, who looked at one another and nodded.

"It is decided then; the wedding will be tomorrow!" Joseph announced somberly.

"Tomorrow is impossible," Miriam objected frantically. "Do you know how much is left to do?"

"There is some advantage to holding it tomorrow," Yeshua tried to pacify his mother. "With a two day celebration, you won't have to cook and bake a week's worth. And, very likely there will be fewer people."

"Are we talking about the same people?" Miriam interjected sardonically. "Mention a feast and free food in the same breath, and every Israeli will fight to get here." She reconsidered the decision and suddenly protested for the opposite reason, "Who is going to eat a week's worth of food in two days?"

"Don't worry," the patriarch patted her hand. "Starting tomorrow no one will rest, sleep or go home until it's all gone. We'll feast around the sundial!"

Next day was the wedding ceremony!

Following tradition the bride wore a beautiful full white dress, bejeweled with Miriam's gold and silver, and a full veil. The dress had embroidered at the bottom large pomegranates, the symbol of the national fruit. She was carried in a litter through the streets of Nazareth. By choice, she held little Lygia wearing a matching dress. Ahead of her litter marched a band, playing joyful music, followed by a dancing group. Flower girls led scattering flower petals ahead of the procession. Anna beamed, enjoying her day of glory.

Meanwhile a few blocks away, the groom's party marched from master Stephanos' residence in the centre of town, meandering through the winding streets. Germanicus, still weak from the wound, was supported by his master, and escorted by the boat crew who enjoyed the loud cheers, especially the attention of the young ladies. The two parties arrived at Master Joseph's house simultaneously.

The wedding party came into the yard to the cheers of guests, the music, singing and applause, stopping under the canopy set up next to Yeshua's workshop.

The boat, sitting upright under the canopy, was covered with white linen and served as the altar, with wine, water and bread on it. Anna opened her veil and spread it to cover Germanicus. The rabbi took Lygia and handed her to Miriam, then lit the seven candles of the menorah. The Star of David hung high on the fence behind them.

The rabbi glanced at Yeshua who stood beside him, both recalling the argument that persuaded him to perform the ceremony. He looked at the couple and knew that Lord Adonai approved. He began to chant signifying the beginning of the holy union.

Yeshua's eyes went to lady Sarah who smiled at him and wiped her eyes. She hoped their union would be as happy as this. It was a lovely wedding. Ben Lebbus was inspired and gave an eloquent ceremony, bringing Lord Adonai's blessing to a deserving couple who promised to serve Him. It was a simple cerimony, touching, yet not overbearing, and above all, brief. All too soon the rabbi declared them to be husband and wife.

Master Joseph immediately stood on a stool and bellowed, "Quiet! My friends, it is our tradition to feast for many days at a wedding. Unfortunately, King Herod ordered us to pay him a visit...therefore, I urge you...no, I order you to eat a mountain of scrumptious food, and drink a sea of delightful wine, being brought to you presently." As he spoke young maidens came out with pots, pans, trays and plates and began to dish out, while boys followed with jugs and goblets, filling and passing them out. Joseph yelled, "I warn you: no one leaves until it is all finished...no mater what Herod says..."

The orchestra began to play; people ate and drank, while heaps of food was being passed out. Goblets were refilled the instant they were emptied.

According to tradition the groom snuck away with the bride into the tent, set up in the furthest corner of the yard. There, in privacy, they were finally able to embrace with nervous giggles and hungry kisses, with promises of eternal love, with heavy panting all unfolding to the accompaniment of music, lively singing and jovial laughter. They lay on the cot where their bodies sought each other and were unified as one. Their heavy breathing and natural desire, caused them to give and receive passionately, until they reached the highest summit of love in a heavenly climax, then lay in each other's arms, exhausted, perspiring, but blessed in love, and thoroughly satisfied.

At length they reappeared and rejoined the festivities, their faces flushed from exertion and love. She smiled shyly, looking down, stealing glances, while Germanicus pranced proudly. Anna's hair which had been so carefully combed and set was now loose and disheveled, and they walked to the canopy where the boat-turned-makeshift-table was covered with food and goblets full of wine. As Germanicus walked, in the Israeli tradition, he held the bed sheet high above his head: evidence of the consummation of the marriage, and virginity of the bride.

Only master Yeshua and lady Sarah were not present, for they stole to the oak tree, where they lay on the grass locked in passionate embrace and kisses. Unexpectedly she pulled him on top of her, and they enjoyed passionate love for the first time that day.

They did not return until dusk to the whispers and teasing of their many friends who had long suspected of their great love and care for each other.

• • •

It was still dark and the last guests were barely out of the gate, when master Joseph hitched the cart to the donkey, threw some straw and blankets on it, then placed some pots and jars of food and water. He brought out the youngest children, still sleeping, laid them on the straw and covered them. Thus they started the long trek to Augusteana. Every family in Nazareth and in the provinces was going through the same motions at that moment. As if guided by an invisible hand they started appearing on the streets. People nodded and grunted tokens of recognition without uttering a word. All one heard were the squeaking and grinding of dry axles as the wheels groaned. By the time they came to the town gate and passed Herod's notice nailed on the post, they saw the caravan far ahead until it disappeared in the darkness, and just as far behind them. It seemed they were fleeing, and abandoning the town to the ghosts. They plodded slowly, solemnly, much like their anscestors when leaving Egypt: quiet, subdued, contemplating the vagaries of life. Their sandals shuffled over the dusty road, reminding them once more they were prisoners tied to the Roman yoke. Eyes rose to the dark universe and the flickering stars as if asking Lord Adonai where was the promised Messiah, the prophesized leader to take them to battle, to victory and long awaited freedom. Then, as if suffering a pang of guilt for demanding too much, they lowered their heads mumbling, "Is a little bit of happiness too much to ask...?"

Yeshua looked into the darkness beyond the town gate and saw dark figures approaching from the bushes, led by master Stephanos and Germanicus, with Benjoseph, Esau, Marcus, Ahmed and Daniel. "You don't have to come," the young scholar commented." The order is for Israelis only..."

"We stood by you in Caesarea..." Stephanos mumbled and joined the file.

The others, gentiles and nationals followed. Yeshua slapped them on the shoulders and continued in silence. They traveled north by east, entering the forest area, descending the rolling hills towards the city on the shores of the Sea of Galilee. As they proceeded more and more families appeared and joined from every direction, as if they were coming out of the earth.

Stephanos, sensitive to the stifling atmosphere muttered to himself, "Why do I feel we are marching to the gallows?" He turned to Yeshua objecting, "We had more enthusiasm marching to certain death in Caesarea."

"There it was our choice. Here we're forced to do it."

In rapid succession the skies brightened from cold blues, through the warm spectrum of browns and beige, until the sun broke above the horizon and began to radiate in all its colorful majesty. But even the warm sun failed to brighten the spirit of the people, as they shuffled along, stooped and forlorn in an atmosphere of defeat. Israeli history was filled with events where they were forced to trek under orders from foreign conquerors: to Egypt, Persia, Babylon, oftentimes to slavery. Now the oppressors lived amongst them but the experience was the same.

Some of the older men, eager to alleviate the sadness, told some off colored jokes, but few people listened and even less laughed. The jokes were crude and the laughter was forced. The witty vibrant humor was lacking and there was none of the spontaneous, contagious laughter that came from the depths of the Israeli heart. Their sarcasm was thinly veiled, poorly disguising the deep hatred they held for their oppressors. The rabbi sensed his people needed inspiration, which could only come from a higher source, and began to sing about their past glories and future hopes. They soon joined him. After a few religious songs he added popular songs of love and hope to brighten their moods.

That morning flocks of little birds perched on high branches and wild beasts of the forests were awakened to a strange sight: a general invasion of thousands of pilgrims, passing through, their voices harmonizing to give glory to the Creator and celebrate life, as if marching to a feast.

They came to the top of a hill and Yeshua stopped, for he saw Auguste-ana in the far distance on the shores of the Sea of Galilee. Although he had never been there before the city seemed familiar. Then he remembered that day, a few years back, when he imagined himself floating over the hills of Galilee, and passing over this city. He recalled one outstanding edifice: a large mansion with shinny copper domes, and a big swimming pool in the yard, with the bluest, freshest water he had ever seen.

While he looked, master Benjoseph joined him, and they started walking together. Neither of them spoke, but Yeshua noticed the school master fidgeting with his tunic, rearranging his belt, sighing and smacking his lips. Obviously, he had something important to say. After waiting a long time he took matters into his own hand, "The sooner you give me their message, the sooner we may resolve the problem."

"How do you know I have a message…?"

"I will tell you what they decided," and proceeded to say it, "'We the Zealots feel that master Yeshua is too sympathetic to master Nehemiah's cause, posing a risk to the organization. Accordingly we forbid him to visit the accused'."

The school master's jaw unhinged, "Almost verbatim…How did you know?"

"Sometimes I find the Zealots are no better than the Romans," the young scholar bristled. "You complain that you're the victim and cry for justice, while you carry a dagger ready to carry out your revenge. I won-der if you had power, would you be any more compassionate?"

Benjoseph knew his friend was correct, but he was given a job and was obligated to perform it. He countered forcefully, "When I went to Tyre I was surrounded by three dozen witnesses against Nehemiah, clamoring for attention. They were eye witnesses, with personal knowledge. I sent away more than fifty others that morning."

"Did you ask if any of them were paid by the aristocrats to bear false witness?"

"What are you talking about?"

Yeshua explained about Helena's abusive marriage resulting in her untimely death, and Sarah's betrothal which led to the bankruptcy of the family. He concluded passionately, "The aristocrats stopped everyone from awarding contracts to Nehemiah, or selling them food. Did those witnesses tell you the family was starving, which forced him into treason to survive?"

"No," Benjoseph confessed, shocked at the disclosure. "Even if it were true, it is no excuse for treasonable actions." Then he pressed his case, "Every person Nehemiah sold, resulted in the man's execution and the suffering of an innocent family. I stopped counting after one hundred: that's one hundred executions."

"He has a right to a defense…to explain," the young scholar pressed stubbornly.

"In any case, I was asked to tell you, you are forbidden to visit him…"

"Why? Do they fear justice or that they will miss a chance for revenge?"

"They fear your closeness to lady Sarah may…help him escape…" Benjoseph almost choked for the words were tearing him apart.

Yeshua walked away enraged whispering, "Lady Sarah was correct: they do not care…!"

They were fast approaching Augusteana, and stopped a couple of hills above it, from where they saw, over the high wall, the spectacular modern city. This was a thoroughly Greek city with colossal, opulent edifices fronted by tall lovely marble pillars. The late Herod, the great, was well known as a builder of many modern cities and a port throughout Israel. His son, Herod Antipas, jealous and desiring to outdo him, constructed Augusteana. Most pilgrims approaching this sprawling metropolis had never seen such massive edifices, and experienced mixed emotions: admiration for the handsomely decorated Doric and Corinthian columns and pilasters, while feeling humble and inferior to the Greek culture, like foreigners in their own nation.

"That's the amphitheatre where they act out Greek tragedies every evening," a well traveled Israeli confided to an old peasant.

"We live tragedies every day in the amphitheatre of our lives," his companion countered with sarcasm.

Another pointed to the large palace near the centre of the city, with shinny copper domes, and a large swimming pool beside it. The estate was surrounded by uniform date palms guarding it like sentinels.

Closer to the pilgrims and immediately inside the city gates they saw a gymnasium and an outdoor stadium, where the youths, sons of wealthy Israelis and gentiles, come out to practice and exercise daily, competing in a variety of popular sports, from javelin and discus throwing, high jumping and running the marathon Many local champions went on to compete in Caesarea, then to Antioch. If they won the championship for the region they continued on to the glory of the Olympiads in Greece.

Although the peasants saw them, they paid no attention to a couple of dozen athletes scantily dressed, sprinkled over the stadium doing warm up exercises.

But Herod unwittingly constructed Augusteana on top of an ancient Hebrew cemetery, making it an unclean city. To the Israelis it was an ill omen, that the city was unlucky, and to be avoided. Before it was completed and consecrated, Emperor Augustus, after whom it was named, died, proving this was a city of bad luck.

Herod quickly changed the name to Tiberias after the successor, Tiberius Caesar, clearly demonstrating Israeli underlings licking the sandals of their Roman patrons.

The pilgrims descended the hills and went as far as the city gates where the merchants quickly set up a gigantic agora, eager to earn handsome profits.

The new arrivals were ordered to remain outside the city gates in front of a platform erected for the occasion. There they set up a makeshift camp. Yeshua looked around the hills and saw the humanity, like a colony of ants, every square cubit covered by caravans.

Soon a loud barking order interrupted his investigation, and he saw Roman soldiers coming out through the gate. They wore full battle dress, with armor, helmets, sheathed swords, spears and shields, and as they came out, one file proceeded to the left side along the wall, the other to the right. There they stood, ready to defend the city.

Next came out a dozen infantry men, followed by officers and centurions, to guard the platform. They were followed by a chariot led by two white stallions. It stopped and a passenger and driver descended, walking up the steps of the platform. One of them, undoubtedly Herod Antipas sat on a large chair. He was a slight dark man with heavy black beard, and a nervous habit, fidgeting constantly. Yeshua recognized the tetrarch's companion, legate Vinicius who came to his house a few months past with the order for the thrones.

With a nervous flick of a finger Herod ordered the proceedings to start. The legate raised his hand and a blare of trumpets sounded to announce the start. The pilgrims were about to discover why they were ordered to come.

A dozen strong, muscular workers came out of the gates, dragging and pushing two male youths bound in chains. As they come out through the agora, their wild eyes darted in every direction, and when they saw the hills covered with people their eyes fixed on the scene, with shock and fright. The two were bare except for loin cloths, and their suntanned bodies were bloody and bruised. Their faces were battered and swollen, their eyes half shut. Yeshua hardly recognized the two brothers, Simon and James, they had seen in the village of Laish only a month past. The crowd murmured and swore as they were being pushed and whipped every time they stopped.

Close behind the youths came more workers, carrying and dragging two giant crosses. At the rear came muscular men with sledge hammers and long spikes.

When the pilgrims saw the crosses, they let out a loud gasp involuntarily. Only one word echoed through the hills, "cruci-cruci-crucifixion-fixion…" until the pilgrims many hills beyond who could not see, knew the punishment awaiting the teenagers. The procession stopped at the platform, a few paces from two holes recently dug.

Suddenly a woman not far from Master Joseph's group shrieked, "No! Simon! James! My God…my sons," she ran towards them. "Don't kill them. Please…in the name of God, don't…"

The boys recognized her and lunged forward, but the muscular men yanked the chains and they fell to the ground. One worker jumped on James, the slighter youth crashing a fist to his head.

The woman almost reached them when a soldier stepped in front, raising his spear sideways between his outstretched hands and thrust it forward, smashing her in the face. She fell on the ground, dazed and bleeding. Yeshua and Miriam ran to her aid, reached to pick her up when a spear pointed at their faces.

"Get her out before I finish her off," the soldier growled.

They grabbed her arms and half-dragged her to the cart where Miriam proceeded to wash her face and console her. They were busy with her and did not see the tetrarch's signal to a centurion who stepped to the edge of the platform unrolled a scroll and began to read:

"Herod Antipas, tetrarch of the Provinces of Galilee and Perea, Greetings;

"My government, with the aid and assistance of our friends and protectors from Rome, uncovered a band of lawless criminals, to wit, Zealots, whose sworn purpose is murder and terrorism;

"The two prisoners Simon and James have freely signed a confession that they are Zealots..."

When the pilgrims heard "Free confession" they yelled and jeered:

"Is that why they're all bruised and bloody?" one man demanded.

"Free confessions, my arse!"

Antipas' face twisted and contorted when he heard the jeers and accusations, and his thin lips tightened into an invisible line. The officers reached for their swords but the tetrarch shook his head nervously, not wishing to risk a riot with him at the centre.

The centurion cleared his throat and continued:

"They were tried according to law, justly found guilty and sentenced.

"Simon and James will be crucified in public, and left on the cross until their deaths. Their bodies shall remain on the crosses as deterrent for all, until their remains rot and fall off to feed the birds and jackals of the fields.

"By the order of Herod Antipas."

When the centurion finished, the tetrarch nodded with a quick jerk and the workers descended upon the young brothers, wrestling them to the ground, and dragging them to the crosses. The youths twisted and fought, with blood curdling screams echoing over the hills and through the forests. Flocks of birds frightened by the terrified screams flew away in panic. Wild beasts in the forest, stopped, looked in the direction of the screams, turned away and quickened their pace.

Although the muscular men greatly outnumbered the two youths, they had a hard time overcoming them. Simon bit and tore off a big chunk of muscle from an assailant's shoulder. James kicked another in the crotch causing him to fall writhing in pain. Yeshua watched the struggle but all he could see were bodies twisting and limbs flinging wildly, with heart wrenching screams. But, being outnumbered and chained, the outcome was a foregone conclusion. A muscular brute crashed his fist to Simon's mouth knocking him senseless, and half a dozen men quickly pinned him to the timber. James, the smaller youth, was easier to subdue. As they held them down an iron spike was placed against the wrist and the sickening strikes of the sledge hammer exploded: "Crack! Crack! Crack!..." It pounded in every ear drum, piercing every Israeli heart.

One of the brothers bellowed like a terrified animal being slaughtered. The loud, surreal, long scream from the very depths of his soul frightened the children causing many to start trembling uncontrollably and crying inconsolably. Mothers pressed them tight against their bosom to protect them from the world. But, the yelling and screaming, the loud swearing and grunting of the workers and the pounding of the sledge hammer assaulted the children's psyche annihilating their innocence. Many months later countless children suffered terrifying nightmares, and jumped at the slightest noise, or broke down crying for no apparent reason. Some who had never done it before, started stuttering. Parents took them into their cots for the night to reinforce love which was so brutally assaulted that day.

Many grownups cried. Others lashed out with the only weapons they had: words.

"You will burn in hell for this," an ancient man shook his skeletal fist at Antipas.

A young mother swore to the heavens, "I will raise every child of mine to live for the day they will avenge your deaths!"

An older lady prayed, "May Lord Adonai give us the Messiah...to drown all of you vermin in the sea!"

The cracking of the sledge hammer assaulted their hearts, and the screams etched their collective memories. Years later when they heard a scream, they stopped whatever they were doing, their bodies shaking, and tears rolling down their faces.

Suddenly the hammering stopped. Yeshua opened his eyes to see a half dozen men lifting each cross. The boys hung precariously like rag dolls, big spikes thrusting through the wrists and ankles. Yeshua was so transfixed by the surreal scene he did not hear Benjoseph until he spoke, "The number climbed to one hundred and two…" He spat on the ground and walked away.

The workers filled the holes with rocks and dirt, and tamped it down carefully. Then they spread excess dirt to look as neat as a new garden.

As soon as they finished, the tetrarch motioned for his chariot, rushed into it and ordered the driver to whip the horses to get him out of there.

The people stood staring at the brothers high against the blue sky. Many had children of the same age and suffered the pains of a parent. The boys' mother lay on the hay in Joseph's cart, dazed and in shock. She did not shed tears, for her eyes went dry long ago.

The rabbi started to sing a religious song about Adonai's people marching to victory. Some people joined, half-heartedly, but after one stanza the voices faltered and they stopped. Their spirits were too broken to sing.

They could not get over the fact that these hills were teeming with tens of thousand of pilgrims, and could easily have overcome less than five hundred soldiers and broken those youths free. If it came to battle they could have torn the Romans apart, limb from limb. But, they did not. For the rest of their lives they felt guilt, saying the boys' blood was on their hands. They did not want a song of victory. They needed silence, and in silence they prayed for the boys to forgive them.

The crosses stood, high against a clear, cool blue sky, so they felt the presence of the Creator watching over the two brothers. After the pilgrims' prayer for them, the boys hung motionless, seemingly at peace, waiting for death.

It was mid-afternoon, the hottest and most oppressive time of the day, and time seemed to have stopped. The skies were a brilliant blue. Parents put their children to sleep in whatever shade they could find and sat down to contemplate. They were forbidden to leave until the boys died, and that could take days. The soldiers stood uncomfortably in their battle uniforms and hot helmets, wet with perspiration, shuffling their weight from foot to foot, leaning on the spears for support.

Yeshua stood transfixed staring at Simon and James, hanging on the crosses, contemplating their lives. He knew, as did every Israeli that these boys were national heroes, and that their grandfather had founded the Zealots and their father had also been their leader. All met untimely violent deaths. He wondered if the brothers attended lyceum, were they forced to suspend their education like him because of economic hardships? Did they have a girl who loved them, whose heart was now crushed? Did they leave plans unfulfilled? Perhaps dreams like his own? As he contemplated an immense sadness seized him, for he knew before the morrow their dreams, and their love, would meld into the infinity of time and be no more.

One of the brothers moved and broke into a coughing fit. Yeshua walked down and stopped under the cross looking up at him. He raised his eyes to the sky above the crosses, "Dear Abba, accept the spirits of these two young brothers whose lives among us were filled with danger and suffering. Forgive them their shortcomings and take them into Your house for everlasting…"

"Young man, you are forbidden to stand here," an officer walked up and interrupted him. "Go back to your people."

"He was coughing…he needs air," Yeshua answered without moving.

The officer looked up and knew Yeshua was right. This was a painful, slow death, where the weight of the body stretched the limbs to the point where the victim was tortured, slowly chocking. Every few moments he had to raise himself by pushing against his nailed ankles, to catch a few breaths, but, being too weak he slid down only to be choked again, until he finally died from asphyxiation.

"He will be looked after," the officer winced shaking his head. "Now go back."

Stephanos came and escorted Yeshua back to his family. The officer went up to a soldier, and said something. The soldier left, and a short time later returned with a heavy iron bar which he swung violently against the brothers' legs. There were loud, sickening "cracks" exploding as the bones snapped, and the bodies sagged listlessly about half a cubit.

Some pilgrims close by commented, "They'll die quicker…less suffering."

The pilgrims started to sing an ancient Hebrew song asking Lord Adonai to lead their souls into paradise and keep them safe forever. Few heard when Simon heaved, coughed, let out a desperate cry to the heavens, then sagged with his head falling on his chest. James died a few moments later. The pilgrims finished the song.

The Israelis were numb with pain that late afternoon as they started to pick up their terrified children and meager belongings, and began the exodus. It would take a long time to rebuild their lives and mend their wounds after the day's chaos.

Yeshua helped his parents, and placed the youngest siblings on the cart, then informed them, "I will stay to bury Simon and James."

"That's against the kings' orders," Miriam argued listlessly.

"I will ask the tetrarch for their bodies," Yeshua replied.

Joseph touched his son's shoulders and nodded.

"I'll go with you," Stephanos offered.

"Me too," James stepped forward.

Benjoseph and the boat crew joined, and they watched their kinfolk leave on the long trek home. Then the young men turned towards the city gates.

"Halt!" The officer barked at them. "You are forbidden to enter the city; tetrarch's orders."

The soldiers guarding the gate stood rigid, ready for action.

"I desire an audience with his Excellency," Yeshua explained calmly. "I will ask for the bodies to bury."

The officer was about to order his soldiers to remove the peasants, when a merchant stepped forward, "You will need frankincense. Take this bundle."

"Take my perfume," another held out a flask.

"Here is cloth to wrap them," another volunteered.

"I'll bring a ladder, and my servants will take down the bodies," another man came forward. "You can inter them in my family cave."

The officer was surrounded by merchants, and the young men. He looked back to the hills and saw dozens of men watching with intense interest. He knew that a wrong word, an unfortunate move would spark a battle. And these thousands of pilgrims would tear them apart. The Israelis have their imperfections but they are not cowards in battle, he thought. He barked an order, "Private Quintus escort these men to the palace!"

Yeshua recognized his friend. He was the one who had brought the iron bar and broke the brothers' legs. Quintus led them into the city and across the large square to the most opulent edifice. From a distance they saw the sun's rays reflecting from the shinny copper domes making it appear the building was in flames. As they went up the marble steps, they saw a large swimming pool with children frolicking and splashing, while women sat around lounging and laughing freely.

The guard listened to their request, frowned, but, entered the building and after a long time returned, announcing, "You have one moment. But, I warn you, the tetrarch is in a foul mood. Speak fast and clearly, and bow...often, and very low."

Inside, Yeshua proceeded to the center of the court until a guard raised his hand. He bowed keeping his eyes on the tetrarch's every movement. Herod sat at the edge of the throne, fidgeting nervously, scowling, fingers constantly tapping the arm rest, "You want the bodies," the tetrarch exclaimed, raising his voice to a falsetto. "Why? Are you one of the bandits?" Before Yeshua could answer, he continued, "Did you not hear my order? They are to hang until they rot, as a deterrent for all Israelis..."

Yeshua bowed carefully, slowly, realizing he must be careful with this nervous man, "Your Excellency, all Israelis were forced to be at the crucifixion. Who is left to be deterred?" Then he mused sardonically, "A wise ruler balances sternness with compassion." As soon as he said it he wished he could take the words back.

The crow feet about Herod's eyes deepened. The court went silent, uncertain how the tetrarch would react to the young man's audacity. Herod did not appreciate uninvited criticism or advice, but admitted the youth spoke soundly. Still he wamted to curb his insolent tongue. While he considered the matter, legate Vinicius approached him and whispered. The tetrarch listened with interest, nodded and smiled faintly, "Are you Yeshua, the son of the carpenter Joseph presently building my thrones?"

"I am, your Excellency," he bowed.

"A carpenter's son presuming to advise me?" Herod queried with sarcasm dripping from his lips like honey. "Are you really a descendant from the House of King David?" Before Yeshua answered the tetrarch launched the next barb, "What next: will you be coming to reclaim your kingdom? Depose me?" He broke into a loud, nervous laughter, which the court underlings echoed. Seeing a chance for revenge he announced magnanimously, "Yeshua, I'll show that I am a compassionate ruler. I will give you their bodies - provided you pay a head tax of one silver shekel for each..." He looked at the courtiers who loudly expressed approval with a grunt or a nod, while he basked in expection of sweet vengeance, certain they could not possibly afford his exorbitant price.

Yeshua was about to object when master Stephanos rushed to his side, grabbed his arm and started to drag him away, at the same time bowing, and spluttering, "Your majesty is very gracious...I will pay...Thank you...Good day."

Herod's face darkened, and his eyes turned the color of hard steel.

Thousands of residents from the city joined the pilgrims who had stayed behind, bringing ladders, water, basins, all the tools, and oil lamps. They took down the bodies and began to wash and prepare them for burial.

Suddenly they heard a thunderous sound of horse hoofs and wheels, raised the lamps and saw two white stallions speeding with a chariot and a Roman soldier inside it. It was heading in the direction of Nazareth.

"Is that not Quintus?" Stephanos asked. "I wonder where he is going?"

"Probably on an errand for his superiors," Yeshua commented as he walked towards his brother James. He put his arm around the younger sibling's shoulder and led him away from the others, stopping by an old fig tree under a canopy of stars. He spoke with a serious tone, "Today when I stood under the crosses watching them die, I was furious with Yahweh," he exclaimed. James looked at him and saw the fires of anger still burning in his eyes. "Why is my heavenly Abba allowing such atrocity to go unpunished? I knew that with a flick of a finger He could pulverize them and save the brothers. But He did not do it. Why?" His voice still betrayed the pain. His breathing was deep and his voice harsh as he relived the inhuman suffering. After a few moments he calmed down, "When I was ordered away from the crosses, I thought about it and began to understand: He wants us to bring about the changes and to stop the atrocities. If we want a better world, we will have to do it."

"So I suppose you are going to start a revolution?" James asked nervously, looking around to be sure no one could hear them.

Yeshua thought about it, and nodded emphatically, "Yes, start a revolution brother James...a revolution without weapons and without violence. We will build a synagogue and welcome all the children of Yahweh in it: Arabs, Romans, pagans..."

"Do you mean you intend to throw away our weapons, and meet a Roman sword with a loving embrace?" James sneered sardonically.

"Love will bring the Indians, atheists, Europeans and all the rest together..."

"Love will get your belly pierced! Moreover atheists don't recognize God!"

"But He recognizes them. Have faith..."

James stopped arguing and reflected for a moment, clearly wavering, "Yes, faith can move mountains…but in this case…"

"Faith is nothing without compassion. We must bring all the Esaus, the dispossessed, Persians, slaves and teach them my Abba's love, charity and forgiveness," the young scholar's voice pressed with a singular passion.

James could hardly believe his ears, "Does that mean you have reconciled with…Yahweh? Is your faith back… renewed?"

"I would not go that far," he bit his lip because he wanted his message to be clear. "Let me explain it this way: my heavenly Abba has no problem with me… perhaps I have a problem…a problem with myself."

"What kind of problem?"

Yeshua took a couple of paces and looked up to the stars, "I do not think I am the right person for God's plans." James rushed to his side ready to argue, but the older brother raised his hand as he wished to finish, "Lady Sarah will be a central part of my life. Today I have chosen you to be the leader our church. I will be the foot soldier, the itinerant teacher…"

"But I am not the chosen one…"

"None of us are…yet we must all work tirelessly for this revolution to succeed."

"Am I expected to guide all the people: gentiles, Arabs, atheists…?" he sounded overwhelmed.

"Did I not say they were created equal, all of them?" Yeshua responded impatiently.

James felt guilty for sounding skeptical, but he was dumbfounded, and far from confident. Would the gentiles want the Judaic religion? If they did, would the priests of the Temple accept them? Would the Israelis? He feared it was too much to ask of them. Yet he was smitten with his brother's vision, an inspiration still far in the future: of different races sitting side by side in Yahweh's house of assembly, worshipping the one and only Creator.

"I like it," James admitted with a smile. "It will take a life time, maybe more, but I'll do it."

When the bodies were prepared, they wrapped each in clean white linen, with perfumed branches and leaves of myrrh and frankincense, and carried them on plank slabs to the burial caves a stadium distant from the city. Thousands listened to master Yeshua's service.

It was a touching service. He looked up to the stars of the universe and said, "Dear heavenly Abba, take Simon and James into Your house and keep them safe until the time when we come to rejoice with You in paradise." Then he turned to the multitude and his radiant eyes traveled from face to face, "I look at you and sense your hearts are hardened with fear and revenge. I tell you truly, since the dawn of time men have reacted the same way: violence with violence, death with yet another killing. If you continue on that path, then Simon's and James' deaths will be in vain.

"But I say: no more. Simon's and James' blood must be the symbol of a new order. Forgiveness and charity shall be their legacy...and your new testament. Meet the tyrants of the world with the greatest weapon - love! Tyrants know terror: they will not fight love.

"Do not be afraid, for love will guide you. From the blood of our martyrs shall spring my church, and a new order."

He looked at his brother, "James, the symbol of our synagogue shall be the cross. And the church shall be in Jerusalem."

He began to walk among the congregants making his major announcement, "Brother James and I will start a new order. He will care for the church. I will travel among the people. But, when I am gone to rejoin my Abba, do not seek for me in plots or burial caves, for you will not find me."

"Where will we find you?" Stephanos asked.

"Search for me in your hearts, and I will be there."

• • •

Daylight was breaking when Yeshua's group returned to Nazareth. From a distance they saw a commotion as people had gathered around the town's gate.

James was the first to point out the problem, "There is something on top of that post."

They looked and saw a round object on it. After coming closer Stephanos gasped with horror, "By Zeus, it is a human head."

They pushed through the crowd until they were directly under the post with Herod's announcement, now soaked in blood.

"It's master Nehemiah's head," Benjoseph exclaimed.

"What happened? Who did this?" Yeshua demanded until a merchant came forward, "I saw everything. I'll never forget it...It was still dark, and I was putting out my merchandize. Suddenly, a roar of hoofs and wheels...I turned and saw two white stallions pulling a chariot, coming at full speed. It stopped right here. A Roman soldier stood in it." He squinted his eyes and continued with confidence, "It was your soldier friend...soaked in blood from head to toe. He held the head high in one hand and his bloody sword in the other. He leaped up the post, and in one motion planted the head up there. Then he screamed, 'Nehemiah, you will never murder again!' He lashed those horses and melted into the darkness."

The merchant wanted to continue, but on impulse, Yeshua leaped up the post, climbing and struggling as it was slippery, splattering blood all over himself. He knew he had to remove it before lady Sarah saw it. With superhuman effort he reached the top, grabbed the head by the hair, and pulled it off. As he was about to start down he heard his name, looked and saw lady Sarah in the crowd running towards him. He froze.

"Master Yeshua," she yelled, "What are you doing?" She stopped when she recognized what he was holding, her hands covering her mouth, then she screamed, "Oh, my God! You murdered my father!"

She gasped, turning waxy white, her eyes rolled up into her sockets, and she fell in a heap.

CHAPTER XVII - THE MIRACLE OF ELLIE

From the dawn of time, Passover which fell around the fifteenth day of the month of NISAN, became Israel's biggest religious feast. All Israelis were expected to make the pilgrimage to Jerusalem. As the day approached the very air in the towns became charged like the heavens before an electric storm. It was all people talked about. Those who could afford to make the pilgrimage were preparing for the biggest adventure of their lives. Pilgrims who had gone in the past, advised them with every detail: which roads were safe from bandits, the location of the best water wells, best camping sites, which gates to enter Jerusalem to avoid Roman guards. They were instructed on how to deal with priests investigating the sacrificial animals, and how to haggle with the money changers in the Temple.

Few peasants from Nazareth could afford the trip. But those who managed to save enough and enjoy the feast, returned with memories of a lifetime.

The less fortunate sent the didrachmon, a half silver shekel, with the rabbi to pay the head tax to the Temple. On the important day they celebrated the traditional meal at home, lifting the goblets with a toast, "Next year in Jerusalem."

Yeshua and Stephanos were preparing to load the animals for the journey when a young soldier arrived from Augusteana. Looking at the sweat on his horse he had galloped non-stop. He handed a letter to Yeshua, "From private Quintus. He is in danger..." the soldier said between breaths and rode off.

Yeshua read it out loud:

"Master Yeshua and friends,

"I hate to involve you in my problems, but I have to warn you. The two Roman trackers who ambushed us, have charged me with being a criminal Zealot, with assaulting and imprisoning them. I suspect they also swore false charges against all of you.

"Leave Nazareth at once, until I persuade my superiors to drop the charges.

"Presently I am in prison for stealing horses and a chariot, property of Rome.

"Quintus"

Yeshua told his friends decisively, "We're going to Angusteana."

Stephanos argued, "We were told to run. Why rush head first into danger?"

"Quintus needs us," the Israeli responded firmly.

The Greek was about to argue but knew he would not listen, so he gave up.

They loaded the supplies, said their good byes and left. Joseph handed his son a pouch of coins with instructions to exchange it and pay the Temple tax.

"We'll have to pick up Lucius," Yeshua said as they were leaving.

"Who is Lucius?" Germanicus could not remember anyone by that name.

"My sacrificial lamb," he replied. "I have to purify myself and the lamb is food for the feast. The rabbi inspected it already and declared it unblemished."

"Unblemished?" Germanicus' eyebrows furled.

"A sacrificial animal must be a perfect specimen. One broken or deformed bone, even a wart could results in rejection," he explained.

"Your God is far too particular for my liking," the Greek smirked sardonically.

"No, the priests of the Temple are," Yeshua sighed shaking his head.

Before leaving they bought some figs in the agora to take the edge of hunger, and headed towards the hills and forests leading to the Sea of Galilee and Augusteana.

That same morning, a few miles to the north, two Roman soldiers, the expert trackers, came out of the forest, heading for Nazareth coming to arrest them.

In the early afternoon Yeshua's group saw the outline of Augustiana in the distance and started to descend. The scholar's mind went back to a few days past, the crucifixion, the burial, and their return to Nazareth. He still shuddered at the shock of seeing master Nehemiah's head, and rushing up the pole to remove it.

The sight of seeing her father's head crushed lady Sarah's spirit and her mind. She was thoroughly distraught, unable to communicate, and sat staring vacantly in space, drifting in and out of shock for days. Except for crying, all she did was gasp and pass out at the mention of her father's name. Her nights were filled with nightmares, necessitating the oil lamps to burn day and night. She refused to eat and her health started to slide to a dangerous state, needing support to walk a few steps. She blamed herself for her father's death and insisted she wanted to die. Then she began to hallucinate and carry on conversations with her dead sister and father. The doctors said that she likely would never recover from the mental breakdown, and if by some miracle she came out of it, her mental health would remain fragile.

Her mother also suffered a complete breakdown from which she never recovered. The servants and slaves took over the family affairs and cared for her young brother and the household responsibilities in exemplary fashion. The doctors prescribed herbs, which when boiled and drunk acted as a strong sedative. It tranquilized the ladies putting them to sleep most of the time.

Yeshua visited lady Sarah but she was in a state of constant bewilderment. He tried to speak to her about their future, but she did not seem to hear. Every day he left more depressed, fearing she may not recover short of a miracle.

In the middle of the second week she began to show some interest in her surroundings, was able to stay awake, and even ate some food. The servants took her off the sedative potion. When Yeshua arrived they announced the happy news, and he rushed to her overjoyed, and impatient to see and hold her.

Alas, when she saw him, her eyes opened wide with fright and she raved out of control, accusing him of killing her father, and screaming until the servants rushed to her. He tried to calm her down but she trembled with fright when he touched her. They quickly gave her the potion to put her to sleep. Then they asked him to leave. For three days he returned and the scene was repeated: at first sight of him, she screamed uncontrollably until the servants scurried to her side. They consulted the doctors, and next day when he arrived, a servant met him at the gate.

"Lady Sarah's doctor advises that you be forbidden to visit with her!"

The young scholar was about to argue when two muscular, ebony colored Ethiopian slaves appeared from the shadows. He decided it was wiser to leave.

He returned every morning only to be told: "No, we will not tell her you are here. Good day."

Desperate, with nowhere to turn he approached Debborah, "You are the only outsider she will see. Take this letter...It's full of good news... Please?"

Her heart ached for him, so she relented and took it. He stood outside the gate waiting. She returned with a shocked look, "I knew I should not have done it," she muttered, "She sensed something was wrong, and when I reached for your letter, her smile froze. She said if I ever tried that again, I would be forbidden in the house."

Yeshua turned without a comment and walked away.

Debborah went in and had a long visit with Sarah, but her mind was on her brother. When she returned home she searched for him to no avail. She suspected he had probably gone to the oak tree, and decided to let him be. But this time he did not return for two days and when she saw him he seemed a different person.

Years later Debborah would say he probably prayed for lady Sarah's recovery, and made a promised to the Lord to make a great personal sacrifice in exchange for her recovery. When he returned, she saw a more somber and melancholic Yeshua. His eyes lost some brightness and he accepted Sarah's decision. He never returned to her gate.

His reminiscing was disrupted when they arrived in Augusteana. They went to the prison, inquired after private Quintus and were told that he was taken to Jerusalem.

"Why Jerusalem?" Stephanos asked with trepidation.

"Tetrarch Valerius Gratus goes there every Passover," the guard droned thoroughly bored. "The tetrarch fears the Israelis may start a rebellion during the celebration..."

The young men discussed rushing directly to Jerusalem when the guard interrupted, "He left a letter for his father...Where did I put it?" He rummaged through a pile of papyrus. "Ah, here it is. He begged this be taken to him."

Yeshua took it, "It only adds one day to the journey. Moreover we promised to see master Hariph about the parchments."

They left immediately. Outside the city gate they proceeded north along the shores towards Capernaum. They walked in silence contemplating Quintus' fate.

"Why did Quintus kill master Nehemiah?" Yeshua queried rhetorically.

"The Romans don't care about foreign spies," Stephanos flicked his hand. "He was arrested because he stole government property: the horses and chariot. Throw in the charges of aiding criminal Zealots, and he is as good as dead."

"We'll tell the Tetrarch those are false accusations," the young scholar argued.

"Your word against Roman soldiers?" the Greek rolled his eyes.

Germanicus broke in, "Maybe we can summon your siccarii friends from Jerusalem to help Quintus break free. Did you not say they're from the city?"

"You're absolutely correct," Yeshua exclaimed exuberantly, then checked himself. "But, I don't know their names, or where they live...all I know is one of them has a Judean accent. In Jerusalem everyone has a Judean accent."

"Like searching for a kernel of grain in the desert sand," the Greek mused.

They continued in the oppressive heat, and their eyes wondered to the boats resting on the beach. Yeshua studied their lines, stopping to admire some closer. Ever since he saw the first sailboat, he felt elated watching them cut through the waves silently. Last year in Capernaum, he often joined as crew, spending the evening ghosting on the lake. He loved the freedom, the endless blue skies and the hypnotic movement of the waves lapping the hull caressingly.

"I think you fell in love with boats," Stephanos quipped.

"I'm searching for that special inspiration the designer felt when he drew the perfect lines," he replied. "It is a rare find. It's the celebration of perfection: when imagination meets reality."

"A perfect line?" Germanicus studied a few boats and shrugged, "A boat is a boat!"

"No more than a person is a person," Yeshua corrected him. "Every person has a quality which defines him as unique. The boat with perfect line is the rarest of gems."

"How can you capture perfect lines?" Stephanos queried genuinely interested.

Yeshua raised his arms to the heavens, "How does one capture a moonbeam? Or the sun rays? Therein is the enigma: you recognize the perfect line when you see it. But nobody can capture let alone describe it"

"Why did you start building a sailboat?" the Greek asked.

"After my sermon they cancelled father's work, and I left the lyceum. But I hated carpentry because it depended on peoples' whims. Then I was inspired about fishing: people have to come to the fisherman if they wanted to eat…"

"Escape and control, the classical response of romantics," the Greek chuckled.

"When our fishermen headed out to the North Sea, they never knew their fate," Germanicus told them. "If a storm caught them, chances were they would perish."

"Fishermen live with a deep fervor and devotion: a continuous struggle of life and death," the Israeli concurred. "Few people are closer to God."

They continued north during the hottest time of day, thankful for every breeze that alleviated the suffocating humidity.

· · ·

When the two soldiers arrived in Nazareth, the old warrior walked up to a merchant in the agora bowing, "May the blessing of the morning be upon you." He smiled and the merchant nodded stiffly. "I am a friend of master Yeshua and bring important news. Can you direct us to his residence?"

Usually the locals would be wary of Roman soldiers and make thorough inquiries before deciding whether to cooperate. But, as master Joseph was on excellent terms with the legate, they saw no reason for suspicion. "Are the news about Yeshua's friend private Quintus?"

"Indeed they are," the old soldier smiled broadly.

"Good soldier, Quintus. Sympathetic to the Israelis," the old merchant volunteered.

The old warrior stretched his lips. "Yeshua just left for Augusteana," the Israeli said.

"Are you sure, old man?" his tone betrayed mistrust.

"As sure as I am of the identity of my mother. He was accompanied by the Greek and his slave. They purchased some figs from me."

The Romans turned and left gruffly. When they reached the forest the young soldier commented, "How will two of us arrest Yeshua's group? Should we not get support?"

"Arrest them?" the old codger gave him an evil smirk. "Who's the only person able to identify them as Zealots? Nehemiah, and he is gone... We'll do better..."

"Are you still planning to...?" the young man asked with fear in his eyes.

"Kill them? Of course! They'll pay for almost drowning us in the wadi; and leaving us defenceless in the forest."

For some time the young soldier had misgivings about his senior partner, but lately began to detest him. They trekked back into the forest and late in the afternoon arrived in Augusteana. The guard told them Yeshua's group proceeded to Capernaum, and they followed. They hardly exchanged a word, the old man planning revenge, while the youth began devising plans to frustrate him.

• • •

Dinner at the centurion Cornelius' was a superb feast compared to the spartan meals the young men usually had. They enjoyed lamb and fish with rich sauces on superb pasta all washed down with fine wine. After the meal they adjourned to the library for dessert.

Cornelius re-read the letter from his son, and folded it carefully, "The charges are sufficiently serious to give me pause...Coupled with accusations of aiding Zealots, and imprisoning Roman soldiers, the penalty will be...death!" He said it with the cold tone of a professional soldier.

Yeshua said they were going to Jerusalem the following day to help.

"Quintus will appreciate your support," the centurion remarked with a sigh. "Master Hariph is helping me retain the leading lawyer in Rome."

Stephanos whose mind was seldom at rest asked, "May I ask an impertinent question?"

"I have never known a Greek to ask any other kind," Cornelius quipped.

"Why does a retired Roman remain in this forsaken, snake-infested part of the world? You can have comfort...a villa in Sicily, ocean front in Corinth. Why here?"

"I'll ask you: Why did you choose Israel in your quest of the Messiah and God?"

The Greek contemplated before replying, "This is the source of God and Creation. Nowhere else does man communicate as personally with the Creator. Moreover, there is God's promise of a Messiah...Imagine, God's representative among men. My mind is exalted at the prospect of finding...Perhaps touching... "

"That's why I chose to stay. This is holy land: equally blessed as it is cursed," the centurion sighed with a chuckle. "Moreover where else can I go? Rome is doomed. Corruption permeates every facet of life. Proud institutions, the Praetorian Guard and the Order of the Tribunes, which only accepted the bravest citizens after a lifetime of service and achievement, now sells membership to the highest bidders. In Rome money is God!"

"Your greatest orator, Cicero said the Roman empire was a ship without a rudder," Stephanos commented, "Four fifths of Rome's residents are slaves. They do all the work and run the nation. If a wise man organized them, they could take over the empire."

"Couldn't someone like the Messiah organize them?" Germanicus mused.

The others looked strangely at the uninvited interruption without pursuing it.

"So you found your paradise here?" Stephanos returned to the subject.

"I'm a fish out of water: a foreigner here and a stranger in Rome," the centurion confessed. He shook his head, but in the next instant recollected more pleasant memories and smiled, "Here I am touched by real happiness every day. Wonderful people, the Israelis: farmers, fishermen, tradesmen...They have so little. But they are happy – here!" He poked his chest with the middle finger. "You are blessed to do Passover with them. This celebration is a spontaneous drama of their faith and tradition."

"Is that the reason you built them the synagogue?" Yeshua could not resist asking.

"That damn building brought me the happiest and most bitter days," he laughed gregariously. "We drew the plans with architects, re-drew, and argued over every stone and ornament into the early mornings. Drank wine, yelling, crying, singing, laughing, above all – arguing. The most minis-cule detail became crucial. You'd think Adonai ordered a specific number of stones, or the height of the building. Then came the construction: every villager stopped daily to inspect and criticize it, driving the stone masons crazy! The architect resigned weekly, and I had to persuade him to return."

They took a short break for dessert enjoying a small bowl of com-pote. As soon as they finished, Cornelius returned to his story, "The ulti-mate irony of that august edifice came when it was completed. I paid for the synagogue, helped plan and build it, and when it was finished I could not enter for the service. I'm an infidel, don't you know?'

Yeshua interjected, "I have decided to modernize Judaism into a uni-versal faith for all the people. You will be welcome in my church."

"I heard about your attempts. Is that why they tried to stone you?" Cornelius teased him. "What will happen to the classical Judaism? Some of their stories are captivating."

"Can you seriously accept circumcision, or rigid Mosaic food laws as fundamentals of a communion with the Creator?" Yeshua countered. "There must be more enlightened and meaningful paths to God."

"What path do you suggest get to God?"

"Love."

The centurion waited for a lengthy explanation only to see the young scholar staring back. He deliberated, then repeated, "Love…Is that it?" When Yeshua nodded, he smiled, "A small word, encompassing heaven and earth…I like it."

After a moment of silence the centurion asked, "Did you find the Messiah? That's what your expedition was about, was it not?"

Germanicus volunteered impulsively, "Absolutely. Personally, I believe he is among us…the people, I mean." He blushed, biting his lips, as he avoided their stares.

"Perhaps the Messiah discovered how ornery his people are, and chose to keep his identity secret." Master Cornellius laughed gregariously.

· · ·

It was the black of night when the two soldiers arrived in Capernaum and went to the centurion's street. The young man questioned the wisdom of the decision, "Why are we stalking them here? If they recognize us, we'll be arrested on the spot. You know how powerful these officers are."

"Recognize us? I can't see my hand in front of my face," the old warrior snapped. This is the perfect time to finish them off."

"Or finish our days in some god-forsaken prison!"

"What do you suggest, since you've become the self appointed genius?"

The young man tried very hard to think of a plan, but all he heard was his partner's deep sigh in the black night, and cringed for another heated argument.

. . .

A few moments later Yeshua's group left the centurion's to go to master Hariph's house, only a block away. Though it was close the walk was a precarious exercise that night.

"I would hate to meet my enemy now," the Greek spoke with trepidation. " I feel like a helpless hen walking into the jaws of the fox."

"He would not have an advantage if you stopped clucking," the slave teased him.

"Are you certain we're going in the right direction?" master Stephanos queried.

"We're close," Yeshua assured them. "There it is; the one with the porch."

"Porch? I can't even see a house," Germanicus complained.

"I don't see which direction you're pointing," the Greek added.

Soon after the Israeli knocked on the door and waited. They heard footsteps and the door creaked open. An oil lamp stabbed the dark first, then a tall, thin man with a long grey beard and graying hair put out his head, and they recognized master Hariph. When he saw Yeshua be broke into a broad smile. But when he saw the earring and a small slit on Germanicus' left ear lobe he remembered the slave. He glanced at the Greek and his smile disappeared. Yeshua knew Stephanos would be in for a rough night.

Hariph stepped aside motioning Germanicus to enter first. The slave stood embarrassed as he never proceeded before his master. Yeshua guessed the scribe's plan and pushed him in, then followed. The gesture caused the Greek's face to darken, and he decided to have words with the host that very night about the proper order of things.

Master Hariph was a scribe, and the only lawyer in the region. His office was in the living room which was filled with scrolls, parchments of leather, papyrus and copper sheets, as well as law books, piled up helter-skelter on two large desks, chairs, stools credenzas and the floor. To find space for his guests he rearranged piles onto the floor. Yet, in this confusion he could easily locate a document or a file. When they settled down, he requested his wife to bring tea and biscuits, over the objection of the guests.

She tempted them with a winning smile, "It's all freshly baked; and your favorites with honey and raisins, master Yeshua." They could not resist the offer, or her smile.

"Master Yeshua worked for me last summer," the scribe explained. "Once you had a dream; to be the High Priest? I hope my hard work did not destroy your dream."

"You could not be more demanding than he," Stephanos quipped. "He's a slave driver." As soon as he said "slave" he cringed, while the scribe's lips stretched.

Yeshua rubbed his chin uncomfortably, "I had to leave the lyceum after the sermon. I ended up working as a carpenter which I hated."

"Being stuck in a tiny workshop, making sieves is hardly carpentry," the Greek interjected. "It's slavery!" Again Stephanos' face turned crimson. The scribe knew from that moment he had a grip on the Greek's mind, but his eyes did not betray his glee.

"So, I decided to become a fisherman," Yeshua continued. "I designed a sailboat which a crew of friends is presently constructing."

"Remember how you disappeared every evening and went to the lake?" Hariph reminded him. "Were you searching for freedom?"

Yeshua nodded with a smile, "I probably was…until master Stephanos persuaded me to trek the the country in search of the legendary…"

"The Messiah," the scribe finished the statement. "Centurion Cornelius showed me letters from Quintus. Most interesting…" That triggered something and he changed topics abruptly. "Have you heard of the charges against him? I fear the matter is hopeless…"

They slumped visibly hearing his opinion. The scribe's wife arrived with the tea and biscuits and seeing them dejected commented, "What a gloomy bunch. Has my husband been telling you his theory about the impending end of the world?" Before he could deny it she added, "Never mind, these sweets will lift your spirits."

They thanked her and proceeded to gorge themselves.

Yeshua explained how he changed his plans from the priesthood, to fishing, to leading the expedition in search of the Messiah.

"Ah, the luxury of youth: making and changing plans at will," the scribe mused. "That is why the good Lord slows time for the young. But you are not finished with the Messiah. There are still two strong candidates between here and Jerusalem: Master Theudas along the Jordan, and Rabban from Egypt...Some swear Rabban is stronger than Samson. Many believe he is the real Messiah."

"Impossible. None of them are the real Messiah," Germanicus protested, but when they turned to him he drew back meekly, surprising himself by his impulsive outburst.

"Can we see some of your ancient parchments?" Master Stephanos returned to the topic which really interested him. "Yeshua said you possess truly rare ones, which may clearly identify the holy man."

"To what do you refer specifically?" Master Hariph queried.

"Everything. We criss-crossed half the nation searching for him," the Greek lamented. "It was like trying to catch the wind. Everywhere they assured us that the next person would be the saintly man. After seeing them at work, they all failed miserably. We don't know who we seek: a divine sage, or a super-human warrior?"

"Ancient prophets interpreted divine revelations not vital statistics," Hariph explained not unkindly. "You have to read between the lines, and make deductions. Perhaps the problem is not with what is being analyzed, as with the analyst..."

The Greek interjected with a sense of wonder as he reminesced, "I met two sages who told me they had traveled to Israel to witness the birth of the anointed one. The birth was marked by a bright star...over a village near Jerusalem..."

"Ah, yes I remember," the scribe assented. "That happened almost two score years ago. Some did assert that was the birth of the Messiah..."

"The story was exaggerated, I am positive," Yeshua interrupted forcefully, but with a defensive tone. "I heard it was a myth." They looked at him surprised, waiting for an explanation. However, he retreated with a lame mumble, "I was told it was an exaggeration of exuberant parents. Their first child..."

Master Hariph returned to his explanation, "There were many prophecies in ancient times and two exceptional ones more recently. But, don't forget, those prophets were not reading from written documents. They were interpreting messages from dreams, séances or geological events. Moreover they were not scholars, but simple peasants with deep inspirations."

"What kind of bizarre reporting is that?" Stephanos replied in a tirade. "The Greeks have meticulous notes of all our great philosophers, scientists, and..."

The scribe interrupted, "Remember when our prophets were scribing parchments, the Greeks were still wearing animal skins and lived in caves. Our holy men were little more than medicine men. Furthermore, living under the Roman boot, only a courageous fool would announce he is the Messiah."

Stephanos nodded, "As the adage says, 'Only the most valiant flea dares to eat its breakfast on the lips of a lion.'"

Meanwhile master Hariph found a couple of old yellow scrolls and unrolled the first one gently, "This one is from Moses...he describes..."

The Greek interrupted him with a flick of his hand, "I've read it: it's too general to be of any help."

He put it down and brought out another, "This was scribed by prophet Zechariah; he offers some description, "He rides triumphant and victorious, but humble and riding on an ass..."

"I knew it," Germanicus' reaction was instantaneous and impulsive. "He favors the humble animal, and is of peasant stock...That's him. That's the Messiah."

"That applies to most Israelis," Yeshua interrupted hoping to deflect attention from him. "Did you decipher the parchments from the cave?"

"I saved the best for last," Hariph smiled coyly. He unfurled it carefully. "These were bone dry, so after humidifying them I copied from the original..."

"What did you do with the originals?" the Greek asked.

"Put them back in the same cave, closed the entrance with rocks and mortar, covered with dirt and seeded it with grass. They will be safe for thousands of years."

"Did you find out who scribed those parchments?"

"Essenes, a religious sect from Qumran, by the Dead Sea. Their prophets spoke of the Messiah." He raised the papyrus and read carefully: " 'An angel will visit a maiden. She will deliver God's child, and the heavens will sing Hosanah. He will suffer at the hands of man, but will conquer death. His teachings will spread throughout the nations.'"

They did not notice, for they became mesmerized by the writings, but Yeshua's face turned white and he felt a heavy pounding in his head.

Stephanos considered the passage for a long time, and when he spoke he weighed every word, "This is clear to some extent: the child born two score years ago was the Messiah...and is presently among us...But who is he? Will we ever find him?"

Germanicus rolled his eyes to the sky. As brilliant as his master was, sometimes he seemed to be living inside an opaque bottle, he thought.

The Greek stood up, "Now if you would kindly direct us to our room..."

"We have a long journey ahead of us," Yeshua could not escape fast enough.

Hariph's demeanor suddenly changed from a docile scholar to a hardened court room lawyer, as he addressed the Greek, "Sit down, I'm not finished with you!" His snarly voice caused them all to freeze, Yeshua in the act of stretching and Stephanos yawning. "Sit down, please," he motioned the Greek who fell heavily on the stool. "What gives you the right to own another human being?"

"I...I paid for him...I mean, my father bought him, and gave him to me as a present," the Greek stared stupefied and completely on the defensive.

The scribe's face darkened and he scowled, as his eyebrows furled touching each other, "You buy a goat, or an ass. They have no souls. Humans have a soul, and you cannot bargain for them."

"I don't want his soul. He can keep it," the Greek tried a lame quip which fell flat.

The scribe's dark fiery eyes remained fixed, staring into his opponent's eyes, "Souls belong to God. And God is the only one they are to serve."

"That's fine with me, as long as he serves me the rest of the time."

The Greek's simplistic replies infuriated the old scholar whose voice took on the hardness of steel, "Beasts of burden were created to serve our needs. People have one master: the Lord. That is why they were given the power of reason and a soul!"

"I already said I claim no ownership to any of those. He can have them all, unhindered. I just want…his time," Stephanos shuffled on the stool uncomfortably, realizing the old lawyer had been sparring, and now would start in earnest to exert pressure.

"Save your lame excuses for your scholarly friends," Hariph countered unimpressed. "When you bought him you imprisoned his body, his soul, his spirit and his future: in short – his entire life. He has no time left to serve his Creator." Then he raised his voice slightly, but firmly, "Give him back his manhood. Let him free!"

"He's not shackled. He is free to serve God - on his own time," Stephanos began to perspire heavily and his brain was in a state of fog and confusion. He knew his replies were shallow, but could not think of substantive answers. Worst of all, he knew the lawyer was sharpening his knife for the final attack.

Germanicus almost came to the defense of his master, but, remembering the recent events with Anna and Lygia, decided to remain an impassive spectator.

Hariph stretched and leaned forward in his chair, like the lion of Judah, which was how he thought of himself in court, "Are you telling me, if Germanicus chose to leave, you would not stop him?" He watched the Greek biting his lower lip and his eyes darting for an escape. He knew he had him in his hand, and was tighting the grip. "If he decided to serve his Creator with his tribe in northern Europe you would let him go?"

The Greek did not respond but foolishly chose to counter-attack, "Recently he found a baby in the woods which he wanted to keep. I did not want it…but I gave in. And, when he wished to marry Anna against…I sacrificed my needs to him!"

Hariph guffawed loudly causing his thin frame to jump, "I expect you would. Germanicus, as a happier slave, will serve you better. Anna, feeling gratified, will serve you. And, together they'll raise the child to please you. Three slaves for the price of one!" He had the Greek in a vice-grip, and from long experience he realized if he eased the pressure gently he may be pleasantly rewarded. He relaxed and spoke softly, "Tonight, at the door, I invited Germanicus in before you. You were angry. Yet, every day he sacrifices his desires to satisfy your whims first and formost."

"You refer to us as enemies," the Greek whimpered with a whining tone. "I value him as a friend – a brother."

"Then why would you enslave a friend, especially a brother?" Hariph asked knowing it could not be answered. He watched the Greek's jaw unhinge, and continued tenderly, "True friends don't treat each other as chattels. I dare say if necessity called, he would offer his life to defend you!"

"He did! He saved my life – twice." Stephanos blurted out, before realizing he gave away the last chance of winning the argument.

Hariph's heart leaped, but outwardly his mask remained as ineffable as the Sphinx. He glanced at Yeshua and with an imperceptible flick of the eyebrows told the young scholar to take Germanicus and vacate the room. The scribe's voice acquired the velvet softness of an angel as he whispered, "Master Stephanos, you are serving the world magnificently, trying to learn God's word, and finding the Messiah. Do you know his first lesson? Love thine neighbor as you love yourself."

· · ·

The following morning the young men said farewell to the scribe and his wife and pressed on. They wanted to cross the Jordan and be on the highway by sunrise.

Germanicus' night had been one long nightmare. He had been unhappy for a long time, but last night master Hariph reopened the festering wound, proving more clearly than ever that his future was hopeless. He dreamt he was out in the water enjoying a relaxing swim, when an invisible force pushed him down. He continued swimming submerged, surprisingly comfortable until he tried to rise for air. Before he surfaced he was pushed him down, again and again. He began to struggle, desperate, suffocating, trying to reach the surface, which he could see, but could not reach. His lungs ached until he thought they would explode. When he looked up he saw his master holding him down, laughing, "I'll never set you free Germanicus, ha, ha ha. Never!"

He awoke in a panic gasping for air, his heart pounding and his entire body wet from perspiration. After some moments he realized it was just a dream and dozed off. But the nightmare returned. The whole night he suffered until morning. When Yeshua shook him to get him up, he let out a scream frightening the entire household.

As he walked he stared at his master with intense dislike, verging on hatred. He feared that if he had a dagger he would finish him off. He resolved at that moment to become a free man, or die trying. Death was better than living as a human chattel.

As they approached the major highway east of the Jordan river the sun broke over the horizon. They stopped to enjoy the surreal view: before them, a mere dozen paces was an endless procession of pilgrims, advancing from the north, proceeding slowly to the south to the holy city of Jerusalem. They were the Diaspora, Israelis living outside the nation's borders, dispersed over the earth. Once every year they made this trek, mingling with locals, gentiles and Roman soldiers.

They wore a riot of colors: blue and orange robes from Babylon, greens and yellows from Persia, orange and black from northern Celecia, mixed with a kaleidoscope of reds, browns, purples of the pilgrims' robes and soldiers' uniforms. Yeshua noticed some groups wore similar colors and guessed correctly that they belonged to one extended family. Some formed as few as three members, others over a hundred people. Interspersed with the pilgrims he recognized merchants with their caravans of loaded camels, hoping to reap a handsome profit at the religious feast. A little further out he saw an entire circus crew: large wagons pulled by camels or elephants, transporting exotic animals from far off India or Africa. Children left their parents and ran to travel with the circus, gawking at giant tigers, growling lions and restless bears, animals that once roamed free in the forests of Israel. Alas, civilization hunted them down and razed their habitats. Acrobats and gymnasts turned summersaults endlessly. A muscular youth with amazing balance walked on his hands for many miles before getting back on his feet.

In dramatic contrast there were cripples, dragging themselves on crutches, others with twisted and deformed, or missing limbs. And there were beggars. All traveled on the annual pilgrimage, searching for a coin or hoping for a miracle.

Yeshua heard an infinite variety of foreign languages: Macedonian, Greek, Gaulish from the west, eastern languages of Syrians, Babylonians and Indians. Most could not communicate with each other though they shared a common Judaic religion. Their universal language was Koine Greek, the language of the empire for over three hundred years.

Finally, as welcome as lepers in a health spa, were the Roman soldiers, travelling with the pilgrims though not a part of them. Tetrarch

Valerius Gratus requested that every fort in Israel send out a few hundred soldiers to Jerusalem to help keep order and quell any rebellions. The commander from Capernaum sent two hundred, composed of infantry, archers and engineers. They marched smartly and rigidly in full battle uniforms with breast plates, shields and plumed helmets a veritable show of disciplined organization. They marched in a perfectly straight line, led by the centurion, proudly flying banners of the empire and the colors of the regiment. They were wedged in at the front and rear by the rag-a-tag, easy going, partying Israelis. The centurion could easily have his soldiers marching at twice the pace but for the fact that the Israelis, in a silent conspiracy intentionally slowed their progress, forcing the soldiers to swelter in the sun every day, confined in the sauna of their airless uniforms and claustrophobic helmets.

The Israelis allowed their children to "run away" and play games of catch, or hide-and-go-seek among the soldiers, bumping and pushing them roughly during the game. They had no idea that the innocent game would soon escalate to a crisis, leading them to the brink of a battle.

Stephanos stared at the endless procession and spluttered with wonder, "Are these snails all crawling to Jerusalem?"

Yeshua nodded, "Every year the pilgrimage is repeated. They say the city swells from two hundred thousand to more than a million for the Passover."

An old patriarch saw them and waived frantically, "Over here! Come join my family." As he waived and called, he began to push his family members out of the way, "Get over. Make room for our guests." Then he motioned, "Get in here!"

Yeshua's group joined and was quickly swallowed up by the humanity. They walked immediately in front of the Roman army. They did not see two Roman soldiers, an old warrior and a youth who had followed them since dawn. They joined the procession immediately behind the army.

The old patriarch put his arm around Yeshua, "My name is Azim. These are members of my family, those are my servants and slaves yonder." He swept his bony arm in a wide semi-circle. Yeshua guessed his extended family consisted of more than thirty members wearing orange and blue colored cloaks. "We spring from Antioch." Then he pointed to an old man beside him, "This is my friend master Micah from Damascus."

"Thank you for inviting us," Yeshua smiled. "These are my friends, master Stephanos, a Greek scholar, and his slave Germanicus. I am Yeshua of Nazareth."

"Welcome to my family," Azim beamed a smile, and turned to Germanicus. "Go and join our servants and slaves. They will take good care of you." He pointed ahead.

Germanicus studied the slaves, deciding on impulse to join them. As he proceeded, a plan began to germinate in his mind: if an opportunity arose, he would try and melt into the crowd, and vanish like a dew drop in the desert.

Stephanos began to enjoy the trek but at first could not put his finger on why, until it struck him. He turned to the patriarchs elated, "I had almost forgotten the pleasure of walking on a level Roman highway. For months I suffered this country's roughest, treacherous roads, if one could call them that, where one could lose one's camel in a rut."

"As I always told my dear wife," Micah pointed to his ladened donkey. "Augustus may be a pompous tyrant, but he gave us fifty thousand miles of the best roads."

"They were not concerned with your comfort," Yeshua corrected him. "Their interest was to move their legions swiftly against us, and to charge high toll fees."

"Like I told my dear wife," Micah again pointed to the donkey. "the best roads which no one could afford to travel."

"Pardon my curiosity," Stephanos asked, "You keep referring to your wife on the donkey, but there is no one on it. Could she have fallen off, and you did not notice?"

Micah chuckled, "Oh no. My dear wife died three years ago. But, it was her dying wish to go to Jerusalem, so I am bringing her bones in that sack."

The Greek looked at the sack next to him and started to distance himself from both.

Meanwhile Germanicus maneuvered himself and the uncooperating camel as subtly as he could between the servants and slaves, separating one from the other. He studied the slaves closely and was surprised that he felt no affinity for them. They were unkempt, dusty and dirty, their hair disheveled and matted down. They were unwashed, and their cloaks filthy. Their foul appearance repulsed him. They seemed like savages, uncivilized creatures from the wilds of Hispania or Lusitania. But he was desperate and needed allies and confidants. He leaned close to one of them and whispered, "I am Germanicus, a slave…just like you. My master is Stephanos, over there," he pointed over his shoulder. The slave looked and found himself staring at the camel. "I want some information about escaping. Do you know of plans…to escape and run for freedom?"

The slave stared at him with disbelief, looked at the others, then they glared at him suspiciously without the slightest hint they understood a word he said. After a long time they began to scoff, slowly at first, then louder and louder, until Germanicus joined them.

Suddenly the slave he had spoken to scowled, leaned towards him snarling, "Do you think we are stupid? Did our master send you to test us…our allegiance? Is that what you are - a spy?"

"No, no, honest, I'm not. Please believe me," Germanicus pleaded.

"Get out! Get out of here before I call your master and tell him what you said…"

Germanicus panicked, "No! Don't do that. If he finds out, I'll…I'll be finished."

"Get out before I plunge this in your traitor's heart," the slave pulled something shiny from his belt which appeared to be a dagger.

He was shocked by the rude reception and veered abruptly to the right, causing the camel to trample the servants and a couple of pilgrims, but dared not stop until he was a great distance from the savage slaves. He trembled the rest of the day from fright and exhaustion. He walked alone, cursing his bad luck, muttering, "I hate slaves. The most ignorant, mistrusting lot…they deserve everything they get…Stupid…"

Alas, many Diaspora who planned and started the trek to Jerusalem did not complete it. For a variety of reasons the sands of time slipped through the hour glass before they were able to go, by which time the lengthy journey, and arduous pace, got the better of their infirm, tired bodies. Many stopped for long rests. Some, like master Micah undertook the journey to fulfill a promise to a dying spouse to bury her remains within the walls of the holy city.

Almost daily one group or another dropped out and was left behind to tend to a sick or dying relative. When the member passed away, they buried him in the lonesome valley under the stars, where the murmuring waters of the Jordan rolling only a few paces away, would serenade him in eternal sleep.

To be sure, not all sick or dying were old and infirm. In the harsh conditions of the time, children suffering malnutrition were weak and sickly, and easily succumbed to illness. It broke Yeshua's heart to see such underdeveloped tots. Too often he saw families transporting skinny children, like living skeletons, with deep coughs, hoping the Lord would provide the miracle of a cure.

No child touched him more than Ellie, a little girl aged eleven, as thin as a dry twig, who was not able to take more than a half dozen steps under her own power without slumping down, wheezing and fighting to swallow some air. Master Azim said that she was as critical and weak when he first met the family in Antioch, but, of late the girl was visibly sliding down.

Back at her home in Corinth no doctor could diagnose her ailment precisely nor prescribe proper medicine, potions or a diet to help her. Professors of science from the university of Athens opined that her lungs were either being consumed by miniscule worm-like microbes, or that her lungs were not fully developed. They could not agree which was correct, and suggested different remedies. Out of desperation her parents accepted both, and Ellie swallowed horrible potions dutifully. Then she battled to keep it down. Alas, the potions not only failed to cure, but complicated her illness. New scientists from the university of Alexandria said the problem was her heart, but were not able to explain what was wrong with it, or prescribe a cure. The parents dared not utter it, but they knew her case was hopeless. They borrowed heavily for the pilgrimage and the last hope: to sacrifice a full grown bull at the Temple hoping a miracle would save their only child.

The family walked immediately behind the Roman army, and pilgrims took turns each day and carried Ellie to the banks of the Jordan so she could watch the children splash and laugh gregariously. When her father could no longer push her small cart daily, an ancient patriarch gave up his place on his son's cart, pulled by an ass, and he walked in pain feigning absolute delight to be able to give his place to such a lovely princess. Ellie's parents adopted him, calling him grandfather, which thrilled him. But, even such kindness and sacrifice failed to strengthen the girl. The older women, with vast experience about the subtleties of life and death, murmured that Ellie would not live to see Jerusalem.

Last night Ellie's condition took a turn for the worse. The pilgrims stopped for the night, setting up camps, to cook and rest. Her father lay her cot outside the tent to give her fresh air and the pale girl lay motionless, her frail chest rising and falling imperceptibly. Only her blinking eyelids twitched showing signs of life. Her mother, in her saintly hope, failed to recognize the presence of death, but the father knew his precious girl was breathing her last. He asked the adopted grandfather to take charge as he stole away to find a rabbi. Wherever he stopped to inquire people recognized him, for the story of Ellie had spread for many miles. People dropped whatever they were doing and came to see her for the last time. They wanted to give words of encouragement, give her a smile or just bring their love and prayers.

When Yeshua's camp heard the news they left the pot on the fire and followed the multitude. Upon arriving Yeshua pleaded to be let through, and squeezed forward until he and his friends stood at the front, about a cubit from her cot.

Yeshua looked down at the frail skeleton, with sunken eyes and white skin as transparent as the thinnest papyrus, and thought of his sister Debborah. The girls were the same age, yet his sister was vibrant, active, full of good humor and the full spectrum of emotions, whereas Ellie lay as lifeless as a rag doll, about to break her parents' hearts. He was tempted to reach out and touch her, pray and ask his heavenly Abba for her health and her life. But, when he looked at the hundreds of people on top of them he froze. He knew if he cured her, he would create a commotion, and not be able to quell the furore and unwanted attention. Moreover the Romans, paranoid about any charismatic leader, would be quick to imprison him. If they thought he posed a risk to the empire, no matter how tenuous their suspicion, they would execute him summarily. They did not suffer any type of leaders among these religious fanatics.

His brain raced to make a decision: intervene or turn away. Torn by pressures to save her life and his own future, his mind became paralyzed. Ultimately he rationalized he could not save everybody.

Ellie's father returned with the rabbi who took one look at her and acted, "She needs air. Move back!" He yelled at the people pushing them. "Move back, all of you. Move! Move away! Can you not see you're suffocating her? Go back to your camps. Move. You're killing her."

The rabbi pushed and shoved them in one direction while the father, utterly desperate, pushed in the opposite direction. At first the curious multitude stood, too sad and engrossed to react, then slowly, as if hypnotized by the presence of death let themselves be shoved away, then began to turn and shuffle away, with tears streaming.

Yeshua seized the opportunity, stepped forward and knelt over Ellie. He took her hand with his left, placing his right hand on her head, gazing intensely into her closed eyes, "Ellie, come back to us. Do not leave us," he whispered, his radiant eyes riveted on her. She opened her eyes, gazed at him, and blinked a few times. "Go to sleep now. Sleep soundly. When you awake you will be well again," he said, and she closed her eyes. An aura of light started to glow about his head, enveloping him as he prayed, "Dear Abba, let Ellie live. She is the only source of happiness in her parents' lives. They need her." A flash of light traveled through his arms and over her body covering it in a shower of sparks. He remained praying for some moments, then stood up, turned away and melted into the night.

Stephanos and Germanicus who had been pushed back stopped when they saw Yeshua kneel over the girl. They heard his prayer and watched the miracle as if hypnotized. The physical transformation overtaking him and the girl, the bright light, the bolt of light which showered her were as incredible as they were ineffable.

Ellie fell into a deep slumber and began to breathe deeply, but strongly and evenly. Then her chalk white cheeks began to take on a healthy rosy color. Her skinny frame, almost all skin and bones began to fill with substantive mass. Stephanos had never seen such physical transformation, and even as he watched her, his intellect told him what he saw was impossible. He was seized with panic and began to draw away. He concluded he must be in the presence of some monstrous, evil, and undoubtedly a supernatural force beyond comprehension, and probably dangerous. He turned to run but Germanicus' powerful grasp stopped him.

"Do not fear, master. This is what I tried to tell you: It is a miracle," he said with wonderment. They stayed and watched it unfold.

Ellie's mother saw Yeshua kneel and pray over her daughter and was touched by the young man's tender concern. But, when she saw his radiant eyes, then the bright light about his head she did not know what to make of it. She leaned over to look at her child to see if she was alright, at first curious about her transformation, then perplexed and finally totally confused. Was Ellie recovering? Was she witnessing a miracle? She jumped up and ran in search of her husband. "Aaron! Aaron," she yelled as she ran every which way in the dusk, "It's a miracle! Ellie...she's fine...

Ellie is fine…Oh, my dear God…" She ran searching for him with tears of joy and delight.

Her husband grabbed her as she was running by, "Mona, what's with this yelling? Are you alright? Is Ellie…?"

"Aaron, it's a miracle," she answered laughing and crying. "Blessed be God…!" She could not stop trembling, looking up to the stars, then at him. "Ellie is cured!" Mona blurted out and kept repeating it, "Ellie is cured…"

"Are you sure?" Aaron was skeptical, starting to wonder if his wife was having a breakdown, as he dragged her back to camp. They were still a long distance from the cot when he saw the girl and stopped. Then he approached slowly unsure of what was happening, or what to do. Never before in her short life did Ellie have such full, healthy, rosy cheeks. He came close, not daring to touch her, "Mona, who did this? What happened?" he whispered with astonishment.

"A very nice young man," she pointed to where Yeshua had been, muttering in confusion. "He's not there…Perhaps…it was an angel…"

"Mona, where is he? What did he look like? Look around, perhaps he is in the crowd," he blurted out the questions as he gazed at spectators still lingering.

She looked at their faces trying to remember. "He was young…like an angel…a pleasant, soothing voice. He prayed, told her to go to sleep… But, I don't see him, I'm so confused." Then she pointed directly ahead, "I think he went that way."

They walked past Yeshua's camp, hoping to see the angel, though neither knew for whom they were searching, or what to say when they saw him.

Two other unexpected spectators stood less than ten paces away also witnessing the miracle. They were the tracking Roman soldiers. Pushed away by the frantic father they had turned to leave, when they saw the aura of light about Yeshua. Curious, they stayed and were astounded by what they saw. Romans were very superstitious and feared he was an evil witch or sorcerer. The old soldier instinctively covered his eyes with his arm warning his young companion, "It's black sorcery. Don't look or you'll be blinded."

They continued to back away, frightened yet curious, and arguing.

"How can that be black magic? He saved that girl. He performed a miracle," the young soldier exclaimed, filled with awe and admiration. "He must be a God."

"Don't be a superstitious fool! It's sorcery," the old warrior yelled. "If you ever say such foolish superstition to your officers, they'll ship you off to the wildest frontier."

They started back to their camp flabbergasted by what they had seen, neither of them comprehending, let alone explaining it.

"I admit it was the most impressive magic," the old soldier mused. "I have seen a prophetic soothsayer in Carthage, drank magic potions in the far corners of Hispania, and saw hypnotic illusions in the Parthian kingdom. This is…supernatural…witchcraft."

They were almost back to their camp when the young soldier excused himself, "Go ahead. I want to go to the river to…wash up." The young soldier went to the bank of the Jordan and sat down. He felt he needed to be alone to do some serious contemplating.

He could not verbalize the nature of the changes he saw with Ellie or Yeshua, but he felt there was a supernatural influence present. His intuition told him he had been in the presence of a God. He knew he could not share this with any of his Roman friends, especially his old companion, but he also knew he could not allow any harm to come to the young God-man. His decision would send him on a collision course with the senior companion, a most precarious situation. He was at a crossroad and had to make a decision: defend the interest of the empire, or protect a stranger who he thought was a saintly man. Faced with the enormous question, he sat, with his head pounding.

When Ellie's parents passed by Yeshua's camp, he was stirring the pot. Mona slowed down and looked his way once, then a second time.

"Is he the miracle man?" Aaron inquired.

She nodded, then reconsidered and shook her head, shrugging her shoulders, "I don't know. It all happened so fast…the burning eyes, a bright light about…Ellie changing. I can't say…" They continued another hundred paces and gave up.

Stephanos and the slave returned to camp, stopping some distance from Yeshua, then approaching slowly. The Greek stared at the Israeli as if seeing him for the first time. Never before in his life had he seen anything he could not reason or explain logically. After an inordinate length of time, he came to two conflicting resolutions: that was the most impressive magic trick, or…a miracle. As he could not explain away the former, he had to accept the latter. It meant they were in the presence of a Deity. Stephanos had long suspected there was a world of gods and angels, where everything was new and different. But how? He was certain that world was alien to humans, perhaps not rational or logical as they thought of it. But, his reason told him it had to be super powerful, capable of exerting extraordinary forces, beyond anything humans could ever achieve.

An idea began to germinate in his mind: how to harness Yeshua's powers, and use it to conquer nations…perhaps the whole world. "We travelled the whole country searching for…for someone who was with us all the time. Germanicus tried to tell me, but I was too…blind. How long have you known…? Have you seen your powers? Do you know the full extent of…? Have you thought about the potential of those powers?"

"I was told on the eve of the expedition," the Israeli replied, as he replaced the lid on the pot. "No, I have not thought about it…I do what I have to… What's right."

"What you did back there was stunning, beyond comprehension… astonishing…it defies logic," Stephanos spluttered like a gushing river. "Do you know what you did?" Yeshua nodded. Stephanos continued stubbornly, "You're the greatest show on earth. You stopped time defeating death, then rushed time to cause her full recovery. You have power over life, death, time and all physical matter…You're God in our midst."

"Master Yeshua, are you a God?" Germanicus whispered with trepidation.

Yeshua was disturbed by the question, but not willing to answer it. He feared the day when he would be discovered and questioned. He sighed, baffled, "I don't know…"

The Greek gushed, "You were born two scrore years ago…you are probably the prophesized child." When he said this, his eyes opened wide as if making a lifetime discovery. "Was master El Sharif the third sage from the east?" he asked, and when the Israeli nodded, he raised his voice declaring eccstatically, "Master Yeshua, you are the Mes…"

"Not so loud," Yeshua raised his hands pleading.

"… the Messiah," the Greek whispered. "Do you know what that means? In your hands you hold unlimited power…to conquer the world….control all nations…"

"I have never even seen any of my miracles," Yeshua shrugged nonchalantly.

"You haven't? Go see Ellie in the morning. By Zeus, you will be flabbergasted." Stephanos leaned over, speaking with a sinister tone. "We have to harness your power to get control. Unleash it when we are ready.

If we organize this, we will be able to defeat every legion in the world. No nation will stop us. We'll control the Roman empire."

"I don't want to defeat legions…or control empires," Yeshua rebelled, taken back by the peculiar shine in the Greek's eyes, who seemed like a madman.

But Stephanos was overwhelmed, drunk by the newly discovered power in their grasp, becoming dizzy, imagining its potential, and refusing to listen. He continued wildly, "Armies will not stand up to you. You'll control the world and all the elements. We'll destroy any nation standing in our way. We'll liberate Israel. Free the world…"

"I never wanted that!"

"Of course you do! The world will be at your feet. Your wishes will be fulfilled; your whims obeyed. You will rule with resplendent majesty. All glory and exultation will be yours," the words cascaded uncontrollably from his lips. It seemed sanity had left him, "But, we have to plan it carefully: first you have to change your name…"

"What's wrong with Yeshua?"

"Tribal! Parochial! To be king, you need a royal name: invincible, something that emanates power…Supernatural - like Zeus!"

Germanicus was shocked with his master's strange behaviour, and grabbed him, "Master, try to control yourself."

The Greek pulled away violently, "Leave me be. Let's see: what's an appropriate name? Jose…? No, too common. Joss? No, it doesn't have the right ring…It has to be magical; a Greek name to bring attention, and silence the room. I have it – JESUS!"

Yeshua considered it shaking his head, "Jesus? I don't know…"

"You'll grow into it," the Greek continued to press, "Something else; a king needs a beautiful wife; like lady Sarah! I'll work on her to quit her pretensions and join forces with you. No one will believe you're godly unless you have a formidable spouse!"

Suddenly Yeshua exploded, "Leave lady Sarah out of this!" He stood up abruptly, leaned over the Greek and scolded him furiously, "I doubt that I'm the person you're searching for, but if I were, I would not have anything to do with your insane plans."

"Sit down, relax; let's discuss this…" Stephanos tried to calm him down.

"Is this what you wanted: to use me for your selfish purpose? If so, you can go back to Greece…" Yeshua threw the spoon down, and walked away furiously into the night.

His angry outburst brought the Greek back to reality. He realized he had overreacted to the fantastic miracle and lost total control. He ran after his friend hoping to make amends, calling out, "Yeshua, wait… please."

Germanicus followed them. Suddenly in the corner of his eyes he recognized two familiar faces: master Azim's two slaves who had threatened him that morning. They were hiding behind some trees, waving him over. He stopped. They beckoned him. He stood undecided, looked at his master who ran after Yeshua. He saw the slaves waving vigorously. He ran, but as soon as he got close, they ran off. He was about to give up when they called, "Psst, Germanicus, over here." When he joined them they explained that they wanted to be sure they were not being followed. They led him deep into the bushes by the river bank, entered through a narrow opening into a clearing deep within the bushes. There he saw dozens of slaves gathered around a fire.

His first impression was they all talked at once and nobody listened. They were loud, boisterous, most were complaining against their masters with deep hatred in their voices. It was a disorgarized anarchy. His intuition warned him to get out, and he turned to leave when a loud voice ordered silence. The speaker barked another order but nothing happened until a slave grabbed Germanicus, pushing him forward. He stood before the burly old man with long grey hair and a bushy beard, with cold eyes fixed on him, "Introduce yourself."

"Germanicus, from northern…" he started.

"Your name is sufficient. You were watched all day," he growled with a raspy voice, then leaned forward chewing every word between his brown teeth, "You are not a spy, are you? We abhor spies. We kill spies!"

"I'm not a spy," he blurted out defensively.

"Shut up! Don't speak until you're ordered to," he spat out, glaring at the new comer who recoiled. "Are you sincere about wanting freedom?"

Germanicus stood frozen and failed to respond.

"Well, are you?" the leader barked.

"Me?…Yes… yes…"

"Do you have any idea how difficult it is to get free? How few succeed?"

Gemanicus waited for an answer, but realized this brute would volunteer nothing unless asked, so he shook his head mumbling, "N-no, sir… How few?"

The leader stretched his mouth in a big sadistic grin. He was going to enjoy shocking the newcomer and all these dreamers with a cold dose of reality. "Sit down," he pointed for Germanicus to sit at his feet, which he did. Then he continued to speak slowly, deliberating, watching their shocked faces, "One slave in ten may succeed. The rest are killed or captured. There are bounty hunters who make a living hunting down scums like you. They get paid handsomely to bring you in - alive or dead. There are thirty of you here. Look around because only a handful will reach freedom!

"To help make your flight to freedom a success you have to learn to survive. We'll break you into many small groups of twos and threes. Each group will run in a different direction to maximize your chances of getting away." He leaned forward with his last bit of advice, "Tomorrow night we'll have our last meeting, and I'll give you the most important piece of advice. After that, it's Jerusalem...and FREEDOM." Everyone cheered at the mention of the word. "Remember the warning I repeat every night: be vigilant and watch each other like a hawk. Many masters offer handsome rewards for you to turn against your brother-slave. Our greatest enemy is the traitor lurking among us, spying, hoping to earn a handsome reward. If you notice anything suspicious do not hesitate," he pulled out a long dagger from his belt and held it up high, stood up and stepped forward. "Let him have it in the heart!"

He plunged the dagger into Germanicus' chest with all his might. There was a loud gasp, and then silence. Only the crackling of the burning wood could be heard.

Germanicus felt a tremendous pain in his chest. His mouth went dry, and he felt a burning sensation. He fell to his knees and felt faint. It was too absurd to be happening, he thought, and two tears formed in his eyes. Would he never see Anna, or Lygia again? Why did it happen to him? Why did he trust them? Everything started to swirl around: the stars, the fire, and the filthy face of the diabolical leader, standing above him...smirking. All blacked out and he fell in a heap.

CHAPTER XVIII - YESHUA KILLS A MAN

The following morning Yeshua went to see Ellie, to see his miracle first hand.

There he saw a large group of people milling about the camp. He overheard some of their comments: the miracle was performed by a rabbi, another said an angel did it then dissolved into thin air. They all guessed, but no one had seen him.

Yeshua realized the story would be told and retold until it acquired the flavor of a legend. He waited until they had left to continue his search. He saw a young girl sitting under a tree playing with a rag doll, and decided she could not be Ellie, as she was healthy and robust. When he looked closer and recognized her dress which had a prominent red rose embroidered on the front, chest high. Was this Ellie? He sat on the grass, his eyes riveted on her. When she noticed him, she lowered the doll and smiled, "Hello," she sang out. He returned her smile. "My name is Ellie. What's yours?"

"Yeshua. I am from the town of Nazareth."

She fixed her eyes on him and stared seriously, "You are the person who cured me." She spoke with a certainty in her voice and started to get up.

"Please, don't leave," he pleaded. "You cannot be certain…"

"Oh yes, I'm positive," she retorted, sitting back on her knees. "I recognize your voice. It's very soft. I opened my eyes and saw you praying… you had a bright halo…"

"Ps-s-t!" Yeshua put his finger across his lips. "Not so loud." He looked around cautiously and spoke in a low voice, "I don't want anybody to know…"

His vulnerability put her at ease. She said in a low voice, "I dreamt about you last night. I was entering a big mansion with many rooms, very bright and full of angels…. There was soft music as I approached a throne.

You sat on it. You said, 'Ellie go back to your parents. They need you.'"
She thought about it and asked, "Was I dreaming?"

"It sounded very real to me," he responded.

She added quickly, "I was not afraid of dying. I knew from the moment
I entered that house, that I would be happy there." She added sadly, "But,
my parents..."

"It breaks parents' hearts to lose a child."

She nodded but did not seem happy, "I felt sad for them. I wish I could
explain to them how happy I was there, but..."

Yeshua was impressed by her mature perception and understanding.
Realizing she had a friend in whom she could confide, she leaned forward,
"Sometimes parents are not very considerate...downright selfish," she
whispered, but when she saw the surprised look on his face, she quickly
added, "Because I am the only child, they would be left alone..." Suddenly
she smiled and asked, "Do you have brothers and sisters?"

"Oh, too many," he rolled his eyes to the sky dramatically. "Four
brothers and two sisters. My favorite is your age, only her hair is darker."

"What's her name?"

"Debborah."

"Debborah. Such a nice name. Does she go to school?"

She did not hear his reply as her mother called her to breakfast and
appeared from behind the tent at the same moment, "There you are, dear.
Come, it's breakfast time," the mother stopped when she saw him. "I
thought I heard voices. Good morning."

"Good morning, my lady," he greeted her with a smile.

"Come Ellie, breakfast," the mother attempted to pick her up as she
always did when the girl was feather-light. Now she was surprised, "My,
you are wonderfully heavy...and healthy; such a blessing." She took her by
the hand instead, addressing him, "I presume you have heard: our wonderful miracle." She smiled. Something made her stop, her eyes fixed on him,
"You seem familiar..."

Yeshua stood up worried and confused, and turned to leave, when
Ellie pleaded, "Don't go yet, please? Mother this is master Yeshua. He is
from Nazareth. He has four brothers and two sisters, and his favorite is
Debborah, and she is my age."

The mother smiled but her eyes remained fixed on him, "My name is
Mona. Will you join us for breakfast, master Yeshua?"

"I must return to camp," he muttered. "Breakfast will be waiting. Good day."

"Bye Yeshua. See you soon," Ellie waved and let out a piercing scream as her mother tickled her ribs, chasing her around the tent. As the girl ran, Mona looked back a couple of times, certain she had seen him before. But where? And when...?

Yeshua returned to camp pleased to see the happy mother enjoying her child. He was surprised by the degree of transformation of the girl, but did not dwell on his extraordinary powers, the extent or limitations of those powers. Nor did he ponder on the nature of the intervention that arrested the disease. It was unexplainable, contrary to the normal laws of nature and human logic, but he did not spend time contemplating it. He accepted that this was precisely the point: it was a miracle, beyond human comprehension, and normal experiences of mortals.

It fell to future generations of scholars, religious and secular, scientists and philosophers to attempt to explain how he transcended beyond this world and for one instant fused the world of man, with some other dimension beyond human comprhension, the world of spirits and faith. This was a world of angels, beyond man's sight or touch, but not beyond the vision of the psyche. It was the world of spirits and the soul. It was the world of the Creator where mortals did not normally enter, but which could transgress into man's physical world at will. Sometimes it did so, as in Ellie's case, to the surprise and delight of humans.

The scholars would argue that he had the gift, the power to call upon that world, and in one instant perform the miracle of Ellie: suspending the passage of time, arresting imminent death, at the same moment rushing the healing process, so what took months occurred in the blink of an eye. It was this bending of time, which was ineffable and incomprehensible to the human mind. But, those who knew that finity and time started with the moment of Creation, knew that special persons had the power to control them.

Not all relied on theories of metaphysics or faith to explain it. Some referred to the position of the stars or studied the innards of fowls, as astrologers and soothsayers did. Over the centuries many elegant, subtle and ingenious scholarly thesis were submitted to dissect, analyze and explain the miracle. Theories appeared and found new favor with generations, while older ones were discarded. Even cynics and skeptics entered the fray, denying the existence of miracles. Some dismissed them as mere illusions, sorcery or outright superstion. Men argued endlessly through the ages, accusing each other, causing irreparable divisions achieving little more than self aggrandizement.

None of those thoughts entered Yeshua's mind. He saw a happy mother enjoying her healthy child, and it was good. When he came to the path leading to his camp, he turned to the river bank instead where he relived the events of the previous night.

After their argument they sat on the bank of the Jordan, both with disorderly thoughts and in confusion. Yeshua despised the thought of marketing himself to the masses, or conquering nations or ruling the world. He looked across the waters in the direction of Nazareth and his thoughts went to lady Sarah. All he wanted was a wife and family...and his heart ached for her. Would she ever think kindly of him? He was never more furious or confused, on the verge of giving up religion altogether. All it ever caused was conflict between races and friends...his thoughts were disrupted by Stephanos who whispered with pain, "I spoke like an idiot...I lost my mind...my sanity...the miracle was such grand, fantastic, godly spectacle that I lost all my senses. I meant well, hoping to use your power for the good...change the world...for the better..."

Yeshua shook his head, "Don't you think I thought about that? But magic and glitter are temporary...and fickle - not permanent changes."

"You have a chance...Why pass up the opportunity?"

"Real changes come from the heart. Only those will pass the test of time."

"Are you back to that...love talk?" Stephanos sounded skeptical.

"When people put their trust in Yahweh, and love one another," the Israeli said, "then they will make changes...lasting changes."

"You're trying to change the heart of man," the Greek replied, "Not very realistic."

"Ever since the truth was revealed, I have thought and started, only to scrap and do it over." He let out a deep sigh, and continued with a tone of desperation, "Sometimes I feel like a painter working in the dark: mixing and splashing paint on the canvass with no idea what color I'm applying or what I am creating."

"We'll have to take control...keeping your identity a secret, of course."

"You're sparring with words. You're saying one thing, but I hear something different."

"You're right," the Greek sighed. "You can't have it both ways: do miracles or keep your privacy." When he saw the Israeli drop his head, he empathized, and put his arm around his shoulder. "Go see Ellie in the morning and you'll understand why people will never stop talking about it. You'll lose privacy but you'll give people hope." He was relieved when Yeshua nodded albeit, reluctantly, so he added cautiously, "Still, you'll have to make some changes…"

"Jesus?"

"Yes, Jesus."

The Israeli broke into a shadow of a smile, "Jesus sounds fine…when I am ready."

They stood up to return to camp, when Yeshua heard loud voices to the north in the bushes, turned and saw a group of men talking animatedly around a fire. He recognized Germanicus, and Azim's three slaves. He wondered why a group of slaves would be meeting in the dark, deep in the bushes, and as soon as he posed the question he knew the answer. He checked to see if Stephanos saw them, but he had started back to camp.

After his reminiscing he returned to camp where Germanicus was preparing breakfast. He looked around and not seeing the Greek, whispered, "Germanicus, is there a problem you wish to discuss?"

"Problem? What kind of problem?" he asked defensively, his eyes avoiding the Israeli. When he sensed Yeshua staring, he protested, "Stay out of my business."

"Last night I saw you in the bushes with the slaves. Have you thought this through? Do you know what it means being part of a conspiracy?"

"It can't be worse than my hopeless life," he snapped back like a cornered animal.

"Everybody has pressures, but that is no reason to react so extremely," Yeshua searched for the kindest words to persuade him.

"What could be worse: slavery or being imprisoned for life?"

"What would master Nehemiah give to be alive today? What about Quintus? Compared to them, you are blessed."

"Me, blessed? Forgive me for not dancing with ecstasy," he retorted sardonically.

"You have a kind master, a wife who loves you, and a wonderful child," the Israeli reminded him. "You do not deserve to be a slave, but, you can earn your freedom."

"That's a fool's dream," he mumbled. "I'll never know freedom… ever."

"Think of your blessings and you will find peace and tranquility in Yahweh's love."

Germanicus snapped impatiently, "Even if I wanted to, it's too late now." He turned and marched away furiously.

He walked a few hundred paces and sat under a tree. His mind was in turmoil and his chest pained. He touched the tender spot where the slaves' leader had punched him violently last night. When he struck him with the dagger, Germanicus was certain he had breathed his last. He grabbed his chest and felt a sharp pain. He checked for blood, but there was none. That's when he realized the leader had eased his grip on the dagger, allowing it to fall to the ground, while striking him with his fist.

Germanicus pondered about last night's confusion. He craved freedom but not with those boors. The leader was a deranged sadist, surrounded by ill-bred simpletons who would prove to be more of a hindrance than an asset. Many were beaten and abused by their masters. After being treated as animals was it surprising they behaved as animals? Perhaps master Yeshua was correct, if he continued with that crowd, he could pay with his life. But, could he turn back? If he tried, they would suspect he had betrayed them and kill him. Either way he was doomed. He knew he was disappointing master Yeshua, whom he revered and loved as his mentor and teacher. It was a love with religious fervor that he hoped would guide his life. Witnessing the miracle of Ellie, he knew he was in the presence of a special man…perhaps a God. It broke his heart to betray him.

He felt just as guilty for letting Anna and Lygia down. He had planned to run to Nazareth for them no matter what the leader said. But, when he reconsidered, he realized that was where the bounty hunters would go. He should run elsewhere and not compromise them. He sat totally confused, guilty for his family, but mostly for Yeshua.

Frustrated, he returned to camp in a foul mood. Yeshua saw that he was disturbed by the violent way he folded the tent, kicking and punching the equipment. The Israeli thought about calming him, but decided instead to respect his privacy. But he also realized Stephanos' life may be in danger, and decided to watch the slave closely.

The pilgrims resumed the journey as they did every morning since the first day: full of energy and enthusiasm. From a distance the fields and the multicolored apparel seemed as soft as the feathers of a bird. A grey haze rose from the Jordan, and flowers shone like flickering stars in the meadows. A vigorous conversation started with excitement, for each step brought them closer to their beloved Jerusalem.

They discussed the importance of the Jordan river to the region, but more importantly to the nation. The river was the lifeblood of the entire valley, not only supporting local farmers and villagers dotting the region, but also a wide variety of wild beasts which were abundant and roamed under the protection of thick bushes and trees. Time was when a great variety of animals crisscrossed the entire country, but most had been hunted down or chased into the shrinking forests.

But the river's real importance was as a living symbol of Israel, interlaced with their history, culture, tradition and deeply rooted in their religion. From the first time ancient Hebrews crossed it, it marked the return of the people to the lost land of paradise. No longer were they the wondering vagabonds of the world, for now they too had a homeland. However, only the most faithful were allowed to cross the Jordan. Moses, one of the most revered figures in Israeli history, questioned the Creator's designs, and was denied passage. The others traversed the river and entered the promised land of milk and honey. The first to cross were the priests carrying the box – the Ark with the Covenant.

Symbolically, the crossing of the Jordan signified washing away of past transgressions and rejuvenation to new life. Poems and songs, too numerous to count, had been scribed by poets and scholars, and leaders such as King David, and Solomon, his son. The haunting songs were enjoyed by the Diaspora who may never see the holy land, or the River. Yet, the Jordan of their imagination loomed bigger than any river in the world.

As the morning sun rose, heating the valley and raising the humidity, it dampened the enthusiasm of the pilgrims. By mid-morning the conversations began to slow and falter, from the zest and enthusiasm of early morning, to a subdued tone. Before midday the faltering conversations consisted of part sentences, followed by intermittent grunts and long periods of silence, a glaring absence of humor, and finally total silence. The noon sun weighed heavy on them like an anvil. Their trek suffered the same fate; from the energetic spring they slowed to a slow shuffle, and ultimately to the point where the oppressive heat made every step appear like the slow motion of a sloth. One by one the groups abandoned the highway for the shade of a tree. Some continued to the cool waters of the Jordan. There they splashed wildly in the refresing water. Like medicinal ointment, it was soothing, relieving and reviving. Within a few moments the pilgrims laughed with ecstasy, singing, frolicking and splashing the miracle of life into the sky.

Through all this the Roman army continued to march like a well oiled machine, oblivious to the changing moods of the pilgrims. That is, until they began to run to the river. Even then the marchers ignored them stoically and continued on. But the ecstatic screams pierced their eardrums, and their eyes darted furtively, catching sight of the distant splashing, laughter and happiness. Then the wet perspiration dripping inside their uniforms became unbearable. Their tongues wiped the parched lips. The march lost vigor, and slowed to a forced walk, their heads turning to the river for longer periods, their eyes and minds wistfully wishing for the cool ointment of the river. Finally the marchers began to falter, the lines became uneven as they bumped into one another. The centurion, realizing he might face a mutiny, wisely barked, "COM-PA-NY – HALT! ABOUT-TURN-RIGHT! – COMPANY…" Before he yelled "FALL-OUT," helmets, armors, shields and lances flew through the air, as they ran, ripping off their tunics, and stripped to their loincloths, they raced to the water. Within moments their screams and laughter mingled with the pilgrims. The highway, now deserted, baked under the fiery sun.

After the sun had long passed the meridian, after the pilgrims ate a lunch and slept under the trees, one by one the groups returned to the road. Before long the proud, poverty-stricken pilgrims were again pressing toward their ancient shrine. They marched until late afternoon, taking advantage of the cooler temperatures. Finally, at dusk they stopped for the night. The Romans took a large space and within moments staked their domain, with banners flying high and proud. Sentries were posted. As if by magic, brown army tents sprand up in six precise rows, a fire started and food being prepared.

The Israelis set up tents and unharnessed the animals while youngsters searched for dried wood to cook dinner, and for a bonfire. After the meal, the parents cleaned up. The youngsters disappeared to play games, or climb trees acting out as jungle heroes.

When the veil of darkness covered the valley, young men took their musical instruments and gathered around the fire, forming impromptu orchestras. They brought lyres, flutes, tambourines or whatever make-shift noise makers and began to play. Men and women formed a choir. Finally, boys and girls took their places and put on dazzling displays of traditional folkloric dances.

A few paces back from the partying pilgrims, peering out of the black night, sat some Roman soldiers, about Yeshua's age. They too enjoyed the festivities: laughing when the Israelis laughed, though they did not understand a word. They swayed to the music, and some beat two sticks together to the rhythm of the songs. Their body language put them in the middle of the party, but physically the two peoples were separated: one in the light and warmth of the fire, the other in the cold of the night peering in as intruders.

For the past few days problems had been escalating between the pilgrims and the soldiers. It all began innocently, when the children began to play, among the soldiers. A few adventurous boys, playing a game of tag, decided it would be more fun to include the area among the marching soldiers. The next few days most of the children ran, grabbing the soldiers as they pivoted around, while fleeing their pursuers. This proved truly ecstatic and more thrilling than running around the bushes, as the soldiers were moving targets, necessitating dexterity and perfect timing to jump from row to row, avoiding getting trampled under the Romans' heavy sandals. The super dose of adrenalin gave the game a new dimension. Moreover, some soldiers, not much older than the boys, joined in and when the smaller tots were in danger of being tagged, they reached out picking them up and swinging them to safety.

More than fifty children spent the day running, screaming, squealing and bumping the Roman marching machine. They disturbed the precision and solemnity of the march, without injuring a child or a soldier. Indeed, the good humored soldiers found some relief from the mindless dreary march. Alas, the stern professionals did not appreciate the intrusion of the brats, or the unprofessional behaviour of their younger mates, and decided to put an end to it. Subtly, they meted out punishment to the invaders by striking them with the backs of their hands, or tripping when bumped. The revenge was so subtle that the children did not suspect it was intentional. Thus, except for the occasional bloody nose or a black eye to a youngster, the game carried on.

After a couple of days they decided the game of hide-and-go-seek among the soldiers would prove more exciting. Next day little tots were gluing themselves expertly to a soldier, or hiding behind moving shields. It was a brilliant idea and succeeded marvelously, especially with the cooperating soldiers.

The stern soldiers complained bitterly, and the centurion promised to investigate. When he saw the invading brats he knew he had a crisis on his hand. At noon he called master Azim and gave a stern warning, "Your undisciplined juveniles are showing disrespect for the Roman flag, and this must stop before your brats get hurt."

"What are you talking about?" Azim asked, baffled by the officer's rude tone.

"Your delinquents are disruping the soldiers' march and endanging the men."

Master Azim promised to speak to the parents. He scolded the mothers, who ordered the children to remain at their heels. They soon learned that it was easier to catch the wind with a net than harness children with words. Soon a more rebellious child broke through the invisible net, and with two others trespassed into forbidden territory. Because there were no repercussions, they persuaded a few more to join and within a day they reconquered the lost territory. Now the games were more exciting because they played in forbidden territory. Young mothers, noticing their children gone, began to search and chase after them among the marching soldiers. Naturally they could not avoid the occasional accidental bump into a soldier, and after a few such contacts, an unspoken conspiracy sprouted of its own volition. The women started swinging their hips and shoulders into the unsuspecting marchers. They bowed and apologized profusely, letting the children escape deeper among the soldiers, giving them a chance to tackle every soldier in the way. It was an amateur opportunity for revenge, for generations of pain and oppression under the boots of the conquerors.

That night the soldiers huddled and planned to exact their revenge.

Next morning the games began slowly and innocently. Soon dozens of children were running helter skelter among them. After an appropriate time the mothers invaded, bumping and tackling enthusiastically. When they went deep in the rows, a soldier gave a signal and closed flanks to prevent anyone from exiting, effectively imprisoning them. Then they

YESHUA: THE REBEL WHO SHOOK THE WORLD

meted out brutal punishment. They stuck out their sandals tripping the children then kicked and trampled them. Desperate mothers jumped on them to protect them, but the soldiers punched, kicked or struck them with their shields, and trampling both. The fathers heard the screaming children but when they looked, all they saw was the front row soldiers stone-faced, in closed ranks, marching. Inside, the gears of the machine were crushing fragile bones, rolling, punching and stomping on them mercilessly. When the soldiers cleared the area, they left behind dozens of children and mothers, strewn on the stone pavement in pools of blood, many with fractured limbs some with missing teeth. A couple of children were critically injured.

When he realized what had happened, master Azim's veins stood out on his neck as he screamed at the centurion, "Monsters! Murderers! Is that what you teach them - to murder women and children?"

"I warned you to keep your delinquents away," the centurion retorted coldly.

That night the young fathers held a secret meeting. They decided to construct a long narrow box, nailed it across the back end of a flat cart, with hinges allowing the top and back side to open along the entire length. They were going to get their revenge.

Next morning the cart travelled ahead of the army with a row of pilgrims behind it to hide it from the soldiers. Pilgrims walked shovels in hand, collecting animal droppings and depositing it into the box, and by noon the box was full. They poured water into it, closed the lid to allow the contents to break down and ferment in the heat. The pilgrims were ordered to continue walking at a faster pace until the Romans were wringing wet, exhausted and on the verge of passing out. Only then they stepped aside, and opened the box releasing the rancid contents which covered the road like a blanket. The pilgrims at the rear pressed the soldiers to march into the slippery, smelly muck.

It was a resounding success. The exhausted soldiers started slip-sliding out of control, bumping and crashing into each other, arms and legs flailing wildly through the air, kicking and knocking each other senseless. Spears ripped tunics and flesh, spearing legs and backs, shields smashed helmets, skulls and faces, knocking out their comrades. They splashed and spread goo over themselves and their partners. The Israelis witnessed some of the most fabulous athletic twists and turns as the soldiers tried valiantly to remain upright. Battered mothers and children hurt from laughing, enjoying their revenge. The Romans' physical adroitness notwithstanding, most crashed violently on their faces or backs.

The unluckiest Roman was the centurion, for not only was he the first to enter the ocean of syrup, but as he slipped into the middle of the fray, his men pushed him around relentlessly where he was unable to escape. He performed the most dazzling pirouettes while his men punished him. A soldier's sandal smashed him squarely in the face and a shield crashed his head. He flew head first into the ooze, his plumed helmet flying high in the air, landing and filling up with the sticky syrup. He landed on his back letting out a loud "U-um-ph!," tried to roll over causing him to slip several times, filling his tunic as he landed on his front, sore, exhausted and covered in foul soup from hair to the sandals. The pilgrims had to hold their stomachs from bursting with laughter when he picked up his helmet and plopped it on his head, the juice running down his face. He glared at them with murder in his eyes. They knew someone was going to be killed.

A big husky youth, father of a critically wounded child stepped forward with a shovel in his hand, "Centurion, we just oiled your marching machine."

The centurion drew his sword, and swung at the youth's head to decapitate him. At the last instant Yeshua stuck out his staff, and there was a loud 'clang', as it deflected the sword harmlessly. "Is killing this man going to solve the problem?" Yeshua asked.

"No! I should kill a hundred of you scum," the officer barked into the young scholar's face. "Get out of my way, or you'll be first."

Yeshua pushed the husky youth out of the way, for he could see the centurion was going for blood. He swung at the young scholar, but Yeshua ducked and stepped back. The officer attacked like a wild animal swinging from side to side to cut him in twain. Yeshua recognized that the Roman was out control: intending to kill at all costs, while leaving his body exposed. The Israeli could easily disable him, but that would offend his officer's pride risking escalating the violence. He chose to retreat bringing the duel to a quick end, allowing the officer to save face. The centurion who had never fought a shepherd's staff interpreted the retreat as proof of his successful attacks, and doubled his efforts. He tried to dismember, cut or pierce him while the Israeli ducked and moved back. When the centurion was about to fall from fatigue, Yeshua quickly knocked the sword out of his hand, and grabbed him preventing his fall.

"Centurion both sides were at fault and both suffered," Yeshua pleaded. "Why not call an end to this?"

"What…do you suggest?" The officer leaned on him heavily, and out of breath.

"Forgive and forget," he replied judiciously.

The centurion stood back looking surprised. His men were thoroughly trounced and embarrassed, he was made a fool of, and this peasant called it a draw. But, he knew they were vastly out-numbered and his men were not prepared to battle. He smirked wryly, went up to the burly youth, ripped the shovel from his hand, walked to the cart and scooped up ooze until it was full. He walked up to the husky youth dumping some of it on his head, some on another who had laughed gregariously and the rest on Yeshua.

"Now we're even," he said, ordering, "COMPANY: to the river - on the double."

The men ran and leapt into the river, and the Israelis joined in. Yeshua followed, but the centurion caught up, and grabbed him by the shoulder, "Watch your back," he warned. "I swear you won't see Jerusalem." Then he ran to join his men.

The Israelis swam upstream of the Romans to avoid the dark rancid syrup oozing off them. That day they enjoyed the swim a little longer, for they arrived to the area where Messiah Theudas promised to part the Jordan as Moses had parted the Red Sea.

After a swim and a bath, the centurion came out for his tunic, when two Roman soldiers, approached him: an old warrior and a youth. The older man bowed deeply, "Good afternoon, centurion. As you see, we are Romans like you. May we have a word?"

The centurion studied the two carefully, before he nodded. They went into a clearing in the bushes where they could not be overheard.

"We saw your duel with the Israeli. His name is Yeshua," the old codger told him confidentially. "We overhead your threat…We want to help."

"We followed him for months trying to capture him," the young soldier explained.

"Two trained and armed soldiers unable to catch one peasant?" he guffawed sardonically. "Why should I join you? I'll carve out his heart and hand it to him."

"He's not an ordinary peasant," the old man protested. "He's…special, a sorcerer with fantastic powers…black magic."

"What superstitious gibberish are you trying to tell me? Get out of my way," the centurion pushed them away unceremoniously.

"Please wait, sir," the young soldier pleaded. "No need to argue over a peasant…The fact is he is a…a gifted trickster. How else could he duel a Roman officer? The point, sir, is that he is worth a hundred gold talents alive, but not a copper penny dead." The centurion looked at them deeply suspicious. The young man had to think fast to persuade him, hoping to save the Israeli. "A sultan or a general will pay a hundred talents for a soothsayer: that's over thirty gold pieces each."

The officer reconsidered the offer, not satisfied and still suspicious. The old soldier quickly grabbed and shook his hand, "Great: it's a deal. We'll follow him, and at the right time…ambush him." Satisfied they had persuaded him, they parted.

Though they shook hands, the centurion decided when they captured him, he would skewer the peasant, so his men would never forget: don't cross a Roman officer.

When they left the old codger put his arm around his young companion's shoulders smirking, "The centurion is a fool. When we capture the Israeli, I'll plunge a dagger into the centurion's ribs and blame Yeshua. Then we'll take him away with impunity."

Back at camp Yeshua and Germanicus were raising the tent when Ellie joined them, "I hope you don't mind. I asked my parents to set our tent next to you. I want to learn more about your sister Debborah."

Yeshua smiled and continued to work. When they finished, the slave left to find firewood while the Israeli and the Greek unloaded the animals and started to plan dinner.

Ellie asked Yeshua in a low voice, "Are you going to tell me how you did…that?"

He looked at her with a blank gaze, wondering what she meant. She stood self-conscious motioning her head towards the Greek, but her hints were lost on the Israeli. Frustrated, she grabbed his sleeve and pulled him towards her whispering so loud Stephanos heard it clearly, "I don't want him to hear our secret!"

"What secret?" Yeshua queried dumbfounded.

"THE MIRACLE!" she exclaimed loudly, and covered her mouth embarrassed.

He merely nodded amused. "My parents took me to the best special-ists," she continued to whisper loudly, "and sent for all kinds of professors of medicine from Alexandria. But no one could help. How did you...?"

Yeshua felt helpless, at a loss for words, and looked to Stephanos for help. But he only shrugged and grinned, enjoying his friend's pathetic awkwardness.

"Ellie dear," her mother appeared from around their tent, "leave the young men alone. They have work to do and don't need you here." She grabbed her hand and began to drag her away. "Please forgive Ellie's intrusion, and feel free to chase her away if she becomes a nuisance." She went a few paces, stopped and turned, "What you did today was very courageous, master Yeshua. Aaron said you saved a man's life and avoided bloodshed." She continued then stopped and turned again, "I watched you closely during the duel, and had a peculiar feeling that we've met. Ever been to Corinth?"

"M-me? N-no...never," he stammered lamely.

"Oh, never mind," she replied leaving. "I'm sure it will come to me. Come Ellie."

They watched her disappear when the Greek elbowed Yeshua with a smirk, "What did I say? It's only a matter of time. Prepare to make your revelation to the world..."

"So the centurion can arrest me?" he interrupted anxiously.

"Tell him you're a philosopher...a pupil of Diogenes."

"He would not know Diogenes from a watermelon. And do not compare me to Diogenes," the Israeli objected tersely.

"Why not emulate the most brilliant mind?"

Unnoticed by them, Ellie had returned again and sat by her tent no more than a few paces away listening intensely, while apparently playing with her doll.

The Israeli sat on a mat where the Greek joined him. "Diogenes encouraged individualism: one man against the world," Yeshua explained. "But, why do you think armies train as a unit? Because united against the foe they are stronger."

"How will you get the riff-raff to join each other? It's their nature to fight alone...disorganized and for selfish reasons," Stephanos countered.

"Is it? Or has a mean society made a mean man?" Yeshua protested coldly.

"To unify them you need a common bond. Where is your bond?"

"Love!" Yeshua exclaimed firmly. "Love from Yahweh and each other."

"They're too busy fighting to survive. When will they find time for your teaching...?"

"I have an eternity," the young scholar countered with finality in his voice.

"Teach them to crush the enemy's skull," a man's deep booming voice interrupted them. "which is what we expected you to do today."

They turned and saw a burly old man in excellent physical condition coming into the camp. They wondered who he was, when they noticed he was being accompanied by masters Azim and Micah. Close behind them came Germanicus with a heavy load of wood. The young men stood up. The stranger with the booming voice continued, "Master Yeshua you should have finished off that centurion. I recognized you as an expert fighter. You were teasing when you should have bashed his skull."

"Enough already!" Master Azim raised his voice, coming between them. "Stop! Let me introduce you so you can argue as friends. This is master Ishmael from Macedonia, a retired soldier. These are masters Yeshua, and Stephanos."

"That is Germanicus, master Stephanos' slave," Yeshua pointed behind the visitors.

Germanicus smiled and started to bow, but no one turned to acknowledge him.

Master Ishmael hardly sat down, continuing his argument, "As an Israeli you must not forget: never pass a chance to kill the enemy, especially their leader. Cut off the head of the serpent and you can finish the body with impunity."

"To what end," Yeshua demanded annoyed, "to stoke more wood in the fire?"

"Is that not what I said?" master Azim interjected with exuberance. "Spill more blood unnecessarily? And don't forget, our side was not blameless."

Master Ishmael raised his voice so it sounded like an explosion, "TO WHAT END? TO KILL THEM! Are you blind? Can't you count? We outnumber them a thousand to one. They kill a dozen of us - we kill them all: fantastic return for a day's hunt."

Yeshua was stunned to hear a man bartering with lives as if purchasing beans in the market. Could he ever persuade such a man to his views?

He decided to try, "When we get to Jerusalem the Romans will slaughter ten Israelis for every soldier. Thousands more lives wasted…for what?"

"To teach them they will pay dearly for every transgression against us," Ishmael shouted with fire in his eyes.

"Fear of retribution is the only thing they respect," Micah echoed the warrior's words. "Apologize to a barbarian and he'll see you as a coward."

"How many times have I heard rabbis pine over our dead heroes as, 'courageous warriors, immortal martyrs,'" Yeshua uttered in a whisper. "Their parents, wives and children fill a river with their tears. But tears won't bring them back…" Then he changed abruptly to an accusing tone, "The saddest truth is that as soon as they are buried, their sons grow up to repeat the same mistakes over and over."

"Bravo!" master Azim applauded. "Say what you will, but master Yeshua prevented hundreds of deaths today… not to mention future repercussions."

"What about our women and children?" master Micah growled, his voice shaking, "Who will avenge their broken bones? Knocked out teeth?"

"An eye for an eye, I say," master Ishmael barked savagely.

"We will be a nation of blind pilgrims within a generation," Yeshua retorted. "Simple adages are for simple minds. Violence begets violence."

Master Ishmael guffawed, "What do you expect me to do: respond to my enemy's violence with an embrace?"

"Precisely: Love thine enemy," Yeshua exclaimed confidently, "the only approach that has never been tried."

Masters Ismael and Micah stared with mouths agape, glanced at each other and broke out laughing. Germanicus kneeling by the fire mouthed the words smiling.

"I could not have said it better myself," master Azim cried out.

"Master Yeshua makes a persuasive argument," Stephanos interjected. "Don't despair if you don't understand it. Think about it. I have been with him for months and still don't grasp some of his ideas. But, when I reconsider them, as strange as they seem there is much wisdom…"

"Why should the Romans love us?" Ishmael interrupted exasperated. "They don't even trust us."

"Have we given them reason to trust us?" Yeshua countered. "The two races are like hunters on opposite sides of an abyss, throwing spears at each other. Why not build a bridge and invite them to come over? We may be pleasantly surprised."

Master Ishmael's laughter broke out into a thunderous guffaw, his baritone voice echoing through the forest. He could not stop though tears came to his eyes, "Thirty years I led an army...Why didn't I think of that? It's a perfect ambush: Build a bridge and invite them to cross. Then slaughter the dogs!" His eyes turned as cold as steel and his voice harsher than granite, "All my life leading men in battles, I saw more violence..."

Yeshua interrupted just as passionately, "And probably caused your share of it. It saddens me that you learned nothing from it." He leaned towards the old warrior scolding him as a teacher would a delinquent student, "I too have seen enough suffering: a senseless slaughter of pilgrims, two youths crucified, a man's decapitated head. There is less violence in the jungles. Yet, what do I hear: Pleas for more deaths?"

"It's the only thing they understand," the Macedonian sneered bitterly. "They only want us for what they can get."

"Let's be the first to offer the olive branch," the young Israeli urged with passion.

"They'll demand the olive tree," Master Micah shouted mockingly.

"Give them two...three if it brings peace."

"They'll take the nation." Master Ishmael snarled.

"They have the nation, yet we have no peace," he protested with a sigh. Then he lowered his voice with inspiration, "As the Universal Creator loves us so we must love one another."

"So now you're going to give them our God?" Master Micah's voice quivered.

"Yahweh belongs to everybody...including the Romans," Yeshua responded.

"How dare you utter His sacred name?" Master Micah's body shook with anger, and foam ran down his chin.

"Mark my words master Yeshua, if the Romans don't kill you, our people will stone you for blasphemy," the Macedonian shook his finger in his face.

"You hypocrites," Yeshua rebuked them tersely. "You hijack the Creator who entreats love, then kill in His name with no conscience. And accuse me of blasphemy?"

"Master Yeshua makes a good argument," Master Azim supported him. The other two tried to argue at the same time, but he raised his hands, "Let him continue."

"People have pillaged and murdered in the Creator's name for too long. I tell you truly, my heavenly Abba cries at every transgression of one man against another."

"What's this? Now you presume to speak for Lord Adonai?" Master Micah spat out, and tried to stand up so quickly he lost his balance. As he bent over he saw a large rock and picked it up. "I'll never stoop so low... as to love pagans...or infidels!"

"Why not? Yahweh loves them," Yeshua responded. "They are also His children."

"What you are saying is truly astounding," master Azim was as surprised as he was pleased by the youth's refreshing ideas. "It needed to be said...and I love it!"

Ishmael stood up huffing and puffing, and thrust his finger at the young Israeli, "A world full of love! What a naïve Utopia. No one will ever live up to that!"

"No one has ever tried," master Stephanos interjected. "They should. Patience and persistence may one day lead to a peaceful world."

"Don't ever come to Antioch," master Micah cried out lifting the rock. "This is the saddest day of my life: to return to my beloved country to be abused and my religion berated." He spat in Yeshua's direction, "Love my enemy! What kind of religion is that? I will avenge the God of the Jews!" He lifted the rock to heave it at the young scholar.

Ellie, who had been listening, leaped up and ran in front of Yeshua screaming, "NO! Don't. He saved my life!"

The three old men looked at her as she embraced him. Then they looked at one another uncertain if they heard her correctly. But it failed to register as master Micah raised the rock to throw it. Germanicus moved in stealthily behind him ready to pounce.

"Leave him be, Germanicus," Yeshua ordered. The slave stopped.

"Hiding behind a little girl," master Micah mocked him. "That's what I expected."

"Throw that stone away," master Ishmael directed. "Let's get out of here."

Master Micah threw it into the fire causing flaming branches to bounce high in the air, as they marched away furiously without looking back.

Master Azim came to Yeshua putting his arm around his shoulder, "I want to apologize for them. I had no idea that they would...I feel ashamed."

Yeshua waved off the incident, but when he spoke his voice betrayed pain and defeat, "I venture to guess the majority of our pilgrims agree with them. So do the Romans. Master Stephanos tells me I'm swimming against the popular current."

"I'll join you," the old man reassured him. "Yesterday I would not believe anyone could stop a centurion from killing. Today I saw it." He turned to leave, stopped and raised his hand as if scribing in the air, 'Love thine enemy,'" he said cheerfully. "I shall have it engraved over my gate." He walked up to Ellie bending over her, "I believe master Yeshua's love saved you." He patted her hair and walked away.

Yeshua stood staring at the fire, thinking about something that had long troubled him. Why could he not explain his concepts more persuasively, and less confrontationally? Could he have explained it differently; more patiently or graciously? He knew he had much to learn if he hoped to influence the masses.

His contemplation was interrupted when he heard shouting in the distance. It sounded like an announcement. Suddenly he felt Ellie pulling at his sleeve, "Master Yeshua, I'm sorry I told your secret. It...it slipped out," she apologized sheepishly.

"We are even now," he grinned. "I saved you yesterday and you saved me today." He listened to the announcement again and told his companions, "Master Theudas is here."

"After seeing your work, no Messiahs could match it," Stephanos replied, then reconsidered, "But we came a great distance. We owe ourselves to see him..."

"I agree," Yeshua said and turned to Ellie. "Go tell your parents master Theudas is coming..." She turned and ran and he yelled after her, "to part the Jordan."

"Wait for me," she called back as she disappeared behind the tent.

People were already pouring out onto the road going in the direction of the announcer. Soon all camps were deserted. The young men joined in, and as they approached one announcer they heard others in the distance giving directions.

Ellie caught up and took Yeshua's hand, with her parents a few paces back. "I'm glad we're alone, because I want to learn more about Debborah," Ellie looked up at her friend, chirping. "What is she like? Is she like me?"

He thought about it, "Before your cure I would have said no," he remarked. "But, seeing you healthy, full of energy and humor, I am beginning to see a resemblance."

"What kind of games does she like?"

"She does not have time for games," he explained. "Being the oldest girl in a poor household, she is busy helping mother: cooking, cleaning and caring for the little ones."

"I couldn't do any of those things because of my illness," she sighed. "Would Debborah like me?"

"I cannot imagine anyone not liking you."

"You always say nice things," she giggled and turned crimson. "Even when those men said nasty things to you…If I had a brother I'd like him to be just like you." She felt special, almost grown-up promenading with her big-brother friend. "Do you have a girlfriend?" Yeshua's thoughts went to lady Sarah, and he wondered how she was, whether she was recovering, or ever thought about him. He had considered writing and telling her about Ellie, but remembered how his letters caused her distress and desisted. His day dreaming came to an abrupt end when he felt her tugging his arm. "Master Yeshua, I asked you a question. Do you have a girlfriend? What is her name?"

"Uh? Oh…oh, it's lady Sarah," he blurted out, then corrected himself. "Only, she does not wish to be my girlfriend any longer…She is angry with me."

"You must have done something terrible," the young girl frowned adding accusingly, "What did you do to make lady Sarah so angry?"

"What makes you think I did something?"

"Why else would she be angry?"

Yeshua glanced at her through the corners of his eyes, "I retract my previous statement: You are very much like Debborah!" But, seeing she was still waiting for an answer he added, "I did not do anything. She suffered a mental breakdown."

Ellie had a vague idea of what he meant, but not enough to ask questions, so she dropped it. They continued in silence, Yeshua daydreaming about beautiful lady Sarah.

As they approached, a young man directed them towards the river where an attendant held a pouch, "One drachma per person: children and old people free."

Yeshua had no money, except his father's coins. Stephanos tossed in three coins and they continued. They joined the multitude and milled around a central point they could not see. People continued arriving and Yeshua guessed there were thousands already waiting. They mingled wondering when the highly praised Messiah would appear?

• • •

Lady Sarah seemed to be recovering well, although she was still weak and tired easily. Debborah visited daily and commented that her cheeks were regaining a rosy color, and encouraged her to eat more.

Her father's mysterious murder bothered her immensely and she could not stop thinking about it. Once she became tired of crying, she decided to investigate as to who killed him and why. She went to the market daily, a center of intrigue and gossip, and learned that he was murdered by a Roman soldier. She wondered for days why would a total stranger murder a famous architect? The logical answer was robbery, but when she received his personal effects nothing was missing. Moreover there had not been ransom demands made, which was common with kidnappers and robbers. Did he have an argument with the soldier? But, the decapitation pointed to a deeper hatred than a mere fight. The murder was too sinister and bizarre, leaving her stymied without leads or answers.

She rummaged through his belongings searching for clues to the mystery. She went through every room, every drawer, boxes, through his extensive library reading his notes, diary and correspondence without finding a name of a suspicious person to help solve his death. Still, she refused to give up. She returned to his office, and dug into the boxes, re-reading every scrap of papyrus. She was rummaging in a box when a servant came in.

"Begging your pardon, lady Sarah, but a Roman centurion, with foot soldiers wishes an audience with you. He said it will only take a moment."

She wondered why Romans would be calling. When she recalled that a soldier killed her father, her intuition told her he may have information, "Show him in please."

She tried to restore the papers and desk to an orderly fashion when the centurion entered, leaving his escort outside. He bowed stiffly. She remained seated, studying him closely, and motioned him to sit down.

"Thank you lady Sarah, but I will only be a moment," the centurion seemed uncomfortable and his eyes avoided her. She was not certain whether he was nervous, or fulfilling an order he thoroughly disliked. He cleared his throat and unfurled a scroll as he spoke, "My commander sends deepest regrets over your father's untimely death, and assures you that private Quintus has been charged and will be punished severely…"

She etched the name Quintus in her memory, the villain she vowed never to forget.

"Is private Quintus from your garrison, sir?" she asked.

"No, my lady. I have been in Sepphoris two years, but never saw him there," the centurion sighed, happy to renounce the killer. "He is stationed in Augusteana."

Sarah found the news strange. Why would a soldier travel all the way from Augusteana just to kill her father? That was intriguing and puzzling, and she vowed to resolve it, failing to hear the centurion until he raised his voice and repeated the question, "I asked my lady if I may read my commander's letter?"

"Oh, yes…please do so…sorry."

He cleared his throat again and shuffled his weight from one foot to the other:

"To the widow and family of the late master Nehemiah,

"Our sympathies and condolences,

"We wish to express our deepest sympathies for the death of the late master Nehemiah. He was a close friend to the Romans and a supporter of Rome. His service to the emperor will long be remembered. He will be sorely missed.

"We will offer a sacrifice of a bull in his memory at the Temple of Mars, Lieutenant Marcus Grottus."

When the centurion finished she felt tears burning her eyes. She knew he was a great architect, loved and revered for his work, and the letter proved it. "Please tell your commander I thank your government," she stopped for the pain almost choked her. "Our people have not sent any..." She could not finish the statement.

The centurion kept his eyes on the floor as he pulled out a fat purse, offering it to her, "My commander sends these coins...for...your father's service..."

She took it. He turned to leave but she had many questions unanswered and was not about to let him escape, "Wait! Please...Is the Roman government going to put up an inscription...a plaque, or perhaps a statue to celebrate my father's work?"

His eyes popped wide as he turned and stared at her as if she had lost her mind, "Pardon? What kind of statue? I don't understand..."

"Perhaps you don't know, but your superiors are well aware...my father was a brilliant architect...deserving of a commemoration."

The officer stood confused, not knowing how to respond. He decided the safest reply was to remain evasive, "I'm sure...Perhaps you should speak to my commander..."

"No, I have you here, and I need some answers," she pressed him with an assertive tone. "Which structures or edifices did my father erect in Sepphoris?"

He felt beads of perspiration on his forehead as his eyes darted furtively, and stuttered weakly, "I'm not aware...I joined Sepphoris...quite recently..."

She glared at him, accusing him with frost in her voice, "You said you have been stationed there for two years. What are you keeping from me centurion?"

He froze stunned, mumbling, "I don't know...I have to go. I...said too much..."

He took one giant step, and got out with a heavy sigh. Sarah started after him but gave up. She remained wondering - Roman authorities paid respects to her father's memory, but, why the money...? Why did the centurion not know any structures he had built? Why was he so evasive? What was he trying to hide? How little did she really know about her father? Why were the Zealots interested in him? Myriad questions came at her from every direction with confusing messages. She realized her investigation was just starting, and the majority of work lay ahead. But, where to start, what to do, she wondered?

. . .

Yeshua's group waited for master Theudas, as thousands more pilgrims continued arriving. They strained their necks to get a good view. But all they saw far to the south along the river bank was a wooden platform, but no one on it. They waited for a long time, until it was getting dusk, but still no word of the promised Messiah.

Finally when it was getting dark there was a commotion and Yeshua craned his neck and saw a handful of men pushing through the crowd. People at the back asked questions and he gave a commentary, "There is an old man...must be master Theudas: an old, stately man, with very long white hair, and a white beard; has a long staff like Moses. He is climbing up the platform..."

Once on the platform everyone saw the stooped old man, fragile, wearing a long white robe which made him appear surreal, like an angel who had just landed. He shuffled to the end of the platform where he stood for a long time. An eerie silence descended upon the valley. All they heard were the gentle gurgle of the Jordan and intermittent songs of the cicadas. They watched as their holy man prayed.

Yeshua saw him raise his head, and whispered, "He is about to start."

Master Theudas raised his arms slowly, holding his long staff in his right hand, as the wide sleeves fell back to his shoulders. With his arms outstretched he spoke in a loud voice giving a command.

"What language is he speaking? Is he not Israeli?" someone asked.

"Hebrew," Yeshua replied.

They did not understand the ancient language, although Yeshua recognized the odd word. But, he clearly understood Theudas' command to Yahweh, "Open the Sea." It was a short, direct speech, not a prayer or supplication, but a direct conversation of a holy man with his God. After he gave the order he stood, frozen, waiting for the miracle. The pilgrims stood with their eyes fixed on the heavens for signs of action. Their eyes travelled from the old man to the heavens, back and forth, waiting.

But nothing happened. They did not know what to make of this. These fervent, almost obsessive religious pilgrims, had spent a lifetime planning, and months on a long, arduous journey to the holy land. Their history, steeped in tradition and the Torah was filled with stories of supernatural miracles, so no one doubted he would part the Jordan.

After a long pause, he closed his hand making a fist, giving a loud order to the heavens, "OPEN THE SEA!" His voice cracked as he yelled expecting immediate obedience. Alas, the results were the same. Finally he lowered his arms and stood, stooped, motionless. His helpers climbed the platform and gingerly escorted him away.

As he shuffled away one of the helpers announced somberly, "My fellow Israelis, conditions are not always perfect for great miracles…If you come back tomorrow… Perhaps the good Lord Adonai was needed elsewhere more urgently…"

The pilgrims accepted the explanation but could not hide their disappointment for they could not return. They expected to be in Jerusalem by tomorrow.

"You go back to camp," Yeshua told his friends. "I'll try to catch up to master Theudas for a word."

"I'll come with you," the Greek said. "Germanicus, go back and start dinner."

The slave returned to camp and put the pot on the fire with ample water, as he was leaving for the slaves' last meeting. Just then Azim's three slaves arrived, startling him.

"I told you, don't come here," he scolded them. "What if my master finds out?"

"Quit worrying," the oldest slave droned. "Your conscience is acting up again."

The intruders got into the supplies, took a loaf of bread and ran off with it.

As they walked Germanicus studied his companions. They complained continuously against their master and swore revenge, but they had no plans, goals or a family they missed. They would scratch each others' eyes out to get an advantage. He worried that he trusted his life to such charlatans, but he saw no way to back out of it.

They turned by the river, entering thick bushes. They were forced to crawl on their bellies becoming entangled. Just when they thought of turning back, they came into a large clear area, where all the slaves were assembled around the fire.

They were restless, and louder than the previous night, being so close to freedom. The adrenalin was rushing, and everyones' nerves were on edge. The leader sensed this and started the meeting, covering the preliminary matters, then went into the most important topic: the escape.

"Tonight is our last meeting. In a day or two, you must plunge into action, and your destiny. The best time to escape is late afternoon or dusk. They won't miss you until next morning, so you'll have a whole night to gain distance. Once you start, keep running. You'll be hunted by professional trackers and killers. They'll travel by donkey, horses, camels and gain on you like this," he snapped his fingers, and they winced. "Travel in small groups, but if you suspect they are closing in, split up. Give yourselves a chance so at least one of you may gain freedom." His eyes travelled from face to face and he savored the fear and terror on their faces. But, he also knew terror was contagious and could freeze their intellect leading to capture and certain death. He had to finish before they panicked, "I'll point to one of you, who will stand up with his companions, and I'll name the gate through which you will escape. Split up and maximize your chances for success." He pointed to one slave who stood up with two others, and he barked, "Horse gate". The second group was told, "Water gate". Another heard, "Dung gate". Germanicus' group was directed to take the "Fish gate".

The slaves began a nervous giddy laughter that masked exposed nerves and jitters, when the leader screamed, "SILENCE," causing them to freeze in mid-sentence. "Idiotic fools, do you want your masters to hear and discover your plans tonight? Maybe you're too stupid to deserve freedom." His glare made them drop their eyes in submission.

When he had their attention he leaned forward with something which he knew would truly terrify them, "Listen carefully. To reach freedom you need money: lots of money." He stopped and watched their expressions change. They were thunderstruck, for few had ever possessed a coin and had no expectation of getting any. He enjoyed their look of horror and enjoyed giving more unpleasant realities, "You won't have food, and without money you won't get any. And no one will hire a run-away slave: it's against the law. You'll be doomed from the start!"

They looked at one another dumbstruck, then prostested all once:

"My dreams...my plans...up in smoke," an old slave cried out.

"I can't...we can't...how can we...?" another mumbled incoherently.

"Why...why did you not tell us before?" a younger slave bawled.

"Are you all stupid sheep?" the leader raised his voice. "You should have figured it out...and planned. Saved. You're all fools! I did not tell you before because you would have robbed your masters, got caught and turned us all in." He glared at them with murder in his eyes. "Tomorrow before you run get some money from your masters. Rob them. Mug them if necessary. Kill them if you have to." He pulled out a dagger hidden in his belt and held it high. "Your assault will create a diversion, and they'll suspect desperate robbers. In the confusion you slip out and run! But don't stop under any circumstances. And remember: no money - no freedom!"

Without a word he stood up and melted into the night.

Left alone the slaves stood stunned. They had yearned for freedom for as long as they could remember. The past few weeks they thought about it around the hourglass. They became obsessed with it. Now, when told kill for it, they shook with terror. Many broke down sobbing.

Germanicus walked back with the others in silence. He seemed to be in a trance. Stephanos was demanding, at times unreasonable, but did he deserve to be murdered? The very question triggered the answer: "Love each other as your Creator loves you."

For the first time in his life he had found something worth living for: an orderly fashion to his life, worthy rules of morality, and concepts which gave him a unique identity and pride. He had found God who loved him, a slave, and saw him equal to his master and the emperor. His faith was his life, and the salvation of his soul. Most importantly it was taught to him by a very special friend: master Yeshua. Germanicus loved him as his religious leader, and would gladly die for him.

He knew if he killed his master he would forfeit everything: his faith, his future, and most important, Yeshua. Yet he had yearned for freedom for as long as he remembered. Master Hariph proved that slavery was wrong. And he pointed out how much Germanicus needed to be free, for himself, for Anna and Lygia. The more he deliberated the more confused he became. If he killed could he ever be free? Could he be happy, with Stephanos' blood on his conscience? Was he willing to lose God, his whole world and all the people he loved?

He did not hear the others bid good night, for his brain was on fire. To sentence his master to death…meant he was sentencing his life to damnation…He sat by the campfire with his head in his hands and sobbed, not for them but for himself.

· · ·

Yeshua and Stephanos waited until the pilgrims left before they were able to walk up to the platform. By that time it was dark and the clouds hid the stars.

Unbeknownst to them three Roman soldiers, an old man, a youth and a centurion followed them. When they reached an area where they were alone the centurion told them his plan, "Let's separate and attack from different directions. I'll attack from the front, you from the right and you the left. Wait for my cue."

They separated and circled the victims as planned, while Yeshua and the Greek continued unaware of the danger.

Suddenly the centurion appeared from the bushes a few paces ahead of them with his sword drawn, "Master Yeshua, I warned you to watch yourself. I'm here for revenge."

The young men stopped. Stephanos raised his staff and held it in both hands in front of them. The young soldier snuck up from behind with his sword drawn and swung the hilt violently, striking the Greek on the head, knocking him unconscious.

"I do not wish to fight," Yeshua replied. "Let's talk. I'm certain we can..."

"It's too late for talk," the centurion interrupted gruffly, stepping forward with his sword raised. "Prepare to die!" He advanced until he looked into Yeshua's eyes and faltered, staring into the burning radiance emanating from them. He drew back, "What's that? Your eyes...on fire...no black magic...I want to kill you..." he stood paralyzed with fear.

The young soldier who had been standing over Stephanos' body yelled out, "No killing. We agreed." Suddenly from the corner of his eye he saw the older soldier coming at Yeshua and screamed, "Look out Yeshua - Behind you!"

Yeshua swung his staff instinctively with all his might as he turned around. It crashed against the old warrior's skull with a loud cracking sound, and the soldier crumpled to the ground like a rag doll. His sword bounced away harmlessly.

The young soldier ran to his fallen comrade raising his head, "His skull is broken...He's...he's not breathing." He stammered with fright. "You... You killed him."

Yeshua dropped his staff and knelt over the fallen soldier.

The centurion took advantage of the confusion and ran at Yeshua, with his sword raised, "Say your prayers; for I'm going to KILL YOU!"

CHAPTER XIX - MESSIAH RABBAN

When Yeshua heard he had killed a man, he dropped to his knees, and lifted the soldier's head, but there was no sign of life. Taking advantage, the centurion swung his sword at the Israeli, but the young soldier deflected the blow. The officer attacked the insolent youth, who fought brilliantly and in one swift move had his sword at the officer's throat, "One move and I'll carve you a new breathing pipe."

"Imbecile, what are you doing? He is the enemy," the centurion barked. "Get away, I'm going to kill him."

"He is saving my friend's life. Get away from him."

"I'll have you imprisoned for this," the officer yelled.

"After he's finished you can do what you want. Now back off!"

The centurion felt the cold steel and stepped back. He swore under his breath as soon as this farce was over, he would finish them off.

Yeshua knew the old soldier was critically wounded when he felt a thick substance oozing from his head. He placed his hand on the soldier's chest and prayed silently. After a while he looked up whispering, "Dear Abba, do not let this old man die. He has not been a good man, but, if given a chance, he will serve You well." He lowered his head and a light began to shine about his head enveloping them. The young soldier knelt down, filled with awe. Stephanos got up, stumbled and came down on one knee. The centurion remembering the Israeli's radiant eyes, backed away.

A pulsating light came down Yeshua's arms like bolts of lightning enveloping them in a shower of sparks. The old soldier's chest rose and he started to breathe.

When the centurion saw this he was terrorized, "What black magic is this? It's...not human." He retreated, "What Satanic powers...from hell..." He started to run, tripped and fell, losing his sword. He scrambled up in panic and ran into the night.

The young soldier started to sob, "You saved him...you gave him his life." He grabbed his friend's tunic and cried.

Stephanos leaned over the old soldier, saw him breathing, and marveled. He knew he was in the presence of a God.

The young soldier grabbed Yeshua's hand gushing with wonder, "You saved him. You brought him back...You must be a God." He showered the Israeli's hand with kisses. "I want to be your servant."

"Do not revere me," Yeshua protested, pulling his hand away. "I killed a man!"

"Self defence," the soldier persisted. "Don't blame yourself, master..."

"What kind of God kills? I am evil..." the young scholar muttered dejected.

"No! You cannot be evil," the soldier grabbed him beseechingly. "You saved the little girl...and my friend. I shall...worship you as my God."

Yeshua tried to pull away but the young man held fast, so he addressed him tenderly, "If you wish to serve me, do as I tell you: forsake all manner of violence." He picked up his staff, raised it with both hands and brought it down on his knee breaking it. He raised the broken halves to the sky crying out, "Dear Abba I beseech forgiveness." He tossed the pieces aside, and turned to the young man, "What is your name, soldier?"

"Appius, my Lord. My old companion is Rufus."

"Appius if you wish to serve God, share His love with every person you meet."

"Love shall be my life. What about Rufus?" he asked the Israeli.

"As he loves his fellowman, so shall he be rewarded," he replied leaving.

• • •

Yeshua walked to the Jordan river, and stood in the water, his body trembling. The reality of his deed struck him, and tears streamed down. He blamed himself for killing wantonly, and his heart ached. He thought he was hypocritical for teaching non-violence then killing. The facts were clear: life was a miracle from his Abba, and once given, must not be taken away carelessly. His character crumbled and he cried helplessly, his spirit totally crushed. He had failed his heavenly Abba again.

He raised his arms to the heavens pleading, "Dear Abba, forgive me. If possible I beg You to release me from this heavy yoke weighing on my shoulders. Let me free. Find someone more worthy to fulfill Your wishes. I cannot do...the mission You gave me..."

He stopped when he heard music from a thousand strings seemingly suspended in the night air. Some clouds began to separate and form into figures of angels. A bright light shone from behind a heavy cloud, radiating shafts of light and glowing upon him.

An ethereal voice spoke, "Yeshua you are the chosen one. Go forth and teach every Man, Woman and Child about my love for them."

. . .

When Yeshua returned, Germanicus dished up a bowl of stew, and cut a slice of bread for him. Then he sat back smirking. Stephanos had told him that the Israeli had killed a man and brought him back to life. He sniggered, unable to resist throwing barbs, "Master says you had a good night: killed a man, then resurrected him?" When the Israeli looked up, he added sarcastically, "Is that what Gods do: preach non-violence, then go out and kill in the night? Where is your staff? Got rid of the evidence of the crime?"

"Your master is correct. I killed…"

The slave interrupted impetuously, "No problem! With your supreme powers why be concerned? What you do you can undo…" He scoffed smugly. "You tell us to love our enemies. The pilgrims worship the ground you walk on. And while we struggle with our conscience, you do as you please. Do these rules apply only to slaves?"

"I did not make myself clear," Stephanos interjected to defend him. "Master Yeshua was attacked…It all happened so quickly."

"That's a feeble excuse," the slave snapped back. "He killed! He said love is unreserved - unqualified. Were those words only for convenience master Yeshua?"

"Appius said master Yeshua reacted instinctively," Stephanos scrambled to defend his friend who sat staring vacantly at his accuser. "It was an accident."

"He kills because he can make it right," the slave countered stubbornly. "Why should I wrestle with my conscience? I can do as you, right, master Yeshua?"

Yeshua guessed the slave's intentions and responded with pity, "What I did was wrong. Do not use my error to excuse your evil plans."

"How do you know I...have plans...?" Germanicus drew back flab-berghasted, wondering how much he knew. "And what gives you the right to judge?"

Stephanos looked from one to the other, uncertain what was the fuss, but wishing to avoid an altercation, raised his voice, "We've heard enough on the matter."

They sat back crossing their arms in an uneasy truce. Stephanos' headache was returning and he reached to touch the tender spot. Soon after, they turned in.

Yeshua spent a restless night full of bad dreams, remembering little of it in the morning, except for the blood: Caesarea, mount Gerezim and finally by the Jordan. Blood accumulated on his hands and ran down the tunic – thick and abundant. Rarely did he feel more tired or more guilty. They broke camp, hardly saying a word, and started for the highway. Stephanos led Lucius, Yeshua had the donkey, and the slave pulled the camel. Germanicus also looked haggard as he too had spent a restless night.

He dreamt that he killed his master. He ran away when Yeshua arrived and revived him. The slave kept running but at every intersection Yeshua and his master waited for him. The other slaves blamed him, so he killed them, but Yeshua resurrected them, and they all chased him until morning.

He sat at breakfast, angry and exhausted. At one point he heard Yeshua mention "Fish gate," and snapped, "What about fish gate? Who told you about fish gate?"

"I was telling your master that every gate in Jerusalem is named for its usage: water gate has a well spring nearby, sheep gate because they bring the animals through it..."

Germanicus suspected that he knew about his plan to run away, and was playing games. How could he hide the truth from one who knew which gate he was to take?

They had almost reached the highway when the slave felt something hard in his belt. He unfolded the material and felt something cold, metallic. He pulled it out: it was a dagger. When did he put it there, he wondered? Then he recalled holding it after breakfast, deciding whether to take it. His mind was so tired and fuzzy that he confused the real with the imagined. He stared at the shiny, cold blade until he realized it was stupid to hold it in full view, and shoved it back in his belt. When he looked up, he saw Yeshua watching his every action. He resumed walking and yanked the camel. But within a few paces the Israeli caught up to him. He felt a cold shiver run up his spine.

"Are you alright Germanicus?" Yeshua sounded concerned.

"Me? Why…yes. Why do you ask?" he avoided making eye contact.

"You seem troubled the past few days," the young scholar remarked, "especially this morning. Are you expecting trouble?"

"No…no…What do you mean?"

"I have never seen you with that," he pointed to the belt. "Why the dagger?"

"You carried a staff…Why can't I…?" he snapped like a cornered animal.

"The staff was for self defense, but it led to trouble," the Israeli explained, then mused. "Do you expect to use it against me, or your master?"

"Stay away from me…I'm warning you!" Germanicus snarled angrily, and pressed ahead, away from his persecutor.

Yeshua remained behind feeling pity and guilt. Pity because he was certain the slave was entangled in a conspiracy from which he could not break free. And guilty because once he let it be known he was aware of the dagger, it may have crystallized his plans. He was more positive than ever it was intended for master Stephanos.

He wondered, should he warn the Greek, or extract a confession from the slave first? Either way would get him arrested, and carted off in chains, to be sold to work in some underground mine or quarry. He had to reconsider his actions.

When they arrived at the highway the Roman garrison was nowhere to be seen.

That day they continued through Jericho, the city of date palms, and turned west walking ever upwards to Jerusalem. Late in the day they camped almost under the gates of the holy city. Many stood transfixed watching the last of the sun's rays kiss the high walls, the roof tops and the center tower of the Temple, before the veil of darkness engulfed the city. As they set up camp they saw the city lights, and their hearts palpitated. They were on the threshold of realizing a lifetime dream. Some stopped in the middle of work and gazed at the flickering lights, as if peeking at the stars in paradise. Truly this was their holy city. Others, overwhelmed by the moment, broke down and cried. Late that night they turned into their cots. But few managed to get any sleep.

Next morning before sunrise Yeshua led a large group to the Mount of Olives, from where they could see over the walls into the city and identify the important structures. The first shafts of light grazed the roof tops, the light reflecting off the spires and turrets as the mantle of darkness drew back. The warm colors of pink sandstone and marble uncovered the splendor of the city. They gasped when a shaft of light shone brilliantly off some brass or copper dome splashing the colors of the rainbow on neighboring buildings.

Ellie's family stood beside Yeshua speechless, their eyes darting from one highlight to another. A little further away stood master Azim with his extended family, and master Micah with his faithful donkey and his wife's bones. From time to time he leaned over and whispered to the bag about the marvels unfolding before his eyes.

"It's like a rose bud unfolding into full bloom before our eyes," lady Mona sighed, filled with admiration. "Like a miracle."

"We had a miracle," Aaron responded. "Are we worthy of another?"

Stephanos who had seen many beautiful cities of the world, stood tall and erect proclaiming with awe, "Jerusalem is worthy of Alexandria... perhaps even Athens!"

Yeshua informed them, "Jerusalem is a complex mixture of history and legends. Ironically the city was first built by pagans who named it after a local god SHALEM. Some say it was built on mount Mariah where Abraham almost sacrificed his son. About a thousand years ago king David conquered the city and made it the capital of Israel. His son Solomon built the first Temple there. It was destroyed. They rebuilt it and the second was destroyed. King Herod started the present one..."

"It's far from complete," Stephanos pointed out.

"The late king started it over twenty years ago. They expect it will take two more generations to finish," the Israeli explained.

"Listen," master Azim interrupted. "Trumpets."

They heard a crisp blare of trumpets from the Temple as if announcing a great fanfare. "It signifies the beginning of another day's religious ceremony," Yeshua said. "Now the priests will start sacrificing a lamb, offer flour and incense, to the music of the orchestra, accompanied by the choir." They heard the harmonizing voices, and the music seemed suspended, along the sun's rays over the city. "After the hymn they will recite the Shema."

Spontaneously they recited, 'HEAR, O ISRAEL; THE LORD OUR GOD, THE LORD IS ONE."

"Is there not a court in the Temple for non Jews?" Stephanos asked.

"Yes," Yeshua confirmed, "but, it is outside of all those railings."

"There is a carving in stone that says, 'FOREIGNERS GO NO FUR-THER ON PAIN OF DEATH,' " master Micah informed him, with a tone verging on threat.

"To the north of the Temple, to your right, is the Insula, the Roman garrison. That high tower is called Antonia, after Marc Anthony. Every year at this time the tetrarch Valerius Gratus, who resides in Caesarea Maritima, comes here with his troops to patrol the city during Passover."

"What's he afraid of, defenseless pilgrims?" master Azim asked sardonically.

"They're afraid the Messiah may show up," Yeshua continued. "As you know Passover is our symbol of liberation from bondage, so the pilgrims believe the Messiah will come at this time to lead them to a war of freedom."

"I heard an expatriate from Egypt is coming," master Azim interjected, "Master Rabban, and they truly believe that he is the formidable Messiah."

"I saw him perform a supernatural feat in Egypt," a young man added. "He uprooted a giant tree, heaving it a hundred paces through the air, without physically touching it..."

"Even Samson couldn't do that," another opined.

"He's coming to destroy the Temple," the young man told them.

"Phew! What's the horrendous stink?" An old lady winced pinching her nose. Many others did the same.

"It's in the yard next to the Temple. The priests slaughter the sacrificial animals, dumping blood, entrails and wastes directly under the Temple where it rots in putrid water," the young scholar explained, shaking his head.

"I thought I heard bleats and bellows, but did not believe it," lady Mona confessed.

"Well, we won't be camping in this poisonous air," master Azim screwed up his face revolted. He looked inside the city and added, "Besides, there is no room..."

"See those dark dots outside the walls?" Yeshua pointed all around the city. "That is tent city. It goes as far as the eye can see. We'll try our luck to the south."

Except for the momentary horrid smell the group was most impressed with their holy city, and considered themselves fortunate to have someone explain it. But no one was more impressed than little Ellie who hung on to the hand of her adopted brother.

"Did you not say you were from Nazareth?" lady Mona sounded confused. "You sound like a Judean."

"My schoolmaster is from here," Yeshua smiled. "Whenever he spoke about the city I wrote everything down and designed it on papyrus…"

Soon after they left and searched for a campsite. The first open space was over a dozen stadia distant from the city, from where they could not see the high walls.

The boys raised master Aaron's tent first. While Stephanos struggled to lift and stretch a corner, the slave came from behind and reached with one hand for the tent, the other for his belt. Yeshua grabbed his hand, and they stood, their hands interlocked, while Yeshua brought up the slave's hand, and saw he held a piece of twine. The Israeli blushed and walked away. Germanicus sighed for it was by pure chance that he grabbed the twine, and not the dagger.

When they finished Stephanos suggested, "Let's go visit Quintus."

"Perhaps I'll bring Lucius and do the sacrifice?" Yeshua wondered.

Stephanos doubted it, but shrugged and they started to leave, when lady Mona intercepted them, "You're not going anywhere hungry. A healthy body is a healthy mind. Come along. I prepared enough for everybody."

They glanced at each other and decided it was easier to give in than argue. Stephanos saw lady Mona staring at his friend, and feared she would not leave Yeshua alone until she solved the question of his identity. This would create a formidable scene and endanger his friend's life. Hence he decided to leave this place as soon as possible.

Yeshua came to the same conclusion, and whispered, "Let's eat quickly and run."

But when they saw the food, they knew they would not be leaving all too soon. It was an attractive meal of a variety of food, simple yet appealing. Mostly vegetables, grains, nuts, raisins and fruits, it was most appetizing and proved delicious. They apologized that they were not hungry, then ate as if starving, cleaning every bowl.

Suddenly lady Mona smiled as if she had seen a sparkling light, "I finally remember where I saw you. I confess, I could not have done it without Ellie's help…"

Yeshua's heart stopped, and he sat frozen with a mouthful, uncertain whether to chew or swallow. Stephanos was already devising a plausible explanation of cases of mistaken identity, and how the more things seem the same the more they are different.

Lady Mona leaned forward oozing confidence, "Some months past a young medical scholar came to our home to diagnose Ellie's illness. I am positive you are that scholar."

Yeshua's eyes darted from her to her husband, then back again.

"I realized immediately you could not be that scholar. He was from Alexandria, had light brown hair and blue eyes..." Aaron clearly disagreed with his wife.

Yeshua concurred with his friend: she would not stop until she uncovered his identity.

Then she sprang the unexpected question, "Were you there to see Ellie's miracle?"

Yeshua almost choked on the food. He started coughing trying desperately to think of an answer, but his mind was blank.

"Everybody within miles came to see Ellie," Stephanos came to his rescue. "We got to know and love her and came to give support..." Then he added unnaturally quickly, "But we did not stay long."

"We did not see anything," Germanicus rushed in as if denying a crime.

"Oh, you should have stayed," she sighed, holding her hands cupped as if praying. "It was the most wonderful miracle..."

Ellie who noticed her friend's frantic look protested frostily, "Mother, must you always talk about that?"

"But, dear, it was truly a marvelous miracle..."

"Still, we don't need to hear about it a gazillion times," the girl interrupted, and turned to the young men. "Are you going to the city?"

"We have an important errand," Yeshua replied relieved with the change of topics.

"Can I come? I won't be any trouble, I promise," Ellie asked, but when they shook their heads in unison she pleaded, "Please?"

Her father hugged her, "They are going to be busy, and you should help mother."

She pouted for a moment, sighing exaggeratedly but in the end obeyed.

Their walk to the city necessitated all the physical dexterity and strength they possessed, not to mention an abundance of patience. They were forced to tread between and around tents, with people sitting or sleeping helter-skelter in narrow paths where they found shade. Children ran bumping into them, terrifying Lucius, animals impeded their progress, and dogs barked defending their territory. Progress was slow and agonizing. Sometimes they entered into a narrow passage, turned and twisted, proceeding blindly, only to arrive at a dead end, then backtracked to take a different route. They came upon busy agoras, with merchants setting up their tables side by side impeding progress altogether. These markets were teeming with shoppers and gawkers, testing, inspecting and bartering all at full volume. Just when they thought they had seen everything, they came upon a circus with an oversized tent with acrobats, fortune tellers, animal shows and wagons with lions and tigers, underfed and in a foul mood, growling at the trainer who snapped his whip, ever cognizant of the danger he faced. There were areas filled with a variety of games of chance and gambling wheels patently crooked, deluding the naïve to bet their hard earned shekel. Over the loud clamor of the announcer inviting people, children screamed with laughter so loud, no one could hear a word. Clowns squeezed through tiny openings searching for children to entice parents to take them to the circus. Mixed in with the humanity, the wares, and animals, mingled a strange variety of smells from rows of kiosks offering foodstuff. Booths dispensed sickeningly sweet beverages of doubtful origin.

As they approached the gigantic walls of the city, they started seeing Roman soldiers, armed with swords traveling in pairs. Most were not older than themselves.

Suddenly there was a commotion and they saw people pushing and shoving, running past them towards the gates. They stood on their tip toes and saw a great congregation ahead. "Where is everybody running?" Stephanos asked a pilgrim.

"Master Rabban, the Messiah is coming," the man replied without slowing down.

They looked all around for a glimpse of the legendary person without success. They started pushing ahead but realized there was a greater likelihood of being crushed with little hope of advancement. They craned their necks and gawked everywhere when someone yelled, "There he is!" They swung around searching, and gave up in frustration. Just when they decided to continue about their business, they saw him.

First came some big burly men pushing to open a path. They were obviously Rabban's body guards. Close behind came a giant, a full head taller than the others. He had a mop of unruly curly black hair and a bushy beard.

"He-he's b-bigger than He-Hercules," the Greek stuttered.

Then the unexpected happened. People caught in the center recounted the events to Yeshua afterwards: "The gigantic Egyptian came to perform a feat of strength. People arrived from every direction to see him. Goliath could not have been bigger or stronger. But, the spies for the Romans and the Sanhedrin informed the authorities and they were ready. Suddenly there was a thunderous explosion of pounding hooves as chariots, cavalry, and foot soldiers rushed at the pilgrims. They tried to turn back and escape. Alas, they were trapped and the Romans slaughtered many without mercy."

Yeshua's group was pushed back into the agora where they remained. Soldiers whipped their horses, charging at the people. Chariots smashed into and ran over the fallen bodies. After dispersing the crowd, they disappeared into the safety of the city. The young men came forward to help the victims. They saw the carnage: people walking about in a daze, some cut and bleeding, others with bruises and welts, many bloody with gashes about their arms or backs, most suffering from contusions. Many lay in agony on the ground in pools of blood. Children screamed for their parents, while mothers ran frantically calling and searching for families. The young men stopped to help the injured, and to console them. But six pilgrims died. The Egyptian vanished into thin air.

After helping the injured, the young men proceeded through the gates and saw Jerusalem in the light. It was a dirty, dingy city with crowded narrow streets, and rows of houses built helter-skelter in every direction. Disease and deformity were evident everywhere as were verminous mendicants. Their progress was slowed by beggars, as everywhere emaciated arms stretched out for a penny. Loathsome sores were displayed in efforts to touch the hearts of passing pilgrims.

Yeshua was touched by the misery and suffering but did not possess a spare coin to give. He stared at the Greek who tossed out many a coin as they headed to the Insula.

Finally they came upon a set of marble steps leading up to a large open area. At the far end was the Roman Insula. They climbed the steps and stood admiring the magnificent sight. It was built on a commanding elevation and dominated the entire city. They were impressed with the mosaic pavement, leading to palatial edifices, the largest of which was a huge rectangular three story palace, with numerous columns fronting it. It was the tetrarch's palace. The wide streets were bordered by flowing gardens and baskets of flowers hanging from wrought iron posts. Sculptured statues of eminent Roman emperors and governors stood proudly on pillars set up intermittently throughout the promenade, like sentries guarding the empire's interest.

Banners of the forts of Caesarea, Joppa, Augusteana and Capernaum, topped by the imperial ensign fluttered in the light breeze, giving color to the teeming courtyard. They were concentrating so intently on the beautiful scenery they did not see two soldiers approach until one grabbed Yeshua's hand.

"Master Yeshua we are very grateful you came to see us," the young soldier Appius fell to his knees. "I told Rufus how you saved his life, and he wishes to thank you"

Rufus grabbed Yeshua's other arm and he too fell to his knees, "I owe my life to you, master Yeshua. How can I ever thank you?"

"You do not owe me anything, either of you," the young scholar pulled back embarrassed, and raised Rufus. "How are you feeling from the...bump?"

"Except for the occasional headache, I am in excellent health, sir..."

"We have been spreading the word," Appius interjected enthusiastically.

"Some look at us strangely," Rufus explained. "Roman soldiers speaking about love? Others listen with great interest. When I retire I'll return to my village to teach our neighbors in Appia about you and the new order."

"It is a pleasure to see you again," Yeshua smiled. "Please direct us to the prison."

Rufus pointed to a low dilapidated building in the far corner between the palatial praetorian edifice and the soldiers' quarters. They went directly to it, entering the dark, humid hallway where Yeshua asked the guard, "Do you have a prisoner named Quintus?"

"The Roman private? Who wishes to know?"

"His friends: Yeshua from Nazareth, master Stephanos and his slave Germanicus. We bring a letter from his father," he held out the papyrus.

The guard did not take it but went up a narrow corridor and returned with a senior officer. "Prisoners sentenced for execution are not allowed visitors or gifts," he said.

"Execution: Quintus?" the three were taken back, horrified. They went outside and stood agonizing as if in a bad dream. Germanicus started to inspect the building for weaknesses. After studying it for sometime he shook his head. The narrow entrances were well guarded, the windows were too high with iron bars, and the building was situated next to the soldier's quarters. Breaking Quintus out was out of the question.

"Wait here," Yeshua told them as he returned to the two soldiers, and called, "Private Rufus, Appius come with me. I'll need your help." When they came he told his friends, "We will go to the praetorian. Hopefully the tetrarch will grant me an audience."

When he asked the centurion guarding the giant door, the officer studied them wondering, what are these riff-raff peasants with a lamb in tow up to? And so, summarily, he refused them entry.

Stephanos walked up uncomfortably close to the officer and whispered as if sharing a great personal secret with a special friend, "Recently, his excellency Valerius Gratus, granted us an audience in his court in Caesarea. He was so impressed with my friend, that he offered him a position of personal advisor." He stared at the officer whose resolve wavered and he started to blink nervously. The Greek pressed his advantage, "Tell his excellency that master Yeshua, of Nazareth, has momentous information to correct a grave injustice… and timely advice which will save the tetrarch's career."

The centurion turned and entered the building like a man on a mission. In short order he reappeared smiling, "Master Yeshua his excellency is waiting. Be quick!"

Yeshua barely reached the center of the large room when the tetrarch greeted him, "Master Yeshua, I did not expect the pleasure of your visit so soon. Come forward," he beckoned the youth. "What brings you here?"

The Israeli bowed deeply, "Your excellency, your prison holds a young Roman soldier, private Quintus." He paused to allow the name to sink in. "He is to be executed. I plea…an opportunity to persuade you to grant him clemency…"

The tetrarch pondered the unusual request, and his eyebrows furled wondering if he had misunderstood the guard? Was he not told he came with advice to save his career? After a long pause he motioned his secretary, "Bring me the charges against private Quintus, and direct the guard to present the prisoner." He took the papyrus, and glanced over it quickly. Then he smiled at the young Israeli, "For a brief moment I hoped that you had changed your mind...my offer still stands and it pays handsomely."

"Your excellency is most kind, but..."

"I understand, you're the oldest and your family needs you," the tetrarch did not hide his disappointment, shrugged and changed topics, "Was I not told you had crucial advice pertaining to my office?"

"Indeed your excellency..." he began, when the guard brought Quintus in.

"Private Quintus," the tetrarch turned to him, "Your friends wish to plead your case." He pointed to Yeshua. Quintus, pale and distraught stared at the tetrarch without reacting. After some moments he looked, and recognizing Yeshua broke into a bright smile. He almost choked but the tetrarch's stern voice jerked him back to reality. "These are horrendous charges...scandalous, unprofessional behavior of the worst kind." He summarized the charges: "Theft of government property; aiding criminal Zealots; assaulting Roman soldiers, imprisonment, and murder...Had you done any one of these in the course of a battle, your officer could execute you on the spot with impunity. The empire will not suffer undisciplined rebels!"

Yeshua saw the tetrarch working himself into a frenzy and decided to interrupt, "With respect your excellency...may I speak?"

"Speak!" the tetrarch, who did not like being interrupted, barked.

The young scholar spoke deliberately, to give the tetrarch time to calm down, and bowed low before addressing the case, "Your excellency, I appeal to your sense of justice and beg clemency for this valiant sold..."

"Your imploring with empty rhetoric is in vain," Valerius Gratus cut him short. "Unless you have a tangible argument with persuasive evidence, you're wasting time!"

Yeshua felt like he was scratching into hard marble with bare fingernails. He had to think fast. In an instant of inspiration, he turned to the door as he continued, "I have evidence that some of the charges are false and malicious. I ask privates Ruffus and Appius to come forward."

The tetrarch was surprised by the unexpected development and demanded gruffly, "Have you two any knowledge about these charges?" They nodded nervously, and he barked impatiently, "Come forward. Hurry up; I don't have all day." They shuffled ahead. "Speak!" he demanded.

Rufus started, slowly and in a low voice, "It is my fault, your excellency. I falsified the charges against Quintus. He did not help Zealots... or assault us...Appius did not want to do it, but...I forced him..."

Quintus stood dumbfounded, wondering what had brought about their confession?

The tetrarch was also stunned by the turn of events, and calmed down, "Appius acquiesced to your deeds, and is equally guilty." Then he turned to Yeshua, "Even so there are still many serious charges to warrant a death sentence. I am not persuaded..."

"I have further submissions, but these are for your ears only, your excellency," the young scholar replied. "May I approach the throne?" The tetrarch's eyebrows furled as he wondered what this remarkable peasant could possibly add, but remembering his timely advice in the past, waved him to approach. Yeshua came up and whispered, "When a Roman citizen is sentenced to death, he has a right to appear personally before emperor Augustus to appeal his case. Private Quintus will certainly be doing that..."

"Don't you think I know that?" Valerius interrupted impatiently. "For his sake I hope he has something more persuasive than your rhetoric..."

"Quintus will tell the emperor how your excellency led Roman soldiers who ambushed and massacred hundreds of defenseless Samaritans on mount Gerezim."

"Are you threatening me?" the tetrarch turned crimson deciding he had wasted enough time on such insignificant matter. The Israeli shook his head. The tetrarch tried to snigger but his grey eyes were a shade paler, "Augustus Caesar will not believe him..."

"An entourage of Samaritans is boarding a bark for Rome as we speak," Yeshua continued calmly. "They will be presenting their case to the emperor...and private Quintus will corroborate their accusations.

"What do you suggest?" Valerius Gratus squirmed on the throne uncomfortably.

"Commute his sentence to banishment. Fifteen years out of Israel..."

Before he finished the tetrarch announced weakly, "I have heard an overwhelming plea, with rare persuasive force for clemency, and I will show mercy. I commute the sentence and banish private Quintus for fifteen years." He glanced at Yeshua who whispered something, and the tetrarch asked, "Is your father a retired centurion?" Quintus nodded, and his excellency added, "You may return if your father becomes ill, or dies."

"Thank you, your excellency…for your mercy," Quintus fell to his knees heavily.

The tetrarch turned to the two soldiers, "Privates Rufus and Appius your punishment will also be banishment." He motioned the guard, "Arrest them. They will travel with Quintus." He looked at Yeshua and flicked his hand shooing him away, "Off with you!" As they were leaving, the Israeli slipped the centurion's letter to Quintus.

Quintus glanced far behind the tetrarch's throne, and saw a young lady who had followed the proceedings, from the stairs. She seemed little more than fifteen years of age, with light curly hair and blue eyes. She stared at the prisoner, and when their eyes met, the corners of her mouth stretched into a smile. She was the most beautiful girl he had ever seen. That night a special meal arrived in his cell with a note. That was how he learned the tetrarch's daughter's name was Veronica.

(Quintus boarded a bark for Rome with the two soldiers, where they remained. By and by emperor Augustus died and his great nephew Tiberius succeeded the throne. Eager to please, he granted an audience to the Samaritans, where Quintus and the two soldiers corroborated the story of the massacre. Valerius Gratus was unceremoniously removed and recalled to Rome. Soon he was posted to command a legion in the wild frontiers of northern Europe. A small contingent accompanied him and his family. Among the soldiers were privates Quintus, Rufus and Appius. Quintus got to know Veronica intimately. But, that's another story.)

From the hearing Yeshua's group proceeded to the Temple. There they stood with awe. It was the most beautiful, massive edifice they had ever seen. As impressive as it appeared from the Mount of Olives, it was truly magnificent when they stood at the foot of the marble steps before the world's most revered structure. It was amply obvious this wonderful miracle of modern engineering was of foreign origin, for its columns and pilasters, the rosy sandstone and imported marble, fairly shouted that it had no relation whatsoever to its mean environment.

Master Stephanos wanted to visit the antiquities shops to search for ancient parchments and gifts in the tourist shops. Yeshua argued against it saying the bazaars were teeming with robbers, "Wait until Lucius' inspection and I will accompany you."

"You'll be there the whole day," the Greek pointed to the long line of pilgrims with their animals. "Moreover I have Germanicus to protect me."

The Israeli knew it was a waste of time to argue, so when they started he grabbed the slave by the sleeve, with stern orders, "Protect your master. I leave him in your care." His radiant eyes seemed to burn into the slave's conscience.

The Greek knew that shops of antiquities contained, in the dark corners, the rarest ancient scripts. Tourists, attracted by the glitter of cheap trinkets, passed over these jewels of ancient cultures. In Babylon by chance he had discovered such a diamond in the rough, prophesizing about the Messiah, which had ultimately brought him here. Now he hoped to uncover other gems. As they entered an area filled with tables, kiosks and tents heaped with merchandize, their progress slowed to a crawl.

Stephanos turned to make certain the slave was close behind, and smiled reassured, "At times like these I'm glad you're guarding my back." They continued at a snail's pace, stopping, inspecting and purchasing toys. After a while he sniffed a strange, smell, "We must be approaching Fish gate. Merchants bring dried, salted fish from great distances: the Great Sea, Arabian Sea, Egypt…"

Germanicus looked around and saw the big gate, making a mental note of the surrounding landmarks. They were stopped by a merchant coming across with his donkey, so the Greek added valuable information, "One goes out that gate, takes the road to the right around the city walls, and at the first intersection takes the path to the north which leads to the Sea of Galilee, thence left to Nazareth: a simple three day journey."

They stopped in antiquities shops where Stephanos inspected numerous parchments: inscriptions on fragile leather skin, writings on copper sheets, and papyrus which he analyzed, verifying their authenticity. Close inspection often proved scripts to have been erased or over-written with false data. He purchased a couple, bought more gifts and started to return via the bazaar.

Germanicus followed loaded down, biding his time until they were returning to the narrow roads by the Fish gate. As they approached he felt his belt and his muscles tightened when he touched the cold blade. He felt his forehead wet with perspiration, and his hands began to tremble. His breathing was shallow, and he felt clammy and faint. He decided if he was going to act he must do it now. A flashback came in his mind's eye: Yeshua did not make those soldiers his slaves. When he saved the old man he spoke of love, not slavery. How could he kill his master using

Yeshua as the excuse? It was clear that he could not. But now it was too late. He had to act or forever remain a slave. He struggled to push all extraneous thoughts aside. His mind screamed: NOW IS THE TIME! He reached for the dagger, when powerful jostling and pushing made it impossible to reach the blade. He struggled, wiggled and twisted every-which-way to no avail. Perspiration ran into his eyes when he finally closed his hand on the cold steel. When he looked up, his master was nowhere to be seen. He panicked. Had he guessed his intention and run away? He searched every which way without success.

Suddenly he heard his name, "Germanicus! Wait! You're going the wrong way."

He turned around and saw his master behind him struggling to catch up.

Master Stephanos took one look at him and was horrified, "Are you all right? You're as white as a sheet of papyrus. Come, I'll get you some fresh air…"

He grabbed the slave by the collar while at the same time pushing with all his might to open a path and advance against the wave of bodies. He screamed savagely, "Open up! Move! I have a sick man who…desperately needs air. Move away…"

Germanicus felt he was at the bottom of a deep well with the top closing in. The lights began to flicker – going out, coming back, going out – his eyes were unfocussing, and his mouth was dry. His breath was shallow and erratic, and all he could think was, this was where he was going to die. His heart pounded so hard he thought his chest would burst. At that moment he smelled the faint aroma of fish, and his mind triggered one desperate thought: FREEDOM! NOW! As he pulled out the dagger he had the sensation the world was revolving before his eyes, for two bearded faces were all over him shoving and yelling into his face, reaching over him. Something flashed. Was it his blade? He heard Stephanos yelling. Everything seemed to spiral and go blurry. He raised the weapon high letting out a blood curdling scream as he plunged the dagger.

• • •

Debborah sat and watched lady Sarah pacing in her father's office, talking incessantly, "I don't understand it. Father was a great architect, and a famous builder. I saw his designs," she emphasized as if trying to persuade her friend. As she explained she drew outlines of imaginary buildings in the air, "I still remember a very high, beautiful structure, with wide windows and big doors, a wide portico, ever so cool..." Then she returned to pacing to and fro, "He explained every blueprint to me as a little child. I sat on his lap and watched his supple hand outlining and explaining every contour: composition, balance, and how curved lines on drawings please the eye. He took me to the edifices he erected in Tyre. They were exquisite, magnificent and aristic. He designed and built this mansion," she swept her arms around the room. "It is a rare inspiration from the gods... He was a perfect man...He was obviously revered by the Romans." She emphasized the statement, then looked out of the window asking the very heavens, "Why else would the commander send that affectionate letter? How do you explain the handsome gift of gold talents except payment in recognition of his genius?" She turned to her friend as if expecting her endorsement. The younger girl nodded weakly, keeping her eyes on the floor. She knew her friend suffered from guilt, causing her to exaggerate his qualities, but she was not willing to disagree. "Yet, if they acknowledge his talents, why won't they raise a statue to him: a small bust, or some dedication, to celebrate his life?" She became worked up and tears flowed as she pleaded, "Let not his memory disappear through the sands of time without a trace that he walked this earth..."

She walked up to Debborah peppering her with questions, "Do you know what I'm going to do? Find out about his most recent contracts: every building and structure. Why should I not erect a statue to celebrate his genius? I'll shout out to the world about him."

Debborah's eyes opened as wide as saucers, and she was not able to hide her fear for her friend, "Wait! Don't over react...Right now you're feeling guilty for his death..."

"Why should I not feel guilty? I caused his death!" she spluttered turning on her friend, "Oh, why do I bother...What do you know? You're just a child..."

Debborah was frantic, trying desperately to take her mind from the morbid topic, and save her from the crushing truth. She did not dare tell her for it would devastate her. Suddenly an idea came, "Lady Sarah, remember when you first moved here, the different things you were learning from Israeli families: weaving, baking and grinding flour? You enjoyed learning our traditions and history; why not do it again?"

"What?" she interrupted, staring at her friend as if she had lost her mind. She scowled and fumed as she rebuked her, "This is the most insensitive suggestion I have ever heard. My father was murdered, and I should concentrate on entertaining myself?"

"Well..." Debborah blurted out unable to think of anything to say.

"You are no help whatsoever. It's obvious if research needs to be done, I'll have to do it," she marched to the door resolutely, saw a servant and a slave in the courtyard and motioned them over. "I want you to go to Sepphoris, and you to Tyre. There you are to make inquiries about my father's work: names of edifices, warehouses, and all types of structures he designed or constructed recently. But, be very careful. Don't ask aristocrats as they hated father. Speak only to servants and slaves. They will be truthful." She opened a small purse and handed them some coins, "These are for food and lodging. Fly and be quick about it. I won't rest until I find out..." They bowed and left. Sarah turned to her friend smiling. "When I find out, I'll celebrate his achievements. They'll revere and envy a great man...a genius. Then I'll have closure...and eternal rest for his soul."

Debborah watched her friend with sympathy and trepidation, and felt tears burning. She wished she had told lady Sarah the truth whatever the consequences.

．　．　．

Yeshua was second in line with Lucius, watching a priest from the Temple inspect the pilgrims' animals. Most of the animals were rejected. He wondered why it was so difficult to approve an animal, slaughter it, take a portion for the priests and return the rest to the pilgrim? Instead, most of them got into arguments some dragged the animals away, while others abandoned them and walked away.

When he finally came to the head of the line, he listened carefully to the pilgrim ahead who had a goat. Just as the inspection started, he felt a tugging of his sleeve. He turned and saw an old, frail, dirty little man, missing most of his teeth, begging, "Can you spare a coin? A penny...anything. I've no home, no job...I need food..."

"I only have father's coins," he apologized. "They're for the Temple tax..."

"I've no one," the beggar pleaded. "I don't remember the last time I did Passover."

"If it's food you seek, wait here. After I finish I'll take you to camp and feed you."

While Yeshua attended to the beggar, a big, corpulent, balding man barged in front of him and waited for the priest. He was obviously wealthy, as he was barbarously festooned with jewellery, a dozen heavy gold chains rounding from his neck to his big belly. Every finger was ornamented with gold rings, as were his ears, and he wore heavy gold bracelets and anklets.

He walked up to the priest, pushing the pilgrim aside, beaming a wide smile, "A thousand pardons for my intrusion, sir. I come from afar, a humble worshipper in the holy Temple." The priest was about to admonish him, when he raised an ornamented hand and removed a ring with a large red gem, which he held up "I need a special chair for the service and a sacrificial animal for my extended family to do Passover..."

Seeing the large stone the priest became mesmerized and his lips began to quiver, "Y-yes, your excellency...Wait right here..." He turned and ran into the Temple.

The beggar saw the bejeweled man, and shuffled towards him, pulling at his sleeve. The corpulent one glanced over and catching a glimpse of the runt, turned away. The old beggar went around and tugged his other sleeve, "Can you spare anything for an old man... a coin, a meal, in the name of Lord Adonai?"

"I have nothing for you," the bejeweled nabob shouted, "Go find some work!"

"No one will hire me, governor. I tried. They throw me out...Please, help."

The fat man frowned, visibly repulsed, grabbed him, literally lifting him off the ground, and heaved him as one discards trash. He landed on his face and rolled through the dust. Yeshua ran after him, and picked him up. Meanwhile the priest returned with a large man whom the young scholar recognized immediately.

"Welcome to Jerusalem. My name is Caiphas," the large man cooed to the nabob. "My father in law is his excellency Ananas, the High Priest."

The stranger held out the gold ring, "A gift for your troubles, master Caiphas."

"No trouble," master Caiphas put an arm on his shoulder, while he deftly plucked the ring with the other, and marched him merrily into the Temple.

Yeshua was so intrigued that he did not notice the priest already inspecting Lucius. The young scholar rushed and volunteered affably, "You don't have to inspect my lamb. It is in perfect condition. Rabbi ben Lebbus went over him thoroughly."

"I'm not your rabbi," he snapped frostily, continuing the examination. Suddenly he roared exuberantly, "Aha! I knew it! On the small of his back he has - A WART!" he announced it as if referring to a terminal disease. "Uncceptable; he's deformed." His judgment was so forceful that Yeshua's jaw dropped. The priest came close, softening his tone, "However, we understand. We raise animals…unblemished. Guaranteed! For a few coins, and your deformed creature, we will provide…"

"I have no money," the young man blurted out with disbelief. "Please take Luci…?"

The priest turned away calling out, "Next! Hurry up, I don't have all day." He pushed the young scholar aside.

Yeshua moved over a couple of paces, astonished by the episode when he noticed the beggar still around and asked, "Are there many of you in need of a Passover meal?"

The beggar nodded dramatically, "I cannot count that high, governor…"

"Take Lucius and enjoy a happy Passover with them," he handed him the twine and walked away.

From there he proceeded directly to the money exchangers' tables to change his coins into silver shekels, the only currency the Temple priests accepted. He did not notice but he was being followed by a young priest in a white cloak. When he passed, the priest commented, "Your generosity will long be remembered, and recorded," master Yeshua.

Yeshua had a strange feeling that he had seen the smiling priest before but could not recollect the circumstances. He stopped by the money exchangers and was shocked to see a long line before every banker. He smiled and congratulated himself when he found one without a single customer. He was waved to the table directly and marched to it. The banker resembled a brigand more than a banker, and demanded gruffly, "How much?"

"Half a shekel…" he mumbled almost inaudibly.

"Speak up," he ordered impatiently.

"Half a shekel," Yeshua blurted out spilling the coins from the pouch onto the table.

Like all the others he brought an assortment of coins from the empire: drachmas, copper pennies, denarii from Rome, Israeli Yehuds, Syrian,

Egyptian and Persian coins and whatever currency customers paid for a carpenter's service. The banker scowled as he inspected them, computed on papyrus, all the while shaking his head and smacking his tongue with a sour expression. Finally he fixed his cold eyes on Yeshua, "You don't have nearly enough. You need the equivalent of twenty Greek drachmas…not counting my commission."

"But, I have no more. What shall I do? "Yeshua replied dejected.

"Go beg for it," the banker shoved his coins back, yelling around him, "Next!"

Before anyone could advance, a man stepped up, put his hand on the coins, and stared at the brigand, "I heard you tell my friend a half shekel costs twenty drachmas?" The banker, not expecting the rude intrusion, nodded nervously. "I come from a banker's family in Corinth, and I know the cost has never been over fifteen." The banker wanted to argue when the man started to pull a scroll from his tunic demanding, "Shall I prove it?"

"N-No, no…" the banker shrank back in his seat visibly perturbed.

"How much is your commission?"

"Eight per cent…sir."

The man counted the coins expertly threw down two pennies and ordered, "Give him his shekel."

The banker obeyed. Yeshua took it and as they stepped back he recognized master Stephanos. The Greek grabbed him by the arm and quickly dragged him away.

"How did you…? What…?" Yeshua was still shaken up. After they cleared the area he grinned cheerfully, "It was fortunate you brought the exchange list."

"This?" Stephanos pulled the scroll. "It's an antique parchment I just purchased."

The Israeli shook his head, then looked around baffled, "Where is Germanicus?"

The Greek sighed and led him towards the Temple explaining, "We were attacked by armed robbers. Fortunately Germanicus foresaw the danger and came armed. His forsight saved my life - once more."

When they arrived Germanicus was bloody from the head to the toes, distraught and shaking like a leaf. Yeshua sat beside him and put an arm around his shoulders, "Your master told me about your brave action. Were you injured? Are you alright?"

The slave sobbed, "I'm fine. M-master Yeshua, I...I killed a man. You warned me, but I did...not listen. I'm sorry. I...I did not mean..." He was totally crushed.

"I explained he was defending me," master Stephanos pressed the slave's arm in gratitude. "Even the police said it was not his fault...They were trying to rob me..."

"Your reaction clearly saved your master," Yeshua tried to console him.

"My intentions were...not honorable," the slave mumbled in tears. "I have forsaken my Creator...You were right...my plans were evil."

Yeshua knew it would take a long time before he would recover from the horrible experience, if ever. He spoke with empathy, "You committed my error. But, you have repented. If you live an exemplary life, and forsake violence, you will be forgiven."

The slave looked with hope, "Do you promise Yahweh will not abandon me?"

Stephanos pulled out a pouch and held it out, "Master Yeshua told me to give you these coins. If we get separated, you have enough to get you back to Nazareth."

Germanicus refused to take it, so his master stuck it under his belt.

Yeshua took him by the hand, "Let's go back and get you out of this bloody tunic."

They started for the camp but Germanicus, still weak, started falling behind. He was still in shock and not thinking clearly. He could hardly believe that the very money he was ready to kill for, was freely given to him. He considered turning and running away, and glanced in the direction of the Fish gate. But, he put the thought aside and followed them. Inexplicably his hand went for the belt and he felt the pouch. Once more his mind was on Europe in the spring, where he could roam free! His mind was in a state of confusion, vacillating: follow his master, or freedom in Europe?

They were almost at the city gate when a crowd pushed them blocking the exit, and started congregating in the area. Yeshua asked why all the commotion and was told, "Master Rabban is coming to demonstrate a fantastic feat of strength."

"We heard that his strength is formidable," the Greek commented rhetorically.

"It should be. After all he is the Messiah," the stranger asserted emphatically.

Just then loud yelling and cheering made everyone to turn to the gate. A group of men pushed through the multitude. Behind them came an old man leading four donkeys pulling a cart, upon which rested a gigantic rectangular marble bolder. The animals pulled with all their might and the axles squealed and squeaked under the heavy load. Behind them four men followed guarding an enormous giant.

"I swear he is bigger than the biggest hero on mount Olympus," Stephanos gushed.

Yeshua's eyes were fixed on the colossal giant as he was studying him. He imagined ancient history must have had cavemen like this: husky, with long curly hair, dishelved and unkempt, his clothes consisting of animal skins sewn together. But when he looked into the giant's eyes, something troubled him. His eyes were set deep in dark sockets, and he seemed to have a vacant stare, like someone whose mind was elsewhere, unhappy with his present circumstances. Yeshua could not decide whether it was boredom or he had deeper promlems of the psyche. While he was debating, the manager stepped forward.

"My fellow Israelis I bid you good day. I have the pleasure to introduce to you the incomparable...the invincible master Rabban, who is quickly acquiring – deservedly - the title of MESSIAH! Today our hero will demonstrate a feat that your eyes will see, but your minds will deny saying - IT IS IMPOSSIBLE! Without touching it, master Rabban will lift that twenty tonne marble stone in the air and keep it suspended above the cart. The power of his mind will defeat gravity. "The manager watched them snigger as their skeptical eyes darted from the giant to the bolder, back and forth and they whispered, "Never! It's impossible!", "That's not a boulder...it's a box of papyrus!" and "It's all a sham!" The sarcastic comments pleased him, for it raised the atmosphere of drama.

"I know what some of you are thinking. That's not a stone; it can't weight twenty tonne; he'll use invisible strings to raise it. We will test and prove all skepticism wrong. I ask eight husky young men, the strongest here, to come forward and lift this boulder." He walked to the bolder and pushed on the thick timber supporting it, but it did not budge. "Do I have eight volunteers?" No one came forward, so he pulled a sizable purse from his belt and shook it, "This is the sound of pure gold and silver. If I can get eight strong men to raise the bolder...the width of my little finger, I will give you the coins."

A legion of strong young men came forward. The manager let the spectators choose the strongest, and placed them two at each corner of the bolder. "Gentlemen get your shoulders under the timber. On the count to three you lift. Ready? Let's count together: ONE...TWO...THREE...AND LIFT!"

They took a deep breath, put their shoulders to the timber, pressed, and pressed... Their faces turned red, the veins stuck out on their necks as they grunted, then their arms began to tremble, and finally their bodies and legs. The spectators held their breaths heaving in sympathy. But, the bolder sat on the cart, as if cemented in place. They rested for a moment and tried again, and a third time, with the same results.

The Herculean youths stood back staring at the stone in awe as if staring at a mountain. Some touched it in reverence, others slapped it as if congratulating a worthy foe, and a few searched under the cart looking for hidden bolts fastening the stone to it. The manager watched with a chuckle, and turned to the crowd.

"Now you will see the strongest man in the world do what they failed. But, he will lift it without touching it: not a hand, a finger, not even a hair. The power of the mind will cause it to rise. Fellow Israelis - the living Messiah: RABBAN!"

The spectators gave him a warm round of applause, and for the first time the giant showed signs of interest, as he took giant strides towards the announcer. He walked around the giant marble as a wrestler stalks his opponent, raising suspense and drama, then stopped about fifteen paces from his foe. He raised his outstretched arms up to the sky, as if receiving super strength from the heavens, then lowered them and pointed at the stone. His finger tips began to twitch slowly, at first one, then another, and another until his hands and arms trembled. Soon his body was quivering as if suffering from high fever. Not a sound was heard. No one moved. Slowly his body quieted, becoming as still as a statue of marble, and the place eerily silent as a tomb. An invisible force seemed to link him to the stone, for it began to quiver, rocking the cart. The spectators gasped. The helpers ran to hold the donkeys, others hung on to the cart so it would not disintegrate.

The impossible began to unfold before their eyes: the gigantic bolder began to ascend slowly, steadily and became suspended in the air. The audience let out loud "oohs" and "aahs," their mouths unhinged. Their eyes were transfixed. The stone floated two cubits above the cart like a sheet of papyrus levitating in the breeze.

The manager teased them, "Anyone who doubts what he is seeing is welcome to crawl under the stone and inspect for cables or mechanical trappings." They scoffed at his idiotic invitation, and nobody ventured forward. The manager walked up to the cart, jumped on and rolled under the stone to the opposite side and back unimpeded. A thunderous applause exploded. Rabban lowered the stone to shouts of approval.

Yeshua watched the colossal man throughout and was amazed at the amount of energy he expended. By the end of the show he was drenched with perspiration. He smiled weakly, happy to have pleased the crowd, but visibly gasping for breath, his hands trembling and his eyes showing signs of exhaustion. The spectators, unaware or uncaring that he was spent, began to chant, "One more time; one more time..." The giant sensed they would not stop until he satisfied their demands, turned to leave. They began to shout abuses: "Is that all you are: a one trick pony?" an old pilgrim jeered. "His gears are worn out," a youth pointed to his head. "You're a fraud," a woman accused him.

The taunting enraged him and he growled like an angry bear. Suddenly he turned to the cart pointing his arms at the bolder and started to lift. Only this time he also lifted the cart and the four donkeys, and when he flung his arms violently, everything flew against the gigantic stone wall of the city. The marble smashed into a thousand pieces showering the spectators, the cart splintered, disintegrating, and the animals crashed and fell helplessly. People were injured by the flying pieces of the cart, the wheels and wood, and started to run panic striken, creating a pandemonium.

Suddenlly they saw the Romans rushing at them. Yeshua realized they had no chance to escape if they remained with the masses. He grabbed the Greek and dragged him to the far wall by to the gate, "We'll try to exit next to this wall. If we fail, we'll have no choice but to return to the square."

He guessed correctly for the cavalry rode at the pilgrims blocking the entrance, then cut them down indiscriminately. Most of the people stood petrified, unable to defend or protect themselves. Women screamed for their missing children. Some were pushed aside, but many were trampled by the rushing people, or crushed under the horses. The Romans chopped their swords cutting limbs and crushing skulls. One old man, panic stricken, climbed on the backs of others, when a sword lopped off half of his neck, leaving the headless body hanging on. Those who could not escape turned and ran towards the horses. Those who survived the first onslaught were crushed by a wave of chariots and mangled under the wheels. The few who survived both were finished by foot soldiers armed with spears. Only the rare pilgrim managed to run back into the square.

Yeshua pushed and squeezed along the wall making slow progress pulling his friend. The best part of being against the wall was that the Romans only attacked the middle. Hence they pushed ahead and seemed to rush out as if caught in a current at ebb tide. Once disgorged out of the gate they yelled at each other to keep moving. Outside they ran for cover among the tents.

As soon as he was safe Yeshua yelled, "Stephanos! Steph…where are you?"

The Greek who hid a few paces away, was seized with panic. He heard his friend but could not reply, sitting curled up, trembling and mumbling, "Here. I'm here…"

Yeshua began to search frantically expecting the worst, until he found him in a dark corner and scolded him, "There you are! Why don't you answer?"

Stephanos stared at him blankly, his mouth moving without uttering a sound. The Israeli realized his friend was in shock, sat beside him, and put his arm around his shoulder, "You'll be alright now. We're safe."

After a while the Greek calmed down and managed a faint smile, "I feel better now. I have never been more frightened." He turned to his friend, "How is Germanicus?"

They stared at one another realizing they had not seen him during Rabban's show, and jumped up calling and searching. They ran back to the gate, "He must be inside," Stephanos cried out. "He will be killed." He started to push against the people yelling, "I'm going in…I have to find him."

Yeshua screamed, "Don't! You'll be killed!" But the Greek pushed relentlessly to get in, so he decided to follow, "Stephanos, wait I'm coming with you!"

. . .

When the spectators panicked, Germanicus was caught in the middle. When he saw the Romans advancing he realized he could not stay there, but had nowhere to run. His only chance was to run at the cavalry. In a fraction of an instant he decided: if he survived he would continue to Nazareth and then to Europe. He knew hundreds would be slaughtered here, and one body more or less would not matter. They would never find him. As he started to run at the horses, he saw far in the distance the Fish gate.

He charged towards the middle at the biggest horse. The Roman instinctively pulled the reigns to avoid him, then brought the animal back to run over him. In that fraction of time Germanicus jumped to the ground to avoid the horse's hooves and the soldier's sword. He rolled on the ground as hooves pounded all around him, and got up behind them unscathed. Before he could react, the chariots were on top of him. He knew from experience these were deadly. Chariots originated in northern Europe, and he had learned to respect and fear them. He dove instinctively into the first space avoiding the hooves. Alas, a wheel struck his left thigh and he felt a sharp pain. When he tried to get up and run to avoid the infantry he felt an excruciating pain. He managed to drag himself a couple of steps and fell to his knees. The last he remembered was a soldier's shield slamming him full in the face. He folded back and fell in a heap.

He did not know if he passed out, or how long he lay there. When he attempted to get up, he could hardly put any weight on the injured leg. He looked back at the Romans who were slaughtering the pilgrims. He turned for the Fish gate, stepping over dead bodies. His head ached, and his face throbbed, and it was bleeding profusely. His left eye was swollen shut. He hobbled and dragged his left leg towards freedom.

Every step of his agonizing progress he thought of Nazareth, his lovely Anna and his beautiful little girl Lygia.

He looked ahead and saw Fish gate. Under it stood the three slaves waiting.

CHAPTER XX - NAZARETH

It was dark before Yeshua and Stephanos returned to camp exhausted and depressed. Ellie ran up rambling, "Where is Germanicus? And where is Lucius?"

"I gave Lucius away," the young scholar muttered. "We don't know what happened to Germanicus. He disappeared…"

"Slaves only disappear when there is work to be done," master Azim disputed with a sardonic tone. "Three of my slaves went missing since morning, and I'll wager the sons of scorpions have run away: perhaps with Germanicus?"

The Greek sat down, too depressed to consider conspiracies, "We stopped to watch the Egyptian when the Romans came. He may be on a slab…with the rest of the corpses."

"We searched everywhere…" Yeshua shook his head dejected.

"Master Azim is correct," master Micah suggested. "Slaves have more lives than cats. Just when you think he has breathed his last, he picks himself up, dusts himself up and walks away."

"What happened to Lucius?" Ellie persisted.

"The priest found a blemish and demanded money, which I did not have," Yeshua was still crossed. "I decided if I could not please the Temple I'd feed the hungry."

"I watched the farse," master Azim shook his head in disbelief. "They used the flimsiest excuse to refuse the animals, then extort wads of money."

"Same with the corrupt money changers" master Micah echoed his sentiments.

Yeshua declared ominously, "If the Temple is not cleansed, I foresee the corruption destroying the Priesthood, and the Temple!"

"Don't get too dejected. Wallowing in hatred is a waste of energy," master Azim decided to brighten the mood, "I purchased a bull for my extended family. There is food for everyone. So let's join all the tables and celebrate Passover together."

"I concur whole heartedly," master Aaron started dragging his table over. "We'll enjoy the holy day as one family."

"Please join us master Yeshua?" the younger members pleaded pulling at his sleeves. Before he could reply, master Azim put his arm around his shoulders confiding, "Our family wants you to lead tonight's ceremony: especially the younger generation."

"Me? But tradition says the head of the family..." he started objecting.

"Do you think I don't know our tradition?" the patriarch interrupted. "They were most impressed with how you dealt with the centurion... Moreover they heard my story so many times, it's as stale as last week's bread."

The youngsters brought make-shift tables, benches and wooden blocks to sit on, and joined them into one long table. Yeshua sat the younger generation in the middle, with the patriarchs at the ends. He placed Aaron's family and Ellie directly across from him, and master Stephanos at a table at the end.

Master Micah saw the Greek's table abutting theirs and objected gruffly, "Get the gentile away from our sacred ceremony. You're going in the teeth of tradition."

"His table is separate from ours," the young scholar replied diplomatically.

"Do you take me for a fool?" Micah barked. "He may as well be on my lap."

Yeshua explained, "The question of distance is a subjective one. For instance, our religion forbids us to work on the Sabbath, including walks longer than two thousand cubits. But wealthy Israelis send servants to deposit worthless personal articles every thousand cubits, then travel great distances...saying they never left their residence."

The younger people guessed where that was leading, and tried to stifle a gleeful chuckle, while master Micah's face turned beet red and his eyes the grey of steel.

Yeshua passed the blade of a knife effortlessly between the two tables concluding, "See? His table may as well be two thousand cubits away."

"The Greek stays," the younger generation cheered with exuberance.

"Master Stephanos is a good man. I am proud to invite him to join my table," master Azim motioned the Greek to come over.

Stephanos who enjoyed the anecdote chose to diffuse the tension, "Thank you but I don't wish to create discord in your fine family."

The goblets were filled with watered down wine, and Yeshua proposed a toast, "Friends, I suggest we celebrate this year's Passover in a novel manner: by honoring the memory of a fine friend and a kind person, the late...GERMANICUS?" He pointed his goblet at a stranger, entering their camp, unsteady, bloody and bruised, his bloody tunic as tattered rags . He was grimy and disheveled, almost unrecognizable.

Stephanos was the first to run and grab him, before he fell to the ground. He cried out exuberantly, "Praise be almighty Zeus: Germanicus – you're alive!"

Yeshua grabbed a jug of water and splashed his face at the same time demanding, "Bring a basin of water, oil and medicine...and clean clothes. I will wash his wounds."

Stephanos and Ellie ran to fetch the items.

Yeshua washed his sores carefully, "Your face is badly swollen. I'll pull your eyelid open. Can you see?" The slave winced but nodded. "Is your nose broken?" he asked moving it gently both ways. The slave shook his head. "Let's look at your head... some bruises, blood, but no deep cuts. Any broken bones or open wounds on the body?"

Germanicus pointed to his left thigh and the young Israeli pressed with his fingers, "There is a deep bruise but no broken bones. What happened? We searched all over."

The slave explained his misadventure in a low voice: running at the Romans, the chariot cutting him down, and a soldier's shield finishing him off.

"It's a miracle you are alive," Yeshua said. "There were thousands killed ..."

Ellie returned with the basin and Yeshua continued to wash him whispering, "You could have run to freedom. What made you come back?"

"When I saw my conspirators, I knew I did not want the life of a fugitive. When master gave me those coins I was free. But I remembered young Jonathan's words: I needed to feel free here first," he pointed to his chest. "I realized I needed my Creator with me...and His love. Then I could strive for freedom. You taught me that."

"Me? I thought I failed you miserably."

"You tried but I was too obsessed to listen. But, I intend to earn my freedom."

Stephanos brought a new tunic, so Yeshua changed the subject abruptly, "Master Rabban has to be stopped. Everywhere he goes he brings death and destruction. If he destroys the Temple which he can do, he will kill thousands of pilgrims."

"Who is strong enough to stop him?" Stephanos posed the question rhetorically.

"Who is foolish enough to try?" a young man corrected him.

"It will take a small battalion to subdue the giant," master Azim conceded.

"Or someone as strong as Samson," a young lady offered. "Someone with supernatural powers...But where can we find him?"

Stephanos and Germanicus glanced at each other then turned to Yeshua. He stared from one to the other and shook his head mouthing, "Not me: no way!"

After washing and cleaning the wounds, the slave joined his master. Yeshua raised his goblet cheerfully, "I propose to celebrate Germanicus' survival, and congratulate him for finding his life's dream." They drank and the young ladies quickly refilled them. Then he told the ancient story, "Traditionally we celebrate the Passover and the Paschal meal, recounting the story of Moses who liberated the Hebrews from slavery in Egypt, and brought them to the Promised Land.

"Moses was born to a poor Israeli family, put in a basket of reeds, and set floating to Egypt for a better life. The Pharaoh's daughter found him, and brought him up in the royal family. As an adult he learned his ancestry and that his people were local slaves.

"According to legend Yahweh ordered Moses to go to the Pharaoh and demand 'To let my people go.' The king refused and a long struggle ensued. Moses brought much strife and destruction to Egypt: he touched the waters of the river with his staff turning it the red of blood. The water stank and the fish died. But the Pharaoh refused to free his people. Next he caused frogs to leave the river and go into the houses. When he touched the dust with his rod it turned to lice in men; and he caused all cattle to die. Each time the Pharaoh became frightened promising to release them, only to recant later.

"Moses continued to battle the tyrant: causing fine dust to grow boils on men and beasts; causing locusts to invade the land and devour everything leaving it bare; and he brought down heavy hail to pound the land,

and burn their crops. And each time the Pharaoh promised to free them and each time Moses stopped the punishment he recanted.

"Moses realized that the tyrant's people must be severely punished. He told every Israeli family to sacrifice a male animal and splash the blood on the door frames. That night while Egypt slept, the angel of death passed through the land and smote the first born male of every household. However it passed over the houses marked with blood. Next day the Pharaoh gave in to the Israeli God and liberated them.

"Our folklore says they left in a rush, fearing that the Pharaoh may give them chase. Therefore they did not wait for the dough to rise, but baked and ate unleavened bread which we will now do." He broke some unleavened bread and ate it, washing it down with watered down wine. They followed his example. He continued, "The Pharaoh chased them. On the shores of the Red Sea Moses called upon God to part the waters and they escaped. Then the seas closed behind them frustrating their pursuers.

"For forty years Moses led them through the desert, searching for the Promised Land. They survived by eating bitter roots of the desert and manna from heaven. Like them we will eat these." They ate chicory, endive, dandelion, snake root, pepper root, horseradish and an egg, wincing for the bitter taste chafed their taste buds.

"They travelled the desert of Sinai, where God gave them the Ten Commandments. When they crossed the Jordan, entering the land of milk and honey, they feasted."

At this point they ate the roasted meat and drank the third goblet of wine.

When he finished, he closed his eyes and recited the Hallel, then asked them to bow their heads in prayer, "My dear heavenly Abba, we thank You for this wonderful day, and the special friends who shared this sacred meal, and ask that Yahweh blesses our special guests master Stephanos and Germanicus…"

At the mention of the forbidden name, two people reacted vigorously: master Micah tensed up gritting his teeth, and lady Mona sat back with a jolt: she recognized the young man's soft voice pleading for Ellie's life. Her eyes popped wide and she stared at Yeshua, pointing and mouthing words without a sound. The others continued praying with their heads bowed, oblivious to her personal drama.

Ellie sensed her mother fidgeting, looked up and guessed what happened. She yanked at her mother's sleeve, put her index finger across her lips whispering, "P-s-h-t! I know…be quiet!" and returned to praying.

Alas, lady Mona could not keep still. She was flabbergasted to find herself sitting across from the author of the greatest miracle in her life. She wanted to shout outloud and share the ecstatic news with the world.

When he finished praying they drank the fourth cup, and Yeshua added with a very solemn tone, "We must remember that the story of Moses is a mixture of folklore and legend, not to be taken literally." They stared at him, with interest and curiosity, except master Micah who did not disguise his hatred. Yeshua explained, "It is inconceivable that my loving Abba would side with one people against another, or kill and destroy…"

At that very instant lady Mona stood up pointing at him, "I know you. You are…"

However Ellie grabbed her sleeve pulling her violently, "MOTHER… sit down!"

But she was drowned out by master Micah who stood up screaming, "Master Yeshua you should be flogged and stoned for your blasphemies. Have you no shame? You address God like a member of your family…and relegate Moses, our greatest ancestor to the dust bin of history. I swear, I'll put a stop to your sacrilege. Before nightfall I'll have you arrested, and crucified before dawn…" He pushed the table away violently overturning everything as he left, bumping and pushing everyone in his way.

Lady Mona sat petrified. She realized that to reveal Yeshua's identity would be sentencing him to death. Instead, she sat flabberghasted and bewildered.

Master Azim's family enjoyed Yeshua's story and his explanation. A young girl commented overcome with enthusiasm, "I liked to hear Yahweh's name. When spoken with reverence, for the first time in my life I felt Him here among us."

"I am glad you clarified Moses' legend," master Azim smiled approvingly. "It always troubled me that we involve Yahweh in our wars of death destruction."

• • •

Early next morning was the celebration of MATZOTH or unleavened cakes. It was the offering of the first harvest of the new season, and all bread and pastry was made from the new grain. It was the celebration of new life, when the pilgrims loved to tell jokes, stories, traditional tales and lessons of irony.

Master Aaron could not wait for a chance to share a story he had heard recently, and fidgeted in his seat until everyone was seated. Then he stood up and started eagerly, "A pilgrim asked a rabbi if he could turn a pot over a scorpion on a Sabbath to prevent being stung. What do you think was the rabbi's advice?" He looked around and when they shrugged he continued, "He said, 'That sounds too much like a hunt, and hunting is forbidden on the Sabbath!' "

The men guffawed, while the women gasped at the prospect of being punished for defending their homes against poisonous creatures.

When the laughter subsided, another patriarch stood up, "A rabbi forbade a cripple the use of an artificial limb on the Sabbath, because carrying the limb constituted work."

Master Azim raised his hands for silence then asked, "Why did God create man only on the sixth day?"

"I don't know. Why?" another queried on cue.

"In case man became too vain, he should remember that even the lowly flea was created before him."

They laughed and cheered, though they had heard the adage many times before.

A young man stood up and recited nervously:

"Yesterday is history
Tomorrow a mystery:
What is today? –
A chance to remake
Yesterday's mistake
Into tomorrow's victory!"

The gay celebration was interrupted when waves of people rushed through their camp heading towards the city. "Why the hurry?" Master Azim asked no one in particular. "Where is everyone going?"

"The Egyptian is here to destroy the Temple," a man replied without missing a step.

A half dozen young men ran through when one of them stopped to announce, "After he razes the Temple he will lead us in war against the Romans. Come join the war!"

"Let's crush the Romans," another yelled pumping his fists as he ran.

They cheered and raised their weapons consisting of clubs, sticks and rocks. Yeshua's group remained undecided, partly because the carnage of the previous day was still vivid in their memories.

After a long pause master Stephanos addressed them with passion, "I don't believe Rabban is the Messiah, but we shouldn't miss this historical event. Just think, the destruction of the Temple, followed by an uprising… We're living in history."

Many young men, eager for an excuse for adventure stood up ready to join.

"I'll go with you," Germanicus stood in pain and shuffled towards his master.

"You're not well…and it's too dangerous," Yeshua argued, only to see them caught by a wave of pilgrims and melt in the crowd. He called out, "Wait for me…"

In the blink of an eye only the oldest women and youngest children remained.

The progress to the city was slow because most pilgrims threw caution to the wind and went on impulse to see the giant's performance then do battle with the Romans. At the gate they pushed and squeezed until they came up to the marble steps directly in front of the giant bronze doors at the central tower of the Temple. The morning service was in progress with over ten thousand congregants overflowing into the square.

They did not wait long before the burly bodyguards pushed making a path for the giant. Close behind came the manager, visibly pleased with the large crowd. Master Rabban came last seemingly uninterested in the chaos and destruction he was about to cause. The manager ran up the marble steps where he pranced back and forth, smiling, and bantering with the audience, while his experienced eyes guessed the number of the spectators: close to twenty thousand and more coming. When the time was perfect, he raised his arms, and one of the guards bellowed, "SI-LEN-CE!"

The manager stood at the edge of the esplanade announcing, "My fellow Israelis, as promised master Rabban, the undisputed Messiah, will use his extraordinary powers to destroy this – King Herod's heathen abomination," he pointed to the Temple behind him. "This monstrosity was designed by Herod, a heathen, and built by thousands of imported pagans. It is the work of Satan. And it must be destroyed!"

"Destroy the heathen Temple, Rabban," an old man screamed.

"Down with infidels and Satanic buildings," a woman echoed his sentiments.

"After that let's get the Romans – Revenge!" a young man in the front screamed.

A pilgrim started chanting, "LI-BE-RATE-US! LI-BE-RATE-US!"

Others joined in and soon the square reverberated to the chant, as if already marching to battle, "LI-BE-RATE-US! LI-BE-RATE-US!"

The clamor of the chant seemed to awaken the giant and he suddenly began to climb up the steps vigorously. Yeshua realized what he was going to do, and impulsively jumped ahead of him, "Master Rabban, you cannot do this. It is filled with people."

The giant, taken by surprise, stepped back and turned to the manager for guidance.

"Don't listen. Do your work," he ordered, turning to Yeshua. "Get out of his way."

The people encouraged the giant, "Rabban - Destroy the pagan Temple."

Yeshua stood his ground, "Listen to me master Rabban: there are thousands in there. Don't kill them…Please!"

The mob threatened the young Israeli, "Pagan lover! Get out before he kills you."

"The Temple is profane. It's Satan's building!" some yelled.

"Kill him Rabban," others demanded.

The manager walked down a couple of steps, grabbed the giant yanking him up rudely to the top. The people were shocked to see that puny man pushing the colossal giant at will. But when he got up to the esplanade they cheered wildly. Rabban flexed his muscles showing off his immense biceps. No one doubted he would destroy the Temple in short order and wanted it pulverized. The chant got louder: "LI-BE-RATE-US! LI-BE-RATE-US…"

Rabban turned to get on with destroying the Temple when he saw the young scholar standing before him. "Get away or I'll break your bones!" he growled.

"Don't do it, master Rabban, please," Yeshua begged, reaching out.

The giant swept his arm as if shooing a fly, sending him flying through the air into the wall, and to the ground. He remained on his knees dazed for some time before getting up. The giant was already gathering his immense power.

Yeshua stood up screaming, "The true Messiah would never murder innocent children." That stopped the giant, as he looked into the young man's eyes, and was caught by the radiant light. "The Messiah saves people, and never kills!" Yeshua continued as if rebuking a child.

"Kill him Rabban," a man in front screamed. "He's a pagan lover!"

"Break his bones," another demanded.

"Get on with it, you big lug," the manager ordered seething with anger. "What are you waiting for, the Romans?"

The shouting and conflicting orders enraged the giant, and he growled savagely towards the sky. He brought his hands up, and started gathering his powers for the assault on the edifice. There was an eerie silence, like the calm in the eye of a hurricane before it destroyed everything in its path. When he pointed his arms at the young scholar, Yeshua floated in the air, like a trifling ornament. The young scholar twisted and struggled to get free like a fly in an invisible web, but to no avail. Rabban twisted and moved his fingers, stretching Yeshua's muscles and bending his bones to the breaking point. His face contorted and he groaned in pain, begging to be released. But the giant roared loudly enjoying the punishment he was inflicting.

"You want to be free?" he asked, and when the young man grunted, he pulled his hands back causing Yeshua to fly towards him, then flung him into the stones. Yeshua let out a piercing scream bouncing off the wall and tumbled on the marble floor.

The giant turned to the spectators who cheered wildly. This was what they had come to see; a combat sport. Blood! It mattered not that the opponents were as unequal as a tiny David against the gigantic Goliath. They wanted blood and he was sating their thirst. They shouted approval demanding more blood, carnage, even death.

The giant returned to the youth who lay on the floor, struggling valiantly to get up. He knew from years of destruction that the young man was on the throes of death. He decided to play with him for a few moments then finish him off.

Yeshua shook his head trying to get his bearings, when he saw the giant preparing for his greatest onslaught. He tried to get up, but his every joint ached and his muscles trembled. He leaned against the wall groaning, "Master Rabban ...don't kill innocent..."

If Rabban heard him, it did not stop him. He let out a blood curdling growl from the pit of his stomach, his mouth spewing foam, "I'll break your every bone...I'll tear you limb from limb."

He aimed his outstretched arms, seized and froze Yeshua, raising and twisting his body one way then the other, and bounced him violently against the wall for the last time. When Yeshua lost consciousness, the giant lost interest in the sadistic game. He turned to spectators letting out a diabolical laughter enjoying the first kill of the day, proclaiming, "I am Rabban, the invincible. I AM THE MESSIAH!" he glared at them inviting them defiantly, "Anybody wants to fight RABBAN?"

Nobody took up his invitation, but continued applauding, whistling and shouting. He scoffed, showing a row of white teeth, perspiration flowing down his face and into his beard. He flexed his muscles. Hercules was not as perfectly chiseled in marble.

Stephanos and Germanicus stood at the base of the esplanade yelling for their friend to get out of there. Each time the giant threw him against the wall they screamed at him to stop, and let him go, but their pleas were drowned by the crowd.

Germanicus started up the steps, "I'm going up to get him..."

Stephanos wrestled and pulled him back, "Don't be a fool. He'll kill you!" The Greek easily pulled him back as the slave was still too weak and sore to fight back.

Meanwhile Yeshua lay on the floor without a stir. Only a bright light appeared deep inside his subconscious, and a familiar voice warned him, "Get up, Yeshua, get up and defend yourself. Go save the people."

He began to stir, almost imperceptibly, struggling with great effort, as every joint in his body seemed disconnected and aching. He stayed on his hands and knees agonizing, then, supporting himself against the stone walls, pushed himself up slowly to his feet. He squinted and saw Rabban showing off to the crowd.

Close beside the giant, Yeshua saw the young priest who had followed him since he gave his lamb to the beggar. Yeshua remembered him, for he was the same priest who had sat beside him in the Temple after the bar-mitzvah, when he was examined by the High Priest Ananas and the leaders of the religious factions: Zohar and Gera. When he saw the priest's smile he regained confidence and strength.

When Rabban turned around and saw Yeshua standing, his smile froze. Nobody had ever survived his beating. His face twisted, "I WILL KILL YOU," he roared shaking like a wild animal.

"Master Rabban, I beg...don't kill children...please..."

But the giant was already summoning his stupendous forces to finish the impertinent youth, and tear everything in his way. Yeshua closed his eyes asking his heavenly Abba to help him withstand the attacks. A bright light appeared about his head enveloping it. He extended his hands to Rabban with the palms up.

When the giant sent out the first burst of energy, bolts of lightning left the young man's arms and a gigantic explosion burst violently on the esplanade. The spectators gasped and stepped back, shocked by the loud claps of thunder breaking off pieces of marble and flinging debris everywhere. For sometime energy rushed from one combatant against the other, bursting like gigantic explosions with deafening loudness and blinding light. Showers of colorful sparks and torn up stone flew in every direction. Balls of fire fell spewing out flame, deflecting and bouncing among the spectators who panicked and tried desperately to escape. They were caught in the gigantic struggle of superhuman forces, which fractured the wall, cracking the esplanade, ripping marble and stone rending it asunder at the fleeing people. Children screamed and ran, followed by mothers trying to stop them. A steady shower of fire and stone rained on the spectators who ran, collided and fell helplessly, getting trampled.

The explosions shook the heavy pillars and the stone walls trembled. The esplanade cracked. The people feared the Temple was about to crumble on them. The giant screamed and cursed at his foe, his face drenched in perspiration. He felt his power shrinking, and tried to muster enough concentration to garner sufficient force for one last attack. But his power was visibly spending and lessening until he could not gather further strength. His arms dropped from exhaustion. "Who are you who can withstand my power? Only one person can match me..."

"I am Yeshua of Nazareth. I was sent to create a new order," he replied exhausted.

The giant fell to his knees, "You are the anointed one. You are the true Messiah!"

They were interrupted by renewed and thundering noise, for the Romans were coming. People who had run away now were returning, to the safety of the Temple.

Germanicus jumped up and grabbed the young scholar, "Master Yeshua the army is here. You must run. Come." He and Stephanos ran along the esplanade toward the gate.

Rabban led Yeshua down the steps, "Run master Yeshua. I'll hold the Romans as long as I can. Pray for me…"

The giant cleared the steps in two jumps and started towards the cavalry.

The young priest grabbed Yeshua's arm and led him down the steps, turned and ran under the esplanade, where he opened a secret door to the Temple ordering, "Follow me." Yeshua realized they would be proceeding into the secret dark passages lit by a row of torches, and stepped into the narrow corridors. Thousands of pilgrims followed them.

They proceeded through the passageways, running from the west to the east side of the Temple where they exited. Outside the priest pointed to a narrow street, "That road will take you to the bazaar where you turn left to the Fish gate. Go out and follow the road. At the crossroads turn north. It will take you to the Sea of Galilee."

He ran gingerly as his right hip was tender and every muscle and bone in his body ached. Yet he dared not slow down. He ran through a maze of crooked narrow streets, grimy and dirty, full of children playing and old men leading their donkeys. A few times he came upon a fork in the road and stopped, uncertain which one to follow. Each time he chose the one he considered to be the major road. After a long and arduous run, he came out in the bazaar. To his left he recognized the Fish gate in the distance. He turned towards it, and in a short time was out. Outside, he stopped and looked back. There were no soldiers in sight. But one could never be certain about them, so he resumed running. He still had a long tricky maneuver through the tent city, but he noticed the aroma: more pleasant than the dingy, greasy stench of the dirty crooked roads. He longed for the crisp clean air and the green hills of Galilee.

• • •

Debborah entered lady Sarah's yard followed closely by the schoolmaster ben Joseph, Esau and Marcus, who walked slowly, and self consciously as if trespassing with unlawful designs. She brought them to the door of the office and told them to wait while she went to find her friend. She soon found servants who located their mistress.

When asked why she was there Debborah did not answer directly, suggesting instead, "Let's go to your father's office. There is important information I think you should hear…"

They proceeded to the office, passing by the young men who stood huddled against the wall. Lady Sarah passed less than a couple of cubits from them without seeing them. Debborah was shocked when she saw this. Lady Sarah was keen, full of interest and curiosity, and always aware of her surroundings. Now she seemed withdrawn, her mind vacant and almost out of touch with reality. The truth of her friend's mental state hit Debborah very hard. She realized her friend was still mentally fragile, masking her infirmity with a strong outward façade. The young girl became anxious, fearing that the news she was about to convey may snap her frail psyche permanently.

She grabbed lady Sarah's arm as she was about to open the door pleading, "I…can't do it. You're not ready…I changed my mind." She turned to leave.

Lady Sarah grabbed and pulled her back, "What am I not ready to hear?" Then she noticed the young men, "What are you doing here? Debborah, what's this about?"

"Nothing," Debborah muttered self consciously. "I had an idea…It was stupid. Forget I even came." She struggled to get free.

Lady Sarah refused to release her and dragged her into the office, "You are behaving like a precocious child. If your intuition told you there was something I should hear, you were probably correct. Are you here to tell me something? Go on, tell me."

Debborah motioned them to come in, although she was still uncertain and confused. She was filled with anger and guilt. She was about to inflict immeasurable pain on a friend whom she loved as a sister, and tried to think of an excuse to stop what she had started. When nothing came to mind, she stood motionless, with tears flowing down.

Lady Sarah pulled her close murmuring, "Why are you crying? Are those tears for me? Afraid you may hurt me?" When her friend nodded, she took her hands to her chest saying, "You don't have to cry for me. I am more resilient than you think…I too have my suspicions…I am ready for the whole truth. So tell me everything…"

Debborah mumbled through tears, "This is…too unpleasant…"

Lady Sarah heard her and tensed up. For some time she had begun to suspect about the circumstances, perhaps some ugly facts about her father's murder. Now she realized it was probably worse than she feared, but refused to flinch, "I have to know. Spare me no pain."

"You should sit down," the young girl whispered.

Lady Sarah walked behind the desk, her hands shaking and sat down slowly. For an instant she debated whether she should hear it, fearing her world could come crashing down. But she insisted, whispering resolutely, "Everything." She took a deep breath, feeling her heart pounding in her throat, she addressed the young men, "Debborah tells me you have something to say…Is it the truth…? I don't want evil gossip." They nodded nervously. She lowered her head repeating, "Then you must tell me, everything…"

They glanced at one another furtively, no one willing to be the first. After a long time Esau stepped forward, "Lady Debborah asked me to travel to Tyre to investigate master Nehemiah's…recent work. I spoke to many…they said…he was not doing architecture." He paused when he saw her expression change to pain, as she lowered her head bringing her hands to her face, and started to cry softly. Esau was not sure whether to continue and looked at Debborah.

"P-please continue…" lady Sarah mumbled.

"He was an informant for the Romans," he blurted out and she looked at him through tears. He forced himself to continue, "He infiltrated political meetings…spied, betrayed…for money. Hundreds tortured…many killed…" Unable to continue when he saw his every word stab her in the heart, he shuffled back to the wall.

Lady Sarah sat sobbing quietly into her hands. Marcus stepped forward but froze, unable to speak.

"Give your report, please, master Marcus," Debborah requested.

"I…investigated in Sepphoris. I learned he did not design, or construct …Then I saw him meeting with a Roman officer in the fort… master Nehemiah took a pouch…a bag of coins…probably payment…"

She looked up, her eyes swimming in tears turned cold, "Did you see coins, master Marcus?" He shook his head defensively. "Did you hear coins?" Again he shook his head. "Did you hear their conversation? How do you know it was payment? I suggest you are making a pre-conceived suspicion fit your conclusion, sir."

"I asked many residents, and they confided that master Nehemiah was an informer. Some saw the officer give him gold talents, and thanked him for a job well done."

Lady Sarah remembered the purse the soldier gave her from the officer, and knew he was telling the truth.

At that moment the servants she sent out to investigate her father's work returned and walked in the door. She took one look at them and knew the answers they were bringing. But she needed to hear it, and she motioned to them to report.

"What they say is the truth…I'm sorry my lady," the servant mumbled.

"It was the same in Tyre," the slave corroborated.

Lady Sarah was crushed. She wanted to fall in a heap and cry. When she noticed the schoolmaster she queried, "Master ben Joseph what hideous news can you add to the horrible accusations?"

"I wish to explain that master Yeshua was not involved in your father's death," he informed her. "He did not capture him, or hold him prisoner."

"But, was he a Zealot…?" she asked confused.

"He fought to save your father's life. He wanted to defend him," he replied.

She closed her eyes, overwhelmed by the news. She whispered, "Thank you for telling me…" They began to shuffle out when suddenly she opened her eyes, and called out, "Wait. Who is private Quintus? Why did a Roman soldier kill father?"

"He is of Roman ancestry," master ben Joseph explained. "But he was born and raised here, and sympathizes with our cause."

She did not understand it, but nodded as she reflected on it. They went leaving her with Debborah. She could not comprehend why a Roman should kill a foreigner who helped the empire. Then she remembered her first days in Nazareth. At first she disliked the people. But, when she got to know their simple way of life, their humor and honesty, and their sincere religious devotions, she learned to love them uncompromisingly. She wondered, could that be the reason which prompted private Quintus' action?

"Your brother was right," she said to her young friend. "The aristocrats forced father to become a traitor." Then she covered her face in her hands and broke down sobbing. Debborah put her arms around her shoulders and held her tight.

• • •

When Yeshua left Jerusalem, he continued at the same fast pace for many miles before slowing down. He mingled with pilgrims returning from Passover, avoiding Roman soldiers. Tired, famished and sore, he finally slowed down to a regular walk. The sun was already beginning its descent when he started to keep a close watch for his companions. He reasoned the sooner he stopped the more likely they were to catch up with him. After all, they had the food and camping gear, and unless they reunited soon, he would spend a long, cold and hungry night. What troubled him most was that he was not even certain they were coming. At one point he considered turning back, but, the prospect of running into Roman soldiers searching for him quickly changed his mind.

When he saw the pilgrims setting up camp he began to panic. Once it became dark he feared they could easily pass without seeing him. He decided to gather wood and start a big fire, to make himself more visible. Then he sat for a long time, his eyes riveted on every trekker. All too soon it got dark and still there was no sign of his companions. He moved closer to the fire to keep warm, when suddenly he noticed some pilgrims who had passed by him unseen. He panicked. How many others had gone by without him noticing? Then he noticed something unusual about the camel; it was limping. Could that be master Stephanos' animal? He decided against it, but got up to investigate anyway, and ran after them. When Germanicus looked back, they ran and embraced as if they had been separated for a year.

At the campsite master Stephanos brought the young scholar up to date, "Master Aaron's family plan to stop in Nazareth for a visit on their way home. Ellie wishes to meet Debborah. Moreover, lady Mona wants a word with you in private."

"Sounds ominous," Yeshua tried to quip to mask his apprehension.

"She knows your identity," the Greek spoke bluntly, but seeing his friend's face turning pale, he decided to ease his mind. "She did not tell anyone, not even her husband. Ellie was the one who told me." Yeshua sighed clearly relieved. "Master Azim is also coming with his extended family. He witnessed your duel with the giant and realizes you are no ordinary person."

"Is he likely to create problems?"

"His family respects and he reveres you. I'm certain he realizes if you chose not to disclose your extraordinary qualities, you must want to keep it private."

Yeshua admitted privately that it was time to make the decision he tried so hard to avoid: keep his identity secret, which was clearly becoming impossible, or reveal his identity once and for all? But at that moment he worried about something much more important, "What happened to master Rabban? Is he alive? Was he captured?"

"After he acknowledged you as the Messiah, he ran at the Romans fighting like a man possessed," Stephanos informed him. "In his first attack he toppled three horses with their mounts, creating a momentary crisis. Chariots toppled over horses, and both went out of control on top of the infantry. The diversion allowed most pilgrims to escape. Many pilgrims joined and turned on the Romans. But they were vastly outnumbered. Still it took six soldiers to subdue him. They tied him up but he flexed his muscles and snapped the thick ropes like rotten thread. They did not bother tying him up again. But, by this time his power was spent. He went as meekly as a child, obeying their orders without argument. When the pilgrims saw him subdued refusing to fight, they turned on him," the Greek finished with a sigh. "They demanded he be killed."

"Really? What did they say?" Yeshua asked deeply shocked by the news.

"They started to chant, 'CRU-CI-FY-HIM! CRU-CI-FY-HIM!' They followed him, taunting and throwing stones. Like hyenas turning on an injured prey!" Germanicus said.

"I sensed that deeply inside he was a kind man, as simple as a child," the Israeli confided evidently troubled. "He was directed to do everything…I suspect his manager is to be blamed for his wanton destruction." After a long reflection he concluded, as if delivering a soliloquy, "The pilgrims obviously hunger for a leader to lead them in battle. If a Messiah appears and refuses to lead them to war, they will quickly dispatch him… Did they crucify him?"

"The last we saw they were taking him to the Insula," Germanicus shrugged his shoulders.

"Probably to try him," the Greek demurred. "By the way, master Micah returned with the police from the Sanhedrin as he threatened…they had an order to arrest you."

"Really?" the young scholar blurted out panicking.

The Greek nodded, "They wanted to drag you to the Priests of the Temple. Take my advice and never return to that city. It's full of fanatics."

"The High Priest warned if I returned, I would leave on a slab."

They looked at each other ominously, but did not say a word. They did not have to.

When dinner was ready they attacked it ravenously. It had been a long hard day, frought with danger. They devoured every morsel of the roast master Azim had gifted them, and scraped the bottom of the bowl, hardly exchanging a word. Their conversation consisted of monosyllables, punctuated with grunts and shrugs between crunching bites.

Afterwards they sat back, happy, with their stomachs full, contemplating the star studded universe. The magnificent sight invited a more philosophical discussion.

"I enjoyed the Passover and the Paschal meal," Stephanos commented graciously. "Are they the same every year?"

"The story of Moses, the angel of death and the exodus remain the same," the Israeli replied. "But the magical stories and folklore vary with each storyteller."

Stephanos chuckled remembering something, "I recognize the story about that fellow Moses. We studied him in Greece, in the lyceum. But, our textbook said the Egyptians got tired of the Hebrew riff-raff and chased them out of the country..." After a moment he laughed gregariously, "Come to think of it, our textbook was from Egypt."

They sat in silence, searching in the stars for an understanding of the universe, for the pulsating stars invited such contemplation. Soon deep yawns were heard more and more often.

Germanicus tossed a question as much to the stars as to his companion, "Master Yeshua, many months ago you told me you had travelled to the moment of Creation. What was it like: the travel...the moment?"

"The first thing you have to realize is that the moment of Creation was very, very, very long ago. To get back there you have to travel through time...to the past. Going directly takes too long, so you take shout cuts, and travel through time warps. You bend time. In a fraction of an instant you cover hundreds of millions of years. Finally you arrive to the era before time and infinity began, indeed before everything. It is Chaos. There I stood beside my heavenly Abba. He brought all matter to a full stop, then, with a gentle nudge sent it outward in all directions. That was the moment of Creation: the beginning of time and finity. Do you know why it is called that?"

He waited for a response and when none came he looked at his companions, and chuckled quietly. They were soundly asleep. He got up, added some wood to the fire, and helped them into the tent. As soon as his head touched the pillow he was asleep.

. . .

As soon as he fell asleep Yeshua felt himself levitating above his cot and out of the tent, rising high above the trees and as high as the hawk soaring in the warm afternoonzephyrs. He sensed someone beside him, and when he looked he recognized the archangel Gabriel, who had journeyed with him back to Creation a long time ago.

They started another journey through time, but on this occasion they travelled to the future. They travelled many years ahead and stopped over Jerusalem. The holy city appeared the same, but the construction of the Temple was much advanced. The city was again overcrowded with the tent city spreading far beyond the horizon again celebrating Passover. However on this occasion it was unseasonably cold and there was snow on the ground, a rare sight in Israel.

There was a commotion at the Insula, and they saw that it was filled with pilgrims. Yeshua and the archangel stopped and hovered over the area. Thousands of people filled the platform, the mosaic pavement, the marble steps and hundreds sat perched on the cement fences. Some climbed up the columns and sat at the feet of Roman emperors' statues, to see the action more clearly.

In the center of the platform stood a solitary man, an Israeli peasant wearing a torn, dirty robe. He seemed to have a crown on his head, but a careful inspection proved it to be a crown of thorns. They descended for a closer view of the events. A few paces from the peasant stood a Roman official, and his cloak and toga told them he was the tetrarch.

The peasant seemed to be on trial and the tetrarch interrogated him incessantly. However, the peasant seemed oblivious to his questions and accusations. By the bruises and blood on his face and his robe, obviously he had been tortured, yet he stood serene and self-assured. After a lengthy cross examination the tetrarch threw his hands in the air and the priests of the Temple took over. They started to throw stones at the peasant, and someone began to chant, "CRU-CI-FY-HIM! CRU-CI-FY-HIM!" The mob took up the chant and the echo of a thousand voices resonated like a drum beat over the city, and into the hills taking on a life of its own.

Yeshua and the archangel followed the peasant as he shuffled along the narrow streets, dragging a cross on his shoulder. They went out of the city gate to a higher hill known as Golgotha, later to be named Calvary. There the peasant and two others were crucified.

In the afternoon the one with the crown of thorns began to heave and breathe with shallow quick breaths. He pushed up against his nailed feet fighting for breath, and let out a piercing cry to the heavens, "ABBA INTO YOUR HANDS I DELIVER MY SPIRIT!" His scream shook the houses and the walls of the city. Birds rushed from their nests. Wild beasts howled in the forests.

Then he died. A long eerie silence followed.

Gigantic thunder clouds rose and turned black, covering the sun and turning day into night. A clap of thunder shook the heavens and bolts of lightning ripped the skies with shattering explosions. The bolts crashed into the ground every few paces forcing pilgrims and soldiers to run for cover. Torrential rains burst and whipped the earth as if to wash off the crime man committed that day against God. When the clouds rolled away an eerie iridescent blue sky remained, with clouds ripped apart as if the heavens were draped with torn rags.

Yeshua noticed a strange development: the cross with the crowned peasant started to grow upwards higher and higher as if it sprouted roots. As it reached the heavens it threw shadows over the land. Where the shadow touched the city walls, the stones ripped apart and crumbled to the ground. The Temple went up in flames. The Insula with the tower of Antonia was razed to ashes.

The living cross threw shadows to the four points of the compass: stretching to the north over Damascus, Antioch and the furthest frontiers of Europe, to the south over Egypt and Africa, to the east over Babylon and Persia, India and China, and to the west over Rome, Hispania and Lusitania. It crossed oceans covering undiscovered continents and as yet unnamed countries.

When they looked at the top of the cross they saw a plaque nailed to it with an inscription in Latin: IESUS NAZARENUS REX IUDAEORUM (Jesus of Nazareth King of the Jews)

As the cross reached the height where he levitated, for the first time Yeshua looked into the face of the peasant with the crown of thorns, and recognized his radiant eyes.

"NO-O! I DON'T WANT TO DIE!" a blood curdling scream filled the tent.

Stephanos and Germanicus bolted out of their cots, rushed to their friend's side, shook and yelled to awaken him. Dogs barked in the neighboring camps. People woke up, and children cried, as Yeshua screamed, "My God, I don't want to die." They begged him to wake up telling him it was a dream. After a long time he came to life, wet with perspiration, trembling and crying, "Dear Abba...don't let them kill..." He shook, terrified to the very core.

"Master Yeshua, it was a nightmare," Stephanos reassured him. "We won't let you die. You will never die."

. . .

They arrived in Nazareth three days later without fanfare. They were three of thousands of pilgrims returning or passing through town. Only master Joseph felt a sense of relief to see his son return safely. The memory of their expulsion from Jerusalem by the High Priest Ananas, and the injunction never to return was still vivid in his memory.

Yeshua's friends noticed a remarkable change in his demeanor after Jerusalem. He became more withdrawn and constantly preoccupied with his life's destiny. His smiles no longer had the carefree zest of youth.

Esau was probably the happiest one to see him. The boat crew had rebuilt the vessel and was putting on the final touches. They eagerly waited final inspection and approval before taking it to the Sea of Galilee for its maiden voyage.

Yeshua complied and in his usual manner gave a thorough inspection, pushing and heaving planks. After he finished there was a long pregnant pause before he smiled, "This will be the sturdiest sailboat on the Sea." There was a collective sigh from the crew. "I congratulate you all, but, mostly Esau," the young scholar put his arm around his shoulder, who stood proudly, his inside bigger than his outside. "This boat will outlast all of us. But, don't forget when you put it in the water it will leak like a sieve. Don't venture far from shore, and take a bailer..."

Miriam who watched the inspection closely, spoke out deeply concerned, "Why did you let them build a boat that leaks?"

"All plank boats leak initially, lady Miriam," Esau explained like an old, experienced shipwright. "But after the wood becomes saturated with water, it swells closing up all seams as tight as a drum."

Miriam did not fully understand it, but was impressed with his confident tone and patient explanation. He is growing into a good leader, she thought.

"Did you not forget something: the boat's name?" Yeshua asked.

"We argued over that for months," Daniel laughed heartily, "but could not come to an agreement."

"I suggested 'lady Sarah,'" Ahmed volunteered. "I thought you'd like that."

"I proposed, 'lady Miriam,'" Marcus added, "more dignified and stately."

Esau returned from the work shed concealing a plaque behind his back, smiling coyly, "One day we had an inspiration and agreed on a name unanimously". He showed the plaque with Hebrew writing.

Yeshua read it out loud, "THE MESSIAH."

Miriam whispered, "Maverick...Magical...Free spirit...I love it. It describes the spirit of a rebel perfectly."

They attached it to hooks imbedded at the stern and started to carry the boat to the cart waiting on the street. "Will you join us?" Esau asked. "We want you to try it first."

"You will not keep me away," he replied. "But, I'll only be able to stay a short time. I must go to Capernaum to give a report to Quintus' father."

They were taking out the rigging when Stephanos arrived with the slave and Anna.

Esau took Yeshua aside for a private word. He had practiced it many times but still started out nervously, "I appreciate the chance you gave me. I confess, there were times I cursed you liberally for dragging me into this...infernal project." He stopped, his emotions beginning to overwhelm him. After he regained control, he sighed, "Anyway, when I realized...I began to appreciate. Thanks for the chance."

The young scholar put his arm around his shoulder, "Your first success. There will be others...But I warn you, you will face much prejudice...but you will overcome..."

"I'll find strength and support from you. I can't wait to join your synagogue," he said with a mixture of enthusiasm and expectation. "There will be a place for me, right?"

The young scholar nodded, "Leader of the congregation..." He wanted to say more but master Stephanos interrupted them.

"Master Yeshua, and you too Esau, please join us," the Greek motioned them, as he pulled out a scroll from his belt. "I have a special announcement to make before this wonderful family. Germanicus, come stand beside me. During our journey I had the singular displeasure of making the acquaintance of master Hariph, the most argumentative lawyer I had the misfortune to cross words with..." he winced as if he had just bit into a bitter lemon. "He convinced me that one person has no right to own another. Then he drew this document of manumission...when everything was said and done, he charged me a whopping sum for it!" Master Joseph's family enjoyed the irony. Stephanos put his arm around Germanicus' shoulders offering him the scroll. "Master Germanicus, I gift you this document: the evidence of your freedom!"

Germanicus stared at his master, his mouth open-wide, too stunned to react.

"Take it," master Joseph urged him. "You're free."

For the first time Germanicus looked at the scroll, but he still did not know what to do. Tears began to well in his eyes as he stuttered, "I-I d-don't deserve it...I- I have a c-confession..."

Yeshua came forward, put his arm around Germanicus' shoulder interjecting, "You are not judged for thoughts or wishes, but for deeds. You have earned it. Take it." He took the manumission and placed it in his hands.

Germanicus looked at Anna, smiled then his expression changed and he became serious, then worried, "But, now I don't have a job. How will I feed my family? Where will we live?"

"What a coincidence," Stephanos smiled nobly, "I happen to be looking for a servant. I'm presently hiring...I pay well, and..."

"I'll take it, if you will have me," master Germanicus interjected eagerly.

Yeshua congratulated them, and started to leave, "I have to catch up to the boat crew, then onto Capernaum..."

As soon as he stepped out on the street, Debborah ran up, "I just spoke to lady Sarah. She is under the oak tree waiting for you."

"How is she recovering?"

"Why not find out for yourself?" she winked with a teasing smile.

Yeshua hurried along the path, his mind filled with trepidation, uncertain how she would receive him or what he was going to say. He thought about her often, his heart filled with compassion and love.

He was still distant from the tree when he saw her, and stopped. He had almost forgotten how beautiful she was. Now, almost fully recovered, she was lovelier than ever.

When she saw him she started to rush to him but checked herself, approaching slowly, unsure of herself, clenching her hands over her bosom. He took her hands, holding them tight for they felt cold.

They faced each other, engraving every detail on their memory. Her eyes swam in his and sparkled.

He smiled tenderly into her eyes, "I am happy to see you recovering so well."

"On the outside. Inside I am cut in a thousand pieces..." she murmured sadly.

They stood looking at each other for a long time. There were so many things they wanted to say, they did not know where to start.

She whispered mistily, "I prayed every night that you would return safely. One hears such strange stories about Jerusalem." Then her eyes looked down and her voice quivered, when she whispered, "Yeshua I must apologize..."

"No. You don't have to," he interjected affectionately.

"I must. I was cruel. I learned the truth about father..." Tears formed in her eyes and rolled down her cheeks. "Can you forgive me?"

"I did not blame him. They starved your family. They forced him into it..."

"Thank you for trying to help him."

They looked deeply into each other's eyes and saw their souls. Their hearts pounded, and their lips trembled hungrily. He put his arms around her and held her tight.

She whispered softly, "I often dreamt about us, although I knew father would never allow it. Nothing can separate us now..."

He placed a finger over her lips and pulled back, "It cannot be, lady Sarah. I am sorry."

"What do you mean? I saw it in your eyes. I felt your heartbeat. Can you deny you love me?"

He did not deny it, but lowered his eyes and walked to the edge of the cliff, explaining with tears in his voice, "I have a mission...a lifetime mission."

"I will help you. Let me share your life...your troubles," she leaned against him.

"I have too much to do, to prepare...to plan...I cannot give you the time, or all the things you deserve..." He pressed his head in his hands, filled with anxiety and confusion as he cried out, "When I start my mission I must travel, without a home, without a bed..."

"I will sleep in the fields with you. I don't want luxury," she threw herself into his arms, holding him desperately, fearing she was losing him. "Yeshua, don't leave me...I need you..."

He removed her arms gently trying to console her, "You deserve happiness... children...a home...I cannot give you..."

She saw her world crumble before her eyes, and began sobbing uncontrollably, heaving and sighing with short breaths. Then she turned on him questioning his agenda, "Is it your intention to create a church where your priests will be forbidden to marry?"

"My priests...and rabbis will be expected to marry," he replied, "But I...I..." He wanted to say more but words failed him. He walked away and she slid to the ground sobbing.

• • •

They did not know it then, but they would see each other one more time. About fifteen years hence, when he became known to the world as Jesus, the itinerant miracle curer and teacher, the Messiah, they saw one another in Jerusalem.

He had just been sentenced by the tetrarch Pontius Pilate, and was dragging a cross on his shoulders, his hair matted and bloody, with a crown of thorns on his head. Blood ran down his battered face. As he shuffled along the narrow road, he came to a sharp turn where he stumbled. As he was getting up he saw a lady in the crowd directly in front of him: a beautiful lady with two children, a boy of fourteen and a girl of eleven. The lady was one of the first converts to his church.

"Yeshua..." lady Sarah called, crying as she reached out to him.

He stopped, glanced at her and for an instant a bright light appeared in his eyes. Then he looked at the children. He recognized the boy immediately - for his striking eyes had a bright radiance eminating from them.

After a moment he turned the corner and continued with the cross.

That afternoon he died on the cross. Lady Sarah sat in the privacy of her study, with an oil lamp on the desk. Torrential rain battered the roof with loud thunder, while lightning brightened the dark rooms.

She sat at the desk with an old diary open before her, the pages yellowed with age. She read a poem written to her so long ago, and set it aside.

She picked up a dry flower which had been carefully pressed between the pages. It was a hibiscus, brown and discolored. Her memory travelled many years to the past when a very special young man gave her the beautiful flower with the pure love of youth. Two tears welled in her eyes and dropped on the flower.

Suddenly the hibiscus began to come to life, swelling into full blossom, regaining its color: a most beautiful rich color – the red of blood.

EPILOGUE

James completed Yeshua's biography while in prison. It was the eve of James' execution in the year 62 AD, thirty years after his famous brother's crucifixion.

James had been relentlessly persecuted by his Excellency Ananus, the High Priest, and brother in law of Caiphas referred to in the Bible. Ananus was also the son of the High Priest Ananas, who had ordered the young Yeshua and his father Joseph out of Jerusalem with an injunction never to return. The present High Priest charged James, imprisoned and tried him for blasphemy for propagating that Yeshua — now known to the world as Jesus — was the son of God, the MESSIAH, and the savior capable of performing miracles and forgiving sins. All of these assertions were contrary to the beliefs of Sadducees, the ultra conservative fundamentalists. Ananus waited until his supporters outnumbered all others in the Sanhedrin then quickly and quietly held a trial thus guaranteeing a guilty verdict. The sentence was death by stoning.

The real reason he persecuted James, popularly known as 'the Just,' was that recently he was popularly elected by the peasants and the lower class to be the High Priest of the Temple. The people, fed up with the antiquated tribal ritual of animal sacrifices and corruption in the Temple, demanded the High Priest be democratically elected. This infuriated Ananus who represented the wealthy ultra conservative establishment: rich merchants, wealthy scribes and lawyers controlling the Sanhedrin. Moreover, James was the archbishop of the charismatic and popular religious sect known as "Cherestians." (Later Christians) The new Judaic sect was growing by leaps and bounds in Israel, and expanding its missionary work beyond its borders. Ananus persecuted him vigorously hoping that by killing James he would destroy Jesus' church.

James oversaw the missionary work of the "Cherestians" from prison, while writing his brother's biography. As he completed each chapter, lady Sarah smuggled it out and hid the book for future generations. The past few weeks he scribed around the sundial to finish it before the sentence was to be carried out.

The morning after he completed it, James was taken to the esplanade of the Temple in chains. His tired eyes swept over the thousands of spectators: the closest were dozens of priests and the wealthiest members of the Sanhedrin; further out were hundreds more of the richest merchants, scribes, lawyers and conservative religious fundamentalists; the rest were hundreds of pilgrims from James' congregation, most of whom he knew well. These were the peasants, servants and slaves, the diaspora, the newly converted gentiles and foreigners from Syria, Greece and as far away as Rome. They had made the long journey to bring their archbishop their love and support.

Beside him, at the top of the marble steps stood the High Priest Ananus, fidgeting nervously with a scroll in his hands, impatient to finish the persecution he had orchestrated so carefully over six months ago. At his feet lay the largest pile of rocks to be used in the execution.

Ananus unrolled the scroll and read loudly to the spectators:

"In this the seventh year of the reign of emperor CAIUS GAIUS CAESAR NERO, of Rome and the Provinces,

"By the authority of the SANHEDRIN, the lawful council and defender of the Jewish faith,

"Master James, of Nazareth, rabbi of a synagogue in Jerusalem, to wit, The Cherestian Church, was charged, duly tried and found guilty in open court of blasphemy for proclaiming the late Jesus of Nazareth to be the son of God, miracle curer, forgiver of sins and the saviour known as the MESSIAH;

"Master James was sentenced by the Court to be stoned to his death, unless he demonstrates remorse and recants his heretic teachings as false and erroneous, and orders his synagogue to cease and desist propagating blasphemies, all to be clearly confessed with remorse, unequivocally and before the public.

"Signed: His Excellency Ananus
High Priest of the Temple."

Absent in the scroll was the fact that the tetrarch did not authorize the meeting of the Sanhedrin, or the trial and that his signature was not on the document. Thus in truth the trial, the sentence and today's meeting were all illegal.

Ananus orchestrated the timing carefully. When the tetrarch Festus died, and before the new tetrarch, Albinius, arrived from Rome, he captured and tried James. James' allies petitioned Albinius who ordered the trial to be postponed until his arrival which Ananus ignored. He was not going to be denied.

Standing over his victim, he smirked evilly, rolling up the scroll nervously, demanding in a shrill voice, "Master James, I am a compassionate man. You can still save your life. Renounce and admit your teachings as false, and heretic, and publicly confess your errors. Do you renounce Jesus?"

The frail old archbishop stretched to his full height, stared at the High Priest replying with an unfaltering tone, "Why do you ask me concerning the son of God? He is now sitting in heaven at the right hand of the Great Power, and is about to come on the clouds of heaven."

The High Priest could hardly contain his glee. He got what he wanted though he knew he could not lose. If James denied Jesus it would be the end of his leadership. If he remained steadfast, it would be the end of James. Ananus got the best of both worlds: the chance to kill his mortal enemy then watch his church wither.

He dropped the scroll, and picked up the largest bolder with both hands, shaking as he raised it high above his head. He screamed as he launched the projectile at the victim's head, "DEATH TO THE BLASPHEMER!"

Ananus' face froze, consumed by irrational hatred as he drove the stone against his enemy's head. There was a loud "crack" with blood squirting everywhere.

James remained standing, his steady gaze riveted on his killer. It was a peaceful gaze, serene and courageous, unblinking, unwavering. That peaceful gaze would haunt Ananus for the rest of his life. With his eyes open, the archbishop tumbled down the steps where the pack of priests and the Sanhedrin spilled their venom, punishing him with stones. But James was dead before he hit the ground.

When the tetrarch Albinius arrived, he removed Ananus for disobeying his order, but no other punishment was meted out.

Thus in AD 62, James, the Just, joined a long line of martyrs of the fledgling church. Yeshua said his church would grow from the blood of the martyrs.

The first martyr, shortly after Jesus' crucifixion, was the Greek scholar Stephanos, who converted and became a devout worker in the new church. He was stoned to death by the ultra-conservative Sadduccees, led by a young fanatic student from Celecia, Saul of Tarsus. Stephanos was later canonized as St. Stephen.

Later in life Saul repented and converted becoming a fervent and tireless missionary of the church traveling and spreading the word and building new churches in Greece and as far away as Rome. He was canonized as St. Paul.

After Stephanos' death, master Germanicus and Anna moved to northern Europe with Lygia. They had many more children, and he became chief of his tribe. He was one of the most influential teachers of Jesus' universal religion in Germany and the Baltic.

Master Esau became a rabbi-priest in the new charismatic synagogue which accepted all believers. He was stationed in Tiberias, and given responsibility for a wide area, sailing the vessel "THE MESSIAH" to the countless fishing villages sprinkled along the coast of the Sea of Galilee.

True to Yeshua's wishes the rabbis and priests of his church did marry. Moreover, women also became priests in the new church. This remained so for centuries until the Roman Catholic Church changed the policy and forbade priests to marry and women to be priests. It is a contentious matter within the church to the present day.

Quintus who had been banished from Israel returned twice. The first time was to visit his sick father. His visit coincided with Jesus' trial and crucifixion. Although he saw the holy man at close quarters he did not recognize Yeshua as the friend from his youth.

The second time he returned as a centurion and the warden of the prison which held James. Again he failed to recognize him as the brother of Yeshua. The Roman badgered and bullied the leader of the Church most cyinnically saying, "If your God is the omnipotent why does He not set you free?" It was not until James miraculously saved the centurion's granddaughter that he acknowledged God's existance.

James' death started a civil war in Israel. At first the battle was one of peasants against the wealthy establishment and the Roman oppressors. In time it escalated to a full war when the Zealots joined, leading the entire nation against the Romans.

They invaded the tiny nation and after a long war, in AD 70 leveled Jerusalem to the ground. The Temple, the colossal monument of King

Herod, took eighty years to construct, stood for seven years, and burned to the ground in one day.

Tradition has it that young Yeshua stood and defended the west side of the Temple when he fought the fierce duel with the giant Rabban. Today the west wall, commonly called the "wailing wall" is the only part of the great structure still standing.

The tiny nation rebelled against their oppressors for the last time in A.D 90. After a short and brutal war, the Romans trounced them and erased Israel from history. They dispersed all Jews throughout the empire, forbidding them ever to return. They erased the name Israel from history books and changed it to Palestine.

After the humiliating defeat, the people without a nation held council, passing many sweeping resolutions, among them, the following:

- The church founded by Jesus the 'Cherestus' popularly known as 'Cherestianity' was excommunicated from the classic religion of Moses. From that day forward the 'Cherestians' were forbidden to enter the synagogues.

With this edict the Israelis hoped 'Cherestianity' would wither like a rootless plant in the desert wadi, and perish under the hot sun.

The fledgling church which was widely persecuted throughout the empire became an orphan without a home. For a time it was in danger of collapsing and disappearing. But the setback was temporary. The priests and congregants met in private houses, caves, abandoned quarries and in the hills, as Jesus had done throughout the hills and valleys of Galilee.

Yeshua knew that a universal faith based on love, charity and forgiveness would find acceptance with all the races and classes without regard for borders. The glue that brought the people together, inspiring them, was that in the Creator's eyes they were loved equally: the peasant with the emperor, the slave with the master. The social bond of love gave them strength and courage. Instead of withering, Yeshua's religion prospered, winning converts in every nation and every sector of life. People yearned for order and morality, in the comfort of God's love. Like the cross in Yeshua's dream, the Christian Churh grew and spread to every continent on the globe, every race and every nation.

But the growth came with heavy penalties: constant persecutions and countless martyrs. In most countries 'Cherestians' were forced to meet underground and invented secret signs to identify one another.

In the Greek Koine language, the common language of the empire, the word "Cherestus" meant both, saviour and fish. Tradition tells us that they had a secret sign to identify one another: one Christian drew a simple design of a fish in the sand. If the other identified it as "Cherestus" they knew they were safe in Jesus' faith and to be trusted.

In the fourth century the Roman emperor Constantine had a vision that the Cross of Jesus should become the symbol of the Roman Empire. He encouraged the bishops to draft a proclamation. In the year AD 312, at the Council of Nicea they did so, and declared that Jesus, the Christ, was the anointed Messiah, son of God. Christianity became the official religion of the Holy Roman Empire.

Thus a young peasant rebel with an inspiration, or in the cripple Jonathan's words - a dream with a vision – gave the Universal Creator back to the people. Christianity became the religion of kings and all the nations.

And the peasant rebel became one of the greatest leaders of the world, teaching God's word – LOVE.

QUINTUS: THE ROMAN JEW

Roman by birth his heart is Jewish, yet both races scorn him. He loves and loses, lives a charming life cheating death many times.

Returning from a lengthy banishment to the wild frontiers of Europe, he attends Jesus' crucifixion without recognizing him as his best friend from childhood. Quintus pierces His chest with a spear and the blood runs down on his hands and arms staining them permanently.

When he crosses the Emperor he is ordered to be executed, and is forced to fight the champion gladiator to the death.

Returning to Jerusalem he becomes the warden of the prison which holds James, the brother of Jesus. He taunts the holy man as a fraud and superstitious fool, until his granddaughter's life is saved by a miracle. For the first time in his life he faces a power greater than Rome—the love of God.

This is the story of a reckless warrior, blinded by ambition, who refuses to recognize God, but who is never forgotten by Him.

10427825R00329

Made in the USA
Charleston, SC
03 December 2011